JORDAN A. SCHWARZ

The New Dealers

Chicago-born at the onset of the "Roosevelt depression," Jordan Abraham Schwarz is Distinguished Research Professor at Northern Illinois University and a Guggenheim Fellow. He has degrees from the City College of New York and Columbia University. His previous books include *Liberal: Adolf A. Berle and the Vision of an American Era* and *The Speculator: Bernard M. Baruch in Washington, 1917–1965*. He lives both in DeKalb, Illinois, and two miles south of Wrigley Field and a few blocks north of the Chicago Historical Society.

ALSO BY JORDAN A. SCHWARZ

The Speculator:
Bernard M. Baruch in Washington, 1917–1965

Liberal:
Adolf A. Berle and the Vision of an American Era

The Interregnum of Despair:
Hoover, Congress and the Depression

The New Dealers

The New Dealers

POWER POLITICS IN THE AGE OF ROOSEVELT

Jordan A. Schwarz

VINTAGE BOOKS
A DIVISION OF RANDOM HOUSE, INC.
NEW YORK

FIRST VINTAGE BOOKS EDITION, MAY 1994

 Published in the United States by Vintage Books, a division of Random House, Inc., New York, and simultaneously in Canada by Random House of Canada Limited, Toronto. Originally published in hardcover by Alfred A. Knopf, Inc., New York, in 1993.

Grateful acknowledgment is made to TRO—The Richmond Organization for permission to reprint from "Roll On, Columbia," words by Woody Guthrie, music based on "Goodnight Irene" by Huddie Ledbetter and John A. Lomax; TRO—copyright 1936 (renewed), 1957 (renewed) and 1963 (renewed) Ludlow Music, Inc., New York, NY. Used by permission.

Library of Congress Cataloging-in-Publication Data
Schwarz, Jordan A., 1937–
The new dealers: power politics in the age of Roosevelt / Jordan A. Schwarz.
—1st Vintage Books ed.
p. cm.
Originally published: New York: A.A. Knopf, 1993.
Includes bibliographical references and index.
ISBN 0-679-74781-8 (pbk.)
1. United States—Politics and government—1933–1945. 2. United States—Economic policy—1933–1945. 3. New Deal, 1933–1939.
I. Title.
[E806.S358 1994]
338.973'009'043—dc20 93-42221
CIP

Manufactured in the United States of America
10 9 8 7 6 5 4 3 2 1

For Linda,
Gene and Fran

The New Dealers were men and women who deeply believed that democratic government could be used for great purposes.

—ARTHUR SCHLESINGER, JR.,
"Aggressive Progressive,"
New York Review of Books,
April 25, 1991

Thank you for letting me see the article for "Common Sense."

I, too, am a philosopher and try to think in terms of a century, as well as in terms of this week and next.

I go further than you do, for I question whether the dark ages in Western Europe from the fifth to thirteenth centuries were really as dark as the usual historian paints them. It might be worthwhile to compare not painting or architecture or literature of the Europe of the sixth century with the Europe of the eleventh century but to compare rather the state of civilization of the mass of the inhabitants of these far separated ages. In the earlier one the mass of the inhabitants were extremely primitive tribesmen—some fixed, some nomadic, organized into small wholly independent units and with little in their heads other than where to get the next meal and how to fight off the neighboring tribe. Their descendants, five hundred years later, had progressed amazingly in brain power, in wider contacts and in most of the beginnings of our modern organized society.

Another thought for you—the only "civilizations" which have really "ended" have been isolated islands like Yucatan and the Incas. They, I fear, perished without transmitting much of their gain to any other part of the world.

—FRANKLIN D. ROOSEVELT
to Theodore Dreiser,
October 5, 1939

Capitalism is that subspecies of all the systems characterized by private property, which carries out new combinations of factors of production and involv[es] the creation of credit. . . . Capitalism is as old as the phenomenon of credit creation.

. . . fiscal demands are the first sign of life of the modern state. This is why "tax" has so much to do with "state" that the expression "tax state" might almost be considered a pleonasm. . . . If the finances have created and partly formed the modern state, so now the state on its part forms them and enlarges them—deep into the flesh of the private economy. . . . The bourgeois tax state of the present time does not exist anywhere as a pure type. Everywhere it is shot through with the elements of the past, everywhere the shadows of future developments can more or less clearly be seen to fall upon it. Yet everywhere this tax state is today the expression of the most creative forces. . . . The tax state is not altogether limited to derived revenues. It has not only the mostly small inheritance of its predecessor, but it can also create its own economic sphere within the world of capitalism and can become an entrepreneur itself. . . . In so doing it does, indeed, transgress its own limits. However, as long as the state has not swallowed all or most of the economy it remains essentially what it was. The decisive criterion is whether, apart from any monopoly position which it might secure for itself, the state does or does not continue to work within the framework of a free economy whose data and methods it has to accept in its own enterprises.

—JOSEPH A. SCHUMPETER, excerpts from
Joseph A. Schumpeter:
The Economics and Sociology of Capitalism,
Richard Swedberg, ed.

Contents

Introduction

AS THIS IS WRITTEN it is nearly three score years ago that some intrepid Americans expanded state capitalism during the New Deal. "State capitalism" is an old term sometimes used pejoratively by Marxists to denigrate liberalism, but for my purposes it is useful—although I alternate it with the term "public investment."[1] Whichever, it describes a massive governmental recapitalization for purposes of economic development, especially in the American South and West during the 1930s. To a lesser extent this book is also about state cartelism, government organizations of industries in order to build a threshold under prices. State cartelism is not as significant as state capitalism because it is not growth oriented, tending to stabilize defensively along static lines that defeat price competition—which may be why cartels fail or at least fall short of goals, and why the early New Deal failed to raise and hold incomes at sustainable levels.

The New Dealers,[2] as they were called during the administration of President Franklin D. Roosevelt, sought to create long-term markets by building an infrastructure in undeveloped regions of America. The New Dealers believed that national economic growth was stifled by the monopolization of capital and manufacturing in the Northeast quadrant of the country—making the South and the West undeveloped countries. They concluded that relief and recovery were stopgap solutions to the problems of unemployment and stagnation; poverty required development through hitherto unimagined quantities of public investment that could inspire labor mobility and private investment. On the eve of World War II, they committed themselves to an expanded consumer-oriented marketplace, but for the time being the burgeoning New Deal infrastructure would cater to the demands of defense. Thus, the New Deal's lasting contribution to America's postwar economic growth is a revolution in expanded credit supported by public capital. The New Dealers planned to increase public demand for homes and appliances supported by plentiful energy and credit. The energy and credit would be made available by government guarantees of increased credit on easier terms for consumers. However, for much of 1945–1990, Washington disguised public investment under the category of defense. For that matter, convinced that they had fashioned models of economic development in the South and the West, the New Dealers exported their concepts of the Tennessee Valley Authority, the Lower Colorado River Authority and the Bonneville Power Authority to an undeveloped world hungry for a taste of the American standard of living. The New Deal contribution to the American century was a public credit that augmented private investment on a global scale.

This is not a book about the introduction of the welfare state. The story of the expansion of the New Deal security state is worth a book by itself, but the focus here is upon the timely opportunism of certain New Dealers who were not interested in recovery or relief, but in permanent improvements of America's capital structure and its standard of living. The Austrian economist Joseph Schumpeter correctly described capitalism as "creative destruction"; the New Dealers sought to make Americans and capitalists everywhere more creative by using public capital to capture and tame the power of rivers and thereby create a demand for refrigerators, milking machines, aluminum, aircraft and atomic energy for even more power and more growth.

My choices of New Dealers are necessarily subjective and probably will not satisfy everyone. Yet I find them interesting and useful in telling a story that buttresses my themes. To this end I have deliberately excluded members of Roosevelt's original Cabinet and those New Dealers most associated with welfare changes. Although New Dealers such as Henry Wallace and Harold Ickes are prominent in these pages, I have chosen to spotlight others who masterminded financial strategies and are usually slighted by historians. What is important to me is that as individuals of this diverse and eclectic group move in and out of the story, their intertwining weaves a substantial fabric with a rich, recognizable pattern. History has a certain continuity, and the 1915–1945 epoch set established precedents and consequences for recent America.

The New Dealers believed that good economics had their foundations in ethics and good spiritual values. To a large extent three followers of President Woodrow Wilson—William G. McAdoo, Herbert Hoover and Bernard Baruch—attributed such qualities to their proposed policies. In a sense these men were the first New Dealers. They consciously tried to improvise a national economy during the century's second and third decades that upheld both the values of community and individualism. Universalists, they did not confine their efforts to American markets. McAdoo, for instance, strove to generate alternative state institutions to the existing systems of national finance, to nationalize them, and to even internationalize them. As Wilson's secretary of the treasury, he played prominent roles in originating the Federal Reserve System and directing American investment interests overseas—and during the war he innovated and/or operated the War Finance Corporation, the Railroad Administration, and the highly creative Capital Issues Committee. Many a New Dealer recalled during the 1930s the importance of what McAdoo created as a Wilsonian.

Hoover and Baruch operated cartel systems during the war in agriculture, raw materials and manufacturing, although such recollections still shock Hooverphiles, most of whom associate individualism with his name. The New Dealers so consciously imitated those systems in 1933 and embroidered upon Hoover's Reconstruction Finance Corporation, that observers such as Walter Lippmann erroneously attributed New Deal origins to Hoover, which is a bit like saying that the city of London resembles Houston. It is true that Hugh Johnson, Baruch's unhappy contribution to the New Deal, modeled the National Recovery Administration after Baruch's War Industries Board. But Johnson knew that he lacked the leverage of war needed to win cooperation from individual enterprises—which the power of patriotism conferred upon Baruch. Also, Baruch used the leverage of military purchasing; poor Johnson lacked control over the parsimonious Public Works Administration. His failure was foreordained.

Jesse Jones is a central transition figure for Democrats eager to promote strategies for Southern and Western development. Through his imperial control of RFC, Jones, a banker and a Texan, innovated the rescue of banks, accepted a role as the New Deal's premier state capitalist, and by the end of the decade reigned over too many agencies as Federal Loan Administrator for recitation here. Those agencies revolutionized the American credit system. Jones's power over public finance rivaled that of the Treasury although he lacked Cabinet status until Roosevelt made him secretary of commerce in 1940—and allowed him to guide public investment in another world war. By that time, however, Jones had been in Washington long enough for the banker in him to surpass the Texas promoter; caution overcame expansion, and Jesse in war was less the New Dealer than before.

Administering the RFC and a multitude of new agencies that proliferated in the 1930s were New Deal lawyers who drew their inspiration for public service and the social uses of the law from Louis D. Brandeis. To a degree Roosevelt himself was a Brandeisian, for both men believed deeply that in times of national stress public leadership called for experimentation and change on behalf of the disadvantaged. The New Dealers believed that government had to take measures that daunted private markets. Brandeis always had been an innovative thinker, which is why as a corporate lawyer he could be useful both to businessmen and to Woodrow Wilson. Indeed, Brandeis was so intent upon being useful and inventive that he always inspired the New Deal lawyers to be likewise. Less inspiring, however, was his spirited defense of noncompetitive small businessmen in an age that called for large organizations to build and manage for growth. Brandeis's acolyte, Felix Frankfurter, taught future Wall Street lawyers that a career of public service was both heroic and rewarding, thereby furnishing Brandeis with disciples and the New Deal with creative managers.

Frankfurter's star pupil, although both would deny that appellation later, was Thomas G. Corcoran. A thoughtful romantic, Corcoran was a former corporation lawyer who believed in the need to reform Wall Street, acted as a one-man employment agency to hundreds of lawyers seeking New Deal posts, coordinated policy for the New Deal, and served as Franklin Roosevelt's political ramrod during the years 1935–38. He also channeled the legal and political genius of Benjamin Cohen, a formidable contribution by itself. Cohen was a brilliant draftsman, negotiator and counselor—every bit the "lawyer's lawyer" that many New Dealers called him. His participation in the writing of the Truth in Securities Act of 1933, the Securities and Exchange Commission Act of 1934 and the Public Utility Holding Companies Act of 1935 made those laws invulnerable to attack by antiregulation ideologues. Together, Corcoran and Cohen achieved Washington status as legends.

What Corcoran and Cohen began, William O. Douglas and Jerome Frank completed: the dismantling of Wall Street's monopoly of control over capital and Washington's integration into the national credit system. An iconoclastic "legal realist" who espoused blending the study of the law with the social sciences, Douglas was a westerner who learned about 1920s corporate finance in Wall Street before embarking upon an academic career via Columbia and Yale law schools that took him to the chairmanship of the SEC, where he established federal supremacy over Wall Street. Moreover, Douglas's almost flamboyant personality appealed to Roosevelt, who made him a policy-making personal crony during the second term. In 1939 Roosevelt, needing a westerner for the Supreme Court to balance previous appointments of a Southerner—Hugo Black—and Frankfurter, nominated Douglas.

Douglas's closest ally in the New Deal was Jerome N. Frank, an experienced Chicago and New York corporation lawyer who gave up a lucrative career to be counsel to the Agricultural Adjustment Administration. Also creative, Frank devised the Commodity Credit Corporation for Jesse Jones and performed assorted advisory roles for the PWA and

RFC until Douglas brought him on the SEC during the New Dealers' soul-searching that accompanied the Roosevelt recession of 1937–38 and sent them searching for new methods of public and private investment to stimulate a consumer economy. In the SEC, Frank served as a conduit of Keynesian concepts for stimulating the economy through innovative stimulation of capital markets. As SEC chairman Frank dismantled the public utilities holding companies. Ever an enthusiast for RFC and state capitalism, Frank coordinated debate among New Dealers from public works pump priming ("compensatory spending") alone to devising original fiscal and credit schemes for stimulating economic growth.

But the Brandeis-Frankfurter disciple who ultimately made the greatest impact upon New Deal concepts of development was an outsider, David E. Lilienthal. He had been a Chicago reform attorney before Governor Philip La Follette appointed him to the Wisconsin Public Service Commission, where the ambitious Lilienthal attracted the attention of President Roosevelt, who appointed him to the TVA board. Only thirty-three when he began the Tennessee Valley Authority's public power program, Lilienthal created a regional public power system that set low energy prices to drive down the national cost of private electricity. Lilienthal preached the liberal gospel that a low cost of electricity to consumers would enhance economic development in rural America, 90 per cent of which then lacked any power. Because the TVA's expanded production of energy called for expanded consumption, Lilienthal devised the Electric Home and Farm Authority in 1933 to extend credit via retailers of appliances to homeowners and farmers eager to wire their establishments and buy low-cost, laborsaving devices—a strategy which Roosevelt made national via the Rural Electrification Administration in 1935.

The author of the Rural Electrification Administration Act in 1936 was Congressman Sam Rayburn from the cotton fields of northeast Texas. Long suspicious of Wall Street's financial power to retard the development of the rural South, Rayburn collaborated with Corcoran and Cohen to write and pass the Wall Street reform bills of 1933, 1934, and 1935—the latter also known as the Wheeler-Rayburn Act. But he was most proud to be the author of the REA. Although New Deal agricultural policy had designed scarcity, REA power and EHFA credit ironically made the farmer a modern producer of abundance.

Rayburn, who rose to become Speaker of the House of Representatives in 1940, was a loyal follower of Roosevelt and the New Deal, but Congressman Lyndon Johnson became Texas's greatest champion of development via New Deal and defense-related projects. Johnson preached as early as 1940 the political success of federal projects for economic and/or defense development. During the war and into the Cold War, Johnson kept the federal largesse flowing to Texas, and its New Dealer development would be associated with the defense and aerospace industries he promoted.

Wright Patman's career prefigured a trend in the politics of the 1930s. A Texan obsessed with the Eastern money power's grip upon Southern economic development, Patman made himself a staunch defender of small retailers by pushing legislation to define fair retail practices in the Robinson-Patman Act of 1936. His advocacy of stabilized competition raised the question of whether it should be based upon price or number of units. When Congress rejected Patman's protection of small retailers as not in the consumers' best interests, the Texas populist survived politically by augmenting his populism with federal projects for industrial development in East Texas.

By the end of the New Deal, Texas and the West were poised for growth. A California contractor, Henry J. Kaiser, known as the New Deal's favorite businessman, had participated importantly in building Hoover Dam, Bonneville Dam, Grand Coulee Dam and other hydroelectric projects that boosted economic development of the American West. When the war erupted, Kaiser launched the RFC-subsidized shipbuilding industry on the Pacific Coast and borrowed additional government funds for a steel plant at Fontana, California, and magnesium and aluminum enterprises in the West. After the war he tried to enter the automobile industry with RFC support, starting Kaiser-Fraser Motors and producing a little car, the "Henry J," which failed to win public acceptance.

New Deal development of the Tennessee Valley and the Pacific Coast inspired reconstruction of Western Europe after the war and state capitalism for undeveloped countries in the Third World. Hydroelectric projects were encouraged by New Dealers in Iran, Egypt, Brazil and elsewhere in Asia, Africa and South America. In the 1960s some liberals justified the American role in Vietnam by assuring doubters that Washington would bring democratic development to Southeast Asia through a TVA on the Mekong River. In a variety of public and private institutions, New Deal–style state capitalism and government-financed military projects proved to be some of America's most exportable products of the second half of the twentieth century.

To some extent the New Dealers went to extremes in exporting their concepts of development against the threat of communism. But they believed passionately in democracy, in expanding liberalism on our own shores and in creating broader economic opportunities within a framework of freedom. In the world of 1940, with militaristic Japan on the march in East Asia, with the Soviet Union in a pact with Nazi Germany to divide Eastern Europe between the two totalitarian states, with Nazi Germany having conquered most of Western Europe in six weeks and standing poised to invade Britain, with all of Europe committed to one authoritarian doctrine or the other, the New Dealers reaffirmed democracy and insisted that liberal capitalism was a viable and dynamic system worthy of the world's emulation. They affirmed that this was not statism but a democratic community at work. Upon reflection more than a half century later, we should conclude that their reaffirmation and reinvigoration of the democratic faith in both the individual and the community deserves our own reaffirmation.

PART ONE

Wilsonians

The Who, preeminently Who,
Is William Gibbs, the McAdoo.
(Whom I should like to hail, but daren't,
As Royal Prince and Heir Apparent.)
A man of high Intrinsic Worth,
The Greatest Son-in-law on Earth—
With all the burdens thence accruing,
He's always up and McAdooing.
From Sun to Star and Star to Sun,
His work is never McAdone.
He regulates our Circumstances,
Our Buildings, Industry, Finances,
And Railways, while the wires buzz,
To tell us what he McAdoes.
He gave us (Heaven bless the Giver)
The tubes beneath the Hudson River.
I don't believe he ever hid
A single thing he McAdid!
His name appears on Scrip and Tissue,
On bonds of each succeeding issue,
On coupons bright and posters rare,
And every Pullman Bill of Fare.

Postscript.

But while with sympathetic croodlings,
I sing his varied McAdoodlings,
And write these eulogistic lines,
That thankless McAdoo resigns.

—ARTHUR GUITERMAN[1]

1.

William Gibbs McAdoo: State Capitalism

The Southern Society of New York

WILLIAM GIBBS MCADOO SOUGHT MONEY and power. When the Great War ended at the eleventh hour of the eleventh day of the eleventh month, 1918, he abandoned his posts as Secretary of the Treasury, Director General of the Railroad Administration, and the four lesser offices he simultaneously held, citing personal financial needs and the inadequacy of his $12,000 salary as his reasons for departing public life. Nevertheless, his name retained its value. In the twenty months that preceded the 1920 Democratic party convention in San Francisco, all speculation concerning the party's choice for president contemplated McAdoo. That he had never run for public office before was beside the point.

The heroes of the Great War were its administrators of the home front. These ingenious organizers, managers and publicists of 1917–18 rallied an unenthusiastic American citizenry to arms in support of a dubious European adventure and adapted a private industrial complex to the needs of public enterprise. Like all good salesmen, they did it by selling themselves to the public. Fortunately for them, the war produced no preeminent American military hero. When the Armistice ended the war without conquest and a conqueror such as Andrew Jackson, Zachary Taylor or Ulysses Grant, efficacious bureaucrats such as Chairman of the War Industries Board Bernard Baruch, Food Administrator Herbert Hoover and McAdoo were political novices, although the war had made them veterans of Washington's bureaucratic politics. Observers considered Hoover and McAdoo the most likely to take to the electoral hustings; Baruch, a McAdoo protégé and a Jew, seemed more intent upon becoming the power behind McAdoo's throne. Nothing limited Hoover's ambitions. Despite the association with Wilson, Hoover, a political loner, declared himself in early 1920 a Republican and immediately became a contender for that party's presidential nomination. All that blocked his path to the presidency was a Republican preference for the likes of

Senator Warren Gamaliel Harding of Ohio; in the other party, Woodrow Wilson stood in McAdoo's way. Both Hoover and McAdoo would be the political stars of the twenties; both represented a new activist role for government in the economy. Yet they were very different men who believed in very different kinds of activism. Hoover brought men of the marketplace together in a corporate body for collective action. McAdoo manipulated the government's finances and used its coffers as public investment that secured and induced private investment. These differences were important, but superficially they represented a consensus for unprecedented government involvement in markets.

Of the two, McAdoo had the greater political viability at the outset of the century's third decade. He was the early favorite in the Democratic race of 1920. "By experience as well as temperament he is an outsider who knows the inside wires," Walter Lippmann astutely wrote of McAdoo. Comparing McAdoo's political instincts favorably to those of British Prime Minister David Lloyd George, Lippmann found McAdoo a remarkable executive "not organized by a class feeling, nor by a set of profoundly imbedded general principles. He is organized by . . . political possibilities. He is bold to seize the possibilities, but prudent not to overstep them." However, as with Lloyd George, a certain reputation for opportunism plagued McAdoo; Lippmann had reservations concerning his ambitions, and so did others.

> He is a projector of concrete programs, and promoter who can reveal to people that those programs embody what they already desire, and he is an administrator of the first order. McAdoo is a man who makes his way in the world, not by conformity but by initiative, not by pull or regularity or even by genius; but by his wits. He is the kind of man who is self-made several times over. He is big at any rate in two dimensions. He has length and breadth if not depth. . . . He is not fundamentally moved by the simple moralities. He is liberal but worldly, he is bold but immediate, he is brave but not selfless. He would win many skirmishes, and make brilliant dashes, and achieve some victories, but for the long strategic campaigning of democracy, it is hard to tell about him.[2]

A dozen years later Lippmann would express similar reservations concerning another Democratic presidential contender named Franklin Delano Roosevelt.

What both attracted and deterred men about McAdoo was his life as a captalist hero. A Southern Cavalier in the Court of the Yankee Dollar, he devoted himself more to transcending capitalist principles than to the

Southern sense of place. McAdoo was born during the Civil War on October 31, 1863, to educated middle-class Presbyterians from Tennessee who had relocated to Marietta, Georgia. The family's experience during the Reconstruction epoch was a familiar tale of property loss and bitter hardship under federal hegemony. His father was a lawyer and, following Reconstruction, a sometime professor of English and history at the University of Tennessee in Knoxville. Following deprivation came struggle. Young McAdoo entered his father's profession, attending the University of Tennessee from 1879 to 1882 and apprenticing with judges and lawyers before his admission to the bar in 1885. However, he proved to be more of a promoter than a barrister.

His first deal was a real estate venture that netted him $25,000. He used the cash to buy a stake in a Knoxville mule-powered streetcar line. Realizing that the success of the line depended upon conversion to electricity, and needing capital for this modernization, McAdoo journeyed north in quest of credit, only to learn that New York bankers were doubtful of the enterprise's profitability. Like other Southern entrepreneurs, he discovered that Wall Street investors preferred putting their funds into regional railroads or raw materials rather than into the development of impoverished Southern consumer markets. Eventually McAdoo found a persuadable Philadelphia banker, but not enough money was forthcoming to convert to electricity; by 1892 the venture had failed, and McAdoo abandoned Knoxville for New York City.[3]

This failed promotion taught McAdoo that every successful venture needed sufficient capital, and that the place to find it was in the financial hub of America: Wall Street. In New York he ingratiated himself into legal partnership with another William McAdoo—no relation. The other McAdoo was building a reputation in the courts as a man of exceptional integrity; he would rise to chief magistrate of the city of New York. William Gibbs McAdoo, as the transplanted Tennesseean styled himself to be distinguished from his partner, was a man of both action and reflection. In the parlance of a later time, he was a "quick study," and what he studied was corporation law and corporation finance. He spent much of his first decade in Manhattan observing and reading, concluding that while Americans lived in a hard social and economic system, he could make it work to his—and perhaps his community's—advantage. And, like many a young man with his eye on the main chance, he had learned that bankruptcy was a new beginning for corporations and that railroads were his favorite corporations. In 1901 he reaped a tidy retainer when he helped reorganize the failed Wilkes Barre and Hazelton Railroad. He was on his way to success, first as an entrepreneur, then as a public man.

McAdoo's energy and apparent idealism made him an attractive personality. Six feet one-and-a-half and lanky in build, he bore a strong resemblance to Abraham Lincoln—except for a very distinctive hawklike nose. He worked tirelessly in any endeavor with a dedication that earned him a reputation for impatience with those of less intelligence or enthusiasm. He could be quick-tempered and pugnacious. Moreover, he did not apologize for his vociferous nature, for he inclined to people with "spirit"; "I do not care for soft, doughy people," he once commented. Colleagues knew him as "explosive" and "voluble"; "McAdoo was a prodigious and proficient cusser," Bernard Baruch recalled. Yet he did it with a soft and pleasant Tennessee accent. In his fifties, McAdoo still cut an athletic figure: he enjoyed occasional games of tennis or golf, ballroom dancing, or horseback riding in the Western style, or driving a motorcar at excessive speeds. The latter suggested an unnerving recklessness that entered his public life.[4]

McAdoo's greatest entrepreneurial venture involved a railroad tunnel under the Hudson River to connect lower Manhattan with New Jersey. Although he later asserted that the idea came to him during his numerous trips between the states by ferry, work on such a project had actually begun back in 1874. Following fitful starts and the loss of twenty workmen's lives, the original corporation expired for lack of capital in 1891, leaving unfinished tunnels beneath the Hudson as memorials to great vision unsustained by adequate credit. Ten years later, McAdoo attempted to revive the project in collaboration with the well-known corporation lawyer John R. Dos Passos. Assured by the defunct corporation's organizers of their cooperation, and of the tunnels' having remained in good shape, McAdoo and Dos Passos obtained the necessary capital to renew construction by wooing some of the most powerful leaders of finance capitalism. A few of them agreed to raise his funds and serve on his board of directors if, to make the enterprise profitable, he would give full-time service as president of the corporation at a modest salary of $15,000. McAdoo would always associate public triumphs with private penury.

The Hudson Tubes made McAdoo famous as their builder and operator. Buffeted by hostility from competing ferries, rails, bankers and politicians, he persisted in creating the Hudson and Manhattan Railroad and its fourteen-story corporate headquarters in lower Manhattan and completed the Hudson Tubes in July 1907; the first train rolled under the river seven months later. At a time when "muckraking" journalists decried the exploitation of workers by greedy tycoons in pursuit of exorbitant profit, McAdoo shrewdly presented himself as an enlightened corporation leader. A popular hostility to predatory capitalists and corporations had been growing at the turn of the century. In 1910, New York City housewives demonstrated against higher meat prices; the following year saw the Triangle Shirtwaist factory fire with an enormous loss of life because employers had sacrificed safety for efficiency. For years the public had read of the railroad robber baron Cornelius Vanderbilt and his "public be damned" attitude. McAdoo proved himself an adept publicist with his "public be pleased" policy. In a magazine operated by a fellow expatriate from the South, Walter Hines Page, McAdoo wrote about how his railroad cared enough about its riders to listen to their complaints, to keep them informed of service changes, to provide them with conveniences in cars and stations, and to practice "neatness and alertness as elements of courtesy."[5]

McAdoo's genius shone when he connected railroads, finance and politics to one another. He understood that the spheres of transportation, money and government naturally overlapped. His success through these insights turned him to thinking about political ventures to remedy social problems. In contemplating the issues of his times he ineluctably depicted Wall Street's monopoly of credit as a major cause of social calamities such as the Panic of 1907. He agreed with most reformers that the pernicious role of the big corporation loomed large at the center of a public debate concerning the nature of America's political economy. The old trustbuster, Theodore Roosevelt, had returned in 1910 from a self-imposed retirement to assume a self-imposed leadership of progressive Republican forces with a restatement of his New Nationalism philosophy—an inchoate proclamation that big business fell into categories of good and evil, the former serving a public interest that perhaps only TR understood. However, the Democratic governor of New Jersey, Woodrow Wilson, at the behest of a Massachusetts lawyer, Louis D. Brandeis, retorted that any unregulated big business endangered competitive markets. A former president of Princeton University, Wilson was accustomed to academic hairsplitting without losing his audience in the argument. While he lacked TR's thundering charisma, clarity was the name of Wilson's game and his New Freedom philosophy appealed to thoughtful businessmen on the make, to entrepreneurs seeking entry to the market but lacking capital—very much as McAdoo saw himself. In Wilson, McAdoo found a self-made man of another order—an intellectually disciplined individual who spoke with a "natural eloquence [that] appealed to the enlightened self-interest and sense of justice of his audience." McAdoo saw much of himself in Wilson: Southern-born, Presbyterian, self-willed, self-possessed, moralistic, and yet passionate; they were outlanders, Corsicans in Paris, who dared to aspire to power at the seat of the empire. But how much power? Although he once wrote of

Wilson, "there is too much outside of the Presidency for an able man to do for any one to break his heart because he cannot be President," McAdoo himself lusted for the presidency with a zeal surpassed only by Wilson's.[6]

The two men met in 1908 when McAdoo visited a son at Princeton. By this time they were both public figures in different arenas, and they quickly realized that their ambitions complemented one another. McAdoo already had hired a publicist to win public acclaim for his message on the need for progressive businessmen to enter the public life of the nation—just the sort of message Wilson wanted to convey. Wilson recognized in McAdoo an experienced manager and a dedicated progressive who would attract a network of enlightened corporation leaders to his own practical idealism.

Both men valued the network of businessmen and professionals they found in the Southern Society of New York. When, on December 17, 1912, Woodrow Wilson stood before an audience of 1,200 cheering members in the ballroom of New York's Waldorf-Astoria Hotel as the first Southern-born President-elect since Zachary Taylor of Louisiana in 1849, he and the Southerners were not strangers to each other. Twice previously in recent years Wilson had visited their annual meetings as a guest speaker and he counted several of the society's members as personal friends, although not all of them aided his pursuit of the presidency.

Founded in 1885, the society for many years met annually on George Washington's birthday to honor the first Southerner to lead the nation. It did not celebrate local or lost causes. These Southerners avoided provincialism, hissed an Alabamian's ungracious denunciation of Northerners, and cheered the name of Abraham Lincoln (McAdoo once toasted Lincoln at a Southern Society gathering as the "greatest man God ever created"). "Sectionalism is dead!" Woodrow Wilson told them, and they nodded in agreement. They were American nationalists to their very core, even jingoists. Undoubtedly many of them agreed with McAdoo that Union General Sherman had done the South a favor by destroying so much of its plantation society as to compel capitalist development via promoters such as McAdoo or to inspire its young capitalists such as McAdoo to seek new lives that took them north. Annually the Southern Society gathered in a fancy New York hotel in the style of New York's high society. Dinner was ritually followed by rounds of champagne, bourbon and the singing of "The Old Folks at Home," "My Old Kentucky Home," a boisterous rendition of "Dixie" and other Southern favorites that suggested fraternity rather than nostalgia. Then, prior to adjourning for dancing with the ladies, they would toast one another and their guests, many of whom were invited Southern politicians. Finally, they would listen to speakers who frequently were New York politicians looking to the Southerners as movers and shakers in southern Manhattan.

Current events sometimes influenced the choice of speakers. Thus, in 1899, American acquisition of the Philippines occasioned an appearance of the Chinese Minister to the United States; the Southerners toasted him as "our newest and nearest neighbor on our western border." Not wanting to show partisanship among new neighbors, the following year they invited the Japanese Minister. Interestingly, the ministers displayed an ironic appreciation that what had been Europe's Far East was now America's West.

Early in his presidential quest Wilson sought to enlist the support of Thomas Fortune Ryan, corporation tycoon and political boss of Virginia's Democracy; but Ryan wanted no part of a reform-minded governor of New Jersey, even if he was Southern-born. Having alienated established Wall Street leaders, Wilson turned to wooing men on the make. McAdoo was then the president of the Southern Society of New York and through him Wilson came to know many of the transplanted Southerners who now considered him their champion. Wilson's first manager in his 1912 campaign for the presidency had been William F. McCombs, formerly of Arkansas, a temperamental lawyer whom Wilson replaced with McAdoo. Another staunch supporter was a former North Carolinian, Walter Hines Page, editor and publisher of the influential journal *World's Work*, who would become Wilson's Ambassador to the Court of St. James. Hovering then in the background as a campaign financial angel was an erstwhile South Carolinian, Bernard M. Baruch. One of McAdoo's closest associates in the society was John Skelton Williams, a Richmond banker who controlled the Seaboard Air Line Railway until he lost it to Thomas Fortune Ryan, thereby making him a formidable antagonist of Wall Street. Williams would serve under McAdoo in the Treasury. When Wilson's Cabinet first assembled in March 1913, half of its members were men born south of the Potomac.[7]

The Wilsonians were nineteenth-century men who frequently thought of public affairs in terms of time and place. Many of them were Southerners born during the Civil War. Although the Reconstruction legacy of defeat and colonial victimization at the hands of a triumphant Northern capitalism profoundly influenced their public thinking, Wilsonian Southerners were more likely to complain against the monopoly of capital in the North than its hegemony over the South. They were entrepreneurs, investors, lawyers and publishers who saw themselves as practical idealists, and disdained idealism of the socialist variety, which they regarded as sentimental or even mawkish. Like McAdoo, they treated their status as pariahs from power with pride—and wore their ambitions as badges of honor rather than shame: they eagerly anticipated the day when they would possess capital and power, both of which they would invest in their native region. "Uprooted, transplanted and urbanized provincials, they lived as exiles in New York," C. Vann Woodward has written. "Insofar as they represented the progressive South, it was the new urban-progressive group which they led instead of the agrarian wing."[8] They were clannishly Southern, but several things set these expatriates apart from most of their brethren back home. For one thing, they did not deplore the federal government, capitalism or even monopoly capitalists. Their credo celebrated businessmen with the wits to embrace social amelioration; it esteemed social idealism, individualism and opportunities to attain personal wealth and national power. Paradoxically, the Southern Society of New York made a network of parvenus into a community seeking expediently to use the collective will of the federal government to advance their individualism.

The Southerners were determined to advance one of their own to any and all national positions, including the presidency. They believed that the nation was looking to them for democratic leadership at a time when the political and social life of Northern cities like New York was increasingly polluted by immigrants and plutocrats. They exulted in 1908 when Woodrow Wilson assailed "privileged interests" and asserted the obligation of government to promote the "general interest"; they applauded Wilson's "radical doctrine" of fostering the "accommodation and readjustment" of class interests in place of class hostility; they cheered his manifesto that "what we seek is the interest of all, of the capitalists as well as those whom capital had too nearly got in its own power." The federal government in Washington was potentially a friend of both the general interest and individualism, not their adversary. Washington thus represented a community interest idealized by Southerners. Wilson's appeal for them lay in the way he articulated their generous materialism with clarity, appealed to their intellects, defined their interests. They thought of themselves as New Dealers without using that term. It is likely that Franklin Roosevelt knew many of them and admired them for their public-spirited credo.[9]

"A Statesman Grafted Upon a Promoter"

AS APPLIED TO MCADOO, the labels "heir apparent" and "crown prince" bore a double meaning: he was both the most logical Democratic successor to Wilson and, beginning in 1914, his son-in-law. At the outset of the administration McAdoo had been a widower. His first wife, Sarah Houstoun Fleming of Chattanooga, with whom in twenty-seven years of marriage he had three sons and three daughters—died suddenly in 1912 at forty-five after suffering eight years with a rheumatoid arthritis that had left her an invalid. The Secretary of the Treasury then began dating the President's youngest daughter, the vivacious Eleanor ("Nell") Randolph Wilson, despite the obstacles of her engagement to another and their twenty-six-year age difference. In the words of her biographer, "The family was not overjoyed." She broke her engagement to the other fellow because she and McAdoo were "simply *mad* over each other." They were married on May 7, 1914, in the Blue Room of the White House.[10]

Wilson's election to the presidency transformed McAdoo from campaign manager to Secretary of the Treasury. The undisputed star of a Cabinet that included the three-time Democratic party standard-bearer William Jennings Bryan as Secretary of State, McAdoo took the lead in advocating preparedness for an American role in Europe's war during 1915, and it was widely whispered that if Wilson did not seek a second term, McAdoo wanted his own shot. When America entered the war in 1917, McAdoo performed heroically in raising capital for the conduct of the war while simultaneously managing the coordination of rail transport. What Wilson really thought of his son-in-law is uncertain but, despite what others said and their personal friendship, he never acknowledged McAdoo as heir apparent or crown prince. This would be one of the tragedies of McAdoo's political life. It may have altered the history of twentieth-century America by delaying the emergence of strong leadership in Washington by more than a decade.

At the top of McAdoo's public agenda was credit reform. Following the Panic of 1907 and subsequent revelations of financial malfeasance, Wall Street sought an American central banker to stabilize the system. Woodrow Wilson had vowed to resist banking panics that left capital more concentrated and less available to those who needed it most. A National Monetary Commission studied the causes of the Panic of 1907 and predictably prescribed greater centralization of money in New York's hands. McAdoo and his fellow Democrats liked the idea of a central banker to stabilize the system, but dreaded locating it in New York. Bankers in the South and the Midwest viewed the agitation for a central banker as an Eastern extension of control via centralization of credit in the House of Morgan. The administration feared that if it left banking reform in the hands of the Senate's and the House's leading financial experts, Nelson W. Aldrich and Carter Glass, then Wall Street control would never be broken. But Secretary of the Treasury McAdoo and his cohorts shared the concerns of the country bankers and the developers on the make. His bias enraged the financiers of lower Manhattan, but they saved their greatest anger for the Federal Reserve bill that evolved over the summer of 1913.

The previous year had seen an investigation by the House Committee on Banking and Currency, led by Arsene Pujo of Louisiana, that revealed how a concentration of New York banks controlled through interlocking directorates the country's major industries—railroads, steel companies, coal mines, public utilities. Pujo found that a handful of New York banks held 341 seats on the boards of 112 corporations worth more than $22 billion. Although J. P. Morgan gave Pujo and the nation his word that character, not wealth, was his principal method of judging creditworthiness—"Because a man I do not trust could not get money from me on all the bonds in Christendom"—it did not seem right that Morgan should be America's self-appointed central banker. A consensus of country bankers demanded that the United States create a central bank outside of New York City. They wanted the proposed Federal Reserve Board of Governors to be in Washington. Moreover, Southern and Midwestern bankers feared that Wall Street might reassert its hegemony during a future administration unless the Democrats institutionalized decentralization. McAdoo agreed to a decentralized system of twelve regional banks headed by twelve executives and nominally independent of both the Treasury and the bankers. He valued the diversity of banking interests. America's central banker would control its gold and currency without destroying peculiar local interests or negating supply and demand. Banks would still fail if they pursued imprudent practices, and depositors would still risk capital with every deposit. A banker's word or reputation was still a depositor's only assurance of security. Even so, a new day in national finance had dawned. The Federal Reserve Act took monetary policy-making out of agrarian politics, allowing the United States to increasingly control world gold supplies or to finance exports to overseas markets. Wall Street, McAdoo commented, ought to like the creation of a government bank through the Federal Reserve Act of 1913; he noted a "growing comprehension on the part of some people in New York of the value of [an] altruistic government agency" managing the nation's finances. Imperial America now possessed a mechanism for imperial banking. It had taken a giant step toward state capitalism.[11]

The Federal Reserve System was a compromise combining centralization in a Federal Reserve Board with regional decentralization in twelve banks scattered in major cities around the country. The creation of the Federal Reserve System was a landmark act. It promised liberalized credit for would-be streetcar magnates in places like Knoxville, Tennessee. Without McAdoo, it would have been a very different Federal Reserve Act. To complete the triumph of liberal capitalism, Wilson made McAdoo the first chairman of the Federal Reserve System.

McAdoo was the undisputed master of the new financial system. His predecessors had routinely deposited Treasury funds in favored banks, but the McAdoo Treasury proclaimed that mobility, selectivity, stability and equity would dictate its choice of depositories. Its announcement that all federal deposits deserved dividends from recipient banks and that the days when banks enjoyed the free prestige and use of the government's coin were over, brought a Midwestern businessman's cheer for McAdoo's "blow in the solar plexus of the money monopoly!"[12] Almost anything involving national finance, such as the Federal Farm Loan Board and the War Finance Corporation, McAdoo quickly snapped up under his almost unquestioned jurisdiction. He converted government finance and central banking into personal vehicles to a bureaucratic empire. It was inevitable that by the time he left the Treasury in late 1918 he would be saluted by some pundits as the "greatest Secretary of the Treasury since Alexander Hamilton." He had brought a new deal to national finance.[13]

The history of the Wilson presidency can be divided into four phases resembling a business cycle. The first, the New Freedom, was marked by the creation of the Federal Reserve System and the adoption of the income tax; Washington's impact upon the national marketplace was indelible. The second phase was dominated by the preparedness-for-war movement, a rising trajectory that made Washington the financier of the arsenal of democracy. The third phase, mobilization for modern total war, witnessed all-out government intervention in every marketplace, domestic or foreign, requiring enormous investment by Washington in the national infrastructure, the state enterprise of war, and manipulation of civilian supply and demand. The final downward leg, readjustment of the economy, saw Washington's retreat from an ephemeral intervention as peace abrogated America's patriotic support for any sustained intervention. Congress wrote the legacy of the first phase into the statute books and the legacies of the latter three phases loomed large in history and in memories.

The Wilsonians launched modern American government in 1913 by dealing a mortal blow to the nineteenth-century wisdom that any mixture of government and enterprise would lead to socialism. Instead, they defined government as the enterprise of last resort. They too abhorred socialism or unwarranted intervention in the marketplace, but when capital was timid or crisis threatened, bold and visionary men in Washington recalled that government itself was enterprise. McAdoo frequently asserted that Treasury revenues should be used in needed projects avoided or shirked by cautious bankers. Thus began the emergence of American state enterprise.

An income tax also was indispensable for America's imperial role. Prior to progressivism the federal government principally financed itself with a high tariff, a tax on commodities entering the country. Southerners harbored an ancient animus against the tariff and sought to end it by reducing rates on protected manufactures and putting most items on the free list. Still, taxes are the price citizens pay for averting anarchy. The Democrats had sought a substitute for tariffs, and since 1909 had campaigned to make the income tax the Sixteenth Amendment to the Constitution. It was necessary, argued Representative Cordell Hull of Tennessee, because "if this nation were tomorrow plunged in a war with a great commercial country from which we now receive a large portion of our imports, our customs revenues would inevitably decline and we would be helpless to prosecute that war or any other war of great magnitude without taxing the wealth of the country in incomes." Dependence upon customs duties was impossible if belligerents disturbed international trade. By 1913 the states had adopted the amendment and Congress made the income tax a part of the government's revenues. McAdoo ever after credited Hull for promoting the most vital fiscal device in the federal government's arsenal. The income tax virtually assured the world that the United States would be a prominent role-player in international affairs. Thus, anticipation of war made the income tax a war tax. And the enterprise of war needed both the capital and the stabilizing potential of an income tax.[14]

The Wilsonians were not warmongers, but they certainly knew that business as usual had ended when Europe went to war in August 1914. As practical idealists, they abhorred war for its unnecessary, irrational and wasteful disruption of markets. War offended both their sense of humanity and their sense of efficiency. Nevertheless, this distaste for war did not cause them to ignore its use in pursuing national interests. Following the initial jolt that markets took upon hearing of the war, McAdoo and Baruch agreed that "an era of exceptional development and stable prosperity" lay ahead, especially, Baruch intoned, "if the uncertainty concerning our ability to defend our possessions were removed by the organization of an adequate defense."[15]

An "adequate defense" required a lot of money, men and materials. McAdoo made himself the administration's leading advocate of organizing that defense, and two interrelated crises dramatized that Americans wanted expanded public investment to meet a crisis. First, amidst the harvesting of the South's largest cotton crop ever in 1914, a bottleneck ensued as cotton intended for export markets found them unreachable in war. As cotton built up in warehouses, its price declined drastically. Although Southerners demanded administration action, McAdoo characteristically insisted that "the people of the South can do more for themselves which the National Government cannot do for them." Prescribing self-imposed crop restrictions long before the New Deal tried them, McAdoo organized a private pool of money to finance the warehousing of cotton; but farmers wanted no part of the debt. So he deposited additional Treasury dollars in Federal Reserve Bank branches in Richmond, Dallas and Atlanta, thereby cheapening credit to farmers, and gradually the price of cotton rose. Millions of Treasury dollars went south in 1915 to make more credit available to hard-pressed farmers, giving that region a lion's share of deposits. McAdoo's actions, along with his public denunciations of banks for failing to aid farmers, kept interest rates low. State enterprise had come to the rescue of private enterprise.[16]

The second crisis grew out of the first: in order to sell cotton abroad, ships to carry the product were needed. However, the demand for ships to transport supplies to Europe exceeded the number of bottoms available. Mighty America needed a mighty merchant marine, particularly at a time when its agricultural output was so great, the war demands for ships so insistent and the opportunity for new markets in South America and the Orient—which the war had compelled the Germans and the British to abandon—so ripe. McAdoo and other Americans decided that "any first-class power" needed both a large merchant marine and a modern navy.

According to theory, if a demand existed, shipping companies would fill it. Still, war requirements overwhelmed the marketplace and cotton exporters sought ships in vain. Additionally, America's Oriental trade saw ships siphoned off for the lucrative Atlantic runs. War created its own equilibrium and American interests dictated a need for a disequilibrium. Pointing to the "violent and arbitrary action" of a few shipping companies who now made effortlessly exorbitant profits, McAdoo sought to bust their "monopoly" with government-built ships that served the needs of American producers. "I am opposed to the government ownership of business enterprises," he maintained, "except in extraordinary circumstances where the intervention of the government is urgently demanded in the public welfare." Wilson too defended a scheme for joint government investment with private capital in American ships as preferable to outright subsidization of private shipping and insisted that he did not want a government-operated merchant marine. As expected, numerous interests assailed McAdoo's bill for "socialistic" shipping, and a congressional fight dragged on for more than a year amid escalating costs to build the government ships. The delay, McAdoo estimated, cost the government a billion dollars more for ships. But it was "the most extraordinary industrial undertaking ever attempted by the United States." The vast majority of the ships would not sail until well after the war, and by then they would cost the U.S. some $3.3 billion to give it about 22 per cent of the world's fleet and about three times as many ships as it had before the war. It would take another war for anything comparable to be attempted.[17]

In McAdoo's eyes, all economic problems stemmed from a lack of financing. Transportation needed capital. During the war a national rail system could not bring cotton or much else to America's Atlantic ports without creating chaos. For years knowledgeable critics had argued that America's rails suffered from excessive competition and regulation; in a national emergency few trains would move without coordination of regional systems or modernization of locomotives, rolling stock and rails. Why was there no coordination or maintenance? In the first instance coordination was anticompetitive and violated antitrust laws. The final word on that had been the *Northern Securities* case decision of 1904, which held that an attempt to consolidate all major Northern rails in a holding company violated the Sherman law's admonition against conspiracies in restraint of trade. In the second instance the railroads depicted themselves as aggrieved victims of democracy when regulators on the Interstate Commerce Commission asked not what the rails could do for America, but rather how many other interests would have their oxen gored by higher shipping rates that the railroads would have to charge for capital improvements. Nobody wanted to pay the price of rail modernization. Needing to be profitable without increased rates, the rails cut costs, which included wages, maintenance and capital improvements. The infrastructure of the United States began its decline for want of internal financing to upgrade services.[18]

In April 1917 the United States entered the war and the chaotic performance of the rails in succeeding months confirmed McAdoo's worst expectations. In early December he pleaded with the President to allow him to assume control of the railroads, labeling "the railroad problem as an essential part of our financial, credit and war problems." Warning Wilson that the railroads wanted "to put upon the Treasury the burden of financing the railroads" without relinquishing control to Washington, McAdoo argued that the government had to be made "an operating partner in the railroads" as a quid pro quo for financing them. Not only could Wilson resolve the railroad problem by exercising his wartime authority to take control of the rails, but its resolution "would strenghten every financial institution in this country and enlarge its ability to help finance the Government's necessities in this time." Simply put, McAdoo said that "the railroad situation is inextricably bound up with the vital and major problem of Government finance." By mid-December his tone assumed great urgency as he admonished the President that "the security markets in New York are very much demoralized" because they feared a government takeover of the roads in which "the rights of bondholders and stockholders will not be protected." McAdoo begged Wilson to do something to allay apprehensions. But whatever Wilson did had to be a comprehensive solution rather than one which left room for uncertainty.

The day after Christmas, 1917, the President announced a governmental Railroad Administration to be run by the Secretary of the Treasury while ownership remained with stockholders. Wilson had asked Brandeis to lead it, but the Supreme Court Justice deferred to an eager McAdoo. As the nation's railroad "czar," McAdoo was careful not to alienate bankers or managers. He was a builder, a planner and a romantic nationalist, but the promoter in him was no threat to private enterprise. His assistance to Southern cotton won him the gratitude of rural bankers. His espousal of government-owned shipping initially enraged shipowners, but years would pass before a glut of ships appeared—and certainly the more imaginative among the shipowners could forecast that Washington would sell its ships after the war at bargain prices and easy credit.

The railroad managers had little to fear and much to expect from McAdoo. Indeed, the Railroad Administration experience of 1918 raised questions as to whether McAdoo had sold out to management. Progressives did not complain about rail unification in the name of patriotism and efficiency, nor did they fault McAdoo for raising the wages and safety of railway labor amid wartime inflation and increased hazards. Besides, higher rail wages also justified McAdoo's instituting higher freight rates. Additionally, he set aside a half billion dollars for badly needed rail improvements. He frequently acted unilaterally, ignoring the interests of shippers on the Interstate Commerce Commission or the state commissions, thereby encouraging a widespread perception of a bias for carriers. The perception was accurate. McAdoo viewed rail problems from the standpoint of an investor. He sought not rail nationalization but standardization and cartelization to stabilize profits. The rails, McAdoo believed, needed capital and coordination, not conscription. But he knew that the approach of peace would raise embarrassing antitrust questions. To meet those thorny questions, McAdoo prepared a proposal for extending government control another five years, thereby deftly postponing the issues of permanent government ownership or control. But he did not evade responsibility for a solution. Confident that it was "impossible, after return to peace, to restore the competitive conditions of prewar days," McAdoo tried to tie the Railroad Administration's extended life to postwar planning of America's total transportation network. Seeking a comprehensive solution instead of economic nostrums that patched the old system, McAdoo brought to the somewhat parochial rails problem a breathtaking vision of a coordinated national infrastructure. But McAdoo had little faith that Congress would appreciate his vision and he resigned from his many administration portfolios before Congress debated his proposals. McAdoo could rightly lay claim to having temporarily saved the railroads—as well as having forecast a later resumption of the railroad crisis.[19]

The Great War's cost to the federal government was ten times more than that of the Civil War and more than twice that of operating the central government since its inception in 1789. As McAdoo noted in December 1917, the war's enormous consumption of capital invaded private capital markets and threatened to deprive corporations of their food for growth. Railroads, banks and utilities were especially pinched. Investment bankers led by Paul Warburg recommended that Congress create a new federal credit institution, the War Finance Corporation, which McAdoo heartily endorsed once it became evident that Wilson had decided to take control of the railroads. Congress, led by North Carolinian Furnifold Simmons, gave the WFC a half billion capitalization and Wilson made it another portfolio for McAdoo's bureaucratic empire. Congress also created a Capital Issues Committee, essentially a voluntary organization of bankers, but it and the WFC did little to supplant banks. The WFC loaned only about 60 per cent of its capital, most of that going to the credit-starved railroads. It and the Capital Issues Committee were there to augment private capital with purposeful state capital. As the war's end came in sight the administration pushed for an extension of the WFC in order to finance overseas trade. Nevertheless, both the WFC and the CIC were important because they lived in the memories of those who administered war finances and went back to Washington in the 1930s. In the words of economic historian Robert Higgs, "So pregnant with political utility was this all-purpose financial rescue mission that it was destined to be revived, not always under the same name, again and again."[20]

Although he usually impressed people with his command of public and private finance, controversy ineluctably attended McAdoo's management of the wartime economy. "We needed broad, sweeping action," observed economist Edwin Gay; "McAdoo had the imagination and the capacity to carry the job through." McAdoo himself noted that the war brought the Treasury "new problems for which there is little precedent."

Historians adopting a monetarist perspective have charged that he resolved those problems with policies and practices that were inflationary. Nobody, however, could accuse McAdoo of indifference to inflation. He initially intended to place expenditures for the war on a pay-as-you-go basis, arguing that it would be immoral to pass its cost along to future generations. That approach proved more noble than practicable. Everyone, including McAdoo, underestimated the enormous costs of U.S. participation in the conflict. He strove to keep the government's debt as much as possible within bounds, so as to minimize its effects both on future generations and on contemporary bond markets. But deficit financing was inevitable. Also, he urged upon Wilson the creation of an Allied Purchasing Mission in order to compel the Allies to pool their purchases in a manner that stabilized prices both for the American government, itself a buyer, and the American marketplace. As custodian of the national exchequer, he did not want to see rising prices which would inflate war expenditures. In sum, he was hardly the crude agrarian inflationist some historians portray.

In fact, McAdoo's relatively sophisticated policies had remarkable success in restraining prices. The greatest price rises between 1914 and 1918 occurred prior to April 1917, a time when McAdoo did not yet have the sanction of a declaration of war for imposing stringent price controls. That gave prices an enormous head of steam. When the surprisingly small increases of 1917–18 are taken into account, the anti-inflation maneuvers of McAdoo and other war managers do not appear fruitless at all. McAdoo did not attempt to hide war costs with inflation. His genius and that of his cohorts are better appreciated if it is recalled that, in the words of a historian critical of him, "World War I was the first major war in which the United States participated as a truly industrialized nation. The new industrial economy thus presented a far different situation to the Treasury than that existing in the Civil War period. It might well serve as a model or proving ground for the financing of World War II and later wars." And it did. A quarter of a century later, the war managers of World War II, skeptical at first that they had anything to learn from their predecessors, conceded that they necessarily had to review the experiences of the managers of 1917. The state capitalist planning of McAdoo and the other Wilsonian war managers anticipated the ideas of British economist John Maynard Keynes. They knew that in a full-employment economy such as war brought about, the best way to spare the public the pain of higher prices was to persuade it (coercion being unacceptable) to restrain consumption and divert discretionary dollars to savings.[21]

McAdoo and Wilson wanted to use the financial might of the Federal

Reserve System, along with America's coordinated rails and enhanced ships, to promote an American trade presence in the Far East and in Latin America. McAdoo depicted the war period as an opportunity to score American gains in overseas markets formerly controlled by warring Europeans. Wilson was not a good neighbor toward Latin America; manipulating Mexico's internal politics and sending American troops across the Rio Grande, as well as occupying and operating the Dominican Republic beginning in 1917, did not promote self-determination. Still, the Wilsonians were the most ardent Pan-Americanists Washington would see until the New Dealers or since then. McAdoo, Edward N. Hurley of the Shipping Board, and others were nationalists intent upon displacing the British and the Germans in South American markets. They were suspicious that while Washington aided an Entente victory and Europe's recovery, the wily British would conspire south of the equator to gain commercial influence in Buenos Aires and other capitals. McAdoo sought to direct American credit into South America in support of American traders, much to the pleasure of Southern editors and congressmen. He organized a cotton loan fund to finance dumping surpluses in markets to the south. He initiated a Pan American Financial Conference in Washington in 1915 to which the leaders of finance from every Latin American country were invited. The frank intent of the conference was to serve notice that while the Europeans had withdrawn from the region, American credits were available to Latin America. For that purpose, McAdoo declared that "It is nothing short of providential that the Federal Reserve system has been established." It had marshalled the credit resources of the United States for such a venture as the economic development of Latin America. Ever the comprehensive schemer, McAdoo linked credit for the Americas with the need for government-built ships to carry America's enhanced trade southward. "It is an undertaking of such magnitude that the government alone has the resources and the power to act quickly and to compass it," he argued. "We can not reasonably expect private capital in this country to engage in this essential undertaking. It is too big an undertaking at the outset for private capital." Security complemented trade in justifying an expansion of state capitalism. In 1915, when he feared that Mexico verged upon economic collapse, McAdoo wanted Washington "to finance her necessities" indirectly by offering "to pay an excessive price for lower California." In the words of a contemporary newspaper, McAdoo's promotions in Latin America amounted to a "financial Monroe Doctrine."[22]

Nobody was a more creative financier than McAdoo. He used every opportunity for expanding Washington's role in the economy. For example, when a conference with representatives of sixty-five insurance companies revealed their reluctance to insure American soldiers in the field because of their need to charge excessive premiums, McAdoo recommended that the government assume the risk to demonstrate its compassion and concern for its soldiers.[23] It was one more financial role Washington assumed in the Wilson years. The Federal Reserve System located the credit hub on Pennsylvania Avenue, and the income tax substantially enlarged federal coffers. McAdoo used those moneys to boost Southern agriculture, to create a national transportation network of modern rail and ships, and to connect these internal improvements to American commercial ambitions overseas. His vision awaited a peacetime application. Ever the promoter who identified his personal interests with those of the community, McAdoo departed Washington in late 1918 to prepare himself personally for a necessary next phase of state capitalist expansion: the quest for a McAdoo presidency.

The Two-thirds Rule

NO ONE DOUBTED McAdoo's ambition. "McAdoo," said Newton D. Baker, "had the greatest lust for power I ever saw." His resignation from his diverse posts for personal reasons shocked most of the capital; "No one suspected it," correspondent Raymond Clapper noted, and it set off a round of speculation. Were the reasons McAdoo gave for leaving Washington—poor health and financial needs—valid? After all, he enjoyed the limelight and his quitting came just when ambitious war managers were jockeying among themselves for the honor of accompanying the President to Paris for the peace negotiations. Didn't McAdoo seek, as Treasury Secretary, to serve Wilson in Paris as an economic adviser, along with Bernard Baruch of the War Industries Board, Herbert Hoover of the Food Administration, and Vance McCormick of the War Trade Board? Didn't his Cabinet post rank him ahead of everyone save Secretary of State Robert Lansing and entitle him to accompany Wilson to Paris? Lack of international experience evidently did not prevent Baruch and McCormick from attending the peace conference. McAdoo's health could have improved substantially from the vacation to which he was entitled; his financial needs in 1919 were attended to by a $15,000 retainer and a $30,000 loan from his friend Baruch—$4,075 of which he used to pay back John Skelton Williams and recover bonds held in collateral.

Charles Hamlin, a Federal Reserve banker who disliked Baruch and feared McAdoo, was inclined to suspect that something was amiss. McAdoo could have lived on loans, had he been as ambitious for the public spotlight as his reputation had it. Although Edith Bolling Wilson confided to the White House social secretary that McAdoo supposedly "worked Heaven and earth" to accompany Wilson to Paris, the president resisted out of fear of being accused of nepotism—although McAdoo's status as his son-in-law had clearly not prevented Wilson from conferring enormous additional responsibilities upon him during the war. Morgan banker Thomas Lamont thought "It would be unfair to say that Mr. McAdoo was disingenuous." Lamont heard from some close unnamed friends of McAdoo that McAdoo had discovered that Wilson wanted a third-term race in 1920, thereby compelling a postponement of his own quest. Admiral Cary Grayson, the President's physician, told Colonel Edward House, Wilson's ubiquitous adviser, that "McAdoo really resigned because he thought the President would bring [Secretary of War Newton D.] Baker over as a Peace Commissioner." Baker himself told Wilson that "Mac's resignation changes essentially the possibility of my going abroad as a member of the peace commission" because two Cabinet officers could not accompany the President to Europe if the Secretary of the Treasury resigned: might not the public wonder who was minding the store in Washington? About all these people agreed upon was that McAdoo resigned with the presidency as his primary consideration.[24]

In 1920, McAdoo represented many things besides ambition for the presidency. He identified himself as a Southerner and the war made him known as a nationalist. In economic policy he was both. Despite his residence in New York City and Washington for nearly three decades, the world identified McAdoo with the New South. And it is true that living in New York City never made a Southerner a New Yorker. The Southern Society attested to that. McAdoo may not have been as "country" as some Southern political heroes, but his appeal to the Southern economic development promoters was real and growing stronger. Conscious that the war obliged government orders to benefit the industrially mature East, McAdoo urged upon Wilson "a definite policy on the part of the Government to discourage such development in Eastern Territory, and to throw all possible additional industrial development south of the Potomac and Ohio Rivers." McAdoo benefited the South, and it followed his nationalist lead. The South identified with the Wilson administration and its powerful Southerners. The war transformed Southern attitudes, historian Dewey Grantham has written; "It intensified the process of nationalization, expanding the role of the federal government, spreading the effect of national regulations and standards, and bringing southerners more fully into the arena of national affairs." Wilsonian policies brought enormous prosperity to the cotton markets of 1917–19. Northern politicians grumbled about this favoritism to the South, and

Republicans used the bogy of "Southern sectionalism" to defeat Northern Democrats in the congressional election of 1918 at a time when the South ironically was bursting with the fervor of "Americanism."[25]

A network of Southerners such as John Skelton Williams of Virginia, Thomas B. Love of Texas and Daniel Roper of South Carolina surrounded McAdoo. Like many regionalists they viewed New York with trepidation and disdain. Because he had made too many enemies in New York, Undersecretary of the Treasury Williams would never succeed McAdoo. McAdoo drafted for his assistant secretary of the treasury a Republican neighbor of his in Yonkers and a partner of the Cravath law firm, and later a Morgan partner, Russell B. Leffingwell. Baruch could have had McAdoo's job for the asking in late 1918, but Baruch—New York City–born, South Carolina–bred, with homes and roots in both—had other plans. Congressman Carter Glass, a Virginian endorsed by Wall Street, got the nod, and Leffingwell played a guiding role until the Republicans returned in 1921.[26]

In Washington, McAdoo had his detractors. The already cited Charles Hamlin, whom McAdoo had nominated for the Federal Reserve Board, called him "brilliant . . . vindictive . . . rather treacherous, vain[,] conceited and wildly jealous of anyone other than him receiving any credit. . . . He is the most selfish man I ever met—thinking only of himself." Some Democrats blamed party losses in 1918 on McAdoo's fiscal policies. His departure from the administration did not make these people more kindly disposed to him. Wilsonians were divided over McAdoo. Baruch and Roper represented a group eager to make McAdoo president. Others were not so sure. With perhaps more hope than judgment, Frank Polk advised Gordon Auchincloss that McAdoo had lost political ground during 1919. Henry Morgenthau, Sr., an erstwhile fund-raiser for Wilson, resisted Baruch's efforts to recruit him for McAdoo's ranks. The *Nation* magazine, while conceding that nobody "ever met the test [of fund-raising for war] more brilliantly, or with greater success than Mr. McAdoo has done," argued, in a characterization not wholly amiss, that McAdoo's sense of democracy was "extremely circumscribed; he is a thorough-going imperialist, eager for a big army and navy and the mailed fist—a sort of Americanized Curzon and Milner without European experience or international vision, but with plenty of American vigor and push added. His election to the White House would be an unqualified misfortune."[27]

McAdoo was still Wilson's unnamed "heir apparent," but any effort by him to obtain the Democratic nomination for president depended upon what Wilson did. Notwithstanding the two-term tradition and Wilson's stroke while campaigning for the treaty and the League of Nations in

September 1919, the incapacitated President still had a third term very much in mind. Perhaps he considered himself the indispensable man. When, shortly after his reelection in 1916, Wilson began to discuss plans for 1920, it put some faithful Wilsonians in a quandary. Like many who were close to both Wilson and McAdoo, Baruch "would not move hand or foot" for McAdoo's nomination until he made his bid official. Although Baruch asserted as late as early 1920 that McAdoo should be the party's next nominee, he sensed that nothing was certain until Wilson officially removed himself from consideration. Loyal to both McAdoo and Wilson, Baruch feared that Wilson was such "a great Colossus that he has dwarfed us all." That left the matter up to the son-in-law who would not openly seek the nomination while Wilson said nothing—although he would not deter others from seeking the nomination for him. All Wilsonians feared any appearance of faithlessness to their stricken leader.[28]

Wilson was a man with a legacy, but not a legator. He let it be known that McAdoo was not "crown prince." On a personal level their relations were good, but points of abrasiveness were noticeable. It was not enough that McAdoo had been among the earliest Wilson backers or that he was one of the most capable and creative of the Wilsonians or that they once had a warm friendship. McAdoo was "Mac" to Wilson's "Governor" and their letters were signed "affectionately." Ostensibly the warmth remained even after McAdoo's unexpected marriage to Wilson's daughter, and McAdoo took care to fill his correspondence with personal details of a happy November-May marriage. But the war altered their official relationship. It made McAdoo more impatient with Wilson's innate caution. Also, it sharpened bureaucratic conflicts with other war managers, and Wilson seemed reluctant to favor his son-in-law even when he deserved approval. Early in the war it upset McAdoo to learn of a Treasury commitment to a program from the newspapers and he admonished Wilson, "It is not possible for me to properly conduct this Department and to deal effectively with the really prodigious problems of finance which now confront the country unless I can be informed about the larger policies that may be in contemplation and be permitted to advise whether or not the necessary moneys can be raised before final decisions are made." McAdoo successfully brought the Railroad Administration and the War Finance Corporation into existence, but his pleas for action suggested a Wilson who was either unwilling or unable to act quickly. Many of McAdoo's personnel recommendations won Wilson's enthusiastic approval, but when McAdoo strayed from the area of finance he frequently found Wilson unmoved by his suggestions. For instance, McAdoo maintained a steady but fruitless campaign through the war for a Bureau of Intelligence to augment the work of the State Department abroad, but in this he was ahead of his time.[29] How these incidents influenced McAdoo's resignation or Wilson's attitude toward the 1920 presidential campaign is not clear; what is evident is that Wilson cared little for McAdoo's ambitions.

When Homer Cummings told him in late May that most Democrats considered McAdoo and Governor James M. Cox of Ohio the front-runners for the Democratic nomination, Wilson "didn't express any preference. Indeed," Cummings carefully noted, "he said he did not want to take the position of dictating anything; he wanted it to be a free [and] open convention." He would get his wish. McAdoo's noncampaign rolled on through the spring of 1920, abetted by polls that had him leading the pack, and gossip that had him winning on the first or second ballot. Without the candidate's blessing, enthusiastic delegates for McAdoo from the South and the West looked to McAdoo's putative floor manager, Daniel Roper. The groundswell for McAdoo startled Democratic state bosses; it augured a genuine draft. Then, ten days before the convention, McAdoo suddenly announced that he did not want his name put in nomination. Roper and Baruch were so devastated that they canceled plans to attend the convention.

But even without McAdoo, the McAdoo movement had a life of its own. At the convention, supporters put his name into nomination and it drew an impromptu demonstration by delegates. The balloting for the nomination saw McAdoo break away to an early lead, followed by Attorney General A. Mitchell Palmer and Cox. After several ballots Cox surged to the lead, but McAdoo's support among Southern and Western delegates held and on the twenty-ninth ballot, McAdoo regained the lead.

Meanwhile, a disheartened Wilson exchanged coded messages with his man in San Francisco, Homer Cummings. Some Wilson adherents wanted to advance the President's name officially in the hope of stampeding the deadlocked convention, but most thought this foolhardy. With characteristic pugnaciousness Carter Glass declared "that he would rather vote for Woodrow Wilson's corpse than for any living man," but saw no chance of the convention turning to a live Wilson. Even the devoted Cummings conceded that this was so.

Increasingly the convention turned into a Cox-McAdoo contest, but under Democratic party rules a simple majority of delegates would not be enough: the nominee had to have two-thirds of the votes. The two-thirds rule began to kill the McAdoo boom of 1920. When the ballots passed forty, the Southern states gradually switched to Cox, until the forty-fourth ballot, at one-forty in the morning of the eighth day, the McAdoo delegates moved that Cox's nomination be made unanimous.

In the judgment of one historian, McAdoo "probably could have won the Democratic nomination in 1920 if he had openly fought for it." Even so, he would have lost to Harding as surely as did Cox.[30]

"I am happy in my escape," McAdoo insisted in the wake of the convention. He regretted the disappointment of his friends, but "We are all young yet, however, and the world is before us." Baruch too expressed "relief" that McAdoo had not won the nomination. It was not a Democratic year. Let the Republicans make a mess of things and the party would be ready for a return to the White House. Meanwhile McAdoo returned to New York freed from loyalty to Wilson and determined to win the 1924 nomination.[31]

Even as a private citizen, McAdoo's involvements were not without national significance. Talented men wanted to work with him, making his law practice a magnet for future policymakers. When he left the Treasury and his several other Washington posts, he went into a New York law partnership with Joseph P. Cotton and George S. Franklin. Cotton had been a consulting counsel for the Federal Reserve Board, counsel to the Emergency Fleet Corporation, and most recently of the Food Administration, where he regulated the meat-packing industry, fixing prices via control over the industry's wartime cartel-like organization, "then a novel idea involving difficult questions of law." (An assistant was the future counsel for the Agricultural Adjustment Administration, Jerome Frank.) Franklin had been counsel for the War Finance Corporation and counsel for the Treasury during the sale of successive issues of Liberty Bonds. The McAdoo, Cotton and Franklin firm dedicated itself to beating every other Wall Street rival in corporation law while keeping its lines to Washington and public service open. Along the Potomac, Hudson and Charles rivers, practicing and teaching lawyers considered it a significant merger of talents. Cotton and Franklin knew McAdoo well; more to the point, they had been themselves law partners almost since 1914, when Franklin had joined the firm of Spooner and Cotton, headed up by John C. Spooner, formerly U.S. Senator from Wisconsin. The firm established a notable record in railroad reorganizations, rescuing several roads from bankruptcy through creative financing or consolidation. Thus, McAdoo Cotton and Franklin knew much about the potential for government investment.

Consumed by political ambition, McAdoo departed early in the firm's career and headed for California and, he hoped, a springboard to the presidency. But Cotton Franklin is significant because the firm continued its Washington associations and to develop many of the policies McAdoo had been identified with before and during the war. Franklin was a Democrat and the firm's workhorse. However, Cotton Franklin's distinguished record mostly grew from the powerful personality of Joseph Cotton. Brilliant, iconoclastic and charismatic, Cotton had been a teacher of English before enrolling at the Harvard Law School where he made editor-in-chief of the *Law Review*. He was known in corporate law circles for the way he uncannily blended idealism and realism. He could have been Dean of the Law School but for the opposition of Felix Frankfurter; yet it was Frankfurter who sent Cotton and Franklin his best students to have them experience corporation law. (One of them in the late 1920s was Thomas G. Corcoran.) Tall, athletic and individualistic, in his office Cotton was apt to be found smoking a corncob pipe with his feet up on a desk, revealing rolled-down woolen socks—neither the appearance nor the demeanor of a Wall Street lawyer. He was easygoing, humorous, casual and ironic, with what Franklin called an "amazing detachment." Interestingly, the much-venerated Henry L. Stimson himself revered Cotton. When President Herbert Hoover made Stimson Secretary of State, Stimson saw to it that Cotton became Undersecretary. Cotton seemed destined for great things, but two years later, amid the crisis of the Great Depression, he died of a rare and painful disease. "You can't realize what a loss to the country Joe's death is," Stimson confided to a friend. "He is the only man who could do anything with the president." Progressives rhapsodized over Cotton's creative mind, but conceded that he had been "far from a radical" and few people could even describe him as even a liberal. He had espoused social change and social justice, believing, like Stimson, in an enlightened conservatism, an effort at amelioration in an epoch caught between hopes for a humanistic democracy and the ruthless corporation. As Cotton once told Frankfurter, industrial progress was inevitable, but it need not take socialistic forms: "It is essential, however, that it shall be an *orderly* progress; that it shall not be accompanied by any social, industrial, or political disturbance."[32]

The concluding years of the Wilson presidency and the emerging years of the Harding reign saw disturbances aplenty. Released from the ingenious devices concocted by McAdoo and other war managers, prices in 1919 soared and workers took to the streets in strikes against the abandonment of social arrangements that briefly had kept their wages in lockstep with prices. Authorities in Washington and elsewhere reacted to the apparent radicalism (some of it encouraged by anarchists and socialists) by deporting its leaders and strapping the society into a straitjacket of "Americanism" known as the Red Scare. The inflation was followed by a severe depression during 1920–21. Led by Secretary of Commerce Hoover, the Harding administration talked its way through the business cycle and back to recovery. But while the industrial scene achieved some tranquillity, discontent overflowed in American agriculture as farmers helplessly pondered their diminished markets, their diminished commodity prices, their diminished incomes and their escalating debts. And then, suddenly, in August 1923, Harding died and Calvin Coolidge assumed the presidency and a new drama involving the Teapot Dome scandal unfolded. Also, Wilson died in early 1924, and at last the world seemed safe for a McAdoo quest for the presidency.

Early in the decade McAdoo realized that the New York State Democracy was not a suitable vehicle for his ambitions. His residence there could not overcome the fact that someone like Alfred E. Smith, born and nurtured in the bosom of the New York City Tammany organization, was preferable to the Southerner McAdoo. Daniel Roper counseled McAdoo that California, where a native son was rare, would be more hospitable to a wandering, rootless Southerner. So McAdoo moved to Los Angeles in 1922 and began a law practice there with J.F.T. ("Jefty") O'Connor, who, a decade later, would be the New Deal comptroller of the currency. Their first client was oilman Edward L. Doheny.

Shortly after McAdoo launched his campaign for the presidency, Eastern newspapers revealed that Doheny was involved with the Teapot Dome crowd, making McAdoo's relatively modest retainer dirty money. Some of his most ardent supporters wanted to call it a day, but McAdoo would have none of that. Needing to make up for his self-restraint in 1920, he intended to fight. His financial angels and other McAdoo supporters were not so sure themselves, although fear of his winning without them kept them bound to McAdoo until the momentous July Democratic convention in New York's Madison Square Garden, where they confronted the supporters of the challenging Governor Smith, who jeeringly chanted, "No oil on Al." The two-thirds rule still prevailed: for nine days and ninety-five ballots neither McAdoo nor Smith could capture the nomination. Only their agreement to withdraw enabled the convention to give two-thirds of its votes to a compromise choice, John W. Davis, Wilson's Solicitor General and a Wall Street lawyer known to be unfriendly to the progressive ideas espoused by McAdoo and the Wilsonians.[33]

In the minds of the Wilsonians, McAdoo had been the one Democrat of the 1920s who linked the party's Bryanite past of the 1890s to its Wilsonian triumphs and promised to make Washington the leader in national life it had been under Wilson. However, even if McAdoo had won his party's nomination in 1924, it is doubtful that he could have defeated Harding's successor, the stolid Calvin Coolidge—though he would have run a better race than Smith or Davis. We can only imagine what sort of a president he would have been, but in all probability a

McAdoo presidency would have been neither as imperialistic as *The Nation* anticipated nor as progressive as both his friends and Wall Street imagined. McAdoo in history is often wrongly lumped with the defenders of the Ku Klux Klan, Prohibition and 100 per cent Americanism. In part, that is his own fault, since he embroidered his Southern identification in the Democratic party at a time when the South represented benighted social perspectives. Nonetheless, it is unfair to him. On certain social issues, such as the role of women, McAdoo was the most progressive politician of his time. He was an original and creative thinker, unafraid of assuming an initiative he believed correct. "Next to Roosevelt, I regarded McAdoo as the greatest humanitarian I had ever known," Daniel Roper recalled. Felix Frankfurter wanted McAdoo to be the Democratic nominee in 1924 because "he is the most sensitive mentality and the most adaptable instrument . . . for dealing with the problems that confront us." Newton Baker, who distrusted McAdoo, agreed with Frankfurter concerning McAdoo's "open and flexible mind."[34] A McAdoo presidency would have been, at the very least, interesting.

In certain respects, McAdoo is quite likely to have led a New Deal without a depression. He was always willing to find new roles for the federal government. While he was too much the jingoist to have evolved a Good Neighbor Policy, it is likely that his trade initiatives would have ushered in a new era of inter-American affairs. McAdoo's nationalism presaged New Deal domestic and foreign programs. In economic policy, for instance, McAdoo, like Roosevelt, was very much the cartelist in agriculture and industry. His relations with labor were good enough to suggest that collective bargaining was on his agenda. He might have hesitated in resorting, as did FDR, to Social Security, but he probably would have been bolder where deposit insurance was concerned. McAdoo did not really espouse government ownership (he opposed Brandeis on ownership of the railroads) except on a temporary basis, so it is unlikely that he would have conceived a Tennessee Valley Authority. Public power was peculiar to FDR. However, because McAdoo was ever the state capitalist, innovative financing was on his agenda. It is hard to imagine a Hoover-like presidency with McAdoo in the White House. "What is government for," he asked during the crisis of 1915. "Is it something in a straitjacket? . . . [Or] is it a flexible instrument in the hands of the people of this country to be used within constitutional limitations for their relief and for their benefit?"[35] In fact, McAdoo might have chosen strife with Congress while in pursuit of his agenda. For it is not that McAdoo was a social reactionary; rather, he was too much the economic liberal. A President McAdoo might have been almost as much of a New Dealer as Roosevelt with a somewhat different, activist program. More so than Al Smith, McAdoo was the principal figure in the Democratic transition from Wilson to Roosevelt.

McAdoo's story did not end in Madison Square Garden. Determined to at last make a fortune before it was too late, McAdoo borrowed at least $55,000 from Baruch for real estate ventures. Baruch carried him on account because he did not want another McAdoo quest for the Democratic nomination. When McAdoo in early 1927 sounded Baruch out on the upcoming race, the old friend advised him to "saw wood and make a living for yourself." In September McAdoo took himself out of presidential races. But he could not stay out of politics.

McAdoo was never a Roosevelt New Dealer, and he did not even support Roosevelt in 1932. Ambitious to go to the Senate from California, he went along with publisher William Randolph Hearst and a multitude of expatriate Texans in the Golden State in endorsing Speaker of the House John Nance Garner for the nomination. McAdoo had known Garner since 1913 as a tough but loyal Wilsonian. Perhaps, too, McAdoo recalled that it was FDR who gave the nominating speech for Smith for president in 1924. McAdoo and FDR had known each other for many years. In 1912 McAdoo offered FDR the collectorship of the Port of New York, which the latter declined; and at McAdoo's urging, Roosevelt had run an abortive campaign for the Senate in 1914. At the 1920 convention Roosevelt had backed his fellow New Yorker, Smith, for seven ballots before switching to McAdoo. And he was ready to support McAdoo in 1924 until Smith asked for his help. Now, perhaps, they could get together in 1932.

McAdoo went to the convention as a California leader for Garner. Three ballots for the nomination showed Roosevelt well ahead of both Smith and Garner, but well short of the two-thirds needed for the nomination. Daniel Roper sought out McAdoo to break the deadlock. Did he want to be secretary of state? Roper asked. "No," McAdoo answered firmly. "No personal advantage must accrue to me, either from our conferences or from anything that happens in this convention." He would deliver California if Garner could have the vice-presidency, and if he could be consulted on patronage in California and on the State and Treasury posts in the Cabinet. Roper delivered and so did McAdoo. The next day he rose and told the convention that he had no wish to see a deadlock like that of 1924; California switched to Roosevelt, moving him past the necessary two-thirds. Listening on the radio in New York, Roosevelt murmured, "Good old McAdoo."[36] In November, Roosevelt would be elected president and McAdoo would be senator from California.*

*In 1936 the Democratic Party abolished the two-thirds rule and thus ended a sectional veto, with profound consequences for 1948 and for civil rights.

During the Depression McAdoo spoke out for giving surplus wheat to the jobless and creating a War Industries Board organization that took "Peace" for its first name. He led an undistinguished career during the New Deal. In 1938 his political career was over and he died a couple of years later, a relic of earlier governmental initiatives that remained very relevant, even if the man himself had ceased to be so.

2.

Herbert Hoover and Bernard Baruch: State Cartelism

The War Managers on the Farm

IN THEIR OWN INDIVIDUAL WAYS, Herbert Hoover and Bernard Baruch sought to apply America's wartime experiences in peacetime. Moreover, postwar turmoil appeared to justify renewed federal intervention. The economic crises of 1919–21—rampant inflation in the first year, rampant deflation in the second—tested the organizational geniuses of 1918. While much of the war organization had been ephemeral, illegal, unconstitutional and, in the end, unpopular, it had won the war with the least possible dislocation of the economy. Were the war experiences so unique as to have no relevance to the peace? The Wilsonians thought not. The stabilization policies of war had great meaning for organizing a durably prosperous peace.

Hoover and Baruch pondered as to how to make their careers vehicles for those policies—or those policies vehicles for their careers. During 1919–21 both men remained officially aloof from the dying Wilson administration and involved themselves only with Wilson's industrial conferences of 1919, gatherings of informed and articulate leaders of industry and government to propose arrangements that satisfied rampaging unions or vindictive employers without saddling Washington with unworkable policies or their administration. The industrial conferences amounted to enlarged task forces of wise men from various economic and political sectors who deliberated on social problems and prescribed nostrums. The concept appealed greatly to both Baruch and Hoover because it lacked accountability. The conference or the committee corporately marketed its prestige to the United States Congress, the only body constitutionally empowered to enact the wise men's prescriptions. If enacted, only the regular executive departments could be held accountable for the success or failure of the proposals. That changed in 1921 when Hoover agreed to head up the Department of Commerce in Warren Harding's Cabinet, while minority party status as a Democrat in the 1920s freed Baruch of any accountability, a role that well suited his style as a free-lancing kibitzer. Hoover too had considered playing the roving wise man, believing that "a few strong men" in private life could contribute to organizing an industrial order, but Cabinet status offered him more opportunities for industrial conferences that educated business leaders as to how to achieve cooperative efficiency while advancing the fame of Herbert Hoover.

Hoover was not the first to perceive that the Commerce portfolio offered great possibilities for industrial innovation. William Redfield, Wilson's Commerce Secretary, amid the crises of early 1919, designed an Industrial Board based on the WIB model. During the war inflation crisis, administrators had endeavored to design a ceiling over prices; during the postwar crisis, Redfield feared a peacetime collapse of prices and wanted someone to fix a floor under them. At Redfield's invitation, Baruch nominated George Peek, a strong-willed farm-equipment executive who had performed brilliantly on the WIB. However, Peek soon found himself embroiled unavoidably in several controversies. The major confrontation involved the Railroad Administration's effort to lower steel rail prices at a time when Peek was organizing steelmakers to defend their high prices. President Wilson disgustedly resolved the conflict by jettisoning Peek's industrial board and permitting a free market to reign. While that was politically satisfying, the free market resolved nothing. Deflation turned to inflation, inflation turned to deflation again, and roller-coaster prices threatened Americans through the early 1920s. An energetic Commerce Secretary, with the WIB strategies as his models, could stabilize the economy.

During the war the WIB had organized trade associations to devise and administer production and price settlements. Alas, under normal peacetime conditions guild government, "a sort of medievalism of industry," as Baruch called the collusive associations, was prohibited by the Sherman Act; if they were voluntary, such associations were illegal. Then, however, a former WIB colleague suggested that if the government encouraged this associationalism by regulating and supervising them through the Commerce Department and the Federal Trade Commission, they would achieve legality. The idea appealed to Baruch: "Why couldn't it be done in peace times?" he asked. Capitalism was an inherently unstable system and if this was price-fixing, Baruch did not shrink from it. After all, didn't the Federal Reserve already fix the price of money? Baruch reasoned, "Price-fixing is like power—it is all right if it is well used; if it is not well used it is bad." For that matter, Baruch hoped to take the concept of market arbitration beyond the legislative branch and out of politics altogether. He wanted "a properly constituted arbitral authority to adjust [prices] with justice and fairness to all." He advanced a new American institution: a "Supreme Court of Commerce" to adjudicate market conflicts among interest groups and render price decisions in the name of efficiency, conservation and cooperation. Competition was a nasty game and when it became most brutal, businessmen would turn to the Supreme Court of Commerce for arbitration relief from excessive competition and overproduction that depressed prices, thereby placing the authority of wise men in judicial robes behind reductions in costs and labor. Needless to say, Baruch's Supreme Court of Commerce scheme aroused either antipathy or apathy, although he got it inserted into the Democratic platform of 1920 and won a hearing for it from the party's nominee, James M. Cox. A month after the election, he took it to Hoover.[1]

The Commerce Secretary-designate found Baruch's notion attractive only because it evaded congressional authority and detestable interest-group politics. Hoover liked to present himself as an advocate of "American individualism," which, he maintained, was reflected in *voluntary* associational activity. But Baruch's proposal reeked of European cartelism. As was his habit, Hoover opposed a peacetime WIB as an issue of great principle. Many Senate Republicans wondered why Harding had to have the arrogant Hoover in his Cabinet, their feelings about him being summarized in one Republican senator's comment, "Hoover gives most of us gooseflesh." However, "Taking into consideration the knowledge he has of things generally," Harding confided to a friend, "I believe he's the smartest 'gink' I know." Hoover seemed to confirm Harding's appraisal. He was a whirlwind of associational promotion. Trade associations proliferated from about 700 in 1919 to over 2,000 in 1929. While much of that organizational activity reflected social and technological developments and would have occurred without Hoover, it is unlikely that it would have happened in that quantity. Moreover, Hoover aggressively expanded the Commerce Department's jurisdiction to infringe upon or absorb many of the bureaus and agencies administered by State, Agriculture and Interior. Ever an able propagandist, he encouraged the press to write about his activities and hail him as "secretary of Commerce and assistant secretary of everything else."

But not everyone in Washington was in awe of Hoover. His command of information and didactic manner won him either adherents or antagonists. A number of Republican lawmakers continued to despise him. Within the Cabinet, Secretary of State Charles Evans Hughes and Hoover respected each other, Secretary of the Treasury Andrew Mellon was wary of the "too officious" Hoover, and Secretary of the Interior Albert Fall (a former New Mexico senator who would go to jail for his part in the Teapot Dome scandal) deferred to him. Others kept a rueful distance from the great engineer—except for Secretary of Agriculture Henry C. Wallace, who dared to resist Hoover's empire-building whenever Hoover crossed his path. On a personal level Wallace found Hoover "bloodless," "stuffy" and "opinionated." Hoover's problem lay in the fact that he knew no limits to "commerce" and translated his omniscience into a bureaucratic imperialism that intruded upon nearly everyone's turf. As he had demonstrated in the Food Administration, Hoover was not a team player. (McAdoo had once complained bitterly that Hoover's Food Administration publicity distracted the public at a time when the Treasury Secretary was endeavoring to launch a Liberty Loan campaign to raise vital funds.) He sought to capture or control industry-regulating agencies in other departments. Wallace died suddenly in 1924, and President Coolidge replaced him with a Hoover acolyte, William M. Jardin. Harding, who died in 1923, consulted Hoover on everything; but Coolidge valued Mellon for his economic wisdom and privately deprecated Hoover as a "wonder boy." By 1928 Coolidge peevishly commented that "that man has offered me unsolicited advice for six years, all of it bad!"[2] Nonetheless, he accepted much of it.

Presidents did not limit the range of Hoover's involvements; the Sherman antitrust law, industrial resistance and his own well-advertised philosophy of government did. Hoover took government beyond laissez-faire but proclaimed his distrust of what he called "collectivism," "statism," and "socialism." He preferred enhancing the powers of private governments, the industrial associations, to maintain WIB-initiated standardization, efficiency and conservation. While publicly extolling American individualism, he acted as the agent of classic cartelism by promoting cooperation in highly competitive industries suffering from pervasive individualism and chronically depressed prices. The press saw this activity as progressive: in an age when the public's appreciation of science and technology's role in society gained, a science of society and organization to match that of the cosmos did not seem out of the question. Hoover practiced the beau ideal of technocracy in the 1920s and extended his sway over every statistical body in Washington. He inherited the Census Bureau in the Commerce Department and broadened its dissemination of data; he pirated the Bureau of Customs Statistics from Mellon's Treasury Department in order to lay his fingers on the pulse of foreign trade; he reorganized the Bureau of Foreign and Domestic Commerce in order to expand the financing of exports; he encouraged the formation of the American Construction Council under the direction of a politician-in-limbo, Franklin D. Roosevelt, in order to stimulate home construction profitability by eliminating waste in the industry; he cajoled the bituminous coal industry into forming an organization to educate operators on modernization and regularization, although Southerners resisted his initiative out of fear that it represented an opening wedge for government control and unionization; he launched programs to expand the nascent radio and electric power industries; and he endorsed public works planning in anticipation of slack times. Hoover never seemed to rest from his frenetic industrial activity, generating seemingly endless conferences that totaled over 900 by 1924, along with 224 active committees.[3]

The industry that most resisted Hoover's cooperative blandishments was agriculture. Wartime inflation had been the farmer's undoing. Coaxed by the Food Administration to produce more crops and reap greater income at artificially higher prices, farmers succumbed to Hoover's inspired appeal to greed. In their haste to produce bumper crops, farmers had scrambled to buy increasingly expensive land and took on considerable debts to do so. Ironically they did not produce much more than usual; calamitous weather made 1917 and 1918 poor harvest years. Only the American consumer's sacrifice through conservation made it possible for Hoover to feed Europe too and even incur surpluses of some commodities. In 1919 the surviving war agencies attempted to market escalating surpluses overseas, but soon gave up in favor of lower consumer prices. The American farmer produced more commodities for world markets now glutted with them. Overall farm prices fell 41 per cent. For corn, wheat and cotton it was much worse than that. Although farm prices in the 1920s were actually 30 per cent higher on average than in prewar years, farmers could not meet their debt obligations (it is estimated that 40 per cent of all farm owners were debtors) and many faced mortgage foreclosures. While the census of 1920 revealed that for the first time in history rural Americans were a minority of the population, the agriculture-related economy still exceeded the nonagricultural sector.[4] This portended widespread economic consequences.

Certain in their minds that their purchasing power was less than that of the manufacturing sector, farmers organized to seek relief from Washington. Business cooperation ideologists such as Hoover and Baruch looked upon the farm movement as a delicious opportunity to instruct these rugged individualists of the soil in lessons concerning the evils of competition and restrictive antitrust laws. The antidote, in their view, lay in prescribing collective action for farmers alone. The Capper-Volstead Act of 1922 exempted agricultural cooperatives from antitrust prosecution, but it remained to be seen if the apostles of cooperation could overcome the farmer's inherent individualism.

Baruch's ties to South Carolina long had made him sensitive to the interests of cotton producers, and shortly after the war Baruch cozied up to farm economists, journalists and political leaders such as Senator

Arthur Capper of Kansas. In December 1920 the speculator went public with a prescription for financing large regional or national cooperatives for storage of commodities until prices were high enough in world markets to warrant sales abroad. Washington could serve as the orchestrator of farm cooperation by selling bonds to pay for warehousing and peddling commodity surpluses overseas. The scheme attracted a wide assortment of farm cooperation enthusiasts. Baruch invested in cooperative schemes to aid tobacco and cotton farmers, matching a $500,000 loan from the state of South Carolina to a corporation for cotton marketing. He ridiculed Hoover's conferences and committees, accusing the Commerce Secretary of more solicitude for bankers than farmers. Both men advocated voluntarism; but as the agrarian crisis persisted, Baruch edged closer to government intervention.

The ultimate issue was the role of the federal government. Farmer discontent with voluntarism found expression in the McNary-Haugen movement for the congressional bill of that name. Its foremost advocate was Baruch's friend, George Peek, a former International Harvester executive and now a part-owner of a farm machinery company called Moline Plow. Although tractors would have considerably improved productivity, many farmers had yet to buy one because of accumulated debts and their reluctance to take on additional debts. In a widely distributed pamphlet, *Equality for Agriculture*, Peek argued that farmers lost income when manufacturers sold in a protected domestic market while farmers vainly sought customers in competitive overseas markets. It was time for Washington to help the farmer as much as it helped manufacturers. The McNary-Haugen bills would invest Treasury funds in a commodity export corporation that purchased surpluses to be sold abroad, thereby shrinking domestic markets and stabilizing commodity prices. That the scheme agitated international markets or instigated foreign retaliation against American manufactures mattered less to these farmers. McNary-Haugenism represented a milestone for those who believed that only the federal government could adequately finance farmer cooperation. In Congress a so-called "Farm Bloc" of Midwestern and Western Republicans pushed the agricultural relief bills that bore the names of the Senator from Oregon and the Representative from Iowa without success. Baruch usually kept aloof from the movement, although he gave it "money and moral support." As 1923–26 passed and the bill did not, Baruch's support for it actually grew. He considered it more important that the government should organize farmer cooperation than to uphold the principle of voluntarism.

A major stumbling block for McNary-Haugenism was the South's traditional commitment to free trade and its fear of losing European markets. However, by late 1926 accumulating stocks of cotton in the South told farmers that foreign markets were lost anyway; in early 1927 Southern lawmakers threw in with the Farm Bloc. By that time a glut of cotton had accumulated in warehouses, and Baruch helped finance the South Carolina surplus. Cooperatives spread throughout the South, and Texas passed a law prohibiting the planting of cotton two years in succession. Southerners came to view the problem as regional and requiring federal help to achieve an "alliance of corn and cotton." Once Peek had complained bitterly that he was "unable to understand the apathy" of some of Baruch's Southern friends in the Senate, but in 1927 and 1928 they joined with the Farm Bloc in passing the McNary-Haugen bill.[5]

Not only did Hoover part company with Baruch on McNary-Haugenism, but he advised Coolidge to veto the bill in 1927 and 1928. The Commerce Secretary argued that it would disrupt international markets and that it marked undue government intervention. "In any event," Hoover had declared in 1925, "if we are to go into socialism I prefer that we do so by the front and not the back door." Importantly, however, McNary-Haugenism and Coolidge's vetoes had made farmer problems national concerns that seemed to be awaiting federal leadership.[6]

Hoover's failure to obtain effective voluntarism in agriculture was duplicated in other atomistically competitive raw material industries such as bituminous coal or lumber. His insistence that the task of raising productivity in the lumber industry belonged to Commerce's Bureau of Standards rather than Agriculture's Forest Service touched off a bureaucratic battle royal with Secretary Wallace. Wallace's death in 1924 gave Hoover a clear field in the country's forests. Confident that if he could corral an industry "so complex and difficult" to discipline as lumber he would eventually command others, Hoover struggled to organize lumber during 1924–25 into a public-private cooperative association. However, he demonstrated that it was easier to standardize lumber than to sustain improved productivity; lumber without Hoover in Commerce remained an extremely cyclical industry and proved immune to effective cooperation.

On the other hand, capital-intensive industries offered Hoover better targets for self-regulation. He organized oligopolistic cooperation in the emerging technological industries of the 1920s such as radio, movies and aviation. The latter especially attracted Hoover. Eager to rid itself of a wartime image as a weapon used by reckless adventurers, aviation wanted to demonstrate safe commercial feasibility. In 1926 the Air Commerce Act provided Hoover with an assistant secretary of commerce for aeronautics and broad control for promoting and regulating aviation. Given license to promote Hoover's cooperation strategy, aviation through its first half century practiced cartelism under a protective cloak of subsidization.[7]

The models of cooperative organization Hoover sculpted in the 1920s did not stabilize the economy when the prosperity decade collapsed in a frenzy of falling prices in 1929–30. The Great Depression further tested his cooperation ideology. If Washington involved itself in recovery, should it be as a banker or as an agent of cooperation—or both? Baruch was less enamored of voluntarism than Hoover and saw nothing wrong with the government "developing foreign trade" through joint financing with exporters. However, federal financing did not entitle Washington to federal ownership. The Transportation Act of 1920 had settled the railroad issue to Baruch's satisfaction by returning the properties to private control; Baruch had feared that wartime nationalization of the rails would lead to nationalization of their sources of energy. "If we take over the railroads," he reasoned, "we must take over coal, oil and power." During the Depression, when the rails again flirted with financial disaster, Baruch hoped for federal credits and consolidation of the rails, not their conscription. Reduced to a few companies, the rails could better attract the extensive investment they once enjoyed and required.

Interestingly, however, Baruch favored further federal funding of the Muscle Shoals hydroelectric development. The WIB had built the northern Alabama dam on the Tennessee River during the war for the purpose of generating power to extract nitrogen from the air for the manufacture of nitrates to be used in explosives and fertilizer. Its peacetime use remained in doubt although everyone knew that Wilson and the WIB also had launched the project in part to boost Southern economic development with cheap fertilizer; its desuetude violated that intent. Baruch hoped that Wilson Dam at Muscle Shoals would provide the farmer with a yardstick for the cost of fertilizer rather than government manufacture of all fertilizer. However, Baruch's ingrained ideological preference for private enterprise made Henry Ford's offer to buy and develop Wilson Dam tempting; he was leery of Senator George Norris's bill for federal development. Indeed, his sentiments then paralleled prevailing Southern sentiments, but by the end of the decade it seemed to matter less who operated Muscle Shoals than that it be operated in fairness and equity and for the economic development of the region.[8]

Baruch and Hoover agreed on associationalism in the 1920s—and why not? For men who prided themselves on their wartime leadership, associationalism amounted to a WIB and a Food Administration strategy in peacetime, except that instead of a blanket organization of industries, they targeted certain raw materials and technologically innovative industries. Yet, for all of Hoover's conferences and committees, precious little cooperation endured.[9] Commercial aviation, for instance, which Hoover called his "personal triumph," was less of a triumph of organization than of subsidization. The Air Commerce Act of 1926 emphasized organization for air carriers, but the Watres Act of 1930 effectively subsidized selected airlines through airmail contracts offered without any competitive bidding that weakened profit margins.

Congress followed a similar policy in the shipping industry. The government struggled to sell off the hundreds of vessels it had built during the war, their prices falling from $200–$250 per ton at cost to $150–$175 per ton in 1921 and only $30 per ton in 1922's depression. Without buyers at even bargain prices, the Shipping Board mothballed the ships and concentrated on regulating the lines through state-sponsored cartelism. Still, without subsidies to aid American lines against foreign-subsidized lines, American ships were almost driven from the seas. Since American enterprise was no match for European state capitalism and cartelism, Congress in 1928 authorized generous mail contracts "intended to convey a hidden subsidy," and authorized bidding procedures that favored established companies. Even then, American shipping could not compete, and the onset of the depression further shrunk credit availability for an industry already in dire need of recapitalization.[10]

Freight carriers were a major concern for Hoover, Baruch and Congress in the 1920s. Cost-conscious shippers usually drove rates lower by encouraging price competition on land, on the seas or in the air. Baruch dreamed of railroad consolidation, but Hoover wanted no part of either antitrust violations or monopolistic contradictions to his cooperative commonwealth. Consequently, anybody involved in foreign trade or air transport was more likely to obtain subsidization than consolidation; but the railroads had neither. Where ideology and self-interest prevailed, state cartelism proved elusive. Wilsonians usually deemed state capitalism unworthy of a free enterprise society, but they expediently wondered how America could maintain its leadership in credit and trade, and pursue imperial dreams in other parts of the globe, without government support via public investment and cooperative organization. Overseas considerations made it permissible to practice state capitalism in foreign trade, specifically sustaining the War Finance Corporation to finance export and agricultural markets.[11] But real markets abroad never matched the dreams of the bankers, the exporters, the farmers, the shipping lines and the politicians.

The greatest market in the world was right here. While the government played as a venture capitalist for Americans lusting for overseas markets, most hardheaded American investors, historian David M. Kennedy has written, "preferred, to a far greater degree than the British, to invest their surplus capital not in Cape Town or Cairo, but in Dallas or Detroit—or in stock market speculation. The Americans, in short, disproportionately employed their profits from the war years to fuel a spectacular expansion of the home economy, rather than extending still farther their position in the world economy." This point is important for what it asserts and what it ignores. In support of it Kennedy quotes a Chicago banker's 1921 view that "Britain's empire is abroad; America's is at home."[12] And so it was. American consumers eagerly snapped up automobiles and electrical appliances for the home and the farm.* Wherever electricity was cheap and plentiful, prosperity followed. But in rural America, especially in the South, Midwest and West, only about 10 per cent of all farms had electricity and in some states less than half of the farmers used tractors or other laborsaving machinery to add to their productivity. Investment in America built an urban infrastructure mostly in the manufacturing East and Great Lakes regions. The rural South and the rural West were noticeably excluded from investments in creature comforts.

The other America understood the importance of investment. The South developed a "business progressivism" in the 1920s that emphasized development through government investment in highways, waterways, power and education. Nor was this movement peculiarly Southern. Wherever business promoters imagined development, one could find a boosterism that gave every town, whether in New England or in Ohio, its very own Babbitt. But, because of their relative proximity to cities, the rural areas of the Northeast and the Midwest enjoyed more "progress" in the form of paved roads and electricity than vaster rural areas abroad in the South and the West (excluding a highly electrified California). There lay miles of dirt roads and the only lights at night shone from kerosene lanterns. In other words, the United States in the 1920s was two countries. One America was developed—marked by great cities, capital, manufacturing, transportation, power and agriculture; the other had few comparable cities, sparse manufacturing, transportation limited to Eastern-controlled railroads or shipping, and electricity (again, Eastern-controlled) that it considered an urban phenomenon. The underdeveloped America hungered for capital with which to make its own

*"Consumers were keen to acquire new items," writes British economic historian Peter Fearon. His colleague and sometime collaborator at the University of Leicester, Derek H. Aldcroft, observes that "a whole range of electrical appliances . . . was *foisted* upon the American public." (Emphasis added.) In either case, the spread of electricity played an important role in American economic expansion in the 1920s. Fearon, *War, Prosperity and Depression: The U.S. Economy 1917–1945* (Lawrence: University Press of Kansas, 1987) p. 53; Aldcroft, *From Versailles to Wall Street 1919–1929* (Berkeley: University of California Press, 1977), p. 197.

improvements. It is this great region—a sunbelt ranging from the Carolinas to the Cascades, containing the industries of cotton and grazing—that yearned for a new deal in state capitalism to compensate for neglect by private enterprise.

The South was not a monolith. Its drive for development varied from place to place depending upon needs and ambitions. Certainly it languished in most of the old Confederacy. In part Dixie owed its inertia to inadequate credit, excessive dependence upon cotton and tobacco, stifling diseases and climate, and an oligarchical political system that encouraged racist repression rather than improvement of the whole community. Although the South emerged from the Great War more national-minded than ever, and its farmers began to appreciate McNary-Haugenism's nationalism, few McAdoo-like promoters stepped forward to guide its destinies. Its political leadership sought improvements, but usually dumped their cost upon the very poor who hoped to benefit by them. Seldom did Southerners look to Washington for funds to fulfill their visions, lest the federal government attach intolerable social strings to its largesse or development attract undesirable elements, as was the case in oil-rich Louisiana and Texas. Instead, conservative Southerners stressed a tradition of voluntarism, demonstrating that self-help among the poor is self-limiting.[13]

No such inhibitions restrained Texas and the West. Twentieth-century Texas was a hotbed of promoters eager to grasp business opportunities through big projects paid for by somebody other than themselves. East Texas was especially fertile for hustlers, from Dallas which had benefited from Washington's 1913–14 decision to locate a Federal Reserve District bank there, south through the poor but ambitious hill country of central Texas abutting Austin and San Antonio to the Gulf, Texans put aside any ideology in favor of using capital—even Uncle Sam's. Houston was a case in point. Seeking to make it the "Chicago of the South," Houston business leaders in the previous century had dredged Buffalo Bayou to fashion a ship channel; in 1902 and 1910 Houston obtained 2.25 million federal dollars for deepening the channel. Houston then promoted itself as a world port for East Texas cotton. When oil company executives wanted to bring their tankers into Houston's port, further dredging with U.S. dollars was needed. By 1930 Houston ranked fourth among U.S. ports in total export tonnage.[14] The Houston success story whetted the appetites of other Texans for their share of U.S. dollars for development.

In the West, entrepreneurs linked the needs for water and energy. Initially Pacific Coast developers and farmers from California's Imperial Valley to Washington State's Inland Empire sought federal dollars for irrigation of arid lands to make farming profitable in the West. Los Angeles's leaders envisioned a major metropolis. Considerable private and public investments in aqueducts for irrigation systems between 1900 and 1920 yielded temporary successes and lasting indebtedness. In the 1920s Westerners attached their quest for water to that for power and built a consensus of interests for federal public works development. In particular, they targeted two great rivers for harnessing their volume for irrigation and energy: the Colorado and the Columbia. Such enormous projects could be funded only by Washington. Without state capitalism they could not even be considered. Without state capitalism the growth of two major cities wisely committed to public power, Seattle and Los Angeles, would not happen.[15]

The ambitions of Texans and Californians interacted with the schemes and ideology of Hoover and Baruch. As Secretary of Commerce and President, Hoover was more directly involved than Baruch, but as a committed Democrat Baruch was more likely to be a state capitalist partisan than Hoover. Party made a difference. Prehensile Texans had played major roles in the Wilson administration. Republican parsimony in the 1920s stifled most Western efforts to pick the federal purse. Although Hoover endorsed California efforts to tame the Colorado, he deemed the quest in the Northwest to dam the Columbia as fiscally irresponsible. Baruch's involvements with Western Democrats made him sympathetic to their cause: voluntarism ended where the need for development began. Moreover, as a Southerner at heart, Baruch could see that the charms of federal public works appealed to his kinsmen. A putative coalition was emerging in the Democratic party among its Southern and Western wings behind the issue of public works. In the 1920s the rationale for federal public works was economic development; in a depression it would have the added force of jobs for recovery. When that happened, the real tragedy of Herbert Hoover in politics would unfold.[16]

President Hoover

HOOVER BUILT HIS REPUTATION on crises, but he was not equal to the great depression that erupted in the first year of his presidency. It was not a wholly unexpected tragedy. Many colleagues in public life saw character weaknesses in him that made them wonder how he would respond to great adversity.

His story is one of mobility and hard work. Born to a poor Quaker family in rural Iowa in 1874, Hoover was orphaned at nine and raised by relatives in Oregon. He graduated from Stanford University in 1895 with a degree in geology amid the worst economic depression to precede his presidency. He worked for a while as a common miner in Nevada before securing an engineering job with a San Francisco firm. Two years after Stanford a London-based engineering firm hired him for overseas assignments that took him to Australia and China. A few years later he was put in charge of operations in China. Biographers argue how much his Quaker background influenced his thought and his life, but nobody can dispute his indefatigable energy, attention to detail and lust for leadership. By 1907 Hoover owned 30 per cent of the engineering firm, selling it the following year to make himself one of the country's wealthiest engineers and one of its best-known. For the next several years he operated as a consultant for mining firms needing capital and mining expertise: like McAdoo and Baruch, Hoover was a promoter concerned with credit markets; like McAdoo, he had learned about banking from the perspective of an entrepeneur. For a while he also acted as a London-based publicist for San Francisco's Panama-Pacific Exposition. By 1914 the Great Engineer had served his promotional apprenticeship and was prepared for life in the public spotlight.

The eruption of war in 1914 found Hoover in London, where he was one of the most visible Americans not working for Washington. When the American Consul General asked Hoover to help those Americans stranded abroad and cut off from funds, Hoover performed the task with dispatch that earned him the gratitude of the Ambassador and brought him to the attention of Woodrow Wilson. Learning that German-occupied Brussels verged on starvation, Hoover created a private relief organization that worked with both London and Washington. Thus began an effort that transformed the Great Engineer into the Great Humanitarian. In May 1917, Wilson summoned Hoover to Washington to organize America's food markets and save them from impending chaos.

The Food Administration created incentives for expanded production and exhorted consumers to limit domestic consumption of agricultural commodities. Posters pleaded for patriotic conservation of food commodities, reminding Americans that "Food Will Win The War" or just beseeching them to "Practice the Patriotism of the Lean Garbage Pail." The Food Administration admonished American families to practice "Wheatless" and "Meatless" days and to use recipes that employed substitutes. The result was a bland diet that led to widespread jokes about "Hooverized" food. "The nation was being drugged by Hooverism," grumbled one Washington attorney who complained about the superficiality of such voluntarism. Nevertheless, Hoover's propaganda effectively stressed the power of consumer cooperation, even if the persuasion of profits ruled production. Promised high prices by the government, farmers increased acreages and bought tractors on credit to take advantage of Hoover's price-fixing schemes, incurring debts that led to a major agrarian disaster. The Food Administration also organized processors to establish their own rules for storage and distribution, effectively skirting the antitrust laws that prohibited cartel agreements. The outpouring of food and the restraint of its domestic consumption were tributes to the organizational genius of Herbert Hoover. He had masterminded a gigantic food cartel.

A moral of the war drawn by an informed public was that government was too important to be left to politicians. Many of the politicians seemed to agree, especially where control of the executive branch was concerned. Both parties sought out Hoover the technocrat, whatever his failings of personality, as a budding political star because he was a savant in economics and bureaucracy and, as of early 1920, had not declared a party affiliation. Democrats, anxious for a dynamic successor to their fallen leader, paid attention when Hoover invoked Wilsonian phrases. Hoover "seems to understand W.W." and his "method of expression reminds you of Wilson," observed Homer Cummings. In truth the clarity of Wilson's words was absent from Hoover's turgid speeches, for Hoover was a wretched writer of awfully awkward sentences. What impressed Cummings and others was that he frequently invoked Wilson's pet phrase "equality of opportunity" in discussions on political economy. As Hoover told a group of engineers in February 1920, "If we would have [the economy] function properly, we must promote the *equality of opportunity* which allows every member of this community to attain that position to which his abilities and character entitle him. To me, therefore, the test of the rightness of any measure is that it shall maintain and build up this *equality of opportunity*, that it shall preserve the initiative of the whole population." Heartened by such expression, the Democrats eagerly sounded out Hoover as to his political leanings. For a time Hoover was noncommital before he finally admitted that he was Republican. That was fortuitous: on the one hand it left the Democratic party in the hands of ardent Wilsonians; on the other it opened the GOP to Wilsonian notions of governmental strategies in the marketplace. Hoover emerged as the spear carrier of Wilsonianism in Republican Washington.

"The nineteen-twenties saw a new breed of economist-politician," writes Robert Skidelsky. Indeed, the usual narrative of American politics in the Jazz Age dwells too much upon the social issues of religion, prohibition and the role of the Ku Klux Klan. Admittedly, the issues were real and writing about them gives the decade much of its readability—also its frivolous superficiality. Economic order through a cartel system or state enterprise remained very much on the minds of politicians endeavoring to integrate into the political framework technological developments that had been retarded and accelerated by the war. That required a new politician with considerable insight based upon both experience and a conceptual synthesis that could win consensus in peacetime. Capitalism was evolving swiftly in the industrial heartland and from the underdeveloped reaches of the American South and West the loud demands for federally assisted development could be heard all the way to Washington. Hoover and Baruch were those new politicians that Southerners and Westerners looked to. In the words of historian Robert Wiebe, "These men started with the scheme they saw about them. They had no vested interest in its origins. Fresh to the task, they longed for an opportunity to build, to integrate, to supervise a much improved version of what they could watch operating directly at hand. The future for a time would belong to them."[17]

Hoover's election to the presidency in 1928 was the triumph of the economist-politician-technocrat. Hoover himself believed that and disdained the ordinary political demagogues in Congress. Few people could look past his arrogance. To his admirers it was an assuring self-confidence. On the other hand, nonadmirers who observed him under pressure before his presidency often wondered how he would handle adversity that persisted. Crisis or not, everyone anticipated from Hoover an active presidency; contrary to popular perceptions, they were not disappointed. It was Hoover's strategy in dealing with the crisis that disappointed many Americans: He employed the voluntary cooperation of private organizations and local governments in administering relief and recovery. Despite unremitting bank failures and rising unemployment, he never conceded that the depression's tenacity suggested the failure of voluntarism. To pleas that he abandon voluntarism for federal programs, he designated legislation as the last resort and resisted Congress until it virtually imposed itself upon him more than two years after the depression erupted. His reluctant consent to legislative activity departed from custom and inadvertently launched the New Deal.

But the depression crisis was unlike the crisis of war which first brought Hoover to public attention. Organizing the public amid prosperity and patriotism was simpler than amid the fear of chaos and failure. Organization of the public amid the depression of 1920–21 had been nearly nonexistent; a quick and sustained manufacturing recovery during 1922–23 seemed to demonstrate the wisdom of restraining federal intervention while exhorting cooperation for relief and confidence for recovery. Unemployment had increased sharply in 1921 to 11.7 percent of the civilian labor force, only to dramatically decline to 2.4 percent two years later.[18] Although the unemployment conference of 1921 had recommended planning of a reservoir of public works to stimulate the economy in future downturns, little actual planning was done by Hoover or Congress. Hoover probably intended the planning to be done outside of Washington by state and local governments. He also sought to educate industrial leaders to the fact that instinctive cost-cutting in a decline is counterproductive. He complimented himself when he lauded the public consciousness of America's economic leadership and assumed that if a depression occurred again, everyone knew his role—including Hoover.

Hoover in the White House was not much different from the ubiquitous bureaucrat in the Department of Commerce; only now he had a license for intervention. Confidence, conferences and initiatives abounded. The initiative he most regretted later was calling Congress into special session in 1929 to deal with his agricultural and tariff proposals. Although Congress did his bidding and created a Federal Farm Board, the board failed miserably to subsidize cooperation among farmers.[19] And the tariff debate lasted into 1930 before the wrangling lawmakers passed the Hawley-Smoot bill in June 1930. The bill imposed the highest tariffs on record, amounting to an economic declaration of war amid a depression. Moreover, Hoover's effort to put Hawley-Smoot in the best light possible was a glaring inconsistency for the man who had lambasted agricultural dumping for its disruption of international markets. Too, Congress was affronted, and denied his bid to allow the President to adjust rates unilaterally as much as 50 percent. Given Hoover's propensity for conflict with Congress, his presidency might have been a failure even without the Depression.

Hoover was not a do-nothing president, but he also was not a New Deal president. He did not abandon the system he had idealized through the 1920s. More conferences with "economic leaders" followed the crash. More voluntary organizations for relief were inaugurated by the White House. If he had not been busy being president he might have headed a relief organization himself. Who else knew more about crisis relief than Hoover? His presidential committees diligently documented the extent and plight of the unemployed while exhorting and coordinating the state, local and private agencies that financed and administered relief. Although there was never enough relief, the President adamantly declaimed against any federal financing and administration of relief, lest they deprive individuals of initiative while unbalancing the federal budget and lowering public confidence in private investment. He resisted any suggestion, let alone legislation, to spend federal dollars for relief or recovery through public works construction. That, he hotly insisted, led to "pork barrel" spending, and its federal administration led to "collectivism." He seemed almost to delight in thwarting or ridiculing anyone's scheme to ameliorate hardship in the depression. As unemployment grew in early 1931 he rejected pleas for a special session of Congress to deliberate upon a depression agenda. He had once made the mistake of calling a special session and was not about to repeat it.

He did all that one could or should expect him to do, Hoover maintained. The circumstances required patience and confidence. To exhibit his own confidence in early 1930 he forecast that in sixty days the depression would be but a memory. But 1930 was not 1921 and the depression did not go away. Still, all agreed that it was most important to sustain a positive psychology. Economies require ritualistic expressions of faith, even when their repetition raises questions that weaken confidence. Prosperity was not just around the corner, but Hoover's confidence made its elusiveness somebody else's responsibility. That somebody was usually Congress, especially after the Republicans narrowly lost control of the House of Representatives and confronted a deadlocked Senate after 1930. Democratic victories in the congressional election were a rebuke to Hoover. Having lost the nation's political confidence, Hoover decided to regain it in time for the election of 1932 by striving to balance the federal budget or laying any failure to do so at Congress's doorstep. The issue of a balanced budget was disingenuous. While Hoover labeled relief advocates as despoilers of confidence and the federal budget, his Assistant Secretary of the Treasury privately conceded that "There seems to be no practical likelihood of a program going further toward balancing the budget."[20]

Congress clamored for relief of the unemployed. Among the leaders for public works relief were Senator Robert F. Wagner of New York and the assistant Republican leader, Wesley L. Jones of Washington State, two men who differed sharply on their approaches to public works. Wagner was a welfare state advocate who distinguished himself from other politicians by cultivating strong ties to unions. He wanted to put the jobless to work, regardless of whether it was done with federal loans or grants; Wagner was not possessed by ideology. Neither was Jones. On Capitol Hill since the turn of the century, Jones was obsessed with the economic development of Washington State, which he hoped to accomplish mostly by obtaining federal moneys for reclamation, irrigation and hydroelectric projects for his constituents. Plain and platitudinous, he chaired the Senate Appropriations Committee in 1931–32, which gave him a strong claim upon such projects. Another senator freshly elected in 1930, Colorado Democrat Edward P. Costigan, bridged any gap between Wagner and Jones. A former Bull Moose Republican, Costigan mixed political and economic strains with his unusual passion for social justice and his normal Western passion for development. Costigan joined with Wagner in 1931–32 to push public works bills that satisfied both Wagner's quest for jobless relief and Jones's perpetual pursuit of federal dollars for development.[21]

This trio and their friends gave Hoover fits because Senate Republicans to whom he looked to resist the public works advocates disliked him personally and politically. Many Republican conservatives supported him only because he antagonized those Western Republicans whom the tory from New Hampshire, George H. Moses, had dubbed "Sons of the Wild Jackass." Westerners were convinced that the party of Lincoln's frontier had become captive to the party of McKinley's Eastern big-business interests, who were intent upon keeping the West primitive. They loved Theodore Roosevelt, with his Western affectations and his occasional thundering against "malefactors of great wealth." Perhaps the GOP would yet spread the wealth of the East. However, in 1930 it had been over a decade since TR had ridden off into the sunset, and Costigan's defection to the Democracy seemed to suggest that it was time for Western Republicans to consider their debt to the party of free soil had been paid in full. Free farmers could not work land so arid that it needed federal engineers to make irrigation. Old-timers such as Hiram Johnson of California and George W. Norris of Nebraska ignored party accountability for two decades while fighting for federal support of public power in the West and the South. In the Northwest the drive for public power bordered upon a secular religion, regardless of party. These Republicans wanted a larger role for Washington in the economy at a time when the nominal leader of their party advocated an associationalism that excluded Washington's direct participation.[22]

Suggestions of a party realignment were out of the question, because congressional Democrats tended to be more cautious than the Sons of the Wild Jackass. Their traditionally Southern leadership was ambivalent toward federal activism. House Democrats had staunchly supported the progressive income tax in the Wilson years, and for a while they fought Andrew Mellon's rebates and lowered tax rates in the 1920s; then they turned to "out-Melloning" the Secretary of the Treasury. Conservatism ruled Democrats late in the 1920s. Representative Oscar Underwood of Alabama sponsored a bill for leasing Muscle Shoals to private interests and Joseph T. Robinson of Arkansas, the Senate's Democratic Leader, fought against its federal development.

Federal aid to cotton farmers was another matter. Western Democrats also tended to follow their own regional interests. Key Pittman of Nevada was a ranking Democrat who forgot fiscal conservatism when Nevada sought federal land reclamation projects. Gradually a Southern and Western alliance for rural development formed in quest of a new deal from the federal government. Certainly it was no more "parochial" than those Eastern interests that opposed it.[23]

Surprisingly, perhaps, the Depression and Democratic victories in 1930 congressional races made conservative Democrats even more conservative. Instead of attacking Hoover in 1931 for indifference to the crisis, they tacitly approved his refusal to call a special session. They preferred to lie low and hope that insurgent Republicans would embarrass Hoover. Here the influence of Baruch showed. Rather than offering alternatives to Hoover's voluntaristic anti-Depression policy, Baruch cautioned the Democratic leadership to "be careful not to get in a position where the Republicans will be able to unload this onus on us." They should not "try to rectify too many things by laws now." Confident that Hoover would self-destruct, Baruch urged that Democrats pass Hoover's program and "be careful not to tie him up. His own people will do that." Another Democrat, Wall Street's Norman Davis, agreed and went further: "We must stop using the Government as an instrument for making money for any classes. Government should keep out of business and business should also keep out of Government."[24]

The centerpiece of Hoover's program was a proposal for a Reconstruction Finance Corporation. This had been prompted when an international crisis of credit threatened in mid-1931 after the collapse of a major bank in Vienna containing a substantial quantity of French funds. American creditors trembled at the prospect of European debts that would not be paid. Hoover proclaimed a moratorium on interest payments to the Treasury, which briefly stabilized confidence. But nowhere was the worldwide depression as extensive as in the United States, and it was here that the credit squeeze most tested the solvency of banks. Moreover, as in December 1917, the railroads' desperate need for capital again aggravated a financial crisis and led economist Jacob Viner to anticipate that Washington again would "promote investment through instrumentalities such as the War Finance Corporation," but he doubted that any federal intervention in the economy would bring a positive turn. To head off congressional action, Hoover initiated conferences with leading bankers. Ever the associationist, he organized a private credit pool of a half billion dollars for the salvation of big banks tottering on the brink of insolvency. However, as Viner anticipated, the bankers had something else in mind. Recalling the war emergency and how McAdoo's War Finance Corporation had supplemented their funds with those from the U.S. Treasury, the bankers wanted a return to the state capitalism practiced then.

Desperate to keep voluntary cooperation in banking alive, Hoover compromised; in return for bankers' organizing a private National Credit

Corporation, he decided in October to ask Congress for the Reconstruction Finance Corporation. (In September, knowing that the Bank of Pittsburgh was failing, Hoover personally attempted to create a local pool to save it: Secretary of the Treasury Andrew Mellon, himself a Pittsburgh banker, refused to contribute; bankers believed that their first obligation was to shareholders, not the community or some mythical ideal such as cooperation.) In January Congress created the RFC with a capitalization of a half billion dollars and power to give loans to deserving banks and other credit institutions, a definition which included the credit-hungry railroads. It evoked an ideological outcry from even those who approved of this "relief for bankers." "I have been called a socialist, a bolshevik, a communist," Senator George Norris taunted, "but in my wildest flights of imagination I never thought of such a thing as putting the Government into business as far as this bill would put it in." A Georgia congressman called it a "most decided step toward communism," and the St. Louis *Post-Dispatch* wondered if the United States would expediently embrace "state capitalism."[25]

The RFC's initial months were sorrowful. Hoover asked the Chairman of the Federal Reserve Board, Eugene Meyer, to be chairman of the RFC, a natural choice since Meyer had headed the War Finance Corporation in the 1920s. For president of the corporation Hoover selected Charles Dawes, a Chicago banker and former vice-president of the United States under Coolidge. To acknowledge Democratic cooperation in creating the RFC, two members of the board had to be Democrats: Senate Democratic Leader Joe Robinson and Speaker of the House John Nance Garner were asked to give Hoover a name each; Robinson chose Arkansas banker-entrepreneur Harvey C. Couch, and Garner tapped his fellow Texan Jesse H. Jones. While the private National Credit Corporation remained virtually dormant, the RFC cautiously loaned its largesse.

The RFC boosted public confidence temporarily, but two factors undermined it. In June, Dawes announced his resignation as president to return to his Chicago bank; a few weeks later the RFC, under regulations imposed by Congress and opposed by Hoover, revealed that Dawes's bank had borrowed $90 million from the RFC. The Dawes loan confirmed popular accusations that the RFC was "trickle-down relief" for the rich. Even in Chicago's financial district, LaSalle Street, cynical lawyers chortled that RFC stood for "Relief For Charlie."[26] The other major factor was the depression's persistence despite more than $1 billion appropriated by the Congress in loans to 4,000 banks, railroads, credit unions and mortgage loan companies.

In those days before the creation of the Federal Deposit Insurance

Corporation, bankers in the United States shared their risks with depositors. In the 1920s alone some 4,500 banks went out of business, although the aggregate level of deposits was unchanged. In 1926, 924 banks had failed. No wonder so many Americans kept their money in mattresses; bank facades were sturdier than their lending practices. Risk was especially great in the rural South, Midwest and West, where nearly 90 percent of all bank failures occurred during the prosperity decade. Bank and farmer indebtedness went hand in hand. Average annual net farm income declined between 1929 and 1932 from $945 to $304. Debt-laden farmers were crushed by the depression. Equally desperate banks repossessed almost one million farms between 1930 and 1934. Big banks welcomed the RFC, but it was too little and too late. Many of them exhausted their RFC loans trying to liquidate their debts (which is what Dawes did); or, arguing that the depression had severly curtailed loan demand, they bought government securities.[27] Either way did not promote economic recovery. And farmers must have wished they had had an RFC to help them liquidate their debts.

Certain that he had met the banking crisis, Hoover now concentrated on balancing the federal budget with additional taxes. Forecasting revenues is usually imprecise, and the uncertainty of business in the depression made it more so; twice already the Hoover administration had fallen short of its revenue targets. With obligations of relief to bankers and others increasing, Hoover decided to make a political stand against additional federal spending and for broadened taxation. The administration pushed for a "manufacturers sales tax" of 2.25 percent to supplement income and customs duties. Democratic leaders, afraid that in a presidential election year Hoover would accuse them of shaking business confidence by not balancing the budget (thereby compelling Washington to make up the deficit by selling government bonds competitive with corporate bonds), decided to go along with the sales tax. Already the Democrats had given Hoover the RFC and a banking bill, making him confident that he could administer "a good licking" to them in November. He even got the Democratic leadership in the House Ways and Means Committee to initiate the tax itself. Speaker Garner, a candidate for his party's nomination for president, was intent upon keeping the onus of the depression off his back. But he miscalculated. Southern and Western Democrats, in alliance with a handful of maverick Republicans, astounded Washington by rebelling against the bipartisan leadership to defeat the sales tax on April Fools' Day, 1932.

What caused such an upset? For one thing, the sales tax was obviously regressive because it taxed the poor on necessaries at the same rate it taxed the rich. Hoover proposed loans to rich bankers and taxes for the poor, an offense to the sensibilities of Democrats who still championed the progressivism of the New Freedom. Ironically, accepting the administration's challenge to balance the budget, Democrats increased income tax rates to such an extent that not even New Deal tax laws would produce such progressive income rates. Progressivism aside, however, regional factors played a role in the sales tax rebellion. Many Westerners were unhappy about having to pay more to a government that stubbornly insisted upon spending less for public works projects to enhance their region's commercial development. On the other hand, Southerners objected to the way the sales tax undermined federalism by innovating a levy that their state governments coveted. Such arguments were not merely states' rights rhetoric. Although few Southern states in 1932 had sales taxes, most of the old Confederacy was desperate for revenues, partly driven by Hoover's dictum that relief and recovery were state responsibilities. State leaders hoped that their revenue salvation would be a state sales tax. A major leader of the rebellion, House Ways and Means Chairman Robert L. ("Muley Bob") Doughton, was among those sensitive to these implications because his brother was a North Carolina state official. They were fearful that their constituents would not tolerate state sales levies on top of a new federal sales levy. Additionally, although most state constitutions prohibited a deficit, a federal deficit, especially in an emergency, was not unheard of.

It was a hard time for politicians. Sales taxes, while easy to collect, reduced consumption and hence the potential revenues that could be collected. Increased income levies were more virtuous because they soaked the rich, but they diminished investment in an already investment-starved economy. Either way, the drive to balance the federal budget in 1932 by taxing consumption or incomes proved to be deflationary in an already deflated economy. Whether to provide work relief, to recover prosperity, or to invest in developing commerce in the rural South and West, politicians would have to tolerate intended or planned federal deficits.[28]

The rebellious coalition wanted to spend the additional revenues from higher income taxes on work relief. Hoover would not hear of it. However, realizing that the conservative coalition upon which he depended for support was in disarray, he decided that by demonstrating courage of economic principle and resisting Democratic spending he might gain politically for reelection in November. His program of voluntary cooperation for job relief was an abysmal failure as state after state, city after city, and agency after agency reported that the demand for succor swelled even as their coffers registered empty. Unemployment was escalating. Standing at 3.2 per cent of the civilian work force in 1929, it rose to 8.7

per cent the following year and soared to 24.9 per cent by 1932. Even these figures tell an incomplete story, because some employers did not fire workers but simply spread the work over a three- or four-day week. Thus, an employed worker could be one on a severely curtailed income.

Breadlines and soup kitchens best testified to the numbers of needy in Depression America. In response to documented need, in June Congress passed a large public works bill, which Hoover vetoed. Arguing that processes of recovery were already in motion and that public works spending would be inflationary after the eighteen months that construction took to impact upon the economy, Hoover assailed this particular bill as "pork barrel" because it lacked projects he considered "reproductive" by encouraging additional investment and commerce, or "self-liquidating" by paying for the projects with tolls or fees. Congress backtracked to satisfy Hoover and pared the bill down. It also mollified the President by stipulating that the public works funds would be distributed by the RFC as loans (at rates that approached the usurious) to state and local governments that would administer the projects. Finally, the loans had strings attached. Hoover mandated that they be repaid by the state and local governments with newly raised, regressive taxes such as user or excise levies. Thus, the working poor would subsidize the jobless poor. And while regressive taxes provided collateral for public works loans to state and local governments, the RFC gave loans to bankers without any guarantees that banking activity would be reproductive instead of self-liquidating.[29] The RFC under Hoover, its critics correctly charged, was a bailout for the rich. The now-familiar accusation of Hoover's insensitivity to the poor was not election-year hyperbole.

"He is living on an island that is getting smaller each day," a friend of the President commented. A morose man, Hoover the crisis manager was not the picture of equanimity in adverse times. He actually tended to be apocalyptic in mood and exhibited signs of depression that depressed others. On May 31 his congressional liaison found him sitting somberly at his desk, "extreme gravity pervading the atmosphere. . . . no ray of light in his eye." The dollar had plunged abroad, and Hoover anticipated it would be followed by yet another Wall Street panic. In answer to an inquiry the President, with "eyes that were almost dead," responded in a subdued voice, "There will be a collapse today." He usually anticipated the worst. Politically he had not lost his will to fight; he had successfully manipulated Congress for most of the year, and now he sat hoping that the Democratic convention would nominate Governor Franklin D. Roosevelt of New York; "Well, I suppose of all those mentioned he will be the easiest one to beat," Hoover sighed. He did not say why he thought that, although much of his conversation focused on two things: Roosevelt's leg paralysis from polio, which Hoover had noticed during a recent visit of governors at the White House, and developing scandals in New York's Tammany Hall. As in his Depression strategy, Hoover erred greatly in plotting his reelection. Other Democratic contenders had little to offer; in the midst of the Depression Al Smith wanted to make Rum and Romanism the issues of 1932, Garner was unknown in most of the country, and Newton Baker, Hoover's personal favorite, was favored by the elites.[30]

Nothing was said in the White House of Roosevelt's pledge in his speech accepting the Democratic party's nomination to give the American people a New Deal. Roosevelt sympathized with Southerners and Westerners who rated relief for agriculture and federal aid for commercial development as high priorities. Even before the depression struck, many Democrats agreed with South Carolina's James Byrnes that FDR "offered the only hope to again get control of the government." Roosevelt's endorsement of public power cheered Montana Senator Burton Wheeler. Senator Cordell Hull of Tennessee took the lead in working for Roosevelt on Capitol Hill. A multitude of Democratic politicians had trekked to Warm Springs, Georgia, where Roosevelt vacationed and treated his paralyzed legs to the soothing waters. Westerners saw Roosevelt as a winner, and "His Southern support, in fact, had as yet little relation to the Depression." Even Western Republicans quietly kept their lines to Albany open as they formed an opposition to Hoover in the GOP. Roosevelt, they believed, was "the only hope for progressivism." For the time being, his "progressivism" simply represented federal activism in promoting the regional commercial development that they had sought for most of this century.[31]

Could a Wall Streeter endorse Roosevelt? Fearful that Roosevelt might be too identified with Bryanites and their losing campaigns, Norman Davis pleaded with Hull not to "let Franklin Roosevelt try to go too far to win the support of the Progressives of the West." But in August, Roosevelt invited Davis to his Hyde Park home, where they had a long conversation. "Frankly and confidentially," Davis later told Walter Lippmann, "I was agreeably impressed by the soundness of his views on some of the most important questions." In October, Russell Leffingwell, like Davis of 23 Wall Street (J. P. Morgan & Co.), decided that he had had enough of Hoover's "lack of economic and social convictions [and] nervous irritability and political ineptitude." Roosevelt, on the other hand, impressed Leffingwell with his "cheerful friendliness and willingness to hope for the best and try to please everybody. . . . It will give relief, I think, to many people to have a pleasant, kindly, well-meaning chap with a pleasing smile in the White House who means to better things if he can. . . . The hungry and the unemployed might be hard to handle this winter if we were in for four more years of the same policies and the same President. When the patient is dying a change of doctors may arouse hope and even that hope may help him to live." Over on nearby William Street, Alexander Sachs of the Lehman Corporation scorned Hoover's attribution of the Depression to "extraneous and foreign influences and [his] hoping that by psychological manipulation and wishful thinking the country could Coué itself out of the depression."[32] Hoover had unwittingly helped shape a broad consensus for Roosevelt.

PART TWO

Businessmen

It is now apparent that there exists a profound misunderstanding between Government (as represented by the New Deal) and Business. The misunderstanding arises from both sides. On the side of Government, the young men of the Administration may be practical theorists but they have no practical business experience. On the side of Business, the average executive is too busy to follow the profound intricacies of modern, interindustrial economics. Hence, to the New Dealer, the hurried Businessman has seemed stupid and stubborn; and to almost all Businessmen, the New Dealer has seemed erratic and untrustworthy. But neither of these impressions is basically correct. *Each arises from a lack of knowledge and information concerning the other side.*

—*Fortune*, 1938.[1]

Shiver me Timbers
Over the Stones,
I, too, have a tale
'Bout Jesse Jones

One morning drear
I had a cold,
And all I needed
Was just more gold.

"O Jones, O, Jones,
Give me some gold,"
And all I got
Was just more cold.

Just then Bill Woodin
Came along,
And joined to mine
His beauteous song.

"O, Jones, O, Jones
Give us some gold,
Or else we'll give you
Back your cold."

As one we sneezed
At Jesse Jones—
He handed out his gold
With groans.

So now we hold
This lovely gold,
We got with groans,
From Jesse Jones.

—The President presents his respects to
the Secretary of the Treasury and to the
Chairman of the Board of the RFC [1933][2]

3.

Jesse H. Jones: The Credit Revolution

Houston

BY HIS OWN TESTIMONY and that of his contemporaries, Jesse Jones was not a New Dealer. Those people who called themselves New Dealers and those who disliked the New Deal considered the Texas developer-banker-publisher too conservative for the label. Aubrey Williams—young, radical, truculent—pronounced Jones "about as sympathetic to the aims and purposes of the New Deal as a dog is to a cat that has just given him a bloody eye." "No one," a *New Republic* writer assured his liberal readers in 1935, "considers Mr. Jones a New Dealer at heart." Still, none other than Franklin D. Roosevelt rated Jones a valuable member of the administration, and one whose value increased even as his disaffection from other New Dealers became more evident. He was a Democrat and it was a Democratic administration. Additionally, he played a decisive role in a key area of the New Deal program. Appearances can be misleading; however the New Deal is defined and wherever Jones's heart was in relation to it, the same *New Republic* writer noted that in the Roosevelt administration Jones had been "more successful than anyone else in avoiding friction inside or outside of his department and at the same time he has managed to keep in tune with the White House orchestra." That was true in 1935, but it would not be so in 1945.[3]

Jones the Democrat was the New Deal's banker for twelve critical years. Aside from the President, he was the single most powerful man in the New Deal, deriving his power from the billions of Reconstruction Finance Corporation dollars he controlled, the financial policies he influenced, the esteem politicians and the press bestowed upon him, and the reluctance of putative enemies to cross swords with him. Most of all, Franklin Roosevelt considered him useful, even when Jones was most devious. New Dealers who wrote him off as a conservative Democrat out of step with a liberal administration usually were expendable; Jones endured. Thomas Corcoran took Jones very seriously, a fact which enhanced his own power as a political broker. Indeed, Jones's story tells us something about power in the New Deal.

Jones's political power flowed from his Texas base. Born to a comfortable Tennessee tobacco-farming family in 1874, Jones struck out on his own at twenty for Texas and his uncle's Dallas lumber business, already one of the largest in the state. Martin Jones had an efficient business: he owned the sawmills that supplied his lumberyards and extracted rebates from railroads hauling his wood to the lumberyards (before the state legislature ended that practice). Uncle Martin initiated the young man into the business, and Jesse quickly demonstrated a managerial and entrepreneurial talent. However, he was restless and adventurous. Soon he relocated to Houston and branched into other enterprises.

He had a promoter's instinct. In an overwhelmingly agrarian state, Jones envisioned a great world metropolis. His imperial city would be Houston, with a population of 27,000 in 1890—fewer people than could be found then in Dallas, San Antonio or Galveston. Although Houston was rapidly becoming a major rail hub for the cotton trade, fulfillment of Jones's vision depended upon a lazy stream called Buffalo Bayou that ran through the heart of Houston to the Gulf of Mexico 50 miles away. Jones and other Houstonians believed that Buffalo Bayou could be deepened and widened enough to bring oceangoing ships into Houston, thereby making it one of the world's great ports—in spite of its close proximity to the port of Galveston, which was plagued by occasional hurricanes. He began to buy land strategically located on Main Street and along Buffalo Bayou and to build houses, hotels, office buildings and all sorts of edifices that generated rent in anticipation of that day when Buffalo Bayou would bring to Houston great ships and the traders who accompanied them. Significantly, all this took capital and all Jones possessed was the lumberyard business, of which he was the executor when his uncle passed on. As a start, he expanded the business and in his first real estate deal persuaded Texas banker T. W. House to extend him lines of credit, using as collateral his uncle's lumberyards. It demonstrated a genius Jones had in dealing with bankers, one that became his hallmark. He opened lines of credit with additional bankers and then made his lines of credit beget lines of credit. Frequently Jones established lines of credit he never intended to use, paying tokens of interest on money he had not invested, simply to maintain and improve an excellent credit rating. During visits to Dallas, Chicago or New York, Jones would stop at a major bank solely to make the bankers' acquaintance and establish a line of credit, usually extended on the basis of other bankers' strong references. As he later said, "As soon as I got a taw to play with, I began buying real estate on long time, and building with no personal obligation on long notes." His reputation among bankers swelled, something which would pay off in the crisis times of the Great Depression. So strong was the Texan's credit that a New York banker once offered Jones $200,000 without any request. In other ways too, he proved expert at using other people's money. For instance, in the panic of 1907 he instructed his lumberyard managers to "crowd collection . . . , push sales for cash," and make purchases only on credit extended by other merchants.[4] Eventually Jones sold all but one of the sixty-five lumberyards he owned and in 1910 he went into banking himself. A millionaire at thirty, he was one promoter who never seemed to lack financing.

Jones and Houston prospered together. He cultivated the Houston business establishment through House (whose brother, Edward Mandell House, lived in Austin, where he invested, wrote, and developed a legendary political relationship with Woodrow Wilson), James A. Baker, a ubiquitous lawyer and later a banker (whose namesake grandson would be Secretary of State under President George Bush), and William Marsh Rice of the Rice Institute family. Together with these men Jones made Houston a transportation center and ultimately the hub for "the whole growing *empire* of the South and the Southwest." He liked to compare Houston to Chicago, a rail hub which had "grown because of that vast *empire* of the Middle West and Northwest." Chicago had a unique vitality that came from its location and the people who manufactured and traded there. And just as Chicago had prospered through the late nineteenth and early twentieth centuries, Jones forecast a movement of capital and people south and west that would make Houston "the inevitable gateway through which the products of this growing southern and western *empire* can best reach the markets of the world." But it was not inevitable. The idea of turning Houston into a deepwater port had been talked about for years without any action. What Jones accomplished was the organization of Houston bankers to seek federal government funds to match local private funds for the 50-mile development of Buffalo Bayou to the Gulf of Mexico (longer than the Panama Canal) as a ship channel, thereby making Houston a world port.

In part, the project was inspired by the digging of the 35.5-mile Manchester Ship Canal in England, which converted that river port into a seaport in 1894. "Houston could go in only one direction—south," Jones's biographer wrote. "He had acquired much property in this line of growth, practically all of which was bought on long-term credit, usually with a separate corporation for each purchase and a small down payment. If the city showed any reluctance to continue in that direction, Jones was prepared to nudge it."[5] The Houston ship channel, built with taxpayer dollars and completed in 1914, added considerable value to the thirty or so commercial buildings, hotels, theaters and department stores Jones erected by the mid-1920s, including a building for his Houston *Chronicle*. Cautious yet intrepid, Jones liked to put up a ten-story building and then add to it later as commerce warranted—his most famous being the deco moderne Gulf Building completed in 1929 (now the Texas Commerce Building). Jones's skyscrapers formed a Houston skyline at a time when skylines outside of New York or Chicago were rare. Soon not even Houston could contain him, as he began to invest in Fort Worth real estate. The cities of Texas were in competition for development, and Jones profited by their civic chauvinism. In 1910 Houston was the third-largest in population, with 78,800. In 1920, it moved into second place behind Dallas with 138,000; by 1926–27 thirty-eight industries put Houston well on its way to becoming a world port thanks to the ship channel. The 1930 census would show Houston with 292,000 people, the largest city in Texas and second in the South only to New Orleans. Much of its growth it owed to Jesse Jones's promotions, which was why Houstonians would say, "Well, we'd rather have Houston the way it is today, with all Jesse's sharp goings-on, than no Jesse and no Houston."[6]

He did not build for the sake of his ego; indeed, he was careful never to put his name on any of his buildings. Nor was his plunge into politics tied to anything but very practical considerations. He knew that government facilitated enterprise. Hadn't the federal government's money paid for half of the Houston Ship Channel and guaranteed the bonds bought by private investors? Government involvement was good for banking. In 1908 he endorsed William Jennings Bryan for president both because he and Houston were Democratic and because he considered Bryan's call for federal deposit insurance a wise move in the wake of the panic of 1907. For that matter, following the panic most Texans favored deposit insurance and in 1910, the year Jones went beyond buying stock in banks to being a managing partner in one, the state of Texas passed a Guaranty Law that was similar to laws passed in other states, and a precursor to the Federal Deposit Insurance Corporation. However, the "jazz banking" of the 1920s—in which banks proliferated, cotton prices tumbled and took high-risk investors with them, and the number of bank failures sharply escalated amid a booming Houston—saw the repeal of the Guaranty Law because numerous small banks had to be bailed out by the fund's dwindling resources. Still, the lesson Jones drew from the experience of two decades was that government regulation stabilized banking, protected bankers from themselves and gave depositors confidence in banks. This last was important: most of Texas was still rural and small-town, and Texans basically disliked bankers, a feeling that seemed well supported by the frequency with which they demonstrated avarice, incompetence and breach of trust. Government regulation and the Federal Reserve System were necessary to build confidence in banks. While bankers were initially hostile to regulation, they usually prospered under its stabilizing influence. As one, then, who recognized the virtues of government regulations, Jones had to ask himself: Why shouldn't a banker be a regulator?[7]

A role-player in Texas politics, in 1912 Jones contributed to the election of Woodrow Wilson and took a step toward power on the national scene. Colonel Edward Mandell House, who fancied himself Wilson's president-maker, brought Jones to Wilson's attention. At various times during Wilson's first administration the President offered Jones the positions of assistant secretary of the treasury, ambassador to Argentina or Belgium and, finally, secretary of commerce. Jones turned all of them down, but he could not refuse a position once the U.S. entered the Great War. Accepting responsibility for raising funds for the American Red Cross in Houston, Jones wrote out a check, took it to James A. Baker, and asked him to match it. Then Jones used Baker's check to get his other wealthy friends to match it with their contributions. In this manner Jones doubled his quota for Houston, and soon Wilson asked him to be director general of the national Red Cross—a key part of the administration strategy of propagandizing the public into "voluntary" social action.

In Washington, Jones directed fund-raising and the distribution of needed commodities, work which soon won him easy access to President Wilson. When the war was over, Jones sailed to England to help organize the International Red Cross. Upon arriving in London, Jones learned that the presidential party, en route to the Paris Peace Conference, had gone to Buckingham Palace—whereupon he headed there to seek out his friend Admiral Cary T. Grayson, the President's personal physician. A "plausible talker," Jones won the confidence of palace guards who had wanted to expel him and was allowed to relax in a public reception room. There he decided to warm his damp feet over an open grate by removing his shoes—just as the royal and presidential party appeared. Fortunately, only Grayson noticed the tall Texan pushing his shoes behind him and trying to cover stockinged feet with his trouser cuffs. "My feet were very cold," Jones explained, "and I did not think these folks hereabouts would object to a man warming his feet when they were cold." A "typical Texas explanation," Grayson called it.[8]

Despite his frequent display of an "aw shucks" manner, few people mistook Jones for a country hick. Some Texans considered him a "cosmopolite" because of the wealthy company in which he traveled and the grand manner in which he lived. It was not an opulent style: Jones displayed his wealth through a quest for comfort and convenience, rather than ostentation. That wealth continued to grow by leaps and bounds. Not only did he add a bank and a newspaper to his holdings, but an insurance company as well. These investments were aided by an ability to recognize talented management in a business and then buying into it. He expanded geographically as well as industrially. In 1921 he planned to build in New York City through a company he called Houston Properties Corporation, telling his friend, Charles M. Schwab, "I came to New York to teach New Yorkers how to pronounce Houston." He built a hotel at Park Avenue and 65th Street, the Mayfair House, and, as he had with Houston's Lamar Hotel, established a home at the top of it. "Jesse Jones is, at heart, as much of an empire builder as James J. Hill or Cecil Rhodes were," Charles G. Dawes cracked; "but he likes to have his empire where he can see most of it most of the time."[9]

Like most wealthy Wilsonians in the early 1920s, Jones prized his identification with the former president. He combined with Cleveland Dodge, Thomas Jones and Cyrus McCormick to create a retirement fund that paid Wilson and later Edith Bolling Wilson a pension of $10,000 a year, there being no government pension then even for a president. Financing a former president's retirement was easier than financing a political party, but Democrats made Jones the party's fund-raiser. Like Baruch, Jones went as a McAdoo delegate to the 1924 Democratic convention in Madison Square Garden, departing disgusted and intent upon a European vacation. However, while McAdoo and Baruch were sailing for Europe, the party's nominee, John W. Davis, prevailed upon Jones to be his director of finance. Because of the prevailing pessimism among Democrats, Jones confronted a meager campaign war chest. Davis was counting upon Baruch for a sizable contribution, but in return for his money Baruch wanted a say in the campaign. When an anticipated $200,000 Baruch contribution turned out to be $25,000, Jones fired off a rancorous letter demanding from Baruch another $120,000 instead of "a miserably small check." "Amazed and hurt" by Jones's "intemperateness of tone and recklessness," Baruch precipitated a feud that surprised most people who had anticipated that two business Democrats would be allies.[10]

Jones remained financial director of the party until the 1928 presidential campaign. After paying off the debts of 1924, he brought 1928's Democratic convention to Houston by writing his own check for $200,000 and promising to build a 25,000-seat arena for it. Although

Senator Tom Connally would snipe, "Jesse later scurried about Texas raising money in order to reimburse himself," Houston celebrated his accomplishment and Texas Democrats honored him at the convention with nominating speeches for president. Still, Jones was respected and feared in Texas, but not beloved. Will Hogg, son of former Texas Governor Jim Hogg, denounced Jones's "stalwart avarice and piratical trading spirit." For a long time many in Houston distrusted Jones, including his former partners. Some Democrats and Texans believed that Jones wanted more than favorite-son nomination at a future convention. In 1928 he did not follow other Texans in distancing themselves from Al Smith, the first Roman Catholic candidate for president of a major party, but he gave only $25,000 to the Smith campaign, the same meager amount Baruch had given Davis.[11]

"He has great sentiment about all of [his buildings]," his wife once remarked. "Every time he passes one, he pats and pets it." Married at forty-six, Jones had no children, lavished attention upon his father's and brother's families, and had no hobbies or interests beyond business and some politics. Horse races, poker or bridge with some whiskey were his only known recreation and vices; he had given up smoking and refused to allow anyone to smoke near him. A robust man, he stood six-foot-two and weighed over 220 pounds, as powerful in appearance as he yearned to be in society. His hair was white by the time he achieved national prominence; one time he was taken for Bernard Baruch, a mistake which neither of them appreciated. While by no means taciturn, he used words sparingly; he was accustomed to having them receive a respectful hearing. He outgrew Houston commercially and was spending more time in New York when the Depression struck. He also had outgrown Texas politics.

Jones was back in Houston during that fateful October of 1931 when the credit crisis that had erupted in Austria a few months earlier threatened to topple the American banking system. His own National Bank of Commerce was sound enough, but the same could not be said of all of the city's other banks when Jones convened a Sunday afternoon meeting in his office of all major Houston bankers. The Depression had already been good to him. In 1930 Jones had bought out Marine Banking & Trust Company and merged it into his National Bank of Commerce (NBC). Others had not done as well in the collapse of the Houston real estate market. Two medium-sized banks were verging upon collapse, their situations made more precarious by probably illegal loans to their owners. A brief survey revealed that most of the city's banks could survive the normal stresses of business, but the merited demise of the two weakest ones could well incite a depositor run that would topple others.

Jones may have yearned for the days of the Guaranty Fund and hoped to re-create a Houston version of it in his offices that Sunday.

The bankers Jones assembled in his office atop the Gulf Building were familiar to one another. In the words of one historian, "Most were either related to each other, close friends, or members of interlocking boards of directors." As bankers, Jones argued, they had a responsibility to the community, and the prosperity of Houston would be assured by their joint action. Among at least some of his hearers, his argument evoked a contrary attitude of rugged individualism. As one banker told him later when he tried to create another pool, "Do not constitute yourself a guardian or a Santa Claus for the community—none of us are in any way qualified to look after anything or anybody beyond our own affairs, and not so well for that, even." (Hoover undoubtedly encountered similar sentiments during his own quests for bankers' pools.) In the end, however, Texas political considerations combined with the economic crisis to make joint action imperative. The state's governor, Ross Sterling, had borrowed from Houston National Exchange Bank more than a million dollars which could not be repaid, a matter of potential scandal. Humble Oil and thirteen bankers agreed to assume Sterling's problem loans. Jones offered to assume the debt of the other troubled institution, Public National Bank, if the pool guaranteed his bank against loss—a prospect which at least two of the bankers resisted, believing that if they agreed Jones "would begin to ask for a little additional protection, just as he did." The prospect of depositor panic kept the bankers talking until five in the morning on Monday, by which time they had agreed that a pool arrangement might save them all a lot of grief. James A. Baker, then on a trip to Massachusetts but in close telephone contact with the bankers, fell in with Jones; "if these two were on the same side, others usually followed." They did. The Houston banking establishment was saved.[12]

How did Jones absorb Public National and its problems? For one thing, he used his personal influence with big solvent banks around the country to assure them that NBC could stand the burden. And with Jones at the RFC beginning in 1932, by 1935 Houston banking profits would return to where they were in 1929—not in the least hurt by a shakeout of competitors in the intervening years. And, while he later protested that his wealth owed nothing to the oil boom that benefited other Houstonians, his NBC "was one of the leaders of early oil lending in Houston." More consolidations and aggressive lending to the oil industry throughout the depression would make his National Bank of Commerce the largest credit institution of Houston.[13]

Events now conspired to draw Jones onto the national scene. Because Hoover could not duplicate the Houston bankers' pool on a national level, the President asked Congress to create the Reconstruction Finance Corporation in January 1932. It could not have been by mere chance that as Congress considered the RFC, Jones, ever adroit at networking, decided to visit some Democratic friends and acquaintances in Washington. His first stop was at the Speaker's office. Jones had known John Nance Garner of Texas, himself a Uvalde banker, since 1917. Hoover was pressing Garner to name someone for the RFC board of directors as a quid pro quo for the Speaker's support for the RFC—just as Jones, the very image of Texas financial sagacity, presented himself. Although Jones modestly suggested the names of a Chicago and a Dallas banker for the RFC board, he appropriately added what any sound Texan wanted to hear, that "the [RFC] directors should realize that most of the country lies west of the Hudson River, and none of it east of the Atlantic Ocean." In other words, the RFC had to be more mindful of the need for Southern and Western economic development and less concerned with European debts from the Great War. Like most Texans, Jones had certain anticolonial attitudes toward Wall Street. A historian has argued well that "class loyalties are the key to understanding Jones," and in this instance Texas bankers were a class unto themselves. Although Jones by 1932 was also a New York resident, he was careful to maintain his base in Houston and raise objections to banker power in New York and Chicago. While in the Capitol, he also visited every Democratic senator involved in the making of the RFC until all of them knew that he and banker Harvey Couch of Arkansas were their choices as Democratic directors on the RFC. Many of the senators Jones visited knew local bankers who knew him. Jones anticipated that the appointment would last for a year, but it turned out that he would be a resident of Washington hotels for the next thirteen years.[14]

The Reconstruction Finance Corporation inspired hope, fear or combinations of those emotions and others. Nothing less than capitalism's survival was at stake. With the private sector in disarray, the U.S. Treasury had come to its rescue. Was this still capitalism? some purists asked. Private enterprise seemed threatened by state intervention in credit markets. Many bankers and old Republicans truly believed in the precepts of social Darwinism and abhorred any intrusion in private enterprise. While Jones ardently defended RFC relief of Charles Dawes's Chicago bank as imperative to spare greater public anguish, RFC detractors from both the right and the left of the political spectrum saw it as "state capitalism," an oxymoron in the eyes of the right, a necessary hypocrisy in the eyes of the left. But opportunists such as Jones viewed libertarianism on the right as an anachronism. The RFC was not quite a year old when Calvin Coolidge confessed to a friend that he "no longer fit in with these times. . . . These socialistic notions of government are not of my day. . . . We are in a new era to which I do not belong, and it would not be possible to adjust myself to it." Two weeks later he died, and an era seemed to pass with him. The new epoch belonged to the likes of Jesse Jones.[15]

Coolidge, of course, was a victim of self-delusion; he imagined more laissez-faire than had ever existed. Instances of government involvement in transportation and banking abounded in the nineteenth century, and, even in the face of a then widespread social Darwinist outlook, government regulation of the rails as well as of food and drugs foreshadowed the coming of the Federal Reserve System and a central banker whose role would be expanded greatly by McAdoo and the Wilsonians during the emergency of war. Capitalism was a utopia sought by capitalists and the next stage of history anticipated by Marxists. But practical men such as Jesse Jones were neither so ideological nor so concerned with theories of capitalism. They welcomed the RFC as warmly as they had the War Finance Corporation, the Railroad Administration, the Shipping Board and the other war expedients. Russell Leffingwell of Morgan celebrated the RFC, whose purpose was "to save the country from a disaster of the first magnitude." Leffingwell thoroughly disliked and distrusted Hoover, accusing the President of indulging in half-truths; he saw Hoover's insistence upon no publicity for RFC loans as a snare: "I like the full light of publicity on everything the Government does," Leffingwell declared—and added, perhaps disingenuously, "I even think bankers ought to have glass pockets." Jones agreed. He maintained that such revelations as the Dawes scandal reassured the public by disclosing the names of banks "who could borrow rather than who had to borrow" and whom the RFC had selected to save. The government had to inflate credit via the Treasury, Leffingwell believed, because the Hoover administration's deficit obliged the issuance of government paper at excessively high interest rates. As Leffingwell reminded Federal Reserve banker Eugene Meyer, a lower discount rate was in order: "This was the war practice; and this is war."[16]

With the creation of the RFC, "We are entering a new, rather dramatic period," State Department economist Herbert Feis had excitedly written; freed from the cant of free enterprise by the use of government loans, "the full jet of our financial reserves will be applied to water the drooping garden." Nonetheless, the dehydrating events of the spring suggested that something more than loans was required. For to what avail did the RFC lend to banks if its loans did not find their way into the economy? What the banks used them for instead was to retire old debts, and also to buy government securities—a practice much less risky than loans to enterprise but one that did nothing for the economy unless the government itself behaved as an investor and entrepreneur. Even the cautious Walter Lippmann was moved to ask privately the next logical question: "If it should appear that private initiative is, for one reason or another, unwilling to use this investment money, is it not necessary to proceed to the next step, which is to stimulate investment directly?" RFC director Jesse Jones chastised bankers publicly for their avoidance of "relending," and accused them of selfishly using RFC loans in ways that strangled recovery.[17]

Amid mounting evidence that loans to bankers would not be enough to reverse the downward cycle, Eugene Meyer resigned in July as chairman of "the Corporation," as Washington dubbed the RFC, to be replaced by Atlee Pomerene, a conservative Ohio Democrat. The election of Franklin D. Roosevelt to the presidency months later excited anticipation that he would enhance the RFC's role. By the end of 1932 the agency had loaned $2 billion, mostly to large banks, but the economic situation was worse. "1933 probably will mark the turning point of national policy, the cross roads on numerous political issues," a young RFC attorney, Thomas G. Corcoran, wrote. "It will be the most important year of either the past decade or the next decade. But 1933 will only fix the trends and will NOT bring permanent settlement of many major issues. It will be a year of semi-timid experimentation, with the 'emergency motif' always uppermost. Permanent correctives will be discussed, indicated, put into tentative shape, but actual adoption of most will be spread out over future years." He forecast that the RFC, "which is a government bank, will acquire new banking functions," thereby assuring "*state capitalism*." With his eye on the main chance, Corcoran considered himself strategically located because "Roosevelt policy on RFC will be to liberalize the law, to make R.F.C. a 'positive agency for business stimulation,' rather than merely Hoover's 'defensive agency for cushioning the deflation.' " He anticipated a credit revolution via "large new government loans" and a "new routing" of investment capital through public channels: "Tremendous growth of *state capitalism* is implied, of course."[18] Testing the political waters of the interregnum, Corcoran mistakenly anticipated that his next boss would be Bernard Baruch. No matter; he correctly foresaw that the RFC would have additional power from Congress to liquefy the system under the leadership of the government's banker, Jesse Jones.

New Capital

FRANKLIN D. ROOSEVELT became President amid the worst peacetime crisis in the history of the United States. One in four workers was unemployed, and in manufacturing states such as Michigan, state governors closed all banks under their jurisdiction to prevent depositors from closing the banks with their withdrawals. Roosevelt's first action was to close all banks under executive powers conferred by the Great War's Trading With the Enemy Act of 1917—the authority Congress had given Wilson and McAdoo sixteen years before—a suitably dramatic first step for the New Deal. But reopening the banks required a restoration of public confidence in them. For five days after Roosevelt's inauguration, holdover officials from the Hoover administration, along with new appointees, New Deal braintrusters, and Federal Reserve officials, conferred informally to work out a banking plan. A special session of the new Congress made the banking plan law in a matter of hours. The Emergency Banking Act of 1933 was the first and quite probably the most important New Deal law. In closing the banks Roosevelt took a decisive step which Hoover had resisted, and in reopening them Congress gave the President powers to safeguard shareholder and depositor interests.

Accordingly, Congress greatly expanded the roles played by the RFC by empowering it to decide which banks could continue in business. Randomly scrutinizing the books of weak banks, the RFC pronounced 5 percent, nearly a thousand, too weak to reopen and so ripe for liquidation. About a quarter of all banks required the RFC's close and careful scrutiny before it permitted unlimited withdrawals from them.[19] Importantly, however, the RFC bestowed Washington's certification for safety upon the remaining banks. Roosevelt's first "fireside chat," on March 12, further reassured the public. As much as it could, Washington had restored America's confidence in its banks.

Reopening the banks with full services was one thing; keeping them open was another. There was now a growing consensus in Washington that the banks needed less credit for their debts and more capital for their investments. Section 3 of the Emergency Banking Act addressed that need for capital by creating what Jesse Jones liked to call the RFC's "bank repair" program, the RFC's purchase of a bank's preferred stock. By commanding banks to issue preferred stock for RFC purchase, the RFC would make itself a major stockholder in banks and virtually move the center of American banking from Wall Street to Washington. The idea for Washington's purchase of preferred stock had been suggested to Jones by Chicago banker Melvin A. Traylor during the crisis over the

Dawes bank in June 1932: "What the banks need is not loans, but more capital," Traylor had argued. The experience of the months that followed seemed to confirm that prescription. RFC loans made debtors of bankers, but Jones preferred to make debtors of entrepreneurs by encouraging them to borrow and inducing bankers to loan. "A dollar spent in the purchase of preferred stock," Russell Leffingwell later reflected, "ought to do as much as $5 or $10 spent in making adequately secured loans." Yet the scheme to pump new capital into banks assumed that bankers had the courage to lend it. Jones, himself an incongruous combination of cautious lender and speculative borrower, now counted upon other bankers to abandon excessive caution and to loan intrepidly against real collateral and for worthy adventures.[20]

The Banking Act of 1933 concentrated enormous powers and responsibilities in the hands of the RFC chairman. What accounts for Roosevelt's appointment of Jones to the post in preference to other likely prospects such as Baruch? For one thing, Jones was familiar with RFC operations and already was a leader on the board of directors. He enjoyed the political support of Vice-President Garner, a considerable influence on all banking legislation. Also, Roosevelt needed someone with Jones's credentials as a conservative banker with an anti–Wall Street bias. The Texan shared with the President a desire to avoid a "tieup with No. 23"—the House of Morgan. Midwestern businessmen such as Robert E. Wood of Sears Roebuck detested Wall Street and hoped FDR would fill important credit posts such as the RFC or the Federal Reserve with men "not bound by the orthodox views of the New York bankers."[21] People like Wood welcomed credit inflation. Finally, Jones himself wanted the job. Only the Treasury portfolio held a greater attraction for him; intent upon control of the government's investment and credit policies, Jones decided to make his name synonymous with that of the Reconstruction Finance Corporation.

Jones never achieved the prominence of other New Dealers. Public attention during the Depression was focused far more on those who gave direct assistance to farmers in distress or the unemployed. Jones's policies, to be sure, also benefited both of these troubled constituencies significantly though indirectly; but his work involved him primarily with troubled bankers, which put him in the company of the villains of the Depression drama. Nonetheless, Jones and the RFC outlasted most of the other major New Deal actors and their agencies. He did not publicize himself as effectively as some New Dealers. Unlike Hugh Johnson of the NRA, Jones did not issue rambunctious pronouncements or stage parades to rally popular support. Unlike Henry Wallace, he asked for nothing as startling as the killing of pigs or the trampling of cotton to increase commodity prices. Unlike Harry Hopkins, he did not dramatize relief with loans for nonproductive government projects. He did not dedicate huge public works projects in the manner of Harold Ickes. But Jones was not shy about bashing bankers and other moguls in public or private, or bragging about it afterwards. Publicly laconic and privately profane, he saved his words for bankers, bureaucrats and congressmen who understood whence flowed the largesse to which capital-starved institutions looked for rescue. He had their confidence. Some liberals accused him of running the RFC as if it were a private banking house when he demanded considerable collateral for loans made at interest rates nearly as high as those of private bankers. But cautious lending practices and tight balance sheets earned him the appreciation of Congress, even when individual lawmakers had to confront unhappy constituents whose dreams of credit for development and reemployment could not meet the RFC's standards for lending.[22]

Jones gained the respect even of many disappointed supplicants: bankers and sellers of preferred stock such as railroads; entrepreneurs at odds with their local bankers and seeking relief or a new start with RFC credit; Southern politicians who fairly oozed with "good ol' boy" fellowship in hopes that Jones would fund their district's developers and promoters; local and state officials with works schemes that would bring cheap electricity to their communities or farm cooperatives; and fellow New Deal administrators who viewed him as not nearly as sympathetic to hard-pressed small farmers or businessmen as they would have wished, but who nonetheless admired his guileful command of finance and politics. He could be an expedient lender; he frequently accommodated schemes of dubious creditworthiness, and liberal New Dealers remained suspicious of Jones's personal coziness with bankers and big business. Ironically, however, the RFC-financed programs such as rural electrification were dear to their hearts and made possible profounder consequences for American society than those of almost any other New Deal agency.

In the early days of the New Deal, however, Jones worried less about what others in the administration thought than about extracting banker cooperation for making loans. During the summer of 1933, he launched a campaign to induce banks to sell their institutions' preferred stock to the RFC. Most banks, however, were unwilling to do so, out of fear that this might subject them to a government directorship and force them to make risky loans. As the summer passed, only a very few bankers yielded to Jones's importunities and sold preferred stock to the RFC. He broadened his public relations attack and used radio time to plead for banker cooperation. When he even wangled an invitation from the

American Bankers Association to address its convention in Chicago on September 5, FDR urged Jones to remind the bankers of Washington's quest for a capital-government "partnership" to expand credit for recovery. However, the banks wanted no more of FDR's partnership than they had wanted of Hoover's cooperation. Indeed, the ABA's president seized the occasion of Jones's speech to harangue him over the Glass-Steagall Act, especially its deposit insurance feature. "Be smart for once," Jones retorted, and, paraphrasing FDR, he admonished the bankers to "Take the government into partnership with you in providing credit which the country is sadly in need of." The bankers sat mute with disapproval. At an ABA party that night, the bankers listened to a talk by a Federal Reserve Board governor and then politely asked Jones for his impromptu remarks. "Half the banks in this room are insolvent," Jones reminded them, "and those of you representing these banks know it better than anyone else." The road to solvency, he argued, now ran through Washington.

Scolding and scaring bankers may have made some of them more sociable toward Jones that evening, but it did not coax from them offerings of preferred stock. What ultimately proved capable of doing so was the need for deposit insurance. Earlier in the year, Congress had compelled the administration to support the proposal for a Federal Deposit Insurance Corporation. Jones's story of how Congress created the FDIC suggests that FDR was at times extraneous, or even an impediment, to the work of the New Deal. In 1932, Hoover had called the widely supported proposal for guaranteeing bank deposits "a lot of rot," adding that "it would make the government responsible for the management of all the banks in the country." FDR's view was not all that different. There was no conservative or liberal or Republican or Democratic position on deposit insurance. Jones himself had favored the concept ever since he'd heard William Jennings Bryan espouse it in 1908 (though he disliked most other aspects of Bryan's economic program). Although the Texas experience with deposit insurance had been a disaster, Jones's friend and fellow Texas banker John Nance Garner eagerly promoted the idea in 1932, to no avail. Big bankers fought it vehemently, wanting nothing to do with putting the government into banking or creating reserve funds to save small banks that did not "deserve" to survive. Roosevelt agreed. "The general underlying thought behind the use of the word 'guarantee' with respect to bank deposits is that you guarantee bad banks as well as good banks and the minute the Government starts to do that the Government runs into a probable loss," FDR told his first press conference. "We all know it is better to have that loss taken than to jeopardize the credit of the United States Government or to put the United States Government further in debt and, therefore, the one objective is going to be to keep the loss in the individual banks down to a minimum, endeavoring to get 100 per cent on [the losses], but not having the United States Government liable for the mistakes and errors of individual banks and not putting a premium in the future on unsound banking." A worthy goal did not justify unworthy means; assuring depositors should not entail insuring rogue bankers. As Roosevelt biographer Frank Freidel reminds us, "since Roosevelt's quarrel with the bankers had been over their recklessness, he wished them to be more cautious, not more daring." Jones, to the contrary, argued that bankers were *too* cautious. In one instance J. P. Morgan ignored his plea to organize a pool to save the failing Harriman Bank, explaining that a banker had no responsibility to depositors. However, Jones's point was that it was to the bankers' advantage to have deposit insurance administered by the government. Although New Yorkers such as Adolf Berle and FDR opposed deposit guarantees, Jones was intent upon teaching them something about politics and the Texas Guaranty Law.

On May 19, 1933, while the Senate debated the Glass-Steagall banking bill, Garner gave his gavel over to a senator and sat down next to Republican Arthur Vandenberg of Michigan. He knew that Vandenberg had been promoting a deposit-insurance amendment to the bill similar to the one Garner had introduced in the House a year before. "Where's that deposit-insurance amendment of yours," Garner whispered. "It's never been out of my pocket," Vandenberg responded. The Uvalde banker left and in a few minutes he was back. "I was just talking to Carter Glass," Garner told Vandenberg. "Next to me, he is the most cantankerous man in the world; but he is in good humor now and I don't think he will fight your amendment too hard." That afternoon the Senate overwhelmingly adopted deposit insurance of up to $2,500. Of course, the key to this was Glass's sudden conversion to deposit insurance. Like Roosevelt, the Virginian had not been stampeded by the banking crisis of March into backing "bank guarantees." However, later that year when Glass wanted an extension of time for repayment of an RFC loan to a hometown Lynchburg, Virginia, bank, Jones instantly complied. Glass knew that a favor always deserved a favor. Years later Garner and Jones chortled about how they'd put one over on Roosevelt and how the New Dealers had embraced *their* reform.

Indeed, for a half century the Federal Deposit Insurance Corporation was a New Deal hallmark and one of the great reforms of the century, because it so stabilized the banking system that the FDIC seldom actually had to bail out a bank. Ironically, it was the oil industry collapse in Texas and rampant incompetence and thievery in the insouciant, deregulated climate of the 1980s that led to the exorbitant savings-and-loan bailout of the 1990s. The 1920s Texas experience with "jazz banking" was here repeated nationwide. Then several critics would recall the prescient words of Franklin Roosevelt.* Had FDR known of the Texas experience? Had the conservative FDR been smarter than the liberal FDR?[23]

On the basis of his Texas experience Jones realized that, as much as big bankers instinctively detested the idea of government-administered deposit insurance, without it they faced a loss of depositor confidence. The Glass-Steagall Act had mandated that to qualify for membership in the FDIC a bank had to be certified as solvent by the Secretary of the Treasury by January 1, 1934. Many banks could attain such certification only by trading their preferred stock for the RFC's capital. A veteran bridge player, Jones knew he held the trump card. In October, at the White House, he confronted New York bankers Eugene Black, Lewis Douglas and Henry Bruere, who were intent upon convincing FDR that Jones could never find the federal revenue with which to carry out preferred stock purchases and make deposit insurance work. They wanted nothing less from FDR than Jones's removal from RFC leadership. Roosevelt, however, was not about to sacrifice a Texas banker to his New York brethren. Following Jones's confident declaration that the RFC would find the more than $1 billion necessary for purchase of the banks' preferred stock to qualify them for insurance, Roosevelt calmly placed a cigarette in his holder, turned to the bankers and declared, "Boys, I am going to back Jess. He has never failed me yet." The bankers emerged from Roosevelt's office, Tommy Corcoran recorded with evident satisfaction, "trying not to look sick, with Jesse ambling behind them trying not to look too triumphant." It gladdened Corcoran's heart to see New York bankers sulking and complaining "that the President had let them down viz. Jesse."[24]

As Jones knew they would, the New York banks soon capitulated and sought RFC purchases of their preferred stock. Smaller banks then fell into line. Still, many recalcitrant bankers counted upon about 2,000 banks remaining "insolvent," and collapsing the deposit insurance system when panicky depositors stormed their doors. Again, Jones outsmarted them. To avert that impending calamity, he persuaded Henry Morgenthau to certify all banks in return for Jones's promise that within six months all of them would truly qualify for insurance.[25]

What Jones was counting on was that deposit insurance would drive

*On the FDIC in 1989, see "Abolish Deposit Insurance" by David Glassner, *Wall Street Journal*, May 5, 1989, in which it is argued that "A system in which all losses are underwritten by the government while profits accrue to managers and owners invites corruption and dishonesty." Also, see "Deposit Insurance Must Go," by James Tobin, *Wall Street Journal*, November 22, 1989, in which the Keynesian economist at Yale asserts that although deposit insurance prevented bank runs in 1933, in 1989 it was "largely obsolete."

big bankers to sell preferred stock to the government for recapitalization and then invest this newly acquired capital in manufacturing enterprises that employed the jobless. Thus, the RFC would virtually underwrite the New Deal's recovery program. Like Hoover, the New Dealers needed cooperative big bankers who ventured their capital. Jones did not want to push the RFC into competition with Wall Street's capital, and he was sympathetic to its complaints that federal deficits unleashed a torrent of government bonds that competed in credit markets with corporate bonds and drove interest rates higher. But his Texas populism—i.e., anticolonialism—overcame banking fellowship. If bankers did not want to lend or take him into "partnership," he would bully them a bit. "It's simple—for a man like Jones," wrote one admiring reporter. "He knows the game and he deals the cards." Denying that he coerced banks, on February 5, 1934, Jones told the New York Bankers Association that he "would be less than frank" if he "did not say that the President would be greatly disappointed if the banks do not assume their full share in the recovery program." Did they need to be reminded that public antagonism toward banking was high? That businessmen were pressuring Congress to expand public credit for private enterprise? "If the banker fails to grasp his opportunity and to meet his responsibility, there can be but one alternative—government lending."[26]

He repeated the threat many times. Also, knowing, as McAdoo had known in 1917, that railroad credit and the well-being of money center banks were inextricably linked, Roosevelt and Jones rated the "railroad problem" as a major concern. In July 1934 Roosevelt asked Jones to get "money at the most reasonable prevailing interest rates" for the desperate Baltimore and Ohio Railroad. Roosevelt believed that the rates charged by bankers were unreasonable; in the end "the cost of money to the railroads must be borne by the people" in the form of higher rates and fares. Jones accused the bankers of "chiselling" by charging the B & O 5.75 per cent for credit, an offer the B & O would have taken but for the President's intercession. Wall Streeters such as Russell Leffingwell earlier had opposed the RFC's meddling in rail financing, but became "reconciled" to the RFC "intervening to save the roads as a transitory measure, faute de mieux." An incensed Jones informed bankers that "since they had run out on the railroads in 1932, making it necessary for the government to come to their rescue, that the government was going to see to it that in the future they gave the roads proper rates and at proper brokerage charges if they were to continue as railroad bankers." Still, to obtain proper costs for money the RFC had to sell its own paper to supplement that of the bankers. But Jones could later boast that he virtually kept the B & O afloat through the 1930s and saved many jobs.

And it was also true that he saved the New York financial structure and its usurious rates; a rail failure would have precipitated a devastating crisis and put Washington into both the banking and the rail businesses.[27]

In the depression crisis Jones had to apply and bend credit principles simultaneously. "The methods used by the promoters of this enterprise seemed little short of dishonest," he once commented when the Comptroller of the Currency recommended a loan to a major Midwestern bank. "It is only with the thought that by overlooking these things a greater good could be accomplished to the depositors of the closed bank that we concurred in your judgment."[28] In banking it was frequently necessary to overlook a lot of malfeasance for a greater good.

Jones did insist upon "some look-in on the management" of borrowers—especially railroads. After all, if management wanted Washington's credit then the RFC "should exact [from the borrowers] intelligent and efficient management." Perhaps he was tougher on railroads because he was a Texan with experience in the lumber business. He demanded from railroads receiving RFC loans that they limit executive annual salaries to $50,000 and that railroads in the South and West transfer headquarters from New York. He was particularly hard on the Southern Pacific, perhaps motivated by its refusal to participate in the Houston pool of 1931, despite the fact that it played a major economic role in the city and had been represented previously among its elite; he could carry a grudge. "You live too far from your tracks," he told officers of the Southern Pacific. "The place for a man to run a railroad is on the line." A railroad man had to know his territory and not just New York's financial markets. Furthermore, he told the Southern Pacific, its acceptance of an RFC loan obligated it to pay no company vice-president more than $21,000 per annum. But he hit other railroads too. Along with a loan to the Chicago, Milwaukee, St. Paul and Pacific Railroad, Jones sent a maximum annual salary schedule for every major officer of that company. He also ordered railroads to fire their outside law firms and use corporate counsel. A loan to a corporation or a purchase of a bank's preferred stock, he reminded them, meant that the RFC guaranteed that its "management shall be satisfactory."[29]

Jones savored a reputation as both flinty and generous. "We are not here to throw good money after bad," a cliché he invoked more times than he could remember. Yet he also aided farmer cooperatives or irrigation districts in the sparsely settled West even when an immediate return was very doubtful. He tried to play no favorites, as when he rescued the cities of New York and Chicago in the summer of 1934. In the first instance Jones got a syndicate of banks to lower a loan rate to the city from 4.036 per cent (6 per cent the first year) to an acceptable 3.75 per cent, saving the city about $3.5 million.

Nevertheless, Jones as a lender was a banker to the core. He usually kept RFC loan rates higher than those of private bankers in order to avoid the accusation that government money competed with private funds. This was the story of the Chicago loan. The city had fallen two years behind in tax collections and between May 1933 and July 1934 its teachers had not been paid. Chicago's banks were useless in this situation, since they themselves were dependent upon the RFC. Congress moved to relieve the teachers' "truly pitiable plight" by extending RFC authority to make loans for teachers "when properly secured." Jones found proper collateral on an entire city block of valuable Loop property owned by the Board of Education and worth a loan at 4.5 percent. In his account of how he rescued the Chicago teachers, Jones omitted the rather exorbitant interest rate.[30]

He held enormous power over American finance. One Washington wag called Jones "the first financial pirate to realize that the new field of opportunity lay in public service." Another journal labeled him "the economic emperor of America." Moreover, his powers grew as Congress and Roosevelt grew confident of his abilities and gave him more leeway in lending. The RFC weighed the merits of each loan applicant, its private alternatives, whether bankers had rebuffed the needy borrower, whether the borrower would create jobs for the unemployed, what other public agencies could help, and—a not inconsiderable consideration—what were the political ramifications of a loan. It was not a promiscuous lender. And Jones usually had the final say about a possible loan. Although many a would-be borrower had congressional sponsors, Jones never hesitated to answer in the negative. If anything, his patronizing rejections enhanced his credibility, independence, and reputation for objectivity. "He handles Congress as if it were composed of overeager children, at times acts as a parental brake on the President, and also likes to play the role of father confessor and Lord Bountiful to friends and employees," wrote Samuel Lubell. Lubell's paternal metaphor was not wide of the mark. As Jones once told a congressman, "Fourteen months in this work has convinced me that our country might be likened unto a big family—some of the children are able to care for themselves—others are not, and usually parents are more patient and spend more time with the latter." Jones personally had never been a parent, but he was a doting uncle. In Washington he was indeed avuncular; he frequently referred to himself, and encouraged others to call him, "Uncle Jesse."[31]

One key to Uncle Jesse's power, other than his "pawnbroker" functions, was his friendship with Vice-President Garner and the way he used it with Congress. Garner, to be sure, was no longer as powerful as he had been in the House; it was he who described the vice-presidency as "not worth a pitcher of warm piss" and he himself did nothing while holding that office to inspire a different valuation. But Garner remained an important player in Texas politics, and even when he moved to the other side of the Capitol, he took with him a great deal of political savvy, respect and ambition. Garner and Jones became fast friends in the 1930s, perhaps because each found so much of himself in the other. They both originated in Tennessee, arrived in Texas at about twenty, and got into banking through other businesses. Garner had taken a more public and less pecuniary course. He had had a career in law and politics in Uvalde in south-central Texas, about 50 miles from the Rio Grande and, following a brief tour in the Texas legislature, arrived in the House of Representatives in 1903. Although he eschewed oratory and seldom introduced legislation, he demonstrated that gregariousness and hard work paid off with his fellow congressmen. In 1911 he became Democratic Whip and in 1913 a member of the powerful Ways and Means Committee, where he distinguished himself as an advocate of progressive income taxation to replace federal dependence upon import duties. By 1917 he had the attention of Secretary of the Treasury McAdoo, who warned Wilson that Garner was "one of our most valuable friends in the House, has constantly upheld the administration, is very influential, and has had almost no consideration at our hands." Wilson and McAdoo remedied that oversight by making Garner the administration's spokesman on finance in the House. That gave Garner real power and in 1923 he became the ranking Democrat on the Ways and Means Committee and Chairman of the House Democratic Committee on Committees, a post which allowed him control over party assignments in the House. He became House Democratic party leader in 1929 and attained the speakership in 1931.[32]

Money also brought power to Garner. His stake in banking came from his wife's inheritance of about a hundred thousand dollars, which he invested in a local bank and later in the stock of about twenty-six other small Texas banks. A very frugal man who lived simply in a Washington hotel with his wife as his secretary (nepotism was not unusual then in Congress and, besides, it was well known that Mrs. Garner was indispensable to running his office), as a banker Garner avoided wild speculations and stuck to loans and modest investments in real estate and a newspaper. He was a small-town Jesse Jones, but very much a millionaire.

That was the unseen side of Garner. The public Garner was the House warhorse, the man who wielded the greatest authority there since the heyday of "Uncle Joe" Cannon, through a bipartisan alliance with Nicholas Longworth, the Republican Leader from Ohio and son-in-law to the late Theodore Roosevelt. The homespun Texan and his aristocratic friend from Cincinnati were "the Damon and Pythias of Capitol Hill." It was they who tapped politicians to be members of the fraternal "Bureau of Education" and join them in a room off the House chamber where they kept an icebox for cooling drinks for themselves and cronies. In Prohibition, the Methodist Garner made no secret of his faith in "striking a blow for liberty," his toast with rye and branch water. Relatively short at five-foot-nine, with large white bushy eyebrows under a white thatch of hair and beaverlike teeth, "Cactus Jack," a nickname which only reporters enjoyed, was a proficient cusser ("Hell's Bells" being only for public consumption), and many of his best expletives were saved for those congressmen who did not follow his elliptical teachings in the Bureau of Education.

To the delight of Texans, Garner opposed Roosevelt for the Democratic nomination for president in 1932. Jones had been Texas's favorite son in the 1928 convention, but Garner's bid was anything but token. Backed by Hearst, McAdoo, a swarm of expatriate Texans in California and a chauvinistic Texas contingent that included Congressman Sam Rayburn and Jesse Jones ("Texans," Jones declared, "have not had an opportunity to render so great a service to our nation since the Alamo and San Jacinto as they now have in offering John Garner for the presidency"), the Speaker ran a distant third in the balloting until it became evident that Al Smith could bitterly deadlock the convention as had happened in 1924. Out of party loyalty Garner then agreed to accept the vice-presidential nomination, although he would have preferred to remain as House Speaker. Once in office, he was loyal too to Roosevelt and the New Deal, keeping any philosophical reservations about it private.

The New Deal brought Garner and Jones together to enjoy each other's "good-fellowship and liberty," poker and drinking. Jones kept Garner abreast of administration gossip and his RFC activities; Garner set aside a room in the Capitol where Jones could "visit" with a senator or a congressman over a drink and exchange some smutty jokes. A reporter noted that Jones was "a prodigious 'visitor' " to Congress who usually got his way on bills important to the RFC. Many of those laws practically gave Jones a blank check on expanded RFC powers, his only collateral being his personal assurance to wary congressmen that he would not spend RFC money on "any of the foolish things you're worrying about."

Neither Jones nor Garner thought of himself as an ideological man. They were Texans, and one aspect of Texas nationalism was a studied disdain for the ostentatious trophies and luxuries of rich Easterners, such as, say, yachts. In a sense they were part of the 1930s cultural conflict in America, much of it regional in nature, much of it based on class, much of it ethnic, much of it religious. Jones and Garner couched their antagonisms along regional and class lines. Early in the New Deal Jones relished outdealing Eastern bankers, after savoring the details of his negotiations with his crony Garner. Although Roosevelt's aristocratic progressivism complemented their frontier distaste for Wall Street, they remained Texas bankers and aloof from the outlook that animated his liberalism. In what seemed to them to be an age of rampant collectivism, Jones and Garner were individualists who mourned the "trend toward a new order of things" and the decline of "the principle of everyone being able to look after himself." (Looking after themselves did not carry over to doing without the FDIC, recapitalizing banks with federal revenues, or federal financing of rural electric cooperatives.) They liked Roosevelt for his good conservative instincts that kept him from "getting too far from the beaten path." Besides, they appreciated that the President was enormously popular with voters and they dared not alienate Roosevelt while Garner still harbored ambitions for the presidency in 1940. By the late 1930s, however, the Democratic party was torn by adversarial political cultures, a fact partly summed up in CIO leader John L. Lewis's 1939 characterization of Garner as "a labor-baiting, poker-playing, whiskey-drinking old man." Garner and Jones reciprocally scorned Roosevelt's liberal acolytes. It was said that in the files of the RFC's press rooms was a heavily underscored clipping with this sentiment: "Too bad John Garner was not nominated for President in 1932. He would have been elected and the country would have been spared the costly, disastrous experiments of the New Deal amateurs."[33] And, as we shall see, the two Texans blamed Roosevelt for the Democratic party's abandonment of the two-thirds rule, by which Southerners could manipulate quadrennial conventions. A deadlocked Democracy was better than one not controlled by the South.

Roosevelt respected Jones's and Garner's ability to make things happen within Congress and in the South, as witness their use of a short, pudgy young Texas newsman named Silliman Evans. How this round bundle of energy entered their lives is not clear, but he was a natural promoter of everything, including himself. Known in Texas for his "colossal crust," for several years Evans followed Texas politicians around the state and federal capitals as a reporter for a Fort Worth newspaper. Eventually he ingratiated himself into the drinking company of Congressman Garner. Soon he was part reporter and part lobbyist for several causes worth his price and his penchant for fun, directing publicity for the Garner presidential campaign, a job that qualified him in 1933 to become Fourth Assistant Postmaster General of the United States.

Jones knew Evans through Garner, and nobody but them could have imagined how Evans would figure in the history of the RFC. It began one day while Evans, Garner and Jones were at Pimlico racetrack and Jones was relating to Garner a tale of woe concerning the Maryland Casualty Company, then quite deep in debt and not worth good RFC money. However, Jones always considered the larger good and, in this instance, a lot of people would lose more money if the RFC could not rescue it. But three people had turned Jones down in his search to find anyone trustworthy to run the company. "Why don't you take this pu'sely-gutted little feller here?" suggested Garner, jabbing his thumb into Evans's belly. Jones said nothing then but gave it serious thought. Back in Washington he made some phone calls before offering the job to Evans. "But I don't know a darned thing about insurance," Evans protested, "I only took one course in algebra and flunked that." "That's what we need," Uncle Jesse said softly, "Nobody who knows insurance would take this job." A few days later Maryland Casualty got an infusion of RFC money and a new president. What Jones wanted from Evans was a shrewd publicist to convince people that Maryland Casualty was recovering and that Evans could keep RFC's money flowing into Maryland Casualty. Evans filled the role well, but he eventually tired of the game and, with RFC money, fulfilled a dream to buy and operate his own newspaper in Nashville, Tennessee (although Jones regularly turned down newspaper pleas for RFC loans and once piously explained to Roosevelt that "the Government should not be in a position to exercise influence on the editorial policy of any publication"). Upon Evans's departure, Maryland Casualty's leadership went to another Jones crony, Stewart McDonald. It was a classic story of what power these good ol' boys possessed.[34]

Jones's power also lay in what he could do for politicians. He understood when a project favored by a congressman was truly needed by all parties concerned and when the congressman simply needed a strong RFC rejection in order to attribute failure to Jones. That was the impersonal side of the RFC's politics. The personal side lay in the pressure for putting friends and relatives of politicians on the federal payroll. William O. Douglas related how Jones filled "one floor of the RFC building with desks, chairs, phones, and a few secretaries. Every political hack he had to hire to placate a senator or congressman was put in that one big room. The new employee would find the *New York Times* on his desk every morning, but he was given nothing to do. He could dictate letters back home, he could telephone to his heart's content, his monthly check for eight hundred dollars or so never failed to arrive—and he never gummed up Jesse's business." Douglas, reformer though he was, understood the need for this nepotism and confessed to practicing it himself.[35]

This technique did not build political power, but by not making enemies it retained power. The need to retain power became all the more important by Roosevelt's second inauguration, when the President's sweep of every state but Maine and Vermont appeared to ensure the ascendancy of the culture of left liberalism. It seemed that the days of Jesse Jones at the RFC were numbered, even if he was then master of a political empire unlike anything the federal government had ever seen.

The Emperor Jones

THE NEW DEALERS TRANSFORMED the RFC from a safety net for big bankers to a catapult of growth for entrepreneurs. "The new role which the Reconstruction Finance Corporation was therefore called upon to perform when the Roosevelt Administration took office was two-fold," RFC attorneys boasted in 1937: "It was given greatly enlarged and diversified lending functions, and it was enabled to cooperate with the new recovery agencies in carrying on their special activities."[36]

Nevertheless, widespread criticism accused the corporation of not living up to its full potential by rejecting valid loan applications and stifling growth when it charged excessive interest for its loans. Both liberals and businessmen accused RFC of dampening entrepreneurial enthusiasm and even discouraging applications for credit. Jones maintained that the problem did not lie with RFC and its cautious credit practices, but with the behavior of the private marketplace. If bankers would lend and businessmen would borrow, Jones argued, then the role of the RFC would expand. He implied that the depression had sapped entrepreneurs of their lust for adventure. Treasury Secretary Henry Morgenthau, Jr., wondered if Jones was just alibiing for his own failures. Envious of Jones as the administration's banker, Morgenthau asked economist Jacob Viner to survey the loan demand situation in 1934 in order to verify the truth of the situation. Not only did the Viner group conclude that Jones's tightfisted policies had contributed to the timorousness of private banking, it also asserted that RFC's credit restraints were responsible for NRA's shortcomings. Roosevelt's response to Viner's report was to create a Morgenthau-led interdepartmental committee to study the policies of all federal agencies involved in investment activity. Confronted with a challenge to his authority, Jones defended himself with figures purporting to show that RFC's rejection rate was not as great as rumored and that the number of loan applications fell far short of administration expectations. Moreover, pointing to a 50 per cent decline in the total volume of mortgage debt between 1929 and 1934, Jones argued that this proved how much liquidity had been added to the market. Of course, a counterargument could be made that it merely meant that bankers were not financing real estate. But Jones used his data to buttress not only pleas for a renewal of RFC's charter in January 1935, but also expanded authority for mortgage loans. Again Roosevelt decided to stick with Jones. The president requested an extension of RFC's time and powers; Congress eagerly complied. The wily Texan had turned embarrassment into triumph.

While the jury was still out as to RFC's fulfillment of its expectations, nobody was uncertain as to Jones's influence on the RFC. He was the corporation. It reflected his personality. Arthur Schlesinger Jr. has written that Jones saw RFC "as a continuing instrumentality for assisting a rising class of new men like himself, promoters and entrepreneurs, to make their initial stake." *Time* observed that "Jones thinks borrowers are the salt of the earth, the optimists, the builders, the men who take chances and thus make the U.S." That was the intrepid side of Jones, but it did not suggest his caution. He knew that a borrower needed sound collateral. "In a more innocent age of capitalism ideas and schemes were considered quite respectable," pundit Dwight MacDonald wrote, "but from his long experience in the RFC Jones has found that men with ideas and no capital are not such good credit risks as men with capital and no ideas."[37]

Nevertheless, Jones continued to argue that the depression had stifled initiative. Applications to the RFC still lagged behind expectations, and commercial loans had to follow suit. The RFC boasted that it loaned billions, but a cursory examination revealed most of the money went to banks and railroads tied closely to banks. The Export-Import Bank, dedicated to stimulating overseas sales of American goods, had loaned only $35 million by early 1937. As for liberating the housing market as Jones promised, the RFC Mortgage Company's high interest rates discouraged loan applications and then approved a mere 10 per cent of the applications it received. In two years it disbursed just $25 million, almost all of it in purchases of Federal Housing Administration mortgages. Stung by criticism that his banker mentality slowed demand, in July 1936 Jones lowered the rates charged by RFC a full point. When this did not increase loan demand, Jones felt vindicated by evidence that whatever RFC's policies were, businessmen were not venturesome. In a sense New Deal liberals began to like his arguments; for his evidence suggested that it was not their policies that were at fault when the depression persisted. The problem lay with bankers who did not lend—what some liberals labeled as a "capital strike"—or that the American industrialist had lost his buccaneer spirit. Jones's evidence not only found a real culprit for the prolonged depression, it also justified expanded or additional programs for economic growth.

However, the debate also raised a question Jones did not want to hear: if business demand for RFC and private loans was not what it ought to be, then were the bankers and the Treasury correct in describing RFC as superfluous? Would the marketplace eventually correct itself without federal intervention? Jones continued to blame disappointments upon the bankers' timidity, but he no more drummed up commercial business than did they. Perhaps, as liberals argued, markets suffered from a paucity of consumers. The business pickup since 1933 had been partly financed internally with corporation reserves. Further gains required additional retail spending, a conclusion which economists said pointed the way to an aggressive fiscal policy—the taxing and spending uses of the federal budget. But the irony here is that Roosevelt clung to the same cautious and deflationary policies as his ill-starred predecessor: he sedulously pursued a balanced budget. Egged on by the orthodox mind of Morgenthau ("Henry the Morgue," FDR called his old friend and neighbor), the President's budget necessarily restrained the flow of federal dollars into markets because a reciprocal flow of dollars into the Treasury was absent. Accordingly, a cautious fiscal policy dampened Jones's enthusiasm for liberal lending. Drawing his loan dollars from the Treasury, Jones would not invest a federal deficit. When Morgenthau carped that RFC was the problem because it cost too much (it had put nearly $11 billion into markets by 1936, already a record for any government agency), Jones the banker proudly noted increasing RFC revenues from debt service and suggested that the agency actually reduced federal debts and helped to balance the budget.[38]

Morgenthau had one insurmountable advantage over Jones: his position as head of the Treasury. The Treasury had been there since the beginnings of the federal government, while Jones headed an emergency agency created for economic reconstruction. Its life was proscribed by its creator, Congress, and had to be renewed upon the conclusion of a two-year term. Nonetheless, RFC had so intertwined itself with other temporary or permanent federal agencies that only a durable recovery could assure its extinction. RFC was an umbrella organization for numerous vital state capitalist activities. It greatly assisted mortgage bankers through the Home Owners Loan Corporation, the Federal Home Loan Banks, and the Federal Housing Administration. Following the economic collapse of 1937–38, Roosevelt asked Jones to create a national mortgage association that would buy FHA mortgages on new homes. The RFC created the Federal National Mortgage Association, "Fannie Mae," which bought FHA mortgages on new construction—thereby acting as a secondary market for them. Jones staffed Fannie Mae with lieutenants from RFC, which gave him virtual control of financing the home construction market since private banking was dormant without it or FHA. At its head he placed Stewart McDonald, a conservative St. Louis businessman and perhaps Jones's closest friend in the administration. Through them, home construction finally returned to pre-depression levels, principally because the New Deal "restructured the private housing market in a way that fundamentally altered the conditions under which Americans purchased and owned homes."

Roosevelt had a passionate interest in home ownership, viewing it as a "right" for the individual American and "a guarantee of social and economic stability" for the nation. The Home Owners Loan Act of 1933, creating the HOLC to refinance mortgages, had been a first step toward his goal. The following year the National Housing Act went further in creating the FHA for the purpose of insuring long-term mortgages at lower interest rates. In the 1920s most mortgages had had terms of five years or less, some calling for periods of up to twelve years, but comparatively few had terms of up to fifteen years. High payments plagued homeowners in the Great Depression, causing many defaults which HOLC sought to refinance with loans backing longer terms. FHA lengthened the amortization period to twenty years, insured new home mortgages and thus drastically reduced homeowners' payments. By 1940 FHA-insured mortgages averaged twenty-three years in duration and would continue to lengthen through the 1940s to thirty years. The result was lower payments for individuals and considerably increased home construction and ownership (also helped by tax laws that allowed for federal deductions of interest and real estate tax payments). It must have been good business: in 1935 only 6 per cent of all mortgages were FHA-insured; by 1950 half of all new home mortgages were backed by either the FHA or the Veterans Administration. Private construction in the late 1930s was more than twice what it had been in 1933, but about half of what it had been in 1929, and it would be the war and the postwar eras that stimulated home construction; in the 1930s the construction industry remained slow due to either slow responses by builders or bank reluctance to lend for real estate. Perhaps builders or bankers had lost their nerve; perhaps the latter, as Jones seemed to suggest, created their own shortage of capital. In any event, without FHA the depression would have been steeper. Through this credit revolution, state capitalism provided for tremendous economic development in the housing markets of America.[39]

The New Deal not only made more feasible the purchase of a home, it also facilitated the buying of appliances and the consumption of electricity which powered the appliances. Another facet of the New Deal credit revolution was the financing of cheap power for the home and farm. In fact, it increased consumer expenditures quite nicely. Following its origins with the TVA, RFC kept the Electric Home and Farm Authority alive as part of its operations because EHFA lent to lenders who financed consumers of electrical appliances for the home and farm—thereby sustaining not only a demand for electricity but all the gadgets dependent upon it and jobs of the people who built them. Significantly, the output of manufacturing in 1937 equaled that of 1929 with the greatest growth coming in refrigerators, washing machines, radios, and vegetables in cans and glass containers that would find their way into refrigerators. Only 516 stores in the United States had had refrigeration capacity in 1933, and that number grew about thirty times by the end of the decade. RFC funded numerous PWA projects that built public power installations for the Rural Electrification Administration, itself a financier of power for small communities and farmer cooperatives; REA got its money from the RFC and by 1940 that totaled $246 million.[40] RFC loans supported such projects as the Bonneville Power Authority, the Oakland Bay Bridge in San Francisco harbor, and a host of public works projects dear to Interior Secretary Harold Ickes. Farmers burdened with debts left over from their land speculations going back to the Great War years enjoyed RFC's funding of its subsidiary, the Commodity Credit Corporation. Although many Americans did not know how RFC influenced their lives, their congressmen did.

None of this soothed Morgenthau. He still blamed RFC's inflation of credit for an absence of prosperity, and when the economy deteriorated in 1937, Morgenthau suspected that the RFC had disrupted business confidence. In a September 1937 meeting he pressed Roosevelt to boost the nation's confidence in the economy by boldly shutting down emergency organizations identified with the Depression and then making a display of government retrenchment by promising a balanced budget to head off additional and undesirable congressional appropriations. Although it would have been a move reminiscent of his predecessor's tactics in 1931–32, FDR "liked the idea fine." The place to begin with the dismantling of reconstruction agencies was with the Reconstruction Finance Corporation. In October, Roosevelt officially ordered Jones not to extend new loans. Jones was not one to stand in the way of balancing the budget: "I'm for that one hundred per cent," he told Morgenthau, adding that "we are up to the closing point with this agency." Perhaps this would satisfy Democratic conservatives, but administration liberals were horrified by an apparent step backward in policy. According to Adolf Berle, now an Assistant Secretary of State and unofficial economic troubleshooter for Roosevelt, state capitalism would be phased out at a time when it was most needed, simply because of "Morgenthau's insane jealousy . . . for Jesse Jones."[41]

Why was the sly Uncle Jesse so agreeable to balancing the budget and eliminating his own agency? Perhaps he knew he could count on his client agencies to protest for him. Sure enough, with the discussion of phasing out RFC came Henry Wallace's complaint that RFC's demise would take commodity credit down with it. Morgenthau turned to Jones for an ally in defense of a balanced budget: "You and I have got some financial sense," he told Jones; "let's stick together on this." While not at all fond of the slow-witted Morgenthau, Jones agreed to this ephemeral alliance. A week later at lunch with Morgenthau and FDR, Wallace averred that RFC could not die because he had committed the Agriculture Department to financing corn crops. Morgenthau laughed derisively, and Wallace snapped that it was no laughing matter because the Midwest would say that Southerners ran the Democratic party. "That's nothing new, Henry," FDR jibed. Although the President still affirmed a balanced budget, Wallace continued to pursue crop financing, which Morgenthau insisted would unbalance the budget by $300 million. Wallace's solution to this anticipated crisis in farm credit was to angrily demand transfer of the RFC's Commodity Credit Corporation to Agriculture; Morgenthau shot back, "You can't have your sales manager and your credit manager in the same person." As was frequently the case, Henry the Morgue would be proven wrong. It signaled a permanent credit role for the federal government.

Jones would eventually lose Commodity Credit, but he would retain the RFC. A few days later, he commented at a White House meeting that if he did not make a particular industrial loan, thirteen hundred people would lose jobs: did Morgenthau think it would be less expensive for the government to put those people on the public works relief rolls? Although Morgenthau would rather see higher taxes than unbalance the budget, Roosevelt understood Jones's not-too-subtle point. "It seems to me that we have to carry out [RFC's] moral obligations and legal directions," the President told the Treasury. The number of jobless was rising again and the elections of 1938 were not too far off.[42]

As the country, not yet recovered from the Hoover Depression, slid into a Roosevelt Depression, the administration groped for new plans. In December a defensive Morgenthau suggested that they consider RFC loans off-budget. In January FDR decided to allow RFC to make loans for self-liquidating projects and utilities. By April Roosevelt fully reversed engines and ordered Jones to resume RFC programs as before, stipulating only that "small enterprises which because of their very smallness find it difficult to interest private credit sources" be favored. For the time being, spending and loaning would be the order of the day in 1938, notwithstanding the lack of adequate revenues. Roosevelt's order transformed the RFC from a temporary agency into a formidable force for state capitalism without any definite time horizon.[43]

As might be expected with such an operator, when Roosevelt revived RFC's lending authority he granted Jones more authority than ever. Jones was one to take advantage of such an opportunity. As he put it in his memoir of the RFC, he "resumed business across the board *at my discretion.*" He liked a lot of discretion. He approached William O. Douglas and observed that the Securities and Exchange Commission was housed in "a ratty place. You deserve a splendid place." He offered to erect a building just for the SEC: "Call it the Douglas building or the SEC building, or anything else you desire." "And the price?" Chairman Douglas inquired. "We'll make the SEC the biggest bureau in the RFC," Uncle Jesse replied. Douglas declined the offer: "It might ruin us, Jesse." Jones renewed the offer several times before Douglas went on the Supreme Court and years later the Justice wondered if thwarting Jones's empire-building had been a mistake; the SEC was in the same ratty place.[44]

For Jones, the revival of his fortunes was welcome but not wholly unexpected. He was serenely confident of RFC's political value for congressmen and his personal utility to Roosevelt. Policy-making is an art that depends upon personalities more than political scientists and Marxists would have us believe, and "in the case of Jesse Jones, personality is closely integrated with policy."[45] Only a personality whose caution inspired confidence could have accumulated as much power over money as did Jones. Personal relationships and public reputations were important to Roosevelt in selecting his administrators to help make policies. The Roosevelt-Jones relationship in that fateful year, 1937, blended camaraderie, respect and fear. They had known each other off and on for twenty years. As was the case for many Democrats, their initial contact occurred during the war and remained occasional through the convention of 1924. Roosevelt made several visits to the Democratic National Committee in Washington during Jones's tenure as its fund-raiser, and Roosevelt, junior to Jones in age and party status, sometimes found reason to initiate communication. In 1926 Roosevelt congratulated Jones on his purchase of the Houston *Chronicle* and denied gossip that he had ever criticized Jones's methods of raising Democratic funds. Addressing Roosevelt as "my good friend" and hailing him as "one of the best assets of our party," Jones cordially agreed that they had no real differences. In

March 1928 Roosevelt made suggestions to Jones concerning Democratic preparations for the coming campaign. Jones deftly assured Roosevelt that every one of his suggestions had been anticipated since 1924. Roosevelt's election as Governor of New York that fall brought an enthusiastic note from Jones ("one of the greatest compliments that has come to anyone in American politics"). As for Jones's support for Garner for president in 1932, it could not have offended Roosevelt any more than Roosevelt's support of Smith in 1924 would have offended McAdoo supporters such as Jones. In the interregnum of 1932–33, RFC director Jones conscientiously kept the President-elect informed of the seriousness of the banking situation as he traveled about investigating troubled banks. It was evident that Jones was eager to work with Roosevelt and be useful to him.[46]

Roosevelt genuinely liked Southern party warhorses such as Jones. He appreciated the votes they delivered in Congress and admired their bucolic sociability, their elliptical storytelling and unhurried gossiping—so different from the intensity of braintrusters or certain urban politicians. Roosevelt was at home in their convivial world: he understood Garner's Bureau of Education without ever seeing it. During the banking crisis of 1933 Roosevelt gave Jones access to his private quarters in the White House and thereafter Jones frequently visited Roosevelt there late at night. As press secretary Steve Early explained, Jones "and the President have long talks which the President finds very useful." That included Jones's advice on financial controversies. Also, Roosevelt was intent upon developing the Southern and Western economies; who would be better able to lead such a scheme than a Texas banker who knew where the votes in Congress were? Because Jones inspired confidence, FDR gave him considerable leeway in RFC dealings. He was in tune with Jones's fiscal conservatism. Also, Roosevelt was concerned to avoid giving him offense, or permitting Morgenthau to do so. Thus, in 1934 he privately told a petulant Morgenthau:

> With a view to personal feelings, etc., I think it would be just as well for you not to instruct Jesse Jones as you did in regard to the interest rate. He is after all the head of an independent agency. If you had told him that I had told you that I wanted the Treasury to charge the R.F.C. approximately what the Treasury has to pay for its money, that would have been enough. I know you will understand.

On another occasion, Morgenthau read into Jones's testimony at a congressional hearing a devious attempt to get his way on policy, and at the next Cabinet meeting the Treasury Secretary scribbled a note to the President accusing Jesse of "trying to force your hand. Am I right?" FDR scribbled back: "*No* because the committee on the hill insisted on asking him questions." Roosevelt liked Jones because he was, said Steve Early, "a Democrat rather than a starry-eyed New Dealer." The distinction was important, and Roosevelt knew who had the clout on Capitol Hill. Politics in their day had very much of a clubhouse atmosphere, and "nigger" stories* or private jokes were zestfully shared, as when Jones wrote FDR that two Democratic officials and their cohorts were wagering as to which of their wirehaired terriers could piddle the most in a given walking distance. Roosevelt responded that if he were in on the wager he could make a lot of money by letting the odds on one dog "go sky-high" and then betting on the other dog.[47]

The Roosevelt-Jones alliance is additional evidence that politics makes strange bedfellows. These very different men each understood what the other required. Roosevelt mugwumpishly appreciated Jones's banker tightfistedness in the same way he tolerated Harold Ickes's ponderously slow spending of Public Works Administration funds. After all, the legend of the Democratic party in their time was still that of how New York City's Tweed ring unmercifully bilked the taxpayers for public construction whose cost far exceeded its worth. Roosevelt prized men of public morality who practiced a deflationary accountability that diligently excluded inflationary unscrupulousness. Given the revolution he was leading in bold federal financing of homes, agriculture and power, Roosevelt needed a man like Jones who reassured more cautious individual capitalists while willingly endorsing state capitalism. On a private level, Roosevelt and Jones bestowed financial favors upon each other with government funds—without greedily feasting at the public trough. Thus, if Jones wanted federal funds to help mark the Texas centennial by building a monument at San Jacinto to rival the height of the Washington Monument, Roosevelt was not one to deny him. Jones liked to consider himself a businessman who was above politics; FDR was all politician. Jones believed he was consistent in his principles, but Roosevelt had to be many things to many people. FDR liked to experiment with government; or, as Jones put it, "In poker the President preferred wild cards

*One "nigger" joke mixed sex and race and went as follows: "Sam Johnson, colored, had a job some distance from home and was only able to come home weekends, usually getting in rather late Saturday night. But one weekend he came in Friday night, unexpectedly and a little late. He had to knock several times before the door was opened. It was a one-room cabin.

"After greeting his wife, he went over to the washbowl, got out his razor and started stropping it. By and by his wife said, 'What yo' stroppin' that razor fo' this time of night?'

"Sam replied, 'Well, if there ain't no nigger under that bed, what fits them shoes I'm lookin at, I'm gonna shave.'" Jones to FDR, ca. November 1936, PPF 703.

and innovations to the kind of straight five-card draw poker most Texans were raised on." So it was in politics. Jones handled Roosevelt's "wild cards" by ignoring them. Years later he would boast about how selectively he enforced many of Roosevelt's orders. William O. Douglas recalled how he once went to FDR to complain of Jones's lack of cooperation. The President called them both in and read the riot act with specific instructions that they were to get together to iron out differences. On the way out Douglas asked Jones when they would meet and Jones responded, "Not now, not tomorrow, never." Then, pointing to his gray hair, Jones said: "When your hair gets to be the color of mine, you'll be wise. You will know that the President is a very busy man. He's so busy that he'll never even remember this talk we've had." The matter ended there. Had Roosevelt staged the scene for Douglas's benefit with the knowledge that Jones would prevail anyway? Even a president had need of the RFC's favors. During the war Jones approved RFC participation in the government purchase of an estate adjacent to Roosevelt's in Hyde Park. But he turned the President down when Roosevelt sought RFC funds to buy the Empire State Building in New York to help out its owners, Al Smith and his friends. By that time relations between the two politicians had frayed; it had become too evident that Jones dearly loved to challenge the President.[48]

A bureaucratic empire as farflung and as popular as Jones's was bound to excite envy in other bureaucratic empire-builders. Following the near destruction of the Commodity Credit Corporation, Henry A. Wallace made up his mind to capture it for the Department of Agriculture. Wallace was known as a somewhat idealistic visionary, but he had learned about bureaucratic politics through his father. Henry C. Wallace, Secretary of Agriculture during Warren Harding's presidency, had been victimized by the all-time champion imperialist, the Secretary of Commerce and "Undersecretary of Everything Else," Herbert Hoover. The experience prepared the younger Wallace to be vigilant over his domain and eager to snatch a bit of someone else's. The Commodity Credit Corporation, Wallace believed, was an agricultural, not credit, agency which he must have under his wing.

The fortunes of history are fickle, as witness the fact that the Commodity Credit Corporation (CCC) is not nearly as well remembered as the Civilian Conservation Corps (CCC) of temporary relief fame or the truly revolutionary Agricultural Adjustment Administration (AAA). Yet, "New Deal credit provisions were probably of more importance to farmers than the crop reduction programs of the AAA," a historian has written. Indeed, Wallace and farmers had come to appreciate the Commodity Credit Corporation's great significance by 1936. Jones's CCC had been the New Deal's agricultural credit arm since 1933, enabling farmers to borrow on their crops, sell the crop if prices rose or leave it in storage if prices declined and await a price rise. It worked so well that in 1938 Congress passed the second Agricultural Adjustment Act, which recognized that CCC was better able to raise prices than Wallace's AAA by setting minimum prices through its loan rates. CCC had become the most politically important New Deal agricultural agency, thanks to its "primary means of stabilizing farm prices and income. . . . Between 1936 and 1938, the Commodity Credit Corporation had become the foundation of a permanent income-support system."[49]

About to lose the Forest Service to Harold Ickes's Department of the Interior under the governmental reorganization bill, Wallace bid for control of the CCC. In June 1938 he proposed reducing the number of directors of the CCC from twelve to nine by reducing those appointed by the RFC from six to three—the Farm Credit Administration and the Department of Agriculture having three each. Jones already had acceded to Treasury's demand that all of CCC's capital be transferred to Morgenthau's domain—a move that made the Treasury a vitally interested ally of RFC. Then Jones negotiated a compromise that reduced the board to ten directors, five of them coming from the RFC. A year later, however, Congress reorganized the executive, with Wallace finally getting his prize, CCC. Nevertheless, he confronted a CCC board whose loyalties lay elsewhere. When Wallace appealed to Morgenthau for help in removing Jones's appointments, Morgenthau struck a bargain whereby Wallace would give information Morgenthau wanted. Wallace did not get all he wanted, but, as Morgenthau explained to his aides, "If I give it to him all at once, I have nothing left to trade with." As for Jones, he accepted his loss of CCC with outward equanimity, but it rankled. No mention of Wallace's triumph appeared in Jones's memoir of the RFC or in his authorized biography. Yet seven years after its loss he bitterly recalled, "We organized the Commodity Credit Corporation and operated it for six or seven years. It got popular and Henry wanted it, and got it."[50]

Jones remembered Wallace's capture of the CCC well because it was about his only political defeat. Also, it came at a time when Wallace was rapidly becoming the darling of New Deal liberals. During the war they would have an epic battle. Jones found himself increasingly isolated at the top levels of the administration. Socially he saw Federal Housing Administrator Stewart McDonald and occasionally went fishing on the yacht of Fred Fisher of the Detroit car body corporation, not exactly the sort of company that would heighten his liberalism. Paradoxically, his associations with businessmen were his ace in the hole. Roosevelt needed the conservative Jones and his influence with businessmen, Southern congressmen and Texas politicos. As *Time* said, "His removal would unloose a roar of thunder in his home state, Texas, and the South, which has received a goodly portion of Mr. Jones's well-distributed loans." FDR communicated his appreciation of Uncle Jesse in 1939 when he balanced RFC's loss of CCC by appointing Jones's assistant, Emil Schram, as his successor at RFC and making Jones Federal Loan Administrator, an umbrella responsibilty that covered not only RFC and its subsidiaries, but all federal investment agencies at a time when the war in Europe and American defense preparedness promised that there would be more such agencies. Ironically, Morgenthau had suggested such a consolidation earlier as a way of getting rid of Jones. Roosevelt adopted it as part of his reorganization plans and justified it on the grounds of "economy," reducing administrative costs.[51] A year later, the President launched his campaign for a third term by taking Wallace on as his vice-presidential candidate. Roosevelt knew that war preparedness would require business participation and less liberal ideology, and he made Republicans Henry L. Stimson Secretary of War and Frank Knox Secretary of the Navy. At the same time FDR asked Jones to take Harry Hopkins's place as Secretary of Commerce.

At last Jones had his desired Cabinet post and his control of most of the state capitalist agencies of the New Deal that now turned their attentions from economic development for recovery to economic development for war. However, Roosevelt wanted Jones to relinquish his leadership of the Federal Loan Agency. Even the temptation of control over the multitude of agencies under the jurisdiction of Commerce could not tempt Jones to surrender the Federal Loan Agency and his supervision of RFC: "I feel this responsibility keenly, and would not like to be taken away from it—for any cause," he told John Nance Garner. In the words of one reporter, "Mr. Jones's own attitude as to the real importance of the job could not have been better put than by his declination to accept the appointment if it meant giving up his place as Federal Loan Administrator." Not even Roosevelt could budge Jones from his control over Federal Loan once his name had been sent to Congress in nomination for Commerce. And Congress approved the dual arrangement with the proviso that Jones get one salary for two jobs; still, "No other man in the Government is able to write his own ticket on Capitol Hill as is Jesse Jones."

Since both agencies were umbrellas, Jones effectively headed the RFC Mortgage Company, the Disaster Loan Corporation, the Federal National Mortgage Association, the Export-Import Bank, the Federal Housing Administration, the Census Bureau, the Bureau of Standards, the

Civil Aeronautics Board, the Patent Office, the Coast and Geodetic Survey—and with the war would be added the Rubber Reserve Company, the Metals Reserve Company, the Defense Supplies Company, and the Defense Plant Corporation. Never had one man possessed so much public financial power in a democratic society. Perhaps only McAdoo, with his control of the Treasury, the Capital Issues Committee, and the Railroad Administration during the Great War, could rival Jones for accumulating portfolios. Jones was, as Dwight MacDonald aptly wrote, "the mightiest state capitalist we have yet produced, ***an economic emperor.***" Since the war gave him an opportunity to add to his empire, Jones and the corporation, Clifford Durr wrote, would leave "a deep impression on the economic structure of the country and, perhaps more than we realize, on present political thinking." State capitalism would thrive nicely.[52]

4.

Hugh Johnson: Raising Prices

HUGH JOHNSON FEARED disappointing Alexander Sachs. That might have surprised many people who knew Johnson and believed the gruff former West Pointer was, as described by his mentor, Bernard Baruch, "a well-developed bully." But Johnson deferred to certain businessmen and intellectuals. "The thing I dreaded most was facing Alex Sachs with whom I had planned so carefully," Johnson later recalled. Yet he had no other choice. For nearly a year he and Sachs had discussed planning schemes for industrial recovery among themselves and with key members of Roosevelt's administration. New Dealers had reached a broad consensus for industrial planning; between Johnson and Sachs the consensus narrowed to what should be planned and how extensive the planning. In June 1933 Congress passed the National Industrial Recovery Act, mandating an ambiguous National Recovery Administration for industrial stabilization and allocating $3.3 billion in public works. As for who would head the NRA, "Hugh, you've got to *do* this job," the President told Johnson. General Johnson was not so modest as to disagree with his commander in chief, even if it seemed an almost impossible task in this national crisis. As an officer in the Army who had once chased Pancho Villa on the Mexican border, he tended to display bravado rather than fear. When his friends congratulated him on the new command, Johnson volubly brushed them aside: *"It will be red fire at first and dead cats afterward. This is just like mounting the guillotine on the infinitesimal gamble that the ax won't work."* At that moment Johnson already believed that NRA could not work. He and Sachs had agreed that industrial recovery called for a necessary union of limited price stabilization and public works expansion programs. However, attending a Cabinet meeting (where he "felt like one accused before the Masked Court of the Venetian Doge"), Johnson learned that Roosevelt would separate public works from NRA and give it to Interior Secretary Harold L. Ickes. "Taken aback," Johnson wanted to decline NRA. Roosevelt saw this and quietly asked Labor Secretary Frances Perkins to "keep Hugh sweet." Johnson rated her "the best man in the cabinet," and there followed a long chauffeured drive through Washington during which Perkins listened to Johnson fulminate against the separation of NRA and public works—but agree to do the job. However, Johnson still had to face Alex Sachs with half a commission.[1]

Why Hugh Johnson? Roosevelt's decision to make Johnson the NRA's administrator appalled Bernard Baruch. "Hugh's got a lot of weaknesses. He's not fit to be the head of anything," he told Frances Perkins. "Hugh's always got to have somebody to keep him in order. He's got lots of ability, but you have to handle it." And Baruch could handle it—which was how Johnson got into the Roosevelt entourage. The day after McAdoo delivered the Democratic nomination to FDR, Baruch walked into Roosevelt headquarters to demand that Johnson be added to the "brain trust." Not wanting Baruch to take his money on vacation to Europe as he did in 1924, the Roosevelt people acceded to his wishes. Baruch did not commit himself to candidates for the nomination, but once the party decided whom it wanted he liked to have influence on policies through his surrogates. Just as his friend George Peek had been Al Smith's adviser on agriculture in 1928, Johnson would be FDR's adviser on industry. Democrats were agreeable because of Baruch's influence in the Senate. Throughout the 1920s he had bankrolled its candidates—mostly its Southern winners such as Democratic Leader Joe T. Robinson of Arkansas, Pat Harrison of Mississippi and Key Pittman of Nevada, the ranking Democrats on the Finance and Foreign Relations committees, respectively. Other friends whose elections were financed by Baruch were rising leaders Alben Barkley of Kentucky and James F. Byrnes of South Carolina. They were known as part of "Bernie's string." Not everyone liked Baruch. Young New Dealers thought him too conservative. Still, as Roosevelt patiently explained to Rexford Guy Tugwell, Baruch "owned" some sixty congressmen in addition to the senators and "that, he said, was power around Washington. . . . Those sixty congressmen had to be kept in line."[2]

Roosevelt took Johnson more seriously than Baruch, a fact that puzzled many, including Baruch. Johnson was a man of excesses: he drank too much, cursed too much and gambled too much. He was a creature of the peacetime Army and might have remained so but for the discovery by General Enoch Crowder that Johnson had a gift for using words. Although hardly scholarly, Johnson loved to read and play with the language. He wrote for pulp magazines on the side and, at Crowder's urging, trained as a lawyer for the Judge Advocate Corps. That brought promotions and, during the war, an appointment to the War Industries Board, where he met his next patron: Baruch. Shortly after the war Johnson resigned his Army commission and entered the farm machinery business with fellow WIB executive George N. Peek. The partnership was doomed at the start because both men were irascible and headstrong; worse, their Moline Plow Company floundered in the early 1920s' agricultural depression. Peek hit the road to campaign for farm relief via the McNary-Haugen plan and Johnson went to work for Baruch as a personal analyst of companies and economic conditions. In the depression Johnson's honesty, insights and craftsmanship shone in reports submitted to his "Chief." His talents surprised academics in FDR's brain trust; FDR found his enthusiasm for government action and ability to speak the businessman's language useful. The President wanted a "driver" like Johnson to lead industrial recovery. Unanswered was Baruch's question as to who would lead the General.[3]

The WIB experience had stayed with most men who had been a part of it, and Johnson's was a case in point. In war the WIB had limited inflation with ceilings on prices; in Depression Johnson wanted to build a floor under prices. Both methods employed industrial cooperation, a euphemism for government-sponsored cartels. Advocates of federal action frequently likened the Depression crisis to the war emergency, but more cautious types such as Baruch suspected that the war metaphor was a trap. A thin line had divided WIB industrial cooperation from government coercion, a line the WIB seldom had to cross because patriotism under fire compelled cooperation with it. As it was, the WIB's actions knowingly violated the Sherman antitrust law's injunction against conspiracy in restraint of trade and got away with it because of the crisis of war. NRA also set aside the antitrust laws; but would business and the courts allow Congress to create a peacetime WIB without external threats to national security? Johnson and Alexander Sachs had considered the absence of the war's moral suasion and had reasoned that public works contracts would serve as incentives for cooperation in the capital goods industries. Now control of public works had passed from them, and Johnson confronted the increased probability of NRA failure.

Without control of public works Sachs foresaw an impending disaster for NRA. Unlike the approach of the plain-spoken Johnson, Sachs's writings on economics were marked by frequent allusions to economic data, philosophy, physiology or the history of western man, thus tending to intimidate rather than inform a reader. Neither uninteresting nor dull, Sachs seldom wrote for a public readership but could pen a vigorous, insightful and even entertaining polemic, if he avoided his usual lengthy and convoluted sentences. Roosevelt usually found Sachs informative and sometimes even persuasive. Actually, Sachs excelled at writing exclusively for a few potential policymakers, whom he cultivated through his Wall Street address. A vain man with considerable effrontery, Sachs numbered among his correspondents during the New Deal years such diverse economic seers as John Maynard Keynes, Jacob Viner, Edward S. Mason, Isador Lubin and Richard Leffingwell. New York *Herald Tribune* columnist Dorothy Thompson practically allowed Sachs to write her columns on economic policies[4]—which made her words as close as he came to finding a general audience.*

His most prominent place in history came about as a result of his continuing contact with Franklin D. Roosevelt, who welcomed Sachs's counsel and his intellectual curiosity about science. It was through the German émigré economist Gustav Stolper that Hungarian émigré physicist Leo Szilard contacted Sachs in 1939, asking him to bring to the attention of the President the fact that Nazi scientists were capable of developing nuclear fission, a necessary step to the manufacture of an atomic bomb. Sachs's response was to draft a letter which Szilard would have Albert Einstein sign for Sachs's personal delivery to Roosevelt. This was the beginning of the American atomic project, and Sachs's proudest moment.[5]

Physically Sachs was a big man with a squeaky voice that reminded some people of the comedian Ed Wynn. Intentionally or not, his manner persuaded many people including those on the *New York Times* that he was the eminent *Dr.* Sachs, though his only degree was a bachelor's from Columbia. He had graduated from Columbia in three years at nineteen, only eight years after his arrival in New York as a Jewish refugee from Lithuania. He then worked as a statistician in the municipal bond department of Wall Street's Lee Higginson & Company for a year before going to Harvard on two prestigious fellowships, spending one year studying economics and social philosophy and another in the law school. He seems to have discovered early in life that brilliance could be acclaimed as evident without credentials to certify it. He worked for Justice Louis Brandeis and the Zionist Organization of America on international problems of the Middle East, which brought him in touch with some of the more prominent Jews in Wall Street. In 1922 he went to work for investor/lawyer Walter Eugene Meyer as an economics and investment analyst, making a small reputation as a contrarian by doubting that the Coolidge prosperity of the 1920s had a firm foundation. He argued that the war had distorted real values and that Republican policies "masked price inflation," and he forecast an overproduction that would reduce real values. Propaganda created a "collective illusion" of well-being in the

*The relationship is not unusual. Journalists frequently deferred to experienced hands in finance for their insights into economic policies. Arthur Krock of the *New York Times* heeded the advice of Baruch, and Walter Lippmann of the *Herald Tribune* had Leffingwell to guide him.

1920s that persisted into the Hoover years and inspired a belief that the country could lift itself out of the depression by "psychological manipulation and wishful thinking." Such erudite, tough-minded, independent judgments attracted the attention of Lehman Brothers, and in 1929 they asked him to organize and direct the economics and investment research department of the Lehman Corporation, their investment trust subsidiary. Sachs kept its funds in cash and when the crash came, he was the envy of Wall Street. Two years later Lehman Brothers elected him to the board of directors, a position he held until his death in 1973.[6]

The unlikely Sachs-Johnson partnership was probably initiated by John Hancock, who had been the Navy's counterpart to Johnson on the WIB before joining Lehman Brothers and becoming its first nonfamily partner in 1924. Although Sachs and Johnson agreed on the urgent need for government help in depression markets, Sachs was not an unabashed admirer of the WIB experience or an advocate of its application in peacetime. He intensely admired American liberalism and wanted no part of anything which mirrored German cartelism and violated the antitrust laws of the United States or the laws of economic man. While Sachs rejected nineteenth-century individualism, he disliked most collectivist strategies, believing collectivism best served agriculture. Following the banking crisis in 1933, Roosevelt attacked the persistent depression in agriculture with a producer allotment scheme; the Agricultural Adjustment Administration, headed by George Peek, would erect gigantic government-supervised farm cartels. Commodity by commodity the cartels employed the government's power to tax and compel cooperation to drive prices up to prewar levels. Roosevelt counted upon higher farm prices to restore farmer purchasing power. Sachs agreed that chaotic farm markets made that strategy somewhat useful, but insisted that manufacturing markets would have to be selectively organized to control production. He warned that widespread restraints upon their output would lead to disaster.

Like the farmers, unemployed workers had champions in Congress. Among them was Senator Hugo Black of Alabama, who introduced a very popular bill for restricting interstate trade to goods produced only by workers working thirty-hour weeks. Sachs and many New Dealers considered the Black bill wrongheaded because it would spread poverty instead of inspiring recovery. But, if they could find no other strategy to demonstrate concern for unemployed workers, then the Black bill would fill the void. Johnson and Peek had collaborated with Secretary of Agriculture Henry Wallace, among others, in writing the agricultural recovery bill. Then Johnson joined a diffuse group of interested parties such as public works advocates, the U.S. Chamber of Commerce, the American Federation of Labor, lawyers, and others, in writing an industrial recovery bill. The strategy of inflated prices had its impact: "As buyers, we are beginning to see some of the practical effects of the industrial recovery bill," Sears's Robert E. Wood wrote; "This bill is going to mean a very substantial rise in prices of manufactured products . . . , which, of course, we will have to pass on to the consumer." Sachs ridiculed the bill as "a conglomeration of purposes, an obfuscation of ends and a stultification of methods." He wanted no part of what he called "monistic planning akin to state capitalism or state socialism"; he sought, he told Johnson, "pluralistic planning for recovery suited to a political and economic democracy. . . . Knowing what I do about the rigidifying maladjustments and autocratic monopolies that have developed from the German cartels and how they contributed to and aggravated the European depression I shudder to think what will follow if we heedlessly embark upon the same treacherous waters without navigation instruments." He warned that, without the lures of public works to stimulate capital goods industries, "the omnibus bill can only be administered by a bureaucracy operating by fiat and such bureaucracy would be far more akin to an incipient Fascist or Nazi state than to a liberal republic." Having said all that, Sachs ruefully signed on as NRA's economist.[7]

Among economic planners, disagreements abounded; where NRA was concerned, they usually fell into two categories: stabilizers and expansionists. Stabilizers saw the depression crisis as a manifestation of overproduction through ruinous unit competition that incited cutting of wage costs—thereby worsening a bad situation; they favored cooperation through organization to restrain output and elevate prices, income and purchasing power. On the other hand, expansionists maintained that the depression had sapped promoters of their entrepreneurial nerve, an interpretation apparently confirmed by the RFC's experience with timid bankers and timid borrowers; instead of fixing prices, "the remedy lay in all-around *expansion* of activity," Sachs wrote. Sachs did not oppose cooperation among producers, for he believed that cartel-like "production restriction and price manipulation are the accepted techniques . . . under orthodox capitalism." A little corporatism was not a bad thing, but he disdained planners such as Rexford Tugwell who would compel cooperation in every sector of the marketplace. Caught between proponents of the "purchasing power fallacy" such as Tugwell and "simple minded laissez faire economists" such as New Era Republicans, Sachs—"a sort of lone wolf New Dealer in the menagerie of economists," as he described himself—cast his lot with planners, hoping to limit cartelist stabilization to a few capital goods industries. Of course, restraint in economic planning needed the fillip of public works spending "to liberate private capital goods." However, early in the New Deal it became evident that public works administrator Harold Ickes was a Chicago reformer more intent upon averting spending scandals than spending for re-employment. Expansionists had to look to the RFC to stimulate private investment when public investment proved excessively cautious. At the same time, businessmen went about organizing NRA cartels with a zeal Sachs deemed undesirable.[8]

Ever the contrarian, Sachs fell out of step with the intensifying demands to codify industries to stabilize production and control prices in the summer of 1933. Also, Sachs thought that Johnson had agreed to oppose price-fixing. "There was a great deal of lack of clicking between Alexander's academic economics and Johnson's opportunism," the ubiquitous Tommy Corcoran observed. But in June the General gave in to businessmen importuning for a textile code that would limit production—a crack in the dam that unleashed a torrent of codes. "At one of the most critical moments in the nation's history," Bernard Bellush has written, "when a great need was to increase the purchasing power of the consumer through immediate expansion in production, jobs and income, the NRA established a restrictionist policy. The precedent was self-defeating, for almost every other industry insisted on similar rights." Admitting to "disillusionment with the fallacious price policy pursued by the Administration and the wrong drift in the process of code making," by midsummer Sachs contemplated resignation. Economies of scarcity made no sense to him because "capitalism is an economy of maximized profit and volume"; the only limit upon output ought to be the absence of profitability, but Sachs found himself isolated when other planners imposed artificial limits upon production.[9] Pleading that the Lehman Corporation needed him, in August Sachs reduced his time in Washington to a half week and began to collect NRA documents for economist Charles F. Roos, who would write its first history. By October his half-time service to NRA existed mostly on paper, and in January he freely admitted to being out of touch with events inside the NRA.[10]

Nevertheless, Sachs kept his lines to the White House open. His reputation as a seer enhanced, Sachs sought all the more influence with Roosevelt. "I do hope to see you one of these days soon." The President welcomed Sachs's "extraordinarily interesting" expertise on industrial matters such as railroad reorganization or public utility funding that directly impacted upon capital markets. Occasionally Sachs sent Roosevelt words of encouragement, but beginning in 1936 he fell out of step with the President's TVA program and tax policies. Roosevelt had remained a stabilizer, while Sachs increasingly sought expansion through private investment.[11]

The once popular NRA soon was in trouble from all sides. By early 1934 Johnson, a whirlwind of action in selling individual codes and the Blue Eagle, was on the verge of a personal collapse from exhaustion and alcoholism. Stories about the General abounded in Washington. His old sidekick, George Peek, told people that Johnson was crazy with power. Once, when Johnson was asked if he harbored ambitions for political office, rather than Washington, he said, he preferred to be "down between Brownsville and Matamoras where the owls fucked the chickens." In one speech he called former Secretary of the Treasury Ogden Mills a "little son of the rich." He denounced a reporter who wrote articles critical of him as having veins with "something more than a trace of rodent blood." Following an incident in which Johnson hurled invective at the estimable publisher of the Washington *Post*, Eugene Meyer, Roosevelt told the Cabinet with amusement that every administration had to have its "Peck's Bad Boy." Yet, it was clear that Johnson needed a handler.

The only person capable of that role was his secretary, Frances Robinson, a diminutive twenty-six-year-old woman who was as ambitious and tough as Johnson. In the eyes of some people she too was one of Johnson's problems. "Robbie" protected Johnson from the world while tending to his needs. She guarded him zealously from intruders upon his time, and sometimes when he was cornered by reporters' questions, he would tell them, "I don't know. Ask the little skirt." Robinson became so indispensable that he eventually gave her the title of administrative assistant and raised her salary three times during 1933, making her the fourth-highest-paid person in NRA. She was a tyrant in the agency. When she discovered a flirtatious secretary who threatened to make trouble, she promised to "tell the bitch where to head in." Donald Richberg, counsel for the NRA, could not have a meeting with Johnson without Robinson present. One time when Richberg managed a meeting with Johnson behind closed doors, she burst into the room and demanded, "What do you mean by locking yourselves away from me in this way?" Because Johnson was a married man who expected his wife to stay home and knit, many in Washington assumed that Robinson had roles beyond those of a concerned aide. Such rumors seemed to be confirmed when Johnson developed the habit of casually changing clothes in the office with Robinson present; or word spread that during a trip to Dallas they reserved an entire floor for themselves and spent much of their time lounging about in nightclothes. Asked by a reporter about their relationship, Johnson evoked titters by asserting that the question hit "below the belt" and then justified Robinson's salary by boasting that she was more than a stenographer. New Deal officials rationalized that without Robinson, the chaos in NRA would have been worse.

In August 1934 FDR, a staunch believer in NRA and Johnson, seemed to tire of its leader and offered him a new assignment. Johnson countered by offering his resignation, which Roosevelt would not accept. But after Johnson speeches laced with antilabor and anti-Brandeis remarks, FDR had a change of heart. Baruch carried the message to Johnson, and in late September a Johnson letter of resignation was accepted with presidential alacrity. On October 1 Johnson delivered before hundreds of NRA workers a florid farewell address in which he compared himself to Christ and Madame Butterfly, quoting in Italian the words on the latter's Samurai dagger, "To die with honor when you can no longer live with honor." He wrote his memoirs, became a newspaper columnist and served as a New Deal critic until he died in 1941.[12]

The departure of Johnson was not yet the death-knell of NRA. Increasingly beset by its own confusion of purposes and policies, NRA had become the object of bitter disgust by former friends in the business and intellectual communities. At issue was the New Deal's overall strategy of planned scarcity. It simply made no sense for NRA to urge consumers to "buy now" when higher producer prices lowered consumer purchasing power or even discouraged manufacturers from producing quality goods. New Deal internal contradictions hurt. By 1934–35 its rural power programs called for increased farm use of energy to make farmers produce more at a time when New Deal price policies dictated production curtailments. An economy of contraction coexisted with an economy of expansion. Referring to NRA cartels coexisting with antitrust laws, NRA economist Leon Henderson conceded that "The elemental conflict between the NRA and the Federal Trade Commission will have to be rationalized." One promoted cooperation, the other demanded competition. How could the New Deal build efficiently through PWA when building materials prices soared through NRA collusion devices? As sometime economic adviser to the Treasury Jacob Viner told Assistant Secretary of Commerce John Dickinson, "I feel myself very strongly that the output restrictions have been extremely important factors in the slowness of recovery, and that recovery will be jeopardized, and in any case seriously delayed, unless and until the government retraces its steps."[13]

"To be sure," Sachs counseled the president, the codes "were ill-advised and, to use a favorite term of mine, diseconomic." Part of the problem was businessmen who craved price protection and price inflation. Of course, some businessmen had succumbed to illusions of stabilization and recovery; but euphoria did not bring prosperity. Nevertheless, NRA had had many virtues. It brought order out of anarchy to some industries such as coal, reduced waste and instituted conservation in the oil industry, improved prices a bit in textiles, implemented a great deal of social legislation in very short time, heightened the individual industrialist's sense of social responsibility and, perhaps most important of all, taught competitive businessmen cooperation.[14]

During a meeting with the President in late October 1934 Sachs concluded that FDR did not yet see that stabilization and expansion were incompatible. Roosevelt was more of a stabilizer than an expansionist and did not yet value RFC policies that broadened private uses of credit; in the long run, however, NRA's restrictionist policies would alienate businessmen and discourage private investment. New Dealers had much to learn concerning the sources, creation and uses of investment. A consensus of New Dealers and businessmen considered economic planning salutary and necessary, but already the New Deal was alienating its business supporters and giving antigovernment elements temporary solace. Businessmen needed planning, but NRA's "semi-planned chaos" cast doubt upon its viability.

NRA's days were numbered. On May 27, 1935, the Supreme Court unanimously ruled that the agency was unconstitutional because Congress could not delegate its legislative authority to a code-writing body and because the particular business in question, A.L.A. Schecter Poultry Corporation of Brooklyn, New York, was intrastate, placing it beyond the commerce clause of the Constitution. The Court's coup de grace brought relief in many quarters. Government-fostered monopolies had alienated many businessmen. Although retailers and some small businessmen still liked the concept of "fair trade" laws and pursued them on state levels and in the Robinson-Patman Act of 1936, NRA had cast into disrepute the whole concept of industrial stabilization; even when World War II justified it during the defense preparedness period, economists and businessmen involved with NRA shied away from price-fixing schemes until well after Pearl Harbor.[15]

PART THREE

Lawyers

•

Some New Deal economists seem to have misread Turner's teaching on the American frontier. He is enormously interesting and very sound; but their inference that because the east and west have met on the American continent and the frontier has disappeared, we are all worn out in our youth, is a perfect non sequitur. To one who is aware of the history of the human race, this country is still a juvenile country. The demands of our people, our appetites and desires are tremendous. They are unappeased. They grow as they are gratified. (I remember that General Motors nearly failed in 1909 or 1911 or thereabouts and it was the opinion of very competent bankers and industrialists then that the motor car production had about reached the saturation point!) Our adventurousness and inventiveness are tremendous. . . . This is a young country and the frontiers of our minds and our achievements and our desires have not been crossed, nor even approached.

— RUSSELL LEFFINGWELL
to Walter Lippmann,
May 24, 1939, Lippmann Papers, Box 84

5·

Louis D. Brandeis: "Isaiah," Zion and Democratic Development

"WELL, WHERE WAS Ben Cardozo?" Roosevelt asked, as he tried to absorb the meaning of the Supreme Court's unanimous decision in the *Schechter* case. His NRA was dead and FDR was angry. The few liberal Justices had voted against NRA. "And what about old Isaiah?"[1] Isaiah was Roosevelt's name for Louis D. Brandeis, the Wilsonian Justice then approaching his eightieth birthday. The first Jewish Justice had the legendary appearance of an Old Testament prophet—tall, spare, ascetic, a furrowed face that seldom broke into a smile because he carried the worries of the world in his head and heart, with a white mane atop it all to give him a dignity that commanded awe. The younger Brandeis had been compared in looks and principles to a clean-shaven young Lincoln. His writings in cases or in journals blended admonitions with righteous denunciations, if his almost biblical wisdom went unheeded; like the Old Testament Isaiah, he mixed "anger with fury, and His rebuke with flames of fire," together with a teacher's plea to "Come now, and let us reason together."

Of all the Wilsonians directly or indirectly influencing policy during the Great Depression—McAdoo, Baruch and Hoover—Brandeis had the greatest impact. He led by intellect, integrity and persistence in pursuit of goodness. Brandeis's ideas demanded a code of ideals and ethics that challenged individual ambitions to strategically search for the heart of the American value system. In a sense he invented the perfect Wilsonian practical idealist—although at times even those who adored him wished he could be more practical and less idealistic. Brandeis was a stern judge of men, which was why generations of law school students viewed him as the beau ideal of a Supreme Court justice. Yet Brandeis the teacher was also an activist who sought to apply laws and ideals to each other—sensitive to the possibility that they may not be compatible. That made him both a radical and a reactionary, an experimenter and a fundamentalist. Whatever the goals and their obstacles, Brandeis's guile and righteous determination were not deterred by barriers that thwarted ordinary men.

Born in 1856, he had spent most of his life in the nineteenth century, but he targeted his values for the coming century, if not for all time. Many people found his espousal of Jeffersonian democracy reassuring, while others derided it as anachronistic. Place had mattered in Jefferson's America. Brandeis hailed from Louisville, Kentucky, in the democratic West; but the study of law took him to Harvard, Boston and New England—an elitest corner of America dominated by exclusionist Protestant aristocrats who did not easily admit a confident young German Jew to their society. Nonetheless, as a corporation lawyer who gave his clients' problems extra attention, Brandeis prospered; by his fiftieth birthday he was worth a million dollars. In part his financial accumulation was due to his genius as a corporation adviser and his reluctance to spend upon anything frivolous. He was not a consumer, conspicuous or otherwise. Visitors to his home were surprised by the modesty, even dinginess, with which Brandeis lived. However, he was not a stingy man; indeed, in certain ways he was very generous. Money allowed him *pro bono publico* service—service in the public interest in the manner of an upper-class reformer. Money allowed him to be a crusader against social injustice and for social goodness. As a corporation reformer, Brandeis wanted businessmen to consider the public interest. "Every act of injustice on the part of rich will be met by another act or many acts on the part of the people. If the capitalists are wise they will aid us in the effort to prevent injustice," the lawyer for capitalists declared.[2]

In an age of big business consolidation he fought its threatening hegemony. He stymied the New York, New Haven and Hartford Railroad's rapacious attempt to buy out the Boston & Maine Railroad—partly because he valued the independence of a smaller, more local enterprise, partly because he correctly detected an evil conspiracy by the larger system to use the smaller's assets to cover its losses. At the same time he sought to protect the working class from a managerial zeal for reducing costs for safety. In *Muller* v. *Oregon* (1908) he persuaded the U.S. Supreme Court to uphold the constitutionality of a state maximum hour law for women factory workers. To alleviate middle-class economic insecurity he proposed an inexpensive savings bank life insurance plan under the supervision of the state of Massachusetts. He was an ideologue. For the 1912 Democratic presidential nominee, Woodrow Wilson, he articulated the inchoate New Freedom philosophy that government should preserve the independent entrepreneur by regulating competition. The philosophy appealed to the consciences of voters fearful of Wall Street's hunger for consolidation of industry. Refusing the grateful Wilson's offer of a Cabinet post, Brandeis shrewdly made himself available on a private basis to the President, serving as an informal brain-truster during the legislating of the New Freedom.[3] His activity was not exclusively covert. He wanted public acceptance of his ideas. Brandeis wrote *Other People's Money and How the Bankers Use It* as a series of articles for *Harper's Magazine* in 1913, but as a book it became a classic denunciation of the evils of finance capitalism and the inspirational guide for a generation of New Deal lawyers.

In 1916 Wilson stirred a storm of controversy by nominating Brandeis for the Supreme Court. Opponents attacked his Jewishness, integrity, honesty and craft as a lawyer. Ignoring the fact that he was one of the most respected attorneys in the country, the American establishment assailed this maverick and his presidential backer; was American society ready for a reformer and a Jew on the Supreme Court? For many in America's social leadership, his reform role was more tolerable than his Jewishness.

That went to the heart of the greatest irony of Brandeis's life. He had only begun to consider himself a Jew in 1912. Prior to his fifties he had been an American and a German-American; then he and Zionism discovered each other, Brandeis finding his Judaism long after Christian America recognized it. Although he had "a rather foreign look, and is currently believed to have some Jew blood in him," a classmate at Harvard Law had written, "you would not suppose it from his appearance—tall, well-made, dark, beardless, and with the brightest eyes I ever saw."[4] Aside from his skill in argument, Brandeis's success owed something to the fact that he had disguised his Jewishness under his Lincolnesque looks. The fight over his Court nomination later revealed hidden hostility toward him as a Jew and magnified the irony of his situation. Although a joiner, he had not belonged to a Jewish organization until 1912, when he became a Zionist. Apparently, his quest for social justice took him to Zionism and his Jeffersonian faith in democracy and individuality brought him to Judaism. Then, like any convert, Brandeis embraced it with an uncompromising and self-righteous zeal: "To be good Americans, we must be better Jews, and to be better Jews, we must become Zionist." Prior to 1912 it had not bothered him that he was, as historian Richard Abrams has noted, an outsider who lacked a political base that came from group loyalty.[5] However, in the instant he became a Zionist, he established a universal base. Among Jews he imposed his direction over an American organization and thereby created it anew. His Zionism appealed to Christian liberals such as Adolf A. Berle, Sr. As Supreme Court Justice, Brandeis accordingly avoided the appearance of any judicial conflict of interest, but he avowed an active Zionism until his death. He seemed to be in a hurry to make up for lost time, thereby suggesting that he had found the key to his life's quest. How could he embrace social justice and not embrace Zionism?

Neither Zionism nor the Supreme Court prevented Brandeis from becoming a secret Washington policymaker. Woodrow Wilson welcomed his covert advice, and Brandeis enthusiastically shared it. For instance, in December 1917 he assured Wilson that although he disliked so much power in one man's hands, McAdoo was capable of handling both the Treasury and the Railroad Administration. While centralized authority went contrary to Brandeis's beliefs, the war demanded expediency and he counseled Wilson that it was right. Besides, Brandeis liked governmental experiments and the war crisis demanded organizational innovations. Later, the conservative 1920s stifled Brandeis. He and Justice Oliver Wendell Holmes, Jr., played the roles of the Court's great dissenters during the decade. While technology in commerce increasingly demanded great concentrations of capital, Brandeis consistently championed competition against monopoly, and decentralization against concentration. He exhorted young lawyers not to be seduced by money and power in large corporations but to seek a more perfect polity in their native states. The onset of the Great Depression seemed to Brandeis to vindicate his antipathy to big business. The 1930s witnessed a revival of Jeffersonian idealism in America, and Brandeis appeared to many young lawyers and politicians as the embodiment of the living democrat.

He enthusiastically anticipated the New Deal. At Felix Frankfurter's urging, Roosevelt made a pilgrimage to Brandeis's house shortly after his election in November 1932 to assure "Old Isaiah" that he would be a progressive president. Rhetorically invoking *Other People's Money* at every opportunity, Roosevelt would both fulfill and disappoint Brandeis's dreams.

New Deal beginnings promised experiments in government that Brandeis found courageous, but their implementation was not always to his liking. At the outset, he lauded AAA's goal of elevating rural incomes and NRA's peacetime introduction of collective bargaining for labor. However, Brandeis was not a stabilizer. Code-making in both agencies simply encouraged big units and public monopolies that obviated competition. Isaiah was a most unhappy prophet. For all of the efforts of disciples Frankfurter and Tommy Corcoran to steer New Dealers to Brandeis's home for counsel, the old man was grumbling "with really husky passion[,] 'I think they're going completely crazy.' " "An unending stream" of New Dealers trooped to Brandeis's home for much of 1933, propelled in part by "such a superstitious awe of his prophetic quality that his disagreement and warnings shake their courage and their conviction and leave them fighting half bewilderedly." Although Corcoran himself swore devotion "to that old man whose judgment I trust beyond that of anybody else in the world," he noted that the Justice's message often demoralized New Dealers. His liberalism seemed out of touch with their collectivism. A year after Roosevelt's inauguration, Brandeis privately complained, "I see little to be joyous about in the New Deal measures most talked about; NRA and AAA seem to be going from bad to worse."[6]

Through Gardner Jackson, Brandeis admonished Wallace and Tugwell in the Agriculture Department that they were driving small farmers off the land and increasing "corporate farming." He threatened "war" against New Deal experiments, a warning not to be taken lightly. Brandeis had known Hugh Johnson during the war and five times during 1933–34 he privately met with the NRA head to counsel restraint in the NRA or its liquidation. Like Sachs, Brandeis was disappointed by Johnson's course. His anxiety increased. He wanted FDR to attack the rich and the bankers with taxes, he told Frankfurter; Roosevelt's advisers "have [an] infantile faith in regulation. The only safety lies in disarming the enemy." In April 1934 Brandeis sent for braintrusters Adolf Berle and Rexford Tugwell, telling them, as Berle reported to FDR, that big businesses "rather than the government were controlling the nation's destinies" and, while he had gone along with New Deal legislation thus far, "unless he could see some reversal of the big business trend, he was disposed to hold the government control legislation unconstitutional from now on." Berle was summoned by Brandeis that summer to visit him on Cape Cod where Berle listened to ideas he had heard most of his adult life.[7] On May 14, 1935, Brandeis sent word to Roosevelt via Frankfurter that the New Deal's "eleventh hour" was at hand. Less than two weeks later the Court struck down the NRA. Brandeis cheered the opinion written by Chief Justice Charles Evans Hughes as "clear and strong—and marches to the inevitable doom." But Brandeis wanted one last word. Summoning Tommy Corcoran, he pronounced, "This is the end of this business of centralization, and I want you to go back and tell the President that we're not going to let this government centralize everything. It's come to an end. As for your young men, you call them together and tell them to get out of Washington—tell them to go home, back to the states. That is where they must do their work." Turning to another messenger, Benjamin Cohen, Brandeis demanded that he go to Frankfurter and see to it that he "understands the situation and explains it to the President. You must explain it to the men Felix brought into the Government. They must understand that [*Schecter*] changes everything. The President has been living in a fool's paradise." Frankfurter understood. "The administration plainly has reached a new stage," he informed Jerome Frank. "From now on it must be to a large extent trench warfare."[8]

Brandeis did not oppose planning in principle, but he rejected stabilization planning for agriculture and industry. Now, in mid-1935, NRA was dead and AAA's turn—if one could judge by Brandeis's tirades against Tugwell's price and income planning for agriculture, and Tugwell's refusal to trim his sails—would come soon. (But when the Court struck AAA down in the 1936 *Butler* case, Brandeis dissented from the majority opinion that AAA's tax upon big corporate processors was unconstitutional.) New Deal internal changes favored Brandeis. The heyday of the stabilizers was drawing to a close. Johnson was discredited, Tugwell was stigmatized as a radical and Raymond Moley had been banished by Hull. The Democrats had triumphed over the braintrusters. Only Berle had been shrewd enough to make himself scarce through temporary RFC assignments while bombarding FDR with "Dear Caesar" letters until such time that FDR personally brought him to Washington as Assistant Secretary of State in the second term. If the regular Democratic party closed ranks with the Brandeisians, the New Deal might still develop a workable program. The President, knowing that an irate business community itched to defeat him in the 1936 elections, needed that coalition of Brandeisians and Democrats.

Brandeis sharpened intellectual debates within the New Deal and earned for himself much awe and antipathy. Few New Dealers outside of the Frankfurter network dared cross verbal swords personally with the patriarchal "Isaiah"; few were brave enough, as were Berle and Jerome Frank, to tell his acolyte Frankfurter or any of his gang of young lawyers that the old man's "atomistic" attitudes toward business were dated. The young attorneys could no more repudiate Brandeis than they could turn against the progressivism of their earliest political convictions, their faith in democracy, their quest for social justice, their beliefs in public service, their Jeffersonian convictions that enunciated first principles of rights and liberties and individualism. As old as Brandeis was, to be young in New Deal Washington meant to know his ideals—to know that he appealed to the better angels of their natures. Whatever ideals they had found in their study of the law or in their practice of the law or in the making of the law they had first found in his published writings or in his briefs or in his decisions. Nobody could reject Brandeis outright. Yet a successful political program requires a consensus, and prophets are not compromisers. Even Roosevelt worried that this great talisman would be a factionialist among friends. By early 1936 FDR would say to a friend of Brandeis: "I always hate the frame of mind which talks about 'your group' and 'my group' among Liberals. . . . I can move only just so fast during any given period, lest a political barrier be thrown up to retard or stop our progress. In the same way with monopolies Brandeis is one thousand per cent right in principle but in certain fields there must be the guiding or restraining hand of Government because of the very nature of the specific field."[9]

Like his actions, parts of Brandeis's ideas were submerged icebergs that the public never saw. Was he merely against big institutions of business and government and for decentralization? Would he have had any impact upon the New Deal if all his true believers had followed his teachings and abandoned Washington for state capitals and other localities to erect a new decentralized democracy? As an avid Brandeisian who reached Washington by way of Wisconsin and Tennessee, David E. Lilienthal knew well that the Justice "encouraged young men from the interior regions to go back to the home communities and build those communities rather than join the rush to the great cities." Stories about this aspect of Brandeis abounded in New Deal Washington. When a young progressive-minded newspaper reporter from Oregon inquired of Brandeis if he could advance their causes by accepting a position in New York City, Brandeis tersely replied, "Stay in Oregon." Similar advice to another young liberal elicited the exclamation, "But Mr. Justice—Fargo, North Dakota!" Another young lawyer cried, "I have no hinterland. I'm from New York City," and the sage responded, "That is your misfortune."[10] Despite these stories Brandeis was not alone in Washington to lobby for his own programs; dozens of young lawyers believing in him flocked to Washington to run the growing agencies that centralized power. He even initiated the Supreme Court practice of taking young men fresh from law school to clerk for Justices, thereby exposing them to the temptations of Washington and centralization.

If he was the object of some sniping, it was because Brandeis asked much of mortal man. If not even he could define the proper size for a corporation, when was it too big? Jerome Frank, a liberal and a corporation lawyer schooled in his writings, maintained that any misinterpretation of Isaiah was the prophet's fault alone: "Emotionally over-charged in his defense of the 19th century American slogan," Brandeis, by his use of the "curse of big business" portrayed himself as "essentially a snob, more interested in the freedom of the spirit of a handful than in the material welfare of the great bulk of our people." Some people accused Brandeis of too much concern with preventing bigness or protecting smallness to care for the consumer or the man without property. Brandeis's defenders often sent doubters to talk to the old man himself, a task made difficult by the fact that he was an aloof—albeit loquacious—person. Contrary to myth, Alexander Sachs pointed out, Brandeis did not defend proprietorships against corporations, nor were the complexities of his economics "identical with the crude and puerile anti-bigness slogan of popular radical journalism." For that matter, differences of philosophy between Isaiah and his acolytes abounded—for one could agree with his premises and dissent from particulars.[11]

Both Frank and Sachs raised significant points concerning Brandeis, indirectly suggesting that few people knew him or his ideas well. Frank's accusation that he was a "snob" suggests that Brandeis possessed an aristocratic worldview that resisted the nouveau riche while saddling the proletariat with a welfare state that deterred socialism. Although Brandeis the democrat was not a Bourbon, that did not preclude him from subconsciously adopting the ideas and ways of the Boston aristocracy he had known so well. It was often said that he could be "more Brahmin than the Brahmins." Frankfurter once told Brandeis, "[Oliver Wendell] Holmes [is] more puritan than you." (Brandeis vehemently shot back: "More so, much more so.")[12] And among the upper classes few issues elicited a consensus for reform as much as the issue of conservation.

In Brandeis's lifetime so much of America had changed. Eighteen states had been added to the United States, and its population had increased by more than 400 per cent. He had witnessed revolutions in transportation and energy, from railroads and canals to automobiles and airplanes, from wood to kerosene to coal to hydroelectric power to petroleum-based horsepower. What would be left when industrial man overran the wilderness? It was a question of economics, exploitation and ethics. While the issue was by no means resolved east of the Mississippi and north of the Ohio, the South and the West were still undeveloped. Most of the twentieth-century conservation debate centered upon the virgin forests, valleys and waters of the West. How were the resources of the West to be preserved and enjoyed by future generations—and by whom would they be enjoyed and for what purpose? Here the issue boiled down to two opposing conservation perspectives: those of John Muir and Gifford Pinchot.

Both agreed that the enemy was industrialism which indiscriminately chopped down trees and tore the earth for coal and metals. There the debate among conservation-minded reformers began: Muir wanted nearly indiscriminate preservation while Pinchot sought to selectively preserve. The debate was fraught with irony: aristocrats adored the stance of the lowly-born Muir while middle-class reformers preferred that of the aristocratic Pennsylvania politician Pinchot. Muir resisted development and a wilderness invasion by the masses; Pinchot would open national parks to the people and instruct the government to control resource development. Like most reformers of his generation, Brandeis addressed the conservation question; but no evidence exists that he ever seriously considered Muir's position. In Brandeis's mind the issue was between laissez-faire or government-controlled development, and he dismissed the former as a license for monopoly.

Brandeis wanted government-controlled development of nonindustrial economies to avoid exploitation of raw materials by big business. He sought to confront the power of the corporation with the power of a government that represented the rest of the community. Government supervision would make corporations responsible—whatever their size. He would police the big and encourage the new—which is why he turned to virgin lands and conservation—to teach promoters and entrepreneurs not to repeat the mistakes of the past that allowed big enterprises to despoil the land.

That was why he involved himself in the famous Ballinger-Pinchot controversy of 1910–11. Essentially the issue was whether the Taft administration through its control of the Interior Department was practically giving away land in Alaska to an investment bankers' syndicate headed by Morgan and Guggenheim interests. Brandeis did not oppose development of this land rich in raw materials: "The people of the United States are entitled to begin to get the benefit and comfort of a reduction in the cost of living which will come from the utilization of Alaska'a treasures," he told fellow progressive Senator Robert M. La Follette. The residents of Alaska were courageous pioneers who deserved the fruits of their labors. Knowing that development required costly transportation and utility systems, Brandeis asserted that the profits needed by investment bankers would make development too expensive for both Alaskans and Americans. Development of Alaska's virgin lands required cheaper money "raised by the people." Washington should invest in Alaska for the benefit of liberal capitalism. Temporary government ownership of Alaska's resources would assure "that the opportunities of earnings of the settlers in Alaska will be the most liberal conceivable." As Brandeis told La Follette:

> My dear Bob: How would this do for the Progressive slogan:
> "Alaska; the land of Opportunity.
> Develop it by the People, for the people.
> Do not let it be exploited by the Capitalists,
> for the Capitalists."

In the words of biographer Philippa Strum, "It is interesting to note how Brandeis, convinced capitalist, hurled that title of opprobrium at others of whose activities he disapproved. The small businessman, to Brandeis, was always a businessman, never a 'capitalist,' a word with which he described those who used other people's capital to undermine economic democracy." Rather than opposing businessmen, Brandeis believed government should protect them "from the grasp of capitalists." He wanted the government to make available cheap quantities of capital for development. Such ideas of state intervention might have made him prone to charges of socialism, but he was evidently not a socialist; he truly believed in individual liberties and disdained all monopoly—whether it was held by a predatory investment banker or a big, indifferent government.[13]

From conservation to Zionism, from Alaska to Palestine was not too great a leap for Brandeis. Both crusades and both undeveloped lands offered him an opportunity to experiment in building a balanced political economy free from grasping investment bankers. "I have been to a great extent separated from the Jews," he told a Zionist audience as he accepted its leadership only two years after he discovered the movement: "I am very ignorant in things Jewish." Indeed, he was. But Brandeis's Zionism reveals Brandeis's political economy. In fact, the people to whom Brandeis most excitedly related his newfound Zionism were gentiles, fellow progressives who shared his fears concerning big corporations. Prior to his embrace of Zionism Brandeis had espoused assimilation of all ethnics, including Jews, disdaining "hyphenate Americans." How did he explain his sudden Jewish nationalism? "My approach to Zionism was through Americanism." He assured American Jews, many of whom were drawn to Zionism by the lure of being associated in a great endeavor with one of the prominent Jews in America, that Zionism did not abridge their Americanism. With Jews from Eastern Europe he liked to drink beer (although he seldom drank any alcoholic beverage) in the evenings and regale them with tales of the Ballinger-Pinchot struggle through which he could introduce his vision of an equitable economic society in Alaska or in Palestine. Brandeis made Zionism a cause for social justice and equitable economic development. Frankfurter later said that Brandeis committed himself to Zionism after "deep searching" and "long brooding"; in particular Brandeis brooded over the plight of progressivism during one of its several seasons of discontent. The summer of 1914 was one such episode and the ultimate moment when Brandeis intellectually committed himself to Zionism. Palestine became progressivism's land of Canaan.

Why did Brandeis need Palestine? Strum tells us that "Creation of the perfect citizen in the perfect state was of course Brandeis's goal and the object of his insistence on education, democracy, and self-fulfillment."[14] To be a Jew in Palestine was to be a pioneer on the frontier. The ideal society would be built by Zionism in a wilderness Palestine. "The same spirit which brought the Pilgrim west is the spirit which has sent many a Jew to the east," he said. He compared Palestine to California. In 1919 Brandeis visited Palestine for the only time in his life, and his enthusiasm for its development appeared justified. "What I saw of California and the Grand Canyon seemed less beautiful than the view from the Mount of

Olives upon the Dead Sea and the country beyond." He forecast that this "miniature California" would be again "a land 'flowing with milk and honey,'" and would grow its industries from agricultural roots without confining development to agrarianism. In what came to be known as the "Pittsburgh Platform" of June 25, 1918, he gave the Zionists six commandments for his ideal polity: equality; a guarantee of "equality of opportunity" by "the ownership and control by the whole people of the land, of all natural resources and of all public utilities"; "All the land, owned or controlled by the whole people, should be leased on such conditions as will assure the fullest opportunity for development and continuity of possession"; "The cooperative principle should be applied so far as feasible in the organization of all agricultural, industrial, commercial, and financial undertakings"; a free public education; and Hebrew as the national language. "Capitalistic exploitation," he told Chaim Weizmann, would require the "utmost vigilance . . . to prevent the acquisition by private persons of land, water rights or other natural resources or any concessions for public utilities." Yet that would be easy because Brandeis anticipated that Palestine always would be small, a perfect size by which "to serve as a laboratory for some far-reaching experiments in democracy and social justice." Palestine would be a model not just of a democratic people but a democratic political economy that would offer Jews market opportunities by blocking investment bankers who monopolized other primitive economies. Palestine would be a model of economic development for the American South and West. Ironically, Weizmann the socialist disdained Brandeis's preoccupation with economic development. Brandeis's Zionists, Weizmann declared, were money-mad businessmen who converted a romantic "folk renaissance" into a soulless "sociological plan."[15]

Indeed, Brandeis's Zionists believed that "the road to a Jewish Palestine is economic." Brandeis shamelessly and incessantly proselytized among Jews for "members and money." He saw nothing crass or demeaning in such promotional activity. After all, the money they raised would be used for development—to purchase land in Eretz Yisroel upon which refugees from Europe would build a Jewish national home. Brandeis and his allies created a multitude of fund-raising and distribution organizations such as the Palestine Development League, the Palestine Co-operative Company, the Palestine Development Council, the Palestine Endowment Fund, and the Palestine Economic Corporation. Through these groups and the Women's Zionist group, Hadassah, Brandeis funneled his contributions and that of American Zionists to Palestine, where it was used for loans to small industry, for consumers' cooperative societies, for low-cost housing, for buying the land for the southernmost port city of Eilat, for harnessing the waters of the Jordan River to produce electricity and irrigate the land, for building Hebrew University, and for the Hashomer Hatzair youth movement to create a kibbutz called Ein Hashofet, "Spring of the Judge."[16] He did not envision American Jews making *aliyah* (the "ascent") to Palestine; they already had prospects for social justice. But he was a colonizer, and from the start he envisioned not merely an Israel of Jeffersonian agrarianism, but one of industrial development from a common pool of capital free from the monopolistic clutches of investment bankers.

From Alaska to Palestine to the Tennessee Valley Authority?* A jump from progressivism to the New Deal had been seen by the New Dealers; and the case for a leap from progressivism to Zionism was ably made by Brandeis; but—from Zionism to the New Deal? Only the Jew-haters, only the Roosevelt-haters, only those who combined both into a "Jew Deal," could have conjured such a farfetched link. Yet it is not far-fetched to imagine that one of the many roots of the New Deal evolved over a quarter century in the mind and machinations of Brandeis and his adherents. Brandeisian New Dealers and Brandeisian Zionists both believed in capitalist planning through a state that made money available to courageous pioneers who dared to build a civilization in the wilderness.

One such Brandeisian was Benjamin Cohen. A progressive reformer during his youth in Chicago, Cohen became a Zionist administrator and fund-raiser who worked closely with Brandeis and Frankfurter. Later, as we shall see, he became a New Deal lawyer distinguished by his work on the National Power Policy Committee and his role in the Wall Street reforms of 1933–35, perhaps the most Brandeisian legislation in the New Deal. To Cohen, Palestine was "an opportunity for the 'planning' of a new country seldom offered in modern times."

> To a cautious, limited degree—in relation to the scientific utilization of its natural resources—Palestine was 'planned' and so intelligently that it is today probably the one economic community in the world substantially unaffected by the Depression. Notable results of this planning were the exploitation of natural potash deposits in the Dead Sea and the extension of the citrus culture which has made the 'Jaffa orange' of growing importance in European markets.

Brandeisians were capitalist planners who preferred agricultural or raw material management to manufacturing. The depression seemed to vin-

*Actually, it turned out the other way. In 1942 Jews from Palestine visited the Tennessee Valley Authority to see how they might develop the Jordan Valley. *The Journals of David E. Lilienthal: The TVA Years* 1939–1945 (New York: Harper & Row, 1964), pp. 594–95.

dicate their biases by demonstrating the failure of manufacturing. But the depression also made planning attractive in ways Brandeisians did not particularly approve. It encouraged planning of a socialist nature too. For while "the Palestine experience gave [Cohen] an unusual tolerance of all kinds of people and of ideas new and old,"

> a sense of reality convinced him of the impracticality of "planning" too closely the detailed future of even a small and homogeneous country. While believing in safeguards against exploitation and against the disturbance of erratic and speculative movements he came to have little sympathy for those who try to force the economic activities of a whole people into fixed grooves. When various proposals for colonization of Palestine were put forward his position was that the advocates of any particular scheme should not be free to carry out their plans but only at their own risk and with their own funds and that they should not be allowed to impose their particular schemes on others who were expected to pay for them.

Cohen's rejection of socialist planning in Palestine was directed against the Weizmann faction of the world Zionist movement. In Palestine or in the New Deal Cohen's planning was cautious. In the words of a biography,

> He is deeply sympathetic toward new ideas and is a believer in continual experimentation. But while recognizing the broadening social and economic influences in government he is too much of an individualist, too conservative in one sense and too much an experimentalist in another, to want to see the economic life of any community completely tied up with, and at the risk of the man-made judgments of, any omnipotent organization, whether public or private. He is equally fearful of both the super-state and of the "private socialism" of super-industry.[17]

Cohen was a Brandeisian philosopher of public policy. He disdained administration, putting his highly valued legal skills to work in service of those who would write and defend laws and thereby make policy. Conservative in his dread of collectivist strategies and radical in his disdain of a financiers' hegemony, Cohen was the leading exponent of Brandeisianism in the New Deal.

Brandeis's ideas, Frankfurter once wrote, were "threads from a pattern."[18] Beyond Zionism, the nonmanufacturing Western and Southern reaches of America offered Brandeis the best hope for a democratic capitalism free from the hegemony of Wall Street. Appropriately, the best of the New Deal came from beyond the northeast quadrant of the United States. At the New Deal's beginnings Brandeis pointed to the administration presence of three Chicago lawyers—Richberg, Lilienthal and Ickes—as evidence of Roosevelt's progressive intentions. To be sure, Chicago was not the hinterlands—except to New Yorkers. But in Congress the most noticeably Brandeisian legislators were men like Senators Burton K. Wheeler of Montana and Hugo Black of Alabama and Representatives Sam Rayburn, Wright Patman, and Lyndon Johnson of Texas, along with other congressmen from Mississippi, Iowa and rural Pennsylvania. Significantly, one did not have to have read Brandeis or sit at his feet to believe, along with him, that too much power was concentrated in the Northeast, that independent and small businessmen did not stand a chance of competing against their big brethren, and that regional economic development depended upon federal leadership in the field of energy. Westerners who sought to experiment with public power development were more Brandeisian than the Harvard lawyers who administered agricultural recovery agencies. The latter espoused centralization and stabilization that yielded bigness. Brandeis had no quarrel with stabilization that saved small businessmen from being driven out by chain stores; the backers of the Miller-Tydings and the Robinson-Patman laws rightly hailed from the South and West and defended local proprietors against Wall Street corporation moguls. But even more heartening to Brandeis than these laws and those which reformed Wall Street, or the punitive tax legislation of 1935–36, was the experimental political economy inherent in the TVA, the Bonneville Power Authority, the Rural Electrification Administration, the Electric Home and Farm Authority, and all the other public power developments of the New Deal. These adventures in state capitalism promised equitable development for those primitive lands Brandeis idealized. These projects would husband the self-determination and independence of the American frontier. That was a key to Brandeis: he was not a Luddite, nor a "Lenin";[19] he was a developer. From the New Deal he wanted cheaper credit, public power and economic growth for a society just beginning to appreciate resources in the South and the West.

6.

Felix Frankfurter: Disinterested Politics

BRANDEIS ONCE DEFINED his special relationship with Frankfurter: "I look upon you as half brother, half son."[1] While this suggests personal warmth and affection, it gives no hint of the extent of their collaboration in public affairs. They were conspirators in reconstructing the quality of American public life and its political economy. The cause of freedom of opportunity justified many of their quests for influence. Brandeis was the prophet, Frankfurter the disciple who gathered in his friend's acolytes. Each had a need for protégés who could celebrate them and their principles. Their heroic and selfish alliance was bonded by genuine love and admiration, because these good men knew how to *use* each other for their own purposes. Brandeis expected from Frankfurter an ideological subservience and, precluded from policy-making by the separation of powers, Frankfurter eagerly performed Isaiah's proselytizing. The "revelation" after their passing that Professor Frankfurter accepted gifts of money from Brandeis to aid his hustling for their causes tells us less about any venality than it tells us about the dearth of financial rewards then for academics and public men in a commercial society.[2] Without Brandeis's remuneration Frankfurter had no money for a pension or his public causes. Only Brandeis's extraordinary patronage prevented Frankfurter's extraordinary service from being lost to history.

Frankfurter deserved his place in American politics and it is likely that even without Brandeis he would have attained it by finding another patron. Garrulous and gregarious, he imperially marshaled his own legion of admirers and was Napoleonic in his use of men. Even before Brandeis entered his life, this five-foot-five Viennese-born Jew, a graduate of the City College of New York, attracted the political patronage of the dean of the American establishment, Henry Louis Stimson, and a clique of admiring Protestants at Harvard Law School. It was Stimson who helped Frankfurter first attain his ideal of public service when the crass commercialism of a New York corporation practice seemed to be all that was available to a young lawyer. At twenty-four in 1906, Frankfurter entered the New York City law firm of Hornblower, Byrne, Miller and Potter, exactly the sort of position for a Harvard Law graduate at the top of his class—even if he was Jewish. When a sympathetic senior partner advised him to change his name in deference to the Protestant world he had entered, Frankfurter changed jobs instead. Stimson invited him to join the office of the United States Attorney for the Southern District of New York, albeit at a lower salary. But money had no meaning to a man inspired by thoughts of making history through public service. Frankfurter stayed three years and then supported Stimson in a quixotic quest for the governorship of New York—which probably convinced both of them that their best exercise of power lay in politics other than electoral. President William Howard Taft consoled Stimson with the post of Secretary of War, and Stimson accordingly brought Frankfurter to Washington as legal officer for the Bureau of Insular Affairs, thereby initiating Frankfurter to games of power on the Potomac.

The breadth of Frankfurter's endeavors made even indefatigable people wonder how many hours were in his day. By the time he completed his first tour of Washington in 1914 he had established intellectual ties with Louis Brandeis and Oliver Wendell Holmes, founded the *New Republic* with Francis Hackett, Walter Lippmann and Herbert Croly, and presided over the "House of Truth," so named by the puckish Holmes because conversation there bubbled with the vitality of young idealistic lawyers and journalists in quest of a fair-minded polity. Frankfurter always led a fast-paced life. Although his published writings drew considerable attention in public and legal circles, they do not form a gigantic corpus; but he also wrote lengthy and numerous argumentative letters and relished spending interminable hours in face-to-face conversation, which he considered an art form. Indeed, even when he was pressed for time, if a letter challenged his ideas he reacted by scribbling in its margins his caveats with arrows and circles highlighting someone else's wrongheaded notions and then sending the Frankfurter-decorated missive back to its original correspondent.

When Frankfurter left Washington to teach at Harvard, Stimson, who had used him as a speechwriter and a political factotum, doubted that Harvard would make the best use of his peripatetic talents for connecting people.* Frankfurter was a natural publicist. More than twenty years later he would sardonically observe that "Herbert Croly was probably right when he said that nature intended me to be a journalist and cir-

*Harold Laski told the story of Londoners introduced to Frankfurter who later ask, "Why is he a Democrat, Mr. Laski?" "Because he is an aristocrat with an infinite sense of pity." "Why does he not want to make money?" "Because most people who have it are vulgar." "Why doesn't he collect books or pictures?" "Because he collects people." Quoted in Joseph P. Lash, *From the Diaries of Felix Frankfurter* (New York: Norton, 1975), p. 36.

cumstances diverted me into a lawyer." Perhaps his prolixity (known as "Felixity") augured a career as a writer. Frankfurter himself conceded that he was "not a scholar qua scholar." Nonetheless, "I do feel very deeply the need of organized scientific thinking in the modern state and, particularly, in a legalistic democracy such as ours, the need of a definitely conceived jurisprudence coordinating sociology and economics." In other words, he was confident that his polemical command of the language of lawyers would sustain him at Harvard and put legal discourse in the business of national policy-making.[3]

War interrupted Frankfurter's young career at Harvard in 1917, but it was a welcome interruption. Frankfurter returned to Washington as secretary and counsel to the President's Mediation Commission, which sought to maintain war production by disciplining labor in a time of rising prices and inert wages. The job involved him in the Bisbee, Arizona, copper miners' strike and the Tom Mooney case in San Francisco, both of which were major causes célèbres for American labor and marked Frankfurter as a sympathizer. The following year President Wilson appointed him chairman of the interdepartmental War Labor Policies Board—where he became friends with a chap about his own age, Assistant Secretary of the Navy Franklin D. Roosevelt. Frankfurter probably surprised some people with his bureaucratic imperialism; "He wants to amplify his jurisdiction," noted an amazed William Howard Taft, then cochairman of the National War Labor Board with Frank P. Walsh. Already Frankfurter was beginning to assert the moral superiority of men who chose public service over private enterprise. Frankfurter thrived on confrontations with businessmen, dismissing them with the comment, "Business men are trained to make money and that is their view point." The wartime public interest required lawyers to assert a national interest over their narrow perspectives.[4] In the 1920s he further invited the stamp of radicalism upon himself by courageously upholding the cause of labor, fighting bigotry at Harvard, denouncing the commercial babbittry that pervaded American society in general and the law profession in particular, and championing the defense of Sacco and Vanzetti, the Italian anarchists accused of killing a guard during a robbery and the alleged victims of Brahmin hostility to aliens and radicals in their Massachusetts. Nevertheless, his "radicalism" never prevented him from serving as a political adviser to Democrats Al Smith and Roosevelt.

Perhaps it is a measure of Frankfurter's radicalism that in early 1932 he preferred Smith for president to Roosevelt. As governor, Smith in the 1920s had stirred the political pot in New York. Also, the Roman Catholic Smith appealed to Frankfurter as a fellow outsider against the Protestant Establishment; Felix suspected that Roosevelt, notwithstanding his own strong progressive record, was intellectually shallow and opportunistic in capitalizing upon his name. Frankfurter had voted for Governor Roosevelt in 1930 in spite of his "limitations": "Most of them derive from lack of an incisive intellect and a kind of optimism that makes him timid, as well as an ambition that leads to compromises. . . . But on the whole he has been a very good governor." Frankfurter appreciated that while Roosevelt would not take his advice carte blanche, the Democratic nominee of 1932 had "his own sense of timing and timeliness" that allowed people of ideas to gain "the eager accessibility of his mind."[5] Roosevelt liked political mavericks like Frankfurter. He valued Frankfurter's brilliance and independent thinking. Thus, when Frankfurter railed against the Columbia-dominated group of academic planners in the brain trust, FDR gave him the same courtesy he gave Baruch's money—the right to nominate a braintruster. Other Frankfurter-inspired appointments to the upper echelons of numerous departments and emergency agencies of the New Deal would follow.

As a recruiter of governmental personnel, Frankfurter was at his legendary best. He had been recruiting bright law students for government posts, law firms and clerkships with Justices Brandeis and Holmes ever since Stimson asked him to organize his offices in New York and Washington. Eugene Meyer too, whether at the War Finance Corporation, the Federal Reserve, or the Reconstruction Finance Corporation, would tell Frankfurter, "I'll take as many first-class men as you will send me."[6]

Frankfurter students were bright and, like their mentor, believers in public service. His reputation was so great that entering Harvard law students knew that being tabbed as a Frankfurter disciple meant much for their careers. James Landis adored him, and David Lilienthal staked much of his budding career as a labor lawyer on Frankfurter's approval. But Frankfurter was not usually accessible to first-year students. Moreover, while he had moments of showmanship as a lecturer, he usually rated mixed student evaluations. A seminar student liked him better than one in a lecture, and it also mattered whether a student concurred with his iconoclastic views favoring labor and assailing public utilities, or was able to withstand a mordant style larded with embarrassing ridicule. Many students did not take well to Frankfurter, and among those was Adolf Berle. After passing Frankfurter's course, Berle was back the following semester and faithfully attended every lecture until an unnerved Frankfurter demanded to know why Berle was auditing a course he had completed successfully. "Oh, I wanted to see if you had learned anything since last year," Berle told him.[7] Among New Dealers it was well known that they were lifelong enemies.

One of his favored students, Alger Hiss, recalled that the "cocky, abrasive and outspoken" Frankfurter was not popular with the majority of students. However, such didacticism weeded out dissidents and helped disciples to revel in Frankfurter's brilliance in his seminars. He excelled in small groups because he was an ingenious nonstop conversationalist. Moreover, truly gifted students, or just the well-connected, along with favored faculty and friends were invited to Sunday teas at Frankfurter's Brattle Street home. There he was "at once the impresario and catalyst," having gathered about him those best able to keep pace with his rapid-fire chatter. Like Brandeis, he always instructed people. In a living room cluttered with magazines and books he flew "like an adult Peter Pan" from journal to journal, from volume to volume, using them as "props of his great performance as a conversationalist." He needed an audience. "Felix has two hundred best friends," his wife, Marion, would observe. Childless, Frankfurter sought out young men to whom he was at once father and friend. Isaiah Berlin recalls him relishing the attention of students at Oxford with whom he "talked with such enjoyment . . . that the young men were charmed and exhilarated, and stayed up talking with him until the early hours of the morning." Sometimes his rapport with students drew the envy of older men, as when Eugene Meyer remarked to Frankfurter with some asperity, "I wish I had only to talk to a lot of young fellows without much knowledge and experience, knowing in advance that I could easily look like a wizard in their eyes." His students were brilliant, if only because he had no time for those who were not. "He loved his protégés," the wife of Mark DeWolfe Howe recalled, "but he also owned them. There was a sweet side to Felix's paternalism, but he didn't care whether what he wanted was good for them." Frankfurter obsequiously flattered the rich and powerful; in turn he loved the attention which his influence earned. "He wants so badly to be liked and thought wise and brilliant," Gardner Jackson observed—and others would have added that he especially craved such esteem from recognizably great men. Still, he treated anyone who made it to Brattle Street with kindly grace and scintillating talk.[8]

Upon graduation the students who had called him "Felix" behind his back had earned the right to address him by his given name or simply as "FF." They would become as legendary as he. Alger and Donald Hiss, Lee Pressman, Tommy Corcoran, Benjamin Cohen, Nathan Margold, Dean Acheson and David E. Lilienthal provided the legal services for a myriad of temporary and permanent New Deal agencies such as the Agricultural Adjustment Administration, the Reconstruction Finance Corporation, the Tennessee Valley Authority and the departments of Agriculture, the Interior and State. Frankfurter's disciples brought with them other FF disciples. He championed brilliant men who were only acquaintances such as corporation lawyers Jerome Frank and William O. Douglas. As for those who did not owe their Washington jobs to Frankfurter, he cultivated them too. He was assiduous in his flattery of talent, flattery which carried the considerable weight of his fame.

A case in point is that of Stanley F. Reed, a Kentucky lawyer whose work for tobacco interests led Hoover to bring him to Washington as general counsel to the Federal Farm Board in 1929. In 1932 Hoover appointed him general counsel to the new RFC, and there Reed made the acquaintance of a young lawyer, Thomas Corcoran, whom Eugene Meyer had given a job on the advice of Frankfurter. By the end of the year Corcoran recommended additional Frankfurter friends and students for RFC jobs because he "has an almost national reputation for being able to find the right men for these public jobs." Paul Freund and other former Frankfurter students later worked for Reed in the Justice Department. In 1935 Reed became solicitor general and Frankfurter congratulated him on "a powerful and closely knit brief in the Schechter case," hailing it as a "real intellectual pleasure." Reed thanked Frankfurter and began to send his briefs to him and to enjoy the professor's praise of their "real quality, lucidity and persuasiveness." In a few months Reed and Frankfurter were on a first-name basis, and soon Reed added a Frankfurter protégé, Charles E. Wyzanksi, Jr., to his staff. "The country is fortunate to have such calm and disinterested judgment and such statesmanlike direction for the guidance of issues of profound moment for the country's welfare," Frankfurter told Reed. It was a mentorship of Reed that would carry over to when they both would sit on the Supreme Court.[9]

Frankfurter's Jewishness and how other men reacted to it determined the extent of his influence. He owed his Harvard position to the fact that Brandeis and several wealthy Jews decided that Frankfurter would be the first Jew to teach at Harvard Law. Ivy League law schools had no shortage of brilliant young Jewish students, but almost never did their faculties have a place for them. Brandeis decided to make him the Jewish pioneer and Frankfurter did not disappoint, although it would be many years before another Jew would teach at Harvard Law. Despite this isolation, Robert A. Burt has argued, Frankfurter sought to be the quintessential insider.[10] The irony is that his appointment established a quota for an outside group while Frankfurter so lacked an outsider's mentality as to be wholly acceptable to his sponsors, to Harvard, and to Franklin Roosevelt.

The liberalism of Roosevelt was important to Frankfurter's influence and the character of the New Deal. Franklin Roosevelt befriended and employed more Jews than any previous president. (And maybe more than any since then.) That does not mean that he lacked a dislike of some Jews or some characteristics associated with Jews. Roosevelt was enough of a liberal to believe that he should employ as many talented people who happened to be Jews as he could, no matter how some people whispered that his name was really "Rosenfeld" or that his program should be called "the Jew Deal." Every New Dealer knew that the larger number of Jewish lawyers in government posts made the administration a target of anti-Semites. Many of the attorneys were former Frankfurter students who had been urged to take jobs in Washington because Wall Street would not hire them. Joseph L. Rauh, Jr., had lined up a position with a Jewish Cincinnati firm until he took Frankfurter's advice to go to Washington. Even there, one did not have to be Jewish to recognize anti-Semitic slurs. Tommy Corcoran warned Frankfurter in England in December 1933, "The Frankfurter-Brandeis-bloc-Harvard-Jews talk is much to the fore." Later in the depression decade a typical comment concerning Jews in Washington went, "You can't find an official in the whole [government] who hasn't got a damned Jew lawyer sitting by him at his desk." Alger Hiss, one of many former Frankfurter students in the AAA, recalled that New Dealers "were well aware that the epithet ["Happy Hot Dogs"] was a demagogic appeal to anti-Semitism, the printable version of the sally in some businessmen's clubs, 'the Jew Deal.' We took this and other attacks lightly."[11]

Lawyers discriminated against Jews because law schools discriminated, and they in turn reflected their society.* For many years Frankfurter fought anti-Semitism at Harvard; when Harvard College instituted in 1922 an indirect quota system on the admission of Jews, Frankfurter branded the scheme as "slimy." The president of Harvard, Abbott Lawrence Lowell, insisted that it was in the best interests of Harvard's Jews that Harvard limit their numbers and restrict less desirable Jews of Eastern European backgrounds. When the Law School tried to base awards on something other than grades, Frankfurter demanded a meritocracy where "Skull & Bones, Hasty Pudding, an H, family fortune, skin, creed—nothing particularly mattered, except scholarship and character objectively ascertained." He dared to fight for the appointment of the

*Lawyers, of course, were not the only professional elites to discriminate. Doctors and medical schools had notorious quota systems. Humanists and social scientists were not different. Scientists were not much more result-oriented. Writing about the Lawrence Berkeley Laboratory during the 1930s, Daniel J. Kevles notes that "Staff recruitment reflected the anti-Semitism then standard in American physics—that is, Jews who conformed to Jewish stereotypes were unwanted, but 'good' Jews were acceptable. . . . The cultural norm at that laboratory was on the whole WASP, western, and insular. Very little of its substantial resources were devoted to assisting displaced European scientists "—many of whom were Jews. "Begetting Big Science," *New York Review of Books,* October 25, 1990, 10.

brilliant Romanian-born Nathan Margold to the faculty in 1928, but Lowell refused to recommend Margold and only eight members of the Law School faculty voted to resubmit the appointment. Thomas Reed Powell told Frankfurter, "The pussagoddamnlimitty of the faculty will come home to roost time and again."[12]

FDR liked underdogs and achievers, and Jewish lawyers certainly filled those bills. He also believed in a society that extended social and economic opportunities. He had been a part of Wilson's "New Freedom" Democratic administration, which, while it was hardly free from bigotry, did see the first Jew elevated to the Supreme Court (Brandeis) and a Jew made chairman of the War Industries Board (Baruch). In politics Roosevelt worked with Jews. His chief adviser in Albany had been Samuel I. Rosenman, who put together the brain trust and later became the President's counsel. Following Will Woodin's demise, FDR appointed a Jew, Henry Morgenthau, Jr., son of a major fund raiser for Woodrow Wilson, to be Secretary of the Treasury. Roosevelt's admiration for Frankfurter was well known. FDR encouraged him to place his students in federal jobs and took genuine pride in appointing Jewish lawyers to his administration. He wanted only the best minds. As someone said, "It just shows you how smart FDR is, to have all those smart Jews working for him." Roosevelt was loyal in his fashion to Jerome Frank, Benjamin Cohen, David E. Lilienthal, David Niles, Abe Fortas and the many Jews who made up approximately 15 per cent of his top appointments. He once told an old Christian friend, "Dig me up fifteen or twenty youthful Abraham Lincolns from Manhattan and the Bronx to choose from. They must be liberal from belief and not by lip service. They must have an inherent contempt both for the John W. Davises and the Max Steuers. They must know what life in a tenement means. They must have no social ambition."[13] In other words, they should hold Wall Streeters and Democratic hacks in equal contempt while wanting little for themselves other than the satisfaction of reform. Of the Jews in the New Deal, however, few knew a tenement home or the Bronx. Cohen and Frank came from middle-class Chicago, Lilienthal from small-town Indiana, and the one who truly knew poverty as a youth, Fortas, had the redeeeming sound of Memphis in his speech.

Roosevelt, like many Protestants, wanted his Jews more American and less Jewish. He believed in quotas. He had been a member of the 1922 Harvard Board of Overseers that set tacit quotas intended to reduce the number of Jews in the college's freshman class from about 30 per cent to 15. Nineteen years later he remarked at a Cabinet meeting that federal employees in Oregon included too many Jews. Later he explained to Morgenthau that he intended to limit the Jewish representation only because it upset Oregon Democrats. He did the same with Catholics in Nebraska, explaining, "You can't get a disproportionate amount of any one religion." During the war he told the French Resident-General of Morocco that restrictions upon Jews in North Africa should be removed, but that "the number of Jews engaged in the practice of the professions (law, medicine, etc.) should be definitely limited to that percentage of the Jewish population . . . [proportional] to the whole North African population." For that matter, he believed an old canard that over 50 per cent of the professionals of Germany were Jews—a source of great trouble to the oppressed. Inevitably, perhaps, Roosevelt supported immigration quotas that limited the number of Jewish refugees seeking asylum in America from Nazi persecution. In fact, Roosevelt once claimed to have told Rabbis Stephen Wise and Abba Hillel Silver that too many Jewish immigrants to Palestine was unwise, asking, "Do you want to start a Holy Jihad?" He sought a balance of Jews and Arabs in Palestine. However, historian Frank Freidel asserts that Roosevelt "was stubbornly pro-Zionist" and in 1945 wanted Ibn Saud of Arabia to approve the entry of 100,000 more Jews to Palestine, but found the King intractable. However, as we shall see in the career of Jerome Frank, creating quotas by limiting the number of Jewish lawyers in any agency was a practice of the time which some Jews themselves followed.[14]

Anti-Semites targeted Frankfurter because it was well known that his students administered the New Deal agencies. But Frankfurter eschewed a position for himself in the New Deal. In 1932 Governor Joseph Ely had surprisingly nominated him for the Massachusetts Supreme Court, a singular honor for the celebrated defender of Sacco and Vanzetti against the Commonwealth. Yet, after a brief period of testing the waters to be certain that the state legislature would confirm his nomination, Frankfurter declined it. Had he accepted, his special activity in the national arena would have been foreclosed because Ely, a Smith loyalist, would have tied him to Roosevelt's Democratic opposition. Besides, Frankfurter considered Harvard Law School to be his calling in public affairs, a point he made to Roosevelt when he declined the new President's offer of the solicitor generalship of the United States. Frankfurter's rejection surprised FDR because the offer was made with the assurance that the New Deal's chief litigator would be a candidate for a Supreme Court vacancy. Nonetheless, he wanted to write laws, not defend all laws, including those he did not believe in—a position that might make him a Court adversary to Brandeis. In other words, as a friend put it, he preferred a role "as a free lance in Cambridge [rather] than as an office holder in Washington wearing a collar." Although Roosevelt promised him "adequate help to free you for other work," Frankfurter knew that the solicitor generalship would leave no time for policy-making. For that matter, he excitedly anticipated a visiting professorship at Oxford during 1933–34 and wanted nothing to interfere with it. Thus, in declining the solicitor generalship he could fill administration posts with former students, all the while maintaining, "I am not in office and have no responsibility for public policy."[15] (A decade later, when he sat on the Supreme Court, he disapproved of Bernard Baruch's gadfly influence "without the necessary responsibility," a role he had relished in the New Deal.)

"A plague of young lawyers settled on Washington," George Peek later wrote following his departure from the AAA. "They all claimed to be friends of somebody or other and mostly of Felix Frankfurter and Jerome Frank. They floated airily into offices, took desks, asked for papers and found no end of things to be busy about. I never found out why they came, what they did, or why they left." Although New Deal enemies portrayed Frankfurter as an Iago, the truth is that Joseph Lash was right: "There was nothing sinister about Frankfurter's role."[16] He had merely expanded a role he had played for two decades for Henry Stimson, Eugene Meyer and others. For that matter, the men he placed in government he did not necessarily own then or later. Friends were not disciples, nor were friends and disciples inalienable.

To be a Frankfurter disciple, it was assumed, meant to be a Brandeis disciple once removed. More perceptive observers realized that one did not guarantee the other. But Brandeis and Frankfurter did agree on labor law and public utilities, both of which Felix taught at Harvard. In the words of Francis Plimpton,

You learn no law in Public U
That is its fascination
But Felix gives a point of view
And pleasant conversation.[17]

Frankfurter's point of view was that public utility holding companies were predatory monopolies. He taught future corporation lawyers to distrust corporations and to avoid at all costs the "legal factories" of Wall Street that protected them. He encouraged his students' sympathy for labor unions, but he was not a leveler. On the contrary, he was an elitist. He always categorized bright people as "first-rate" and mediocre people who disagreed with him as "third-rate." An avowed intellectual, he demeaned the businessmen whose dependence upon lawyers he cultivated. Lawyers at "first-rate" centers like Harvard were superior intellects to any men. Men of ideas, he urged Eugene Meyer, should not succumb to "traditional American" anti-intellectualism, arguing that the depression crisis needed "more and not less theory, in the systematic and disinterested pursuit of understanding." "Disinterested" was a favorite adjective of his and lawyers had to be disinterested enough to favor government over business. Anyone who sneered at braintrusters and professors in government only reinforced "the conventional American system of political patronage and political improvisation." The power of ideas had to prevail over the power of wealth or the power of democratic politics.

Frankfurter exuded confidence that the intellect of lawyers made them better suited for dealing with the Great Depression than businessmen or even economists. The depression ought to have humbled "the damned economists," he told economist Jacob Viner in 1932, diminishing their "awful swagger" and talk "about 'the new economic era' and what statistics prove; in too many instances they have managed to produce a strange coincidence between money-making and 'science.' " Economists, he charged, excessively venerated "a maker of money, which apparently validates ideas." Viner retorted that Frankfurter was "a little unfair" with his generalizations; economists were "even less standardized" than lawyers and not every commentator on markets was qualified to be called an economist. But intellectual generalizations were Frankfurter's stock-in-trade: Thus, he surprised Undersecretary of the Treasury Arthur A. Ballantine in 1932 with news that "preponderating economic opinion . . . had crystallized into a definite program"—albeit it had yet to reveal itself.[18]

Frankfurter collaborated with former students in writing the Securities Act of 1933, a law intended to generate truth in Wall Street, and then set sail for an Eastman Professorship at Oxford. He fairly tingled with anticipation as he prepared for his year in England. For, as the English would learn, this American "was a genuine Anglomaniac" with a "childlike passion for England, English institutions, Englishmen." Isaiah Berlin has recalled that "The English . . . could do little wrong in his eyes. . . . In general, he liked whatever could be liked, omnivorously, and he greatly disliked having to dislike."[19]

Among those British he especially admired were Fabian socialists. Several of FF's students flirted with Marxism in the 1930s, and some joined the Communist party. But not Frankfurter. While students may have found his alleged radicalism congenial to theirs, his anticapitalism was almost aristocratic or Bohemian. He had no coherent social scheme. The story is told that his Harvard colleague Thomas Reed Powell once spent an evening listening to various lawyers and businessmen complain that Frankfurter was a radical before he expostulated, "Felix, a radical? Hell!! The damn fool is wearing out his heart trying to make capitalism live up to its pretensions." Indeed, Frankfurter thought that investment banking had "nothing to fear and everything to gain" from the securities law he had helped to write. His radicalism took more from his British friend and gadfly Harold Laski than from Karl Marx. Laski, a lecturer at the London School of Economics, had taught at Harvard during 1916–20 and, although more than a decade his junior and an ocean apart, took upon himself the task of playing Frankfurter's mentor in matters of state and capitalism. "America cannot live half slave and half free," Laski pontificated in 1934 while Frankfurter was at Oxford; "control capitalism is a contradiction in terms. Therefore, either you have got to go backwards to a kind of industrial feudalism or forwards to a much greater increase in socialised economic life. . . . Roosevelt is standing proof of Lenin's insistence that you cannot go make greater reforms unless you have a theory and an end you want to reach." Frankfurter's enthusiasm for Laski mystified some young New Dealers.[20]

Frankfurter did not subscribe whole to Laski, but in a nebulous way he wanted to control capitalism to the extent that American society would tolerate it. He rejected a dictatorship of the proletariat, for he abhorred any dictatorship other than that of philosopher-kings such as himself. Once, when his Fabianism provoked a listener to ask, "Since you believe those things, why aren't you a Socialist?" Frankfurter shot back, "Because I cannot compress life into a formula." The man of ideas was too much the realist to envision a direction for all markets. He simply believed that fairness of markets called for public sectors such as road-building and public ownership of utilities.[21] That found a responsive chord in Roosevelt and others of their generation. Since the first decade of the century Americans increasingly suspected that market capitalism exploited the public in industries where competitive producers depended upon noncompetitive utility services. If regulation by disinterested states and the federal government failed to achieve fairness in utility ratemaking, then Washington had a duty to directly enter those markets. With parts of America still awaiting hydroelectric power, Brandeis believed that only state, local or federal governments could provide it for remote and sparse businesses whose usage brought utilities no great profit. And Frankfurter was no more a socialist than Brandeis.

Nor was Frankfurter any more a socialist than John Maynard Keynes, the British economist who avidly played the stock market. Keynes, in Frankfurter's eyes, symbolized all that was great in English intellectuals. He had known Keynes since the Paris Peace Conference of 1919 and had arranged for his *Economic Consequences of the Peace* to be published in the United States and serialized in the *New Republic*. He followed Keynes's career as a polemicist on British economic policies in the 1920s with "unbounded admiration." Shortly after Roosevelt's inauguration the

New York Times serialized Keynes's analysis of the depression and his prescription of public works spending; it soon appeared as a pamphlet in New York, with an assist from his unpaid literary agent, Frankfurter. Of course, Keynes's ideas perfectly dovetailed with Brandeis's campaign for expanded public works spending. A month after he arrived at Oxford Frankfurter met with Keynes and soon prevailed upon him to use his influence via an "An Open Letter to President Roosevelt" that would appear in the *New York Times*. In the letter Keynes deplored the higher prices generated by NRA and AAA while recommending a stronger program of public works. Roosevelt must have seen Felix's fine hand behind Keynes's letter, for he wrote Felix at Oxford, "You can tell the professor" that the Keynes prescription did not allow for the fact that "there is a practical limit to what the Government can borrow." In the spring Keynes visited America to receive an honorary degree from Columbia, an occasion Frankfurter saw as an opportunity to bring the great economist together with the great leader. Letters from Oxford crossed the Atlantic to prepare the way for Keynes, but, although the meeting with FDR took place, it disappointed the participants. While both men professed to their intermediary that they had "a grand talk . . . which was fascinating and illuminating," Roosevelt took up an unexpectedly large part of the hour with discursive conversation; in the remaining time the professor concluded that the President lacked adequate economic literacy while FDR wondered if the professor was more of a mathematician than a political economist. Not everyone shared Frankfurter's esteem for Keynes. "Nobody has been wrong on as many things as Maynard Keynes," Eugene Meyer asserted. Frankfurter accepted such good-humored carping about Keynes from that source, a respected friend for more than two decades, but it is probable that a junior critic would have been written off as third-rate by Frankfurter.[22]

The year in England confirmed Frankfurter in his biases. It reinforced his mugwumpish faith in a strong civil service system based on the English model. "He has a passion for good, disinterested, inconspicuous work in government," Joseph Alsop observed following an interview. "He is full of stories illustrating the superiority of the British system, . . . also full of bitter little quotations of second-class American statesmen [who demean government service]. . . . He literally froths at the mouth and begins to squeak at the thought of the waste and inefficiency, the graft and stupidity in the American system of administration." The problem, as Frankfurter saw it, was that too few good men had tried government service. He had not recently come to that conclusion. Back in 1913 he had been working for Taft's Justice Department when the Democrats came to Washington for the installation of Woodrow Wilson. Frankfurter and his cohorts invited the new Attorney General to dinner to tell him the government's legal arm should be above politics. "What you say is all very well," James McReynolds finally declared, "but I'm afraid you know nothing of public life. You don't see the ninety-six United States senators, all clamoring for patronage in my outer office." "May I suggest, Mr. Attorney General," Frankfurter responded, "that you allow the ninety-six United States Senators to block your vision of the ninety-six million citizens of the United States." A quarter century later Frankfurter would recount the exchange for visitors who needed to be reminded that little had changed either in Washington or in his thinking.[23]

For people who doubted that government lawyers were as good as corporation lawyers, Frankfurter liked to say, "It's a curious thing how public service destroys the taste for private business" and quote John Stuart Mill to the effect that "Mediocrity ought not to be engaged in the affairs of state." "We can no longer afford to do without a highly trained, disinterested governmental personnel," he lectured. He was confident that the New Deal had "more intelligent and more purposeful and more disinterested men in the service of the government than there has been for at least half a century." He took a lot of credit for that improved state of affairs. As he told Jerome Frank, his government lawyers possessed "imagination and disinterestedness." His emphasis on "disinterestedness" is curious: it presumed that if one was not a businessman or a lawyer for corporations he was "disinterested." Of course, not everybody equated a disinterested New Dealer with competence and savvy. Eugene Meyer told Frankfurter that his young lawyers "have come pretty near [to] wrecking the country, and some of their performances, while high-minded, do not reflect glory on you as the highly 'practical' man I know you to be."* (Men like Meyer and Stimson saw Frankfurter as "practical" or as "moderating," not the radical of the *New Republic*.) When Meyer observed in 1934 that "radical" New Dealers such as Rexford Tugwell made Americans "jittery," Frankfurter loftily suggested "that it would take a score of Tugwells to perturb the stamina and placidity of English business and financial men." Yes, Meyer shot back, but Tugwell "would not be in a position of power in England to do so."[24]

Upon his return from England Frankfurter found the New Deal at a standstill. Its cartels agitated Brandeis and its lawyers agitated businessmen. Frankfurter met with Roosevelt at the White House on August 29

*They were old friends, but Frankfurter's constant boasting of his young New Dealers' successes grated on Meyer's nerves. He recounted a particular reform effort of young government lawyers more than a decade before and concluded with asperity, "I am only mentioning this because I want you to realize that in spite of everything that the country was not born on the 4th of March 1933." Meyer to Frankfurter, May 18, 1938, Meyer Papers, Box 22.

and 30, 1934, for nearly five hours, and, echoing Laski, told the President that he faced an "irrepressible conflict" with business. While FDR agreed that he faced a "war" with business, he disagreed with Frankfurter's prescription for massive federal spending on public works financed by massive federal borrowing. FDR could not be a Keynesian. Still, the next phase of the New Deal promised to include a larger role for Frankfurter. Roosevelt, he assured Brandeis, "knows all about Tom and Ben," a reference to Corcoran and Cohen, two of his major collaborators on the Securities Act and then his favorite Washington protégés: "F.D.'s needs and Tom's and Ben's abilities may give us a real opportunity."[25] Nineteen thirty-five would be a Brandeisian year.

7·

Thomas G. Corcoran: The Fixer

"CONJUNCTIONS OF DREAMY, intellectual Jews and effervescent Irishmen may have occurred before but never more effectively than in Corcoran & Cohen."[1] So wrote a *Time* staffer in a journalistic cliché that was repeated again and again in the depression decade. Once the press penetrated their "passion for anonymity," Corcoran and Cohen made excellent copy for the Fourth Estate. In truth these Frankfurter protégés were a potent team of counsels for the New Deal, their alliterative names enhancing their caricatures. Thomas Gardiner Corcoran was a gregarious political dynamo; Benjamin Victor Cohen was a thoughtful legal craftsman. They even looked their parts. Corcoran the Irishman had a jutting jaw and a ready smile; Cohen the Jew wore glasses and looked scholarly somber. "Tom is optimistic and bouyant—Ben is pessimistic and discouraged," went a typical description. "Tom talks with rapid-fire eloquence—Ben with a hesitant drawl. Tom skips rapidly from one subject to another—Ben tracks each idea to its ultimate lair. Tom makes everything crystal clear in five minutes—Ben points out a problem's complexities for five hours. Tom loves the great outdoors—Ben loves the lamp and the cloister. . . . Tom is robust—Ben is pale." Eugene Meyer thought that Cohen made "an impression of a much more intelligent and less emotional personality than Tom Corcoran," but to those who knew better Corcoran was a powerful legal intellect, a shrewd political strategist, and a stabilizing force among young New Dealers. Yet, for all their differences in personality Corcoran and Cohen were devoted to one another and made each other more effective. The press called them the "Gold Dust Twins," a nickname inspired by an advertising slogan for a cleanser.[2] Preferring to operate well beyond the gaze of the press, Corcoran and Cohen wrote the 1933 Truth-in-Securities Act in comparative anonymity; not until they clashed with prestigious Wall Street lawyers in writing the SEC bill of 1934 and the Utilities Holding Companies Act of 1935 did reporters recognize their impact upon the New Deal.

Corcoran in Washington performed as Frankfurter had done when he worked for Stimson: he brought the right people and agencies together.

He had aggressively pushed his way into an RFC job when George Franklin declined Eugene Meyer's offer in 1932 to leave Cotton Franklin. Corcoran had two reasons for wanting to leave corporate practice for Washington: the depression had reduced his salary at Cotton Franklin, and he recalled Frankfurter's celebration of government service. He believed that in the depression Washington was where the action would be—or ought to be. Having run a personal placement operation for lawyers in New York in the manner of Frankfurter, Corcoran took his talents to Washington; in a few years he recruited some 300 to 400 lawyers for a wide variety of agencies and departments. Claiming a closeness to Brandeis, Frankfurter, Jesse Jones and eventually Roosevelt himself, Corcoran unhesitatingly wielded considerable influence in New Deal agencies and departments. Also, he teamed with Cohen to write laws that would stand the test of constitutional challenges and of history. At great risk he immersed himself heavily in party politics, virtually building an organization of Washington lawyers that projected an alternative to the party hacks inhabiting the Democratic National Committee and both Houses of Congress. Yet he professed no political ambitions for himself. Not until World War II did Corcoran express personal ambition; for the time being he wanted no more than an opportunity to make history and then take his friends into a New York law practice such as Cotton Franklin.

Tommy Corcoran found the road to power soon after Congress created the Securities and Exchange Commission in 1934. Roosevelt surprisingly nominated millionaire plunger Joseph P. Kennedy to be the SEC's Chairman, and Kennedy smartly solicited the law's authors, Corcoran and Cohen, for their unofficial services as counsels. Liking to entertain from his big rented home on the Potomac, "Marwood," Kennedy invited Corcoran and Cohen to a party. It is doubtful that Cohen went, but the effervescent Corcoran was quite the party man. However, warned by Frankfurter never to become a tippler on the Washington party circuit, Corcoran hit upon a device that allowed him to be the life of the party while deterring offers of highballs: an accordion. Having played piano in an orchestra as an undergraduate at Brown University and coming from a musical family, Corcoran, standing before a mirror, easily taught himself to play the accordion and brought it to Kennedy's party. The president's secretary, Missy LeHand, was enchanted by his playing. LeHand invited Corcoran and his squeezebox to a White House party where he played sea chanteys and Irish songs. Play "The Wearing of the Green," the President requested. Corcoran charmed Roosevelt, whose fondness for nicknames led him to dub Corcoran "Tommy the Cork"; it was the beginning of a warm partnership.[3]

Born in 1900 in Pawtucket, Rhode Island, to a conservative lawyer's family, Corcoran had been a brilliant student at Brown, graduating at the top of his class with a major in English composition. At Harvard Law School Frankfurter made him a protégé; "he was such an admiration of mine," Corcoran later recalled. Their friendship led to Corcoran's designation as secretary to Supreme Court Justice Oliver Wendell Holmes, the greatest honor Frankfurter could bestow upon a law graduate. In Washington, he became Holmes's "little jewel," as a newspaper reporter tagged him, reading to the aging Justice, as all his secretaries did, from Montaigne and Dante, two of Corcoran's favorites. "Of all his secretaries Tom was the dearest to Holmes," Frankfurter told FDR. Corcoran himself told how Holmes described him as "quite noisy, quite adequate, and quite noisy." He idolized Holmes, and for the rest of his life Corcoran quoted Holmes on the law and on life itself. In 1927 he went to Cotton Franklin to learn about Wall Street, and Joseph Cotton became another Corcoran icon. Later it would be rumored that Corcoran was bitter at Wall Street because he lost money in the 1929 crash; he did lose money, but it was in a pool operation to save a large investment trust that failed anyway when the pool manager absconded with the funds. In 1932, following Cotton's untimely death, Corcoran decided to escape from that "house of bondage" (Frankfurter's double entendre for a Wall Street firm) to the RFC. Frankfurter had idealized government service for Corcoran, but now he feared that as an "incorrigible romantic" Corcoran might be disillusioned by Washington. "Don't be disappointed if at the end of a few months you will find fallible and finite human beings fallible and finite," he cautioned the worshipful Corcoran. "Thank your maker, or yourself, that you found one Holmes and one Joe Cotton all in one lifetime." At the RFC Corcoran specialized in loans for municipal power plants, perhaps out of a distaste for private utilities acquired from Frankfurter. He anticipated that his role and that of the corporation would change decisively when Jesse Jones assumed RFC's leadership and the New Deal began. Years later, having ignored Frankfurter's admonition against seeking intellectual heroes in Washington, a confused Corcoran commented, "To have in your intellectual inheritance Holmes, Roosevelt, Cotton, and Jones is—indigestion." Significant was Corcoran's omission of Frankfurter and Brandeis; that is a story in itself.[4]

In the New Deal Corcoran was almost slavishly devoted to Brandeis and Frankfurter. He echoed Brandeis's injunctions against bigness and the NRA, and advocated public works; like Frankfurter, he praised Harold Laski and John Maynard Keynes, solicited readers for the writings of David Cushman Coyle, and gloried in disinterested government service; however, his Irish ancestry saved him from Anglophilia. But Corcoran's influence went far beyond that conferred by his identification with Brandeis and Frankfurter. As early as late 1933 some Democrats were a little afraid of Corcoran's "extra-curricular activities in 'running the government.'" In the RFC Jones gave him responsibility for the purchase of banks' preferred stocks; later he transferred his attentions within the agency to financing the Coast Guard and still later to financing the Electric Home and Farm Authority and other aspects of public hydroelectric power. He helped convert the RFC from a nominally bipartisan agency to one more tuned to New Deal programs for state capitalism—which is what it became under Jesse Jones. However, by 1934–35 Corcoran became a ubiquitous New Deal operative with only a nominal portfolio. The RFC provided Corcoran with an office and a secretary, the beautiful Peggy Dowd (whom he finally married in 1940). He acquired several New Deal hats: the official one at the RFC; the personnel hat, from which he constantly drew names of lawyers for a myriad of positions in departments and agencies; the counselor's hat, the one he shared with Cohen and others in writing laws that reformed Wall Street; that of presidential braintruster, the man who almost lived at the White House and wrote presidential speeches that virtually made administration policy; and the political ramrod, the hatchetman who drove the president's agenda ahead of what the Democratic party sometimes seemed willing to follow.

During 1934–38 it seemed that almost nobody save Harry Hopkins was closer to "the Skipper," as Tommy affectionately called the President. Roosevelt and Corcoran shared a dislike of utility holding companies and a desire to tightly regulate them. Also, they were "both sanguine, volatile, warmhearted men. They are impatient of obstacles," an astute reporter wrote, "fertile in expedients for surmounting or circumventing those obstacles. They do not admit the impossible. If you can't do a thing one way, they maintain, you can do it another. Their minds are quick, flexible, subtle. Corcoran has not, of course, Mr. Roosevelt's gift of swaying great masses of men, but he is almost as persuasive in personal conversation." Raymond Moley, Adolf Berle and Sam Rosenman still wrote speeches for Roosevelt, but in 1936 Corcoran supplanted Moley. In the climactic campaign speech at Philadelphia in which Roosevelt said, "Governments can err, presidents can make mistakes, but the immortal Dante tells us that Divine Justice weighs the sins of the warmhearted in different scales," those who knew Corcoran knew the author of those words.[5]

The New Deal lawyers were Roosevelt's party and Corcoran their chairman. Pariahs in any local, state or national Democratic party organization, Corcoran and Cohen made themselves vitally useful to Congress. Men such as Senators Burton K. Wheeler, Hugo Black and House Majority Leader Sam Rayburn used their legal craftsmanship and quick minds. What characterized them was their devotion to the public weal: they were antiparty, antipatronage, anti–interest group as defined by their "disinterestedness", and pro–civil service, pro–public interest, pro-regulation of business and pro–government development of the economy. The New Deal lawyers who followed Corcoran and Cohen were experts, technicians in democracy, beholden to nobody but the president and the Constitution—and they knew that the latter was subject to changing interpretations. They were indispensable in running the government. They sneered at party chairman James Farley: in the words of one lawyer, "Farley could furnish you four hundred stenographers, but not four hundred lawyers."[6] They were reformers, moralists, pragmatic in behavior and in their choice of goals. The lawyers boiled their biases down to an ideology, a liberal system of ideas that drew its strength from a crisis conviction that government must do for people what they could not do for themselves individually; government collectively was the people. They were intolerant of big business, Wall Street, political hacks and interest group representatives. Ironically, while they celebrated the emerging power of an expanding federal government that promised to lead to a better life, they increasingly were aware of their own political impotence without the popularity of FDR. Nobody had elected them but Roosevelt—whom they worshipped. Corcoran and Roosevelt conspired for a realignment of like-minded liberals into the Democratic party to reduce the influence of Farley, Baruch, Jones and other conservative manipulators of Congress; they would get Congress and the party behind Roosevelt.

Self-consciously infused with what reporters Alsop and Kintner called "caste spirit," an attitude of identifying themselves against older entrenched power groups, "The young men in the government in the 1933 to 1935 era ate, slept, and constantly talked the topics of their jobs," one of them, Charles Wyzanski, remembered: "There was constant communication among these people, an enthusiasm, an energy, an awareness of fresh problems and a feeling that one really counted and that what one did was very important." Corcoran husbanded an esprit de corps by converting a rented house in Washington into a meeting place, a sort of intellectual center. The idea for the house had come to him when Cohen threatened to return to New York in quest of a more stimulating environment. Corcoran needed Cohen and wanted him to be comfortable in Washington. But the dining room in the house on Thirty-fifth Place proved to be too small for the throngs of lawyers drawn to it. They leased another house on R Street, which reporters tagged "the little red house" both for its "radical" occupants and its appropriate color. But it too became so crowded with lawyers that Tom and Ben went to eat downtown. In recruiting "the Corcoran Gallery" of lawyers, so-named by the press for the famous Washington art museum, Corcoran stressed their shared convictions and the desirability to place at least two of his lawyers in an agency where intellectually "They take fire from one another." Also, the group reinforced an attitude of all work and no play. When young Joseph Rauh, fresh out of Harvard Law, joined the Corcoran group in mid-1935, a story made the rounds about one New Deal lawyer asking another what he was doing in his office at midnight on a Saturday and being told that he was "writing home." "Oh," exclaimed the first lawyer, "a half day." Corcoran saw to it that although they were young, they were not rowdy. A self-professed "Puritan," he insisted upon their abstinence from alcohol (especially among Irishmen) and no partying; their work ethic had to put that of their enemies to shame. Their only evident vice was a $300 per month telephone bill and their greatest virtue, in the eyes of their supporters, was a passion for anonymity.[7]

It seemed that nobody was more passionate for his anonymity than the very private Benjamin Cohen. If it had not been for his pairing with Tommy Corcoran, Cohen might have been overlooked by all but connoisseurs of great legal talents. The son of an immigrant peddler from Poland, Cohen was born in Muncie, Indiana, in 1893. At an early age his family moved to Chicago, where he enrolled at the University of Chicago at sixteen. He went through college in three years and by twenty-one had earned a Phi Beta Kappa key, a Ph.D. with honors in law, political economy, and political science, a J.D., and the reputation of being very political-minded, reserved, studious and self-effacing. Politically he identified himself with the Bull Moose Progressives and their local leaders, lawyer Harold Ickes and professor Charles Merriam. Ever the scholar, Cohen then went to Harvard and the embrace of Felix Frankfurter. They were made for each other. "I never thought of going into private law practice," Cohen later recalled. "My decision was for a public career in matters relating to law." However, he always seemed to be searching for meaningful work, and Frankfurter gave his life some needed direction. "Felix liked to arrange things—mainly good things," Cohen noted. In the words of Joe Lash, Cohen needed someone like Frankfurter because he "lacked a presence that dominated and commanded. He read, analyzed, understood better than everyone around him, and his sweet nature made him a delight to those who appreciated intelligence and sensitivity, but the ideas and visions that thronged his brain required others to bring them to fruition." In 1917 Frankfurter placed him with the Shipping Board, whose counsel was Edward B.

Burling of the Washington firm Covington Burling. But it was not government service that drew Cohen abroad in early 1919. At 77 Great Russell Street Cohen beame a mainstay in the London Zionist offices and did not return for over two years. He remained a part of the Zionist movement through the 1920s and 1930s, organizing the Palestine Cooperative Company that would later become the Palestine Economic Corporation. Through Brandeis he learned the role of planning for economic development. Then he took Burling's suggestion and focused on corporate finance. Living frugally and managing a corporate receivership, Cohen invested with moderate success in the Chrysler Corporation, pointing with delight at every Chrysler that passed on the street. And he spent a large part of his time working pro bono for women's organizations concerned with child labor legislation.[8]

Although no government lawyer was as respected as Cohen, he never had a prominent position in government because of his palpable Jewishness. He was modest, but confident of his skills, and most people agreed that he deserved any office conferred upon him. He had been considered for an SEC commissionership in 1934, but prominent Jewish lawyers and bankers opposed his appointment out of fear that it would escalate anti-Semitism. Although Brandeis, Frankfurter and Judge Julian Mack pleaded with Roosevelt to ignore those Jews—for whatever reason, Cohen was not nominated. In 1937 FDR discussed with Morgenthau whether Cohen should be used in the Attorney General's office or the SEC; without knowing Cohen, Morgenthau preferred the former, where a Cohen would be less conspicuous. A year later Harold Ickes suggested to the President that Cohen should fill an important vacancy in the Treasury, and Roosevelt responded that Ben was "a good man but he questioned the wisdom of appointing a Jew under Morgenthau." A Jew should not have a Jewish counsel, whatever the attorney's qualifications. Ironically, when C. C. Burlingham discussed the solicitor generalship in 1941, he thought that Tommy Corcoran should be disqualified because he was "too coarse and crude," the Jewish stereotype, while Cohen was quite different: "He is the type of Jew that I like best, a gentleman." But it went to neither Corcoran nor Cohen, as the capable Charles Fahy got it. A soft-spoken Southerner, Fahy had attended Notre Dame, taken his law degree from Georgetown and served as general counsel of the National Labor Relations Board for five years before becoming assistant solicitor general. During Fahy's leadership the NLRB hired more Jewish lawyers than any other agency of the government. Few people thought that the NLRB had too many Jews; few people knew that Fahy's mother was Jewish. But Cohen was very obviously Jewish and that was why Roosevelt denied the solicitor generalship to him. Although he knew how the game of quotas was played, Cohen tried to be above it. As he told one of the game's most assiduous practitioners, Jerome Frank, "I don't know that the figures regarding the number of Jews in Government service is available. . . . In some respects this talk about the number of Jews is all wrong, and the more we talk about it the more confused we become. The problem is the type of men in public service without regard to their race or creed." Such clear thinking was unfashionable in those days.[9]

It was Frankfurter, of course, who brought Cohen into the New Deal. He recommended Cohen to Eugene Meyer for an RFC job, but it did not work out: "He is more interested in the legal principles than in a great administrative grind," Meyer reported. Cohen wanted to write laws, not administer them. Cohen's first exposure to the New Deal came when Edward Foley, representing some Army engineers and public works experts who were anticipating Roosevelt's push in public works, sought a general counsel; again Frankfurter recommended Cohen. Later in 1933 Cohen would inform Frankfurter that he wanted to leave the PWA because "I am as you know without real influence on fundamental policies and I have no hankering for the general run of administrative work, no matter how important it may be in itself."[10]

Cohen revealed little of himself, but once Corcoran knew his talents, he ebulliently forecast that one day his friend would be nominated for the Supreme Court—and few who knew Cohen as the "lawyers' lawyer," a most respected legal technician, could disagree. All the lawyers wanted Cohen to read their briefs or articles. In April 1933 Raymond Moley cast about for someone to write a corporation finance law to correct Wall Street abuses and called Frankfurter, who immediately saw that it was a major opportunity to influence a reform New Deal. With his fellow law school professor James N. Landis in tow, Frankfurter entrained to Washington where he had Cohen meet them and the three went to Tommy Corcoran's apartment. Corcoran and Landis knew each other from Harvard, but wondered what the Cohen contribution would be. Soon they discovered what Frankfurter already knew, that Cohen was familiar with the disclosure provisions of the British Companies Act, which would be their model. Frankfurter returned to Cambridge, and the drafters began a long labor to find formulas that would outwit the Wall Street lawyers scanning their handiwork for loopholes or violations of the Constitution. At times differences among them arose and at one point Cohen threatened to pull out, but Corcoran called Frankfurter to mediate a problem and calm him. Over the next few years clashes between the mercurial Landis and the pedantic Cohen would be a common occurrence and would keep Corcoran busy with exhortations to both to keep working. Sam Rayburn spearheaded their handiwork through the House, and on

May 27 Roosevelt signed the "Truth in Securities" Act. It was a beginning for reform of the financial system.[11]

Despite the bias that limited the uses of Cohen and Corcoran, Washington's Protestant Establishment had decided it needed them. A cultural revolution was at hand. "What was once thought of as an inexorable social deficiency was reformulated in terms of behavioral characteristics, and, as a consequence, a non-WASP could achieve prominence by exhibiting WASP behavioral patterns," G. Edward White observes. "If non-WASP lawyers were professionally qualified and properly WASP in their behavior, they could achieve prominent positions hitherto reserved for WASPs."[12] That did not mean Frankfurter's Jews alone. For he had sent not only Corcoran but another Irishman, James Rowe of Montana, who served in several agencies before he became White House counsel late in the decade. Corcoran and Rowe kept up an Irish camaraderie that promoted such other Irishmen as Edward H. Foley, Jr., of upstate New York and a graduate of Fordham Law School. "The Irish are a sentimental race," Rowe liked to remind Corcoran.[13]

Frankfurter embarked for England in the fall of 1933, but not without directing New Dealers to discuss all personnel matters with Tommy Corcoran, "a shrewd person generally [who knew] a good deal about Washington ways." At the same time he instructed Corcoran to visit Brandeis at least once a week for intellectual guidance. Corcoran was everywhere in Washington: counseling with Alexander Sachs on the best way to finance credits for small businesses, lining up a public relations adviser for David Lilienthal at the TVA, "clearing every problem of judgment" with Brandeis, securing jobs for Raymond Moley's in-laws with the National Park Service and the Civilian Conservation Corps ("he pounded me pretty petulantly all the way but that's done") and even placing secretaries in offices where they could be useful conduits of information. In the first year of the New Deal Corcoran carved out the political leadership that would be evident later. In late 1933 he and Cohen set up their lawyers' quarters and, following the passage of the Securities and Exchange Commission Act in the spring of 1934 the press picked up on their activities. Evidence of their influence excited Frankfurter. "Dear Little Boys," he addressed them; "what darling children you must be to have wormed your way not only into the heart but even into the mind and will of the President of the United States, so that he says what you tell him to do." Just think, Frankfurter exulted, "he lets you think for him and even act for him!"[14]

Frankfurter's humor aside, the fight for the SEC made Corcoran and Cohen known throughout Washington. Corcoran's reputation for clout was sealed. "The word went back to the White House that by God I could handle myself [and] I became known in the White House as a guy who could go down and be a front-line fighter," Corcoran remembered. "Roosevelt liked that kind of guy and little by little, I was the guy who handled all the tough ones on the Hill." He already was known among the agencies that proliferated in New Deal Washington as the key man to see about staffing them with lawyers. Until then he considered himself a temporary resident of Washington, even declining an invitation to join a club because he expected his stay to be "prospectively short." When visibility added to his prominence and power, he did not shun it. Officials in Washington could pick up a ringing phone at any time to hear a New England accent barking into the earpiece, "Hello, this is Tom Corcoran calling from the White House." It certainly got one's attention, even if the call did not originate from 1600 Pennsylvania Avenue. It added to his influence in the RFC. Investment bankers seeking to save Kelly Springfield Tire Company from bankruptcy approached him for RFC assistance, and other businessmen also sought him out for the corporation's special attention. In 1935 he seemed to do everything, from writing speeches for Harold Ickes to heavy lobbying for the important Public Utilities Holding Company bill. The fight for the latter was bitter, but it added to his reputation as the President's spear-carrier.

Loyalties were made in that fight, especially loyalties to those Congressmen who stood by Roosevelt and against the billions in wealth of the utility holding companies. Rayburn had led the fight against the holding companies, and if he wanted the Red River Project in Texas for power and conservation, then Ickes and Corcoran did their damnedest to get it. In 1936 Corcoran was especially sensitive to the fact that the holding companies pumped millions of dollars into primary campaigns for conservative Democrats and into the 1936 election coffers of Republicans running against liberals first elected in 1932 or 1934. Even in Northern states such as Maine the "power trust" went after Roosevelt Democrats, who looked to Corcoran to save their seats. Loyalty to Roosevelt and the New Deal were Corcoran's sine qua non, and Congressman Edward C. Moran, Jr., of Maine's second district understood that when he declared, "I've nailed my flag to the New Deal and, with proper national support, I predict my re-election." Many of Moran's fellow Democrats had hard fights in 1936 and some ran too far behind the national ticket for a return to Congress. A few liberal freshmen Congressmen, such as Maury Maverick of San Antonio, Texas, survived, but Congressmen D. J. Driscoll of rural Pennsylvania and Edward C. Eicher of Iowa needed lots of Corcoran's "proper national support" in the form of campaign contributions he solicited from new sources such as David Dubinsky, president of the International Ladies Garment Workers Union.

Corcoran sent speakers to help Driscoll; in Eicher's unusual case, the Iowan pleaded with Corcoran to *prevent* a PWA grant to the town of Morning Sun to create its own power system competitive with the Iowa Southern Utilities Company, "a very square-shooting concern" that already provided the town with cheap electricity. Both men lost: in 1937 Driscoll would be appointed to the Pennsylvania Public Utility Commission and Eicher headed back to Washington for a career as an SEC commissioner and a 1941 nomination as Chief Justice of the United States District Court for the District of Columbia. Corcoran saw to it that loyalty to FDR had its rewards.[15]

Corcoran also made alliances in the press with such disparate persons as Russell Davenport of the Luce magazine *Fortune*, and the radical chief editorial writer of the New York *Post*, Isador "Izzi" Feinstein. Feinstein and Corcoran first got together in May 1936 when the newspaperman went looking for administration help in civil rights cases. They subsequently enjoyed a friendship of favors—Corcoran soliciting Feinstein for a job at the *Post* for Samuel Beer, to write four speeches on the Supreme Court and civil liberties, to write editorials denouncing the Court on power cases and to support Robert H. Jackson for governor of New York. In turn Feinstein used Corcoran's political clout to get his father's temporary job at the Philadelphia Mint made permanent and to secure living and traveling expenses from Frankfurter and retailer Lincoln Filene while he drafted a book on the Constitution and minimum wage legislation. In the light of the different directions their careers would take during and after World War II, when Feinstein became the radical journalist I. F. Stone and Corcoran became a Washington lobbyist and corporate lawyer, theirs was a curious combine that belonged uniquely to the era.[16]

Cohen had hoped to get the job as general counsel of the SEC, but when Kennedy gave it to John J. Burns, it made Cohen available to be Ickes's general counsel for the National Power Policy Committee in 1934. Cohen made the NPPC more than the obscure committee it could have been and gave it impetus that brought about the Bonneville Power Authority. In his heart, and in Roosevelt's too, there should have been more power administrations, but NPPC had no administrative authority. Cohen made NPPC's office on Eighteenth Street a place where the young lawyers of the New Deal could repair to in quest of his avuncular advice. Significantly, however, it was where Cohen et al. drafted the Public Utilities Holding Company Act, which sealed his reputation for drafting genius; it was perhaps the most critical law of the New Deal. A lawyer for the utilities, John Foster Dulles, patronizingly conceded that Cohen was a "very bright young man [but] a misguided idealist." Still, the decision to go after the utilities was Roosevelt's. "F.D. is really hot on the holding cos. and for drastic action," Frankfurter told Brandeis in early 1935. Indeed, in a meeting with utility company executive Wendell Willkie, when Roosevelt was asked, were "any further efforts to avoid the breakup of utility holding companies . . . futile?" Roosevelt tersely responded, "It is futile."[17]

The assault on the holding companies completed FDR's reform of Wall Street, although a monumental fight for TVA and public power remained. The trio of laws beginning with the Securities Act of 1933 sought to prevent financial abuses similar to those of the 1920s and to reduce the menace of concentrated financial power. Between 1932 and 1934 the Senate Banking and Currency Committee had investigated financial practices with no other purpose than to spotlight the corrupt practices that had resulted in the loss of millions of dollars by investors. Led by a pugnacious cross-examiner and politically ambitious general counsel, the Sicilian-born Ferdinand Pecora of New York City, the committee so relentlessly pursued the moguls of Manhattan that J. P. Morgan, Jr., would complain that he felt like "a horse thief." This inspired the Truth in Securities Act of 1933, which gave Washington the right to regulate the honest sale of stocks—a goal long sought by Roosevelt, who saw self-regulation or state regulation as ineffective. (Interestingly, Roosevelt probably also recalled that William G. McAdoo's Capital Issues Committee first supervised Wall Street in 1918 as a wartime measure; a bill to continue regulation of the sale of securities died in 1920.)[18] The 1933 law passed Congress easily. Rayburn and Vice-President Garner gave indispensable leadership. Yet it was but a modest step; Frankfurter did not want to suffer defeat in the New Deal's first clash with Wall Street. Indeed, he and several of his former students opposed creation of the Securities and Exchange Commission. SEC's birth, concludes one historian, "in a sense, was an accident."[19]

But the Pecora Committee and an FTC report suggested that Wall Street reform was impossible unless the New Dealers went after the utilities. In 1932 three holding companies controlled 45 per cent of the electricity privately generated in the U.S. When combined with thirteen other holding companies they controlled 92 per cent. Control of these companies in turn depended upon excessive debt-to-equity ratios in which financiers sold bonds that devalued shares held by the public. The technique of using bonds to circumvent the ownership of equity holders was not too different than the "junk bond" exploits of corporate raiders in the 1980s. The greatest scandal associated with the holding companies had been the collapse of Samuel Insull's paper empire of Midwest utilities and Insull's flight from the United States to avoid prosecution. Added to that was the fact that accounting practices then were such that any realistic appraisal of the properties' value or profits was nearly impossible. The holding companies were financial empires of a few men. "I am against private socialism of concentrated private power as thoroughly as I am against governmental socialism," FDR declared upon receiving a report from Cohen's Power Policy Committee recommending the end of all holding companies. "The one is as equally dangerous as the other; and destruction of private socialism is utterly essential to avoid governmental socialism."[20]

Following passage of the Public Utilities Holding Company Act, the lawyers plotted its defense against an anticipated Wall Street assault on its constitutionality. The corporations' principal target was its Section 11, the controversial "death sentence" provision that empowered the SEC after January 1, 1938, to reduce a holding company to a single electrical system unless it could be shown that geographical or economic logic existed in a multiple systems company. In writing the death sentence Corcoran and Cohen rejected arguments by those who called for the abolition of all holding companies, preferring to push for contiguous utilities. "Down with scatteration!" was a battle cry that defined the enemy as far-flung utilities from Maine to California under one corporate head. "In the broadest sense, the Holding Company Act gave the SEC power to refashion the structure and business practices of an entire industry," historian-lawyer Joel Seligman has written. Following the Supreme Court's decision that NRA was unconstitutional, the New Dealers anticipated a test of the utility holding company act. They were not disappointed.

Seventeen days after it became law, the utility industry announced that it had retained Wall Street lawyer and 1924 Democratic presidential nominee John W. Davis, along with former Secretary of War Newton D. Baker and former Solicitor General James M. Beck to test its constitutionality. On behalf of a dentist who owned $2,500 worth of utility stock, Davis petitioned a friendly Baltimore Federal District Court judge to declare the law unconstitutional. Although SEC Chairman James Landis denounced the proceedings as a "sham," the conservative judge did not disappoint Davis, thereby precipitating a torrent of utility company suits to prevent enforcement of the provision that utilities had to register with the SEC by December 1, 1935. Landis and Cohen, now augmented by experienced prosecutors Robert H. Jackson and Lawrence Fly, swiftly counterattacked by filing a complaint in the New York federal court of Judge Julian Mack, a friend of Frankfurter and former employer of Cohen. The complaint's target was the Electric Bond and Share Company, the second-largest holding company, covering thirty-one states from

Florida to Washington. By filing before lawyers for the utility could get their complaint into court, the SEC lawyers chose not only a court but the law's provisions for defense. In January 1937 Judge Mack ruled that two sections of the law were valid and that the utilities had to register. Several did, but not until the Supreme Court upheld the law in 1938 did its enforcement proceed apace—and then under the tough-minded leadership of a new SEC chairman, William O. Douglas.[21]

By that time many Democrats had wearied of Corcoran's ramrod political leadership. FDR himself quite clearly approved of and encouraged Corcoran if only because Tommy the hatchet man enthusiastically deflected criticism from the Skipper. During the fight over the Utilities Holding Companies bill, Republican Representative Ralph Owen Brewster of Maine took the House floor to accuse Corcoran of threatening to stop construction of the Passamaquoddy Dam unless Brewster voted for the death-sentence provision. The House Rules Committee investigated the charges, and Corcoran responded that in a conversation with Brewster he had merely raised a question as to whether Brewster could be trusted to support the "Quoddy" legislation, which journalist Ernest Gruening verified. In the words of *Time*, "With cold, lucid, driving fury, [Corcoran] tore Ralph Brewster's tale to shameful shreds." "Dear Tommy—Stout Fellah! FDR" a pleased President wrote Corcoran. While Corcoran wanted public attention to spotlight the fierce holding company lobby that influenced Brewster's turnabout on the bill, what gave credibility to Brewster's tale was Corcoran's growing reputation for political brashness. On the one hand, Corcoran's fierce loyalty to the President was admirable. "Whatever Rubicon he crosses, I will follow," he would say. On the other, it rankled some Democrats that Corcoran expected everyone to follow him without question.

It was so in 1937 on the administration plan to "pack" the Supreme Court. It was so on an administration effort to reorganize the federal bureaucracy. It was so on the Wages and Hours Bill of 1938, in which, it was said, Corcoran kept a tally of Senate votes—vowing revenge against those who voted against Roosevelt. It was so in the subsequent attempted "purge" of conservative Democratic Senators during the primaries of 1938. It was so during a push to make Robert Jackson governor of New York as a stepping-stone to advancing Jackson as FDR's successor in 1940. It was so when Corcoran abruptly launched a drive for a third term for FDR. He made every fight for FDR a jihad. ("It will be the sword or the Koran," predicted one Democrat. "No," quipped another, "it will be the sword or the Cor-coran!") When a former comrade from Wall Street attacked FDR's spending policies in 1938–39 as "Economic Masturbation," Corcoran shot back, "I don't care for this smart alec like horseshit of yours." With a network of friendly political reporters throughout Washington hanging on his every word, he could destroy or make reputations. But politics also costs money and Corcoran could bring contributors together with winners. Claude Pepper credited Corcoran with his winning the Florida Senate primary in 1938 because Corcoran funneled contributions by Boston millionaire Lincoln Filene, United Fruit Company president Samuel Zemurray and others into the war chests of Democrats. "Tom, old fellow, I will never be able to thank you enough for what you did in the campaign," Pepper wrote. "Yours for progressivism until age and good fortune shall harden our spiritual arteries." They were crusaders together for liberalism.[22]

In Wall Street and in the Democratic party there were many people who wanted to prove that it did not pay to be too smart. Wall Street accused Corcoran and Cohen of seeking "revenge" against the exchanges for their losses in 1929 (Cohen's were rather ordinary), but that was nonsense; in the words of an observer, "They know that 'Wall Street' is not a person, but an aggregation of thousands of people, good and bad, most of whom lost as much in the crash as they did themselves. They want to reform the system, not take revenge on it." Some Democrats considered them too young to call the shots in Washington (in 1935 Corcoran was thirty-five and Cohen was forty-two, and combined they had been practicing law in private life or government for more than a quarter century); five years later an irate citizen would write FDR that "these two boys have had a lovely time for the past few years but it is time for MEN to be in key positions now." It was true that unlike electoral politicians they had not paid their local political dues. Even the liberal Henry A. Wallace stubbornly opposed the purge of 1938, which targeted Guy Gillette in Wallace's home state of Iowa. "I didn't like Tommy Corcoran's maneuvers," Wallace said plaintively some dozen years later. Former Secretary of Commerce Daniel Roper of South Carolina, a longtime party war-horse, told Wallace and other sympathetic Democrats that he could not get along with Corcoran and intended to do something about it at the party's 1940 convention. Senator Gillette estimated that Corcoran had alienated about thirty-five Senators. "It is obvious that Tommy will have very little value when it comes to winning an election," noted a satisfied Henry Wallace.[23]

Between 1933 and 1940 Corcoran had gone from obscurity to fame and power and, finally, vilification. The New Dealers Corcoran brought to Washington combined idealism with hardheaded practicalities so readily that observers alternately considered them naive or cynical. Get on board "with mushy people down here," Corcoran invited a young fellow Irishman from Wall Street named James Forrestal. They would prove that toughness and ethics were compatible in the financial marketplaces of America. But conservatives like Eugene Meyer grumbled: "Many New Dealers do not understand . . . that being righteous isn't always identical to being right." Judge Learned Hand, who by Arthur Schlesinger, Jr.'s reckoning "liked the New Deal but not the New Dealers," once commented: "The Filii Aurorae make me actively sick to my stomach; they are so conceited, so insensitive, so arrogant." Rightwingers dubbed them "the Georgetown revolutionaries" or "Thinkers of almost legendary existence whose skill at totalitarian induction makes neophytes of the former Regimenters." But that ideological chasm was small compared to the evident power rift among Democrats, where party chairman James A. Farley resented the way the New Dealers hoarded jobs in the new agencies among themselves and did not share with the party. Did the party belong to its regular workers and elected officials or to a bunch of intellectual lawyers who, representing only themselves and the President, threatened to establish an ideological discipline that excluded dissenters? "We don't know how many times we've been asked by tired Democrats as we've wandered about the country: 'Who's running the party these days, Jim or Tommy Corcoran?' " wrote one reporter; the Corcoran Democratic party "is pretty well convinced that the sun has set permanently on the old-fashioned political racket. They may be too optimistic." Indeed; Harold Ickes admired Corcoran's assumption of authority and the way he "keeps us liberals from being frozen out and he gets things done." A sympathetic Joseph Alsop, a distant cousin of the Roosevelts, believed that "the New Dealers' intellectual liberalism was a healthy force in American politics," but doubted that the Democratic party could continue to win if it was dominated "by a small group of rather obscure appointive officials in Washington." By the late 1930s Alsop and others wondered about Roosevelt's political legacy: would FDR leave a split party in 1940? "As cousin Alice [Roosevelt Longworth] says, 'Roosevelts and history both repeat themselves.' "[24]

Corcoran and Cohen helped Roosevelt win the third term in 1940, but the Democratic party wanted no more of them. In trouble with Congress, Roosevelt told Corcoran in 1940 to "stop this New Deal talk." FDR was intent upon using the war to unify the nation and jettison the divisive New Deal. What was left for Corcoran and Cohen? They had grown tired of the amorphous roles that seemed their destinies and yearned for positions of responsibility; but Roosevelt and others now kept them afar. In early 1941 Corcoran became a father and James Rowe drafted Roosevelt's congratulations, hinting that Corcoran would have a position in the growing war setup. Corcoran expressed yearnings for security and prestige in a defined administration role, but Roosevelt seemed torn between recognizing his loyalties or his liabilities. Corcoran set his eyes on the solicitor general's office for expressing his unheralded legal talents. In the White House Rowe told the President, "Most people have forgotten it, but Tom is a brilliant legal scholar and, what is more important in a Solicitor General, has a felicity and clarity of expression both in formal and informal talk surpassing any other lawyer I have ever heard in court." Rowe had to concede that Corcoran probably could not be confirmed without a political fight in Congress. Corcoran sought support for his quest from members of the administration and even from the Supreme Court, but studiously and noticeably avoided Frankfurter—of whom it was said that he disapproved of Corcoran's visibly political role. Frankfurter, now on the Court, viewed Corcoran as "nothing but a political fixer." He showed Cohen a letter to Corcoran he did not send, confirming his opposition to him as solicitor general on the grounds that he lacked "temperament" because of his political proclivities. By September all of Corcoran's friends realized that he would not get the post.

What would Corcoran get? After Pearl Harbor William O. Douglas sent word to the President that Corcoran would take any government assignment FDR bestowed upon him and abandon the lobbying retainers that had come his way. But no offer from the White House was forthcoming. Harold Ickes thought that nobody wanted a personality as strong as Corcoran's in their organization. Months passed without Roosevelt and Corcoran even seeing each other. In late 1942 Roosevelt told Henry Wallace, "I wish I had Tommy back. He has not called on me in a long time. Why doesn't he call? I suppose Tommy is too busy making money. They say he is making it hand over fist." Indeed, Corcoran busied himself with war contractors like Henry Kaiser, frequently visited a sympathetic Harold Ickes, and satisfied himself that he was both making money and helping the war effort—even if some journalists called it cronyism for personal profit. Although FDR hoped Tommy would get back into public life once his debts were paid off, in 1944 Francis Biddle brought to the President's attention the fact that the U.S. attorney's office in the Southern District of New York was vacant, and suggested that Corcoran could give the job "real intelligence and leadership." But, inquired FDR, would the Senate approve his appointment? Biddle said that preliminary soundings indicated a favorable vote. Still, Roosevelt had politics on his mind and was cautious, although he declared, "I will appoint Tom the day after election." Did he make the offer? If he did, would Corcoran have removed himself from his Washington connections to be a prosecutor in Manhattan? A week before the 1944 inauguration he went shopping for Roosevelt's old assistant-secretaryship of the Navy via Secretary of the Navy James V. Forrestal, an old Wall Street friend. All we know is that Corcoran remained one of Washington's fabled lobbyists.[25]

Cohen was heartbroken when Corcoran did not get the solicitor-generalship and briefly considered pursuing it for himself. Part of Cohen's problems was his uncertainty as to his own future. James Rowe believed that Cohen was Corcoran's "only anchor to windward," but for all of his stability, nobody could find a niche for him that did not put him in tandem with Corcoran. Cohen went to England at Ambassador John Winant's invitation, a role that suited his growing interest in foreign affairs. But he was soon home amid rumors that he would replace Jerome Frank as Chairman of the SEC. FDR agreed to give Cohen a vaguely defined position as administrative assistant reporting on defense problems, but Cohen wanted something more substantial. He was one of the most creative minds and best draftsmen in Washington and he lacked a portfolio. In early 1942 Harold Ickes reported him as so "utterly listless and discouraged" that he seemed capable of suicide. For a while FDR thought about making Cohen assistant to the Attorney General, a position that called for handling patronage. Rowe knew something about patronage and something about Cohen: they did not mesh. "He has been a steadying force in the administration," Rowe told his chief, "and now he is becoming just a bit of a prima donna himself." That did not sit well with Roosevelt. In 1942, when Attorney General Francis Biddle and FDR discussed a Supreme Court replacement for James Byrnes, who had resigned to administer the war effort, Biddle suggested Charles Fahy, Dean Acheson, and Benjamin Cohen—and Roosevelt immediately said that "Ben would not do." In terms of legal scholarship he would have been an excellent appointment, but with Frankfurter there it would not look good to have two Jews. Byrnes, however, already had sought Cohen's legal talents. Cohen would have no shortage of responsibilities during the war as Byrnes ran the Office of War Mobilization and Reconversion with Cohen's aid. Cohen was at the Dumbarton Oaks conference, and in early 1945 Roosevelt suggested that he become an assistant to the new Secretary of State, Edward Stettinius; but Cohen demurred, saying it was "abundantly clear to me that I am not really wanted in the State Department unless I wish to accept some undefined, subordinate position." When Byrnes became Secretary of State under Harry Truman, Cohen was never far from his side. And what prominent role Cohen played in American recognition of Israel in 1948 is still unclear, for as long as he lived, Cohen, unlike Frankfurter after Brandeis's passing, remained a staunch Zionist.[26]

In the years to come it was said that Tommy Corcoran became conservative while serving as a notorious business lobbyist in Washington.

Cohen remained true to liberal causes and played roles in the civil rights movement and other activities. Old New Dealers shook their heads at the mention of Corcoran. But Cohen would not discuss Corcoran, and it was said that every Thanksgiving Day you could find him at Corcoran's house.

8.
William O. Douglas: The War Against Wall Street

COLUMBIA UNIVERSITY HAD its impact upon the New Deal's initial Hundred Days (Moley, Tugwell and Berle), Harvard Law influenced the first term (Frankfurter, Cohen, Corcoran, et al.), but Yale Law School dominated its latter stages. The Yale people were Westerners who never attended Yale: Jerome New Frank of Chicago, professors William Orville Douglas of Yakima, Washington, and Thurman Arnold of Laramie, Wyoming. What distinguished them and Yale were their "legal realism."

Legal realism owed much to a revolt against traditional formalism in teaching law. At Harvard it took the form of Frankfurter's inchoate sympathies for the working class and hostility to utilities. But Frankfurter was the exception on the Harvard law faculty. While he excited generations of bright students with an appreciation of law as something more than the march of logic and precedent, his approach remained mostly an enthusiasm for social uplift through administrative law in government or a contrarian defense of labor and radical rights. Frankfurter taught students to loathe the "legal factories" of Wall Street that served big business. Alternatively, lawyers could and should serve the public interest in government. Yale Law admired Frankfurter and could sound very much like him, as when Dean Charles Clark wrote in 1932 that "the corporation of the past decade must give way to the public counsel of the next."[1] Nevertheless, Wall Street expected products of Harvard and Yale Law Schools to serve corporate interests and most did not disappoint. Many Frankfurter products acquired a taste for the expensive billing techniques of the big firms or, like Ben Cohen, navigated solo through the storms of corporate law.

What distinguished legal realism was its assertion of an objectivity that conformed with social realities. An early twentieth-century intellectual explosion in the social sciences inspired legal realists to integrate findings in social behavior with developments in the law. Legal realists focused upon markets: what especially concerned them was the creation and growth of corporations through finance. They defended basic principles of capitalism, arguing that Wall Street usurped the best ethical and competitive values of the marketplace. "The Yale thesis, crudely put, is that any judge chooses his results and reasons backward," Arthur Schlesinger, Jr., wrote. "A wise judge knows that political choice is inevitable; he makes no false pretense of objectivity and consciously exercises the judicial power with an eye to social results."[2] Given this air of expediency and moral righteousness, perhaps we should not be surprised that legal realists enjoyed a political following in the capital-starved South and West and that two of the most forceful exponents of legal realism were sons of Protestant ministers, William O. Douglas and Adolf A. Berle, Jr.

Douglas and Berle shared much in terms of their legal emphasis and moral universe. They first encountered each other in 1927 when Douglas joined the Columbia law faculty as a fugitive from the big Cravath firm; Berle had elbowed his way into Columbia Law while maintaining a small practice in Wall Street. They both knew corporation finance well enough to doubt its honesty. Both were worshipful of Brandeis, but there their similarities end. Aided by his wife's inheritance of an old family fortune, Berle established an independent corporate practice. His greatest ambition was to make an impact upon the world of ideas by promoting an iconoclastic quest for a modified capitalistic system that eschewed excessive individualism without embracing Marxist collectivism. Combining a downtown law practice with an uptown academic career, Berle promoted his ideas through journals of informed liberal opinion such as the *New Republic* and professional legal journals.

Berle used a friendship with William Zebulon Ripley of the Harvard Business School, an influential force in railroad regulation and financing and author of a much discussed book, *Main Street and Wall Street*, to gain a Laura Spelman Rockefeller Foundation grant to study corporations by combining legal and economics scholarship. Needing an economist he teamed up with Gardiner C. Means, a former textile manufacturer turned economics graduate student, in writing *The Modern Corporation and Private Property* (1932), a book that electrified the worlds of academe, law and policy-making. Historian Charles A. Beard hailed it "the most important work bearing on American statecraft" since the *Federalist Papers*, Brandeis cited it in his significant dissent, *Liggett* v. *Lee* (1932), and *Time* in 1933 called it "the economic Bible of the Roosevelt administration." Legal realist Jerome Frank forecast it would "rank with Adam Smith's *Wealth of Nations* as the first detailed description in admirably clear terms of the existence of a new economic epoch." Of course, yesterday's revelation is today's cliché. What Berle and Means described was a big corporation culture in which a concentration of 200 corporations, according to Means's data, dominated American wealth and power, virtually constituting an economic government in themselves. Berle argued that a handful of managers controlled the corporations through a variety of financial strategems. Thus, he maintained that corporation managers usurped the more democratic, broad-based ownership of shareholders. An oligarchy of managers threatened liberal capitalism. *The Modern Corporation*'s conclusion read like a manifesto to the investing public to seize the federal government and use it to create an alternative control lodged in Washington that reasserted the rights of property for shareholders. At the same time the federal government had to direct public investment to areas of the national marketplace suffering from underinvestment through indifference by the Wall Street tyranny.[3]

Douglas was jealous of Berle's fame in 1933. Although a year before Berle's splash as a New Deal braintruster Douglas had complained that "Some of the stuff this boy Berle has been getting off is not only bum law but also very very poor theory," he thought well enough of it to invite Berle for appearances before his seminars at Yale. Douglas had left Columbia for Yale Law School in the wake of "the battle of 1928" between Columbia's legal realists and its traditionalists over the choosing of a law school dean; Columbia's autocratic president, Nicholas Murray Butler, had selected a traditionalist, and Douglas responded by accepting Dean Robert Maynard Hutchins's offer to teach at Yale. His reputation as a teacher was mixed: some considered Douglas an exceptionally well-organized and demanding teacher; others discerned a lack of "any spark or flair" in his lectures and a tendency to ask questions for the sake of embarrassing students. He was a "mean son of a bitch," a student recalled. Cynical and ambitious, Douglas was ambivalent toward academic life. Like Berle, he was an academic parvenu who projected ideas that seemed more innovative or radical then rather than now. Just as Berle had linked the somewhat abstract world of law to the marketplace, Douglas likewise assigned his best student, Abe Fortas, to study a particular social problem in Chicago. He also concocted an experimental curriculum that combined Yale law courses with Harvard Business School courses. Dean Hutchins adored such innovations. When Hutchins left Yale for the University of Chicago's presidency he tried to take Douglas with him, explaining that he was "the outstanding law professor in the nation." Yale countered that offer by making Douglas Sterling Professor of Law at a salary of $20,000, more than it paid the dean.[4]

Douglas became a favorite among New Dealers in part because of his Horatio Alger rise to prominence from poverty through hard work. He had been born in 1898, in Maine, Otter Tail County, Minnesota, a western part of the state dominated by Norwegians, Germans, Swedes and Finns. It was an arid field for his father, William Douglas, an evangelical Presbyterian minister from Nova Scotia. The family moved on to

California and Washington State in search of a favorable climate and pulpit for the sickly Reverend Douglas, who died at forty-seven when his son was only five. Raised in Yakima, Washington, by a stern mother trying desperately to make ends meet, young Bill always worked to make any sort of money. More important to his mother than making money was academic achievement, and Douglas, who possessed a photographic memory and a capacity for hard work, proved himself a star. Whitman College in Walla Walla gave him a full tuition scholarship and he supplemented it by working at a jewelry store during the academic year and picking Yakima valley fruit during the summer. At college he was again an outstanding student. Upon graduation he taught for two years at Yakima High School, but he was ambitious to become a lawyer. A friend suggested that he enroll at Columbia Law School. He got into Columbia without difficulty, but to earn his way there Douglas took a herd of sheep by rail to Minnesota, then hoboed to Chicago, and finally spent what little he had on a coach ticket to New York City, where he arrived with six cents in his pocket. He borrowed money for registration at Columbia and then went out and got a job teaching a business law corespondence course. Of course, he proved himself the academic equal of Easterners at Columbia, graduating second in his class.[5]

He was an attractive man, standing about five-foot-eleven, his lean appearance giving the illusion of greater height. His tousled, unkempt sandy hair, with its home-cut look, and steely blue eyes suggested a rugged Western air that appealed even to Wall Street. The Cravath firm hired him out of Columbia, in spite of the fact that, as John J. McCloy later recalled, "he looked like he had come off a hike. He was not one of the usual Brooks Brothers set. In fact, he looked like a singed cat. . . . He talked about his background and how hard life had been."[6] At Cravath, Henderson & de Gersdorff, Douglas worked sixteen-hour days and distinguished himself in the reorganization of the troubled Chicago, Milwaukee and St. Paul Railroad, a financial disaster that greatly benefited its bankers and lawyers and taught Douglas a great deal about Wall Street. Exhausted from his work on the case, Douglas took an eight-month leave to set up a modest practice in his native Yakima. But the town had more lawyers than it had retainers, and Douglas, realizing that Yakima would waste his talents, returned to Cravath. He also taught part-time at Columbia for a couple of years until it offered him a full-time position in 1927.

But Yale was more to his liking. He had greater freedom for legal research, preferred New Haven for its small-city living in which to raise a family of two children, and he enjoyed the rollicking friendships of two Westerners, Wesley Sturges and Thurman Arnold. "Douglas was a Westerner," Abe Fortas recalled meaningfully. "He either worked or played." And when the Westerners played, whether at poker or games they invented, they played very hard. Fortas recalled liquor-filled barbecues with the boisterous trio which turned into a hunt for snipe in a New Haven park. Stories of their pranks were legion at Yale. As they became budding public personalities Arnold devised a celebrity game and assigned points ranging from one hundred for a mention in a *New York Times* editorial down to one point for a mention in a speech. They told of the time Sturges and Arnold were to speak at different locations and each received a telegram signed by the other requesting that the speaker mention them by name; each assailed the other for stooping so low for a point in that manner—but, of course, the real prankster was Douglas. We can imagine their envy in 1932 when Adolf Berle not only scored high on their scale with *The Modern Corporation*, but also became a Roosevelt braintruster.[17]

Sturges was the most reticent of the trio, Douglas was its cagiest mischief-maker, and the glib Arnold was its most zealous self-publicist and in private its greatest hell-raiser. Arnold's background was quite different from Douglas's. Seven years older, Arnold was the son of a well-to-do Wyoming rancher-lawyer who sent him to Wabash College and Princeton. He earned his law degree from Harvard in 1914 and practiced in Chicago until his Illinois National Guard unit was mobilized for duty on the Mexican border in 1916 and then World War I service. In 1919 he returned to Wyoming and settled down on a homestead in the mountains. A Democrat in Republican country, Arnold ran for the state legislature in 1920 and was the only member of his party elected to the body. He made it an enjoyable experience. After the Republicans nominated their candidate for Speaker, Arnold rose to nominate and second himself, following which he solemnly told the body that "Some irresponsible Democrat has put my name in nomination for Speaker. I wish to withdraw." To his delight, the press services carried the story throughout the country. Fearing boredom in the legislature, he ran and was elected mayor of Laramie. At the same time, Arnold prospered as a rancher and attorney. In 1927 a friend from law school days remembered him as a brilliant student and recommended him for Dean of the University of West Virginia Law School; Arnold decided to leave Wyoming because "I had gotten all out of it I could." At West Virginia he introduced several courses, which attracted the attention of Hutchins's successor at Yale, Charles Clark. In 1930 Clark offered him a professorship at Yale. Two years later the irreverent Arnold pronounced his own studies "bunk" and told Clark "we had been kidding ourselves."

Asked for his personal philosophy, Arnold the prankster would say, "I am always getting up a philosophical defense for an opportunist point of view." Disarmingly handsome with a mustache that gave distinction to his titles and accomplishments, Arnold was a compulsive cutup who loved to shock audiences. He was Yale's most entertaining teacher, partly because students never knew what he might do—whether it was bringing his dog to class or reading chapters from his forthcoming book, *The Folklore of Capitalism*. "He had the element of the unexpected," Edward H. Levi recalled. In a small seminar Arnold seemed to babble, some students thinking it was because his mind leaped ahead of theirs and others thought him just crazy. Ever an iconoclast, Arnold insisted that "Given industry, enthusiasm and a good personality, unpopularity for a while is only a sign that a [young professor] is working out his ideas. Immediate popularity simply means he is a copy-cat." Arnold was an original. "A law school is an institution designed to make simple things appear complicated," he liked to say. Teach someone how to use the law library and "The rest of being a lawyer is just argument." " 'Teacher,' " Fortas reflected, is "a poor and inadequate word to decribe his role in academia"; he was a provocateur. Espousing the social sciences as tools for studying law, he seemed to attack the economic system, an impression reinforced by his 1937 book, *The Folklore of Capitalism*, which rose to seven on the bestseller lists. But Arnold's basic message could be best summarized in an impromptu talk he gave a women's organization: "The trouble with modern civilization is that we are getting away from fundamentals." They loved it. And he meant it. An assistant in the Justice Department, Milton Katz, believed that he was "deeply devoted to the old-fashioned economic order." Arnold knew that conservative words could sound very radical to some and radical words could sound conservative to others. As Eugene Rostow put it, "If his economics were not systematic, nor informed by a grasp of monetary theory, his ridicule was devastating." Eventually his fame and Douglas's patronage would make Arnold Assistant Attorney General and head of the Justice Department's Antitrust Division, where in five years he undertook 215 investigations and launched nearly half of the antitrust litigation since the Sherman law's inception. "Arnold's passion as an antitruster," Fortas said, "stemmed directly from this basic, humanistic attitude—a Westerner's dislike of suppression, a Westerner's commitment to the openness of life." His antitrust activity amounted to another demand for a more liberal capitalism.[8]

Differences among New Deal lawyers centered upon Yale's scorn for the law as taught at Harvard. While Yale legal realism concurred with the Brandeisian call for experimentalism in public life, and Yale professors admired Frankfurter for his assault on formalism, Frankfurter correctly interpreted their applause as less approval for him than an attack upon Harvard. In the words of one Yale product, "Almost every class would start: 'There is a New York rule, and a federal rule and a Massachusetts rule.' And of course we were against the Masachusetts rule because that was the Harvard rule. It was a marvelous pattern . . . You had a ready-made dialectic." Another bragged that "the Harvard people tended to look upon us as unsound maniacs, and we in turn looked upon them as sort of antiques whom time had passed by." The Yale attitude disturbed Frankfurter; and when push came to shove he loyally defended Harvard. How could the legal realists proclaim cavalierly, "The law is bunk"? Frankfurter called such sacrilegious flippancy "overjazzing," a cynical "smartaleck, wisecracking attitude" that masked an inferiority complex toward Harvard. Gradually the Harvard-Yale battlegrounds shifted from law journals to the Supreme Court, where Douglas continued to twit Frankfurter unmercifully and Frankfurter retreated further toward a defense of formalism. In the New Deal, however, Harvard and Yale lawyers set aside trivial differences in the cause of disciplining big finance and expanding government's power to grow the economy.[9]

Led by Douglas, the Yale lawyers were more interventionist. In 1932 William O. Douglas sedulously cultivated Frankfurter, congratulating him on an old article that Douglas had recently discovered. "Truly, Felix," he wrote, "there are passages in the article which for sheer beauty and style have seldom been equaled in legal literature." (Frankfurter enjoyed these compliments, but in later years he privately called Douglas "the most systematic exploiter of flattery I have ever encountered in my life.") Roosevelt's appointment of Jerome Frank to the AAA in 1933, at the behest of Frankfurter, gave the Yale legal realists opportunities to crack the New Deal. Arnold and Sturges got part-time service at the AAA. As an expert on the law of corporation finance, Douglas carved his own niche. With the introduction of the securities bill of 1933, he confided to Frank and Frankfurter that he would like to be a securities regulator. "I think there is a splendid opportunity for adventurous thinking and planning in that field," Douglas wrote Frank. But the law was weak on administration, and Felix would not endorse Douglas to play with it. Douglas needed another avenue to Washington.[10]

At first, Douglas celebrated the Securities Act of 1933, but when nobody called him to Washington he tacked. A prodigious writer and academic entrepreneur, between 1931 and 1934 Douglas wrote or coauthored five casebooks and nine law review articles on bankruptcy and corporate and securities law. Two of those articles, coauthored with Harvard Business School professor George E. Bates, criticized the 1933

Securities Act in the *University of Chicago Law Review* and the *Yale Law Journal*. Another of his articles in the *Yale Review* reached a somewhat broader audience. He knew, he confided to Jerome Frank, that they would "not be particularly pleasing to my good friend, Felix Frankfurter." But, he asserted, the time was ripe for innovation because "Felix and his common law are not going to pull us out of this hole." In advance of these publications he warned Frankfurter, then abroad in England, that he would bring to bear the light of legal realism upon the law. "I saw just enough of the horrors of Wall Street to know that adequate control of those [corrupt securities] practices must be uncompromising," he told Frankfurter. The securities law had to be judged according to "the actualities of life," even if criticism might be construed "as an advocacy of the cause of the goddam bankers [and] an effrontery to you and the noble cause you serve." His sympathies, Douglas claimed, lay with the small investor, with widows and orphans. Frankfurter, without seeing the articles, insisted that Douglas should not fear offending him: "For heaven's sake, Bill, are we dealing with ideas or throwing spit balls at each other? Suppose you did disagree with me, even on a major public or legal matter. What the hell?" However, Frankfurter suggested greater conservatism toward Douglas's interest in a federal incorporation law. It augured too much intervention, too many "devices for running the whole continent from Washington." Rejecting Douglas's "passion for [administrative] control," Frankfurter advanced the taxing power "to curb the mischief and abuses of corporate activities." Among disinterested gentlemen there was room for disagreement, Frankfurter maintained. Then he received one of Douglas's articles. "What's the big idea, Bill?" he tartly demanded. He accused Douglas of a "bleeding heart [for] persecuted houses like J. P. Morgan and Kuhn, Loeb." Rejecting his "realism," Frankfurter demanded that Douglas bring his "head and heart into alignment."[11]

Douglas accused New Dealers of not going far enough. The securities law's authors—Landis, Cohen and Corcoran—had written an "inadequately drawn or misconceived nineteenth-century piece of legislation." Choosing his strategy and words carefully, Douglas labeled it insignificant except as a "symbol" of a shift of political power. The law called for "supplementary legislation dealing directly with the forces which must be controlled if high finance, as Mr. Berle would say, is to be the servant not the master of society." Douglas not only invoked Frankfurter's nemesis, Berle, as an authority, but he also ridiculed the law for timidly protecting the investor. The law, Douglas said, "falls far short of making significant progress because of the really *superficial* way in which it covers the object of its *control*." Comparing it unfavorably to the "more thorough going programme of stabilization" in AAA or NRA, Douglas proposed a cartel to regulate the finance industry. After all, he wrote, during the Great War William G. McAdoo's Capital Issues Committee had regulated the issuance of new securities, something New Dealers should be "astute enough to follow . . . and provide a similar type of *control* for peace-time financing." Endorsing a revival of the Capital Issues Committee, Douglas told Jerome Frank that his "criticism of the Securities Act is chiefly that it does not have any of the characteristics of that kind of *control*." Significantly, Douglas embraced Berle's key word in *The Modern Corporation*, "control," and demanded "regulation by industry with supervision by government." Douglas, like Berle, advocated consolidation by big finance and the railroads, in general "a more thorough-going control" over business by the government. "It seems to me that a fascist system is almost necessary," he ominously told Frank, adding for emphasis, "Felix and his common law are not going to pull us out of this hole."[12]

A master of argument, Douglas must have chortled over Frankfurter's confusion. At times he seemed as intent upon confounding Frankfurter as accomplishing anything else. Calling himself just an innocent "country lawyer," he would remind Frankfurter of his superior experience in Wall Street. "Just because I have a deep understanding of corporate finance do not infer that I am an Ivy Lee [publicist] for Wall Street," Douglas admonished. High finance was a tiger that needed taming. "I hate to see (even more than you do) the shift of power to Washington," Douglas wrote, but federal incorporation was "a damn convenient" device for social control when "hooked up with the commerce and taxing powers." Frankfurter had to answer certain key questions: "What should be destroyed? What types of holding companies do you want? What room should be left for the little fellow, the Henry Fords of the future or the corner grocery store of the next decade?" Scorning legislative compromises, Douglas insisted upon control of Wall Street by a federal administrative body. Failing that, he would not be adverse to seeing "the government [go] into the investment banking business." Thus, Douglas neatly blended arguments for corporatism, liberalism, and failing all else, state capitalism.[13]

"What made you a great authority on administration?" Frankfurter snapped back. Why had Douglas made himself "the chief scholarly source of attack against the Securities Act"? Was he playing Frankfurter for a "sap"? Why did the dissembling Douglas write Frankfurter "privately how deeply you agree with us [when] publicly, somehow or other, you come out the other way"? Douglas drafted a six-page single-spaced defense that he let sit a week and then condensed to two pages. "By all that's

Holy, you are making a Red out of me," it began. "And I do not think you will like the brilliant hue." In the unmailed letter Douglas was eloquent.

> Merely a formula for telling the truth to people who have already seen the stark reality of ruin and despair is idle and fruitless. Let's face the reality of the need for control. Then let's devise our administrative machinery to fit it. If you had seen, as have I, rooms filled with broken old men, despairing and wailing women—tear-stained victims of high real estate finance in New York—you would be moved to righteous wrath. And to treat that crowd only to truth about securities would seem such an empty gesture as to lead you to lower your yellow flag and to wave my reddish one and move swiftly to the goal of a more pervasive control. Certainly you would not make it more difficult, more expensive, more hazardous for indignant citizens to be their protectors and seek to salvage for them something out of the wreck. By God, Felix, it's all wrong.

"So-o-o-o-o-o-o-o-o!" Douglas concluded. "We have to prepare here for the Labor Party program of England, only on a grander scale." They needed to educate the public as to "the best and worst in capitalism" and erect a control to deal with the latter. In the end, Douglas hinted at Fabianism, but he might have been animated by fascism.

Ironically, Frankfurter's protégés, Corcoran and Cohen, fell into step with Douglas three months later as Congress created their Securities and Exchange Commission. And within a week of the SEC law's signing, Douglas asked the Connecticut congressional delegation and Jerome Frank to back him for a spot on the administrative commission. Instead, SEC counsel James Landis asked him to lead an investigation into unethical and illegal manipulations of bankruptcies and receiverships by protective and reorganization committees. Douglas eagerly grasped the consolation prize. In one last exchange with Frankfurter he was brief, humble and cordial: "My office is on Wall Street. But so is that of each member of the Yale law faculty. My hair, however, is not red. Is not this long deferred frontal attack ever going to materialize? Very few country lawyers like myself have ever survived your assaults. But I am willing to take my chances and risk such tail feathers as I have." Circling the first sentence, Frankfurter scribbled in return, "This I had suspected." The ambitious Douglas had penetrated Frankfurter's skin and now would use Felix's fame to make his own. He would even be more closely identified ideologically with Brandeis than Frankfurter had been.[14]

Perhaps one of the more startling facts about the career of William Orville Douglas is that fourteen years after he passed the bar exam FDR nominated him for the Supreme Court. His speedy rise among the ranks of the lawyers suggests he was among the cleverest of the New Dealers. In part he took advantage of Frankfurter's obvious need of adulation while masking his own considerable ego. An adroit duelist with words, Douglas usually concealed his goal. After all, one did not campaign for the Supreme Court while in his thirties. Perhaps Douglas had something bigger in mind.

Certainly he proved to be an aggressive administrator. He no sooner got the job as an SEC investigator than he demanded of Jerome Frank that Abe Fortas be released from AAA to work for him. Together again, mentor and student, Douglas and Fortas were tireless in uncovering financial abuses by bankers, bond houses and their counsels, which they later summarized in an eight-volume detailed report marked by Douglas's thoroughness. Even Felix saluted its "resourcefulness in examination, and, above all, the fearless clarity that followed trails, wheresoever they led." When SEC's first chairman, Joseph P. Kennedy, left it about fifteen months after its creation, Landis succeeded him and a vacancy opened on the SEC. Again Connecticut went to bat for Douglas, and this time Corcoran and Cohen added their influential voices to the chorus. Landis's choice, SEC counsel John J. Burns, declined any interest, and suddenly the national press discovered William O. Douglas.[15]

The games he played with Arnold and Sturges in New Haven had prepared Douglas for some self-promotion in Washington. Wanting FDR's attention, he used the SEC's Trading and Exchange Division to come down hard on Wall Street's sleazy practices. An adept political animal, in the summer of 1936 Douglas combined an attack on the New York Stock Exchange with a spirited defense of administration fiscal policy. He timed this to answer attacks by business and Republicans during an election year, something certain to attract the admiring attention of the President. And just to make sure that FDR noticed him, Douglas wrote to thank him personally for his appointment to the SEC. Before long Douglas received an open invitation to the White House.[16]

While Landis on the SEC seemed to accommodate the New York Stock Exchange, Douglas shrewdly articulated a philosophy of capital that courted Wall Street's hostility. In a lecture at the University of Chicago, an institution founded by John D. Rockefeller, Douglas proclaimed that "Irresponsible, laissez-faire democracy is dead everywhere" and assailed financial " 'termites' who practice the art of predatory or high finance." His speeches rang with populism and indirectly paid homage to Brandeis.

> High finance has the following characteristics. In the first place it is nothing but a game—a game played for large stakes. Those stakes

> are *other people's money* or control over *other people's money*. Under the aegis of high finance, business becomes pieces of paper—mere conglomerations of stocks, bonds notes, debentures. Transportation, manufacture, distribution, investment become not vital processes in economic society but channels of money which can be diverted and appropriated by those in control. The farmer with his raw materials, the laborer whose blood and sweat have gone into the steel and the cement, the investor and the consumer who are dependent on the enterprise, become either secondary rather than primary, or inconsequential rather than paramount. Business becomes not service at a profit but preserves for exploitation. The basic social and economic values in free enterprise disappear. For such reasons one of the chief characteristics of such finance has been its inhumanity. Its ruthlessness has precluded consideration of human values. Its predatory nature has excluded regard for all social values.

In March Douglas spoke to the Bond Club of New York and, in the words of *Newsweek*, "shocked Wall Street with a heated attack on present underwriting methods." He alliteratively assailed the "destructive domination" of industry by bankers who usurped "the rights of the great body of investors." A month later at American University in Washington he stressed a significant theme: "capital waste." America in 1933 had confronted a dichotomy of Wall Street's "lawlessness" and Washington's "control," and had chosen the latter. Precedent for the control of capital reached back to 1917 and McAdoo's Capital Issues Committee, created then in order "to conserve capital and resources for the purpose of winning the war." However, "capital waste" still prevailed without effective SEC administrative control, which could be aided by a federal incorporation law to protect investors' interests. Was this too much government control? Americans, Douglas insisted, should have confidence that administrative agencies "will be as much the champion of our liberties as the courts." Complicated modern corporate finances compelled novel responses by government: "An inventive liberalism is the only safeguard against regression or smug complacency."[17]

Douglas's "inventive liberalism" reminded business critics of European corporatism. Arguing that the SEC's new regime stifled the freedom to trade, Alexander Sachs pleaded with Landis, Corcoran and Cohen that the SEC would defeat the cause of recovery by destroying investor confidence, accelerate monopolistic tendencies and, by "irrational overregulation," broaden absentee ownership and bureaucratic management. Russell Leffingwell, himself a lawyer, faulted the SEC for an "overlegalistic approach" that created jobs for lawyers and deprived others of jobs. Through 1935–37 the New York Stock Exchange hoped that if it ignored the SEC it would go away. Failing that, it hoped that after 1940 a Republican administration would consign the SEC to an asterisk in the history books. Landis practiced self-restraint toward the NYSE, but in 1937 he resigned to return to Harvard Law School as Dean. In September, Roosevelt gave the SEC's chairmanship to Douglas.[18]

He got the job by being loyal to FDR and tough on Wall Street. He had staunchly defended the Court-packing plan—thereby enhancing himself in the eyes of Tommy Corcoran and the Skipper. At a time when New Dealers knew that Wall Street viewed them as mushy sentimentalists, Douglas cultivated the image of a ruthless liberal. On his appointment to the chairmanship he told a press conference, "What kind of a bird am I? . . . I think that I am really a pretty conservative sort of fellow from the old school. . . . I am the kind of conservative who can't get away from the idea that simple honesty ought to prevail in the financial world." The SEC, he said, would not intervene in markets that maintained "those standards that the best elements in business and in finance adopt for themselves" and promised not "to accomplish by indirection what Congress never empowered us to accomplish." Douglas assured investors of brevity and intelligibilty in prospectuses, segregation of functions between brokers and dealers, and regulation of investment trusts. He was the third chairman of the SEC, he reminded people: the first consolidated rules protecting the rights of investors, the second taught the SEC how to get things done, "and we're now going to go ahead and get them done."[19]

The SEC might have been ineffectual without Douglas. "No other SEC chairman ever addressed so many fundamental problems simultaneously," its historian has written. "Not all of Douglas's initiatives succeeded. But his chairmanship was the most accomplished in the SEC's history, in part because it articulated a coherent policy framework for federal corporation law that was to guide the next two generations of corporate reform efforts." He was "concerned with the preservation of capitalism." He was "the investor's advocate." He did not seek an SEC hegemony over capital. He wanted financiers to write their own rules and, through the exchanges, enforce them. He brought self-government, an NRA, a financial code authority by which the NYSE regulated itself under SEC supervision, to Wall Street.[20]

As *Business Week* astutely appraised him, "Douglas differs from Landis in one basic respect. Landis likes to be liked. Douglas is not so apt to try to please. . . . Douglas is impatient with all forms of subterfuge. . . . To sidetrack him with bypaths will be bad tactics. It will arouse his suspicion, rather than charm him with finesse. Yet no radical changes impend. As a lawyer, he has profound respect for the orderly way of accomplishing things." Indeed, Max Lerner warned liberals that Douglas sought a modest "reconditioning" of markets: "That will sound to most Wall Street men, and even to most liberals, sweepingly radical. But when stress is laid upon the word 'reconditioning,' it becomes clear that if his plans are radical, it is only in an ethical sense."[21]

Douglas's moment came as the New Deal was in retreat. Stock prices had fallen by a third in the two months prior to his ascendancy as chairman, prompting him to disclaim any link between market behavior and Washington actions. In 1937–38 the Roosevelt depression was at its worst. More than six million people were added to jobless rolls. Charles Gay, the president of the Stock Exchange, blamed the debacle on the SEC, and most of Wall Street wanted to agree. Alexander Sachs attributed the recession to "too much and too amateurish regulation and interference with the process and the flow of capital." To appease Wall Street, Roosevelt asked Douglas to lower margin requirements and to nominate a member of the Exchange, John W. Hanes, to the SEC—balanced by the simultaneous selection of Douglas's liberal friend, Jerome Frank. Douglas agreed: "I think the two of them will pretty well distribute the weight in the boat." He assured Frankfurter, "We are going places."[22]

The need for Washington's reform of Wall Street had become self-evident. Gay had been elected president of the exchange as a reformer in 1935, but his hostility to Douglas hinted at an intent to stall the SEC until the Republicans won in 1940. However, a reform faction within the exchange believed that only a rapprochement between SEC and NYSE could stabilize markets in 1938. But, when that faction by itself could not end the corrupt practice of privileged trading by members, Douglas decided to lend reform a hand. On November 23 he threatened that if the exchange did not curtail preferential short-selling, the SEC would intervene. "In a market in which there is such an enormous public interest—in which not only 300,000 small traders but 10,000,000 investors have a stake, it is essential that no element of the *casino* be allowed to intrude and that all such elements be obliterated," Douglas declared. Six days later the exchange announced a six-member reorganization committee composed of three exchange reformers, led by young William McChesney Martin and three outsiders, including Adolf Berle. The committee quickly recommended limitations on short sales and reorganized control of the exchange to admit brokers—a blow to the power exercised by floor traders and specialists. Significantly, the committee report also repudiated the exchange's propaganda blaming the SEC for low prices.

By January 31, 1938, the exchange implemented the reforms. *Fortune* praised the SEC leadership as of "extraordinary importance to anyone who believes in the capitalist system," and published an article by Douglas's Yale friend Fred Rodell extolling Douglas's efforts "to get the Exchange with him instead of against him."[23]

But an old guard faction led by former exchange president Richard Whitney still held sway in Wall Street. Whitney, a classmate of FDR's at Harvard, had once arrogantly labeled the exchange "a perfect institution." Not even Douglas was prepared for Gay's private revelation to him in March that the perfect institution had secretly censured its former leader for misconduct and possibly illegal activities. The next day Gay stopped trading on the exchange floor to announce the suspension of Richard Whitney & Company for insolvency. However, the exchange did not admit that Whitney had committed a criminal act. "This was not a fraud in securities practice," an SEC official countered: it was not the kind of financial irregularity which the SEC could eliminate; "it was nothing but out-and-out stealing by the most respected and prominent of all the figures of the financial world in the country." That was obvious to others. New York County District Attorney Thomas E. Dewey arrested Whitney for grand larceny in misappropriating $105,000 in securities, and the state issued another larceny indictment for stealing $153,000 from the New York Yacht Club. Although Whitney quickly pleaded guilty to both charges, Douglas knew that the whole thing went deeper. After all, the indictments against Whitney overlooked his embezzlements from a Stock Exchange Gratuity Fund to provide death benefits for members: he had stolen over a million dollars from it. Who else was involved and who had known about this and for how long?

SEC attorneys investigated and found that over a twelve-year period Whitney had borrowed over $6 million (without collateral) from sixteen exchange members and at least eighteen other people had turned him down for loans. It was evidence that Whitney was "broke and borrowing money all over the street." Whitney's brother George had gone to the venerable Thomas Lamont of the House of Morgan, and Lamont had come across with over a million dollars to cover the Gratuity Fund thefts. That left both George Whitney and Lamont open to federal charges that they conspired to obstruct justice by covering up a crime. But the Justice Department, to Douglas's consternation, refused to prosecute. When the NYSE did not discipline Lamont, it proved, Douglas said, that there is "one law for the very powerful or wealthy and another for those of little wealth and influence." It was a "white-wash." So Douglas cleverly exploited the scandal. As he remarked to an aide, "Political and economic power only rarely diverge, and when they do, you must move quickly."

Through the spring of 1938 Douglas practically blackmailed the exchange into cooperation with threats to reveal what the public still did not know about Whitney. He even campaigned for its election of reformer William McChesney Martin as president, wrapping his arm around Martin after one SEC–NYSE meeting and boasting, "Here's a fellow I can really work with!"[24]

Franklin Roosevelt might have said the same of Douglas. At a time when some New Dealers were tiring of Tommy Corcoran, Douglas combined in some ways Corcoran's political toughness with Frankfurter's intellectualism. And he had the sociability of Hopkins. Sometimes in the late afternoon Roosevelt would call over to the SEC and ask Douglas to come over for a relaxing chat in the Rose Garden. He included Douglas in the presidential poker group. Their senses of humor complemented one another. Following Douglas's ascent to the Supreme Court, the cartoonist Herblock noted its youth by showing the Justices huddling and one of them saying, "Let's phone the cabinet members and see if we can get up a ball game." Douglas sent it to Roosevelt with a note "sounding you out informally on the proposition." It stirred Roosevelt's imagination. His counterproposal for a baseball game between "the Administrative Oligarchy and the Judicial Hierarchy" called for a Cabinet battery consisting of Secretary of State Cordell Hull and Interior Secretary Harold Ickes; the Court battery would be Chief Justice Charles Evans Hughes and Justice James C. McReynolds, a pair ten years older than that of the Cabinet. "Finally," Roosevelt wrote, "we insist that your 'nine' waive in advance any judicial authority over umpires' decisions and that in publicity after the game no minority opinions be filed." Douglas retorted that FDR's proposals were "a body blow to judicial supremacy," and proposed that the President and Speaker of the House Sam Rayburn serve as umpires. But FDR was too involved to umpire: "I am ready to confer with you at any time as to what proportion of the gate receipts will go to you and me as Managers." By this time their correspondence reached into the football season, and Roosevelt suggested that Douglas draft judges from the lower courts for an eleven. Douglas declined football and opted for "that ancient, wily game" of poker: "You can furnish the deck." FDR retorted that Douglas's "Nine Old Men still have that dreadful inferiority complex that descended upon them during the athletic season of 1937." He did not let go of the sports metaphor, preferring ice hockey to poker; besides, "I ask you, do Baptists play poker?"[25]

At the SEC Douglas also became an economic adviser to FDR, coaxing the President out of his habitual fiscal conservatism in the spring of 1938, recommending electric utility expansion, taking on special assignments such as railroad reorganization, and creating through the SEC the

Temporary National Economic Committee. Warmly supporting Douglas's war with Wall Street, Roosevelt encouraged him to expand the SEC's range and its enforcement of the Public Utilities Holding Act. He liked Douglas's fearless and earthy style—a "hard hitter" in journalistic vernacular. If somebody in the SEC voiced a concern for offending a Wall Street big shot, Douglas would say, "Piss on 'em." He knew that FDR considered securities legislation "one of the major accomplishments of my administration." Joseph Alsop noted Douglas's "dog-like devotion to the President." It was devotion that anticipated a reward. Importantly, Alsop also noticed Douglas's sense of political rivalry with the Corcoran group: "He criticized the political acumen of the group rather sharply" and carefully kept his distance from "the hot dogs." "Their real value," Douglas shrewdly commented, "was as galvanizers, animators and technical advisers, and he seemed to think that they should never have become political at all. He said that in his opinion no member of the group . . . qualified to be a political leader."[26] Douglas, who had never run for office, saw himself as a potential political leader, and used his own aloofness from party politics to enhance his political availability.

At a time when Corcoran's star was on the wane and even Frankfurter was thinking that Tommy was nothing but "a fixer," Douglas had the right enemies: Wall Streeters. On March 20, 1939, Roosevelt nominated Douglas for the Supreme Court. The Court was always on New Dealers' minds, a circumstance brought on by the extraordinary governmental experiments of the past six years. It was bad enough to lose NRA and AAA, but danger to the SEC, the utilities law, TVA, Social Security and other New Deal laws remained as long as the Supreme Court remained unreconstructed. Roosevelt had had no opportunity to nominate a justice during his first term. That inspired the ill-fated Court-packing plan of 1937, which in itself prompted a Supreme Court reorientation on New Deal legislation as the Court decided to follow the electoral returns of 1936. Then Justice Willis Van Devanter resigned. Roosevelt replaced him with Senator Hugo L. Black, a staunchly liberal Southerner who had led the fight for the utilities holding company law. Other justices retired or died, and Black was followed by the nomination of Stanley Reed, the Solicitor General from Kentucky who had first come to Washington under Hoover, and—the moment that New Dealers long had anticipated—the nomination of Felix Frankfurter for the Supreme Court. On January 11, 1939, Harold Ickes was lunching at the Interior Department with Attorney General Frank Murphy, another future Justice, when Corcoran burst in with two magnums of champagne to celebrate the moment when his mentor won nomination for the Court; soon the joyous party grew to include Harry Hopkins, Robert Jackson (another prospective Justice), David Niles, Missy LeHand, Peggy Dowd, and Douglas. In his diary Ickes captured its significance: Roosevelt had "solidified his Supreme Court victory, and, regardless of who may be president during the next few years, there will be on the bench of the Supreme Court a group of liberals under aggressive, forthright, and intelligent leadership." Of course, that assumed that Frankfurter would be the Court's leader.[27]

A month later Brandeis retired. Douglas had seen that coming. Already he had informed Roosevelt that he would leave the SEC to return to Yale and its Law School deanship that September. Three days before Brandeis's announcment Douglas made a very Brandeisian speech (he sent Brandeis a copy) that assailed certain big corporations as "a menace to the ideals of democracy." With Frankfurter already on the Court, Douglas bid to alert everyone that he too was Brandeis's intellectual heir. Of course, Douglas later asserted that he had not even given the Court a thought. Indeed, the odds for his getting the nod were not great. It was well known that FDR wanted a Westerner there and that Senator Lewis Schwellenbach of Washington had the inside track; Douglas was only a Westerner transplanted to Connecticut. Also, he was forty and only one Justice (Joseph Story at thirty-two) had been younger. Finally, what politicians spoke for Douglas?

Douglas waged a vigorous sub rosa campaign for himself. The day after Brandeis resigned he wrote to the Attorney General, the Speaker of the House and the chairman of the Democratic party, requesting autographed pictures of each for his wall. He also sent a flattering letter to pundit Walter Lippmann. More directly, he wrote to fellow Whitman College alumni among Washington State lawyers for endorsements. When Schwellenbach supporters tried to get Washington State legislative endorsement of their man, they were beseiged by Douglas backers who demanded a place for their candidate alongside Schwellenbach in the endorsement resolution. At the same time, Douglas's friends, Corcoran and Frank, worked on independent Republican Senator William E. Borah of Idaho and got from him a ringing public endorsement of a Douglas nomination. When the *New Republic* called Douglas's liberalism into question, Douglas vehemently blasted Wall Street to underline again his liberal credentials. Additionally, on March 12 he invited Harold Ickes, who frequently saw the President, to lunch with his own booster, Robert Hutchins of the University of Chicago; Ickes came away confident that Douglas was "more than willing to go on the Supreme Court." That paid off when Ickes lunched with Roosevelt and, sensing that the President favored Schwellenbach, the Interior Secretary heaped abuse upon Schwellenbach's legal and intellectual abilities. Accordingly, on March 19, Roosevelt called Douglas with the news that he wanted him on the Court. Few people believed that that would be the last stop for young Douglas in Washington.[28]

For all Douglas's derision of Corcoran, he emerged in the 1940s as Corcoran's candidate to succeed FDR. Liberals loved Douglas; the Court could not contain him. In 1940 he exhorted Roosevelt to run for a third term, suggesting for vice-president Senator Frank Maloney of Connecticut (a longtime friend and political supporter of Douglas), although he surely knew that FDR was not about to take on a Roman Catholic running mate or someone from a state bordering on New York. Whenever liberals wanted one of their own for a tough wartime administrative job, Douglas's name immediately sprang to mind. A more visible place had to be found for him in Roosevelt's administration. While Roosevelt could not decide what to do with Corcoran and Cohen, in September 1941 FDR, in Douglas's words, asked Douglas "to be the top guy in the defense work—to take it off his neck; to be his alter ego." But Douglas did not want leadership of a pressure-filled defense organization where, he said, "the fat cats would be entrenched" and the President would be under constant pressure to overrule a liberal Douglas. He hoped that Roosevelt would appoint Ferdinand Eberstadt, a Cotton Franklin alumnus, to a defense post so that Douglas could work through him. Most of all, Douglas did not want to leave the Court because not only was he happy, but he was certain that his departure would make Frankfurter happy. Delighting in angering Frankfurter, Douglas easily provoked him with taunts and challenges to his intellectual authority. Meanwhile, Corcoran, alienated from Frankfurter, began to push Douglas for president or at least vice-president. Knowing of those "in the president's inner circle [who] whisper that this is a big chance—that it will lead to the 1944 nomination," Douglas averred that he was "not a bit interested in running for any office." He had been mentioned already for the 1940 ticket, only to be scratched because party leaders considered him too much of an unknown. Although Douglas told other confidants that he would remain on the Court "for keeps," he said nothing publicly: his mischievous mind enjoyed all the points he piled up in the publicity game. If Douglas wanted the second spot behind FDR, he was unwilling to resign from the Court and fight for it. And in 1944 Roosevelt and the politicians made certain that only an available politician would get it. The game went on following Roosevelt's death and Truman's ascendancy. "Douglas inspires fanatical loyalty in some people and absolute mistrust in others," Arthur Schlesinger, Jr., astutely wrote.

> He has executive vigor, intelligence, simplicity, and considerable charm; but he is also wary by instinct, highly ambitious, and fond of intrigue.

> Douglas' position is complicated by the fact that few believe he has abandoned his presidential aspirations. No Justice gets better publicity. His special appeal is to "hardboiled" liberals who propose to escape the usual sense of liberal futility by concentrating on results at the expense of scruples.[29]

After 1948 liberals seemed to tire of Douglas's game and he settled down on the Court for the longest run in its history.

9.
Jerome N. Frank: Public Investment

IN 1932 JEROME NEW FRANK joined the Yale Law School as a research associate, a position whose tasks included transporting illegal liquor from New York to Arnold and Douglas. Hailed and denounced as the author of the widely read *Law and the Modern Mind* in 1930, Frank distinguished himself in the eyes of the Yale faculty by advocating experimental laws that blended precedent with Freudian psychology. In applying Freudianism to the law Frank already had a fellow believer at Yale in Douglas, who had been psychoanalyzed because of migraine headaches by Dr. George Draper of New York. (Draper also had been Franklin Roosevelt's physician in the 1920s.) Douglas considered Draper "the main seminal influence in my life" and kept in mind Draper's advice "Find your kindred spirits in the law and they will help you find your lodestar." Jerome Frank became one of those kindred spirits in Douglas's life.[1]

Frank was one of the most extraordinary corporation lawyers in America. In the words of his biographer he was "a creative, witty, and brilliant man, but one deeply troubled, conflicted, and ultimately insecure." An eclectic person, never certain where his many talents were put to the best uses, Frank became a lawyer to please his father, a Chicago lawyer. He graduated from the University of Chicago at nineteen and dutifully went on to be one of the two highest-scoring graduates at its Law School in the prewar era. (The other? Ben Cohen, of course.) The Franks were a very musical family, but Jerome also had a strong literary bent; in 1914 he married a poetess, Florence Kiper, three years his senior, and joined a Chicago literary circle that included Carl Sandburg, Sherwood Anderson, Ben Hecht, Floyd Dell and John Gunther. He tried his own hand at writing a novel, never finished it, and ultimately branded it "a neurotic effort." Nevertheless, Frank made himself one of the mainstays of Chicago's politically active intellectual circles that also included social science professors Charles Merriam and Paul Douglas. At the law Frank verged on genius, beginning his practice with Levinson, Becker, Cleveland and Schwartz, a medium-sized Chicago firm specializing in corporate finance and reorganizations for major banks, railroads and industrial corporations—his reputation for creativity in corporate reconstruction reaching to Wall Street. Although married and a father by the time the U.S. entered the Great War, the restless Frank decided he "ought to do something" patriotic and volunteered to work with the Food Administration, where he worked with the similarly intellectual Joseph Cotton, then Herbert Hoover's man in charge of purchasing food for export to the Allies. While Cotton already knew Frank from corporate reorganization cases, another common thread ran through their careers: they deeply believed in public service.

Belief in public service was part of the Chicago intellectuals' credo and imbued careers such as Cohen's even if they left Chicago. When Frank returned to Chicago in the 1920s he voluntarily worked with Mayor William E. Dever to acquire the street railway system for the city, a plan foiled by electric utility magnate Samuel Insull. Known for his brilliance and enormous energy ("Being married to Jerome is like being tied to the tail of a comet," his wife once observed), Frank possessed remarkable patience as a negotiator, a phenomenal memory, exceptional powers of analysis, and a very creative mind. His volubility revealed a fecund and insatiable intellectual curiosity. Unlike most of his colleagues, he had not entered corporation law to become rich; money seldom motivated him until he had needs. So it was that when his daughter suffered from a psychosomatic paralysis of the legs, he left his Chicago practice and moved the family to New York in quest of psychiatrists who could help her. (The intellectually curious Frank ineluctably insisted that he also undergo analysis.) With his experience and reputation Frank easily caught on with Wall Street's Chadbourne, Stanchfield & Levy. As a partner once commented, "It's worth $50,000 a year to us to have Jerry around just to hear him talk." The family lived in Croton-on-Hudson and Frank commuted to lower Manhattan, spending an hour each way on the trains either reading books or writing *Law and the Modern Mind*.[2]

Like many corporation lawyers or investment bankers. Frank's work in the marketplace made him an economic philosopher. A liberal who believed in expanding market opportunities, Frank was startled by the Great Depression. The collapse of markets seemed to be a watershed event that gave extra meaning to his life. Pondering how Hoover might counter unemployment, Frank disdained the Hoover administration's drift; in 1931 he told a partner that "intelligent and clear-headed leadership is badly needed" and that it was not being asserted. At first his ideas blended Theodore Roosevelt's New Nationalism with market Freudianism. He wanted "a courageous program" to make a "self-conscious, integrated, national capitalism as efficient as it possibly can be." To achieve this extensive design, he prescribed "the concentration of credit." At a time when a specter of hegemonous capital terrorized other men, Frank asserted that a "Conscious, integrated, world capitalism would become consciously benevolent" by achieving greater efficiencies that it shared with labor. A democratic capitalism could give "its workers advantages which Russia can probably not begin to give to its workers for at least a hundred years." Such "enlightened selfishness" required planning.[3] While other liberals detested big utility holding companies, Frank proposed consolidation of industries and creation of "super-holding companies" to enable a few nationwide banks to direct credit and manipulate interest rates. Like British economist John Maynard Keynes (whom he read and admired), he would nullify the antitrust laws. Frank always interacted with ideas about him, grasping or rejecting every economic notion that floated his way, which is why Berle's book with its prescription for greater government planning of industry excited him. "With the present drift of events, we may soon come to state capitalism (via the R.F.C. or something like it)," he told Felix Frankfurter.[4] The concept fascinated Frank. The corporation gathered capital for its development; at a time when the national marketplace no longer seemed to grow, why shouldn't the government take the role played by corporations and use public capital to create additional entreprenurial opportunities and jobs? Washington should lead in developing credit markets.

As in 1917 Frank in 1933 decided that the emergency required public service. He was forty-three, with a family and a splendid Wall Street income, which his associates considered him "a damn fool" for giving up. But his quest for a job in the government delighted Frankfurter. As he told Frankfurter, "This crisis seems to me to be the equivalent of a war and I'd like to join up for the duration"; the war served as a New Deal benchmark for bringing economic order out of market chaos. Frankfurter responded that "If you get a curious offer, don't reject it without considerable reflection." Frankfurter knew enough about Frank to know that he could be both impetuous and contemplative: "Frank has two sides of him—the playful, dialectic, argumentative side, which is very much the minor part of him; and the penetrating, practical-experience talent for bringing results to pass in the world of affairs. . . . He is widely read in the modern literature of economic and social thought, and has simply a fiendish appetite and capacity for work." Soon Assistant Secretary of Agriculture Rexford Tugwell called to offer Frank the position of solicitor for the Department of Agriculture. But Democratic National Chairman James Farley confused Frank's father with an old Chicago political enemy and objected; Tugwell then persuaded Frank to become General

Counsel to George Peek and the Agricultural Adjustment Administration. It was a fateful move.[5]

When Peek recognized Frank as a lawyer for Chicago banks that had liquidated his failed company, Moline Plow, he wanted to get rid of him immediately. But Secretary of Agriculture Henry Wallace stood firm, and Peek settled into an uneasy collaboration with Frank. Seven stormy months later the volatile Peek left the AAA to become FDR's foreign trade adviser. Peek's successor, Chester Davis, brought no biases against Frank to the job and got along well enough with his counsel. For in spite of Frank's reputation as a sharp corporation lawyer, his experiences with the Food Administration and agricultural corporations made him more knowledgeable about agrarian concerns than most farmers expected from Chicago and New York barristers. Importantly, he knew that farmers desperately needed credit, and ever the state capitalist, he innovated the RFC's Commodity Credit Corporation, the most accomplished of the New Deal's agricultural agencies. However, Frank also outspokenly challenged AAA's planned economy of scarcity, which sought to drive prices higher and benefit producers. When he championed the interests of consumers, sharecroppers and tenant farmers against the interests of food processors and producers, Frank elicited farmer demands that he be fired along with some of his staff. This time Wallace knuckled under to pressure and executed what became known as the "purge" of AAA.[6]

The erstwhile Chicago and New York practitioner had champions at Harvard and Yale law schools. Not only did Frank hire on a special assignment basis three friends from Yale—Arnold, Sturges and Fortas—but he also put on his staff numerous Frankfurter students from Harvard: Alger Hiss, Lee Pressman, Nathan Witt, and Corcoran's brother, Howard. The latter deed did not win Tommy's undying friendship: one of the lawyers, an alcoholic with a dislike for him, toured the bars of Washington with stories of how Frank called Corcoran "seven different kinds of a louse." An irate and revengeful Corcoran began feeding the press stories hostile to Frank. Ever direct, Frank decided to have it out with Corcoran and, although he could not reach the peripatetic presidential adviser, he left word with Cohen that his "bastard friend ought at least to have the courage to tell his enemies what he thought of them to their faces." Corcoran got the message and came around; a shouting match ensued, and the two came close to heaving inkwells at each other. While the Frank-Corcoran imbroglio remained legendary among New Deal lawyers, in the end they became good friends when they discovered a mutual admiration for the late Joe Cotton.

Having demonstrated a genius for public finance, Frank briefly found a home in Jesse Jones's RFC as a special counsel on railroad reorganization and also as a part-time counsel to the Public Works Administration. In 1937, along with Morris Ernst and other liberals, he founded the National Lawyers Guild as a liberal alternative to the conservative American Bar Association. (But, like many New Deal lawyers who started the guild, Frank abandoned it in 1940 following a fight with radicals and communists.) In 1937, when both Frank and the New Deal seemed to be at loose ends, William O. Douglas persuaded Roosevelt to appoint Frank to the Securities and Exchange Commission. In the midst of the Roosevelt recession of 1937–38, Frank used his base in the SEC to play a creative role in setting an administration course of economic expansion. However, by then Frank also had come to the conclusion that he wanted more out of life than a place in Wall Street or in the ephemeral New Deal: with unusual personal ambition he decided that he wanted a place on the federal bench.

Frank was known as a liberal's liberal. For him America had no place for any benighted racial, ethnic or religious discrimination or any mindless faith. A proudly assimilated Jew, Frank took his Americanism seriously and wore his Jewishness lightly. He believed that America's strength was its diversity. Under Frank the AAA employed some sixty lawyers. As historian Peter H. Irons notes, the early New Dealers assembled government legal departments as if they were putting together law firms. On principle they wanted the best graduates the prestigious law schools could offer, regardless of ethnicity. In practice, however, that meant hiring a lot of Jews because Jews led their classes out of proportion to their numbers at Harvard, Yale and Columbia, and many of them could not breach Wall Street's discrimination practices. When Frank first hired lawyers for the AAA, he simply sought the best of Frankfurter's students while making it clear that he did not want "too many Jews on the legal staff." He appreciated Lee Pressman, he told Henry Wallace, "an exceptionally able lawyer. . . . However, he is a Jew." Another lawyer he wanted, Arthur Bachrach, was "unusually skillful in assisting in handling a legal staff. Unfortunately, Bachrach is a Jew." Fortunately, Frank had interviewed several other lawyers who "would be excellent additions to the staff; only one of them is a Jew." Part of this sensitivity to Jewishness reflected Frank's eagerness to show Wallace his political astuteness; a Jewish chief counsel wisely should not hire other Jews if he could avoid it. The handicapped should not hire the handicapped. When somebody commented that Frank's lawyers included an exceptionally large number of Jews, he instantly disputed that: of the over thirty lawyers then working for AAA, including himself, only five were Jewish. "Indeed," he assured Wallace, "I have taken such care to discourage Jewish applicants that I have gained the reputation among my non-Jewish friends at Columbia, Yale, and elsewhere, of being anti-Semitic." He boasted that he had rejected "at least half a dozen very able lawyers" for no other reason than their Jewishness. When he sought to recruit lawyers it "very much embarrassed" him "that a very considerable number of the particularly able lawyers available for such work were Jews." Hiring them "might cause comment unfavorable" to AAA. Ordered to hire "the ablest lawyers available," Frank advised his assistants "to recommend lawyers who are not Jews." In a story he told about himself, Frank refused to appoint three Jewish lawyers, admonishing assistant Frank Shea, "Goddam it, Frank, I've got to be careful. You've got too many Jews in here now. The people will begin to say that I'm just selecting Jews." This prompted Shea, a Catholic, to accuse Frank of blatant anti-Semitism. Indeed, Frank set the tone for his young lawyers. One of them, Adlai E. Stevenson, a genteel graduate of Princeton University and Northwestern University Law School, noted a feeling among AAA lawyers "that the Jews are getting too prominent."[7]

Although Frank owed his entry into the New Deal to Frankfurter, they clashed frequently over personal and policy matters. When he blamed his firing from AAA upon Frankfurter, Frankfurter loftily lectured Frank that "public life is warfare, that it is always permeated by people who are in Holmes' phrase, fired with a zeal to pervert, that the luxury of letting one's mind roam through one's tongue is a luxury that can't be indulged in, and that there are lots of things that can be and should be done but shouldn't be talked about." Frank did not care for Frankfurter's insightful but patronizing remarks: "It has irked me beyond words to be judged unjustly and superficially by you of all people," Frank countered. He insisted that he did not wish to personalize their quarrel: was it not symptomatic of philosophical differences, he asked, in which Frank aligned himself with Tugwell, Berle, Marriner Eccles, Senators Robert M. La Follette, Jr. and Edward P. Costigan, and others against fellow New Dealers Frankfurter, Corcoran and Cohen? And if he was correct, Frank said, "it is unwise not to try to reconcile those differences as far as possible. For those differences may have important consequences in the next few years."[8] Curiously avoiding mention of his Yale friends—Douglas, Arnold and Fortas—in his roll call of dissenters with the Frankfurter crowd, Frank made certain that it was understood that this was more than a Harvard-Yale argument. Frank's intellectual alignments confused more than enlightened, but he no doubt was correct that policy differences among New Dealers raged.

Frank made astute policy distinctions and had a talent for setting the terms of a debate over economics. He understood that all New Dealers subscribed to a belief in a need to have the federal government manipulate the economy. But for what purposes and by what means? To achieve growth or stability? Having read widely in the economic literature of the time, Frank was attuned to the ideas of John Maynard Keynes, the subject of numerous discussions in the salons of the New Deal even before Frankfurter arranged for the *New York Times* to publish his open letter to Roosevelt. Of course, Keynes did not need Frankfurter to act as his American publicist. Older and more conservative Wall Streeters such as Norman Davis, Thomas Lamont, Russell Leffingwell, Alexander Sachs and Walter Lippmann had made Keynes's acquaintance at the 1919 Paris Peace Conference and had followed his subsequent career and writings with respect, albeit not necessarily concurring with his prescriptions.

In this country Keynes had his imitators and popularizers. Unfortunately, Frankfurter discovered the writings of David Cushman Coyle, a civil engineer who worked in the Public Works Administration and wrote books and articles advocating increased government economic activity. *Time* said that he had three reputations, "engineer, eccentric, economist," and left little doubt it was most impressed with the middle one. Coyle's hybrid Keynesianism appealed to Frankfurter and Corcoran, who in turn tried to peddle it around Washington. People like Russell Leffingwell considered Coyle's ideas "monetary moonshine" and while most critics were polite, more sophisticated types such as Frank were unimpressed by Coyle's nebulous calls for more public works. "I am skeptical as to his broad sketchy surmise," Herbert Feis told Frankfurter, and so were others.[9]

That was the problem: a new consensus for economic action by the federal government had replaced the old consensus for inertia, and about all that Coyle had going for him, besides the enthusiasm of Frankfurter and Corcoran, was his subscription to the consensus. But that was no longer at issue among New Dealers. Public works had been tried, and at issue was what additional strategies ought to be attempted. The debate was not confined to New Deal lawyers such as Jerome Frank. In fact, the converted included a surprising number of economists and businessmen. Inevitably, they comprised a network of overlapping circles that grew increasingly corporate as the New Dealers struggled to sharpen their understanding of the expanding economy during 1933–36 and the recession economy of 1937–38.

One such network dating back to 1931 was an organization of businessmen disenchanted with Hoover's inaction. Calling itself the Committee for the Nation (to rebuild prices and purchasing power through planned monetary inflation), it was led by James H. Rand, Jr., the president of Remington, Rand, and its directors included Frank A. Vanderlip, a New York banker, Vincent Bendix of the Bendix Corporation, Henry A. Wallace, and Lessing Rosenwald and Robert E. Wood of Sears, Roebuck. Wood, typically, was a Republican who voted for Roosevelt in 1932 and 1936, despite his misgivings about certain New Dealers. ("It is equally repugnant to me to be on the side of Ogden Mills and Hoover as on the side of Tugwell and Dubinsky," he told the President.) One of its coordinators was economics professor Irving Fisher of Yale, an advocate of price "reflation." Another supporter was publisher Frank Gannett, who supported "managed currency" as a way "to increase the purchasing power of the masses." Many of its members were single-issue cranks.[10]

They achieved a dialogue with other businessmen such as Utah banker Marriner Eccles, whom Roosevelt appointed as a governor of the Federal Reserve Board. When the committee's secretary, Edward A. Rumely, accused Eccles of "lip worship to capitalism," Wood scolded him that Eccles's outspoken support of government spending was something he could support. What offended right-wingers like Rumely was Eccles's almost casual anticipation of "some form of 'modified capitalism' in which government controls and regulation will be extended rather than restricted." Eccles liked to say that one thing which made him an unconventional economic thinker was the fact that he had not been to college and was a country banker; but John Nance Garner, another Western country banker suspicious of Wall Street types, also had not been tutored on college economics and was a much more intuitive person. Indeed, the Federal Reserve's economist, Lauchlin Currie, called Eccles "an inveterate theorist [who] did not always recognize that he was talking theory and was allergic to anything that too obviously looked technical or academic. He never, for example, read any of Keynes." Still, many people would hail Eccles as an advance agent of Keynesianism because in 1934 he declared publicly that balancing the federal budget was "of wholly secondary importance" to spending for public works. However, Eccles did not then like the new credit agencies such as the RFC, or the financing of homebuilding and TVA in competition with banks and private utilities. "He feels that if the government takes over all credit facilities, the nationalization of credit is much more dangerous than anything else," Wood observed. Listening to an Eccles monologue, Alexander Sachs noted that "he made it perfectly clear that in his opinion the day of laissez faire in America is definitely done; that a system of 'modified capitalism' is the only alternative to complete collectivism; that it will be necessary for the government to accept the responsibility for creation of the new order to the extent that business fails to assume it." Sachs, Douglas and Frank found Eccles "quiet, unassuming, keen, of quick mentality and by no means superficial"—possessing "more strength and stability" than most of their colleagues.[11]

In the same category of pragmatic conservatism looking to the federal leadership was Jacob Viner, a special assistant in the Treasury to Henry Morgenthau, who looked to the Federal Reserve Board as "a place to exercise a little central planning." Viner was one of the most respected senior economists to work for the New Deal. He did not approve of everything attempted by the New Dealers, but did prefer occasional failures to inertia. As his student Herbert Stein has written, Viner "did not find in the literature, and did not accept, the idea that being 'for freedom' answered all the policy questions that have to be answered." Morgenthau was comfortable with Viner, who could reinforce both balanced budgets or deficit spending, believing that planning and liberty were compatible.[12]

But that still left it to the New Dealers to discover what planning the new consensus wanted. Younger New Dealers looked to Lauchlin Currie for guidance. Currie, an iconoclastic economist who buttressed Eccles's instinct for public works, was the ringleader of young economists from Harvard and Tufts universities who challenged academic orthodoxies. A Canadian from the London School of Economics who had failed to get tenure at Harvard because he departed from monetary theory to propose exotic remedies employing fiscal policy, Currie attracted the attention of the eclectic Viner, who brought him to Washington in 1934. Although Currie later achieved fame or notoriety as the first of the Washington Keynesians, his faith in countercyclical fiscal policy antedated Keynes's publication of *The General Theory of Employment, Interest and Money* in 1936: "As early as 1930 I began to feel that . . . the Government should embark on a large scale public works program and not try to cover the current cost by taxation, i.e., deliberately incur a deficit." Nevertheless, American intellectuals, including economists, dubbed him Keynesian out of need for the crutch of British approval of the unconventionally practical. (Country bankers and Canadians apparently did not need British intellectual approval.) Currie enlivened New Deal policy discussions with Frank, Cohen, Corcoran, Berle and government economists such as Isador Lubin, Gardiner Means, Thomas Blaisdell, Robert Nathan, Louis Bean, Paul Appleby and Mordecai Ezekial. Moreover, as Frank recruited lawyers for AAA, Currie, in John Kenneth Galbraith's words, "ran an informal casting office," recruiting economists for the Federal Reserve and other agencies, including Alan Sweezy, Richard Gilbert (who became Harry Hopkins's chief economic adviser), Walter Salant and Galbraith. All of them formed an informal president's council of economic advisers before there was such an institution. According to Lubin, the group's task was "to collect facts, raise questions, point out probable trends, and make recommendations." Some recommendations ignited a "violent argument," as ensued when Ezekial "favored virtually scattering money from airplanes," while others sought to finance public works. Importantly, Currie was not dogmatic and did not espouse public works exclusively. He picked up new ideas and in turn instructed Eccles in them, which led the Federal Reserve to advocate in 1937–38, among other things, liberalized credit for mortgages. Additional participants in Currie's new economics came from the National Resources Board, which Roosevelt converted into a think tank of advanced economic polemics for thinkers such as Albert Gaylord Hart, Alvin Hansen, J. M. Clark, Arthur Gayer and Beardsley Ruml. Hansen too became a leader among some New Deal economists because of his espousal of Keynesianism at the height of the critical debates of the late 1930s—and because he dared to do it at Harvard. But a good polemic needs a good publicist and that was where Ruml excelled.[13]

Eccles appointed Ruml director of the Federal Reserve Bank of New York, despite the fact that he was neither a banker nor an economist. But one would have been hard put to discover Ruml's true profession; he had a doctorate in psychology from the University of Chicago, briefly managed personnel at the Scott Company, moved on to the Carnegie Corporation for a year, where he made philanthropic foundations connections, and then became director of the Laura Spelman Rockefeller Memorial, which he converted into one of the biggest supporters of research in the social sciences. In these positions he suggested to his contacts that he was one of the great original and creative minds in America. In the Rockefeller orbit, President Robert Hutchins made him dean of the Social Sciences at the University of Chicago in 1931, but the faculty rejected Ruml's idea for unifying departments. He lasted three years in academia, and then Percy Straus offered him the post of treasurer for the department store R. H. Macy. Obviously businessmen were more persuadable than professors. When he was asked what difference he found between operating a department store and a university, Ruml replied, "The great difference is that in business the problems are intellectual." He added: "If things don't work out in business, it affects profits. If things don't work out in a university, it affects nothing. It is the difference between frustration and futility." A rotund man with a nearly perpetual smile, he loved classical music, scotch and avoiding exercise. "I spent many years getting into condition for a sedentary life," he said, "and, having gotten into condition, I never broke training." For all his wisecracks, Ruml was the ultimate useful man to both the Rockefeller coterie and New Dealers because, as Leon Henderson observed, his sometimes misbegotten but challenging ideas provoked challenging thoughts in others. But he remained, as Broadus Mitchell said, merely a "publicist."[14]

"B," as nearly everyone called him, was clever with numbers and economic concepts. At Macy's he financed its expansion and its introduction of installment credit. He thought in terms of consumer purchasing and consumer debt. The concept of using debt to encourage economic growth endeared him to New Dealers. In 1937–38, he argued, economic problems involved not the restraint of purchasing power, but its enhancement. Roosevelt appointed him in 1935 to serve with Frederic A. Delano and Charles E. Merriam on the Advisory Committee of the National Resources Committee. It discussed the planned development and use of land, water and other resources; planning was what organizations usually expected of Ruml.[15]

The Keynesians made economic planning in hard times a major fiscal problem requiring more taxing and spending, but many conservatives and businessmen saw taxing and spending as fiscal mischief. All agreed, too, that in taxing and spending, timing was important. By common agreement the economy had begun to grow again in 1933–36. Then came the decline of 1937–38: why? Many economists believed that to a large extent the Roosevelt recession was due to, in Ruml's words, "a retreat from civil works . . . begun too soon," or regressive taxes such as the Social Security tax, state excises, or perhaps even the undistributed profits tax, born in improving times, now the reason for declining times, the bête noire of many businessmen. When unemployment suddenly soared in 1937, one businessman wondered if conditions had reverted to 1931; no, responded Jacob Viner, but the situation was "fairly comparable to that in the spring of 1933." Robert E. Wood reported that in March 1938 "purchasing power is off everywhere" and feared that if it lasted another ninety days "it will be very difficult to avoid another downward spiral." If only the President could be "more conciliatory and friendly with business as a whole," he confided to Henry Wallace. "The great majority of businessmen are really scared to death. . . . What we need in this country today is for capital to get to work, and, badly frightened capital will not get to work." More vitriolic was Alexander Sachs, who, from his perch in Wall Street, termed the downturn "*a planned depression* in the sense of its being the calculable though undeliberated result of misplanning and mal-administration in our governmental policies and measures." Keynes agreed with Sachs that the economic slump was "synthetic" rather than cyclical because it seemed based upon "a peculiar kind of new crisis of confidence"; the President had to be "reasonably kind to business." Administration proclamations of pump-priming and congressional passage of a generous capital gains tax, along with moves to liquidate the undistributed profits tax, brought an apparent upturn; by July Wood could describe himself as optimistic and expecting a decrease in unemployment by the fall. But, he asked Harry Hopkins, "how long can we hold it?" It was so easy to create a recession within a depression that it raised serious questions as to the fragile nature of the economy and the durability of any recovery. Indeed, examining economic data in late 1938, Frederic A. Delano was moved to tell his nephew the President that "real danger of another depression in 1940 exists; . . . I think it is important for us all to realize the hazard of repeating the occurence of 1937." If 1929–33 had been a searing experience, 1937–38 was a learning experience. And the lesson of the latter pointed not to inertia but to the wrong kind of action: taxes.[16]

Morgenthau and his aide Herman Oliphant had wanted the undistributed profits tax to compel corporations to distribute profits which investors could reinvest. At first some businessmen, such as retailers, were indifferent toward the undistributed profits duty. In the words of Robert Wood, "There are two sides to this tax on corporation surpluses question, and I am not prepared to say which is the proper side." Although Eccles endorsed it with an antibigness Brandeisian rationale, old Brandeis himself preferred a graduated corporate income tax as the more direct antibigness approach. Sachs tried to bring Keynes into the controversy, and Keynes allowed that "It seems to me clear that the tax on undistributed profits only operates as a deflationary factor if the additional dividends are saved by those who receive them." More Keynes was not prepared to say, explaining "that I am inclined to attach more importance to the failure of durable investment to develop, and less to such factors as the undistributed profits tax, than you do." And that left Americans with a shortage of investment, no matter who or what was responsible. Many businessmen disliked the undistributed profits tax not only because it was badly timed, but also because it targeted too many victims with a shotgun effect. It had passed in 1936 because of big Democratic margins in Congress and the disciplining effect of the presidential election. Afterwards, businessmen mobilized and others who had not paid too much attention gave it some scrutiny. By the time the recession hit in September 1937 the tax was in jeopardy as business opinion took the offensive. Sachs summed it up to his own satisfaction by telling Marriner Eccles that the undistributed profits tax had "anti-capitalistic features" because it stifled emergent and growing enterprises. Businessmen needed a climate of confidence in which to invest.[17]

For a long time certain New Dealers had accused bankers of a "capital strike" by withholding investments. Certainly Jesse Jones (and even Hoover before him) encountered much evidence of banker timidity that defied Washington appeals for credit cooperation. In 1935 Treasury economist Harry Dexter White could say with confidence that "The cry of 'loss of confidence' is largely a smokescreen let loose by certain conservatives who are traditionally opposed to almost *any Government expenditure,* who object to any increase in taxes, who are too shortsighted to know that the perpetuation of the present level of unemployment consitutes the most dangerous threat to their own interests." But in 1937 timid capital argued that FDR had made it timid. Ferdinand Eberstadt, for instance, argued that the undistributed profits tax made "expansion out of earnings . . . extremely costly, with the result that in many cases it seems advantageous to obtain such funds through public financing." And that put corporation bonds in competition with public bonds, adding to business timidity. Whatever the argument's merits, it had a force that had been absent before the tax act of 1936.

By consensus, there was a "capital shortage." To what or to whom it could be attributed was a matter of debate, but common sense increasingly dictated that the White House could not deny existence of the shortage. Popular perception, whatever its reality, had it that investment was down because taxes were up. Therefore, Roosevelt had to be friendlier to business by lowering taxes. "Taxes have already reached the point of diminishing returns," Thomas W. Lamont of 23 Wall Street told FDR; "You and you alone can, I believe, say the words that will pretty nearly end this menacing situation." Roosevelt's troubles stemmed from the fact that a Wall Street–hating Midwestern retailer could concur with Wall Street's assessment. "The trouble is," Robert E. Wood wrote, that [Roosevelt] does not understand the economic system under which we live and has some inexperienced, immature economic advisers." New York banker Fred I. Kent, who had long known FDR, seconded that judgment and tried to educate Roosevelt with lengthy (one went thirteen pages) letters, most of which were either ignored or answered briefly and tartly. On a more reasonable level, Eberstadt argued for a diminution of duties while conceding that "there can be no diminution of government spending without a catastrophe."[18]

The "capital shortage" argument not only led to cries to kill the undistributed profits tax but also calls for more public investment. The permanent federal institutions most concerned with this revolution in spending and lending were the Treasury, the Federal Reserve and the Securities and Exchange Commission. The latter gave Jerome Frank an opportunity to involve himself more deeply in the discussions and policymaking of state capitalism. Through the winter of 1938 Frank informally met to discuss programs at the homes of Senator Robert M. La Follette,

Jr., of Wisconsin, a longtime friend of public works, Paul Appleby, administrative assistant at the Department of Agriculture, and Mordecai Ezekial, Agriculture's Economic Adviser. The group also involved Eccles, Currie, Harry Hopkins, Leon Henderson, Harry White, Isadore Lubin, Louis Bean, Aubrey Williams and Henry Wallace, among others. The group arrived at an easy consensus to spend on public works, but it paid careful attention to the investment potential of the RFC, FHA and the SEC, hoping that the latter would "reorganize the capital market to make it a capital-issuance agency instead of a roulette wheel." The National Resources Committee also served as a formal discussion group and through Henderson, Williams and Ruml figured prominently in Roosevelt's decision to increase government spending without much attention to the budget. Currie was happy "with the main outlines" of the program, but disapproved of its "hastily improvised" nature. Appleby too suspected that a public works program, "unless carefully planned in advance, is apt to be wasteful."[19]

Aware that the public was no longer enamored of public works spending, the New Dealers increasingly turned to financing expansion through various credit schemes. Essentially they concurred with businessmen that the system needed additional infusions of capital. In large measure. it was Ruml who contributed to a New Dealer–businessman rapprochement by bridging the gap between planners and free enterprisers. "Private investment houses are at present unable to meet the existing needs for equity capital for new enterprises of corporations, large and small, old and new," wrote Ruml. Public investment was imperative. Arguing that "A compensatory [budget] policy is not new to American experience" and that "the competitive capitalist system has been sustained from the beginning by federal intervention to create purchasing power," Ruml tried to make businessmen accept New Deal manipulations of fiscal policy. In particular, he insisted that "Purchasing power must again be created by the federal government." As Ruml averred, "the prior issue of balanced budget versus compensatory budget has been pretty well disposed of," a compensatory budget making good business sense. That cleared the way for an aggressive federal fiscal policy. Given a choice between "whether the orientation of intervention should be toward the producer or toward the consumer," Ruml came down decisively in favor of the latter. Through 1938 he furiously worked up three memos, which he disseminated through Jerome Frank and other New Dealers. Beginning with the proposition that "The competitive capitalist system under democratic political forms has come upon evil days," Ruml prescribed some general steps for expanding purchasing power. In particular, he sought to remedy a capital shortage and boost employment through the creation of what he called twelve investment trusts, capitalized by the RFC and operating in the twelve districts of the Federal Reserve System.

Frank was among those impressed by Ruml's ability to speak both the New Dealers's language and that of businessmen. Moreover, Ruml's twelve trusts proposal brought Frank and the SEC into the picture by giving the trusts full authority to buy, sell and exchange securities in order to attract capital within a prescribed Federal Reserve district, thereby strengthening the equity positions of corporations and directing capital to "sections of the country where such capital is scarce." The trusts would augment, not supplant, other investment institutions such as banks and insurance firms—although Ruml conceded that competition between the trusts and private organizations was inevitable. A federal deficit to boost national income was unavoidable, but the deficit would be created by federal loans to supplement private investment, thereby raising personal income and government revenues in years to come. In these ways, Ruml said, "the solution of the unemployment problem must come with a much higher average standard of life, a standard of life that in large measure will be embodied in consumers' goods." Businessmen would profit by the deficit because of lower taxes: "The possibilities of real tax reduction are much better under a compensatory fiscal policy than they are under a balanced budget policy." More efficient national management would be brought about by making the Bureau of the Budget a major implementer of policy.[20] Although Ruml's twelve trusts proposal would not see fruition, it advanced the concept of using the federal budget to expand credit and investment.

Ruml moved New Dealers like Frank rightward. In 1938 Frank clashed with SEC economist Paul P. Gourrich, a Kuhn, Loeb analyst whom either Kennedy or Landis had brought into the SEC in 1934. In many respects, Gourrich's thinking resembled Ruml's, but he lacked Ruml's facility with language. Analyzing Wall Street's mood as "strangely reminiscent of 1931–1932," Gourrich also argued for regional lending banks to augment timid private bankers. Washington's investing was important because "Such risk now can be carried only by the Government." But Frank detected in Gourrich an unreconstructed economist because he attributed part of the recession to tax policy inhibitions of the investment markets. Making it plain that Gourrich ought to pay more attention to Lauchlin Currie than bank economists, Frank demanded that Gourrich furnish "*data to justify that statement.*" Gourrich interrupted a vacation with his family to answer the SEC Commissioner, arguing that the undistributed profits tax had forced corporations into a billion-dollar "overdistribution" of dividends that reduced reinvestment. The unusual brevity of Frank's response suggests that Gourrich had made his points. Indeed, the tone of Frank's memos took on an almost contrite, respectful, less-belligerent quality. Frank seemed to realize that indeed there were frightened investors in America whose fears were not entirely due to ignorance.

Other New Dealers also got the message. When Paul Appleby suggested that the government endeavor to boost private equity capital with an "Intermediate Investment Bank," funded by the RFC, Frank thought it well worth considering and passed it along to Corcoran. Frank's comments that business would have to rely more on equities than on bonds, on diluting shares rather than running up debt for capital, brought hearty agreement from Wall Street economist Elisha Friedman and the ever-cautious Jacob Viner. Eventually all of these thoughts would generate part of the abortive Works Financing bill of 1939.[21]

The government's quest for business capital was not the road to ruin or totalitarianism. The language of the new economics had to be modified to make a compensatory budget concept more acceptable. Perhaps, as Louis Bean suggested, "it is time for us to drop the phrase 'government spending' and to adopt another phrase including the word 'investment.'" The New Dealers would have to educate the electorate and their representatives for new economic thinking. "If we can't do that," Bean mused, "then one might raise this question: If Italy got its Mussolini in 1922 and Germany its Hitler in 1932—can we escape in 1942?" Or, as Harry White forcibly put it: "God help us if we are still around after 1940 when the [next economic] break is expected and we have no program to trot out and have not even taken precaution of educating public opinion to support the program we would then like to trot out."[22]

Nineteen thirty-nine was a critical year for democracy. It was the year that that "left wing legend," Jerome Frank, replaced Douglas as chairman of the SEC. Since memories in financial markets are short, the tempestuousness of his AAA tenure was remembered and forgotten was his brilliant career as a corporation lawyer. Wall Street also quickly forgot Douglas's alleged harassment of it and now conceded that Douglas had restored stability to the markets. Reminding corporation lawyers that he was one of them, Frank built upon Douglas's legacy by likewise assuring conservatives that, while he expected Wall Street to play by SEC rules, he would prefer that it enforce its own rules. The most conservative SEC Commissioner, John Hanes, departed for a post in the Treasury and wrote Frank that "Your judicial and fair-minded approach to our many problems has completely won my admiration."[23]

Frank's personality, not his policies, set some teeth on edge. He relished polemics and seldom accepted criticism as readily as he gave it. He could not leave an argument alone.* Nevertheless, many people loved Frank because he was warm, boisterous, brilliant and honest.† But he was not a radical, being only to the left of the Republican party and Wall Street. As a liberal he disdained extremes, believing that "right and left wing alike make false assumptions about us." Frank would be SEC chairman for two years, during which he enforced the Public Utilities Holding Company Act's death sentence. He left for the seat he coveted on the Second Circuit Court of Appeals in March 1941. By that time the SEC legacy would be nearly complete and the commission itself relegated to relative obscurity during World War II. Still, Frank and Douglas played a vital prewar role in freeing securities markets for the development of a competitive public utility industry.[24]

Meanwhile, events and advisers such as Frank persuaded Roosevelt that 1939 required additional appropriations for public works, which now included spending for defense. New Deal economists wanted an expansionist compromise: public investment in big-ticket items and a tax reduction to spark private investment in little-ticket items. But conservatives were not ready for the escalation of spending unless it began with the de-escalation of taxes. "Most business leaders would never abandon the hallowed ideological position of the balanced budget, but never again would they opt for a corporate-tax increase when they could settle for a larger deficit," a historian has written. "If New Dealers can be better described as deficit spenders than as Keynesians, businessmen can best be viewed as deficit taxers." Businessmen and congressional conservatives overturned the undistributed profits tax in 1939. At the same time discussion of more broadly based taxes, including income and sales taxes revealed a drive to balance the budget in regressive fashion. In the absence of a balanced budget and with a need to increase spending, the government could meet its obligations to all creditors only by borrowing via the sale of bonds. Corporations always borrowed from banks and the public to cover debts: why shouldn't the government?

*Frank's biographer tells how between June 1931 and January 1932 Frank and City College of New York philosopher Morris R. Cohen "exchanged thirty-odd letters often ten to fifteen pages long, each blaming the other for straying from the point, being obtuse, and resorting to 'inexcusable abuses of the privilege of friendly correspondence.'" Robert Jerome Glennon. *The Iconoclast as Reformer: Jerome Frank's Impact Upon American Law* (Ithaca, N.Y.: Cornell University Press, 1985), p. 23.

†Gardiner Means once disagreed concerning Frank's integrity. "You are a god-damned son-of-a-bitch," his letter began following a reading of Frank's book *Save America First*. "It is one thing when the National Industrial Conference Board misquotes my writings . . . but it is a different matter when a Commissioner of the SEC and an ardent New Dealer misrepresents my position." "Them is strong words," Frank responded in an uncharacteristically brief and subdued letter, and said he would answer Means in a subsequent edition of the book. Means to Frank, June 27, Frank to Means, June 28, 1938, Frank Papers, Box 33.

That meant that expedient businessmen, conservatives and New Dealers endorsed a *planned* federal deficit to increase investment.[25]

Public investment was evident in 1939, not only from the expansion of the defense establishment, but also from the administration's proposal for "splending," the Works Financing Act of 1939. The bill would have had the RFC loan an additional $2.8 billion to a variety of government agencies to spend upon highways, electrification, conservation and assorted public works projects. It had many origins. Secretary of the Treasury Morgenthau apparently wanted it because he preferred lending that sustained an illusion of a balanced budget to outright spending that offended conservatives. Moreover, he liked to hint that the cautious Jesse Jones had not been doing his job and needed to loan more. Of course, although Harry White called "splending" the application of a new principle, it was merely an extension of the credit revolution begun in 1933. Other spear-carriers for the bill were Eccles and Currie in the Federal Reserve, who wanted lending and spending on the railroads via a railroad equipment trust. Frank, Ruml, Ezekial and all the others who had been braintrusting in groups meeting in various homes (what *Fortune* referred to as "the Cohen circle" on the assumption that Cohen was its chief administration spokesman) all pushed the Works Financing Plan to make the RFC the engine of economic growth. To expand investment, lending via the RFC was in, spending for pump-priming was out.

Importantly, however, the man who would administer this largesse was unhappy with it. Jesse Jones did not like the implication that the RFC had not done enough and told Congress that he did not need more funds. He did not cotton to liberal criticism that he was a passive lender instead of one who used money to open up opportunities by making funds available through low rates. It was true that Jones did not loan unless he was asked and then loaned against secured collateral at rates, although lower than private market rates, that brought RFC profits. When Congress rejected the "splending" bill in the summer of 1939, Roosevelt and Morgenthau blamed Jones. An exultant Alexander Sachs called it "a vote of no confidence in the president's program" and asserted that it marked "a turning point in American history." Conservatives certainly had reason to rejoice. But a month later Europe would go to war and the United States would be "splending" anyway. Public investment through federal budget deficits would become an American way of life.[26]

10.

David E. Lilienthal: Making America Over Again

"People's Lawyer"

"I DON'T KNOW a more interesting job—short of the Presidency—than yours," Felix Frankfurter told David E. Lilienthal.[1] He meant it too. As a director of the Tennessee Valley Authority, in charge of its power projects and general counsel, Lilienthal spearheaded an agency that competed with Wall Street's holding companies, espoused Brandeisian experimentation and economic development, and planned nothing less than the social transformation of a whole region of the United States—if not the whole country. Long before the U.S. embarked upon a national program of public investment, TVA had embarked upon regional public investment. As TVA, Bonneville, and other power projects demonstrated, regional programs were more politically acceptable in 1933 than any national planning. Ironically, about the time that public investment regionally lost favor in 1938–39, national economic development for reasons of defense gained favor.

Of all the Frankfurter-trained lawyers in the New Deal, Lilienthal was perhaps the most paradoxical. Although one would not discern it from Frankfurter's praise in the 1930s, Lilienthal had not been his favorite—even if he consciously followed the career pattern prescribed by Brandeis and Frankfurter. Alone among Frankfurter's disciples, Lilienthal did not entrain for Washington, but launched a lucrative practice as a utilities and labor lawyer in Chicago which he then forsook for an eighteen-year career in public service that took him to Madison in Wisconsin, Knoxville in Tennessee and Tupelo in Mississippi. He was more Brandeisian than most New Deal lawyers. While sincerely articulating an intensely idealistic role for government in regional development, Lilienthal was far from naïf; he was intensely ambitious for control and recognition, revealing ideals and plans so openly as if to suggest a total absence of guile. But adversaries and allies learned to appreciate young Lilienthal's political cunning. He almost single-handedly altered the trend in energy and economic development in this country. Lilienthal built the Tennessee Valley's electric power capacity beyond what anyone anticipated and sharply lowered energy costs, thereby hastening the South's economic development and, by example, that of the West—giving rise to the sunbelt. Moreover, Lilienthal, an extraordinarily gifted publicist, gave TVA ideological underpinnings that appealed to both advocates of federal development of public power and right-wingers who appreciated enhancement of business and individualism. By the end of the decade he would contemplate the possibility that he had invented "public businessmen," an oxymoron describing those who derived their capital and assets from government investments. Finally, he provided the New Deal with its only exportable product—the TVA ideology of state-planned and capitalized democratic development, an alternative to totalitarianism. Nobody better rationalized state capitalism than Lilienthal. "How do you do it, dear Dave," Frankfurter once asked, "how do you manage to have the angels of light regard you as a social reformer and the hard-boiled Mr. [Arthur] Krock [*New York Times* columnist] see in you 'the builder, the engineer, the business man'?"[2] It would not be the last time someone wondered about Lilienthal's paradox.

A half century after William Gibbs McAdoo failed to make electric trolleys profitable in Knoxville, David Eli Lilienthal accelerated development of the Tennessee Valley with federal moneys, promotional skills, political acumen, and a universal imagination that surpassed McAdoo's own enormous vision, ingenuity and salesmanship. Lilienthal was a contrarian in love with contradictions—maintaining that from TVA's centralized authority flowed decentralized administration, from the overhead planning genius of its engineers and experts issued "Democracy on the March," from its federal funds cascaded a cornucopia of private wealth, and from FDR's decision to build TVA emerged political leadership that eschewed partisanship. When he departed from TVA, and much later the Atomic Energy Commission, he capitalized on a reputation for successful planning and administration of economic development and established a private global business that modeled Third World countries such as Iran upon the development example of the American South. These pursuits gave him the remuneration absent during his government years and homes in Princeton and Sutton Place in New York City.

In some respects, Lilienthal may have been the quintessential Brandeisian. More than any other Frankfurter student he hearkened unto Brandeis's preachings of public service: he worked for government at the state level far removed from Washington and made war against private corporations that selfishly exploited America's natural resources and monopolized its economic development. Such a career called for a tough and determined outsider who could pull levers of political power—as

Brandeis had done. Like Brandeis and Frankfurter, Lilienthal traveled in the company of presidents of the United States, leaders of corporations and countries, and a host of internationally powerful men—acceptance that depended upon his capacity to make himself useful and welcome. He went to Wisconsin as an outsider chosen to regulate its utilities. He went to Tennessee as an outsider picked to plan its economic development. He was born an outsider. The first child of Leo and Minna Lilienthal from Austria-Hungary, David arrived on July 8, 1899, in Morton, Illinois. His father was a merchant who tried his luck in a succession of Illinois-Indiana towns during the turn of the century, eventually settling in Michigan City, Indiana. Tall, handsome and extremely verbal, young Lilienthal enrolled at DePauw University in Greencastle, Indiana, where he demonstrated versatile talents as an athlete, a debater, a campus politician and an academic achiever. He briefly considered a career as a writer but instead took his ambitions to Harvard Law School. Lilienthal's enormous energies would always find an outlet in his writings for law journals and journals of opinion. He liked to think that he had the capacity to move people and reshape history with his oratorical and writing talents, and perhaps he had. Ever introspective, without shyness or an inclination to hide his natural confidence—a confidence that amounted to vanity—he began at an early age to keep journals in which he set down personal thoughts and observations; naturally he converted this habit of a lifetime into a late-career publishing venture. Dave, as he liked to be known, was never so introverted as to be bashful. "Ambition" was a word and a trait he flaunted, as if he were unaware that others might be wary of Cassius's lean and hungry look. He was an intense competitor, relentless, whether in his quest to become student body president, valedictorian, to win oratory contests, elections or sports events. He also flaunted idealism in a way that made most people ignore the way he used idealism to advance his career. His liberalism had an artful nonpartisanship almost bereft of righteousness. With an appealing personality the sycophantic young Lilienthal courted famed liberals such as Brandeis, Frankfurter, Frank P. Walsh, Donald Richberg, Philip and Robert La Follette, Jr., Franklin D. Roosevelt and numerous others. Significantly, they too rated themselves as outsiders from American circles of social power; they too sought to use government to achieve greater social equity.[3]

Lilienthal collected patrons. In his first year at Harvard he tried to make Felix Frankfurter a prize in his collection. The strikes and labor turmoil of 1919 made Lilienthal a workingman's sympathizer—well, sort of: "Although my sympathies now as before are with labor," he insisted, "I am trying to preserve a balance—to suspend judgment until I am competent to judge." He chose not to enroll in any movement to advance labor's cause: "For the present I want to be a *student* of the problem. . . ." He lacked any passion to alter the established social order. In other words, socialism did not attract him. He abhorred its "large chunks of sticky, syrup-like sentimentalism": "Too much passion is being lavished on dreaming of the revolution—too little thought expended on how it will be made a sane, happy, orderly revolution—a road upon which Progress can safely travel yet onward—not a pitfall into which she shall fall, there to writhe in the blood and hideousness of disorder and strife." At a time when many labor supporters turned to socialism or syndicalism, Lilienthal stayed with melioration. So did his declared heroes, labor lawyers like Brandeis, Walsh and Clarence Darrow—men "who have aided the cause of the working class." Lilienthal had not yet defined his progressivism, but Harvard Law "thrilled" him daily with its "intellectual strife." Its courses, especially Frankfurter's public utilities class, helped fix his liberal perspective. In his quest to "get such a man as Brandeis or Walsh interested in me and my ambitions," he wrote flatteringly to Walsh and approached Frankfurter. "I do not care to be a corporation lawyer," he assured Walsh. He wanted to be a "people's lawyer" like Brandeis. Telling Frankfurter there was "no one better in the country better qualified than you" to help him find a niche in the labor movement, Lilienthal gained some of Frankfurter's attention, but not the warmth and enthusiasm he bestowed upon his prize pupils. Frankfurter rationed his affection and it was Lilienthal's misfortune to be a classmate of the brilliant Nathan Margold, who was, like Frankfurter himself, born in Central Europe (Romania) and a graduate of the City College of New York. Thus, even in Frankfurter's circles, Lilienthal was an outsider. He would not become "Dave" to the professor nor would the professor become "Felix" until after the student had entered public life in Wisconsin. Still, Frankfurter avowed admiration for Lilienthal's "deeply burning fire" and referred him to various jobs; but on a personal level he remained tepid toward Lilienthal.[4]

Something about Lilienthal put Frankfurter on his guard. Perhaps it was the younger man's indifference toward his Judaism which suggested to Frankfurter that Lilienthal's enthusiasms needed the measure of time. Frankfurter did not test his Jewish students as to their Jewishness, lest they apply the same test to him and his "shiksa," as he referred to his non-Jewish wife, Marion Denman Frankfurter. While not religious, Frankfurter did not deny his Jewish identity. But Lilienthal's religion was American liberalism: it gave him the freedom not to be a Jew.

Lilienthal's greatest faiths were democracy and development. He treated his Jewishness as if it belonged to his parents' European past and had nothing to do with his future as an American. His Jewishness was a dead historical fact and not an inherited and/or current belief system. In American liberalism the Lilienthals found an antidote to European pogroms. But, ethnic violence in America during the Great War suggested that the world was not ready for liberalism. At a DePauw chapel assembly during the Great War Lilienthal used an oratorical contest to speak on "The Mission of the Jew," in which "after reading on and brooding over these unspeakable sufferings of my people for months," he felt compelled to speak with "an emotion and a passion I hardly believed I was capable of." It was strictly theatrical. Later he confessed that he had "traded on my religion in college with my college oration. . . ." Like the good lawyer he would be, he used his Jewish origins to win the sympathies of his liberal audience and the contest. Much later, the rise of Hitler in Germany and the revival of anti-Semitism in America during the 1930s had little impact upon him. "I do get spells of worry about the consequences of . . . anti-Semitism," he wrote in 1939. "But very few of the evil things that are going on in the world . . . have affected me directly." Later that year he personally encountered a Jew-hater who launched into a tirade on how Jews had ruined Miami, Florida. Lilienthal remained silent: "There was really no occasion for my making a scene. . . ." On a personal level he seemed as comfortable with Christianity as with Judaism. But every so often something would jog his memory of Judaism. Once, when Bernard Baruch told him that he would be going to services on the anniversary of his father's passing, Lilienthal had a flash of recollection and thought, "How completely I have missed all that tradition; there are times when I feel I have fallen between two stools, in a manner of speaking."

He could not recall any encounters with anti-Semitism while growing up in Valparaiso, Gary or Michigan City. On the other hand, at law school he found himself disliking "the cliquing of Jewish fellows." He preferred "to select my friends without any consciousness of their origins." A job interview with a Cleveland law firm intruded upon his liberalism when the interviewer brought up the subject of his Jewish heritage, which Lilienthal forthrightly conceded; later he supposed that he did not get an offer for that reason. But the incident did not otherwise disturb him. Years later at TVA he heard that the utilities tried to stir up anti-Semitism, but "it didn't take fire" because he overcame it by refusing to be like those Jews who "are unduly sensitive, for example, to books about Jewish foibles or characteristics. . . ." He stymied anti-Semitism, he believed, by insouciance to it and through service to the cause of humanity. Believing that anti-Semitism existed only among the poor, he went among the poor to promise their uplift. Humanism would thwart anti-Semitism. Although Henrietta Szold, the founder of Hadassah, the women's Zionist organization, was Lilienthal's distant cousin, he disdained the movement's lack of "diversity." He preferred a melting pot for humanity.[5]

Lilienthal found his diversity in the law and in liberalism. After Harvard Law, when he applied for a job with the noted Chicago lawyer, Donald R. Richberg, his references included Walsh, Frankfurter, the president of DePauw, Dean Roscoe Pound of Harvard Law and Evans Clark, a labor economist—a formidable list presented to a formidable employer and potential reference. Richberg was made to order for Lilienthal's list. An ardent political activist, Richberg had long advocated a social science approach to law that resembled Brandeis's. Richberg's practice attracted Lilienthal because he represented workers and consumers against utilities and railroads. In 1922 Lilienthal began to help Richberg with railway labor cases. In order to draft a railway labor bill, Lilienthal researched extensively a variety of issues such as industrial arbitration, mediation and conciliation—work that formed the basis of the Railway Labor Act of 1926. He also prepared briefs for Richberg to argue before the Supreme Court and assisted him as national attorney for the La Follette progressive campaign for the presidency in 1924. It gave him a taste for politics. Working with Richberg was "very pleasant and very stimulating," but Lilienthal could not support his wife and child on a salary that lacked "the certainty which a man with an ambitious family needs for his peace of mind." Not only did Lilienthal strike out on his own in 1926, but to supplement his practice he researched for Commerce Clearing House, a legal publisher, compiling and digesting decisions on state rate regulation of utilities in the *Public Utilities and Carriers Service*. It was a learning experience for him. Most of his clients were lawyers who defended the utilities against state regulators, thereby assisting "big, bad attorneys who taught the 'power boys' how to mulct the public." Lilienthal finished a good part of the work in two years and then turned to Frankfurter for advice on using his new expertise on utilities, how to beat the utilities at their own game.[6]

Lilienthal converted that expertise into a lucrative Chicago practice. One of his cases under retainer to the city of Chicago won a $20 million refund from the telephone company for its customers. He adroitly negotiated his way through state utility regulation, a delicate process involving a company's credit standing, its role in local economic development, and complex corporate devices such as the superregional holding company. In litigation and through articles in law journals and progressive magazines he built a reputation as a crusading liberal lawyer. The reputation was important for his ambition, which was why he decided in 1931, "in the face of real difficulties, mostly financial," to accept the offer of the newly elected Governor of Wisconsin, Philip La Follette, to join the state's Railroad Commission, with the promise that Lilienthal's first task would be to draft a law expanding and strengthening the commission's regulatory powers and changing its name to the Public Service Commission. The appointment of an outsider was significant. The state of Wisconsin had signaled its defense of the public interest against state utility exploitation. But Lilienthal's fellow lawyers were certain that the thirty-one-year-old had, in the words of William L. Ransom, Chairman of the American Bar Association's section of Public Utility Law, the requisite "courage, brains, character and . . . fine idealism which has characterized his career."[7]

It is not too much to say that the eyes of every utility regulator in America were on Lilienthal in Wisconsin. He was well aware of their interest in him. Indeed, Lilienthal used the Wisconsin position to bring himself to the attention of longtime carriers of the public power tradition such as Morris Llewellyn Cooke and Cooke's friend Governor Franklin D. Roosevelt of New York. Lilienthal acquired a heroic reputation by just accepting the Wisconsin position. Richberg and at least two other lawyers had declined it, presumably because its $5,000 salary was insufficient for the troubles that threatened. But one man's troubles were another man's opportunity. Knowing that nothing could have gratified Frankfurter and Brandeis more than taking up the cudgels of utility regulation, Lilienthal marched to Madison confident that he would make his reputation as a champion of progressivism. Indeed, in a few months he dominated the commission, led pitched battles against the utilities over rates and became a marked man for conservatives. Still, he was careful not to offend businessmen. Although his style caused a few utility executives to label him a socialist, Lilienthal thoughtfully eschewed public ownership of the utilities. Among antiutility reformers Lilienthal sided with those who espoused tougher regulation without the problems of public ownership. Lilienthal even opposed discussion of public ownership at a conference of progressives. But he was an aggressive regulator—so aggressive that he had the temerity to demand that the president of the state's largest utility substantially reduce rates; as anticipated, the demand was rejected. Lilienthal expected his stay in Wisconsin to be brief because the state legislature would never approve his reappointment. When a conservative defeated Governor La Follette in the 1932 Republican primary, Lilienthal had an excuse to seek a position in the coming Democratic administration in Washington.[8]

"Roosevelt knows of your qualities and experience," Frankfurter assured him. Lilienthal also had such regulators as Joseph Eastman of the

Interstate Commerce Commission and Frank R. McNinch of the Federal Power Commission aiding his quest for a job in the New Deal. Throughout early 1933 Lilienthal toured the East to ostensibly discuss policy changes in Washington with McNinch, Walsh, Frankfurter, Brandeis, Richberg, Senator Robert M. La Follette, Jr., Milo Maltbie and James P. Bonbright of the New York Public Service Commission, and others who might be well situated to pick up rumors concerning the new administration's regulatory policies. Would he land on the Federal Trade Commission? Would the increasingly incestuous interlocking of the holding companies and big finance bring about a Federal Utilities Commission? Anticipating the latter, Lilienthal drafted and circulated a bill for creating such an agency, but none was in the offing.[9]

Instead of regulation, Roosevelt chose to attack the conundrum of high utility rates by setting a federal example—or, as he liked to call it, creating a "yardstick" for the cost of power. He asked for and Congress created the Tennessee Valley Authority with nearly a blank check for its three directors. Roosevelt designated Arthur Morgan as Chairman of the TVA's directors and commissioned him to find the other two directors, defining one as a Southern agriculturist and the other as an advocate of public power. After a false start, Morgan decided upon the president of the University of Tennessee, Harcourt A. Morgan, a scholar of the boll weevil and a man rich in Tennessee contacts as a second director. Looking for a public power man to be the third director, in late May Morgan met with Lilienthal in Chicago. Lilienthal "inclined" to it. Although he was not a Southerner, he wrote Frankfurter, "I know something about the prejudice against the outsider because of my experience here." Backed by public power advocates like Senator George Norris and several Southern newspapers, Lilienthal took the job with an understanding that he would concentrate upon development of power and protect it as TVA's counsel. Frankfurter rejoiced: Lilienthal would dominate TVA because "Morgan will not be a real leader." That old warhorse for public power Morris Cooke agreed: At last, "Something is sure to happen."[10]

"White Coal"

ARTHUR MORGAN HAD BEEN among the few engineers to endorse federal development of America's waterways for power. Franklin Roosevelt thought that made him a good choice to head TVA. South of the Ohio and west of the Mississippi Rivers, Roosevelt believed, a broad consensus prevailed for federal leadership in the economic development of the United States. The issue was whether Morgan could organize regionalism in the Tennessee Valley and give it a national voice. Another advocate of cheap public power for development, Ezra F. Scattergood, Chief Electrical Engineer for Los Angeles, did not think Morgan was the right man. Scattergood warned the President that Morgan lacked the integrity and "aptness [for] putting to use the [Tennessee's] power for the benefit of those states" through which the river coursed.[11] Time would prove him correct.

Los Angeles looked out on the Pacific, but in Scattergood's eyes its growth needed federal development of the Tennessee Valley. Reciprocally, TVA's origins as a power project were in the West. It was not a mistake that in the group Roosevelt invited in early 1933 to view Wilson Dam at Muscle Shoals on the Tennessee and hear his nebulous plans concerning the valley's development were Senator George W. Norris of Nebraska and Ezra Scattergood of Los Angeles.[12] The federal government ostensibly had built Wilson Dam during the Great War in order to generate power for nitrate production to manufacture explosives and fertilizer, but President Wilson also emphasized its importance for Southern economic development. In 1933 a coalition of engineers, conservationists, agriculturists, Brandeisian lawyers, local promoters and political advocates for federal irrigation and hydroelectric projects in the arid and sparsely settled reaches of the West viewed Tennessee Valley development as an opportunity to spur other regional or local growth schemes.

For more than a quarter century Scattergood and his friends in Los Angeles believed that the growth of the City of Angels required plentiful and cheap public power. In 1906, when Los Angeles was a city of about 160,000 people, it decided to bring water from the Owens Valley, 255 miles away, via a gigantic aqueduct system. By 1928 imperial Los Angeles had a population of 1,200,000 and covetously cast its eyes about for additional sources of water to support its prosperity. Knowing that current sources of water could sustain 2,000,000 souls, the city fathers—including Scattergood—decided that Los Angeles would grow in excess of that figure. The more water Los Angeles had, the more it had to have. It needed nothing less than the water of the Colorado River over a hundred miles away. And the Colorado's development needed the cooperation of seven states tied into the Colorado River basin, as well as the financing and coordination of the federal government. The site for a dam to harness the water and energy of the Colorado already had been selected by federal engineers at Boulder Canyon, Nevada.[13]

Arid California needed water for its agriculture. Without irrigation it could not populate its interior. Also, water provided cheap power for farms and coastal cities. The state had been far-sighted and had planned for that need. In 1924, at a time when more than 90 per cent of American farms lacked electricity, in California "It is no unusual thing to see a new farm cottage completely equipped with electrical appliances—lights, vacuum cleaners, sewing and washing machines, water heater, cooking stove and refrigerator—at the same time the electric pump is installed to pump water, to irrigate the land, to raise alfalfa, to feed electrically milked cows in the electrically lighted barn." "California," an industry journal observed in 1912, "is the birthplace of real long-distance power transmission on this continent." Northern California exploited Sierra Nevada mountain streams for the cities of San Francisco Bay and the central valley, which "awaited the arrival of energy to relieve the constraints of their growth. They would spring to life dramatically as the transmission lines reached them, a situation not unlike that which occurred when canals and railroads first spread in the United States." By 1912 California already ranked second to New York in the generation of power.

What made so much electricity available to most Californians was a World War I decision to pool all the power of the state through a single administrator, an arrangement that lasted three years and connected hydroelectric plants under one organization through the 1,200-mile length of the state. Although California coordination later lapsed into localism, the availability of cheap power remained. In the United States in 1924, 35 per cent of all dwellings were wired for electricity; in California 83 per cent of all dwellings were wired! The cost per kilowatt hour for electricity in the U.S. was $2.17; in California it was $1.42. A tenth of all the electric energy generated in the U.S. was generated in California. At night Los Angeles "became a wonderland of light." Californians attributed their growth and prosperity in the 1920s to cheap electricity—a moral that the rest of the country could not fail to heed: "Industry means energy and as the fuels increase in cost hydro-electric power cannot fail to become more and more in demand." California demanded growth, growth demanded cheap power, and cheap power demanded water. In the words of one writer, "Electricity is such a vital thing that the job of continuing its development cannot be permitted to stop and there is no reason why it should stop."[14]

Scattergood heartily agreed. As the czar of Los Angeles's electric energy, he headed the largest municipal-owned power system in the world. Typically of Los Angeles, Scattergood was not a native. With an engineering degree from Rutgers University in New Jersey, Scattergood had taught at the University of Georgia and took a wife from one of the Old South's best families. When his health was threatened, Scattergood took himself to Southern California and a private engineering practice before joining the city government in 1909 as the chief electrical engineer under William Mulholland.

Angelenos did not oppose free enterprise, but ownership of water and electricity pitted the city against private corporation interests. In early twentieth century Los Angeles a millionaire reformer named John R. Haynes had led the movement for municipal ownership in the name of cheap energy required for commercial and industrial development. Engineers Mulholland and Scattergood were no less promoters of economic development than the Chamber of Commerce. But not everyone agreed with their advocacy of municipal ownership. In 1911 Scattergood fought off private efforts to get the city out of the power business, prevailing principally because he persuaded businessmen to endorse cheaper municipal power as opposed to the higher rates and more uncertain service of Southern California Edison. In 1924 Scattergood vanquished the last strong offensive by the private utilities and soon thereafter organized a coalition to build a dam at Boulder Canyon on the Colorado River. The dam expanded power output upon which the city could sustain growth. Scattergood's Municipal Bureau of Power and Light incessantly reminded Angelenos that their prosperity was inextricably linked to municipal power: "Anything less than full support of the City's water and electric investment by any citizen is disloyalty to the deliberately established policy and purpose of Los Angeles." As the historian of southern California has put it, public power "was a dogma demanding assent." Los Angeles businessmen accommodated municipally owned power to their free enterprise ideology.[15]

More power through the building of Boulder Dam called for federal financing. Ironically, a major participant in the Boulder Canyon decision was that public celebrator of American individualism Secretary of Commerce Herbert Hoover. Although Hooverphiles inflated his role, the real heroes of the Boulder Dam story were the Director of the United States Reclamation Service, Arthur Powell Davis, and a pugnacious Congressman from the Imperial Valley named Phil Swing. Swing wanted the Colorado's water for his agricultural district via the federally built All-American Canal. However, Davis, the engineer and builder of several dams and water projects, opposed piecemeal development of the Colorado and insisted upon comprehensive plans for flood control, aqueducts and hydrolectric power. Davis argued that Boulder Dam's construction would be paid for by the companies that supplied power for the growing cities of southern California. The states in the Colorado basin—California, Arizona, Nevada, Utah, Wyoming, Colorado and New Mexico—held conferences during 1922 that involved the Reclamation Service of the Interior Department. But Hoover, ever the bureaucratic imperialist, asserted his authority as an engineer and represented the federal government. Declaring that "Scenically as well as industrially we can be better off through the civilizing of our rivers" Hoover built his reputation as a progressive, although he lost interest in all rivers but the Colorado. Still, Ezra Scattergood shared with Hoover a concern for the Colorado and represented Los Angeles's interests at the conferences.[16]

Seven states signed the Colorado River Compact at Santa Fe, New Mexico, on November 24, 1922, although Arizona's legislature opposed it. That did not impede the project because six were needed to implement it. Engineers surveyed the river and, although it would always be known as the Boulder Canyon Project, selected Black Canyon near Las Vegas as the site for the dam. Phil Swing wrote the bill for its construction, but opposing Boulder Dam was an unlikely coalition: Arizona congressmen who accused California of a voracious thirst for its water; publisher Harry Chandler of the Los Angeles *Times,* who feared that the development would drain water from 830,000 acres he owned in Mexico; Eastern lawmakers who saw no reason for their constituents to fund development of the Southwest; and Utah's Senator Reed Smoot, who depicted it as an effort to drive private electric utilities out of business. While businessmen and farmers in the Compact states pushed for the project, the opposition delayed congressional approval until its fourth try in 1928. Not until Hoover was President would the digging begin in 1930. His Secretary of the Interior, Ray Lyman Wilbur, apportioned the water and power among the interested parties, Los Angeles getting favored treatment. In the words of historian Donald Worster, the Colorado would become "a managed ditch running meekly from its headwaters to its mouth under the strict supervision of the federal engineers."[17]

An Englishman, J. B. Priestly, visited the construction site and pronounced it "the soul of America under socialism." But building what Wilbur named Hoover Dam was a magnificent exercise in state capitalism. "The Boulder Canyon Project would be the most ambitious government-sponsored civil engineering task ever undertaken in the United States," its historian reminds us. It was then the biggest dam built anywhere and it captured the imaginations of the best civil engineers and earth movers. Its construction exceeded the resources of one contractor. Westerners were eager to break the construction dominance of the east; six Western contractors, taking the name Six Companies—Utah Construction, Morrison-Knudsen, J.F. Shea, Pacific Bridge, McDonald & Kahn, and Bechtel-Kaiser-Warren Brothers—formed a consortium to bid on the project. It marked the entry of the Bechtel and Kaiser families into the world of big-time construction. Federal money paid for everything, including the creation of a workers community in the Nevada desert called Boulder City. When Congress threatened to tighten the Boulder project's purse strings, Hoover the depression budget balancer pleaded for its exemption, lest it bankrupt the Six Companies. President Franklin D. Roosevelt dedicated it in 1935. Other dams would follow as individually and together the contractors would build Parker Dam downstream on the Colorado and Bonneville and Grand Coulee Dams on the Columbia. Here were the beginnings of the manufacturing industries that would flourish in California during World War II. Here was the industrial transformation of the West.[18]

Southern California was hardly alone in the West with its obsession with water for reclamation and power. However, in the Sacramento Valley of northern California the problem was less one of aridity than persistent flood. Its proposed solution was flood control financed at least in part by the federal government. The Flood Control Act of 1928 spotlighted the Mississippi Valley crisis of the previous year and included the Sacramento Valley for federal succor. In the 1930s Henry Kaiser would begin the cement company that bears his name in order to partake in the building of Shasta Dam and resolve the flooding problem of the Sacramento.[19]

Outside of the Sacramento Valley the West was usually arid, compelling Westerners to seek a federal solution to their paucity of water. Eastern Washington was a regular petitioner for irrigation assistance, and an Illinois lawyer named Wesley L. Jones set up a practice in Yakima and made the issue a vehicle for his political career. Elected to the House of Representatives at thirty-four in 1899, Jones set his eyes on a Senate seat by constantly pushing the Reclamation Service to consider federal irrigation projects in Washington State. In 1905 the Reclamation Service began building reservoirs in Washington. Somehow, though, nothing was done concerning the Northwest's greatest resource, the Columbia River Basin. By the late 1920s California and even Idaho and Oregon surpassed Washington in obtaining federal funds for irrigation and power. At last some Washingtonians, led by the Columbia River Development League, began to push for a federal project at Grand Coulee. Jones—now Senator Jones—along with Senator C. C. Dill, urged Hoover to make a study of the Columbia, which predictably recommended a dam at Grand Coulee. Congress supported a dam in principle in 1930, but Hoover pleaded federal poverty in the depression even as he poured millions into the Colorado project. Dill, a Democrat, extracted a pledge of support from Roosevelt in 1932. For eastern Washington farms, most of which still did not have electricity, public power offered the promise of abundance. Washington's private utilities opposed public power and refused to spend on stringing lines to rural homes. It remained for the New Deal to electrify most of rural Washington.[20]

In Seattle, however, the city was in the power business. Its Scattergood was J. D. Ross, who had fought the utilities for more than two decades. Working for the city since 1903 on a salary that averaged about $6,000 annually over three decades, Ross converted Seattle citizens to a gospel of cheap, clean and efficient electricity sold by the city. Seattle wired houses for free and then installed model electric ranges and water heaters. As Seattle's manufacturing grew in the 1920s, the city found customers for its low rates. Ross claimed in 1926 that his City Light had 83,000 customers against Puget Sound Power and Light's 25,000. By the 1930s Seattle had more electric ranges than any city in the United States. When Mayor Frank Edwards, working at the behest of the private utility, suddenly in 1931 dismissed Superintendent Ross, the City Council rejected all nominations to replace him. A young liberal, Marion Zioncheck, then collected enough signatures to force a recall election and, although Edwards had been elected twice by the largest majorities for mayor in Seattle's history, the voters overwhelmingly turned him out; the acting Mayor immediately restored Ross.[21]

Easterners had fewer energy concerns than Westerners. Public power was not a prime issue in New England, except in the rural areas of the Connecticut River Valley where half the farms lacked electricity.[22] However, power was a critical matter in the backroad regions of Pennsylvania and New York. The prophet of public power in Pennsylvania was Morris Llewellyn Cooke, a high-minded engineer-progressive who believed that government "must guide and direct the advancement of society." A graduate of Lehigh University in mechanical engineering, Cooke had married Eleanor Bushnell Davis of Germantown, whose wealth and similarly liberal views enabled him to aspire to reform society. As an advocate of scientific management he targeted utility companies for their inefficiency and corruption of American life. In 1911 at thirty-nine he was appointed Director of Public Works for Philadelphia by Mayor Rudolph Blankenburg. While Cooke improved efficiency by reducing patronage and paperwork, he outraged a Philadelphia Electric Company official who accused the self-righteous Cooke of believing he was "the only honest man in Philadelphia." During the war Cooke worked for the Council of National Defense, an experience which further convinced him that public ownership was necessary for cheap electricity. In the 1920s he crusaded for governmental control and development of power, earning the admiration and friendship of George Norris, Felix Frankfurter and Franklin Roosevelt.[23]

An ally in Pennsylvania and fellow advocate of "Giant Power" was Gifford Pinchot, a longtime crusader for conservation. Pennsylvania elected Pinchot governor in 1922 on the promise to push Giant Power as "a plan to bring cheaper and better electric service to those who are still without it." Pinchot hoped to sway the electric utilities with the power of his reason and rhetoric by creating the Giant Power Survey Board and its advisory committee of Henry L. Stimson, William Allen White and Arthur E. Morgan. He chose Cooke to lead the survey. Giant Power appealed to utility engineers and managers with its proposals for using advanced technology, large-scale power plants, wide-area grids of transmission lines, and interconnection with other regional producers. But the nagging questions of ownership and control remained: the Pinchot-Cooke forces wanted strict state regulation of power to limit profits and the rights of ownership. Only a tenth of Pennsylvania's farmers had electricity and Cooke would compel the utilities to provide rural service at low rates that disregarded utility quests for profit. Vociferous industry opposition defeated both Giant Power and Governor Pinchot in 1926. Nevertheless, the cause of publicly owned power took on a new note of urgency.[24]

One aspect of Giant Power that appealed to conservatives was the interconnection of private utility companies into larger units. The Great War experience with coordination of power had proved the progressives' point concerning its efficiency. But how could they accomplish coordination without the government meddling suggested in Giant Power? A publicist-engineer and sometime friend of Cooke named William S. Murray had proposed in 1918–19 a concept he dubbed "Super Power," and in 1920 Congress appropriated money for a survey of its feasibility. Its advisory board included utility executives, engineers and Herbert Hoover. Discussions dragged on through 1921 because the board could devise no way to achieve interconnection without some form of government regulation. But the utilities and Wall Street, led by Electric Bond and Share, promoted their own form of interconnection without regulation: holding companies. Following the political success of Pinchot and Giant Power in Pennsylvania in 1922, Hoover kept Super Power alive through conferences that made it appear to be an alternative to Giant Power's regulatory interference. As Pinchot put it, "Super Power is the name chosen by the electric magnates for their own set up of a nation-wide electric monopoly." (Meanwhile Hoover achieved interconnection in the power-hungry Southwest because the utilities there needed federal development of the Colorado River via Boulder Dam as much as did Los Angeles.) The holding company movement in the utility industry swung into high gear during the late 1920s.[25]

Giant Power also interested Westerners such as Los Angeles's Scattergood, who had served as a consultant for Cooke during the fight for Giant Power and had urged Cooke to emphasize that public financing would "result in much cheaper money and, therefore, lower cost" than private corporations could provide in rural areas.[26] In a world where the utilities assumed that few rural customers existed for their product, public power advocates wanted to take their vision of low-cost electricity beyond the cities of America. Washington, they insisted, could raise capital more efficiently for rural development than could private corporations. The federal government had built great dams like Roosevelt and Boulder to harness the powerful flows of America's rivers. They argued that when private utilities organized holding companies such as Electric Bond and Share and Commonwealth and Southern, that proved that the private quest for economies of scale in energy transmission led to unregulated monopolies whose exorbitant rates stifled industrial development for cities and left farms in the nineteenth century. They also pointed out that private utilities seldom used water power, the cheapest and most efficient form of energy. On opposite sides of the continent, Cooke and Scattergood insisted that American manufacturing and farming could not afford the holding companies' expensive energy.

With Coolidge in the White House and Hoover waiting in the wings, advocates of public ownership in the late 1920s attacked the increasing concentration of utilities in holding companies. Progressives depicted accelerating Wall Street speculation in utilities as evidence that finance capitalism now sought exorbitant profits through the excessive rates electric utilities charged consumers. Who would regulate the holding companies? State public service commssions could not because the courts ruled that holding companies which owned public utilities were not utilities: "In other words, the holding company device operates in such a fashion as largely to defeat the purpose of security regulation." "Nothing like this gigantic monopoly has ever appeared in the history of the world," ex-Governor of Pennsylvania Gifford Pinchot exclaimed—his words invoking the cartoon imagery of a giant spider with control "over the daily life of every human being within the web of its wires." This inspired the *New Republic* in 1926 to call for some courageous and imaginative politician to dramatize the fact that electricity "is too high or not available" and make it a political issue. Less than a year following the defeat of Governor Pinchot, the *Literary Digest* found that the issue of high utility rates seemed to grow as rapidly as the consumption of power. Western and Southern Senators were especially eager to thunder against the "Power Trust." Even the conservative *New York Times* had to concede that the fact that the five largest holding corporations controlled half of the American electric power industry was worrisome enough to imagine that "the end will be one gigantic corporation, which will furnish power from coast to coast."[27]

But the utilities were safe as long as Hoover was in the White House.

Felix Frankfurter argued that, notwithstanding Hoover's support for Boulder Dam, Super Power demonstrated opposition to federal regulation or development and "instead of Mr. Hoover educating the electrical industry, the power interests have educated Mr. Hoover." An energy revolution could accelerate America's economic development, but Frankfurter feared that its growth would be arrested if electric power remained in the hands of a few venal interests. "Without the control of adequate public safeguards," Frankfurter warned, "power development will repeat the disastrous history of transportation development—overcapitalization, wasteful competition, needless duplication of equipment, receiverships, undesirable consolidations, instead of a directed development of the generation, transmission and distribution of power."[28]

But politicians had to educate the public to this need for development. Some observers doubted that the public even cared about electric power. Few people cared about water power and utility control, wrote one cynic; "a debate on whether or not seven cents a kilowatt hour is exorbitant for electricity in the home" would not disturb public apathy. Events within the industry appeared to confirm that judgment. Municipal ownership of power distribution in the 1920s began to look like the wave of the past. Although municipal ownership of utilities had grown from 728 in 1900 to 3,083 in 1923, by 1927 the number declined to 2,198. At the same time the number of private utilities sharply declined too as the holding companies bought out small units. Even so, Los Angeles, Seattle and Tacoma continued to generate and sell power; San Francisco, Cleveland, Detroit and Jacksonville generated their own power for distribution by private companies. But many cities preferred profits to politics in their administration of energy. Smaller cities sold their generating plants to private industry for prices considerably below what they cost. Public interests were supposedly protected by state regulatory bodies in thirty-six states. Although states with regulation had lower rates than states without regulation, state regulation, even in Wisconsin, lacked experienced and knowledgeable leadership. Still, opponents of holding companies charged that the utilities were overleveraged pyramid schemes and that public bodies could finance a power plant at lower credit rates; but "For the present, private enterprise is riding high in the saddle."[29]

The depression and the elections of 1930 revived public power as a political issue. Demand for power amid the early depression stagnated, and utility debts surpassed an anticipated cash flow; the holding companies turned to consumers to pay higher rates. But Pennsylvania returned Gifford Pinchot to its governorship. Oregon and Washington elected men opposed to utilities and even voted to consider the joint development of the Columbia River. Nebraska, Colorado and Alabama elected George W. Norris, Edward P. Costigan and John H. Bankhead—all advocates of federal power development. In addition to Pinchot, Governors Franklin D. Roosevelt of New York, Philip La Follette of Wisconsin and Wilbur L. Cross of Connecticut were elected on vows to oppose higher power rates. "There is no doubt about it," exulted a partisan journalist, "the power issue has arrived." Amid declining business conditions, businessmen as consumers of electricity preferred public power to cut their costs. John Fahey, former president of the United States Chamber of Commerce, put it this way in 1929: "As a businessman I would prefer private ownership, but when the public cannot obtain the best possible service at the lowest possible cost, the advantages of private ownership disappear." Even a friend of President Hoover ruefully agreed that the tide against public power had turned.[30]

Of all the public power victories of 1930 the most encouraging was the re-election of Roosevelt. Al Smith had first put New York in the public power column when he endorsed developing the water power of the Niagara and the St. Lawrence rivers. Smith extolled water power as "white coal," a reference to the more expensive Eastern dependence upon mined coal for fuel to generate electricity. Early in the 1920s Smith espoused state ownership and operation of hydroelectric power as the only way to assure its fair and equitable transmission. When the Republican-controlled State Water Power Commission threatened to turn over the state's rights to the St. Lawrence to the Frontier Corporation (owned by General Electric, Aluminum Company of America and du Pont), Smith unflinchingly scotched the plan. Big business viciously branded him a socialist, but GE's Owen D. Young defended Smith when his company was no longer interested in selling electricity to consumers. Also, Young knew that, rhetoric aside, Smith wanted New York to generate power—the costly end of the hydroelectric business—and leave transmission and distribution of power to private business. The climax of the New York story came in 1929 when Wall Street's House of Morgan, through its United Corporation, jumped into the holding company game by acquiring Niagara Hudson, Public Service of New Jersey, Columbia Gas and Electric and other companies that controlled more than a third of the electric power production in twelve states. With magnificent arrogance, Morgan kept United's books private and filled its board of directors with Morgan partners and cronies. Morgan dared New York State to contest his bid to control hydroelectric power, confident that he controlled Republican legislators. It was the sort of challenge that could not be ignored by Governor Franklin Roosevelt.[31]

"It is our power," Roosevelt declared in 1929, "and no inordinate profit must be allowed to those who act as the people's agents in bringing this power to their homes and workshops." The state, he maintained, had the right to dam its rivers and harness their power. He vowed that the state would assert its rights of transmission and distribution of power only if private utilities scheduled unreasonable rates. He also called for a state power authority to bring cheap energy to the undeveloped St. Lawrence region. In 1929 the Republicans killed Roosevelt's power proposals, but he rebounded the following year with the same proposals for state generation *plus* transmission. To dramatize the choice between private and state development, Roosevelt compared home costs for electricity in Ontario under provincial power as opposed to home costs per kilowatt hour in Albany or Brooklyn. Government provided cheaper electricity. This time Niagara Hudson chose not to contest state creation of the New York Power Authority. Roosevelt appointed Frank P. Walsh as its Chairman and four other trustees including Morris Cooke. The authority decided to have the state develop the St. Lawrence in cooperation with the federal government and Canada. But the Hoover administration's cooperation was not readily forthcoming. It was easier for Roosevelt to deal with Tories in Ottawa than Republicans in Washington—especially if Hoover anticipated that FDR would win the Democratic nomination for president in 1932. Nevertheless, "You have vindicated courage in government," an elated Felix Frankfurter wrote the Governor. "You have also achieved the indispensable, correct first step in working out a socially sound water power policy." Momentum on the issue of public power development had shifted decisively.[32]

To be sure, not everyone agreed with Frankfurter about Roosevelt. In the words of one observer, "Roosevelt had broken completely with Wall Street and his presidential aspirations became a threat to the utility monopolies. He had branded himself a socialist." The utilities warned the public to beware of "new statutes and new theories," the head of Niagara Hudson arguing that lower rates would come from the corporation's "sound economics and able, public-spirited management." Martin Insull of Chicago's Commonwealth Edison pleaded with the public to balance consumer interests with those of investors who sought a fair return.[33]

Ironically, public power advocates insisted that the far-flung holding companies had made it a national issue by violating certain business principles: "Vast power combines, illogically assembled over a number of areas, are dangerous both to good service and to investors," wrote one engineer. "Private enterprise is fully adequate and able to carry out an efficient power policy in each area provided enterprises are loyal to their own areas and do not attempt to build overmastering financial and franchise combines."[34] Yet the holding companies in New York controlled vast noncontiguous entities that defied the original local nature of the utility. Led by the house of White Weld & Company, Wall Street erected giant paper organizations whose capacity for intimidation of the public seemed unlimited. White Weld's president, Philip Cabot, envisioned "national electrical highways . . . chartered as toll roads under private ownership and management." The National Electric Light Association, the utilities' trade association, bombarded Americans with propaganda for private enterprise, less municipal ownership and less regulation. But the holding companies had made power a national issue, and if Wall Street's greed knew no boundaries FDR would dramatize the issue when he became a candidate for president.[35]

And where else was a local power fight more nationalized than at Muscle Shoals, Alabama? Ownership of its power plant remained one of the hot political issues of the 1920s. Henry Ford had offered to buy and operate it—evidence to some people that power production had become one of the great industries of the postwar era. The heroic opposition by George Norris of Nebraska had left Wilson Dam's power in limbo, except for the federal contract to sell its energy to the Alabama Power Company. In January 1933 FDR revealed his plans for Muscle Shoals at Florence and at Sheffield, Alabama, declaring, "The development here is national and is going to be treated from a national point of view. It is going to be my purpose to put Muscle Shoals on the map."[36]

Roosevelt made the issue one of private versus public costs for economic development, something which the South was not indifferent to. Regularly returning to his adopted home in Warm Springs, Georgia, for treatment of his legs, paralyzed by polio in 1922, Roosevelt had seen in the 1920s the rise of considerable industrial promotion in the agrarian South. Southern states had embarked upon spending progams for roads, water and sewer systems, and schools in bids to make themselves more attractive to manufacturing. Many states and communities viewed cheap hydroelectric power as the key to their economic development,* leading one newspaper to observe that the South "is not eager to turn off the power that makes it grow." Growth was an obsession in the urban South.

*Did electricity actually improve the cost efficiency and productivity of industry? While Americans hungry for power accepted it as an axiom then, an economic historian argues that it has not been verified empirically. Significantly, however, he asserts that "technological change was responsible for a substantial portion of the rise in capital's [income] share and the decline in labor's share" by reducing energy costs. Firms were encouraged to "move toward more capital intensive and less labor intensive means of production." Hence, Wall Street's interest in control of hydroelectric power via the holding company for increased productivity. Arthur G. Woolf, "Electricity, Productivity, and Labor Saving: American Manufacturing, 1900–1929," *Explorations in Economic History* 21 (1984), 176–91.

Southern cities had a singular objective, the Atlanta *Constitution* declared: "Expansion! Expansion! EXPANSION!" They equated growth with cheap energy. Towns and counties looked to Washington for low-cost loans to build their own power distribution systems and further local entrepreneurial ambitions. Writing in 1924, the director of the North Carolina Geological and Economic Survey noted that "The demand for water power throughout the region is considerably in excess of supply. Many progressive municipalities are becoming seriously concerned at seeing industries located elsewhere and the growth of their own cities retarded by lack of power." In 1930 Crisp County, Georgia, completed its own power plant after a seven-year legal and political fight against the Georgia Power Company and established a rate schedule 10 per cent lower than the company's. Georgia Power countered by slashing its rates to the county by 35 per cent, whereupon the state Public Service Commission ordered the company to show cause why it should not share the same reduction with the rest of the state. Insisting that such a cut would bankrupt it, Georgia Power procured an injunction from the courts to prevent the commission from viewing the company's books. It seemed to be a glaring example of the need for a competitive public power corporation which might provide a governmental "yardstick" to measure the true profits of utility companies.[37]

Muscle Shoals, where the Tennessee River ceased to be a barely navigable waterway to become inaccessible at a plunge of 134 feet in northern Alabama and a rocky stretch that lasted for 37 miles, had been a natural object of local concern long before the war. In the nineteenth century nothing came of federal plans to build a canal parallel to the river. Shortly after the inauguration of William McKinley in 1897 a group of Florence, Sheffield and Tuscumbia, Alabama, businessmen organized the Muscle Shoals Power Company and requested congressional permission to construct a canal and a hydroelectric plant. But the Alabama promoters sought more control over the canal than representatives from other states thought that a private company should have over a public development. And there was some doubt on the part of the promoters that the hydroelectric project would be profitable enough. Still, led by Representative John H. Bankhead of Alabama, Congress passed the Muscle Shoals bill only to run into a veto by President Theodore Roosevelt in 1903 on the grounds that it set a significant federal power policy in a happenstance manner. By now the issue achieved national attention as Frank S. Washburn, president of the American Cyanamid Company in New York City, in quest of a low-cost source of electricity for producing nitrates, joined forces with a local promoter, J. W. Worthington of Sheffield, to form a power company and begin another round of legislation. However, in the progressive era the emphasis was on conservation rather than exploitation and one powerful House Republican, Theodore E. Burton of Ohio, vigorously opposed all private monopolies. A "partnership" concept evolved in which the government would build the plant and lease it to a private company. By this time Wilson was President and Midwestern Republican senators accused the Democrats of "pork-barrel" favors. The partnership idea died. Not until the National Defense Act of 1916, with a provision authorizing a federal power development for production of nitrates for explosives, did a Muscle Shoals dam achieve reality. Importantly, it, along with the Hetch Hetchy Act of 1913 for developing a site at Yosemite for the benefit of San Francisco and the Water Power Act of 1920, articulated the will of Congress to develop resources for the benefit of all people and not just private companies. That principle would be tested in the 1920s and again in the New Deal with the focus upon Southern economic development using Tennessee River power.[38]

"A.E.": Honesty, Contumacy and Democracy

A LONER ACCUSTOMED to making arbitrary decisions, Arthur Ernest Morgan did not take well to organizational politics—or any politics. He was a self-proclaimed idealist. Early in his life Morgan had decided to seek out "ultimate values" and to devote himself to the welfare of mankind. In St. Cloud, Minnesota, where he was raised, the bright young Morgan opted not to attend college but instead to apprentice himself to his father, a land surveyor, and begin a career in drainage projects that would make him one of the best known hydraulic engineers in America. Largely self-taught, he developed a stiff-necked and self-righteous attitude toward bosses, clients and rival engineers, especially those who carried credentials from some prestigious institution of engineering. Notwithstanding his stubbornness, Morgan also was recognized as indefatigable, scholarly, methodical, thorough and innovative. Dissatisfied with the water control laws of Minnesota, Morgan crusaded to change them, thereby establishing himself as an expert on flood control laws. The states of Arkansas, Mississippi, Ohio, Colorado and New Mexico consulted him, but his greatest triumph came when he revived at the Miami (Ohio) Conservancy District a dormant engineering practice of using flood control reservoirs instead of a dam. The Miami project also pioneered the use of spillways and worked out a complete classification system for national records of flood rainfall and runoff.

Importantly, Morgan was a conservationist. His dams were intended to preserve the land from rampaging waters and irrigate it with controlled waters. Significantly, perhaps, at each of the five reservoirs at Miami he erected a granite block with an inscription, "The dams of the Miami Conservancy District are for flood prevention purposes. Their use for power development or for storage would be a menace to the cities below." In the words of his biographer, the statement "sounds judgmental, even defiant, in rejecting electrical power."[39]

His quest to preserve the rural world he idealized led the tall, lanky Morgan in several different career directions. At a time when Southern and Western cities yearned for growth, Morgan idealized the small community, which he felt was threatened by the onslaught of electric power development and manufacturing. Early in his life he read Edward Bellamy's *Looking Backward* and embraced the novel's advocacy of a utopian socialism; much later he wrote a biography of Bellamy. A charter member of the American Eugenics Society, Morgan believed in a planned society and sought a milieu that would allow him a free hand at planning. In 1919 he accepted the presidency of the nearly bankrupt Antioch College of Yellow Springs, Ohio, whose prosperity he thought he could revive through self-sufficiency. He never generated the self-supporting industry that he believed the college needed, but his idealism—expressed through his writings on social planning and uplift in *Antioch Notes*—attracted the attention of Eleanor and Franklin D. Roosevelt, among others; that added to Antioch's endowment and gave the college a sense of community and mission. Morgan boasted that Antioch, unlike some other small denominational colleges, did not educate "reformers and preachers, but entrepreneurs." Antioch students were scrupulously honest, and Morgan intended that they would bring that honesty to the economic and political world about them. When the local Dayton Power and Light Company charged excessive rates, he had Antioch and Yellow Springs build their own generating plant and operate it despite pressures from the company that threatened Antioch's financial support. He insisted he was not idealistic, but merely honest; the difference between idealism and honesty was that the latter allowed a man to control his destiny. He was merely honest.[40]

When Roosevelt announced his plans for TVA, Morgan immediately saw it as an opportunity to apply his ideas on social planning and self-sufficiency in a controlled environment. Unaware that former Governor James M. Cox of Ohio, who had picked him to build the Miami Conservancy District, had recommended him to FDR, Morgan was surprised by the President's offer of the TVA chairmanship. "But, Mr. President, you do not know me," he protested. "Haven't I been reading *Antioch Notes* all these years?" Roosevelt responded. "I like your vision." Morgan listened to Roosevelt expound upon his own vision for an hour and a half and agreed to take TVA's chairmanship—provided that it involved no political patronage. "There is to be no politics in this!" Roosevelt exclaimed, pounding his fist on the table for emphasis. He asked Morgan to recommend his two fellow directors, a Southern agriculturist and a public power advocate.[41]

Morgan's first choice for a Southern agriculturist was a Southern industrialist, George G. Crawford, president of Jones and Loughlin Steel Corporation in Pittsburgh, formerly of Tennessee Coal and Iron. Roosevelt rejected Crawford, and Morgan then suggested Harcourt A. Morgan of the University of Tennessee. A Canadian from the University of Guelph, Ontario, Morgan was an entomologist who had been chairman of the Department of Zoology at Louisiana State University and had long experience in working with Southern farmers on such problems as the cattle tick and the cotton boll weevil. He went to Tennessee in 1905 to direct its agricultural station, and in 1913 he became dean of the college of agriculture. A vigorous sixty-six, Harcourt Morgan was a popular and logical choice among county farm agents and farmer organizations because he had crusaded throughout the state for crop rotation, diversification and erosion control. Later, the antipolitical Arthur Morgan characterized Harcourt Morgan as "one of the most powerful figures in the South, though he nearly always chooses to be behind the scenes."[42] Within TVA Harcourt was called "H.A."; Arthur Morgan was "A.E."

Finding a suitable public power man was more difficult. Roosevelt suggested J. D. Ross of Seattle City Light and E. F. Scattergood of Los Angeles. Both men, of course, ran their city's own power facilities and were ardent promoters of their city's industrial development. Arthur Morgan rejected them for their "personal traits and methods of operation" that suggested potential conflicts with Morgan over "programs and policy." Morgan wanted no part of their public ownership of power dogma. Lest he alienate Rooosevelt, who obviously knew both by reputation and wanted one of them, Morgan claimed to prefer a public power man who cooperated with private power such as Llewellyn Evans, builder of Tacoma's public power operation; but he passed on the mild-mannered Evans, as did Roosevelt too. Anticipating utility resistance to TVA, the president wanted a scrapper for public power. Told to touch base with Justice Louis Brandeis, another reader of *Antioch Notes*, Morgan first heard the name of David Lilienthal. He checked on Lilienthal's credentials and was told that he was bright but ambitious: "He will steal the show!" Still, with time running out on Morgan's coast-to-coast search for a public power man suitable to Roosevelt, he had little choice but to take Lilienthal.[43] Lilienthal was TVA's power man.

Arthur Morgan generated divisions at the outset. While Harcourt Morgan and Lilienthal busily wound up their other affairs, Arthur Morgan made several key decisions that got TVA off to a spectacular start. As Chief Engineer and temporary General Manager, he took control of Muscle Shoals from the Army Corps of Engineers and set in motion plans to build a dam at Cove Creek, naming it for Senator George W. Norris. At the same time, however, he proposed a bizarre ethical code for employees that suggested to Lilienthal and Harcourt Morgan that their chairman was "impracticable and highly visionary." Still, they cooperated with the honest man. Other proposals also suggested an otherworldliness. They approved his social plans for self-sufficient communities of skilled yeoman whose primitive industries produced native furniture. TVA also would organize and enlighten agrarians as to the correct way to manufacture and farm—but it did not, as "A.E." proposed, deprive a farmer of his land if he did not cultivate the land correctly. Arthur Morgan's benevolent despotism even conjured up a special currency for his isolated valley. Tennesseans were hostile to such arrogance. "I do resent, on behalf of my people, and for myself," wrote Senator Nathan L. Bachman of Tennessee, "the suggestion that we are in need of a new cultural civilization, which you continuously advocate in your addresses." Lilienthal ridiculed the older man's fatuousness. Photographs of Lilienthal at TVA occasions often show him with a smirk suggesting contempt. (Knowing of Arthur Morgan's hatred of patronage, Lilienthal loved to tweak Morgan on how many Antioch people held TVA jobs.) If Lilienthal saw humor in TVA, Arthur Morgan did not. "Humor's dangerous," Morgan believed. "A man of dignity and responsibility must beware of it."[44]

From TVA's start, Arthur Morgan was the board's odd man. He might have done better in Herbert Hoover's administration, where his preference for rule by "consensus" was more acceptable. He defined "consensus" this way: "Consensus of judgment would not mean taking formal votes on the 'one man, one vote' principle. Consensus of judgment may be arrived at by the deference of the many who do not know to the superior judgment of the few who do." Morgan wanted a consensus that deferred to the hydraulic engineer. But his other two directors were strong-willed, and the board divided philosophically over power policies: Chairman Arthur Morgan versus Harcourt Morgan and David Lilienthal. The latter two insisted upon votes on public development of power, which they won. To create the illusion of a consensus Arthur Morgan made their motions unanimous; only after two years of that did he bitterly abandon consensus and become a minority on the board. For three years FDR and the press treated the public division on the TVA board as a personality contretemps and played down its significance for New Deal policy.[45]

Each of the directors brought a passion to TVA. Arthur Morgan found satisfaction in planning a small-unit primitive economy for the Tennessee Valley. He created the model town of Norris, Tennessee, in the hope that he could shelter the rural South from twentieth-century technologies that called forth great organizations such as big corporations or municipalities. Four years older than the President, Arthur Morgan was more the nineteenth-century man than Harcourt Morgan, a decade older and so much more worldly. While Arthur Morgan had the commitment to planning that FDR admired, he expected planning to be shielded from the democratic politics Roosevelt thrived upon. Harcourt Morgan was a scientific farmer intent upon agricultural experiments with phosphates instead of nitrates to conserve the soil for a greater yield. A democratic, cajoling, wise neighbor, Harcourt Morgan encouraged local agricultural leaders to dominate TVA's agricultural decision-making process to the disadvantage of poor farmers in the valley. Lilienthal was the crafty lawyer who set his sights on providing cost-efficient public power as a cheaper alternative to the Wall Street–run local operator, Commonwealth and Southern Holding Company. He compelled utility holding companies to reduce rates by providing consumers with public alternatives. He would make TVA an experiment in capitalist planning.

"It began life in 1933 as a multi-purpose project," historian Thomas K. McCraw reminds us, "with missions involving flood control, fertilizer development, promotion of the region's economy, construction of an inland waterway, and generation of hydroelectric power." And it left a "grand legacy" that

> lives on, in the flood control system, so well designed that the Tennessee River can be shut off like a kitchen tap; in the 650-mile inland waterway from Paducah to Knoxville, providing an avenue for inexpensive barge transportation; in the architectural grandeur of almost all TVA water projects, and some of the steam plants as well; in the verdant valleys that once ran dirty with washing topsoil; in the enhanced living standard made possible by regional electrification; and, perhaps above all, in the example that this kind of superior achievement could be accomplished in the public sector, not for profit but—as the plaques on all its projects say—"For the People of the United States of America."[46]

McCraw saves an important point for last: TVA produced cheap electric power intended to have *national* significance. Even without the Great

War, sooner or later the dam at Muscle Shoals would have been built because of the ambitious local promoters of industrial development. But the New Dealers gave Wilson Dam a *national* vision—and Congress enthusiastically concurred. Congress in 1933 made TVA an example and a resource for Americans in all regions. Every congressman who voted for it did so knowing what TVA power potentially signified for his district or state. "All this is TVA as Congress contemplated it and as Lilienthal sees it," reporter Jonathan Daniels wrote in 1938. "Never doubt that. But never believe either that power in TVA is incidental. Flood control and navigation, national defense, even cheap fertilizer are the incidentals. *TVA is power.*" Daniels roughly tallied federal spending on TVA and concluded that "half the total investment now is in power and the investment in power is greater than the investment devoted to any other two of the important purposes contemplated in an integrated river development." TVA was the keystone in the New Deal edifice of restructured control of electric and financial power in order to promote economic expansion in all America. "TVA began," Daniels argued, "as a weapon in the power fight."[47]

Roosevelt disdained electric holding companies as overcapitalized and inefficient organizations that profited exorbitantly without giving service. The best way to demonstrate the truth of this, he believed, was to create a rival public operation to provide more service at less cost to the consumer. These issues of marketing electricity transcended the Tennessee Valley and caught the attention of all who believed cheap power was necessary for local economic growth. Their hopes now rested with Lilienthal and his organization. Shortly after assuming his post in the TVA, Lilienthal encountered Governor Pinchot. The sixty-eight-year-old Pinchot congratulated the thirty-three-year-old Lilienthal on his appointment and the younger man confessed his awe of the task. "You will succeed," Pinchot assured him; "you have the right point of view." Lilienthal understood.

Arthur Morgan did not have the right point of view. When Lilienthal went to the TVA board's first meeting at Washington's Willard Hotel, he heard Morgan report that he had given Commonwealth and Southern president Wendell L. Willkie his personal assurance of TVA cooperation. Lilienthal was aghast. He wanted to compete, not cooperate, with private utilities. Numerous holding company scandals suggested the hopelessness of cooperation with men who valued utilties as personal "profit machines" rather than for their service to the community. Lilienthal wanted TVA to compete by selling government-generated power from Wilson Dam to customers serviced by utilities and those without any power at all. Lilienthal hoped for "voluntary relinquishment" to TVA of territory served by utilities, but he knew that that goal ran against "every reasonable expectation." The national importance of the coming conflict was underlined by Cooke who told Lilienthal to "Go ahead and do Uncle Sam's job without promising any private interest anything." Cooperation as preached by Arthur Morgan defied experience with the utilities.[48] Assailing a bland five-page policy memorandum on power production, Lilienthal ridiculed Arthur Morgan's proposals as "unscientific, impractical, [serving] no public interest, [and] opposed by time-tested public men" such as George Norris. Morgan quickly retreated and thereby confirmed Lilienthal's control of TVA power policy.[49]

Roosevelt was TVA's architect, but Lilienthal was its engineer. A visionary himself, economic multipliers danced through Lilienthal's brain and often embroiled him in running controversies with Arthur Morgan. One such fight concerned the Tennessee Valley Associated Cooperatives. When the Chairman organized TVAC to implement his dream of local self-sufficient producers throughout the valley, Lilienthal demanded that Morgan's cooperatives convert to manufacturing that consumed more TVA-generated power, employed more people and developed "new industrial opportunities." A horrified Arthur Morgan disdained manufacturing; he was content with growing beans and canning them. So Lilienthal and Harcourt Morgan branded Arthur Morgan's TVAC "an inappropriate TVA activity" and withdrew their support.[50]

"I am in favor of public ownership wherever it can compete in fact with private ownership," Arthur Morgan once told Morris Cooke. "In that I think we are all agreed."[51] But Morgan was devious in his disdain for the public tradition in the generation of electric power. Since he was a closet Bellamy socialist and venerated Senator George Norris, that is surprising.* Arthur Morgan's preference for the primitive led him to eventually side with big utility holding companies against his own TVA. Their indifference to rural markets for electricity complemented Morgan's quest to isolate rural markets from what he considered the terrors of manufacturing and growth that accompanied electrification.

But Harcourt Morgan had to oppose Arthur Morgan as both a scientist and a politician: he valued electricity's prospects for improving agricultural output and rural living; he also knew that his rural constituency wanted to produce abundant crops for the outside world and enjoy the

*Norris let him down. When Morgan's assistant, Gordon R. Clapp, investigated political patronage in TVA and brought in evidence embarrassing to Lilienthal, Morgan took it to the Senator, who refused even to review it, sternly telling Morgan, "We need the president. We cannot get along without him." As Morgan recalled sorrowfully, "from this time on he tended to treat me as an enemy." Morgan did not understand that TVA's power policies were more important to Norris than issues of honesty. The most honest man in American public life had rebuffed Morgan's quest for honesty.

creature comforts of clean power.* Harcourt Morgan enabled Lilienthal to promote TVA as "Democracy on the March," by emphasizing local decision-making in agriculture. He believed that Tennessee would gain from public power and recoiled in horror from Arthur Morgan's endorsement of utility holding companies to retard development rather than enhance it. That isolated Arthur Morgan in TVA and left him only the utilities as allies.[52]

Lilienthal planned to capture utility-held markets for TVA via competitive rates that appealed to consumers. As a Midwesterner only a decade removed from Harvard Law, he sought lawyers and engineers to aid him who could not be taken for "city intellectuals" in Knoxville. In particular, he found a chief electrical engineer in Llewellyn Evans, one of the men Arthur Morgan had avoided in his quest for a director of power. Evans had "made the Tacoma municipal plant what it is," and Lilienthal saw him as one of the few "qualified engineers (not merely God-sakers) who are concerned only for the the public interest." Evans had brought a clear-eyed approach to the TVA task. Having managed a low-cost power plant that gave the same low rates to residential users it gave to big industrial plants, unlike private utilities, Evans would be greatly responsible for devising the low rates for which TVA would be famous.[53] Also, his management skills would enable the three directors to build an organization as free from political influence as possible, although Arthur Morgan never conceded that fact. Several TVA employees went on to brilliant administrative careers elsewhere in the government, and two rose to be chairman of the TVA.

TVA's promise of economic development enthralled Southerners and Westerners. Lilienthal's announcement that TVA's rates would allow municipalities to charge 2–2.75 cents per kilowatt hour astonished the nation. Numerous small cities from South Carolina to Texas petitioned the RFC for loans to set up their own transmission lines and distribution systems. Although Jesse Jones could not make such loans then and was reluctant to do so if he could, TVA inspired demands for low rates. The national average was 5.5 cents and Tennessee Electric Power charged 5.8 cents and Alabama Power charged 4.6 cents. How could TVA justify such low rates? At a time when average annual usage was 595 kilowatt-hours, and TEP averaged 612 while Alabama Power averaged 793 hours, TVA usage would have to rise to 1,200 hours to make such low rates pay. Fortified by Evans's calculations, Lilienthal gambled that TVA would

*Of course, expanded production ran counter to AAA's economy of scarcity to raise prices, just as TVA's quest to increase production of electricity and sell it at lower rates ran counter to NRA's manufacturing economy of scarcity to raise prices.

induce increased consumption and that the volume of usage would somehow justify the low rates.

Indeed, TVA's low rate attracted customers. Tupelo, Mississippi, the hometown of Representative John Rankin, the sponsor of the TVA bill in the House, began to buy TVA power in February 1934. Lilienthal pressed Commonwealth and Southern to cede whole counties in Mississippi, Alabama and Tennessee to TVA, threatening C & S with competition via TVA transmission lines from Wilson Dam. Moreover, Norris Dam would sell TVA power in C & S territories. Already several towns in this area prepared to follow Tupelo and bolt the C & S system. Wendell Willkie offered TVA a deal; in early 1934, in return for TVA power from Wilson Dam and its promise not to invade additional C & S markets, he gave TVA options on C & S franchises in northern Alabama and eastern Tennessee, an offer Lilienthal found "exceedingly favorable to us."[54] However, when C & S reneged on the promised territorial options, Lilienthal threatened to encourage the Public Works Administration to make loans to municipalities wishing to build their own systems. (The RFC now could finance the PWA for such projects.) Knoxville, the largest city in the area, voted 2–1 to sell bonds for buying its utility from Electric Bond and Share Company, the New York holding company, and building a competing plant. The PWA gave Knoxville a loan, inspiring Willkie to strike another deal with TVA in August 1934; but again he welshed.

C & S's strategy called for containing TVA's power at Tupelo and a few places in Mississippi and Alabama. TVA did not accept such limitations, but the area served as TVA's "yardstick." Roosevelt himself was the foremost advocate of measuring private costs for commodities sold to the public sector, having been a governmental customer for metal plate for battleships as Assistant Secretary of the Navy in the Wilson administration. He never felt that he knew metal plate's true cost. Now he felt that the cost of power at Tupelo in 1934 would "be copied in every state of the Union before we get through." Formulas would be devised covering TVA costs. Nevertheless, TVA did not publish a "yardstick" based upon its rates until 1937.

Could state capitalism measure costs in private capitalism? "Hell," an engineer for a utility exploded, "if that's a yardstick, I'm a New Dealer."

> It's not a yardstick; it's a club. They get their money from Uncle Santy and no interest charged. We have to borrow ours from the public and pay what it costs—five per cent and up. And TVA pays taxes—that's a joke—$67,000 for the 1937 fiscal year. Do you know what a private company with an investment the size of TVA's would

have to pay? I'll tell you: damn near $3,000,000. TVA's financial statements show no charge for depreciation. They keep the real size of their investment—on which they've got to earn something to save their faces, if not Uncle Santy's money—down by a mumbo-jumbo allocation to flood control and navigation. They send their mail free. The government prints their pretty picture books. They get reduced freight rates. Maybe it's a detail—a damn big one—but they ride their damn cars all over hell and gone and pay no auto taxes at all. And when they want to take a whole town of customers away from us, they lend the city fathers—or give it to them—the government's money, or Handsome Harold Ickes does it for them. And that's the yardstick set up in odor of civic sanctity to show the dear people what the utilities ought to be charging them if we bastards weren't cheating them. And the saps eat it up.

You can't blame the people. They don't care who freezes their ice cubes. If the government pays the Tennesseans' power bills, you can't expect the Tennesseans to complain.[55]

In the end, the engineer knew that he would win the yardstick battle and lose the power war: any way he sliced it, public power was cheaper to the consumer. In a free market in which government was a competitor, utilities had to lower rates or lose customers. Willkie knew that, as the engineer put it, TVA's cheap power was a club at the head of C & S.

But TVA's cheap power also did the utilities a favor. When C & S companies in the South reduced rates in October 1933, they began to increase revenues for the first time since 1929. TVA data proved that lower rates brought more consumer usage and additional volume. Lilienthal called TVA rates "regulation by example," noting that private utilities as far away as Oklahoma and Colorado attacked TVA rates because regulatory knowledge of them compelled the utilities to lower rates. Farther west, Ezra F. Scattergood did not need TVA's example because he had set his own in Los Angeles. As he wrote in 1933, "The influence of the municipal system of Los Angeles . . . together with smaller municipal systems in California, has necessitated gradual rate reductions on the part of privately owned utilities."[56] The yardstick may have been an accounting farce, as utilities charged, but they could not deny that lower rates were not only possible but profitable.

The trend away from municipal power in the 1920s owed something to a lack of capital for such projects; in the 1930s the Public Works Administration financed new municipal power projects to reverse the trend. By mid-1935, 495 local governmental units had applied for PWA loans to build their own power plants; 145 requests were granted. PWA loaned money to nine cities in Alabama, two in Mississippi and eight in Tennessee to build facilities to receive TVA power. All of these projects brought utility lawsuits aimed at preventing the sale of TVA power to the cities. Eventually the cities prevailed in the courts over the utilities, but not without engendering considerable tensions between public and private agencies.[57]

The bitterness reached into the TVA leadership. Arthur Morgan opposed TVA competition and sought Lilienthal's removal to end it. In 1935, while utilities attacked TVA's yardstick in Mississippi, Morgan tried to recruit one of the agency's lawyers, Herbert Marks, to do "a friendly but independent and critical study" of the cost of public power at Tupelo. Marks viewed Morgan's request as an undisguised effort to document hostile utility arguments. Morgan was a "saboteur" and fatuous to think that Marks, a former Frankfurter student, would do the utilities' work.[58] Still, he knew that an opportunity to get rid of Lilienthal was approaching. At TVA's beginnings the directors staggered their terms and Lilienthal drew the short one that would end in May 1936. In the fall of 1935 Morgan lobbied Roosevelt to replace Lilienthal; the President led him to believe that he was supportive. In February 1936 the Supreme Court ruled that TVA had the right to transmit power to towns from Wilson Dam, a considerable victory for Lilienthal—but its significance seemed to escape Morgan. A month before Lilienthal's term expired, Morgan threatened Roosevelt that if Lilienthal was reappointed he would resign. But Lilienthal was a more adroit lobbyist than Arthur Morgan and had been prudent in his relations with Congress. He hired Marguerite Owen, Senator Norris's former secretary, as TVA's extremely effective Washington liaison to aid in the public relations war.[59]

To Arthur Morgan, Lilienthal's successes at TVA masked "hard boiled selfish intrigue." He never understood the public power network in Washington politics or Lilienthal's use of it. He knew that Lilienthal confided constantly in Senator Norris and others, but Morgan never appreciated Lilienthal's importance to Roosevelt, Norris and the cause of public power. "Morgan," Louis Wehle observed, "was not skilled in the ways of politics and politicians." The significance of lower electric rates, greater consumer usage, and its meaning for Southern and Western economic growth seemed beyond Morgan's comprehension.

Roosevelt reappointed Lilienthal, and a disappointed Morgan did not resign. The President had his own idea as to what was at stake. As he wrote to "my dear Arthur," 1936 was an election year and Lilienthal's removal would be seen as "the first victory against your fundamental beliefs and mine [that] TVA is the first of, I hope, many similar organizations and that we are in the formative period of developing administrative methods for a new type of governmental agency." TVA would be a prototype of other valley authorities to follow. Ignoring Morgan's threat, FDR told Lilienthal that although Morgan "doesn't understand the power issue at all, [he] has a great soul." FDR wanted no changes at TVA. "Now next year we are going to have some more authorities," the President said, and both Lilienthal and Morgan had to remain and make TVA a model for them. Southern and Western economic development was at stake. During one meeting Roosevelt looked Lilienthal in the eye and said portentously, "You and I will be gone one of these days. . . . We will have a chance to affect the course of these things. If we fail, they may be set back, but the issues are there; and we may be faced not only with economic revolution and social revolution," and at this point he jabbed his finger at Lilienthal, "but political revolution."[60]

Still unaware of what Lilienthal's appointment signified, Arthur Morgan now deluded himself into thinking that Roosevelt would transfer Lilienthal out of TVA following the 1936 election. He did not seem to realize that FDR enjoyed TVA's war with C & S. Roosevelt told Willkie "with gusto" that he would not yield to C & S demands to limit TVA's territory. Meanwhile, Lilienthal, now aware of Morgan's effort to get rid of him, exacted revenge by bringing E. F. Scattergood from Los Angeles as a special consultant, knowing full well that Morgan despised Scattergood. (Only two years before, Lilienthal had rejected Scattergood as a consultant.) Embarrassed, Morgan took "a much needed rest" and departed for a while.[61]

In moments of despair, Morgan fled the scene of defeat—this time back to Yellow Springs, where he was "rusticating and trying to make up his mind what he ought to do." He schemed to find a way "to checkmate Lilienthal." In the words of a friend, Morgan was "a tired and overwrought man who should have a long rest." Morris Cooke counseled Roosevelt to ask soap manufacturer Samuel Fels, a friend to both the New Deal and to Antioch College, to help keep Morgan in line. Roosevelt agreed and wrote Fels to "advise Arthur 'to keep both feet on the ground.' " In the meantime, two of Morgan's aides abandoned him and went to Lilienthal with tales of Morgan's machinations. When Morgan returned, Lilienthal wrote:

> Instead of coming back refreshed, his soul aired of its suspicions, jealousies and hatreds, he is worse than ever before. He looks like the wrath of God—dark bags under his eyes, nervously tight as a drum, thin. Been brooding and planning all that time. I think he is sick.

Indeed, Morgan was subject to emotional and physical illnesses when he was under stress. In those moments, he once wrote,

> the front part of my head, just back of my eyes, feels as though it were in high fever, and in that limited area there is a sense of extreme physical discomfort. I find difficulty in controlling the course of my thoughts. That is, I cannot dismiss a subject from my mind, but it "runs away with me," keeping me awake at night. There is a lack of control which inclines me to lose my temper or to talk too much.

Later he went to Florida for six weeks, his biographer calling it a "breakdown." In each case he returned filled with strategies for retaliating against his tormentor, Lilienthal. TVA's chairman was at war with TVA.[62]

But so was Wall Street at war with TVA. The erstwhile New Dealer Alexander Sachs had his own plan for blocking TVA's expansion. Visiting the White House on behalf of Lehman Brothers to explain to Roosevelt why the utilities feared TVA competition, Sachs tried to persuade the President that it made no sense to expand Southern hydroelectric energy when "an inadequate market for available power" existed and that construction of additional power plants would discourage capital markets from investing in private utility construction. To counter FDR's concern with power's exorbitant cost or absence in most of rural America, Sachs broached the idea of a pool for public and private utilities to reduce costs and rates through economies of scale. He echoed Brandeis that a power pool was a "social invention." Roosevelt was conciliatory. Like Sachs, he wanted to avoid "open warfare" with the utilities. Sachs conferred again with the president on June 8, August 11 and September 16, after which FDR called a conference on September 30 to discuss securing "abundant cheap power." Ever the experimenter, Roosevelt embraced the power pool idea.[63]

Sachs envisioned a public-private pool that would integrate TVA into a mixed power system designed to restrain public growth and make utilities more attractive in capital markets. The pool idea appealed to Roosevelt because he liked capitalistic planning for stabilization. Also, the plan, as did everything in TVA, had national portents for the integration of competitive energy systems across the country. But Lilienthal understood his own mission to be that of building a public system and correctly suspected that the unification of public and private systems was a scheme to limit TVA and municipal power expansion. The utility holding companies had stepped up their attacks upon TVA in Congress and in New York, averring that public power set back economic recovery by sowing uncertainties in investment markets. Utility lawyers and engineers privately appealed to Roosevelt and New Dealers to listen to financial reason, Russell Leffingwell summing up the arguments of Wall Street by declaring, "If you want private companies to take electricity to the consumer, you must let them make some money and sell some stock."[64]

The pool proposal placed Lilienthal on the defensive. Although he viewed it as a diversion of TVA's quest for power markets, its appeal to Roosevelt silenced Lilienthal. He reminded the President and congressional friends of TVA's mission, accomplishments and prospects, but he dared not attack the pool directly. On September 12 he got from Roosevelt a promise to permit TVA expansion in return for which Lilienthal bowed to Willkie's request *not* to sell power to Chattanooga after a referendum ordered the city to buy its power from TVA. Lilienthal wanted PWA to give municipalities loans, hoping that Memphis and Jackson would build systems that purchased power from TVA and that C & S opposed the loans.[65]

Meanwhile Sachs tried to align Basil Manly, Vice Chairman of the Federal Power Commission, and Democratic lawyer Louis B. Wehle, Brandeis's nephew and a putative expert on public corporations, behind a moratorium on TVA "intrigues" for expansion. Sachs offered to curb utility lobbying in Congress against TVA appropriations in return for a prohibition on additional TVA-encouraged municipal ownership.[66] At a conference of interested parties,* Willkie accused TVA of stealing utility customers and Lilienthal asserted TVA's right to sell power to a municipality and the municipality's right to choose from whom it would buy its power. Sachs insisted to the President that the utilities had a standstill agreement preventing Lilienthal from selling additional power to TVA area towns for three months. When Wehle commented that "Dave would be quite a problem," Roosevelt interjected, "Oh, he will do no instigating."[67]

But Arthur Morgan did his own instigating. Morgan went to the power pool conference armed with a 22-page memorandum drafted by a former chief engineer of the Middle West Utilities Company. Although Morgan insisted that the utility engineer also had advised TVA, that did not diminish the fact that Morgan had mimeographed the memorandum in

*The President selected the conferees, a distinguished group including Lilienthal, Morgan, Willkie, Manly, Cooke, Wehle, Sachs, Preston Arkwright of the Georgia Power Company, Samuel Ferguson of the Hartford Electric Light Company, Chairman Frank McNinch of the Federal Power Commission, Frederic Delano of the National Resources Committee, Owen D. Young of General Electric, and Russell Leffingwell of the Morgan interests (who could not attend, and partner Thomas Lamont served in his stead).

New York, instead of at TVA's Washington or Knoxville offices, and secretly sent a copy of it to the McGraw-Hill Company, publishers of the trade publication *Electrical World*, and the *New York Times*. George Fort Milton, editor of the Chattanooga *News*, a TVA supporter whose paper was boycotted by the utilities in favor of the *New York Times*'s subsidiary the Chattanooga *Times*, accused Morgan of "treason" to TVA. But Morgan had been liberated from any New Deal loyalties. Speaking to the American Economics Association on December 30, Morgan castigated "the socially irresponsible Napoleonic complex which dominates some so-called reformers"—"Napoleonic" being his code word for Lilienthal. Also, he sent an article to the *New York Times* that read like a utility position paper. In the words of Morris Cooke, "Dr. Morgan is out of effective sympathy with New Deal power activities."[68]

Both Morgan and the utilities aroused Roosevelt's ire in December when a federal judge enjoined TVA from any expansion while he studied its constitutionality. The decision grew out of suits launched in May by nineteen private companies in the Tennessee Valley against TVA in federal district court. Lilienthal had argued that the suits were violations of TVA's standstill agreement with the utilities and used the decision to withdraw TVA from pool negotiations. Roosevelt still wanted the pool but agreed with Lilienthal that the utilities sought to litigate TVA to death. He was especially incensed that the injunction broadly covered "every angle of the situation." With TVA fighting for its life in the courts, Roosevelt now doubted the good faith of the utilities and declared the power pool negotiations at an end on January 25.[69]

Lilienthal now seized upon mounting evidence of Arthur Morgan's collaboration with Willkie to push for the Chairman's dismissal; but Roosevelt confounded him by taking no action against the treacherous Morgan. Amidst the court reform fight of 1937, the President's mind was elsewhere.[70] Unhampered, Morgan escalated his war against TVA with an article in the *Saturday Evening Post* that impugned the honesty of his fellow directors, something Roosevelt could not ignore. Cooke answered Morgan in a *New Republic* article which he first cleared with Roosevelt: was it all right with the President to attack his TVA Chairman? "Go the whole hog," ordered the exasperated Roosevelt. The Morgan situation had so deteriorated that when TVA confronted the utilities at a trial before a three-judge federal panel, general counsel Lawrence Fly and Special Assistant John Lord O'Brien, concluded that TVA's own Chairman could not be a trusted witness in its behalf.[71] What they did not know was that Morgan secretly conspired with a sympathetic Alexander Sachs on a TVA minority report to Congress challenging TVA's "yardstick."[72] For most of 1937 TVA tried to ignore its Chairman. But by the end of the year insouciance turned to irritability. "He's so haywire that one has to be ready anyhow for surprises," Herbert Marks suspected. "His TVA record is no subject for a congressional investigation. It needs a psychiatrist. And if he keeps it up much longer, the rest of us may need one, too."

Part of the frustration stemmed from the so-called "*Berry* case," involving claims by a group of Tennessee Democrats that they had to be compensated by the government because it had flooded their land, which was rich with marble, in order to build Norris Dam. TVA worked out a legal procedure for remedy with the Berry group, but Morgan vehemently protested that because Berry had been a New Deal appointee, at stake was not the value of a claim but the propriety of a group of public officials compensating another federal official with government money. Indeed, evidence showed that Berry group had acted in bad faith, a discovery that prompted Morgan to accuse his fellow directors in court of dishonesty because they had been anxious to settle with Berry as soon as possible. On March 1, 1938, the Berry claims were thrown out as worthless, Morgan claiming vindication and a need for Congress to investigate TVA's dishonesty.[73]

"What in hell are we going to do about Arthur Morgan?" the President finally asked Lilienthal on March 3. Lilienthal disingenuously hinted at his own resignation to relieve Roosevelt of embarrassment. "Don't be silly," the President snapped. "The only embarrassment is the embarrassment of having a befuddled old man on our hands." Recalling the Jimmy Walker case of 1932, in which the then Governor Roosevelt had held court on charges against New York Mayor Walker of corruption until Walker resigned, Roosevelt decided to take the same tack with Morgan. But the President should have known that Morgan was not Walker, that what worked on a politico did not apply to a moralist convinced of his own rectitude. He ignored Lilienthal's insight that "disagreement with [Arthur Morgan] is frequently considered [by him] evidence of dishonesty." Morgan reluctantly attended the hearing on March 11, sitting passively while Roosevelt questioned him. When he did respond, he was incoherent. His clearest argument was that Roosevelt's court had no standing because only Congress could judge the TVA and Arthur Morgan. (The TVA law allowed the President to terminate a director without Congress's permission.) After six hours Roosevelt had heard little from "my dear old friend" Morgan except nebulous accusations that his tormentors were evil men. "I am disappointed," Roosevelt admitted. Morgan thanked FDR for his "fine consideration."[74]

Sensing that the Morgan denouement might not be like that of the Walker case, Roosevelt demanded that Morgan either prove his charges of dishonesty or resign. Morgan politely refused. What could FDR do? If he abruptly ended the hearing, Morgan "would continue to give the idea he *still* had no confidence in my fairness and only the Congress would be fair." So Roosevelt concluded the second session on March 18 by declaring Morgan guilty of having "obstructed and sabotaged" TVA, as well as "contumacy," defiance of the President's questions. When the President concluded by demanding that Morgan resign or be fired, Morgan answered that his removal was not in the public interest. With that he left Washington for Yellow Springs. A beaten FDR, still lacking Morgan's resignation, fired "the old man" and made Harcourt Morgan Chairman of TVA. (Lilienthal took it over in 1941.) A year later Roosevelt would remember sadly "that disgraceful, that humiliating scene we put on here."[75]

With many lawyers eager to challenge the constitutionality of Morgan's firing, the Democrats decided upon a congressional investigation of TVA management. Alexander Sachs hoped the publicity would make Morgan a national hero and expose TVA as a "reckless and planless socialization of power, . . . a sort of governmental East India holding company" run by "crypto-fascists."[76] But for more than six months in 1938 a congressional committee bored the nation with its tedious investigation. Arthur Morgan mumbled for nearly six hours that TVA was guilty of intellectual dishonesty but he produced nothing damaging to TVA. In the end, *Time* correctly concluded that the hearings proved that TVA was more important than its personalities.[77]

While Congress investigated TVA, Lilienthal bought out the C & S–owned Tennessee Electric Power from Willkie and gained the Knoxville market from Electric Bond and Share. Politics and financial markets motivated the holding companies to take advantage of state capitalism. The election of 1936 made Willkie more tractable by putting Roosevelt in the White House for four more years. Also, holding company defeats in the courts confirmed TVA's staying power. Most importantly, C & S decided that a deal with TVA was in its best financial interests. "Its Southeastern properties need new capital to meet maturing obligations and to construct new facilities," wrote one journalist in late 1936. "While the TVA conflict remains unresolved, these properties cannot take advantage of the present cheap money market to save themselves millions by scaling down their interest charges." He forecast that "the Roosevelt Administration will be ready to dicker in earnest with [the utilities] on a program aimed at the ultimate conversion of the Tennessee Valley into an area of exclusive public ownership and operation, the change to be achieved without loss to those who actually have put money into the development of the private companies now in the field."[78] In March 1937

Willkie privately hinted that he would consider selling TEP because "the period of cheap money may pass" without C & S acquiring additional companies. Willkie later indicated that if he could not buy companies, he may as well sell them—even to the government, if the price was right.

But TVA was growing without the TEP properties. Following the dissolution of the injunction prohibiting TVA from accessing new customers, it added Chattanooga, Jackson, Trenton and Paris in Tennessee, Tuscumbia and Guntersville in Alabama, Middlesborough in Kentucky, and was negotiating to sell its service to other towns and counties. Sheffield, Alabama, and Memphis and Knoxville were building their own power systems to run off TVA transmission lines. Also, TVA had its first big industrial contracts with Alcoa and two other manufacturers. The valley's economic growth had begun.[79]

Nonetheless, the resurgent depression of 1937–38 strengthened Wall Street demands that TVA relent in its competition with private power and allow utilities to raise capital for expansion and improvements. Lilienthal retorted that investors preferred monopoly power: whose monopoly would prevail—the holding companies or the government's? In January a federal court upheld the constitutionality of TVA and dealt a blow to the prayers of its enemies. Still, FDR could not ignore complaints from the investment community.[80] Willkie hoped to sell all of TEP to TVA, but Lilienthal did not want to swallow more than TVA could chew. TVA negotiated for TEP through 1938. When Electric Bond and Share agreed to sell its Knoxville property to TVA, Lilienthal knew that "Mr. Willkie is now isolated." But not until the Supreme Court ruled TVA constitutional in early 1939 did Willkie discuss a figure New Dealers found reasonable.[81]

When Willkie asked $78,600,000 for TEP, Lilienthal was inclined to take it without haggling. From his home in Norris, Lilienthal conferred by telephone with the President on February 4, 1939. FDR demurred. "Do you think it's all right, Dave?" he asked. "If you want to get a few million dollars less the thing to do is to go straight to J. P. Morgan & Co." Lilienthal dreaded a protracted negotiation. The timing was right; they had political and financial support in Nashville and Chattanooga, where the company had fought a vicious battle to win a referendum and was trounced 3 to 1. Chattanooga's power plant, when operated, would ruin TEP. Ominously, however, sentiment in Congress was shifting against public power. Although public power was stronger than ever in the Tennessee Valley, Texas, the Pacific Northwest and other parts of rural America, utility propaganda gained in Congress. The administration could not afford to delay purchase of these utilities. Lilienthal called

Willkie in New York and told him it was a deal. "I think it has all been on a fine basis," Willkie replied.[82] Congress gave TVA bond-issuing authority and at a ceremony for the benefit of newsreels on August 15, Willkie and Lilienthal staged an exchange of a check and deeds to consummate the transfer of TEP to TVA—Willkie mugging for the cameras by looking astonishingly at the check and exclaiming, "Dave, this is a lot of money for a couple of Indiana boys to be handling."[83]

In New York Alexander Sachs interpreted the "far-reaching significance" of the settlement as a victory for the decent Arthur Morgan because Willkie had fought off "confiscatory" power to obtain a fair price.[84] But Sachs and other Wall Streeters deliberately overlooked the commitment of New Dealers to democracy. While not always sincere, modest or intellectually honest, Lilienthal saw nothing wrong with government investment for development and personally opposed anything that limited individual freedom, whether it was utility holding companies or totalitarian governments. In his way he was an entrepreneur. In 1939 he already dreamed of a private practice that would bring him a fortune. More than one person noted that not a lot of difference in personalities existed between Lilienthal and Willkie. TVA and the public power tradition were in retreat. To survive TVA had to defeat a ruthless combination of utilities, holding companies, Wall Street investment bankers and the *New York Times*. It succeeded in compelling a lower price for electricity throughout the South and those states reaching through Texas to California and on up the Pacific Coast to Washington, making that region more attractive to manufacturing. Roosevelt intended TVA to be a forerunner of other river valley developments, and demands from the Central Valley of California, the Arkansas River Valley and the Missouri River Valley encouraged him to think about those additional areas for development. However, political signs already suggested in 1938–39 that TVA would not be repeated. "Splending's" failure in the spring of 1939 compelled Roosevelt and Lilienthal to emphasize the importance of TVA's advancement of democratic life in the valley. Roosevelt wanted to tour TVA in 1940 to highlight its democratic dimensions, but other matters interfered. Lilienthal proclaimed an end to TVA's power phase and channeled his combative energies to resisting Harold Ickes's efforts to absorb TVA into the Interior Department and to finding places for TVA in defense mobilization. TVA's days of growth lay ahead of it. Still to be answered was the question: had TVA threatened or extended democracy?[85]

EHFA: Consumer Credit

THE NEW DEALERS did not like certain capitalists, but they had nothing against capitalism. *Fortune* liked to say that it understood the New Dealers, without necessarily approving of them, and knew that they intended "to make capitalism work. . . . *by taking hold of the system from within rather than by policing it from without.*" Thus, if an excessively competitive industry could not prevent declining prices, New Dealers were prone to organize an industrial cartel to stabilize prices, as they did in agriculture; and conversely, if competition was lacking and an industry tended toward inefficient concentration, New Dealers sought to create competition in behalf of consumers and growth. In the event of capital deficiencies they were prepared to pursue public investment planning to make them up. Ineluctably this brought down upon their heads the wrath of many businessmen, but, as *Fortune* noted, "It was not over the preservation of capitalism that the New Dealers and their opponents clashed. It was over the appropriateness of the means offered to preserve it." Most New Dealers were instinctively capitalists. For instance, in the same letter in which TVA lawyer Joseph Swidler discussed the fight against the utilities, he also disclosed that he was selling corporation stock "to take advantage of a temporarily high market level."[86] New Dealers prided themselves on knowing capitalist economics well enough for their own best advantages and for others. Eschewing greed and fear, they sought to humanize the system without destroying it. They did not boast much about their altruism, because each New Dealer fancied himself a hard-boiled character as apt to collaborate with as fight against evil utilities and their hired lawyers in order to serve humanity.

They were building a capitalism with a human face. They would make capitalism work more fairly and equitably for middle-class investors, consumers and workers. They fancied themselves virtuous businessmen. David Lilienthal copied for his files a press description of himself and Willkie in which Willkie was described as a "new kind of politician" because he was described as a businessman who ventured into politics and Lilienthal was a "new kind of business man" because he ran a public business worth half a billion on a salary of a $10,000 "for the excitement of it and old fashioned impulses about public service." Lilienthal's public service impulse masked something in his personality that aligned with his corporate enemies. "Lilienthal is a hard-bitten, hard-working empire-builder with a crusading zeal different in direction but as cold as the elder Rockefeller used to have," a Baltimore journalist remarked. "It is probably true of him, as some of the power tycoons, that had destiny faced him in the right direction, he would have made an excellent Wall Street raider and bear-market operator."[87]

In these extraordinary times Lilienthal found himself managing a big business with a big difference: it organized things for people that they could not do for themselves and did it without any thought of its profit. While some businessmen argued that this would lead to paternalism or worse, New Dealers insisted that TVA need not lose its consciousness of democracy. TVA's most paternalistic leader was Arthur Morgan because he was the least responsive to politics. Morgan failed to determine what residents of the valley wanted or to persuade them of what he wanted. On the other hand, Lilienthal and Harcourt Morgan preached and practiced democracy through widespread organization of cooperatives and popular programs. "We must learn how to *decentralize administration,*" Lilienthal wrote. "The citizens' participation in the exercise of *centralized authority* must be increased. That is our only safeguard in this modern world."

The last sentence is a key to their thinking. Aware of the monstrous ideologies then ravaging Europe, the New Dealers made certain that TVA was not totalitarian fascism or communism. They were crusaders for liberalism, the only intelligent alternative to Hitlerism or Stalinism. In valley areas untouched by power companies, TVA encouraged the democratic creation of rural cooperatives to enable people to obtain cheap electricity. But the cooperatives were a local decision. "It's strange," a visitor told Jonathan Daniels, "but all these men you meet in the TVA talk about democracy with the same solemn but casual devotion as you will hear from all sorts of people in Germany about the Nazi program."[88]

At a time of totalitarian pomp and projects in Europe, New Dealers asserted that democracy too could build great projects for the people. Since rural Americans could not provide low-cost electric power for themselves, the New Dealers felt justified in subsidizing public corporations to deliver the service to have-nots neglected by the utilities. The Reconstruction Finance Corporation substituted for Wall Street as a source of capital for enterprises distributing cheap electric power. TVA was state capitalism, but capitalism nevertheless. But who would buy its electric service unless the citizen had need for it by being able to afford wiring and appliances that made him a consumer? Credit would have to be made available to the consumer. Anticipating this problem of an excess of electricity and a dearth of demand, Lilienthal contrived one of the New Deal's more ingenious public corporations: the Electric Home and Farm Administration.

TVA's success depended upon selling electricity. Finding customers in the poverty-ridden rural South who could afford electricity and felt a need for appliances that used the power generated at Wilson and Norris dams and elsewhere was TVA's central concern. And if such people existed, the utilities should have serviced them. But poverty and the utilities left the Southern countryside in the dark. Llewellyn Evans's apparently arbitrarily low rates for TVA electricity conjured up a theoretical demand; a real demand remained to be discovered or created. TVA could bankrupt itself seeking consumers of power at rates that brought inadequate revenues. The utilities counted on that. They knew that only 3 per cent of all farms in the Tennessee Valley had electricity and that its farmers in the boom year of 1929 averaged less than $1,000 income. "Unless consumption shot upward, the low rates were certain to fail, and the TVA power program was doomed to become the laughingstock of the utility industry," historian Thomas McCraw has written. "That Lilienthal, Evans, and their advisers well understood the risk makes their decision the more remarkable, and the more admirable. This was just the kind of experimentation the federal government had promised, and that it alone—unlike the private power companies—could afford to take, even during an economic depression."[89]

The magnitude of such an experiment inspired Lilienthal's imagination. He envisioned not only a best-case scenario in which TVA would sell its surplus power, but also where it would provide the engine of economic growth regionally and nationally. "The crux of the whole matter is a lack of purchasing power in the hands of the people—people who have an insistent and overpowering need for goods which our idle factories and idle capital and idle men and women are capable of producing," Lilienthal wrote. TVA's generation of electricity could emerge as the American economy's great multiplier if Washington could generate consumer credit. However, the creation of consumer debt went counter to a society's personal habits of thrift—as well as Lilienthal's own personal values. Later he reflected upon the irony: "My abhorrence of getting into debt is rather amusing since it was I who so greatly stimulated installment buying, a form of getting into debt, by the creation of the Electric Home and Farm Administration, with the object of getting the easiest possible terms in the purchase of electric appliances—and very successful it has been, too, at that."[90]

It was a limited success—necessarily limited. When TVA produced energy for industry, businessmen appreciated its low cost; but when EHFA put the government into the business of financing the sales of appliances, retailers resented the competition. EHFA began in January 1934 and consciously kept a modest profile. Few reporters wrote about it then, and few historians have written about it since. Yet it endured until 1943, when the war rendered it quite superfluous. Its limitations were a tribute to the caution of its creators and the resistance of both its beneficiaries and its adversaries.

Lilienthal did not discover by himself the multiplier magic of electricity. Household appliances, especially refrigerators, were a big business in the 1920s. The amount of steel used to manufacture refrigerators rose from 1,000 tons to 88,000 tons during the prosperity decade. Consumer spending stimulated increased production, and, according to Michael A. Bernstein, "It was the fact that the shift to this new pattern of spending was taking place when the crash intervened, and that the economy was therefore blocked from sustaining the transition, that is essential to an understanding of why the slump continued for as long as it did."[91] Bernstein's point is that the modern consumer economy was in its adolescence during the 1920s and that the Great Depression interrupted and retarded its maturity. He correctly assumes that no adequate private initiative existed to renew its growth. Indeed, appliance manufacturers and utility executives blamed each other for high prices and high rates that restrained consumption of electricity. The New Dealers were cognizant of the problem.

By executive order under the authority conferred upon him by Section 220 of the National Industrial Recovery Act, President Roosevelt created the Electric Home and Farm Authority on December 19, 1933. Promoted by Lilienthal as a "reemployment and recovery" agency, EHFA was basically a finance corporation, its original name being "Electric Appliance Corporation," a Delaware corporation. A December 13 White House conference attended by Herman Oliphant of the Treasury Department, Director of the Budget Lewis Douglas, Attorney General Homer Cummings and the Chairman of the Reconstruction Finance Corporation, Jesse Jones, had decided to take a million dollars from the $3.3 billion appropriation for the NIRA to promote the sale of electrical equipment. After that initial funding the RFC would bankroll EHFA by as much as $10 million, charging no more than 4 per cent interest. The participating agencies agreed that

> The primary purpose of the corporation will be to increase the domestic consumption of electricity in the areas served by the Tennessee Valley Authority and competing utilities. It will seek to accomplish this result by securing manufacturers of heavy use electrical equipment to make standard high-grade electrical equipment available at prices much below any heretofore prevailing, by securing from the utilities arrangements as to rates on current which will make the use of such appliances economical, and by securing from the utilities agreements as to handling of collections and reverts which will make these items much less expensive than heretofore. . . . The appliances will be sold through the regular outlets.[92]

The three directors of the TVA became the board of directors for EHFA, but since Lilienthal controlled power he controlled EHFA.

Responses to EHFA varied from enthusiasm to caution. The fiscally conservative Lewis Douglas characteristically feared it would create a precedent for "additional huge Government financing." Nevertheless, Douglas supported EHFA because he too wanted to sell a lot of electric appliances to consumers. A "terribly excited" Felix Frankfurter thought that the announcement of EHFA "may well be the beginning of a tremendous thing," and he advised Lilienthal that to run the agency he needed a businessman who can be "trusted with responsibilities in an enterprise that looks like business, but isn't."

Significantly, Lilienthal designated himself as that businessman. With characteristic confidence he already had negotiated with General Electric Corporation on the manufacture of low-cost appliances that would be sold with EHFA financing. In March he went to New York to dicker for low-price appliances to EHFA customers in return for high-volume sales for brave manufacturers who believed EHFA estimates that it could induce a million and a half appliance sales. The sticking point, as industry leader Frigidaire pointed out, was that EHFA violated NRA prices by demanding lower appliance prices. At a time when NRA recovery policy called for price maintenance, TVA's and EHFA's low price policy suggested that an alternative route to restored prosperity lay not with scarcity but abundance. EHFA contradicted 1933's conventional economic wisdom. Yet Lilienthal realistically appraised the Tennessee Valley's poverty and backwardness and concluded that high prices retarded its development. Likening EHFA to the marketing of Ford Model T's, Lilienthal looked to the mass purchase of appliances at low prices and installment loan rates, using EHFA-subsidized wiring in homes and barns, to raise the Tennessee Valley's standard of living.[93]

EHFA pioneeered cheap money. Before the Federal Housing Administration hit upon lower rates, lower down payments, lower payments and longer terms to finance home-buying, EHFA cut consumer credit rates on appliances, slashed payments in half, and extended contracts by a third. But such shrewd marketing by a government agency created all sorts of problems. Its announcement that power companies would sell EHFA-approved and EHFA-financed appliances elicited a torrent of protests from retailers who feared a competitive government–utility combine. With more than 90 per–cent of EHFA-financed appliances sold through utilities, Lilienthal blamed this on manufacturer reluctance to finance retailer sales of appliances with loan guarantees while utilities eagerly used their cash to promote appliance purchases. Lilienthal's remedy was a request that RFC create a collateral trust fund to expand retailer installment sales.

EHFA chose Tupelo, Mississippi, as the site of an all-out effort to demonstrate that low electric rates, low appliances prices and available credit could increase usage of electricity. In July 1934 Lilienthal boasted that in six months Tupelo had increased its consumption of power by 83 per cent over the previous year. EHFA expanded the program to other parts of TVA's area and soon the Tennessee Electric Power Company led all other utilities in the country in increased kilowatt hour consumption per customer; utilities in the valley showed the greatest increased use of home appliances. The states of Tennessee, Georgia and Alabama, as documented by the trade publication *Electrical World*, were first, second, and eighth in the nation in the largest increased use of electricity. [94] With the cooperation of seven refrigerator manufacturers, nine electric range manufacturers, eleven electric water heater manufacturers, and 300 independent retail dealers, EHFA achieved "really spectacular" results by reducing interest charges and prices on appliances. Significantly, EHFA justified TVA's lower electric rates. Employing a campaign similar to NRA's "Blue Eagle," TVA exhorted consumers to buy EHFA-approved appliances that showed an emblem of a man's hand grasping a lightning bolt with the legend "TVA—Electricity for All." Later in the 1930s, as EHFA grew more national in scope, the city of Austin, Texas, put flyers into utility bills that depicted Uncle Sam declaring, "I'll carry your appliance purchases."[95]

Roosevelt showcased EHFA success at Tupelo by visiting it in November 1934 and telling newspaper reporters he wanted people to know about EHFA "all over this country." A few days later at Warm Springs Roosevelt told Lilienthal that in order to influence electric rates across the country, he wanted EHFA to go national. That meant removing it from TVA leadership. Ever the believer in economic growth through electrification, Lilienthal heartily agreed. Accordingly, he drafted a memorandum for Roosevelt in which he laid out the goals of an expanded EHFA; the President returned it with a handwritten message, "Take this up with the other gov. agencies. F.D.R."

Although RFC would take over the national direction of EHFA, Lilienthal saw many benefits for TVA. One was that it spread the gospel of cheap power. Another was that if the Supreme Court should rule TVA unconstitutional—a real fear in the wake of the 1935 decision that NRA was unconstitutional—separating it from TVA would save EHFA to carry the cheap-power message. Financing of appliances would be assured through the RFC, Congress having authorized it to lend up to $300 million to EHFA for that purpose. EHFA collaboration with municipal power cities such as Los Angeles would leverage demands for lower appliance prices. On July 20 FDR pronounced Lilienthal's plan for the EHFA "sound" and suggested that he take it up with Jesse Jones, Morris Cooke and Frank McNinch. Within days EHFA's directors resigned to make way for a new group composed of George R. Cooksey, Cooke and Tommy Corcoran—the latter to play a key role in the new EHFA as its advocate in RFC. "No objection FDR Aug 1 1935," the President scrawled at the bottom of a memorandum proclaiming the design of a new EHFA.[96]

With the move of EHFA headquarters from Chattanooga to Washington, Cooke, who then headed REA, replaced Lilienthal as head of the national EHFA. That was a mistake because Jesse Jones ignored EHFA while it remained under Cooke's control. Cooke complained to Roosevelt and on October 5 the President wrote a memo: "Jesse - Corcoran - Lilienthal - Cooke - Ben Cohen - To meet with me and start the enlarged E. H. & F. A." FDR loved EHFA more than anyone in government, but he recalled Lewis Douglas's fear that it would be a budgetary burden. It needed money without going to Congress and that meant going to Jesse Jones. Moreover, Cooke had unnecessarily embroiled himself in a squabble with Jones's crony Stewart McDonald of the Federal Housing Administration over which agency should insure loans for the purchase of electric appliances for homes and farms. It was not a fight that Cooke could win. When Jones and Marriner Eccles of the Federal Reserve Board sided with McDonald, Cooke struck a deal with them: McDonald retired from the appliance loan business, Cooke retired from the EHFA (he remained in REA), Emil Schram of RFC assumed the leadership of EHFA, and Corcoran policed EHFA on behalf of the White House. Thus, the financing of electricity consumption fell to a Texas banker, Jesse Jones.[97]

In 1935–36 EHFA's future was uncertain. FDR seemed more concerned with budgetary and political constraints than financing electricity. In the void between the Cooke and Schram reigns, its trustees ran EHFA while Roosevelt tried to reduce its administrative costs by assigning its loan functions to private agencies. Informed that those arrangements would reduce EHFA administrative expenses from $150,000 per month to $15,000, the President "expressed his great pleasure . . . , saying that the sum saved could well be used by him in his budget making work." An exasperated Cooke feared that EHFA was "gradually dying."[98]

But Roosevelt would not let EHFA die, and he knew that Jones and Corcoran would make it thrive. Of course, Jones was hardly the sort of banker to make installment loans on appliances. In 1934 he had disdained such a role for RFC. This did not mean that he was uninterested in EHFA. A national mandate and a place in his empire suited Jones just right. He viewed EHFA with the eye of a frontier promoter. Perhaps he could boost his reputation with liberals by helping poor people without alienating conservative friends with fiscal irresponsibility. Perhaps too he took note of the fact that EHFA could have an impact upon national financing complementary to Stewart McDonald's FHA. Indeed, EHFA compelled General Motors Acceptance Corporation to extend terms on Frigidaires to thirty-six months, the time allotted for payments on appliances by EHFA.[99]

Jones made EHFA self-supporting and raised EHFA's weak standing with Congress. The very capable Emil Schram headed its adminstration. Corcoran, who fondly called EHFA "Little Eva," sat on its board and personally kept Roosevelt apprised of it. Importantly, Jones maintained TVA–EHFA principles, which meant investing RFC cash nationally in behalf of "the low-rate idea" only with utilities that practiced "progressive low-rate-high-volume programs." Thus, in early 1936 EHFA finally became truly national with forty-one cooperating utilities and 409 appliance dealers in ten states from Florida to Nebraska selling eleven types of appliances from seventy manufacturers. EHFA encouraged utilities to lower rates on the promise of additional sales volume. Also, EHFA's expansion complemented the economic growth encouraged by its cooperating agencies—TVA, FHA and REA. EHFA financed a consumer purchase when the customer selected an EHFA approved appliance, paid at least 5 per cent of the price and agreed to installment terms approved by EHFA (5 per cent interest in 1936), the unpaid balance being a loan to the dealer from EHFA. Because EHFA financing functioned only where electricity rates did not exceed maximum or "accepted" levels, EHFA could claim that in every community where it operated it had been "an important influence in the reduction of interest rates by national finance companies." As Corcoran liked to point out, EHFA was a "pilot plant" that drove down national consumer interest rates. Like TVA's impact upon electric rates, EHFA credit competition worked to reduce consumer costs.[100]

EHFA retained numerous problems. Utilities still competed with retailers to sell EHFA appliances; one Georgia utility had to remind employees that its load-building program mattered more than who sold appliances. Significantly, amidst the turmoil of the New Deal's war with utilities, Georgia Power valued EHFA cooperation that demonstrated, in the words of an EHFA report, "the Government's fundamental intentions toward the private utility industry are intelligently helpful, not destructive." However, some EHFA-approved appliances were of such inferior quality that they incurred service problems before the consumer fully paid for the appliance; and that also raised questions as to responsibility for repairs. In areas where utilities gave both electric and gas service, utilities demanded that EHFA finance gas appliance purchases too in order to maintain the company's investment in gas mains, etc. (EHFA announced on May 23, 1939, that it would finance gas appliances.)

But by mid-1937 EHFA could claim 1,102 retailers who sold appliances made by 137 manufacturers in 20 states serviced by 99 utilities. In other words, EHFA's activity approximately doubled during 1936–37.* Most of all, EHFA congratulated itself that its credit " 'yardstick' . . . has been an undeniable factor in a general revision all over the country of installment credit terms in favor of the ultimate purchaser."[101]

The Roosevelt recession of 1937–38 did not interrupt EHFA's expansion. Deciding that it was wise "not to tighten up on our credit terms on . . . electric appliances because the vast untouched market for such appliances . . . cannot be saturated in a foreseeable time," EHFA kept loaning and reported "a constantly increasing demand" for appliance financing, demonstrating that "Government credit assistance of this kind can be effective in holding up business volume in a difficult period." EHFA "helped to maintain employment" by steadying demand for appliances. Although its number of delinquent accounts increased through the fall of 1937, EHFA extended them and the number of delinquent accounts peaked in January. In this way the EHFA played a small and unheralded role in the countercyclical efforts of the New Deal.[102]

Nonetheless, events overtook Lilienthal's offspring. In 1941 the defense program preoccupied Congress, Emil Schram left the RFC and the EHFA for the presidency of the New York Stock Exchange, and Director of the Budget Harold Smith suggested that EHFA lending functions cease, "consistent with other efforts of the Administration to free industry for defense needs." In other words, rather than encouraging production of low-cost appliances to use low-cost electricity, the country needed power for manufacturing war materials. The U.S. would have to trade a growing economy for one of waste. FDR bowed to the inevitable and requested Jesse Jones to terminate lending. By 1943 all its outstanding loans were paid off and EHFA faded into the lost history of the New Deal.[103]

EHFA administrators claimed success. In 1938 Corcoran proudly listed it as one of his three accomplishments in Washington, citing EHFA's "extremely efficient management [which showed] a remarkable record of

*Two months later it was operating in 21 states with 106 utilities and 1,527 dealers of appliances from 139 companies.

actual financial profit on its loans."[104] However, other liberals argued that EHFA had been too businesslike and accomplished too little; conservatives saw it as more government competition which weakened rather than strengthened markets. Both arguments were wrong. By financing appliances in predominantly rural areas and in small cities south of the Ohio and west of the Mississippi where electricity was still a novelty, EHFA deserves applause for improving the standard of living. (Besides Tennessee, Georgia, Mississippi and Alabama, it was strong in rural Minnesota.) Only Los Angeles among major American cities enjoyed EHFA, and we may presume that Ezra Scattergood had something to do with that. EHFA's impact might have been greater had it served utilities that combined electric and gas services earlier in the decade. Also, it was not until 1938 that EHFA began to finance contracts for wiring houses. Its data suggest that without the war EHFA would have continued to play a role in economic development. By June 30, 1938, EHFA served 31 states, 206 utilities, 175 retailers, and 175 manufacturers. On June 30, 1939, 353 utilities, 3,203 retailers and 281 manufacturers collaborated with EHFA. A year later, June 30, 1940, EHFA operations included 553 utilities, 4,855 appliance dealers and 405 appliance manufacturers. Just before it was discharged for the war in 1941, EHFA operated in 37 states with 657 utilities and 5,604 appliance dealers.[105]

In setting a standard for the cost of electricity and the cost of appliances and their financing, EHFA did not have to reach every potential appliance customer. If EHFA's direct influence seems limited, we must remember that private business would have throttled EHFA if it was more competitive. Also, EHFA was administered by businessmen after 1936, and at no time did it ever hope to gain more than a 20 per cent share of the retail appliance market. It influenced by example. As one economic historian has observed, "The trade was aware of EHFA's presence, and it is surely correct to conclude that finance companies hesitated to boost charges while the Authority lurked on the horizon." In fact, as early as 1936 EHFA officers knew that EHFA actually had a "revolutionary effect . . . on the installment financing field." Big firms lowered down-payment requirements and lengthened minimum monthly installments. EHFA compelled a liberalizing of credit for ordinary families in America. As it boasted, "A primary objective of the Authority is to offer adequate installment financing for the purchase of electric and gas equipment to families in the medium and low-income brackets. The success of the Authority in this purpose is indicated by the fact that during the fiscal year 1940, approximately two-thirds of the purchasers using the financing services reported their monthly incomes at less than

$150.00."[106] That was no mean accomplishment. In the darkness of the Great Depression, EHFA comforted many families with low-cost radios, refrigerators and power for all sorts of unexpected conveniences. It also pointed the way to postwar economic growth that benefited ordinary people.

PART FOUR

Texans

If all our states were in the same condition as Texas, I would feel very comfortable because business is exceedingly good down there. The state has enormous resources and a young and ambitious population.

—ROBERT E. WOOD to Brendan Bracken, February 18, 1938, Wood Papers

He was a New Yorker and an Easterner. But one of the first tasks which he set himself was the raising up of the South, economic problem number one, still suffering from the destruction of capital in the War between the States. He was an Easterner and a New Yorker but the second important task he set himself was to bring to the West the electric power, the rural electrification and the water which it needed to grow. And the West and the South will forever love him—and follow where he led.

—LYNDON B. JOHNSON, May 30, 1959, Hyde Park, N.Y., address file, FDRL

11.

Sam Rayburn: Rural America's Champion

TEXAS GREETED THE NEW DEAL with the sort of enthusiasm all good promoters have for a good business deal. Although most Texans held their noses when it came to the social welfare and labor aspects of the New Deal, they adored Franklin Roosevelt's public investment agenda. They also enjoyed the political power that came with being a Democratic state that regularly returned its representatives to the House in a time of a Democratic congressional majority. They recalled that Texans had been well represented in House and Senate committee chairmanships during 1913–19 and savored power once again. With John Nance Garner in the vice-presidency, by the late 1930s Texans controlled at least twelve major committee chairmanships in the House and in the Senate. They were proud that Jesse Jones ran the RFC. Against the outside world a Texan's first loyalty was to a fellow Texan. In the words of reporter Thomas Stokes, "Texans still remain Texan first." But all this Texas power in the New Deal did not portend a love feast. Texans were individualists even before they were Texans, and when the choice was among Texans, it was every man for himself. The New Deal drove a wedge between Texans. All of them gained enormously from Roosevelt's first term, but when Roosevelt began to court labor unions, ignore or refuse to condemn industrial sit-ins, propose a "Court-packing" reform of the Supreme Court and liberalize the Democratic party, some Texans, including Garner and Jones, wanted to take back their party from the Roosevelt-worshipers. They were Southerners who did not take kindly to Harvard-trained lawyers, labor unions or Negroes. But most Texans ignored the liberals and enjoyed state capitalism to the fullest. A new generation challenged its leaders. "The older men are 'through,' " Tommy Corcoran declared with all the certainty of a youthful outsider.

The 1940 Democratic Convention inflicted wounds upon Texans where there had been abrasions. National Democrats rejected John Nance Garner's bid to succeed FDR, conferred a third nomination upon the President, and sent the Vice-President home to exile in Uvalde.

Texans may have loved FDR, but they began to doubt Democrats. Texas Democrats were divided. Even before the Texans reached the Chicago convention, New Deal Texans had embarrassed Garner by denying him the state delegation's chairmanship and its favorite-son vote for the presidency. Jesse Jones blamed Sam Rayburn for this discourtesy when he won more Texas delegate support for the chairmanship than Garner. Rayburn, once Garner's protégé and now the New Dealers' favorite Texan, supposedly wanted Roosevelt's nod for the vice-presidency on a third-term ticket, but Henry Wallace got it instead. Working frenetically behind the scenes for Rayburn was a young New Deal Texas congressman named Lyndon Baines Johnson. Although Tom Corcoran exulted that Roosevelt's Texans triumphed in 1940, he knew enough about politics in the Lone Star state to appreciate that little had been settled. At issue was political power in a rapidly growing state: "Local control of the Texas situation is desperately important." (Years later another Irishman from New England, Tip O'Neill, would generalize it more succinctly: "All politics is local.") Texas New Dealers knew that Democratic support of the Roosevelt administration was often "as thin as the liberalism of a Texas congressman." And nobody knew it better than the man who best represented Texas New Dealers, Sam Rayburn.[1]

Samuel Taliaferro Rayburn, twenty-four days older than FDR, reflected the rural political economy of East Texas. Texas New Dealers such as Rayburn, Wright Patman and Lyndon Johnson came from its cotton fields, piney woods, and arid hills—populistic politicians intent upon improving the lives of the poorest farmers. More conservative Texans such as Garner and Hatton Summers also came from rural Texas, but Garner was a banker and Summers reached different conclusions than New Dealers. Maury Maverick was a New Dealer but, hailing from an urbane elite class of San Antonians, showed more interest in civil liberties than economic development that benefited the underclass. Jesse Jones understood the New Deal better than Maverick, but he disliked much of what he understood. Rayburn, however, knew farming and that was where most of his North Texas constituents could be found. Like Jones and Garner, he was a first-generation Texan hailing from Tennessee. At five his parents brought Rayburn, the eighth of eleven children, to Texas and indoctrinated him in a hard-shell Baptist faith in work and personal integrity. But cotton farming on 40 acres barely sustained the Rayburns, and when Sam was eighteen his father gave his blessings and the family savings ($25) for the young man's education at the normal school at Commerce. Afterwards Sam taught school for three years in rural Texas. However, the teacher's first love was politics and at twenty-four, aided by seven brothers who campaigned for him, Rayburn won election to the state House of Representatives by 316 votes. In Austin, he combined the study of the law with a legislative career, and by 1911 he earned both a law degree he would never use and the speakership of the House. The following year, at thirty, Rayburn won a seat in the United States House of Representatives in the same election that sent Woodrow Wilson to Washington as President of the United States. Early in his Washington career Rayburn demonstrated some independence of his party's leadership, but he was still a Democrat and an organization man. Power in the House called for organization: leadership of the House called for patience and a perseverance that brought seniority. His climb to the speakership of this House would take twenty-eight years. And then he would hold it over twenty years—longer than any other Speaker.[2]

Rayburn was known as a moody man. Portly at five feet six inches, laconic with a nearly expressionless moonface and a balding head that the six-foot-four Lyndon Johnson loved to pat or kiss, Rayburn occasionally revealed a nice smile and a sense of humor; but he was never known as a gregarious person. A shy man, he disliked "swank," usually avoided parties, seldom played the raconteur, and when he tried to tell stories revealed some very dated jokes to small groups of people. He avoided publicity like the plague and seldom spoke in the House. In Texas he was much more relaxed than in Washington. In the House he often took a seat in the back of the chamber, taciturnly observing the proceedings; when his expression showed emotion it was apt to be a scowl, and when he felt crossed by somebody his temper was short and his profanity heavy. His judgments of House members could be harsh. "He's a shit-arse, and I'd rather be a train-robber than a shit-arse," he once said of New York Republican Hamilton Fish, Jr. But seldom did he say much that a newspaper reporter found interesting or significant. In 1930 Rayburn was distinguished in the House only by his longevity. "In politics," he would say, "unless you can wait, you are lost."[3]

Rayburn hated to lose. And he was patient. In his entire career he served on only one committee, the Interstate Commerce Committee, which he intended to chair because his hometown, Bonham, was a "hamlet on a branchline railroad." When the Democrats organized the House in December 1931, Sam became its chair. What he did not say was that he connected railroading with its financing; he retained an unusual interest in Wall Street. He had many friends in the House, but few of them were socially close. John Nance Garner had been his mentor, which meant that Rayburn respected the traditions of the House. Of course, he qualified for membership in Garner's "Bureau of Education." He liked bourbon and branch water, knew how to "strike a blow for liberty," played cards for the fun of it, and spoke worshipfully of Robert E. Lee and his father's service in the Confederacy (three pictures of Lee adorned his office walls). Sometimes he went fishing in Maryland with other congressmen, the rule being that no political talk was allowed: "Why'n hell don't you stay in Washington if you want to talk that way?" he would ask an offender. He smoked about a pack of cigarettes a day, maybe two in times of stress. He had been married briefly in 1924 to Metze Jones, sister of fellow Texas Congressman Marvin Jones, but it did not take (he was forty-two and she was twenty-seven and it was said that she objected to his social drinking); it was dissolved within months. He thereafter remained a bachelor devoted to unmarried sisters who kept his house in Bonham.

According to a Texan who was acquainted with him since about 1910, the most important thing to know about Rayburn was that he was sentimental and expected loyalty. A story Rayburn probably told about himself described how as a young teacher with no money in a small town and in need of a place to sleep, he had been refused by large rooming houses; but a man who ran a small shop offered him a room. Years later he returned to that town as the leader of the U.S. House of Representatives to a great reception and invitations from bankers and other leading citizens to stay with them; but Sam chose to remain with the old man who had taken him in when he had been poor and friendless. Sam was a loyal Democrat too. One of his favorite sayings was "You can't forget the rock from which you are hewn."[4]

Rayburn denied that he was a member of a "lower House" of Congress; he called it the "popular branch" of government. He never considered a run for the Senate; he wanted to be Speaker of the House. Sometimes in talking with colleagues his eyes would take on a faraway look and he would say, "Now if I can get to be Speaker of the National House. . . ."[5] His name for the institution revealed a lot about his politics. He saw national economics with the eyes of someone who had worked the cotton fields of East Texas. He stayed with the Interstate Commerce Committee because every cotton farmer believed that railroads charged exorbitant rates to haul their cotton and that railroad finances were too closely tied to venal investment bankers in Wall Street. Early in his career he had crossed swords with Woodrow Wilson and the House Democratic leadership over railroad finance and tariff legislation. Although he lost these battles, it did not take the populist out of him. He bided his time through the 1920s and tended to his district. He had learned that to get along one had to go along—an aphorism often attributed to him. He respected individualism and democracy. He had opposed Woodrow Wilson on the draft in 1917, vowing to vote against it even if 90 per cent of his district supported it; when he capitulated and voted for it, he explained that "ninety-five per cent of my people favor it."[6] Loyalty, democracy and individualism: These principles were not at odds with one other. He managed John Nance Garner's 1932 run for the presidency, but when Roosevelt became President, Rayburn became one of the most loyal of the President's congressional followers, in part because he appreciated FDR's empathy with Southern agrarianism.

Few Southerners respected the young New Deal lawyers, but Rayburn, to his surprise, did. In turn, they valued Rayburn's economic populism and political caution. Neither side knew much about the other when Frankfurter, Corcoran, Landis and Cohen responded to Rayburn's plea for help in improving a weak "Truth-in-Securities bill" proposed by the administration. The lawyers wrote one, and Rayburn's assistant molded their version into acceptable legislative shape. Then the Texan held a hearing in which the estimable John Foster Dulles led a battery of highly reputable Wall Street attorneys to challenge it. The lawyers had assumed that Rayburn knew little about securities, but they were ignorant of his history: he had led the fight during the Wilson years to bring railroad securities and bonds under the jurisdiction of the Interstate Commerce Commission. Although he knew very little about the bill's particulars, he assured Landis that he would do "whatever job I thought was right to do." Knowing that Dulles was there only because Wall Street opposed it, Rayburn launched negotiations with the attorneys by emitting a string of obscenities intended to convey his contempt for Wall Street power. A month of hearings passed with Ben Cohen ever present at his side; then, in a six-hour meeting, Rayburn got unanimous approval from his committee. It happened so quickly that Rayburn confessed he did not know whether it was "because it was so damned good or so damned incomprehensible." Then he maneuvered it through conference with the Senate by getting prior consideration of the House bill, thereby demonstrating an exceptional mastery of men and procedure.[7]

He came from a part of the country that long had held grievances against the Northeast. Yet that unexpectedly made him an eager collaborator with the young Harvard lawyers. He sought alliances and, although he was a Southerner and they were Yankees, they were all outsiders where Wall Street was concerned. When he found that one of the more junior New Deal lawyers—James Rowe—was from Montana, he made it a point to tell him "that there is not a hell of a lot of difference between Texans and Montanans." Both were sparsely settled and colonized by New York capital. But a Texan was still something special, a leader among Southern and Western Democrats. "Jim," he would proclaim during a breakfast chat he had at his apartment at the Anchorage, an apartment house slightly above DuPont Circle, where he hosted breakfasts or dinners in his two rooms for young lawyers or congressmen, "you know, your state reminds me a great deal of Texas. I think in about another generation you will be as civilized as we are."[8]

Roosevelt's eagerness to fight Wall Street and reduce Texas's colonial dependency upon the money power won Rayburn's admiration. In the 1934 fight for the Fletcher-Rayburn stock exchange bill, Rayburn encountered what he called "the most vicious and persistent lobby that any of us have ever known in Washington." Wall Street, in a major assault upon the New Deal, bombarded congressmen with bogus constituent letters to create an illusion of massive public opposition. Yet Congress retained key portions of Cohen's draft and brought the Securities and Exchange Commission into being; Landis lauded Rayburn as a "strong man." Douglas, Corcoran and Cohen fondly dubbed the SEC the "Rayburn Commission."[9]

But the fight over the SEC was mild compared to the fray that erupted in 1935 over the public utilities holding companies bill. Utility executives, investment bankers and bar association officials attacked the measure with a vehemence that had not been seen before. Although Wendell Willkie of Commonwealth and Southern (C & S) demanded that Congress distinguish between the honest holding company and its less scrupulous brethren, Rayburn dismissed the distinction because there was "no realistic and far-sighted way to handle the relation of these private empires to the people other than by their ultimate elimination." Because Wall Street had discovered that Cohen could adroitly draft legislation unlikely to be overturned by any court, the fight against Rayburn in Congress took on an air of desperation. Wall Street was determined to keep the holding companies bill off the books, and Rayburn was determined to use the big New Deal majority gained in the 1934 elections. However, Rayburn lost control of his committee when two conservative Democrats joined forces with Republicans to threaten the key "death sentence" provision. A sectional battle erupted with conservative Southerners allying with Easterners to decisively beat down the House's holding company bill. Conceding that he had lost control of the House, Rayburn, with Garner's aid, forged an alliance with Senators Burton K. Wheeler of Montana and Alben Barkley of Kentucky and, after a fight of several months, prevailed.[10]

Roosevelt and Corcoran did not forget the House Democrats who faced down the enormous onslaught of utility-lobbying on the holding company bill and courageously supported the death sentence; neither did the utility companies forget them. Outside money flooded New Dealer districts as the utilities sought to defeat them in 1936. Even Rayburn confronted a candidate running on the slogan "Sam's been there long enough." Just because he had been there a quarter century was no reason to force the fifty-five-year-old Rayburn into retirement before he had attained the acme of his ambition: the speakership.

Following the 1936 election Rayburn took a decisive step toward the speakership. Garner's successor, Henry T. Rainey of Illinois, died in 1934 and, despite Garner's influence in behalf of Bureau of Education reliables Rayburn and John McDuffie of Alabama, Joseph W. Byrns of Tennessee won the speakership and William Bankhead of Alabama became heir apparent. But the setback brought Rayburn some national attention, and in Washington it was whispered that "the president calls him 'Sam.'" Then, in the last days of the 74th Congress, Byrns died. Bankhead succeeded to the speakership, in spite of illness that had kept him from carrying out the majority leader's duties. His aide had been John J. O'Connor of New York City, and now O'Connor loomed as the front-runner for the Democratic leadership. However, despite the fact that O'Connor's brother, Basil O'Connor, was Roosevelt's former law partner and that about half the House Democrats favored O'Connor, the President signaled that he wanted the loyal Rayburn in the job because FDR had not forgotten that as Chairman of the House Rules Committee O'Connor had refused to report a rule on the death sentence provision of the utility holding company bill. At a crucial caucus vote of Pennsylvania House Democrats in December 1936, Rayburn won, 18 to 6, the vote binding House members to the unit rule. Garner returned from Texas unexpectedly early and immediately met with Rayburn and told waiting reporters, "I am for Sam Rayburn 200 per cent." Observers guessed that half of that endorsement spoke for FDR.[11]

When an Associated Press reporter interpreted the close Garner-Rayburn relationship as one that would not interfere with Rayburn's loyalty to Roosevelt, he received a wire from Rayburn congratulating him on his ability to read between the lines. The Bureau of Education was now his. It included John McCormack of Massachusetts and the Ways and Means Committee, the conservative but loyal Eugene Cox of Georgia and Fred Vinson of Kentucky—the "smartest national politician I have ever known"—high praise indeed from Rayburn. Although Rayburn remained on cordial terms with Garner and Jesse Jones, a gap between them was opening. It would test Rayburn's old loyalties.[12]

Rayburn prided himself on his liberalism, but on labor issues he tended, like most Texans, to be conservative. However, he was proud of his role in the New Deal's credit revolution. And when it came to public power, Rayburn's populism was evident. Next to Morris Llewellyn Cooke, no other man more deserved the designation "father of REA." As a sentimental man he was proudest of his sponsorship of the Rural

Electrification Act of 1936—which promised to bring electricity to farms throughout the South and the Midwest, the sections with the least rural electrification. He fervently believed that electricity would take much of the hardship out of living and working on the farm. "I want my people out of the dark," he frequently declared. "Can you imagine what [electricity] will mean to a farm wife to have a pump in the well and lights in the house?" REA, he predicted, would "make the farmer and his wife and family believe and know that they are no longer the forgotten people, but make them know that they are remembered as part of—yea, they are the bulwark of the Government." Later he boasted that REA brought electricity to 9,032 farms in his district alone. When utility companies branded REA as unfair government competition that amounted to socialism and insisted that they would bring electricity to the farms of Texas, Rayburn scoffingly retorted, "When free enterprise had the opportunity to electrify farm homes—after fifty years, they had electrified three percent." He would bring electricity to the other 97 per cent.[13]

"Southerners were fiercely devoted to rural electrification," writes the historian of the REA. "Living in preindustrial conditions, but surrounded with the resources to modernize their life [sic], southerners saw federal intervention as the answer. They knew, too, that since their region had such a high proportion of small, poor farms, power companies would not enter the rural market and public action was their only hope." Only a few well-to-do Southern farmers could afford electricity. Power companies charged farmers exorbitant rates for the service, insisting that lines cost them up to $2,000 a mile to service a few customers. Of course a farmer's home had to be wired before he even began to buy appliances and laborsaving devices. Little wonder then that individualistic farmers joined electric cooperatives that allowed them to buy service collectively. Even then, only fifty cooperatives existed in 1935 and they were mostly in the Midwest.[14]

Sam Rayburn and Morris Llewellyn Cooke fought for rural electrification, but in a very real sense, however, George Norris and TVA were its true originators. "The greatest development yet undertaken by the TVA," Mississippi's John Rankin proclaimed, "is that of rural electrification. We expect to light every home in that section of the country and to give the farmers electric lights and power." In early 1934 Cooke proposed a plan for rural electrification of all American farms via cooperatives and low-cost government financing along the lines of EHFA. Importantly, Cooke did not rule out participation by private utilities. The following year, Roosevelt created the REA via an executive order and put Cooke in charge of it. Roosevelt intended it to be both a relief agency and a lending agency, but the first decision Cooke made was to make it an agency of electric development. A hundred million dollars was allotted to the emergency agency, which then would decide who would get it. When Cooke asked the utilities for a plan to bring about rural electrification, they disappointed him by proposing to electrify about a quarter million farms at a cost in excess of REA's budget. Casting for other means of attaining his goal, he turned to farm cooperatives. Across the Midwest, led by Murray Lincoln's Ohio Farm Bureau effort, farmers organized cooperatives to petition REA for loans to bring about rural electrification. REA moved too slowly for them. It spent only $9 million on fifty-five projects, hardly more than an exploratory operation. Nevertheless, popular demand would move REA along.[15]

When Corcoran and Cooke wrote a bill to expand REA and give it additional duties, Rayburn insisted upon shepherding it through the House. George Norris took charge of it in the Senate. Although they both sought increased federal funds for rural electrification, they disagreed over whether private utilities ought to be allowed to participate, Rayburn favoring a conservative policy of nonexclusion. They worked out a compromise whereby utilities could participate, but preference for loans would be given to cooperatives. Congress gave REA a life of ten years and RFC funding of $50 million a year for the first two years and $40 million for each year thereafter.[16]

REA put the New Dealers in the business of raising rural standards of living. Modeling itself on the Alcorn, Mississippi, cooperative of the TVA and the EHFA, REA made itself a lending agency that would bring power to the American farm. A provision in the Norris-Rayburn Act of 1936 stipulated that REA allocations would be apportioned among the states annually by the number of *unelectrified* farms—thereby favoring Southern and Midwestern states with the fewest electrified farms. As Cooke explained to the President, "hereafter we will not loan simply on 'miles of line' but on the percentage of farms connected in a given area"—the areas without favored over those with power.[17]

With REA, moreover, the New Deal took another step away from the economy of scarcity that had marked NRA and AAA. Advocates of stabilized prices were not yet in retreat, but planned economic expansion emerged as a New Deal theme. Under Cooke REA neither agitated against nor sought utility cooperation. Casting about for a deputy administrator, Cooke hit upon John M. Carmody, former chairman of the NRA's Bituminous Coal Labor Board. Early in 1937 Cooke resigned from REA's leadership and Carmody became the Joshua who would lead American farmers into the promised land of electrification. Carmody understood REA's mission as a multiplier for economic growth. As he later wrote,

Idle people were given employment. Demand for poles put men to work in forests and preparation plants; copper and aluminum rolling mills went to work again; one transformer factory, long closed, devoted full time to REA orders, others part time. It meant thousands of carloads of transportation on many railroads. A new demand was created for radios and all manner of electric appliances. All of this began in 1937 and expanded rapidly while I was Administrator.[18]

At the time Carmody took charge of REA it had been described as "one of the most complete failures among all the Roosevelt Administration's undertakings." Nevertheless, Carmody, in his words, "settled the issues there and then, threw the hatchet out the window and really began to build lines instead of talk and argue." Importantly, he signaled a shift away from loans for private utilities that promoted little expansion to cooperatives eager to build rural lines. To do this he had to overcome two Cooke aides, engineer friends from Philadelphia, who believed "We cannot go on the theory of taking electricity to every farmer that wants it—obviously not." Carmody viewed them as obstacles. They were "completely devoid of imagination, faith in the future, or confidence in the integrity of farm people." He didn't change personnel, but he did change the organization's direction.

As with EHFA, the FHA and the Commodity Credit Corporation, Jesse Jones in RFC acted as the REA's banker. So great was the demand for REA loans and so pleased with Carmody's administration was Jones that more RFC millions were made available for REA loans. "A husky two-fisted Irishman," Carmody had had a varied business career in Elmira, New York; West Virginia; Cleveland; Cuba; Russia and New York City in the coal and iron industries before his expertise as a labor relations man attracted Harry Hopkins's attention and earned him an invitation to work in the Civil Works Administration. He was serving on the National Labor Relations Board when Cooke picked him as his successor. A native Pennsylvanian, Carmody's pugnacity often reminded New Dealers of Hugh Johnson. A committed public power man, Carmody had considerable staying power in the New Deal no matter how many people he occasionally offended with his brusque manners. Most importantly, he got things done. It was not long before he began deluging Southerners such as Senator Hugo L. Black with announcements that REA had signed a loan contract to build 359 miles of lines for customers in five counties for the South Alabama Electric Membership Corporation, a loan to the city of Athens, Alabama, for constructing 65.6 miles of distribution lines, and similar loans to other county cooperatives. In Carmody's native Bradford and Tioga counties in Pennsylvania, REA's chief obtained quick results from its loans: Three farms attached their dairy herds to milking machines and expanded their poultry businesses through a local cooperative that marketed their eggs. One farmer boasted how he made $20 more a month on poultry alone.[19]

Through its preference for loans to cooperatives, REA stimulated numerous grass roots movements throughout rural America. Yet REA's early indifference to cooperatives retarded electrification in places like Otter Tail County, Minnesota. In the fall of 1935 sixty-five farmers in this western Minnesota farm county met with the state commissioner of agriculture to organize a cooperative and elect a leader, fifty-one-year-old Albert R. Knutson, an energetic electricity enthusiast. Knutson had been pushing to no avail for electricity for Otter Tail County farmers since 1929; by the end of 1935 the Lake Region Co-op Electrical Association began to sell stock at $2 a share. In April the cooperative made the first of three applications for a loan and each time REA turned it down either because its request was too large or not large enough or that the rates charged by a local utility where the farmers would buy their electricity were too high. When Carmody took over REA in early 1937 the cooperative was frustrated but still determined. Knutson worked with Senator Hendrik Shipstead to bring Otter Tail's case to the attention of REA as the co-op's membership passed 1,300. On July 13, 1937, REA announced that it would loan Otter Tail farmers $125,000 to bring in electricity. Over the winter, routes were designated and new members were recruited. It surprised many farmers that for only an initial membership fee of $5 they could have electricity. In March the first electric meter was installed. Washington loaned the cooperative another $252,000—$10,000 for local financing of wiring and plumbing of houses. By the end of 1938 Otter Tail county had 226 miles of wires and 240 electrified farms where 750 people lived. An additional loan of $400,000 allowed the co-op to expand into adjacent counties. Electrification proceeded apace in rural western Minnesota, and Albert Knutson became a full-time project superintendent. "No New Deal program was more popular with farmers than the REA," Otter Tail County's historian has declared, "and nowhere was electricity more important than in a dairying country." Years later residents recalled that electricity had transformed them into producers of plenty: as one farmer put it, "I'd say that there would be no surplus of milk today if there was no electricity on the farm." Inside the farmhouses families put away their kerosene lamps: "Lights were the biggest change." Another farm wife later recalled, "I didn't have to carry water, any more. I used to have to carry all the water for washing clothes and I'd heat it in the boiler on the cookstove." Some things did not change: Otter Tail County continued to vote Republican.[20]

Most of REA's successes were not recorded in such personal terms.

Washington usually quantified its impact upon rural America. Thus, we know that in 1935 only 1.7 per cent of Louisiana farms enjoyed electric power and by 1939 REA had financed eleven projects that ran 2,700 miles of lines to over 9,000 farms, over three times the number of farms with electricity as four years before. In Montana REA financed construction of 756 miles of lines to give 2,463 farm families electricity. Only one in nine Colorado farms had power in 1935; thanks to REA loans to local cooperatives, one in four had it by 1940.

Historians usually note such triumphs with the comment that "Private firms had fought this change all the way." Indeed, we have John Carmody's word that "Private utility lobbies fought rural-electric cooperatives bitterly." Arkansas Power and Light Company, led by Harvey Couch, who had once been a director of the Reconstruction Finance Corporation and who ran his Arkansas businesses like a feudal lord, opposed REA projects in the state. While Carmody tested the demand for electricity in rural Arkansas, the University of Arkansas encouraged farmers to organize cooperatives. Couch tried to persuade REA to finance the building of company lines, but Carmody would not hear of it. When the Arkansas Public Service Commission guaranteed rates lower than those charged by Couch's utility, Carmody allotted $2 million for hundreds of miles of distribution lines that would carry power to be sold at wholesale rates that compelled low retail rates from the company.

The Iowa situation was similar. There the utilities charged such high rates that few farmers could afford electricity. Also, Carmody discovered that the Iowa Farm Bureau was "in cahoots" with the companies to discourage cooperatives. He decided to build REA's own generating plant—which evoked a storm of protest from Iowa politicians; the outcry subsided when farmers and county agents cheered the news. REA constructed two generating plants in Iowa for distribution co-ops, and on one of them was inscribed the motto "OWNED BY THOSE IT SERVES." Considering that REA usually stimulated growth by influencing competitive private utilities to lower rates and profit through increased users and usage, it surprised Carmody when private enterprise fought the co-ops, and he wondered, "Is there no way of persuading businessmen and professional men that these cooperative enterprises are creating new wealth that spreads throughout the community?"

Across the Mississippi in Illinois, the Farm Bureau's Earl Smith, "a power in Illinois," insisted upon high-cost private power and opposed farm cooperatives. His farm already was blessed with 60-foot poles painted green that carried his electricity above the trees. "Any wonder Earl could see the private power point of view and express it forcefully?"

Carmody reflected. But Illinois farmers organized and over Earl Smith's protests put in a generating plant a short distance from his green poles.

Down in Alabama the Cherokee County Electric Membership Corporation ran into classic utility intransigence. In early 1937 it asked the Alabama Power Company to provide service for all the county in return for which the cooperative would secure all right-of-way easements to enable the company to build lines without interruption and at a low price; the power company refused. The cooperative then turned to the REA and requested funds to construct its own lines. The farmers would get their power from TVA over some 30 miles of transmission line. So Alabama Power began to build "spite lines" in areas the cooperative intended to serve. The cooperative then offered to buy the company's 40 miles of lines; the company rebuffed that offer too, and the cooperative served notice that it would build its own parallel lines in competition for customers. In desperation Alabama Power sought an injunction against the cooperative to prevent it from wiring the entire county and endangering its own investment of $91,000. A federal court threw out the petition, and the cooperative proceeded to sign up hundreds of customers.

Under Carmody REA preached a stubborn faith in democratically organized and operated cooperatives. Yet the REA people were tough-minded realists and recognized that not all of their cooperatives were democratic. A case in point was "Georgia 51 Newton," a relatively small project that virtually became the private property of C. V. Ellington, its president, manager and recipient of a $100,000 REA loan which benefited him without any guarantee that cooperating farmers would repay it. An REA administrator, Boyd Fisher, decided that Georgia 51's farmers required his special attention—but it was not easy to convince them that REA offered something special. For one thing, a group of farmers who originally had signed up for the project went over to the Georgia Power Company. Faced with either appropriating more money for additional territory or conceding that Georgia 51 was a loss, REA sent a supervisor to persuade Ellington's customers "that we had really made the loan for them" and that they should run the project. Additionally, some farmers objected to paying a $5 membership fee for power they already enjoyed courtesy of Ellington. Nevertheless, REA persisted and eventually "the consumers came together" and an REA-backed slate of directors voted out the Ellington crowd. By early 1940 Georgia 51 was a financial success. Not only was it self-supporting; it had repaid the REA loan, had a bank balance of a couple of thousand dollars, made a loan to its host city, Covington, enjoyed a customer density among the highest in the region, and had repaid REA $300 for the supervisor's salary and expenses. All of this, Boyd Fisher was certain, was "a tribute to what farmer cooperative management can do when the members are given a proper form of constitution and bylaws and are instructed as to their rights and duties."

Giving proper instruction in every aspect of the rural electrification movement was the REA's monthly publication, *Rural Electrification News*. The *News* carried many messages concerning the uses of electricity on the farm and in the home, stressing that the more people who subscribed to power and used convenience appliances, the more affordable electricity was for everyone. Thus, a University of Illinois extension specialist in dairy husbandry described how "electro-farmers" saved money in dairying by grinding grains for cows, pumping the enormous amounts of water cows needed to consume each day, running the milking machines, cooling the milk with refrigeration, and heating water for washing and rinsing dairy equipment. Electric brooders became the rage on Midwestern farms. Emma Waltz of the North Central Electric Cooperative in Attica, Ohio, reported how she used her brooder "for keeping the pigs warm and contented" and in Indiana seventy-seven electric brooders used power from the Kosciusko Rural Membership Corporation to increase production of eggs. Another article with photographs told of how young farm women improved farm living and relieved household drudgery through the use of electric irons and electric roasters. A member of the Utilization Department of the Pioneer Rural Electric Cooperative of Piqua, Ohio, reported that he increased sales of electric ranges through "kitchen parties" in which an electric range company contributed its product, the cooperative contributed food and a housewife contributed her kitchen for a demonstration of meals to be cooked on a range. REA Oklahomans used electricity for drilling for oil. REA *News* also boasted of instances of quick restoration of service following a Minnesota tornado or how a cooperative came to the rescue of Wayne City when the Central Illinois Public Service Company's generating plant broke down.[21]

After twenty-eight months of Carmody's leadership, President Roosevelt surprised him by announcing in May 1939 that the independent agency would be subsumed under the Department of Agriculture—another triumph of bureaucratic imperialism for Henry Wallace. An angry John Carmody resigned rather than see REA "get thrashed around by people who know nothing of the history of the enterprise and who see in it only something with which to exploit or to enhance their own official and personal prestige." He had doubled the number of farms with electricity during his tenure, building 226,000 miles of lines and twenty-six generating plants across forty-four states, nearly 90 per cent of the REA loans going to farmers' cooperatives. Roosevelt, under pressure from Senator George W. Norris and not wanting Carmody's departure from the federal government, asked him to assume leadership of the new Federal Works Agency, a consolidation of the Works Projects Administration, the United States Housing Authority, the Public Roads Administration, and the Public Buildings Administration; Carmody would make it the principal builder of America's infrastructure for defense in the coming years. Although REA became embroiled in intramural political warfare within Agriculture over farm, business and public power interests, it never bogged down until electricity reached almost every farm in America. It was a tribute to the principles of cooperative independence inculcated by Carmody, its championing in Congress by Sam Rayburn, George Norris and others, and the exigency of war that came with the 1940s.[22]

12.

Lyndon Baines Johnson: Politics and Projects

AT THE HEIGHT of the New Deal the darling of New York and Washington liberals in the House of Representatives was Maury Maverick of San Antonio, Texas. A passionate civil libertarian from Texas aristocracy, Maverick got an inordinate amount of publicity in the Eastern press for a freshman congressman. He adored newspapermen, demanding their attention by buttonholing reporters with the promise of an entertaining story for their attention. "Did I hear you were a newspaperman?" he might ask an acquaintance. "I am a propagandist. . . ."[1] And he was. Nationally syndicated columnists such as Robert Allen and Drew Pearson and Rodney Dutcher printed his stories. First elected in 1934, he eschewed party loyalty, sometimes asserting that not even FDR moved quickly enough for him. Built somewhat like the short and chunky Fiorello H. La Guardia, the former Congressman from New York's East Harlem who also endeared himself to reporters and won the New York City mayoralty in 1933, Maverick sometimes was called "the Texas La Guardia." He liked to shoot from the hip when he spoke, which made him quotable. "I agree with Father Coughlin in almost everything but his manners," he once told the press. "I favor social justice, but I don't like social bad manners."[2] He was the only Southerner in the House of Representatives to vote for the Gavigan antilynching bill of 1937. The South, he wrote, had to take on a "national vision." It had to free itself of colonial subjugation and prevent its natural and human resources from being drained by a rapacious Northern capitalism while it was "robbed by cotton speculators, utilities, big-town and small-town money lenders." Southerners, Maverick declared, should not oppose federal labor laws while they hypocritically accepted federal dollars for development.[3]

He was never an ordinary Texan or congressman. In 1935 Sam Rayburn and Tom Corcoran took the freshman to the White House to meet Roosevelt and charm the President. On June 11, 1936, in the midst of his primary fight for re-election, Maury Maverick brought Franklin Roosevelt to San Antonio, where the President told a crowd estimated at 75,000 that "on every occasion I have seen him for the past two years I have been promising my good friend Maury Maverick to come to San Antonio." It was heady stuff for the peppery Texan. He told a San Antonio audience, "Frankie and me are pals and out in front of the Alamo we had our picture taken. . . ."[4] In the words of a biographer, "he now considered himself a national figure." He launched a national speaking tour and eagerly accepted offers to speak as far away as Massachusetts and Minnesota. In 1937 he staunchly defended the White House plan for reform of the federal judiciary, more popularly known as packing the Supreme Court. He championed the President's executive reorganization plan. In the Texas delegation only Maverick, Sam Rayburn and Lyndon Johnson supported the wages and hours bill. In San Antonio these measures cost him political friends. It was said that Maury had "gone national" and had abandoned the Alamo. He blithely ignored constituent letters and telegrams assailing his support of Court-packing and unions. In a town that treasured its cheap labor, Maverick's prounionism and support of the minimum wage was anathema. In 1938 the Democratic machine put up a well-connected Paul Kilday against Maverick. Maverick was desperate to show how his friendships in Washington had brought federal projects to San Antonio. An incumbent should not have had any trouble in the Democratic primary, but Maverick had little on his side but truth and Franklin Roosevelt. With his wealthy erstwhile friends avoiding him, Maverick raised little local campaign money and solicited $10,000 from Michael Straight of the *New Republic*. He pleaded that he could still win in Bexar County if Roosevelt would speak in San Antonio of "my many virtues, my pious character—and also how much [federal] dough I got for San Antonio." So Roosevelt came to San Antonio again to speak for his "friend" and to announce a $3,588,000 federal grant for slum clearance in the Hispanic neighborhoods. Still, Maverick lost to Kilday by 493 votes out of over 49,000—a stunning reversal of his 7,000-vote plurality two years before.[5] In the words of a pro-New Deal Austin newspaper, "Maverick was ostentatious, with an eye to the headlines, addicted to impulsive and frequently embarrassing comments with a peculiar knack for drawing the fire not only of New Deal opposition, but on occasion from some of its friends."[6]

The lessons of Maury Maverick's political career were not lost upon Lyndon Baines Johnson. The young Congressman from the Tenth District of Texas, a rural district adjoining Maverick's Twentieth, had first-hand knowledge of Maverick's career in the House. When Maverick first ran for Congress in 1934, he borrowed Johnson from Congressman Richard M. Kleberg, who lacked opposition in his primary. Known to be a very savvy House secretary, Johnson assumed a major role in Maverick's campaign, allegedly buying Mexican votes on San Antonio's west side for Maverick. Following Maverick's arrival in the House, Johnson instructed Maverick's secretary, Malcolm Bardwell, on how to organize a congressman's office, answered Maverick's queries on how to interpret proposed legislation, and saw to it that Maury's brother, Albert, got a choice patronage job in Kleberg's district. Later Maverick would inscribe a photograph of himself, "To Lyndon Johnson, who got me started."[7]

Johnson, who won his own House seat in 1937 when he was only twenty-eight, viewed Maverick as someone who violated all that was common sense about Texas and House politics. Johnson made himself a staunch New Dealer, and what marked a New Dealer in his eyes was not only a willingness to use the resources of the federal government to improve the standard of living of all Americans but to recognize that its political accomplishment required a certain deference to senior lawmakers. In the House Johnson, unlike Maverick, kept his silence. He let his voting record identify him as a New Dealer. Meanwhile, Maverick's career confirmed for Johnson that what wowed New York and Washington liberals guaranteed a brief political career in Texas. It was no sin to be a New Dealer in Texas if one understood that it entailed following the program and strategy of a Sam Rayburn.

He rammed that point home hard when, in 1939, White House counsel Jim Rowe questioned his friend's politics: Johnson explained, "You know, look where your old friend and my old friend Maury Maverick is, he's not here. The first problem we've got is to get re-elected. I don't want to go that way." Another time when Rowe pressed Johnson to be more visibly liberal, Johnson retorted, "Now look, don't forget our friend Maury. I can go so far in Texas. Maury forgot that and he is not here." Reflecting on these words from the vantage point of decades of subsequent political activity, Rowe mused, "You can be a Wright Patman or a Sam Rayburn or Lyndon Johnson as a congressman, but you can't get too far out of line down there." Johnson "lived to a certain extent by the dictum that the first duty of a politician is to stay in office." A politician either lived by the expectations of his constitutents and the institution in which he served or he ultimately faced failure and defeat. "The fellows who try it the other way—" Johnson believed, "the Mavericks, Marcantonios, etc.—do not last long." Johnson intended to survive and thrive. He reflected the hard-boiled realism, craftiness and guile, blended with an almost maudlin idealism, typical of many New Dealers and downright endearing in the 1930s. Corcoran, who also epitomized the idealism and realism of a New Dealer in his own personality, said of Johnson in 1940: he "has taken over all the [New Deal] strength Maury Maverick once had on a much more intelligent plane."

Texas politicians kept clear of labor liberals. One day Johnson learned that the *New Republic* intended to profile him along with other New Deal congressmen. Knowing the magazine's close identification with New York liberalism and knowing that Texans believed in guilt by association, Johnson was filled with consternation. He could not prevent the journal from writing what it pleased, but he decided to neutralize that association by having a union leader assail him. So Johnson called Rowe's wife, who worked for the International Labor Organization in Washington, and pleaded, "Lib, you must have some friend in the labor movement. Can't you call him and have him denounce me? [If] they put out that special supplement that I am a liberal hero up here, I'll get killed. You've got to find somebody to denounce me!"

Johnson, as Rowe put it, "quite early seemed to know where the buttons for power were."[8] He had an instinct for politics that amounted to an obsession. It came naturally. His father, Sam Ealy Johnson, Jr., had served in the Texas House of Representatives, where he had met Lyndon's mother, Rebekah Baines, a young reporter covering Austin politics because her father too had served in the Texas House. Both parents traced their Texas roots back to the 1840s and 1850s and their Southern origins back to Tennessee, Kentucky and Georgia. But right after they were married Sam abandoned his political career for farming on Johnson family land along the Pedernales River in the hill country west of Austin. It was hard country, sometimes arid and sometimes flooded when excessive rains turned the Pedernales into a rampaging stream. Lyndon was born, August 27, 1908, on a farm near Stonewall, and when he was five the family moved to Johnson City, where he received his schooling. That was important to a college-educated mother with aspirations to gentility and intellectuality. His father speculated in land and, caught between the vagaries of climate and markets, found scant success. Debt followed Sam Johnson through much of his adult life. He tried politics again in 1917, winning a special election for the Texas House of Representatives and retaining his seat until debts and poor health again compelled his retirement in 1924. Like Sam Rayburn, Lyndon Johnson knew mostly hardship and failure and both drew the moral that state and federal governments ought to help those who farmed to help themselves. Politics should be a profession in service to humanity. However, Lyndon Johnson may have drawn another moral—that decency alone was not enough and that the extent of one's service to the community depended upon individual success in political and economic markets.[9]

As with Rayburn, education figured prominently in Lyndon Johnson's youth. After putting off college in favor of a brief adventure in California, Johnson began his political education at Southwest Texas State Teachers

College at San Marcos. He was not an academic star; but then he probably never sought such stardom. He gave more time to the school's debate team, newspaper and yearbook. Also, he used his father's political connections to cultivate a warm friendship with the college's president, Cecil Evans. Eager to experience the world beyond the academy, he got a leave from his studies and his first job in Cotulla, teaching seventh and eighth grades in an all-Hispanic school. His first constituents were the Hispanics of South Texas that Anglos like Johnson were supposed to despise; he drove himself relentlessly to give them the best education they would ever know. Already he exhibited the quality of extending love to people at the lowest level and attracting their loyalty ever after. After nine months, in which he made himself a hero to the downtrodden of Cotulla by his unstinting determination to raise them up via an education, he returned to San Marcos to finish his degree, to resume his former extracurricular activities and to engage in some campus politics. In education and in politics his success was in part due to his organizational leadership and his devotion to individuals who gave their reciprocal loyalty. Although he could be politically devious and early on displayed a capacity for exaggerating his own importance, most acquaintances saw him as a very warm and gregarious person. He was generous with affection and favors, expecting only the same in return. Importantly, at least one biographer assures us that "these relationships were not hypocritical."[10]

In 1930 Johnson took his bachelor's degree in education into depression America. His debate skills earned him a job at Sam Houston High School in Houston and there his leadership abilities earned him a raise, another contract and the personal lifelong political fealty of two student debaters. That summer his obsession with politics involved him in a campaign for a candidate for the state Senate. Zealously organizing two counties, Johnson so impressed the victorious state senator that he recommended Johnson to the newly elected Congressman Richard Kleberg who sought a congressional secretary.

Johnson arrived in Washington on December 7, 1931, the first day in session for the momentous Seventy-second Congress. He quickly showed powerful talents for observing, questioning, flattering and an almost limitless chutzpah. Kleberg, one of the wealthy owners of the immense King Ranch, had a diffident attitude toward a congressman's multitudinous roles. Johnson eagerly filled what might have been a service void for Kleberg's constituents in Texas's Fourteenth District while making important contacts with other congressmen through their secretaries. He ran a model congressional office, one principally concerned with tying new governmental agencies to district grass roots through service. Little wonder then that Maverick sought out Johnson. Many people sought out young Johnson when he impressed them with his extraordinary insight into the workings of government.

Six-foot-four-inches tall, lean but deceptively strong, Lyndon Johnson possessed inordinate ambition. In 1935, when Congress created the Works Progress Administration (WPA) and from that appropriation Roosevelt mandated the National Youth Administration (NYA) under a liberal Alabamian, Aubrey Williams, Johnson obtained the NYA state directorship for Texas through a budding friendship with Sam Rayburn and left Kleberg in the hands of his younger brother, Sam Houston Johnson. Heading back to Texas to coordinate WPA's youth employment, Johnson never doubted that his return to Washington would be imminent and as a congressman himself. For the time being he was in the business of fashioning public works and distributing patronage, two vital parts of any accomplished politician's career. It taught him the importance of works projects in politics. In Austin Johnson encountered Alvin Wirtz, a lawyer and politically well-connected former state senator, and made him chairman of NYA's State Advisory Committee, a job that made Wirtz Johnson's personal political consultant. Tireless as usual, Johnson planned schoolyard construction and roadside parks projects totaling over a million dollars and employing about 15,000 youths throughout Texas, thereby building a mini-bureaucracy into a field operation with a budget of $133,000. In every county of Texas a young man knew that he owed his job to Lyndon Johnson. However, unusual for a Texas politician, Johnson spread the benefits of the federal largesse across the color line. Quietly he saw to it that black students received more than their usual share of jobs, that black college students got scholarship aid, and that Texas NYA had a nominal black advisory board. But he trumpeted this liberalism selectively in Washington, not Austin.

On February 23, 1937, Congressman James P. Buchanan, whose Tenth District included Johnson City, died. Johnson saw this as his main chance. Neither his age, twenty-eight, nor the fact that he was the least known of several anticipated candidates, discouraged him. Johnson decided to run in the April 10 special election. Alvin Wirtz agreed to support him because he had concluded that his only hope of completing his pet project, the Lower Colorado River Authority for flood control and power, begun with Buchanan, lay with Lyndon. Despite the fact that he hailed from the least populous county in the district, they expected Johnson to win by a plurality, a majority not being needed because the unscheduled election would have no runoff. Johnson needed to capitalize on FDR's popularity in the district by distinguishing himself as the President's man in Texas. He targeted the few liberals in Austin and in the countryside and mobilized them as few Texas politicians could. Additionally, he made it known that this New Dealer knew how to get projects for his needy constituents. Significantly, he passed the word among blacks that his services as a congressmen would be available to them. In private meetings with black leaders he asked for their votes (a rarity in Texas—even Maury Maverick engaged in "nigger-baiting"), promising to recognize their voting rights and include them in federal programs such as hot lunches: "I think I can help you," Johnson said, words that few blacks ever heard from a white politician in Texas. Aided by oil company funds raised by Wirtz, Johnson ran an exhausting campaign and wound up in a hospital bed on election day as a result of a bursting appendix. Still, his personal contact with voters paid off in the light turnout—Johnson carrying his own county and the city of Austin, winning over 8,000 votes of the 29,000 cast.[11]

Roosevelt took notice of the Texas congressional race because it suggested a test of his presidential popularity. In May the new Congressman who so zealously championed the New Deal met the vacationing President in Galveston and entrained with him to Fort Worth. Indeed, upon returning to Washington Roosevelt called Corcoran and told him, "I've just met the most remarkable young man. Now I like this boy, and you're going to help him with anything you can." Even before arriving on Capitol Hill, Johnson had the President's mantle, his promise to ask the powerful Carl Vinson to support Johnson's bid for a seat on the Naval Affairs Committee, and assured access to the White House via Corcoran. The word went forth and soon Secretary of the Interior Harold Ickes reported that Roosevelt had told him "that in the next generation the balance of power would shift south and west, and this boy could well be the first Southern President."[12]

The "boy" did not wait upon others to introduce him. The former congressional secretary knew which doors he needed to open himself. Soon Ickes, Corcoran, Harry Hopkins, leaders in Congress, journalists and others became part of Johnson's network. He moved fast, both because he faced another election in a matter of months and because he had an agenda to meet. That meant service to his district, and to Johnson it meant fulfilling a quintessential New Deal agenda: economic development for his district and his state and his region and his country through government investment in capital projects that created jobs, economic opportunities and improved living conditions for all Americans. To a lawyer-promoter such as Alvin J. Wirtz and contractors-promoters such as Herman and George Brown of the firm of Brown and Root, Johnson's pursuit of re-election and development dovetailed nicely with their interests. And Johnson never questioned their right to profit through government contracts that benefited the community at large. They were builders bringing wealth to themselves and their neighbors—his constituents. He believed in service to all, questioned nobody's motives and expected nobody to question his. Finally, Johnson's friends were outsiders in Texas politics and Texas business, New Dealers by virtue of having been left out of other deals involving the Establishment represented by those other New Deal Texans—Jones, Garner and their allies. Getting nothing from Jones and Garner, men like Wirtz and the Browns made common cause around Lyndon Johnson in their bids for wealth and power.

Johnson seldom said anything for the *Congressional Record*, but he let his New Deal votes speak for him. He supported public power, work relief, conservation, agricultural price supports, and the Fair Labor Standards Act. In a matter of months he won re-election in the Democratic primary and the general election without opposition. His re-election brought satisfaction to the White House, Sam Rayburn, House advocates of public power and the business promoters who looked to him for federal support of their interests. Winning re-election every two years might bring him a very long and useful career, and like Rayburn he would rise to be a leader of the House. But many people sensed in him too strong an impatience, ambition and urgency for him to limit his political career to a House district in Central Texas. Conquest of the state itself was a worthy goal, even if it entailed a struggle against the entrenched interests of old Jesse Jones. And who knows, perhaps Roosevelt, who well knew the ambitions of the South and the West because he manipulated them so much to his own advantage, correctly forecast a population shift in response to economic development of those regions by his presidency, and the greatest political beneficiary of it would be "that boy" from Texas, Lyndon Johnson.

But in 1937 that was all far in the future. Johnson knew that his first task was to secure appropriations for completing a dam begun by his predecessor's influence in behalf of the Lower Colorado River Authority, of which his friend, Alvin J. Wirtz, was Chairman. The LCRA reflected unrequited local ambition for economic development that antedated the New Deal; Wirtz shrewdly made it his personal cause. Because the river flooded, interest in controlling it via a dam went back to central Texas's earliest settlement. By the late nineteenth century the city of Austin wanted control of the Colorado for electricity too. Without power, Central Texas would remain a backwater that lacked industry and creature comforts, as well as conservation of the soil to prevent floods and erosion.[13]

The father of the LCRA was Alvin Wirtz. Born in 1888 in Columbus,

Texas, of parents from Virginia and Alabama, Wirtz had been a small-town lawyer most of his adult life, practicing seventeen years at Seguin in Guadalupe County, a town of 6,000. He was a large, affable man inclined to listen much and say little. But when he spoke he always commanded the listener's attention without appearing to be particularly imposing. In an adversarial situation, he disarmed people with the understatement that he was a country lawyer and ignorant of certain complex matters or the worldliness and sophistication needed to deal with them. Of course, this pose worked especially well with non-Texans. In both business and politics Wirtz moved with a catlike agility, preferring the shadows, where he could manipulate people or a contract. He was elected to the state Senate in 1922 for the first of four terms, becoming president of that body in his second term. In his own words, "During service in the Texas Senate and as Chairman of the Committee to which all tax measures and general legislation was referred, and through general representation of clients having state-wide interests, [I have] become familiar in a general way with varied problems of business throughout the State."[14] In other words, he knew where a lot of political skeletons were buried. Although he served as a delegate to the Democratic National Conventions of 1928 and 1932, he was not known to be favored by either Jones or Garner; nevertheless, both of them had to reckon with his influence in central Texas Democratic politics.

Like them, Wirtz necessarily mixed business and politics. Like them, he bought stock in and served as a director for local banks and insurance companies. Those institutions enabled local capital to generate development without big-city banks or state and federal governments helping it. Wirtz's principal interest was in riparian rights, ownership of land adjacent to water—important to parched Central Texas. When Samuel Insull of Chicago sought to bring his electric utility holding company empire to Texas, he found a valuable local partner in Wirtz. They built six dams along the Guadalupe River to harness its hydroelectric power and then Insull began to build a big one on the Lower Colorado. But Insull pulled out when his paper empire collapsed in 1932, leaving Wirtz as general counsel, director and receiver of corporations whose growth depended upon the completion of the Colorado River dam. In 1934 Wirtz persuaded the Texas state legislature to create the LCRA with the half-finished dam as its cornerstone. Then Wirtz headed for Washington to secure PWA funds for what was then known as the Hamilton Dam. In the Capitol his sponsor was Congressman Buchanan, chairman of the Appropriations Committee; Roosevelt, always interested in a "partnership" with the states, local governments or industry that furthered development, not only supported the completion of what was now being called Buchanan's Dam, but the building of another dam 21 miles downstream at Marshall Ford. Although construction of the second dam began, the necessary funds had not been appropriated when the influential Buchanan died. Fortunately, during his tour of the Capitol Wirtz also encountered Congressman Kleberg's secretary, Lyndon Johnson.[15]

Counseling the young Johnson on Lone Star politics, Wirtz urged Johnson to forgo a vacation upon the adjournment of Congress and return to Central Texas and show his constituents how he had procured federal tax dollars for his district. Success at getting appropriations for the LCRA, a postmastership for a political friend, and a host of projects for Austin including slum clearance and a new municipal building would assure Johnson retention of his seat without a primary fight and "we won't have to go through a campaign next July." Through Johnson's Washington network of influential people, Wirtz relied upon him to get the necessary funding for Marshall Ford Dam and additional dams. Johnson made a coalition with Sam Rayburn and Judge Joseph Mansfield, Chairman of the powerful Rivers and Harbors Committee on Capitol Hill, Corcoran in the White House and the RFC, and Abe Fortas in the Interior Department. Johnson learned quickly to appreciate the uses of Washington lawyers who blended the talents of Harvard "Hot Dogs" and Yale "legal realists" in behalf of economic development in Central Texas. Two thousand jobs were immediately riding on the funding for construction of Marshall Ford Dam, and untold thousands of jobs hinged upon the LCRA's completion. However, an obstacle in the way of federal funding was LCRA's peculiar combination of private and public power. At the dedication of Buchanan Dam Ickes served notice that he wanted power from LCRA "at substantially [low] TVA rates" to encourage municipal ownership of power. Wirtz was eager to comply because it not only meant additional funding, but it also had the "considerable strategic value" of taking away business from the high-rate Texas Power & Light Company. LCRA obtained funds from Ickes's PWA and at the critical appropriation vote for Marshall Ford Dam, Rayburn threw his influence behind it. He was glad to do it, Sam Rayburn told Alvin Wirtz. "I think Lyndon is one of the finest young men I have seen come to Congress," Lyndon's father figure–adviser in Washington assured Lyndon's father figure–adviser in Austin. "If the District will exercise the good judgment to keep him here, he will grow in wisdom and influence as the years come and go." Wirtz shared Rayburn's letter with Johnson, who immediately saw it as good political capital: "Make use of it [in Austin] and maybe we can get away to Mexico for that rest."[16]

Shortly after Congress gave the green light on LCRA, Johnson issued a victorious press release trumpeting LCRA's importance beyond flood control or local power. "The power is there," he declared. Texans now could "turn the vicious Colorado which for centuries has gone whooping and snorting down the valleys on its sprees of destruction, into the quiet ways of work and peace." The opportunities for Texas farmers were enormous:

> There are hundreds of farm houses all over Central Texas where the smoky lantern and the stifling kerosene lamp are still the chief sources of illumination and elbow-grease still the principal motive-power [sic] although this is the Twentieth Century and not the era of Noah's Ark. There are dozens of small towns, farm communities and little cities that have no light or power at all.
>
> Now there would be no dearth of cheap power.
>
> The supply will be enormous and the cost small. Adequate financing for building connecting lines and all proper purposes, including even such auxiliaries as pressure water systems and plumbing for homes and barns, is available at low interest on long terms.

Rural Electrification Administration officials were prepared to finance cheap power for LCRA if the farmers of Central Texas undertook to organize themselves into cooperatives. Johnson exhorted them to organize: "Everybody benefits. There is work for the jobless, cash for materials, and power for all. But if no one makes a start, no one can benefit." Alvin Wirtz pleaded with communities to buy power from LCRA. At a meeting of LCRA directors in Washington, where they and Johnson impressed Ickes and other public power advocates that LCRA would bring low rates to Central Texas, word came that Kerrville and Fredericksburg in the hill country and Waco and Temple to the north would buy their power from LCRA; a satisfied Wirtz declared, "I think we are ready to go places." Indeed, the gospel of cheap power generated by LCRA quickly spread as far away as Fort Worth and Huntsville to the political benefit of Lyndon Johnson.[17]

At a time when Maury Maverick was the darling of national journals based in New York and San Antonio politicians circled his dying political career like buzzards over mortally wounded prey, Lyndon Johnson was the toast of Austin and, more than anything, wanted re-election without opposition. It was apparent that he would have his wish. In May, with less than two months before the 1938 primary, Wirtz, who would not let Johnson rest the previous year, now asked Johnson to let him know when Congress would adjourn, "and your latest ideas about the vacation."

Johnson was one of eight Texas congressmen (out of twenty) without primary or general election opposition that year.

How did he accomplish that feat? Two weeks before the primary Johnson summarized for the benefit of Mayor Tom Miller of Austin what he had done for that city in only fourteen months in the House. As written by "An Austin Business Man," it went:

> Our city hall project was dead. He brought it to life and sent a check for $112,000 in an outright grant to carry it through, providing for a $250,000 city hall. Our water supply was in danger of pollution and he got us funds to put 300 men to work cutting and burning timber in the Marshall Ford Lake bed and got a $140,000 federal grant to pay the bill. He has during his entire first year in office kept 1000 persons in Travis County at work on WPA projects, thereby putting $40,000 a month into Austin trade channels. He secured radio beam service for our airport to prevent accidents like we had last year. He secured improved mail service for Austin. . . . [He] made it possible to construct the Austin dam and got $2,500,000 to do the job, after years of waiting. When our children were dying with infantile paralysis he brought expert counsel and assistance from Washington through the Public Service. We hoped for $5,000,000 to construct the Marshall Ford Dam and he got us over $7,000,000. He got the first housing project in the nation for Austin, where $750,000 will be spent to put idle skilled and unskilled workers back on payrolls and provide better homes for our people. He obtained $29,000 to remodel the old federal building and kept federal payrolls from moving from Austin. Wednesday he obtained a $33,000 grant for a fire alarm system for Austin. While other members of Congress are vacationing he is in Washington and will remain for some time yet working on a $36,000 grant for an incinerator, $600,000 to improve and extend the school system and $150,000 for the waterworks and electric transmission lines. Every county in this district and our trade territory has got this kind of service from their Congressman. . . . That's why the ten counties in the Tenth District will always be ahead of the others. Austin business has been better and will continue to grow better as these projects develop fully and are given constant assistance and stimulation by our Congressman who has in a short time made a record for determination, efficiency and speed in handling the needs of his district.

And there were lots more projects for Austin and the hill country—adding up to $70 million by Johnson's own estimate. Few lawmakers availed themselves and their districts of every benefit conferred by Washington. Johnson did. Among White House insiders such as Corcoran and Rowe, or PWA insiders such as Ickes and Fortas, whose jobs required them to satisfy congressional requests, they knew how skillfully and completely the thirty-year-old Texas Congressman used what the federal government offered after only one year in office. "He got more projects, and more money for his district, than anybody else," Corcoran recalled. Johnson was "the best Congressman for a district that ever was." At a time when many Southern congressmen reluctantly accepted government projects as inconsistent with Southern individualism, Johnson wanted the farmers and the promoters of Central Texas to know what governmental benefits were available to them. When a businessman friend complained that New Deal programs deprived him of his individualism, Johnson said, "What are you worried about? It's not coming out of your pocket. Any money that's spent here on New Deal projects, the East is paying for. We don't pay any taxes in Texas. . . . They're paying for our projects." Assailed for accepting federal dollars, Johnson shrewdly fell back on typical Southern and Western anticolonial justification for New Deal public investment. Texans wanted "some electric power which doesn't have to run through the cash register of a New York power and light company before it gets to our lamps."

That Christmas a thankful Johnson sent his Austin mentor an effusive letter of gratitude and to Corcoran a big wild Texas turkey that had "wandered all over the hills around Marshall Ford lake snatching juicy acorns where they lay." In 1938 Lyndon Johnson had wandered all over Capitol Hill snatching juicy New Deal acorns where they lay. And he would be back in 1939–40 to improve upon that performance.[18]

Nobody was more eager to make use of Sam Rayburn's Rural Electrification Administration than Johnson. In part that was because the hill country of Texas contained many poverty-ridden farmers ignored by utilities such as the Texas Power & Light subsidiary of the Electric Bond and Share holding company based in New York City—additional evidence that Texas anticolonialism was not unfounded paranoia. The story of those Texans living without electricity, and how power altered the lives of the hill country people, and how Lyndon Johnson led the fight to create the Pedernales Electric Cooperative and even went to the White House to convince the President that he ought to waive the rule of membership density for the PEC to obtain an REA loan, has been told elsewhere.[19] It also points up Johnson's reluctance to rest upon his laurels or to be content with conquering the House.

Lyndon Johnson was not a disingenuous liberal because he knew what it meant to be "our kind of folks . . . a consistent liberal." The core of

Johnson's liberalism was to see to it that government performed for his constituents in Texas. In 1939 that enabled LCRA to buy out Texas Power & Light with the aid of RFC loans in sixteen counties, a distinct triumph for public power in Texas. LCRA provided additional low-cost power for Central Texas and even lower rates for many of those communities that already enjoyed electricity. Also, a $7 million PWA loan built LCRA transmission lines throughout the district. "Every newspaper in the district has gone out with a story giving you credit for the new rates," the operating manager of LCRA reported. Johnson himself claimed credit for "keep[ing] Tenth District money in the Tenth District, instead of paying big fees and dividends to officers and holding companies east of the Alleghenies"—another victory for Texas anticolonialism.[20]

Instead of Wall Street exploiting the Texans, the Texans exploited Washington. By late 1938 Johnson turned his attentions from roads and other works projects to bigger game: the military. It began innocently enough with Johnson pushing the War Department to consider purchasing its electricity for Fort Sam Houston from LCRA. However, Johnson also targeted bigger military game: a naval air station for Corpus Christi, which was in Congressman Kleberg's district—but would justify a seat for a Texas congressman from a landlocked district on the House Naval Affairs Committee chaired by Carl Vinson of Georgia. The military was about to become a gigantic public works program for all congressmen. In 1938 Roosevelt had proposed the creation of a two-ocean fleet, with the emphasis upon building a naval air capacity. Johnson wanted the Corpus Christi Naval Air Station to be built by Brown & Root, the Houston road builders now constructing LCRA dams and fast becoming major benefactors of Johnson's ambitions. With Vice-President Garner now quietly opposing New Deal programs and publicly pushing his own 1940 candidacy for the presidency, and with Jesse Jones as a silent partner, political considerations operated here: Johnson and the Browns did not want the Corpus Christi Naval Air Station to be built by W. S. Bellows—who, in the words of George Brown, "built the San Jacinto Monument, a world of dormitories at A & M College, and several large office buildings for Jesse H. Jones' interests." The White House had to give it to the Browns because they were attached to Johnson's interests and, as Corcoran put it, "Lyndon Johnson is the best there is in Texas."

FDR sent an additional message to Texas: He made Alvin J. Wirtz Undersecretary of the Interior. Secretary Ickes at first did not cotton to Wirtz, but a letter from Maury Maverick persuaded Ickes that the appointment of Wirtz would help liberalism. Johnson put an exclamation mark on the appointment by telling the press, "It is good that the talent he has expressed in Texas development will be made available to the whole country." It made Wirtz the second most powerful Texan in the administration next to Jesse Jones and signaled to Texas Democrats that Lyndon Johnson was a name to reckon with. The fight for benefits from increased federal spending was on: Garner and his friends regularly denounced New Dealers for their reckless government spending, but now Garner and Jones sought to distribute some of the largesse to friends such as Bellows. As Johnson puckishly put it when the House debated the increased lending power of Jesse Jones's Export-Import Bank, part of his Federal Loan Administration empire, "I am afraid if we don't put a stop to this business of making loans and grants to everybody who wants them, we will bankrupt the country. Jesse called me out in the lobby to see him today and greeted me rather cordially. I think he was rather cordial with everyone because he really wants the $100,000,000. It's all right to spend, but the thing that provokes the fuss here is who does the spending." Never, as we shall see later, were truer words ever spoken by Lyndon Johnson.[21]

The New Dealers decided to make a fight on the issue of who controlled federal spending in Texas. In the spring of 1940 Garner's pursuit of the Democratic nomination for president ran into trouble in the Wisconsin primary and elsewhere. Rayburn, now Speaker, challenged Garner for leadership in Texas by winning the chairmanship of the state's delegation to the Democratic National Convention from Jesse Jones. His vice-chairman of the delegation was Lyndon Johnson. Moreover, when the convention polled the Texas delegation as to its choice for vice-president, Rayburn defeated Jones a second time. "Lyndon Johnson and Sam Rayburn ran things at Chicago to suit their own purposes," Jones groused to Garner. In Washington Alvin Wirtz rejoiced over a report that Harry Hopkins would resign as Secretary of Commerce and would be replaced by Jones because "If this is offered to Jesse, it will be in the nature of trading him position for power. I think the New Deal would like to have the RFC in other hands, and this would be a neat way of accomplishing it." But Jesse outfoxed FDR when he insisted upon taking all his Federal Loan responsibilities with him to Commerce and got Congress to back him.[22]

"Local control of the Texas situation is desperately important," Corcoran warned. "Right now there are mutual acrimonies splitting the Texas crowd which offer an extraordinary opportunity to get control. *The opportunity will only last a short time if not availed of.* If you move fast you can crystallize a new leadership in Texas around your man, Lyndon Johnson,—a permanent leadership. If you wait, the old crowd will get together and the job may be impossible." Johnson was the New Deal's stalking horse, Corcoran assured Roosevelt. To build up Johnson's reputation, he should be given a national visibility. Indeed, Roosevelt earlier had asked Johnson to head up the REA, but the Texan declined to take himself out of the House in the waning months of Roosevelt's second term. Should Roosevelt make Johnson another offer? Corcoran thought so:

> The reasons are these: (1) Johnson is energetic, imaginative, soft-spoken and skillful as a political manager and will give a focus through whom the younger New Dealers can cooperate with the leadership of the Democratic National Committee. Johnson has no contest in his District. There was no filing against him in the last primary. He therefore has time to give the job as well as energy. He won an enormous victory over the utility companies in Texas with the Buchanan Dam and the attendant rural electrification projects.
>
> (2) Johnson was the real leader in the fight for you in Texas and is the symbol of your interest in Texas. He is an extraordinary symbol of the clean young fellow in politics. Handsome, able,—and two years ago the State Administrator for the National Youth Administration. He can pick up the youth symbol as very few people can.

Although Corcoran even promoted Johnson to replace Jim Farley as Chairman of the Democratic National Committee, Johnson and Rayburn decided that he should help elect Democratic congressmen via the Congressional Campaign Committee. The White House considered this extremely important because of the beating it had taken in the previous Congress. Johnson's task would be to see that New Dealers were re-elected to the next House.[23]

Like most New Dealers, Johnson operated best with a telephone in his ear. Money was his first priority and in a week he raised $45,000 for Democratic candidates via the Brown brothers of Brown & Root. The races in Illinois, Indiana and Missouri especially concerned Johnson because Democrats could lose twelve, five and three seats respectively; and each of the Democratic congressmen wanted campaign money, projects and a Roosevelt visit to boost their candidacies. Johnson's gloomy report showing "a definite downward trend in the Middle West" was corroborated by Department of Agriculture statistician Louis Bean, who interpreted Gallup Poll data as suggesting a parallel with 1916, when Wilson did poorly in the Middle West and won the election on the coasts, again during a time of preparedness for an impending war. Rowe and Johnson decided that districts not getting a Roosevelt visit would be assured of projects.[24]

What kind of projects? In an Oregon swing district, liberal Nan Wood Honeyman was fighting to regain a seat she had lost in 1938: to help her Johnson drafted both her request for presidential aid and a presidential reply. In both drafts Johnson connected the political importance of New Deal works to the defense works projects then under way—and the local impact of the projects. "The Portland area, like the rest of the Pacific Northwest," Johnson wrote in behalf of Honeyman,

> is beginning to notice its transformation into the industrial empire those of us envisioned when we planned and fought for the development of the Columbia River. The new contracts for the sale of electric energy being entered into by the Bonneville Power Administration will make even more rapid this change in the essential characteristics of this region from a source of raw materials to an important producer of necessary defense supplies.
>
> In keeping with this change in the economy of the Portland area, I believe a study by competent authorities of the military defenses in this area should be undertaken. The Far Eastern situation makes this region doubly important to our national defense effort—a fact further substantiating your faith in the soundness of the development you brought about on the Columbia. I do not pretend to military expertness, but the news from Europe regarding the bombing of industrial centers—of power supplies and aluminum works, in particular—makes expertness unnecessary in analyzing the importance of the Portland-Vancouver region at this time. The defense plans for this region must keep pace with its economic and strategic importance.

And then Johnson had Roosevelt answering Honeyman,

> It was good to hear from you again and to receive from one who had fought shoulder-to-shoulder with me for the Columbia developments a picture of their present usefulness to our national defense program.
>
> The suggestion you make, that the change in the characteristics of the region may require a change in the plan for its defense, is a good one. I am asking both the Army and the Navy to study the situation in the Portland area and to report on suggested additions and betterments to our defenses there.[25]

It was bravura performance. Knowing of the Northwest's love of its public power, its quest for industrial development, its fear of Japanese expansion in the Far East, Johnson sought to rally its boosterism the way he appealed to Texas promoters.

In the 1940 congressional races, Lyndon Johnson had seen the future of American politics. The Roosevelt association still had magic, money was still the mother's milk of politics, and now Democrats had to consider something else: public works projects could help elect congressmen, but defense contracts had become public works. Johnson had bet Rowe that the Democrats would lose less than thirty seats in the House and Johnson won—in Rowe's words, "And how! Is my face red!" But then, Rowe did not have as high or accurate an impression of Johnson's ability as did Johnson.

Three months later Johnson repeated for himself and Central Texas some of what he had to say for Nan Wood Honeyman and Oregon. He reminded the President of the LCRA's power for development:

> The presence of this abundant supply of water and power, coupled with the raw materials available such as oil and sulphur, should make the area around Austin particularly attractive for the location of a munitions plant or a similar defense industry. In Baytown there is a toluol plant; Houston has been designated as the site for a $15,000,000 steel mill; in Dallas and Fort Worth there are to be aircraft manufacturing plants. The existence of these plants should make the location of a defense industry in the Austin Area even more advantageous.

Public power and development for defense were on Roosevelt's mind too, as when he told Dave Lilienthal that "those early struggles [for TVA] and . . . the bitterness they engendered [were] . . . a small price to pay for TVA's present usefulness to national defense." Senators and congressmen deluged the White House in 1941 with pleas to get defense site locations in their districts and states—and to get the favorable publicity attendant to it.[26] The New Deal's public power for state capitalist development of regional economies would be the engine of World War II.

The role of defense projects in politics would be evident in Texas when Senator Morris Sheppard died suddenly in the spring of 1941, thereby necessitating an immediate election to determine his successor. Johnson was eager for the race. Despite all his New Deal activity he was one of the least-known candidates statewide. No matter; again Johnson could mobilize for himself the image of the President's candidate—the New Deal's man in Texas, the man who could deliver defense projects. The Senate had long been on Johnson's mind, as well as on the minds of the contractors who looked to him to secure their share of federal projects. George Brown and Wirtz wanted Johnson to run and saw Sheppard's passing as "opportune" for Johnson. Later Wirtz resigned his Interior Department post to return to Texas as Johnson's campaign manager.[27]

For Johnson to make the race, he needed to neutralize the Texas influence of Jesse Jones. And he chose to confront Jones by demonstrating that he could deliver defense spending benefits. Johnson and Wirtz counted upon White House support because of "the licking they gave the Garner-Jones crowd in the pre-convention fight." They were the only liberals in Texas, the only alternative to the power of Jesse Jones. They accused the other possible liberal candidate, Texas Attorney General Gerald Mann, of owing his office to support by public utilities (in fact, he was known as a strong antitrust liberal). They made a Johnson race in 1941 part of a fight for a liberal Democratic party in Texas. Initially, the only challenger to Johnson besides the weak Mann was Congressman Martin Dies, whose principal talent lay in depicting a ubiquitous communist conspiracy against Texans. But the Dies candidacy faded more rapidly than did Mann's. Roosevelt and Rowe wondered where Jesse Jones would cast his influence.

They had many bones to pick with Jones, such as his alliance with Garner, his hostility to Texas liberals and his work in behalf of conservative businessmen on Capitol Hill. Rowe, the son of a Montana Democrat frequently at odds with party leadership there, identified himself with public power advocates in the Pacific Northwest and saw Texas as another battleground between conservatives and progressives. For his part, Roosevelt recalled the swarms of businessmen who descended upon Washington in 1917 and anticipated that the inexorable march toward war in 1941 would bring to Washington businessmen dedicated to reversing the New Deal. It was perhaps unavoidable that, as he put it, "in some of these new [war] production agencies we are employing dozens of men who have hated the Administration and fought all constructive change for years." But he did not want Jones employing anti–New Dealers in "the regular permanent agencies of the Government" such as the Department of Commerce.[28]

Jones always was a special problem. Roosevelt could not fire him without offending certain Texas Democrats and alienating the Southern leadership of Congress. Moreover, Roosevelt preferred to have troublemakers inside the administration rather than organizing the opposition against him outside. Besides, he used Jones for personal favors which only a man of great wealth and power could bestow upon him at a presidential request. But Roosevelt would not tolerate Jones's blatant insubordination or being outfoxed by Jones, as he was when the Texan went to Commerce and took his federal empire with him. Roosevelt saw the 1941 Texas race as an opportunity both to erode Jones's Texas base and to strengthen New Dealers in Texas and in the Senate.

If Roosevelt's only concern was the vigor of a Johnson campaign, he need not have worried; in the parlance of a later era, Johnson was a campaign junkie. Ironically, nearly three decades before another generation mobilized to bring down the Johnson presidency in the legendary 1968 campaign, Johnson had demonstrated the efficacy of the "new politics" practiced by the New Dealers. He had but to announce his candidacy and hundreds of young people in the NYA and elsewhere across Texas volunteered for mailings and door-to-door solicitations in his behalf. He generated a young persons' crusade: if Johnson won, he would be at thirty-two the youngest senator. Additionally, he had a hold upon old politics: money. He paid for the posters young campaign workers put up all over Texas with money given and solicited by his contractor friends who benefited from New Deal projects, the Brown brothers of Brown & Root. As the candidate best identified with Roosevelt, Johnson could promise what only the federal government could deliver: projects. New Deal and defense projects worked two ways for Johnson: first, they repaid debts to communities and contractors for votes and campaign funds; second, they informed have-not communities and contractors that they had to join the bandwagon to get a share of projects. Indirectly Johnson threatened subcontractors to contribute or find their bids blacklisted. He flaunted his direct line to the White House at every opportunity. "Could you get me some kind of wire on munitions plant on Brazos River near Possum Kingdom Dam or near Waco," Johnson would plead in telegrams to Rowe. Here was a budding military-industrial complex in Texas.

Eventually Gerald Mann caught on to what Johnson was doing and tried to appeal to Texas chauvinism and anticolonialism. However, Mann was ineffective. Suddenly, the enormously popular Governor W. Lee ("Pass the Biscuits, Pappy") O'Daniel jumped into the race. A former radio personality in Texas, O'Daniel had won two elections for governor when he decided that he wanted to be senator instead. He turned an inexorable Johnson march to the Senate into a real horse race.[29]

"Where is Jesse?" Jim Rowe rhetorically asked FDR. Jones had "to do something affirmative" for Johnson or risk diminished influence in Texas. Moreover, his loyalty to Roosevelt would be tested by his support of Johnson. Asserting that everyone else in the administration backed Johnson (which Jones labeled "misinformation"), Rowe accused Jones of secretly urging Governor O'Daniel to run for the Senate. Although Jones denied the allegation (saying that he merely had "asked [O'Daniel] if he expected to run," a question from one of the most powerful Democrats in the state that was more than academic), people close to Jones endorsed O'Daniel, tantamount to a signal to other Democrats. Rowe accused Jones of implicit disloyalty—the only cause for which Roosevelt could fire Jones without creating an unnecessary firestorm in Congress and in Texas. Feeling the heat, Jones, via his Houston *Post*, invited Roosevelt to more directly assist the Johnson candidacy and soon after endorsed Johnson. Jesse had "arrived at last!" Rowe exulted.[30]

Rowe and Roosevelt built a Texas consensus for Johnson by securing endorsements from such diverse people as Fort Worth newspaper publisher Amon Carter, Secretary of State Cordell Hull (who held the respect and affection of many Southerners), president of the Social Security League of Texas D. C. McCord, and congressman Paul Kilday of San Antonio—the corrupt archenemy of Maury Maverick—whom Harry Hopkins personally promised "everything except the south portico of the White House" in return for his support of Johnson. In the waning days of the campaign an exuberant Rowe telegraphed Johnson, "O'DANIEL WENT INTO THE LYNDON DEN HE MET THE SAME FATE AS DIES AND MANN HE WENT FROM BAD TO WIRTZ OUR LYNDON IS THE NERTS." Rowe's celebration was premature. O'Daniel narrowly defeated Johnson when rigged East Texas returns rolled in. The Texas Brewers Institute wanted to send O'Daniel to the Senate rather than see him appoint more prohibitionists to the Liquor Control Board. As such the brewers virtually stole Johnson's election.[31]

Nevertheless, Johnson's race and those he masterminded in 1940 demonstrated a crucial connection between electing New Dealers and well-placed defense projects. When South Carolina too had a special senatorial election in 1941 and Governor Burnet Maybank ran as a loyal New Dealer, Jimmy Byrnes asked Rowe "to make sure that word was quietly passed to the [War] Department to do everything they could for Maybank." Roosevelt approved the request, and the War Department promised Maybank to study Greenville, South Carolina, as a site for a shell-loading and bag-loading plant. It was the Lyndon Johnson defense project technique that worked so well in the 1940 races. In the future, defense projects would be as political as public works.[32]

13.

Wright Patman: The Last Brandeisian

A RUMOR MADE the rounds following the death of Morris Sheppard that, in addition to Johnson and the others, Congressman Wright Patman of Texas was considering a race for the vacant Senate seat. If he had run, a Patman candidacy might have reduced Lyndon Johnson's New Deal vote. While Washington insiders marked Johnson as the more effective New Dealer, few doubted that Patman of rural East Texas was the more outspoken New Dealer. Although Patman did not vote for the Fair Labor Standards Act of 1938 and seemed to be more Texan than New Dealer, many considered him as populistic or left-wing in his hostility to big corporations as any Democrat in the House. Like Rayburn, Patman had a long-term mission. Hailing from the piney woods section of East Texas, where, it was said, the occasional patches of red soil so closely resembled Georgia that many a Georgian had settled in the nineteeenth century to raise cotton, Patman had many of the characteristics of Southern populists. Patman differed from Texans such as Johnson because he was combative on the House floor almost from the day he arrived. Like Rayburn, Patman attacked the power of big Eastern banks and corporations that exploited Texans, scolding and defying concentrations of money. He did not assail them because they were big, but because they were unfair in monopolizing their trade. This quest for fairness in the marketplace marked his career for decades after the New Deal.

John William Wright Patman was born in a two-room shack at Patman's Switch, Texas, on August 6, 1893, to a family with origins in Virginia and Georgia. His father, John Newton Patman, was a poor tenant farmer and part-time blacksmith. The Patmans were devout fundamentalist Baptists whose faith cast doubt upon the righteousness of all who disagreed with them. One of the first things Patman learned in life was that he had to attain an education to escape poverty and find truth and salvation. "My father was a farmer, and earned a little extra by repairing cotton gins, but we were always poor," Patman remembered. "Neither of my parents had much education, but my mother was an ardent student of the Bible." Riding 6 miles on horseback each day and working as a school janitor to attain a high school education, Patman found time not only to gain a love of history, geography, mathematics and literature, but to organize a school debating society and to graduate as his class's valedictorian in 1912. For three years he worked and saved his money in order to attend law school at Cumberland University in Lebanon, Tennessee, then reputedly one of the best in the South and one which emphasized ideals, values and civic responsibility. Sharing a four-room shack with two other men, he worked hard to support himself at his studies. The year he graduated he passed the Texas Bar and began a brief legal career in Hughes Springs. He joined the Army in 1917 but never saw action abroad. After the war he married and settled in Linden, Texas, and like most young lawyers shopping for clients he joined organizations with civic purposes. In 1920 he stood for the Texas House in the Democratic primary and won Cass County by almost 2 to 1.[1]

In the House he made the acquaintance of Sam Ealy Johnson and his tall young son. Patman revered the elder Johnson as a straight-shooting legislator who worked hard for his agrarian constituents. In turn, Lyndon would later tell people that when he was first elected to Congress his father advised him, "Son, when you get up there in Washington you're going to have to vote on a lot of issues you won't have had time to study up on. So when you don't know how to vote, you pass until you see how Wright Patman votes and vote like he does, because he always votes for the people." Patman's integrity was tested early when the Ku Klux Klan injected the race issue into East Texas politics. In spite of the Klan's popularity there during the early 1920s, Patman assailed it as "un-American" because of its disrespect for the law and sponsored a resolution in the Texas House to condemn and denounce it; however, the House tabled the resolution, 69 to 54. When the Klan sponsored a Baptist preacher with Klan sympathies to address the House, Patman led a fight against the resolution endorsing the speaker. The Klan harassed Patman, ran a candidate against him in the 1922 election, but failed to defeat him. In the next legislative session the energetic and articulate Patman sponsored bills to aid public education and agriculture—and to prohibit a farm corporation from vertically integrating, which foreshadowed some of his later anti–big business activity. In early 1924 the governor of Texas offered Patman the post of district attorney for Bowie and Cass Counties; Patman accepted and moved to Texarkana, where he showed extraordinary moral and physical courage as a prosecutor, winning election in his own right. With Baptist zeal he waged war against Texarkana's notorious red light district, enforced Prohibition and rooted out gambling and graft. When rumors spread that certain elements had hired a hit man from Chicago to take care of Patman, the Governor sent in Texas Rangers to protect him and Patman himself packed a pistol.

In 1928 he ran for the U.S. House of Representatives, vowing to fight for farmers and against big corporate influences in the Treasury, the Federal Reserve and the Federal Trade Commission—political targets for the rest of his life. However, to win he had to beat incumbent Congressman Eugene Black, a veteran of fourteen years with strong supporters in Congress and in the district. An aggressive and tireless campaigner, Patman accused Black of indifference to the interests of veterans and farmers and of not originating any significant legislation. But Patman was especially indignant that Black had voted for the Railroad Act of 1920 to benefit the holders of railroad securities, Wall Street bankers. Finally, Patman asserted, fourteen years in the House was enough for any man. "Give a Young Man a Chance," was his slogan; the young man won by 3,000 votes and would serve forty-seven years in the House of Representatives!

Patman's district then included eleven counties with a population of about a quarter of a million. It was so poor that in 1935 it was estimated that less than two thirds of 1 per cent had ever filed an income tax return. Beginning his tenure in the special session of 1929, Patman announced that he would not "regard the House as a morgue where new members must lie on a marble slab for several sessions" to attain the right to speak. A few months into his career he introduced a bill to give an immediate cash payment to war veterans of the paid-up life insurance promised them in 1924. As the veterans' bonus would cost the government the astronomical sum of $2 billion, Patman proposed issuing new currency to pay for it—a proposition that correctly revealed him as an inflationist. The veterans' bonus bill failed then and again in 1932, when it provoked a massive veterans' march on Washington and a riot that President Hoover put down with military force. In 1935 Congress finally passed the veterans' bonus over President Roosevelt's veto. Branded as a "funny money man," Patman ignored John Nance Garner's orders to desist, persisted in pursuing inflation and paid the penalty for his populism—he was denied a seat on the House Banking and Currency Committee for eight years and, he calculated, found his ascendancy to its chair delayed by sixteen years.[2]

Patman vehemently depicted monopoly of capital as this country's greatest sin and the farmer its principal victim. Monopolies in banking, he insisted, bred additional monopolies in manufacturing, distribution and even retailing, which went to the heart of woes endured by small-town merchants. In 1932 he generated a House investigation by charging that the Federal Trade Commission had created in 1928 a cottonseed cartel by encouraging the six largest corporate buyers of cottonseed to fix bids while prohibiting commodity warehousing that would withhold crops until a better price could be achieved. Eventually Patman would see the cartel's breakup. A defender of "independent business," he endeared himself to constituents and fellow Democrats by attacking Republicans for "making the rich richer and the poor poorer." Patman seized every opportunity to assail Secretary of the Treasury Andrew Mellon, climaxing in a 1932 demand for his impeachment on the grounds that the Pittsburgh banker–shipper–aluminum and oil magnate's interests were directly benefited by decisions he made in the name of fiscal policy or public works. Others had attempted to spotlight Mellon's conflicts of interests before, but few went about it with Patman's diligence. Nor did it hurt that the Great Depression created an atmosphere more receptive to Patman's charges that Mellon had "illegally acquired more property" than anybody was entitled to possess. When the impeachment effort ended in Hoover's appointment of Mellon to be Ambassador to Great Britain, Patman branded it a "presidential pardon."[3]

Patman supported the New Deal, but he also set his own Brandeisian agenda. Until we have evidence suggesting otherwise, we have to assume that Patman was Brandeisian by instinct rather than persuasion. Although he may never have met Patman, Brandeis had articulated democratic capitalist sentiments that were congenial to the rural South from which Patman hailed. Patman saw the world through the eyes of another Texas farmer–small businessman intent upon defeating big corporations, Wall Street financiers that fostered them, and federal corporate structures that protected and enhanced them. At stake was economic individualism and the protection of the petite bourgeoisie. In particular he defended proprietary retailers against chain stores.

Although chains such as the Great Atlantic & Pacific Tea Company had been around since the nineteenth century, an anti–chain store movement did not exist until the mid–1920s, when the chains enjoyed a boom along with the rest of the economy. Southerners bought from chains, but some independents cultivated their hostility by trying to convince shoppers that Aaron Montgomery Ward, Richard W. Sears and Alvah C. Roebuck were blacks. In 1930 high school and college debaters argued the proposition "Resolved: That chain stores are detrimental to the best interests of the American public." Patman's region was particularly active against the chain store system. In Shreveport, Louisiana, less than 50 miles from Texarkana, a broadcaster importuned against "sending the profits of business out of our local communities to a common center, Wall Street, [and] closing this door of opportunity [to those] who entertain the hope of their children becoming prosperous business leaders." He forecast that chains would foster "an economic system which will destroy every vestige of individual initiative and personal incentive to progress." Although Piggly Wiggly was a Southern chain founded in 1919 in Memphis, elsewhere in the South and up in the Midwest local groups organized to defend local grocers against outside competition. "Keep Ozark Dollars in the Ozarks," they pleaded in Springfield, Missouri. By 1930 Georgia, Maryland and North Carolina had enacted laws taxing chains by the store. When the Supreme Court upheld Indiana's graduated tax on the number of stores in a chain it touched off a wave of anti-chain store taxes. But then the Court struck down a similar Florida law in *Liggett* v. *Lee,* despite a heroic dissent by Brandeis, who asserted that the state had a right "to protect the community from apprehended harm" by an "experiment" in law meant to foster "equality of opportunity." Of the twenty-seven states with remaining antichain laws, eleven were Southern or border states, the toughest being Louisiana's. Wright Patman sought to nationalize their impact.[4]

NRA codes reflected the most common complaints against the chain system by outlawing the practice of loss leaders and other competitive threats to price maintenance. NRA's Hugh Johnson agreed with Patman and others that if the chains "cannot be checked or at least controlled by the people who serve them for pay, then the few human beings who really do control these powerful and massive organisms will not only conduct them with no more reference to the common good than they elect, but they will also control the government to such purpose as they choose." Implicit in this New Deal thinking was the assumption that economic organization and power would be translated into arbitrary political power. Although the number of chain outlets declined by almost a quarter during the depression decade, at the same time independent grocers banded together to form cooperative distribution networks, their number more than doubling in the 1930s. An organization calling itself the Progressive Food Dealers Association ("Organized for the Protection of the Independent Food Distributor") inveighed against a lack of code enforcement and the "unethical tactics of the chain gang." Asserting that "the NRA has done nothing for the small business man," the organized independents demanded NRA protection. But the demise of NRA reversed the trend toward price stabilization.

Seeking to fill the void left by NRA, the general counsel of the United States Wholesale Grocers' Association wrote a bill instructing the Federal Trade Commission to outlaw quantity discounts, brokerage payments and advertising allowances. To introduce it he sought out the House's champion of small business, Wright Patman. Patman, encouraged by independent grocers and wholesalers, had been investigating the American Retail Federation as a front group for the chains and knew enough tales about the A & P and Woolworth and how they connived with big manufacturers to undersell small competitors. "To restrain and restrict tendencies toward monopoly," Democratic Leader Joe T. Robinson of Arkansas introduced the wholesale grocers' bill in the Senate. The National Association of Retail Druggists, a trade organization dedicated to "fair trade" laws, mobilized druggists on behalf of the bill. NARD's Washington lobbyist, Rowland Jones, Jr., sought "free play of competition between the largest possible number of competitors in any given field," but that did not mean that chains would be allowed to compete. Thus, the organized independent wholesalers and retailers opposed price competition and wanted an unlimited number of competitors. Alternatively, congressman Emanuel Celler of Brooklyn, New York, opposed the bill because it would victimize consumers by fixing prices and eliminating price competition that benefited consumers. While some economists called the Patman-Robinson bill "another part of the drive for security," retired persons in St. Petersburg, Florida, complained that NARD sought to victimize consumers and wage earners with higher prices that stifled re-employment. However, in 1936 Congress passed the Robinson-Patman Bill.[5]

Indicative of the small retailers' passion for price-fixing, the organized independents also wanted a national law exempting certain price maintenance agreements from antitrust prosecution and got it in the Miller-Tydings law of 1937 as a rider on the District of Columbia tax bill. The law encouraged price-fixing by the states. Although NARD considered the Miller-Tydings law vital for upholding "fair trade" laws in every state, and it credited Patman with playing a major role in winning reluctant administration approval of it, it is interesting that Texas is one of three states that never passed a fair trade law.[6]

More than anything else, Patman wanted a law to "strike directly at chain stores" in the same manner as the states, via taxes on the number of stores owned by a chain. Arguing that such a tax was not intended to destroy the chains, although it would "cause them to reduce the number of stores they own and give other people, especially local citizens, a chance," Patman introduced his bill to tax the chains in 1938, along with seventy-three cosponsors. No other bill so threatened to change the character of American retailing. If Patman's bill passed, the A & P claimed, it would have to pay a tax of $471,602,000 on a profit of $9,119,114; Woolworth asserted that its tax would be $81,048,450 on earnings of $28,584,944. NARD was ecstatic, its lobbyists promising Patman to "be in with both feet in any direction you decide upon," and trade association journals such as *Farm-Town Hardware* beat the drums for his bill. Patman promised that his taxes on chains would deter concentrations of wealth in the hands of Huntington Hartford of New York City, owner of the A & P, and thwart the "destruction of local communities" by the absentee ownership of outsiders. He depicted this as a cultural war between the colonizing chain stores headquartered in Northeastern cities and the oppressed small-town merchants of the Midwest and the South. "It is right that the invader should pay invasion taxes . . . ," Patman asserted. "The interstate chain store must go."[7]

But, as evidenced by Congress's repeal of the Undistributed Profits Tax in 1938, anti–big business fervor had subsided. The Roosevelt recession also took its political toll. Yet Patman did not notice that the proposed tax on chain stores was in trouble. A tall, heavy-set, pink-cheeked man with glasses and curly hair, Patman's smallish facial features gave him a somewhat cherubic look of political innocence—an impression he reinforced by communicating sincerity in crusading for the underdogs of the marketplace. Yet, he had a streak of vanity. The success of his drive for the Robinson-Patman Act went to his head and caused him to overestimate his power to rally citizens in defense of little retailers. He thrived on publicity, making national lecture tours during 1936–37, obviously relishing the adulation of small-town grocers, druggists and hardware dealers who flocked to hear his message assailing the conspiracy of capital in New York City. His newspaper clipping service deluged him with hundreds of editorials celebrating the Robinson-Patman Act. "Literally millions of persons are deeply interested in what this Act really means," he exulted. "My correspondence on the subject has been overwhelming." He enthusiastically paraphrased economist Roger Babson to the effect that Robinson-Patman "is one of the most important laws that has ever been enacted by Congress concerning business." Confident that the public wanted his analysis of the law, Patman shopped around for journals interested in an article by the lawmaker. Knowing of the penchant of sympathetic liberal New York publications to denounce Wall Street, he tried selling an article there: the *New Republic* turned him down, but the *Nation* bought him. Then, in late 1938 the press revealed that the nation's largest drug wholesaler, McKesson & Robbins, had "sponsored" Patman's earlier lecture tour "to consolidate the sentiment of retailers, manufacturers and businessmen generally behind the Robinson-Patman Law." Although Patman insisted that a New York lecture agency had arranged his tour, it was obvious that the big wholesaler had a stake in supporting business ties with many small independents. Additionally, a Connecticut legislator pleaded guilty to accepting a McKesson & Robbins bribe to promote passage of a state fair trade law.

The revelations fueled a strong chain counterattack upon the integrity of the antichain drive.[8]

Even without these "scandals," the drive for the tax on chains had stalled. For one thing, the chains had powerful and articulate allies in this fight. The American Farm Bureau Federation, the National Grange and the National Council of Farm Cooperatives opposed the tax on the grounds that it would restrain produce distribution and reduce consumption by raising prices charged in supermarket chains. At House Ways and Means Committee hearings, consumer groups joined the National Association of Manufacturers in denouncing the bill. Noted economic historian Caroline F. Ware testified that the tax would cost millions of chain store employees their jobs. Also on the list of opponents of the chain tax bill were the American Federation of Labor, the New York City Federation of Women's Clubs, and the Twentieth Century Fund. More witnesses testified against Patman's bill than for it. The Patman bill's troubles multiplied when thirty-two of its seventy-three cosponsors went down to defeat in the election of 1938. Administration New Dealers abandoned Patman. Henry Wallace and Harry Hopkins attacked the bill publicly. Liberals were divided between saving the small businessman or lowering prices for the consumer. Reacting to Morris Ernst's strong Brandeisian antitrust argument, the SEC's Jerome Frank argued

> Now what is (1) the number of small shopkeepers injured by A&P as compared with (2) the vast number of consumers aided by A&P? Comparatively very small, isn't it? So you're a snob—more interested in letting a comparatively few small grocers enjoy the fun of running their own businesses [with most of them going bankrupt, which is lots of fun!] than in promoting the welfare of millions of consumers who badly need to have their meager purchasing power increased.

Besides, Frank opportunistically noted, the current Temporary National Economic Committee investigation, for all its rhetoric about monopoly and concentration of economic power, reported surprisingly little trust-busting sentiment in its mail.

The Patman bill could not pass. Finally, on June 7, 1939, Robert L. Doughton of North Carolina, the long-time Chairman of the House Ways and Means Committee, along with Majority Leader Sam Rayburn, informed Patman that other "urgent and pressing matters" commanded the House's attention and that debate on the tax would be put off until January. Patman knew that the administration wanted no part of his tax. Ever a believer in conspiracies, he bitterly assailed Agriculture Department official Milo Perkins for getting "in bed with the chains," Secretary of Commerce Harry Hopkins for surrounding himself with "chain store men," and Roosevelt's son John for taking a job with the president of the American Retail Federation in Boston. Patman renewed his antichain tax in 1940, but New Dealers and the House studiously ignored it.[9]

The war brought political and economic changes, and Patman adjusted. East Texas hungered for economic development, which mobilization offered. The East Texas Regional Chamber of Commerce campaigned to build a steel plant in Longview to fabricate pipelines for the booming oil industry and to use long-dormant local iron ore deposits. But the boom threatened overcapacity in peacetime. Patman later told how he and other East Texans petitioned Dallas and New York bankers for loans to build a pilot plant and were rejected because the major steel companies and their New York banker friends opposed it. Jesse Jones's Reconstruction Finance Corporation subsidiary, the Defense Plant Corporation, came through for Patman, as one Texan helping another, to get around New York's stranglehold on credit. By 1943 the wartime boom in Texas created enough of a regional market to justify organizing the Lone Star Steel Company. Rayburn and Patman helped Lone Star build a plant at Daingerfield for converting native ores to pig iron—using surplus power from Lyndon Johnson's Lower Colorado River Authority and Sam Rayburn's Denison Dam on the Red River. Defense industries sprouted all over the state during the war thanks to $1.6 billion of government money, far and away the most invested in any Southern state. However, most of it went to the Houston-Gulf area or Fort Worth's aircraft industry. East Texas wanted an integrated steel mill at Daingerfield, but Eastern steel industry leaders maintained that any such plant built with $35 million of government funds would be superfluous and amount to wartime "pork-barrel" spending. As Chairman of the House Small Business Committee Patman vowed that the steel plant would be built in Daingerfield "even if I have to go to the President." At a ceremony lighting the coke ovens of Lone Star Steel's blast furnaces, Speaker Sam Rayburn threatened, "If we can get [the loan] approved any other way, we'll get 'em by the throat and throw 'em just like bulldogging a Texas steer." Even if Texans were left with a postwar plant that produced surplus steel, they believed that one of the big companies would buy and operate it rather than endure charges of violating antitrust laws. In the words of *Business Week*, steel industry executives "feel that they'll be damned if they do and damned if they don't. If they buy the plant, they'll be accused of monopolistic practices. . . . If they don't buy the plant they will be charged with failing to aid in Texas' industrial development."[10]

While Lone Star Steel and other projects related to defense and the paper industry remained dear to Patman's heart, nothing surpassed his devotion to "fair trade" laws.* Although the Robinson-Patman Act proved confusing and nearly unenforceable in its very first year and was practically ignored thereafter, Patman and the NARD still celebrated its silver anniversary in 1960. Even Patman conceded privately that the antitrust laws were more effective against the chain stores than Robinson-Patman. As for fair trade laws, twenty-three states enforced them as late as 1963. Advocates even maintained that the fair trade movement grew stronger in the early 1960s when Senators Hubert Humphrey of Minnesota and Homer Capehart of Indiana introduced a bipartisan "Quality Stabilization" bill in 1962—a voluntary national fair trade measure. But the racing inflation of 1965–1980 doomed any remaining fair trade laws. Patman himself concentrated upon attacking banks, foundations and the Federal Reserve.[11]

*There is one final bit of irony in the story of Wright Patman. The modern equivalent of the A & P chain store bogey of the 1930s is Wal-Mart, led by the late, folksy Sam Walton and headquartered in Bentonville, Arkansas, not more than a hundred miles from Patman's Texarkana. Its specialty is competition by price, a facet of American consumersim that has enriched it. Today we have numerous instances of Wal-Mart underselling independent retailers and truly bankrupting them in small towns all across the rural South and Midwest. In one case Wal-Mart, after exhausting the competition, decided some years later that the market was insufficient and closed its store—leaving the town without a merchant to sell pharmaceuticals or some items of clothing. A half century after the New Deal the advocates of "fair trade" had lost the battle for rural America, and the number of people leaving it for cities, suburbs and exurbia suggests that twenty-first-century rural America will see ghost towns where market towns once thrived.

PART FIVE

New Dealers Abroad

Roll on, Columbia, roll on,
Roll on, Columbia, roll on.
Your power is turning our darkness to dawn
Roll on, Columbia, roll on.

Green Douglas firs where the waters cut through,
Down her wild mountains and canyons she flew,
Canadian Northwest to the oceans so blue,
Roll on, Columbia, roll on.

Other great rivers add power to you,
Yakima, Snake, and the Klickitat too,
Sandy, Willamette, and Hood River too,
Roll on, Columbia, roll on.

Tom Jefferson's vision would not let him rest.
An empire he saw in the Pacific Northwest.
Sent Lewis and Clark, and they did the rest.
Roll on, Columbia, roll on.

At Bonneville now there are ships in the locks.
The waters have risen and cleared all the rocks.
Shiploads of plenty will steam past the docks.
So roll on, Columbia, roll on.

And on up the river is Grand Coulee Dam,
The mightiest thing ever built by a man,
To run the great factories and water the land,
It's roll on, Columbia, roll on.

—WOODY GUTHRIE,
"Roll on, Columbia" (1941)

14.
Henry J. Kaiser:
New Deal Earth and Money Mover

How the West Was Built

THE PROLETARIAN TROUBADOR Woody Guthrie wrote these visionary words in the spring of 1941 while he languished on the Bonneville Power Administration's payroll. He intended them to delight a world and a time in awe of men who moved rivers in order to capture their energy for industry and trade. Wanting economic development, Westerners yearned to harness the power of the Colorado and the Columbia for the benefit of Los Angeles, Seattle and all the farmers, merchants and would-be entrepreneurs between Puget Sound and San Diego harbor. The promotion of industrial growth on the Pacific Coast inspired images of "shiploads of plenty" tying up at docks adjacent to neon cities ablaze with the dawn of great factories that lured masses from Eastern cities to be fed by fields of abundant crops. The soaring dam structures that diverted water and captured power at Boulder Canyon, Bonneville, Shasta, Fort Peck and Grand Coulee thrilled Americans from Washington State to Washington, D.C., with their beauty and their anticipation of power for enterprise and jobs. Moreover, their planners and builders were solicitous of nature, including ladders on the dams to be sure that the salmon could go upstream to spawn. They did not fail to imagine an adverse environmental impact from their altering nature, but they were supremely confident that they could and would improve upon the wilderness and benefit men without harming nature.[1] For the primitive West lusted to become the industrial West.

Still, if the trepidations of some economic thinkers and businessmen of the early 1930s were correct—that the manufacturing frontiers of the country were finite, that Americans had reached the limits of economic development, that their markets had attained capitalist maturity in the East—then little would be new in a New Deal for the West. In the words of one Chicago manufacturer during the Roosevelt recession, "While I like the idea of private property and rugged individualism, my common sense tells me that the U.S. is growing older, that it is now passing into middle age and that the design for living which was followed during its youth can no longer be applied."[2] It seemed to some that liberal capitalism had yielded to the cartelistic collectivism of NRA and AAA. Had a new phase of historical economic development begun? Were Western promoters too late to enjoy industrial capitalism?

Such questions aroused and energized the peculiar chauvinism of Westerners. They recognized that the absence of Western growth meant continued colonial subservience to New York. An element of Western belief missing from Guthrie's song about their majestic Columbia was their hostility to the East. Like Texans, the people of the Pacific Coast were optimistic, anticolonial and resentful; they wanted their share of the economic pie. "The people here will mesh their assets and their strength and wage a united fight to expand the tremendous industrial potential out of the Columbia River Valley," a Bonneville Power publicist forecast. "The West must make its voice heard now rather than take it lying down, against the danger of the East. . . . It must work together to abolish the wanton old system by which the West ships raw materials three thousand miles East, then gets the finished products from those materials shipped back three thousand miles." Feeling exploited economically and ignored politically, Westerners made resentment and grievances an ingrained part of their culture. In defense of their "regional self-interest," Pacific Coast representatives in Washington, D.C., demanded more federal expenditures for Western roads, irrigation, reclamation, and power projects on the Columbia. "They aimed at harnessing the region's water resources and improving its production and distribution systems to promote economic development and growth," historian Paul Kleppner writes. "And, of course, by securing federal funds they also aimed at reducing their region's dependence upon eastern bankers and industrialists."[3] Nothing better suited the ideology of the Brandeisians who sought to redirect American capital from the glutted vaults of New York to a primitive Zion awaiting development. Even those New Dealers who had never seen the Pacific shores were Westerners at heart. They would make the Federal Treasury the West's best banker.

The Columbia River originates in British Columbia and flows southward through eastern Washington before it lurches westward for about 300 miles to define Washington and Oregon as it empties into the Pacific. Although the two states had long recognized the Columbia's apparently unlimited potential for cheap, clean energy for industrial development, nobody did anything about it until the 1920s. Observing California's and especially Los Angeles's rapid growth through exploitation of the Colorado's hydroelectric power, business and agricultural groups in the Pacific Northwest wondered if they should imitate it. They knew they could, if they tried; after all, somebody estimated that 41 per cent of all the latent hydroelectricity in the United States lay in the Columbia Basin. Additionally, they had a foundation for low-cost power; across the nation about 20 per cent of all power systems were publicly owned, but in the Pacific Northwest that ratio reached 50 per cent—evidence of a collective will for development. In the state of Washington, a strong tradition of public power prevailed in the Seattle-Tacoma area. The Columbia River Development League, based in Washington and hoping to build a dam at Grand Coulee to sell its power and irrigate the surrounding farmland, had launched a campaign in 1918 for statewide support. But the West lacked capital for development. As in the case of Westerners with designs upon the Colorado, the route to Columbia River development detoured through the United States Congress for a larger share of federal capital. In 1924 a Democratic politician named Homer T. Bone tried to turn legislative attentions to public power, but arguments over Prohibition enforcement drowned him out. Still, thanks to Republican Senators Wesley Jones of Washington and Charles McNary of Oregon, the 1925 and 1927 Federal Rivers and Harbors Acts included recommendations for a system of dams on the Columbia. In 1931 and 1932, Congress rejected appropriations for the dams, but they attracted the support of Franklin D. Roosevelt.

Washington State Democrats were some of Roosevelt's most ardent supporters at the 1932 convention, and in a campaign speech at Portland on September 21, 1932, Roosevelt vowed that his presidency would initiate hydroelectric power development on the Columbia. As with his conception of the Tennessee River, Roosevelt stressed regional development, declaring, "This vast water power can be of incalculable value to this whole section of the country. It means cheap manufacturing production, economy and comfort on the farm and in the household." The Columbia River's uses figured prominently in the 1932 Washington State race for the U.S. Senate between Jones and Bone. Jones espoused federal dams to irrigate eastern Washington while Bone wanted public power's low rates for manufacturing. Although the power issue carried Bone and Washington Democrats to victory, it did not cross the Columbia to help Oregon Democrats. McNary sought federal development of the Columbia River but he wanted private utilities to distribute and sell its power. The public-private conflict sharply divided Oregon Democrats and left them a minority party during the New Deal.[4]

The men who were building Boulder Dam had more than passing interests in the Northwest's 1932 elections. Henry J. Kaiser and his Six Companies cohorts in the Colorado River venture could count upon more jobs for many Western conservation and power projects, thanks to

Washington and Oregon lobbying for such projects, if Roosevelt were president. But Hoover shied away from federal development of the Columbia River. A man like Kaiser might otherwise be apolitical, but as one of the few Western contractors experienced in such big projects and eager to keep his men working, he became a New Dealer.

Kaiser would be recognized in an administration not known for favoring any businessmen as the "New Deal's favorite businessman." He served the purposes of Harold Ickes at the Interior Department and at the Public Works Administration to implement big projects for the West while Jesse Jones at the Reconstruction Finance Corporation bankrolled them. Ickes and Tommy Corcoran learned to love Kaiser's zeal for new projects, and a skeptical Jesse Jones made concessions to Kaiser's ambitions. A road builder and a dam builder through the 1920s and 1930s, Kaiser demonstrated a versatility for any industry late in the decade when he constructed his own Permanente Cement Corporation in order to ensure an adequate supply of material to build California's Shasta dam. When the New Dealers shifted gears in preparation for war, they found Kaiser eager for shipbuilding, fabricating steel, and manufacturing aluminum and manganese. Almost any industrial problem excited his enormous industrial curiosity.

New Dealers saw Kaiser as a great blessing. Had he not existed, they would have had difficulty inventing him. They needed to demonstrate that public investment could do the job that private bankers shied away from. The crusades for development of the West and against the Axis threat afforded them opportunities to prove what government could do. They were antimonopolists, yet believers in bigness, who doubted the efficacy or wisdom of the antitrust laws. War, history told them, increased industrial concentration, remembering as did Roosevelt that the mobilization of 1917–18 put too much money in the hands of too few businessmen, contributing to a maldistribution of wealth that led to the Great Depression. Kaiser was different from the big corporations, whose efficiency would be needed in a war mobilization again. He thought big, acted big, and proved to be a humanely liberal businessman sympathetic to unions and considerate of his employees' health problems. New Dealers wanted him to be the beneficiary of mobilization in 1940, not those businessmen who were the enemies of the New Deal. For instance, building an air force would require enormous quantities of aluminum and manganese—which would further enrich the Aluminum Company of America unless an alternative to the ALCOA monopoly could be created. In an age of state capitalism, the monopolist's competitor was Henry J. Kaiser.[5]

Kaiser was a Western Horatio Alger story. Born a few months after

FDR's birth in 1882 to poor German immigrants at Canajoharie, New York, he early exhibited entrepreneurial skill; at twenty-five he decided to seek his fortune in Spokane, Washington, where he became a salesman for a paving contractor. However, Kaiser quickly perceived that the automotive revolution then sweeping the West would bring prosperity to more people than Easterners who assembled cars and supplied their parts for sale in places like Spokane. Throughout the Pacific Northwest towns and counties were paving roads with revenues from user taxes—thereby making motorists pay for their roads as they bought their fuel. But motorists demanded good roads, thereby inspiring a revolution in public finance to accelerate road-building; Kaiser saw his chance and by 1913 formed his own construction company. In 1921 the restless Kaiser headed south to California in quest of fulfilling its burgeoning need for highways.

"Find a need, and fill it," he liked to say—and he adeptly practiced it. A contractor had to avoid idle time for his machinery and crews; "Before you work yourself out of the last job, line up a bigger one to pull yourself out," Kaiser said. Kaiser's appetite for jobs grew. Based in Oakland, California, he extended his lust for projects over thousands of miles; one of his more famous jobs was building a 300-mile stretch of highway through a primitive part of Cuba. Many a builder overextended himself and fell victim to bankruptcy because projects involved unanticipated costs, but Kaiser had a genius for devising ways to save money on labor and materials after he underbid competitors for projects. For example, to conserve time he put rubber tires on wheelbarrows and hitched them to tractors and he replaced ordinary gasoline engines in tractors and shovels with more efficient diesel engines. Even the mugwumpish Ickes admired Kaiser for saving the government money by bringing Boulder Dam to completion well ahead of schedule through the innovation of specially designed machinery.

Also, he shrewdly negotiated his contracts. In 1931 the executive committee of Six Companies, Inc., elected Kaiser its chairman and its contact man in Washington. "The Washington assignment was of critical importance in determining the ultimate direction of Kaiser's career," his biographer has written. "From the day he got off the train in the nation's capital as official representative of the Six Companies in 1931, Kaiser assiduously cultivated cordial relationships with important government decision-makers. Even before Franklin Roosevelt was inaugurated in March 1933, Kaiser was recognized as a businessman who knew the bureaucratic ropes in Washington." Like the Brown brothers of Texas, Kaiser befriended useful lawyers and politicians. He contributed to political campaigns and built a "sumptuous" visitors' cottage at Hoover Dam for the use of political VIPs. He made alliances with Ickes, Jones, and when the ubiquitous Corcoran left government service he knew that he could have a retainer from Kaiser. But all the friendships in the world could not bring him government contracts unless Kaiser performed quickly, acceptably and free from the graft frequently associated with the building trades. New Dealers expected Kaiser to be simon pure.[6]

Other jobs followed. In 1933 Kaiser won the contract for Bonneville Dam, 40 miles east of Portland, where the flow of the Columbia River was five times more powerful than the Colorado and where spring rains brought floods to wipe out many man-hours of work. Kaiser's son, Edgar, would later recall that Bonneville was "without question, the most difficult construction job we ever built." In 1934 Kaiser sought the contract for Grand Coulee Dam. At Grand Coulee the Columbia at low level carried more water than the Colorado at flood stage, thereby calling for a structure so big as to dwarf the spectacular Boulder Dam. He lost the contract for preliminary work on Grand Coulee but in 1938 won the assignment for building its superstructure. The dam they built there has three times the bulk of Hoover Dam and required Kaiser's men to devise a special trestle costing $1,400,000 to pour $36,000,000 worth of concrete. Also, his organization made the pilings for the Oakland–San Francisco Bay Bridge.[7]

Kaiser demonstrated too that government funds could generate competition in monopoly industries. The builder knew something about covert cartels. "It used to anger me to see the cement companies gouge the little contractor," Kaiser recalled. "Cement represented a major part of his costs, but there was nothing he could do about it." But Kaiser was big enough to do something about those costs. When he lost the contract in 1938 to construct Shasta Dam at the head of the Sacramento River, an angry Kaiser bid to supply the dam's cement from a plant to be built at a location rich with limestone deposits on Permanente Creek in Santa Clara County. He infuriated the big cement companies because his low bid lacked a plant from which he could produce—but Interior Department officials loved the fact that his price undercut other identical bids by twenty-two cents. But could Kaiser deliver on schedule? When the other companies compelled a railroad to charge him exorbitant rates to haul sand and gravel, Kaiser outfoxed them by rigging a 10-mile conveyer belt to carry sand and gravel at nine cents per ton less than the railroad. He erected the Permanente plant, then the world's biggest, in six months. Although Kaiser lost money on the Shasta contract, selling cement to other contractors gave him a small profit. Most of all, the Shasta deal added to his goodwill with Ickes and other New Dealers. "If Kaiser's life can be said to have a turning point, it was then," a California railroad man observed. "He licked a tough bunch. From then on, he wasn't afraid to tackle anything."[8]

Impressing Ickes was important to Kaiser because of all the New Dealers he dealt with, Ickes was the man Roosevelt chose to build the infrastructure of the West. The President had wanted a Western progressive Republican senator to be his secretary of the interior and czar of public works. Known for their political probity and hunger for federal development of the West, FDR envisioned Western progressives and promoters participating in a party realignment in which the Democratic party emerged as the liberal party. But when Roosevelt sounded out Hiram Johnson of California and Bronson Cutting of New Mexico, neither wanted to leave the Senate for the Cabinet. Johnson recommended Ickes, a Chicago lawyer who had labored for the causes of conservation and political reform for many years; only a few months before, Ickes had led a quixotic effort to have the GOP nominate Gifford Pinchot for president over Hoover. Ickes himself figured that that endeavor caught Roosevelt's attention and that his Western interests qualified him to be commissioner of Indian Affairs. Only after he heard that Johnson and Cutting had rejected it did Ickes set his sights upon Interior.

Something about the political exploitation of Chicago's development and industry's economic exploitation of the West made Ickes an unalterably indignant and self-righteous good-government man. Initially an investigative reporter, Ickes had turned to law in a quest to purify Chicago politics. Long before David Lilienthal's arrival, Ickes too had been Donald Richberg's associate in law and politics. He managed the abortive campaigns of reformers John Maynard Harlan and Charles E. Merriam for mayor, worked actively for Theodore Roosevelt for president between 1912 and 1916, for Hiram Johnson for president between 1920 and 1924 and, finally, performed the 1932 comic opera Pinchot effort. Fortunately, he abandoned the GOP in 1932, thereby entitling him to dream of a New Deal appointment on February 21, 1933, when he joined several people waiting to speak with the President-elect at his New York City home. As Ickes was ushered in, Roosevelt began to to tell him of his priorities for interior secretary, concluding with the declaration, "You and I have stood for the same thing, and I think that Harold Ickes of Chicago is that man." But Roosevelt needed a day to touch base with Democratic and progressive senators. The next evening Ickes returned to find him with Jim Farley and Frances Perkins. Turning to Perkins, Roosevelt said, "I'd like the Secretary of Labor to meet the Secretary of Interior."[9]

What was it that Roosevelt thought he and Ickes stood for? It was an uplift reformism that eschewed radicalism and stressed moralism in public life. While not absolving politicians of blame for political corruption, Ickes agreed with another reformer's comment that "Political corruption in the United States is an incident in the history of commerce." Big business corrupted America's public life. With some acerbity, Ickes once declared, "It'll take a quarter of a century for Illinois to get over [Samuel] Insull." However, as with most progressives, condemnation of businessmen did not signify espousal of socialism. In fact, Ickes favored public ownership of utilities only because utility moguls corrupted otherwise honest regulators. "He would rather have a municipal plant even if it costs a little bit more to operate," Joseph Alsop observed, "so long as the poisonous influence of the utility is removed from the municipality."

As expected, Ickes ran Interior and the Public Works Administration with a conservative zeal for avoiding any taint ("corruption is a word which recurs very regularly in his talk," Alsop noted). He proved to be a tough and nasty administrator, and when he could not have his way he could throw himself into a "sort of Donald Duck type of rage." Paranoid, he detested his peers and persecuted his subordinates, turning his department into what one lieutenant called "a regular OGPU," the acronym then for the Soviet secret police. He personally hired private investigator Louis Glavis, who more than two decades before had been in the middle of the Ballinger-Pinchot controversy. It was evident that Glavis was there to spy on Interior employees. One man in the Power Division would end his telephone conversations with, "Listen in, Glavis, I don't give a damn." Another would shout into the phone, "I hope your damned ears drop off." Needless to say, department morale was low, but eventually Ickes and Glavis alienated each other.

Although he was an eighteen-hour-a-day workaholic, Ickes found time for extracurricular activities. Before long all of Washington knew that the Interior Secretary had a mistress. Ickes's marriage to Anna Wilmarth Thompson had been unhappy for some time prior to his arrival in Washington, and he soon had a sexually gratifying affair with an Interior Department employee. "She enjoyed intercourse and she could give as well as take," Ickes happily recalled. But then her jealous boyfriend began sending anonymous letters to Ickes and to newspapers, compelling Ickes to inform Roosevelt about the letters, "without admitting or denying they were based on facts." Appreciating a man's need for a discreet affair, Roosevelt ordered the Secret Service to investigate the writer of the letters.[10]

Eight years younger than Ickes, FDR may have underestimated his ambitions. The "Secretary for the West" proved to be one of the outstanding bureaucratic imperialists and political manipulators in an administration noted for them. Henry Wallace, whose father had learned about agency-grabbing from Herbert Hoover in the previous decade, once persuaded Ickes to take a vacation, during which Wallace convinced Roosevelt to transfer the Soil Erosion Agency from Interior to Agriculture; Ickes flew into a rage when he returned. In later years during an after-dinner speech to administration officials, with Wallace present and squirming in his chair, Ickes recounted how he ended his absence only to find Agriculture trucks carting away Soil Erosion files from the Interior Department. However, once burned, Ickes did some burning himself, embittering Secretary of State Cordell Hull by insisting that the overseas sale of helium came under Interior's banner and feuding with Harry Hopkins when Hopkins garnered Congress's 1935 works appropriation into the creation of another relief agency, the Works Progress Administration—an acronym chosen, Ickes was certain, to confuse Hopkins's relief agency with Ickes's recovery agency. He was a superb feudist. He brimmed with undisguised contempt for Secretary of Commerce Daniel Roper and Postmaster General Jim Farley because they were "political hacks."

Viewing Ickes as "a combination of Foxy Grandpaw and the Terribly Tempered Mr. Bangs," Tommy Corcoran got much political use out of him. Although the petulant Ickes threatened to resign several times during the course of a dozen years in the Cabinet, Roosevelt confided to Corcoran that he valued the Secretary for his loyalty, as well as his willingness to be a "valuable hatchet man for the administration." Indeed, Ickes yearned to be Roosevelt's pit bull. Soon after taking the leadership of Interior, he renamed Hoover Dam Boulder Dam. Detesting Hoover, Ickes righteously believed that the name had been a Republican political trick. (It was the practice since Theodore Roosevelt's presidency and through Woodrow Wilson's tenure to name federal dams for presidents who began their construction.) Also, at Roosevelt's request, Ickes tried to remove Robert Moses as head of New York's Triboro Bridge Authority, but Moses fought back until Ickes backed down. Still, Ickes enjoyed the attention newspapers gave him when he delivered slashing speeches written by Corcoran and Cohen attacking conservative Democrats or rich Americans. In 1936 Senator Joseph Guffey of Pennsylvania asked Ickes to make a campaign speech in his state because, as Corcoran said, "Ickes always puts on a good show." He not only had mastered political invective but he realized "that he must throw more people to the lions to keep the crowd interested."[11]

Ickes thought that every New Deal initiative for public power should result in an agency, authority, administration or bureau which would be lodged in the Interior Department. If Jesse Jones was the czar of credit, Ickes expected to be the potentate of power. As Bonneville neared completion in 1935, Senator James J. Pope of Idaho put forward a bill for a Columbia Valley Authority modeled upon TVA, but the whole concept of regional development came under fire in the Pacific Northwest and in Congress. Ickes demanded that Bonneville Power be placed under his jurisdiction. Roosevelt cared less about bureaucratic fights than the concept of public planning for America's great river valleys and a low price for energy to encourage their economic development. Rather than give in to Ickes directly, the president created a low-profile committee to hammer out a national power policy chaired by Ickes. The National Power Policy Committee, with Ben Cohen as its general counsel, included Morris Cooke, Frederic A. Delano, Robert Healy and Frank McNinch. Of course, they were no match for the pugnacious Ickes.

Beginning on January 19, 1937, the NPPC held a series of meetings and hearings in Ickes's office. Roosevelt directed the committee to obtain a "uniform" pricing of power: "This does not mean identical rates in every part of the country but it does mean uniformity of policy." The issue centered around the Bonneville Dam Kaiser was building. The Washington State and Oregon Planning Boards had gone on record for low-cost power "to create opportunities for the economic development and use of the great hydro-electric power resources of the Pacific Northwest, now largely going to waste." Almost all congressmen from the Pacific Northwest denounced proposals to have the Bonneville Power Authority and private utilities pool their power distribution, demanding instead that public agencies have priority to buy power at low rates. To the suggestion that the Federal Power Commission market Bonneville power, Frank McNinch denied that the FPC could act as both regulator and retailer. Cohen drafted a bill for Bonneville's operation which, not surprisingly, adopted most of the recommendations of the Pacific Northwest Regional Planning Commission—with the notable exception of its proposal for an independent corporation. Instead, the BPA would have the authority to build more power facilities and sell power as a bureau in the Department of the Interior. Ickes appointed Bonneville's first administrator, J. D. Ross of Seattle, a man certain to keep the price of power low for developing industries. He had scored a notable victory, but, as we shall see, that would not content him.[12]

The NPPC's work had implications for all the West. Two powerful advocates of power for the Southwest, Ezra Scattergood of Los Angeles Power and Light and Senator Key Pittman of Nevada, demanded that the Bonneville legislation be tied to modifications of Boulder Dam's contracts for power and thereby make more of it available for less cost. Four Western states—Colorado, Utah, Wyoming and New Mexico—accused Los Angeles of seeking additional federal subsidization of Southern California electricity while they were "treated as step children of the federal government." When Pittman threatened to delay Bonneville legislation if he could not remove this "discrimination against Boulder," the administration separated Boulder from Bonneville by promising an investigation into their rate differentials; the president would designate an agency to make the study: "Of course, we will pull for the Interior Department for this assignment," Ickes said. Deciding that he did not want a fight with Ickes, Scattergood tacked and called for interconnection of all power projects for West Coast development—modestly offering that the credit for the idea go to the President.[13]

Although nearly unknown to the public, Scattergood was one of public power's most effective friends. He could be troublesome to New Dealers because he was among the most insistent local promoters of federal benefits. Los Angeles may have been the only city at the time to employ a full-time lobbyist in Washington. Also, Scattergood maintained a fund for "promoting industries in Southern California and for advertising and the general commercial development of that section of the state," which Henry Kaiser, among others, contributed to. Sometimes when Scattergood wanted legislation, he was not above blackmail. For instance, knowing that Nathan Margold, Solicitor for the Interior Department and part of the Frankfurter network, aspired to a judgeship, Scattergood once reminded Corcoran "with complete frankness which has always characterized our conversations and relations" that he had ways of influencing the votes of Midwest Republican senators. In that instance as on other occasions, Scattergood got what he wanted. When J. D. Ross died suddenly in 1939, Corcoran carefully consulted Scattergood on Ross's successor. Modern Los Angeles would owe much to the New Deal and Ezra Scattergood.[14]

Public power in the New Deal needed local boosters such as Scattergood and J. D. Ross of Seattle. Ross counted upon Bonneville to expand the Seattle market. As in Los Angeles and the Tennessee Valley, Bonneville would reduce rates to private power companies who then would pass the reductions along to businesses and enjoy a swelling volume of business, thereby passing "the advantages of Bonneville to their customers." Surveying in 1939 the potential for the region's industrial development, the Pacific Northwest Regional Planning Commission and the Bonneville Power Administration anticipated considerable population growth. That was before war erupted in Europe: the onset of the defense preparedness program would make those anticipations appear modest. However, as with TVA, in 1939 New Dealers moderated their ambitions for public power because, in Cohen's words, "political conditions are different from what they were in the early days of T.V.A." While public power in the Pacific Northwest was popular and "not a novel experiment" there, Cohen shrewdly judged "it dangerous to give the impression that we are bent upon driving out private power." BPA would have to be content with compelling through low wholesale prices low consumer rates.[15]

Heavy industry in the West required two things Washington could deliver on: capital and energy. The energy was provided by nature, if men were wise enough to capture it. The funds were provided by the federal Treasury. The start-up money for Henry Kaiser's cement business came from Bank of America, itself heavily indebted to the RFC, making Jesse Jones directly and indirectly Kaiser's banker. Kaiser thrived because he hired clever and loyal men and because he usually had money in the pipeline from a government job. Corcoran, who played a prominent role in facilitating federal contracts for Kaiser, depicted the New Deal's businessman as one of the few entrepreneurs in America who dared to think big. He believed that Kaiser justified all of the administration's state capitalism: "If we could find one financier who thought as Henry Kaiser does, we could show the world that our ideas will work."[16]

"Dreamers With Shovels": The New Dealers at War

COMPETITORS AGREED that Henry Kaiser possessed enormous creativity as a businessmen, but many also argued that his genius owed much to Uncles Sam's financing. Either the works projects of the New Deal or the Reconstruction Finance Corporation funded his fecund dreams of enterprise. But not all of his schemes earned a blank federal check. Harold Ickes, Jesse Jones and Franklin Roosevelt could be tightfisted and choosy—and many of Kaiser's mental blueprints never even saw a drawing board. Still, his detractors insisted that he was not a true free enterpriser; Kaiser had seized and built upon "an important truth. It was that 'you could operate on government money.' " Indeed, in World War II he pushed his way with Uncle Sam's eager support into the shipbuilding, and steel, aluminum and magnesium industries. He initiated those enterprises. While U.S. Steel and ALCOA sniffed disapprovingly that he did it with government capital, to his credit he showed enormous nerve in rushing in where supposedly wiser heads feared to go. Other builders lacked his audacity. "As a contractor I like to put my money into a specific job, and pull out," said Felix Kahn, a Six Companies partner who did not follow Kaiser beyond earth moving. "I didn't like the idea of freezing my capital in a steel mill." Admittedly, only in wartime could Kaiser have entered manufacturing with Washington's money. In the postwar era, another builder predicted, Washington would withdraw as a customer and if Kaiser sought to remain in manufacturing "he will have to have either government or public money."[17]

As evidenced by the fate of the Works Financing bill of 1939, New Deal state capitalism would have been reduced in the 1940s without the war—a victim of politics and its own success in creating growth and recovery. The New Deal's zenith had passed quickly. The Roosevelt recession of 1937–38, the errant court reforms, and the confused tax policies of 1935–39 stymied New Dealers. Although the economy rebounded nicely from the recession, administration programs engendered shock and bitterness among some Democrats, alerting New Dealers to fears that if another downturn erupted soon it would destroy them politically. Also, a resurgent electric utility industry joined with its financial partners in Wall Street to put the New Dealers on the defensive: could and should public investment supplant private investment? The issue seemed to climax in the spring and summer of 1939 as most New Dealers retreated from reliance exclusively upon public funds without corresponding incentives in indolent private markets. Conservatives in both parties threatened to abort any more river valley imitations of TVA, leaving some liberals, including FDR, to encourage local and regional boosters to change congressional minds concerning the Missouri Valley and other power projects. TVA and its friends throughout the country rightly pointed to its successes, but the message a congressional majority sent was that TVA would stand as an isolated monument to a moment that could not be sustained or reproduced. Still, the West had seized the moment. Scattergood and Ross got Bonneville to build massive grids that carried additional cheap power throughout the far West; Los Angeles and Seattle would be great cities. But BPA would never be TVA. Slightly more than six years after they had begun to make the world over, the New Dealers were exhausted and in search of legacies; without Roosevelt they probably were moribund. In an increasingly hostile world, it seemed likely that if Roosevelt bowed to the two-term tradition and retired, the New Deal would enter a period of consolidation or even retrenchment. If a Democrat won the presidency in 1940, he would likely have to be more conservative than the New Deal leader—even if his name was Franklin Roosevelt. But World War II's eruption in Europe on September 1, 1939, rescued the New Dealers and allowed them to believe that the world still needed practical dreamers of federal enterprises.

It is a cliché that the war and not the New Deal restored prosperity.

The war also rescued from potential eclipse Franklin Roosevelt's presidency and quests for projects that used, expanded, justified, and perpetuated principles of state capitalism. The war convinced many liberals that New Deal projects had been on track to prosperity and that public investment accelerated an ineluctable American abundance. By comparison, federal outlays during the war made the enormous spending of 1938–39 appear minuscule; they also pointed the way toward grander projects for development. Westerners especially took heart from the looming industrial necessities of war and the Japanese threat in the Pacific to proclaim that the New Deal had been America's rehearsal for a war mobilization. In 1940 John Carmody, formerly of the Rural Electrification Administration and now Administrator of the Federal Works Agency, published a booklet celebrating seven years and a billion dollars of New Deal spending for projects to create "highways, hospitals, power plants, and scores of other types of public works of military and civil importance." Now development and defense were the same. Later David Lilienthal recalled that "the fall of France [in June 1940] made it clear that TVA must be converted to war."[18]

Attitudes toward government planning swung violently during 1939–41 between the imperative for a collective defense and the fear for individualism's decline in an increasingly totalitarian world. New Dealers had averred that state capitalism both venerated a collective will and excited individual opportunity; the totalitarians inadvertently proved that the New Deal had been on the right track after all. America suddenly realized that it needed certain New Deal projects. What had been a battle every year in Congress for a TVA budget became a cakewalk in 1941. New Dealers dusted off plans for regional development in the styles of TVA or Bonneville for the Missouri and Arkansas River Valleys and the Central Valley of California. America's Arsenal of Democracy had to grow and it needed power. In 1940—with Western Europe ground under the heel of fascism, the Soviets capturing the Baltics, Japanese militarism on the march through East Asia—great New Deal projects fulfilled America's material and ideological needs. American liberal capitalism told the world's democratic remnant that public investment created magnificently productive works while it reinforced individualism as an alternative to totalitarianism. Liberals throughout the world celebrated TVA and Bonneville as monuments to a democracy's virility at a time when totalitarians scorned liberalism as futile and effete. Through 1941 public investment poured forth an enormous quantity of ships and planes from a Southern and Western infrastructure the New Deal had built in the previous decade.

Like the colonial South and the preindustrial West, the American military establishment of the 1930s lacked adequate investment and development. Less than 2 per cent of the gross national product was spent on the military. Nobody wanted militarization of the economy. Businessmen feared defense preparedness as reviving WIB-NRA regulations administered by a huge government bureaucracy. New Dealers dreaded regulations written and administered by big businessmen to favor great corporations whose scale gave them the illusion of efficiency in the manner of the Great War. The Nye Senate Committee investigation of 1934 confirmed that munitions manufacturers and bankers had profited handsomely from war—even if it could not fault the WIB for that. Although Roosevelt promoted partnerships with business in public enterprises such as electric generation, liberal New Dealers suspected that war enterprises would make them junior partners. FDR scuttled the business-backed War Resources Board of 1939, insisting upon defense preparations directed from Cabinet departments; if he needed any emergency setup, he would originate it in the White House and make it consonant with New Deal principles.

Could the Arsenal of Democracy be built by the New Deal earth movers? As early as 1937 Kaiser and Steven Bechtel of the Six Companies saw that the river projects would not go on forever and confidently asserted that their principles of organization would work in industries other than dam construction. They had begun to direct their attentions to shipbuilding following a 1933 investigation by Senator Hugo L. Black's special committee that found "fraud and extravagance" in the allotting of mail contracts as indirect subsidies. Black argued that Washington had paid out $3.5 billion to build a merchant marine that had not been self-supporting since 1891. Nevertheless, "without government aid the merchant marine would die a none too lingering death." In 1935 FDR asked Congress to forgo the usual "subterfuge . . . of disguised subsidies to American shipping" via mail contracts; he would call "a subsidy by its right name." Roosevelt hoped that "direct financial assistance . . . would be exposed to public view" and reduce federal expenses through candor. Nevertheless, Roosevelt characteristically did not recommend to Congress any specific legislation, allowing nationalism, interest groups and a spirit of economic development to assert themselves. Indeed, that old friend of an ambitious merchant marine, William G. McAdoo, then a Democratic senator from California, emerged as a leader of the drive to encourage a West Coast bid to build ships and to extend American commerce throughout the world. Congress asserted that American flag ships had to be built in American yards with American materials and labor. To implement these and other mandates, it created a Maritime Commission which Roosevelt, to spotlight its importance, put in the hands of his erstwhile SEC Chairman, Joseph P. Kennedy. Kennedy's prominence inspired *Fortune* to devote an entire issue to America's maritime and captured the attention of Kaiser and the Bechtel group. Expecting to reform the industry and move on, as he had done with the SEC, Kennedy vowed that the Maritime Commission would replace fifty vessels a year, but not add any ships that anticipated war duty. Then he departed the Maritime Commission to become an appeasement-minded Ambassador to Great Britain. He had not replaced a single ship. Shipbuilding under the Maritime Commission did not commence until January 1939 and then it was limited to the East Coast. It was up to Kaiser and Bechtel to shift Washington's perspective on the industry.[19]

Teams of British purchasing agents trekked to Washington in 1939–41 to assert the urgent need for ships to ply the North Atlantic with materials for Britannia's defense. In response to a Maritime Commission call for bids to build shipyards and cargo ships, Six Companies entered a partnership with Todd Shipbuilding. In December 1940 the British ordered sixty freighters, half of which would be built in Maine, the others on the West Coast at Richmond, California, amid "a vast sea of mud." Although no ships had been constructed on the Pacific Coast between the wars, Six Companies, led by Kaiser, also built shipyards in Los Angeles, Portland and Houston. The Maritime Commission and the Navy provided the financing. To the delight of Anglophiles, liberals and cost-conscious administrators, the Westerners emphasized speed in construction without sacrificing quality. It drove the Eastern shipbuilding craftsmen to distraction when Kaiser and his fellow Westerners conceptualized the business as akin to erecting a dam or assembling a car. Still, they spent just 196 days to build their first Liberty ship instead of almost a year, the time it normally took to build a freighter in Maine; moreover, by 1943 Kaiser cut that time to 27 from the laying of the keel to delivery. Fifty-two per cent of all American ships—over a thousand—built in the war came from Pacific Coast yards. Although the tanker *Schenectady* sank in the Willamette River (Kaiser blamed it on defective steel), ships built on the Pacific Coast were durable. Instances of ships constructed in warm Pacific waters sinking in frigid Russian and North Atlantic waters were dramatic, but rare.[20]

Such feats and others made Kaiser a celebrated figure in wartime Washington, and he bulled his way through the capital's china closet in quest of federal contracts. "How he covers the ground that he does is beyond me," an admiring Harold Ickes wrote. "No wonder the country has welcomed Kaiser with open arms. . . . Kaiser may be the miracle man to turn the war for us." Needing steel plate for his shipbuilding operations, and aided by Los Angeles lobbyists directed by Ezra Scattergood, ever intent upon Los Angeles's growth, Kaiser used his shipbuilding assets to obtain credit to build a blast furnace and steel plate plant at Fontana, California, the first steel plant in the West. But Fontana's output depended upon the War Production Board cooperating on supply of materials. When steel executives at the WPB gave Kaiser a runaround on the steel he needed for the war effort in September 1942, he took his story to an understanding Westerner who hated monopoly, Assistant Attorney General Thurman Arnold. At issue was regional and corporate competition, and Western economic development—all of which required new sources of capital.[21]

The need for new credit brought to mind the Reconstruction Finance Corporation. Ensconced in the Commerce Department and enjoying his role as Uncle Sam's banker, Jesse Jones could have been the William Gibbs McAdoo of World War II. Strangely, the thought never seemed to occur to him. The Federal Loan Administrator had not lost any of his imperial instincts, but he rejected external encouragement of RFC expansion, as his response to the Works Financing bill of 1939 suggested. Jones liked to show his independence of liberals and Roosevelt. He did not like Texas liberals such as Wirtz, Rayburn and Johnson, and Garner's ignominious departure from Washington made Jones rely even more upon conservative businessmen and Southerners for friends and allies. In the words of *Fortune*'s editor, the RFC was now "the fourth branch of government" by virtue of its powerful command of credit. RFC could generate economic growth or stave off bankruptcy, as it willed.[22] More cautious than ever, Jones was neither imaginative nor ambitious. New Dealers should have been grateful for that.

But they weren't. In May 1940 the President's National Defense Advisory Committee described an urgent need for aircraft and Roosevelt asked Congress for 50,000 planes. The NDAC also pointed to an absence of aircraft manufacturing capacity that only Washington could finance—a job for Jones's RFC. Along with other administration "all-outers" sympathetic to British needs, RFC lawyers Clifford Durr and Hans Klagsbrunn drafted a bill to give the agency power to finance aviation expansion, although nobody expected Jones to appreciate their initiative. As Jerome Frank once said to FDR concerning his proposal for financing, "Inasmuch as Jesse Jones does not like suggestions from outside sources, it might be well . . . not to tell him that it comes from me." But, with the fall of Paris to the Nazis and Britain's isolation in Europe, events overseas could not wait upon Jones. Previously the RFC loaned only against a borrower's collateral and potential profit; however, the law FDR approved on June 25 gave RFC powers to loan for national defense through corporations it created. During the summer of 1940 the RFC originated the Defense Plant Corporation, the Defense Supplies Corporation, the Metals Reserve Corporation and the Rubber Reserve Corporation, subsidiaries headed by a trusted apprentice of Jesse Jones.[23]

Jones either resisted or did not seem to realize that Congress had made him the principal banker of war preparedness. Accustomed to the old art of horse trading ("I can tell a damned peckerwood first time I lay my eyes on him. Can't you?"), he did not seem to appreciate that he had no time for negotiation. Moreover, it made him uneasy that in defense a company's sole business came from government spending. He let his longtime RFC lieutenant, Emil Schram, run the Defense Plant Corporation with a free hand—which was why, at a January 1941 press conference, Jones "pretty nearly fell out of his chair" when Schram announced a long list of expensive projects for DPC financing. Schram moved RFC and its subsidiaries quickly into war mobilization—DPC investments amounting to $500 million by the spring of 1941. Jones's caution contrasted sharply with Schram's alacrity. "Is Jones of Texas a great national asset or is he in fact a bottleneck?" *Fortune* asked.[24]

It was no time to be niggardly. When Jones reported that the Senate Finance Committee supported borrowing $500,000,000 for defense, FDR responded, "OK—why not $1,000,000,000? Time is of the essence!" Evidence that Jones missed the point came when he insisted, "We are negotiating contracts all the time, and we do it as rapidly as good business warrants." But it was not time for good business. For the first time since the early days of the New Deal Jones was stung by congressional criticism (the Truman committee in the Senate, which investigated waste and bottlenecks in the defense mobilization) and a normally sympathetic *Business Week*. Eugene Meyer's conservative Washington *Post* declared that "The plain truth is that Mr. Jones fell down rather badly on the job." The day Jones read that editorial, he encountered Meyer at a party. Words were exchanged, Jones grabbed Meyer, who was at least five inches shorter, and shook him until his pince-nez fell to the floor and shattered. Jones was not a man that the press cared to affront: when he threatened reprisals against attacks by Drew Pearson and Robert S. Allen, Pearson decided "to lay off Mr. Jones, because of his charges of malice."[25]

But Schram soon left to become head of the New York Stock Exchange; it was said that Jones maneuvered the appointment. Although that did not slow down DPC investing in aircraft plants, Jones made a fool of himself by betting on a continuous supply of natural rubber from overseas and refusing to build synthetic rubber factories: "Why put all that money into plants making rubber that would cost 40 cents a pound when you can get it for 18.5 cents in the Far East?" In 1942 Japanese conquests cut off the Far East and the U.S. confronted a rubber shortage Jones was unprepared for. One story heard in New York had a warehouse full of rubber burning down and Jones saying, "Well, we shall collect the insurance, shan't we?"[26]

Additional embarrassments followed Jones in the aluminum and magnesium industries, which provided the key materials in aviation. Incensed liberals feared that war orders would enhance ALCOA's monopoly. The coupling of ALCOA's economic power with the government's power of priority was "outrageous," Leon Henderson believed. Ironically, ALCOA had been among the first corporations to benefit by cheap government-produced power when it set up plants in the TVA and Bonneville regions. Nevertheless, the administration knew that ALCOA allowed the Germans to outproduce the U.S. in lightweight metals by at least five to one by adhering to cartel agreements with Berlin's subsidized aluminum industry. Moreover, Jones personally negotiated a loan to ALCOA for a plant to be built in Canada for aluminum to be mostly sold in the U.S. Under pressure from the Justice Department for antitrust action, the DPC funded competitors with ALCOA such as Richard Reynolds and Henry Kaiser. And when Clifford Durr left the DPC for the Federal Communications Commission, the Justice and Interior Departments increased their surveillance of DPC contract negotiations in order to encourage new producers of aluminum and magnesium. Reynolds Metals won loans to begin its own production in Alabama and Washington State. Harold Ickes made a special point of bringing a fabricating plant closer to raw materials and cheap power in the Pacific Northwest by pressuring the DPC to finance Kaiser Aluminum in the Bonneville region. Indeed, the DPC launched Kaiser and Reynolds in the aluminum industry, investing more than $400 million in them and ALCOA. Kaiser and Ickes directed most of this money to the Pacific Coast to fulfill its visions of enormous industrial development. Still, Jones invested the bulk of government funds for aluminum and magnesium with ALCOA, which could deliver quicker than its nascent rivals. Only toward the end of the war could Kaiser buy government-owned plants dirt cheap with RFC loans under the benevolent eye of the Justice Department.* Inevitably, making aluminum and magnesium made Kaiser think of manufacturing planes. He went into partnership with Howard Hughes, but their experiments never achieved more than demonstrating that one could build a larger aircraft of lightweight mate-

*During the war the government instituted unsuccessful antitrust suits against ALCOA, and by 1956, thanks to postwar antitrust litigation and wartime competition, ALCOA controlled only 43 per cent of the industry's primary capacity.

rials (the "Spruce Goose") and make it fly. Kaiser also dabbled in erecting synthetic rubber factories.[27]

Notwithstanding the Howard Hughes venture, Kaiser's most spectacular wartime failure was in magnesium. From the RFC Kaiser obtained over $9 million, and from the Army and the Office of Production Management he got an important "Certificate of Necessity," which gave him a tax write-off—"amortization"—of his magnesium plant in five years instead of the normal period under the American tax laws for plant depreciation. He owed this last plum to the collaborative efforts of Tommy Corcoran, Ben Cohen, Averell Harriman of the National Defense Commission, and Ickes. But Kaiser pinned his initial efforts upon an Austrian chemist named Fritz Hansgirg who had developed a process for magnesium's manufacture.* Unfortunately, the FBI jailed Hansgirg as a dangerous alien in December 1941; even worse, the cost of his process proved much greater than other means of producing magnesium. Magnesium never returned the profit for Kaiser that he got from other metals. Although Jesse Jones asserted that Kaiser went into metals production mostly to escape excess profits taxes on his shipbuilding, Kaiser never pretended to being an altruist; he was a businessman and the West's agent of change—self-consciously fostering industrial development on the Pacific Coast because he was a regional promoter.[28]

With the aid of his corporate public relations men and the awe of reporters accustomed to business types who eschewed any soft-minded liberalism, Kaiser became one of the most written-about men during the war, shrewdly playing upon his legendary exploits and fame. Roosevelt liked what he saw and encouraged members of his Cabinet to consult with Kaiser on economic planning for the postwar era. Although Kaiser disclaimed an interest in politics, a wartime Gallup poll found that 8 per cent of those Americans who were asked which public figure not in politics might make a good president, named Kaiser—ranking him just behind Generals MacArthur and Eisenhower. Some Democrats considered him for vice-president in 1944.[29]

In part, Kaiser furthered New Deal regionalism and the success of New Deal regionalism stimulated acceptance of state capitalism. Nothing

*For his services on just the magnesium matter, Corcoran charged Kaiser $100,000 and 150 shares of Todd-California Shipbuilding Corporation stock. Kaiser to Corcoran, June 4, 1941, Corcoran Papers, Box 496. Corcoran boasted to Drew Pearson that his Interior Department connection secured Bonneville Power for Kaiser and denied it to ALCOA—which netted him fees of a half million dollars. But Corcoran did not reserve his services exclusively for Kaiser. Lyndon Johnson's friends George and Herman Brown also benefited from Corcoran's "advice, conferences, and the negotiations" over shipbuilding contracts—for which they paid him $15,000 in 1943. Pearson Papers, G131; Corcoran to George Brown, November 18, 1946, Corcoran Papers, Box 49.

was more responsible for Western industrial development. Companies like ALCOA and U.S. Steel resisted building plants in Texas or on the Pacific Coast without government capital—and then they doubted their survival in peacetime markets. Kaiser changed many minds about the Pacific Coast during and after the war. But the South had nobody comparable to Kaiser.

David E. Lilienthal, that erstwhile Midwesterner, was the New Deal's strongest champion of Southern development—besides Roosevelt. Now secure in TVA following battles against the utilities and against Arthur Morgan, Lilienthal envisioned Washington's quest for aircraft in 1940–41 as an opportunity to take TVA into a new era of expansion. Like the champions of Bonneville and the West, Lilienthal reasoned that planes would be built from aluminum produced by using immense quantities of cheap TVA power. He hoped to enlarge TVA's consituency by promoting the idea of a governmental "aluminum yardstick" by which TVA would build an aluminum plant using its power to drive down the cost of ALCOA's precious industrial metal. However, he found to his chagrin that War Production Board officials were less interested in aluminum's price than in its quantity.[30] Even so, TVA's popularity had risen so swiftly that Congress bestowed funds upon it for projects the lawmakers and TVA knew little about, such as a "mystery plant" to be built at Oak Ridge that would use twice as much TVA power as did all of Memphis and would necessitate building another dam. Of course, that TVA energy would bring forth atomic energy. TVA invaded the war business in so many ways justified by national defense. By 1943 TVA alone employed more than 40,000 people, making it one of the largest government agencies of the time.[31]

Power remained TVA's principal business—which was why Harold Ickes coveted it for his power trophy closet along with Bonneville. And the war made TVA all the more desirable. In this respect, Ickes, who wanted public power to end monopolies among private utilities, would make the Interior Department a holding company of federal power authorities. As Petroleum Coordinator and Chairman of the National Power Policy Committee, Ickes enjoyed titles and policy leadership, but no administrative functions. It disturbed him that the defense need for more and cheaper power led to agitation for creating additional regional authorities for California's Central Valley, for the Arkansas River Valley or for the Missouri River Valley. It made Ickes want TVA all the more: at issue was whether the new projects would develop independently along the TVA model or, like BPA, become part of the Interior department—where Ickes wanted all energy agencies. Lilienthal had known enemies in Arthur Morgan and Wendell Willkie, but none like Ickes. Among the members of the 1941 Cabinet, Ickes was arguably FDR's favorite, its most vocal liberal and its most determined bureaucratic imperialist—as Henry Wallace and Jesse Jones could attest. On the other hand, by his choice of Knoxville for TVA headquarters, Lilienthal was a Washington outsider (which was somewhat to his advantage because it gave him the aura of being close to the people), disliked by certain congressmen, pathologically hated by Senator Kenneth McKellar of Tennessee, and only enjoyed access to the President by his leave. Still, Lilienthal had important friends in Felix Frankfurter and George W. Norris, the hero of the TVA story, without whom there would be no TVA or power yardstick.

To get TVA into Interior Ickes had Corcoran and Cohen lobbying for him; Lilienthal hoped to build a backdraft against their fire with a propaganda barrage. TVA was not just power, Lilienthal argued; it was regional development through "decentralization of administration." Through magazines such as *Fortune* and *Survey Graphic*, through correspondent Marquis Childs of the St. Louis *Post-Dispatch*, Lilienthal declaimed that TVA's decentralization was democracy in action. It was "something Dave and I have talked about frequently," Roosevelt said; "the damned newspapers have made it out that TVA is simply a power agency. Now that isn't the fact. We aren't just providing navigation and flood control and power. We are reclaiming land and human beings."

But Ickes did not see it that way. Claiming to be "hurt" by his ingratitude for all that Interior and PWA had done for TVA, Ickes accused Lilienthal of "just being selfish." More than a quarter century Ickes's junior, Lilienthal thought that he was almost "whining" when he pleaded that TVA in Interior would make for "sound organization." When California tried to turn its Central Valley into a TVA, Ickes insisted the project had to be in the Interior Department, not independent. But it was 1941, mobilization was feverish, and Lilienthal had additional allies in Federal Power Commission Chairman Leland Olds and Julius Krug, his former aide and now Chief of Power for the Office of Production Management. Knowing that Ickes had told columnist Drew Pearson, "If the President continues to follow Lilienthal and his gang on this proposition and continues to humiliate me, he is going to have to choose between my resignation and Lilienthal," and that Ickes "resigned" regularly, Lilienthal rejected a compromise proposition Cohen and Abe Fortas carried. "We have capitulated," Cohen blurted out. "Why can't you accept our surrender gracefully?"[32]

Ickes still could not be power czar. Lilienthal was protected by Roosevelt's personal commitment to TVA and their bond in the fight against the holding companies. Although they publicly insisted that TVA was more than a power project, in private the conspirators congratulated themselves on building the largest single American power company in 1944—an important contribution to the war effort. TVA would continue to grow after they passed from the scene and by the early 1970s it would produce about 10 per cent of all the electricity in America. As intended, while TVA did not redistribute wealth, it did add wealth, it did transform race relations and it did set a standard for low energy rates that helped produce economic development for the South. Whatever else it did, TVA promoted economic growth. It was a romance Roosevelt and Lilienthal shared. Following publication of Lilienthal's book *TVA: Democracy on the March*, Roosevelt wrote, "Truly I am thrilled by it. It puts clearly so many of the things which we have been striving for that it is in a sense an epic of what you call 'dreamers with shovels.' We all really belong in that category."[33]

Lilienthal's victory over Ickes was also significant because of a New Deal commitment to Southern economic development. Ickes did not think of expanding TVA's uses, and Roosevelt probably understood that. But development was important to Roosevelt. In response to Clark Foreman's suggestion in 1938 that the President appoint distinguished Southerners to survey and dramatize the economic needs of the South, FDR not only did that but wrote the introduction to its manifesto, *Report on Economic Conditions of the South*, in which he declared the region to be "the Nation's No. 1 economic problem." Ickes would not have hindered TVA's and the South's growth, but he lacked Lilienthal's daring creativity and penchant for planning. Ickes's PWA had been notoriously hesitant, while Lilienthal's TVA had been opportunistic. Ickes liked control more than leadership. TVA needed Lilienthal's imaginative leadership. Ironically, Ickes compelled Lilienthal to sharpen his apologia for TVA into a polemic of purpose—a defense against centralization, bureaucratization and totalitarianism—which gave TVA greater international importance.[34]

But the real story lay in how TVA facilitated government spending in the South. The South's poverty was palpable as well as legendary. Although the South dominated congressional leadership during the New Deal and could have captured a large share of public investment, it also had both a tradition and an aversion to federal spending. Which states did New Deal state capitalism benefit? New York, the most populous and the richest, received the most federal dollars during 1933–39. Midwestern states too did very well as every one of them made the top sixteen where New Deal dollars were spent. The only Southern state among the top third benefiting most from New Deal expenditures was

Texas, which was sixth—a tribute to the power and ambition of Jones, Garner, Rayburn, Johnson and Patman. California was fourth, showing that funds tended to go where the population was—except that the South did not claim its share. Without Texas, the Southeastern states, with almost a quarter of the American population, received less than a fifth of New Deal expenditures. On the other hand, the West, with a little more than a fifth of the population, obtained more than a quarter of federal appropriations.

Spending does not tell the whole story on regionalism in the New Deal. The New Deal also accelerated the federal government's loan business via the RFC, the Commodity Credit Corporation, the Rural Electrification Administration and other agencies. The state that benefited most from loans for banks, housing, agriculture, construction of power facilities, public works, consumer purchases, etc., was, not surprisingly, New York. But it is significant that the other states to make the most of expanded federal loan programs were, in order, Illinois, California, Ohio and Texas. The agricultural Midwest, together with California and Texas, borrowed the most for its economic development. The Southern states obtaining the most loans were Louisiana and Tennessee, fifteenth and sixteenth on the list. The Midwest liked to bank at the U.S. Treasury rather than Wall Street, but the South was not much interested in federal capital. And, if we list creditor states on a population basis, we find that the heaviest borrowers were the sparsest states such as Nevada, Montana, Idaho and the Dakotas. Interestingly, California was the ninth largest borrower on a per capita basis and Texas and Louisiana were sixteenth and seventeenth. And, if we examine where Jesse Jones put the bulk of the Reconstruction Finance Corporation's loans on a per capita basis, we see that California and Nevada headed the list—Louisiana, Texas and Tennessee being eighth, tenth, and twelfth, respectively. Finally, adding up all New Deal expenditures, loans and insurance allocated state by state on a per capita basis, we find that the real winners were the Western states with the fewest people. The only populous state among those most benefited by New Deal capital was California—tenth on a list in which the preceding nine were all mountain and plains states. As was the case with expenditures, when the matter of federal credit is included, the big winner in the New Deal was the West.

This finding suggests that Harold Ickes and Jesse Jones were the busiest of the New Dealers. It is also apparent that Roosevelt had determined upon economic development of areas where the amounts of raw materials were high and public investment on a per mile basis was low. In his 1932 speech at Portland, Oregon, Roosevelt had pledged that his administration would pursue regional development of the West, and he made good on his pledge. Moreover, the West during the New Deal saw the opportunity and aggressively made its case. Its leadership lusted for federal funds. And California's prominence in grabbing for federal expenditures or loans suggests the success of its unheralded booster and public servant Ezra Scattergood. On the other hand, Western acquisitiveness is in sharp contrast with the peculiar languor of Southern leaders. No wonder Roosevelt considered the South to be the nation's number one economic problem in 1938. Given a sympathetic President and control in Congress, the South missed an opportunity to feed at the federal trough.[35]

However, a new era dawned in 1938 in which federal dollars for economic development went hand in hand with dollars for national security. The Defense Plant Corporation, the RFC's offspring, was a major dispenser of the federal largesse at the outset of war in Europe. Ohio, Michigan and Pennsylvania received the most plants and other projects from the DPC—being the states where the steel and automobile industries were concentrated for manufacturing tanks, jeeps, planes and ships. What is startling is that Texas received the third highest amount of dollars spent by the DPC—another tribute to the political efforts of Jones, Johnson, Rayburn and Patman. California was only the eighth largest recipient of DPC dollars.[36]

The South and the Western states did not especially benefit from a situation in which speed of government expenditure mattered more than location. With in excess of 25 per cent of the population, the South received only 21.6 per cent of all federally financed manufacturing facilities and only 10.6 per cent of the alternative sources. And those figures include Texas—which alone produced 41 per cent of federally funded synthetic rubber. The South gained production capacity during the war, but, in the words of historian George B. Tindall, "Throughout the war the South remained more campground than arsenal." Thus, it won 36 per cent of the total spent on military facilities for the continental United States. It got 17.6 per cent of the national expenditure for war plants.[37]

The war benefited Texas far beyond any other Southern state. The value added of Texas manufacturing as a percentage of Southern manufacturing during 1939–45 rose from 14.4 to 17.3, displacing that of the leader in Southern manufacturing, North Carolina, which fell from 17.3 to 13.6. Moreover, the wartime economic growth for Texas created a trend that gathered momentum after the war. The data on per capita personal income by state as a percentage of the U.S. average (100) for the years 1934, 1944 and 1954 suggest both regional redistribution and additional enrichment.* Texas grew from 67 to 81 to 85. Two decades later it would be at about the national average while the industrially mature states of the Midwest and East would be approaching it from the other direction and the South would be slowly rising toward that elusive parity. Thus, on the one hand, a north-south regional redistribution was effected, but the rich Westerners still kept well ahead of poor but developing Southerners.[38]

The New Deal did work profound changes in Dixie. The South's industrial output in 1939 was less than it had been in 1909; Southern industrial growth was flat for the 1930s. Nevertheless, thanks to the New Deal, economic historian Gavin Wright tells us, "The economic underpinnings and social glue that had kept the regional economy isolated were no longer present in 1940." Rather, the New Deal had begun to integrate the South into the national economy. The era of the Southern promoter, when investment meant more than white supremacy, had erupted. The seeds of civil rights were planted and, "As distant as these changes seemed in 1940, the economic bases were already there before World War II." However, the only Southern state in 1980 with a per capita income above the national average was Texas. Its aggressiveness seemed downright un-Southern.

While most Southern states sought federal dollars with some indifference and lesser success, a few began to raise capital with which to induce industry to relocate there. In 1936 Mississippi began a modest program called "Balance Agriculture With Industry" (BAWI) to subsidize industrial relocation. Although the state remained poverty-stricken with little real economic growth, the concept of bribing corporations to relocate caught on among other Southern states. In the 1960s, writes a historian, "Socialistic and exploitative as it might be, the BAWI approach to industrial promotion had become a bandwagon, and Mississippi's competitors for industry were jumping on." Other lures for industries such as exemptions from state taxes—negative state capitalism—were devised.

Still, the real fillip for Southern economic growth came from a new and federally fostered racial climate and billions of federal dollars for highway, defense and space programs. When it came to celebrating the interstate highway system, Texas and its wide open spaces led the way as it stood to gain more funds than any other state but New York. The Airport Act of 1946, championed by a Lyndon Johnson who would win his Senate seat by helicoptering around the state, gave Texas more dol-

*Thus, New York's share of per capita income declined from 162 to 129 to 121 over the two decades, and California likewise declined from 140 to 132 to 122, while Illinois remained stable around the same number. North Carolina grew from 58 per cent to 64 and then to 69.

lars for airport construction than any other state. In 1940 Southern state governments depended upon federal grants for 14 per cent of their revenues; in 1955 20 per cent came from Washington. That the South did not truly exploit federal and state public investment until the 1960s is a tribute to its individualistic ideology, its conservatism, and its lethargy. The New Deal, via TVA and REA and other programs, had erected an infrastructure upon which it built during the war years. Cheap hydroelectric power brought additional industries such as aluminum to the South and a rising standard of living. Not until the introduction of cheap natural gas during the 1950s did TVA and Bonneville have competitors for their power for aluminum production. But Southerners showed little initiative to develop their resources prior to the 1950s. Conscious of Southern needs because of his family origins, Robert E. Wood of Sears, Roebuck made special efforts to locate stores and suppliers in Southern states. Nevertheless, federal programs and the South's increasing receptivity to them put the region on a course for growth in the 1960s—making for what Gavin Wright calls "an amazing economic spectacle." The once detested federal government had become the South's favorite banker. "Our economy is no longer agricultural," William Faulkner declared with maudlin finality in 1956. "Our economy is the federal government."[39]

How the federal government transformed the South is also a human story. Jack Temple Kirby relates one such tale:

> Out in Titus County, Texas, Mr. and Mrs. Dewey Blackstone, a young white couple, purchased a 61½-acre farm in 1938 with FHA assistance. The following year the Rural Electrification Administration turned on the electricity, and the Civilian Conservation Corps, yet another New Deal agency, fenced most of the property and sodded a pasture at no cost to the Blackstones except for fencing materials. A federally subsidized tractor owned by the county then terraced most of the crop for thirteen dollars.[40]

The Blackstones' experience succinctly dramatizes how federal capital enhanced individualism in the South. Yet it is another Texas tale, symbolic perhaps of Southern agricultural decline despite the TVA. When California farmers embraced machine cultivation during the war, the South began to produce proportionately less cotton nationally. Following the war California farmers eagerly bought more mechanical harvesters than did Southern planters. In the West 94 per cent of all cotton farmers used tractors as against 42 per cent in the Mississippi Valley. Again, while the South suffers by comparison, tractors did revolutionize farming there and make it much less labor-intensive. Between 1935 and 1970 more than thirteen million people, more than 20 per cent of its population, left Southern farms. In part, the cities lured them; "Southern cities emerged from the war brimming with federal dollars and optimism," an urban historian has written. Once the only major Southern metropolitan area, New Orleans found itself pressed by Atlanta, Miami, Charlotte, Memphis and, of course, the Texas cities of Houston, Dallas–Fort Worth and San Antonio. But it is also likely that many of those erstwhile Southern farmers headed west for Phoenix, San Diego, Los Angeles, San Francisco—and maybe even the wetter climes of Portland and Seattle.[41]

The New Deal's westward movement of dollars inevitably attracted people like Henry Kaiser who had their eyes on the main chance. Subsidization of the aircraft industry following the Air Policy Commission hearings and report of 1947 for military and political reasons led to a boom in California and Washington State. "An alliance of politicians, military officers and airplane industrialists, acting through the military establishment, has fostered the world's pre-eminent military and nonmilitary aircraft industry," writes historian of technology Thomas P. Hughes. "Since Pearl Harbor the level of [government] investment has been so considerable, the number of workers so large and the deployment of human and material resources so great that airplane manufacturers have built up an enormous momentum." The impact upon California from this heavy aircraft and other military spending is profound. Historian James L. Clayton asserted in 1965 that "defense spending has been the primary reason for the extraordinarily rapid expansion of industry and population in California since World War II. . . . Without these massive outlays, California's manufacturing growth since World War II would probably have been about one-third, other things being equal, and her net in-migration about one-half its present level." American emphasis upon security in the Pacific led to more investment on the West Coast. The war in Vietnam, an economist testified in 1967, "followed the traditional lines of concentration [of public investment] on the south and west."[42]

The Exportable New Deal

HENRY KAISER DID NOT lack imagination or courage. Cynical reporters, accustomed to businessmen dependent upon lieutenants for their originality or verbal facility, were frequently surprised by Kaiser's loquaciousness and global visions. "Kaiser talks incessantly and usually in a semi-evangelical fashion," a reporter noted in 1941.

In my talks with him I have never been sure whether he was an extremely clever super-salesman or a man with a mission. Perhaps he is both.

He talks to everybody who will listen to him about his program for America: hundreds of thousands of planes going all over the globe, a super-highway system, tens of thousands of merchant ships built more cheaply than ever before. Essential to this revolution is light metal. From sand and gravel he has turned to aluminum and magnesium.[43]

But could Kaiser compete against ALCOA or any other existing giant corporation without a government interest? And what would be the consequences of his failure? Put another way, could postwar Western manufacturing survive without him? Somewhat belaboring the obvious in 1944, a special assistant to Attorney General Francis Biddle, Edward H. Levi, a former Thurman Arnold student at Yale, described the problem of industrial concentration and its postwar implications for the West Coast, predicting that the West would suffer "a serious unemployment problem if the war-time industries are not converted to peacetime use and, [lose] its most important opportunity to develop industries of its own, free from Eastern controls." Kaiser would have to spearhead continued Western industrial development and diversification. In 1945 the government owned many of his cement, gypsum, shipbuilding, steel, magnesium, aircraft and aluminum plants, and the industrial future of the West depended upon Kaiser's purchase—with RFC credit—and operation of them. Fortunately for Kaiser and the West, the federal government was a banker addicted to his interest payments on previous loans. Also, it was intent upon maintaining world dominance in commercial aviation, making the aircraft industry in the Seattle region a promising market for Kaiser metals. Finally, the Kaiser organization itself considered ventures into helicopters and automobiles.[44]

Kaiser never lost his creativity or nerve. Studying a market, he dared to imagine a place in it for himself. Just as he anticipated the automobile's need for roads, the West's need for cheap power from its rivers, the war's need for ships, his worker's need for decent and inexpensive health care, the aircraft industry's need for lightweight metals—so Kaiser anticipated a postwar housing and automobile market. If he could build ships the way he had built dams, why could he not build cars the way he had built ships? Teaming with a former car salesman named Joseph Frazer, Kaiser in 1945 invaded the oligopolistic automobile business, confident that American savings would pour into a car market that had not seen new vehicles since 1941. The public's purchase of $43 billion in government war bonds was not debt, Kaiser declared; "That is pure venture capital." He anticipated a booming housing market, especially in his beloved California. Returning veterans would want government financing through the FHA and other programs. However, he would discover that building homes was not like building ships or cars. Although he constructed thousands of Kaiser Community Homes between 1945 and 1950, they amounted to a small fraction of the market. Housing was not an industry where a few competitors divided an oligopoly. Housing involved real competition, and it soon drained Kaiser's enthusiasm.

Such was not the case for automobiles. After the war there would be seven million fewer cars on American roads than were there in 1941. As late as 1946 *Fortune* estimated that "every week from now until 1948, literally thousands of cars will drop dead somewhere in the U.S." Beginning in 1942 Kaiser had studied the international automobile business and decided he would build a $400 *Volkswagen*, dubbed the Henry J, for the ordinary American. Kaiser envisioned a small, lightweight, automobile that might get 100 miles per gallon of gasoline. Although it would carry just two passengers, Kaiser reasoned that because individualistic Americans did not willingly carpool, autos capable of carrying six but driven by a lone commuter were inefficient and wasteful; and he speculated that many Americans agreed with him. In July 1945 Kaiser and Frazer announced the formation of their company and the sale of stock to the American public (something Kaiser had never done before; it went against his Western distaste for Wall Street), and demonstrated a model car with features well ahead of their time, front-wheel drive and torsion-bar suspension. To build it Kaiser and Frazer bought the RFC's Willow Run, Michigan, aircraft factory. Ever the Westerner, he also purchased a California aircraft plant for Pacific car distribution. With the fame of Kaiser behind it, Americans snapped up Kaiser-Frazer stock and its price soared. However, history did not favor Kaiser-Frazer. In 1920, 120 companies assembled cars; in 1941 only ten remained—the Big Three accounting for 90 per cent: would Kaiser-Frazer follow the rest to an auto buff's museum?[45]

At first Kaiser-Frazer produced overpriced cars, not the "people's car" Kaiser had promised. But Kaiser got away with it because he accurately gauged the American appetite for vehicles. By late 1948 Kaiser-Frazer was the fourth largest automaker. The little Henry J, with its front-wheel drive and aluminum body, was a marvelous car, even if it was disappointingly expensive. It was also Kaiser's first venture without the government as a principal investor and customer, and steel and auto executives expected the arrogant Kaiser to fail. But critics conceded that he made the most of his postwar opportunities, in part because he had put together an outstanding organization of hard-driving Westerners intent upon showing Easterners that they could compete. Also, the government's threat of antitrust action prompted General Motors to give the fledgling automakers technical and material assistance with gear boxes. Five years after the war Kaiser could boast that he had paid back all government loans. But Kaiser-Frazer hit hard times and when private financing fell through, it had to call upon the RFC for help. Other Kaiser industries did better. The Korean War gave Kaiser Aluminum a big boost when the government underwrote the industry's expanded production for thirty months. Kaiser again used his aluminum and cement companies as collateral to acquire additional capital for Kaiser-Frazer, selling government-guaranteed bonds instead of more stock that would dilute equity. Kaiser-Frazer's costs were not under control. For a time the Korean War kept the automaker afloat, along with a General Motors subcontract. But peace came in 1953 and Kaiser-Frazer was in trouble. In 1955 its management closed all operations but the Jeep business it had acquired from Willys-Overland, and gave stockholders shares in other Kaiser industries. Well into his mid-seventies, Kaiser focused his energies upon housing and hotel developments in Hawaii while the company moved on to what it knew best—construction of government-funded projects in Australia, India and elsewhere.[46]

It was said that Kaiser "might easily get over-extended, but never with his own money." "Money is a problem with us—it always has been," a Kaiser manager once observed, "but so far it has never stopped us from doing anything we wanted to do." For a quarter century Kaiser had lived at the public trough, fulfilling the ambitions of New Dealers and his own. Through New Deal, war, postwar readjustment, and Asian wars again in the 1950s and 1960s, the Kaiser organization flourished with government capital for dam construction, shipbuilding, Western steel and aluminum fabrication, and finally, automobile manufacturing. But manufacturing without adequate capitalization was difficult even if the business press loved Kaiser more than ever. He still found new opportunities by doubling Hawaii's hotel capacity and becoming the biggest landowner in the Waikiki area as he bet that the islands would draw vacationers with the advent of jet travel in the 1960s.[47]

But Kaiser in Hawaii was in semiretirement. The earth movers of the 1930s passed from the scene—although not completely. Big projects relating to America's infrastructure still existed. An occasional Western dam needed construction. The Interstate Highway System, beginning in the mid-1950s, gave local and regional builders much needed federal dollars. The arrival of commercial jets and the passing of ground-based interstate travel required construction of expensive modern airports. Congress funded a subway system for the District of Columbia and the San Francisco Bay area. But the communist threat abroad and the space program called forth the biggest ventures for earth movers. National defense required all sorts of construction at home and bases abroad. Moreover, anticommunism justified U.S. loans to undeveloped nations who sought to achieve growth such as had been attained in the South and West through well-placed injections of state capital.

"The TVA idea" was the first message America sent the world concerning democratic development during the war years. In a world overrun by fascism, nazism and communism, Washington needed to dramatize liberalism as a viable alternative to totalitarianism. And, as an envious Harold Ickes correctly told a 1945 press conference, David Lilienthal was "one of the best propagandists in the business." During the war Lilienthal adroitly marketed "the TVA idea" as a model of economic development for the world. He wrote articles, made radio speeches and buttonholed journalists to expound upon TVA. Foreign visitors from colonial countries or Europeans from a decimated continent traveled to Knoxville where Lilienthal impressed them with tours of TVA that inspired visions of their own future economic development or reconstruction. TVA was a beacon for a world tired of depression and war. As Lilienthal wrote in 1942,

> there is an amazing amount of interest in the application of the underlying TVA idea to the international situation, particularly the problems of reconstruction and full employment through resource development and otherwise. Especially is there the keen interest in our innovations and experiments in management methods, as applied to the new problems that are emerging in foreign countries. China, the Danube River Valley, India, Africa, Latin America, and so on are among the parts of the world from which observers have studied the TVA from this point of view.

Certain that "this TVA idea and the methods we have been working out may soon find themselves in a global forum," Lilienthal rehearsed the TVA idea again and again with Mexicans, Zionists, Chinese nationalists and British imperialists. He repeated it in conversations with Henry Wallace and FDR, in his letters, articles and private journals. The message won a favorable reception among those peoples wanting to believe that democracy and directed development were compatible. "The TVA, in recent months, is receiving an acceptance as an American institution (like the Panama Canal, say, or the blue plate luncheon) that is really quite remarkable," he exulted to a journalist. "I have, of course, been gratified to watch the growth of enthusiasm in this country and abroad for TVA," FDR wrote to Tennessee Congressman Estes Kefauver.

> You and I can remember when TVA was denounced as one of this administration's wild ideas. It does not seem wild now even to those who damned it most loudly at first. But it is, as it was, a great American idea. It is still disturbing, of course, to old advocates of the exploitation of resources without much concern for people beside them. It still disturbs, too, those who do not understand the meaning of TVA as an instrument by which big government need not be absentee government.[48]

Lilienthal put his lyrical enthusiasm for the TVA idea into a book for all the world to be stirred by it. In 1944 he published *TVA: Democracy on the March*. Deep in a war against authoritarianism, he glowingly celebrated democracy. At a time when again questions were asked as to how a democratic government could fashion effective mobilization for war, he asserted that efficient and democratic organization truly reflected the yearnings of humanity. At a time when Americans wondered if demobilization would result in unemployment, he called TVA a model for liberal economic development to create postwar jobs. His book was a pragmatic manifesto that celebrated history; a program for the middle way between communism and fascism, rather than anticipation of a utopia. With the disingenuous disclaimer "I am an administrator and not a professional writer," Lilienthal wrote his exposition with the eloquence that only a self-assured proselytizer could muster:

> *This is a book about tomorrow.*
>
> My purpose in writing today is to try to cut through the fog of uncertainty and confusion about tomorrow that envelops us. . . .
>
> This book then is about real things and real people: *rivers and how to develop them; new factories and new jobs and how they were created; farms and farmers and how they came to prosper and stand on their own*. My purpose is to show, by authentic experience in one American region, that to get such new jobs and factories and fertile farms our choice need not be between extremes of "right" and "left," between overcentralized Big-government and a do-nothing policy, between "private enterprise" and "socialism," between an arrogant red-tape-ridden bureaucracy and domination by a few private monopolies. I have tried in these pages to express my confidence that in *tested principles of democracy* we have ready at hands a philosophy and a set of working tools that, adapted to this machine age, can guide and sustain us in increasing opportunity for individual freedom and well-being.
>
> This confidence that *it can be done* [his emphasis], . . . is based

on ten years of experience in the Tennessee Valley. Here the people and their institutions—among them *the regional development corporation known as TVA*—have provided just such a demonstration of the vitality of democracy. It is that ten years of actual experience . . . that reveals the promise and hope of tomorrow for men *everywhere*.[49]

Building upon the nationalism of Henry Luce's "American Century" and the globalism of Henry Wallace's "Century of the Common Man," Lilienthal mixed the chauvinism of American exceptionalism with the optimism of American internationalism. It was the "can do" spirit of the New Deal at work. Within a year *TVA: Democracy on the March* was translated into twenty languages and published as a cheap paperback, then a comparative rarity. The eminent British scientist Julian Huxley proclaimed that the TVA idea "has already found its way into the world's general thinking," especially as it related "to the planned development of regions of greater backwardness, like parts of Africa." Economist Herman Finer published his own study of TVA to demonstrate that it had "lessons for international application." In the words of C. Herman Pritchett, "The TVA has proved to be the New Deal's most exportable product."[50]

Over the years the book attracted the sort of attacks that are reserved for classics. Critics complained that Lilienthal confused decentralization with democracy because Harcourt Morgan allowed local elites to control TVA agricultural policy. The most common charge was that TVA practiced racism. Lilienthal himself, for all his self-congratulatory tolerance and goodwill toward blacks, did nothing to threaten the South's segregation of the races. Jim Crow was alive and well under TVA. That permitted Rexford Tugwell to jibe that "TVA is more an example of democracy in retreat than democracy on the march." Of course, it could not have been anything else at that time or else TVA would not have won its hard-fought appropriations from Congress.[51]

But the future of New Deal–style economic development overseas did not lie just with the TVA model. Indeed, another wartime Washington bureaucratic feud that forecast the exportability of the New Deal, like the Ickes-Lilienthal duel, was the conflict between Jesse Jones and Henry Wallace. Most of the press saw it as a titanic fight between a conservative Democrat and a liberal for what remained of the New Deal's tattered soul. But it did not take much insight to realize that the New Deal would fare better overseas than it would at home.

The Jones-Wallace feud began when in 1940 FDR gave Jones responsibility for the development of strategic and critical materials with instructions to deny the Germans or the Japanese what they needed to wage war. But in 1942 Roosevelt characteristically split the job by creating the Board of Economic Warfare under Vice-President Henry Wallace's leadership. Wallace portrayed his task as one of building a liberal alternative to the conservative departments of State and Commerce under Cordell Hull and Jones—thereby giving his bureaucratic buccaneering a distinctly ideological flavor. If he hoped to rally liberals such as Ickes to his standard, Wallace needed to mend fences with the aggrieved Interior Secretary from whom he had pirated agencies. His aide, Milo Perkins, paid a courtesy call on Ickes, whose hostility was evident: "You do not like Wallace," Perkins said; "No," Ickes righteously replied, "I do not. I don't like any man whose path in Washington is strewn with the maimed bodies of men who were his friends."[52] But Ickes knew that liberals had to close ranks against Jones—the most insidious supporter of big business in the Cabinet.

Wallace's crusade for BEW and against Jones was a fight for New Deal–style international development of areas such as Latin America. Roosevelt wanted to spread America's economic influence in former colonial regions of the world, although he did not consider Wallace his best political vehicle. Thus, while the President gave Wallace authority for economic warfare, he left the checkbook with Jones. As Attorney General Francis Biddle put it, "It really comes down to the ability of Wallace to get vigorous and active action against the State Department on the one side and Jesse Jones, who still wants to keep control on the other." Wallace had greater moral authority than clout. Ickes and Henry Morgenthau rallied to his side in the belief that a Wallace-Jones fight would decide whether the postwar American economy would be guided by New Dealers or big business. Morgenthau knowingly warned Wallace that he would have many conferences with Jones that would accomplish nothing because Jesse was a "terrible staller," but Wallace loftily asserted that "the importance of the times were such that Jesse simply could not stall."[53]

But Jones proved too powerful and crafty. In most cabinet meetings he sat inscrutably silent, Roosevelt either ignoring him or addressing questions at him that Jones evaded without any presidential follow-up. "Jones is literally a law unto himself," Ickes commented. In 1942 FDR proposed a separate corporation to buy South American assets and prevent Axis ownership of them; but Jones blocked administration adoption of it because it duplicated his own authority. Lacking interest in international problems, Jones brought in Houston cotton broker Will Clayton to run his empire abroad. He relegated BEW to an overseas intelligence role without any substantial operational function except for occasional purchases of raw materials or chasing small-time chiselers who defied the American embargo against the Axis. As Jones told John Garner, BEW administrators wanted "a check book of their own" but they operated with such money as Jones allowed them. Wallace complained mightily to Roosevelt and others about this, but was helpless to do anything by himself. Nevertheless, he and Perkins won liberal loyalties with Wallace's "Century of the Common Man" speech in New York's Madison Square Garden and Perkins's public attack upon Jones—which backfired because it made Perkins appear divisive at a time when Americans cherished solidarity of purpose. Despite their left-wing public images, Wallace was basically an agrarian businessman and Perkins, in the words of Ernest K. Lindley, "has intense faith in the ability of American engineers and businessmen to step up production all over the world. Given a free hand, he probably would have put Americans in direct charge of most of the mines, forestry operations, and industrial-crop plantations of Latin America, Africa, and the Middle East." Lindley did not perceive any "fundamental issue" between Jones and Wallace, except that Jones was decidedly less evangelical about America's overseas role.[54]

Jones kept BEW powerless and frustrated into 1943 by manipulating congressmen and controlling money BEW needed to buy critical materials overseas. When the Jones-Wallace fight finally came to a head in June and July with public attacks by each upon the other, Roosevelt settled it by taking BEW leadership away from Wallace and creating an Office of Economic Warfare (later the Foreign Economic Administration) under Leo Crowley. To console liberals, FDR deprived Jones of a few minor parts of his empire. The alleged compromise satisfied only Jones. "Franklin D. Roosevelt has again run out on his friends," mourned Wallace supporter I. F. Stone. Significantly, the *New Republic* wondered if the settlement meant that Wallace would be stricken from the Democratic ticket in 1944. Nevertheless, Wallace's failure was his own; Roosevelt's interest in expanding liberal capitalism abroad had not diminished.[55]

Roosevelt apparently felt a need to keep on cordial terms with Jones, making certain that the Texas banker was solicitous of the needs of small business or the interests of Americans in overseas markets. Thus, as he once wrote Jones on the subject of the American President steamship lines,

> there will be many places after the war which will be inaccessible to American business unless the Government still has something to say about it. For example, if you are a shoe manufacturer after the war and want to start a line of sale in Liberia, how will you get

there? The people there don't wear shoes but might be taught to do so if a good American salesman came into their midst. I have been there.[56]

Roosevelt also hoped to make the Democratic party a vehicle of international liberal capitalism. But tensions between Jones and FDR climaxed in 1944 when Texas friends of Jones, anticipating an FDR bid for a fourth term, organized Democratic "Regulars" in alliance with Governor Coke Stevenson and seized control of the state party convention. After they passed a resolution calling upon the state party's electors in the Electoral College to vote independently of the national convention, New Deal Democrats led by Alvin Wirtz and Lyndon Johnson bolted the Texas Democrats and in a rump convention declared themselves "Loyalists." The Regulars were led by George Butler, the husband of one of Jesse Jones's nieces, but they denied that Jones had anything to do with their revolt. In conversation with Roosevelt, Jones pointedly said that he could not control Butler any more than FDR could control his sons—reminding the President that Elliott Roosevelt had seconded Jones's unsolicited nomination for the vice-presidency in 1940 when FDR wanted Wallace. In August the Democratic national convention resolved the fight by splitting the Texas votes between Roosevelt delegates and supporters of the conservative Virginia Senator Harry F. Byrd. It also replaced Wallace with Senator Harry Truman of Missouri, which "very much pleased" Jones. Jones, in a front-page editorial for his Houston *Chronicle*, endorsed the Democratic party electors and sent a clipping of it to Roosevelt. However, Roosevelt probably saw it as an affront because Jones also urged a restoration of the two-thirds rule at the Democratic National Convention, a slap at FDR. In Washington it was rumored that Jones quietly worked for the Republican nominee, Governor Thomas E. Dewey of New York, who had promised him a Cabinet post if he won.[57]

Roosevelt had a score to settle with "Jesus H. Jones," as he called Jesse behind his back, and he would make Wallace the beneficiary of his anger. After the Democratic convention Roosevelt promised Wallace any Cabinet post except the State Department and pointedly remarked that if everything went well on November 7 Jesus H. Jones would be the first person to go. With that cue, Wallace piped up, "Well, if you are going to get rid of Jesse, why not let me have Secretary of Commerce with RFC and FEA thrown in? There would be poetic justice in that." Roosevelt swiftly agreed. At the first postelection Cabinet meeting, Roosevelt declared that he was mad and would stay mad, glaring all the while at Jesse Jones. "He is out to get J.J.," thought a delighted Wallace.

On December 20 Wallace and FDR agreed on the reorganization of Commerce and the RFC to provide easier credit for small business and foreign trade expansion. By this time Wallace made sure that half of Washington knew he would get Commerce. On January 11 Jones sent the President a news clipping intended to mollify him by announcing that RFC now would look more kindly upon small business loans. But on Inauguration Day Roosevelt sent Jones a letter telling him that because Henry Wallace had been a good trouper he deserved a Cabinet portfolio—and Henry wanted Jesse's Commerce job. How would Jones like an ambassadorial post, FDR asked? Jones's reply was swift (it had probably been drafted weeks before). Declining any job abroad, Jones played his best card: "For you to turn over all these assets and responsibilities to a man inexperienced in business and finance will, I believe, be hard for the business and financial world to understand." Roosevelt would hear that theme again.[58]

Following the Inauguration Day exchange of letters, Jones met with Roosevelt at twelve-thirty the next day. According to Jones, Roosevelt asked him to choose between an ambassadorship to France or Italy. When Jones declined both, Roosevelt offered him Marriner Eccles's job at the Federal Reserve, but Jones again declined. He made it clear that he wanted to remain as Federal Loan Administrator. Roosevelt could give Commerce to Wallace, but Jones intended to deprive Wallace of the loan agencies.[59]

As Jones anticipated, the switch at Commerce "stunned" business, said *Business Week*. Businessmen did not like Wallace and Congress, which had specifically conferred the Federal Loan Administrator's job upon Jones, would not allow it to go to Wallace. "Make no mistake about it," the *New Republic* averred: "this is a fight against Roosevelt and the New Deal." It was. Wallace told the Senate Commerce Committee hearing on his nomination that he intended to pursue a program that guaranteed jobs and broadened public investment. Called to testify on Wallace's nomination, Jones painted him as, in *Time*'s words, "a sincere but somewhat aimless dreamer who might be all right as an amiable philosopher but who should be kept at least a mile away from a balance sheet." Senator Walter F. George of Georgia introduced a resolution divorcing the Federal Loan Agency from Commerce, and the committee voted 15 to 4 for the George resolution and 14 to 5 to deny Wallace the Commerce Department itself. Both the Senate and the House upheld Senator George by whopping 74 to 12 and 400 to 2 votes, a humbling rejection of Wallace as Federal Loan Administrator. However, the Senate approved Wallace as Commerce Secretary minus the loan agencies, 56 to 32. Eventually Fred M. Vinson became the Federal Loan Administrator.[60]

The Wallace-Jones fight was about many things—two tremendous egos, the future of liberalism and the Democratic party and the next direction of state capitalism. Increasingly hostile to any state capitalism, Jones disdained the New Deal trend of fiscal policy. It was not by accident that Texas Regulars favored the nomination of budget-balancing Harry Byrd at the 1944 Democratic Convention. Had these been the only differences between them, it is likely that FDR could have lived with Jones. But the Texas Regulars incident revealed a blatant grab for political power by Jones and everything else suggested his opposition to an exportable New Deal.

The disposition of fiscal policy in the reconstruction of postwar Europe made these men adversaries. Thus, when Roosevelt offered him ambassadorships and a role in reconstructing European economies, Jones "told the President that I was not in complete accord, or even sympathy, with his plan to give those people everything we have, probably to the point of bankrupting ourselves."[61] While Jones thought state capitalism had gone too far, Roosevelt believed that its overseas experience was just beginning. A European Recovery Program—a Marshall Plan—was in the cards.

The RFC had been giving overseas loans for a long time via the Export-Import Bank, which Jones controlled with a country banker's hostility to international markets. The war in Europe demanded more attention paid to this side of the RFC ledger. The State and Treasury Departments desired more U.S. loans to undeveloped countries as a way of capturing their raw materials markets while the Europeans were preoccupied with fighting. Harry White in Treasury, along with Adolf Berle in State, wanted an Inter-American bank. Beguiled by the wealth of Latin America's raw materials, White asked Morgenthau to "force the issue of real aid to Latin America" because the region presented "a remarkable opportunity for economic development." All it needed, White argued, was U.S. capital and technical know-how. Alas, in 1940 two thirds of the Latin-American countries rejected Washington's developmental loans. Berle and White then turned to bilateral loans through Jesse Jones's Export-Import Bank.[62]

Of course, Jones ran Export-Import as if it were his personal bank. Originally established in 1934 to facilitate trade with the Soviet Union, it was besieged by other countries for its capital. As usual, Jones was a cautious lender, especially to companies (countries) whose credit was questionable. He liked to keep the bank "a small-fry institution," lest anyone dare to suggest that it was attempting "to play Santa Claus." Frequently he objected to particular overseas loans, but he acceded when Roosevelt took a personal interest, as in the case of a $2 million outlay for additional road construction in Panama. If the RFC could finance the development of hydroelectric power for American farms, it could do likewise for Uruguay—especially since it meant completing during the war a plant begun by the Germans. But, so notorious was Jones's parsimony that during a 1940 Treasury discussion of the disposition of a loan to Chile, White half-facetiously recommended that they "See which way Jones votes and vote the other way." With Eurasia increasingly closed to American trade, Roosevelt urged Jones "to give sympathetic consideration to Latin American products in the procurement of strategic and critical materials for the defense program"; "When buying in foreign markets for defense needs, it is my earnest desire that priority of consideration be given to Latin American products and I so request." FDR also ordered Jones (marked in his own hand, "secret") to make loans of $12 million to build Latin American airfields that would benefit the Pan American Airways Corporation. To avoid responsibility for exporting state capitalism, Jones made Will Clayton his deputy for buying raw material stockpiles and sealing off the Axis from all strategic materials in the Western Hemisphere. However, Clayton performed so aggressively that he later moved from RFC to the State Department. In 1945 Congress separated the Export-Import Bank from RFC and launched it upon an extended career in overseas state capitalism.[63]

During 1943–44 FDR fixed his attention upon postwar economic agreements requiring international cooperation. Instead of one big international conference as occurred at Paris in 1919, the Allies held a series of meetings at Bretton Woods, Dumbarton Oaks, the United Nations Conference at San Francisco and the International Civil Aviation Conference at Chicago. The last in particular sent a message to the world: the U.S. expected to be the principal manufacturer of aircraft, builder of air fields, and banker for international commercial aviation development in the postwar world.[64] In every case the U.S. linked world prosperity to its interests. America would exercise its state capitalist responsibilities through agencies such as the International Bank for Reconstruction and Development (the World Bank), the International Monetary Fund and a proposed Inter-American bank. About three quarters of all Export-Import Bank loans had gone to Latin America while it had been in the clutches of a Texas banker, but its postwar career would not be confined to any one part of the globe. Although it recognized that Southern and Western economic development was hardly complete, Washington applied the state capitalist lessons of 1935–1945 to postwar development abroad. During early 1944 Henry Wallace had toured China and Siberia, spotlighting East Asia as a developing market. Businessmen in the Bonneville region anticipated "a great industrial empire" emerging from World

War II in America's Pacific Northwest that would flourish for years to come because "the markets in the Orient and Siberia will offer almost unlimited opportunities."[65] Nonetheless, Wall Street investors were not as interested in unstable and risky developing countries south of the equator as they were in investing in the known and growing Southern climates of the United States. But certain businessmen and some liberals were intent upon expanding liberalism overseas in the New Deal tradition of state capitalism.

One of those interested in evangelicizing the gospel of New Deal development to the developing world was David E. Lilienthal. In January 1946 President Truman appointed Lilienthal Chairman of the special State Department Board of Consultants to develop an American plan for international control of atomic energy which drew up the Baruch Plan for submission to the United Nations. In October he became the first Chairman of the U.S. Atomic Energy Commission. He left the AEC in 1950 for a career as a consultant to investment banker Andre Meyer of Lazard Freres & Company and David Sarnoff of RCA. Lilienthal's greatest stock-in-trade was his leadership at TVA, which brought him back to the business of economic development—ever at the cutting edge during the Cold War because it would save Third World areas from famine and possible communist revolution. In 1955 he founded the Development and Resources Corporation with Gordon Clapp, Lilienthal's manager at TVA.

The TVA idea retained its magic. Harry Truman, for instance, saw his Point Four program as a TVA for the world. " 'Now here is the finest opportunity for development in the world' (pointing to the valleys of the Tigris and Euphrates)," he told Lilienthal in 1949. " 'They have to know how to do things. We can show them that. Then here' (northern India) 'and here' (the Parana, in S. America, and the great plateaus of Brazil) 'and here' (the Belgian Congo). And so on and on—and Alaska. His eyes snapped, he was happy. 'We might even use an atomic bomb to change the course of some river.' " Another time Truman and Lilienthal imagined a TVA on the Yangtze River in China.[66]

Lilienthal always inspired others, by his words or merely his presence, to imagine a TVA or some form of economic development. After all, much of the world in the mid-twentieth century had less electric energy than rural America had had in the 1930s. Also, Lilienthal's enhanced connections with Wall Street and the World Bank brought him invitations to consult on government projects to develop the Indus River Valley of India and Pakistan, the Cauca Valley in southwestern Colombia, and the Khuzistan region of southwestern Iran. But TVA certainly opened doors for Lilienthal. As Walter Lippmann once remarked, "TVA is a magic word all over the world, wherever you go." Overseas, however, it was not democracy on the march. In some cases local military men and politicians used the TVA idea for land speculation with American and World Bank funds. That is not to say that the masses would not be benefited. As one Colombian told Lilienthal, his country's "democracy" was *for* the people, but it would not be *by* the people. Lilienthal himself was of two minds on the topic of democracy and development: Although projects for economic growth could be initiated from above by autocrats such as his friend the Shah of Iran, they had to be sustained by the participation and the enrichment of the masses. By the mid-1960s the limitations of New Deal–style development for the rest of the world were evident to Lilienthal. "What has all this come to for the underdeveloped countries—all this sincere effort, these billions of dollars granted or loaned or invested, these volumes of plans and mountains of expert advice or direction?" he asked rhetorically. "The answer, one must realistically and reluctantly admit, has been grave disappointment and frustration. The gap between the richer and the poorer nations has not been narrowing, but widening." He might have added that development within countries had widened gaps among their rich and poor.[67]

Lilienthal was not the only New Dealer to preach American-style economic development overseas. In 1945 Adolf Berle went to Brazil as U.S. ambassador, a post he believed entitled him to begin to promote Treasury financing of the Sao Francisco River project, "an attempt to do something roughly analagous to the TVA in the Sao Francisco valley." He forecast that it could supply electricity to the entire northeast region of Brazil and a score of years later when Berle revisited northeastern Brazil it was served by "a government-owned [electric] company along the lines of the TVA." New Dealers were always welcomed in energy and capital-starved developing countries. Economist John Kenneth Galbraith went to India as President Kennedy's ambassador. Richard V. Gilbert, who had worked for Harry Hopkins, served as an adviser to the government of Pakistan. Lauchlin Currie, following his role as an author of the charter of the International Bank for Reconstruction and Development, strangely became a victim of McCarthyism and migrated to Colombia, where, as a businessman, he became an adviser to the Colombian and Venezuelan governments on development deals with Lilienthal's firm. And who else but Lyndon Johnson would tout a plan for economic development of the Mekong Valley of Southeast Asia via hydroelectrification? Beginning in 1957 the United Nations Mekong Coordinating Committee spent well over $100 million in a decade to develop a plan which Lilienthal scornfully dismissed as "nothing remotely resembling the comprehensive unified report TVA published in 1936." A TVA on the Mekong was doubtful, Lilienthal thought, because the river flowed through four Asian countries and the committee's report reflected the "crazy managerial patchwork" of the UN; he didn't bother to mention the wars raging over much of Indochina during the 1960s.[68]

Much of the construction for development overseas was handled by American contractors—the very ones who built the West: Kaiser, Bechtel, Morrison-Knudsen and Brown & Root. The Republican builder—Bechtel Corporation, Henry Kaiser's former partner in Six Companies—profited enormously from New Deal state capitalism. By World War II the firm had entered its second generation of Bechtel family leadership under Warren's son, Steven. Like Kaiser, Bechtel built ships during the war in collaboration with another Californian, John A. McCone, and it made both of them very rich. Unlike Kaiser, Bechtel avoided manufacturing and never went public for capital. Bechtel built oil pipelines, beginning with the Canol project linking the U.S. to Alaska, an industry that expanded enormously after the war at home and abroad. Its projects included pipelines for the Canadian and Saudi Arabian governments, building sewer systems, roads, power plants and airports for the Saudis at Jeddah and Riyadh, an electric plant in California, an oil-processing complex in Indonesia, an iron-ore extraction plant in Venezuela, numerous infrastructure projects in Yemen, Kuwait, Lebanon, Iraq and Iran, gaseous-diffusion plants at Portsmouth, Ohio, and Paducah, Kentucky, and, with McCone, transporting oil for the Navy from the Middle East to the U.S. During the war Bechtel had helped construct nuclear facilities at Hanford, Washington. In 1949 Lilienthal and the Atomic Energy Commission gave Bechtel the contract to build a Nuclear Reactor Test Station west of Idaho Falls, Idaho, an experiment that put both the AEC and Bechtel in the business of encouraging utilities to convert to atomic power. Several managers left the AEC for jobs at Bechtel, and John McCone became AEC Chairman in 1958, creating an AEC-Bechtel relationship that was, in the words of Connecticut Senator Abraham Ribicoff, "so incestuous, it is impossible to tell where the public sector begins and the private one leaves off." It brought Bechtel the contract to build the first major nuclear power station at Dresden, Illinois, for Commonwealth Edison, and many other subsequent nuclear plants in the wake of the Atomic Energy Act of 1954—most of them government-subsidized for developmental purposes. Indeed, most of Bechtel's work was funded directly and indirectly by the United States government. Bechtel built three coal-fired plants for South Korea, more mining complexes in South Africa, Chile, Mauretania and Ireland, pipelines in Germany and Switzerland, hydroelectric plants in New Zealand, Newfoundland and Quebec, fertilizer factories for Algeria, refineries for

Libya, and the San Francisco Bay Area Rapid Transit System (BART). The builder aided countries seeking Export-Import Bank aid for development. In the words of a former Bechtel director, "The South American general who needed $60 million to build a pipeline usually didn't have any idea where to go for his financing or what elevator button to push when he got there. [Our] job was to point the way and help him put together the necessary paperwork." In this way Bechtel made itself the beneficiary of low-interest, government-guaranteed loans to developing countries who, in the context of the Cold War, needed development to improve their standard of living, and might otherwise succumb to communism or turn to the Soviet Union to help them build an infrastructure and industries. In the 1960s, however, much of this work went to Brown & Root for military and space projects that came from Washington via Lyndon Johnson. While Bechtel cursed this downturn in business, Richard Nixon's election in 1968 put the fox in the chicken coop when Congress greatly increased the Export-Import Bank's capital and Steven Bechtel became a director of the bank.[69]

The Cold War encouraged the exporting of all sorts of state capitalism. The Iron Curtain across Eastern Europe continued Washington in the business of government-to-government loans which had begun in 1941 with lend-lease. With a poverty-stricken and war-torn Europe apparently on the verge of electing communist governments, the U.S. pursued the reconstruction of Europe with the Marshall Plan in 1948, which committed the U.S. Treasury to an eventual $15 billion in low-cost loans. The next logical step came with the founding of the North Atlantic Treaty Organization (NATO) and the increased militarization of the Cold War. While restoring European industry had the highest priority, President Harry Truman, perhaps motivated by the "loss" of China, in 1949 proposed Point Four economic assistance targeted for development. Republicans immediately saw "New Deal" written all over it and demanded that it be killed or used to facilitate private investment guaranteed by Washington—although American business was unwilling to invest in undeveloped countries. Yet Point Four technicians, with comparatively little in congressional appropriations, did a social task in undeveloped countries during the 1950s that anticipated the Peace Corps of the 1960s. Through the Point Four program the U.S. imported raw materials and built airfields and highways in Afghanistan, Jordan, Saudi Arabia, Thailand and Vietnam. Following the departure of its conservative Secretary of the Treasury, George Humphrey, in 1958, the Eisenhower administration fiscally expanded overseas state capitalism with the creation of the Inter-American Development Bank, additional funds for the Export-Import Bank and encouragement to the World Bank to support developing countries' projects.[70] Right-wing Republicans may have had some justification in suspecting that Ike was a closet New Dealer.

Much of this public investment overseas was, of course, motivated by fears of communist expansion and much of it was driven by military considerations. America's military-industrial complex flourished both as part of the drive to stem the march of communism and to continue where Congressman Lyndon Johnson left off in 1940—identifying New Deal public investment with spending for defense. "Our military organization today bears little relation to that known by any of my predecessors in peacetime, or indeed by the fighting men in World War II or Korea. Until the latest of our world conflicts, the United States had no armaments industry," Dwight Eisenhower observed in his 1961 Farewell Address as president. "This conjunction of an immense military establishment and a large arms industry is new in American experience." He had an appreciation of the enormous changes in the government's role that had occurred during his Army career and the greater changes that they portended. On the one hand, necessity supported those changes.

> We recognize the imperative need for this development. Yet we must not fail to comprehend its grave implications. Our toil, resources and livelihood are all involved; so is the very structure of our society.
>
> In the councils of government, we must guard against the acquisition of unwarranted influence, whether sought or unsought, by *the military-industrial complex*. The potential for the disastrous rise of misplaced power exists and will persist.[71]

Perhaps Eisenhower emitted that cry from his heart because he was otherwise powerless to stop the complex's political and bureaucratic growth. During his presidency he had hoped to restrain its growth with policies that emphasized relatively low-cost nuclear retaliation and by harping upon the economic dangers of inflation from excessive government investment and spending. But his own service, the Army, plus unemployment-conscious Democratic politicians and economists, opposed his public investment niggardliness. James Tobin, a Keynesian at Yale, assailed Eisenhower in 1958 for a "solicitude for the budget that has weakened us in conventional arms [and] has enabled the Soviet Union to catch and surpass us in the realm of nuclear weapons and rockets." As Eisenhower delivered his admonition in 1961, his successor, John F. Kennedy, surrounded himself with economic and military advisers whose counsel echoed Tobin's. Not only would they expand public investment in military bases and hardware around the globe, but also in the interstate highways and space race accelerated during Eisenhower's watch. The Soviet-launched satellite in space, *Sputnik*, Tobin declared, "will be well worth the blow it has dealt our national pride if it frees national policy from the shackles of fiscal orthodoxy."[72] In point of fact, however, it had been freed long ago, in the New Deal.

In later years Clifford Durr would tell liberal listeners that he had innocently played an important role in the origins of the Cold War military-industrial complex. Of course, an obvious relationship between New Deal public investment and DPC loans for defense existed and was the source of some controversy. Would Americans spend for defense projects the way they spent for peacetime public works? At a September 17, 1940, meeting at Washington's Mayflower Hotel, economist Lawrence Dennis heatedly charged that New Dealers had resorted to defense spending as a "new W.P.A. project" and that liberals should not confuse public works spending with the grim business of building a defense. While some liberals conceded Dennis's point, others such as Jerome Frank argued that, because it would lift the national standard of living, defense spending was socially desirable. To deny defense spending's social purposes was fascistic, Frank asserted. Indeed, even a conservative investment banker such as Ferdinand Eberstadt had begun to like overseas state capitalism. Looking to a postwar era in late 1944, Eberstadt proposed that the RFC "share a part of the burden of loans made by local banks to small or new business up to a limit, say of $100,000." He knew that this "suggestion of government aid in solving these problems may cause concern" in Wall Street, but Eberstadt insisted that because "Government has borne a large measure of the credit risks in our economy, why should it not also give support where needed in peace times?" Although they despised New Deal state capitalism, the war convinced men like Eberstadt it was "more constructive to accomplish something with Federal aid than nothing without it." Immediately prior to the war Eberstadt had denounced public investment as inhibiting private investment and economic expansion; but the war experience signaled public and private investment compatibility. In the next decade he would lead the charge for continued public investment in the aviation industry. With or without Keynes, a revolution in public attitudes toward state capitalism had occurred. Overseas exigencies demanded it.[73]

Afterword: Development's Contraction

THE SUCCESS OF NEW DEAL economics during 1940–1965 compelled conservatives to reassess fiscal and monetary orthodoxy. The New Deal's credit revolution, for instance, merited a reappraisal of international credit policy. Challenged around the globe militarily and politically by aggressive Eastern communism, liberals assailed that stodgy community of bankers for not innovating more generous policies toward the developing nations. As Franklin Roosevelt had urged Jesse Jones, liberals beseeched bankers to alter their anachronistic lending habits to better reflect the credit power of the world's richest country. It made no sense for money center banks to insist that good loans still required good collateral from the poor, liberals averred; even the World Bank, a development institution, sought a triple-A rating. "For the countries needing development most urgently," David Lilienthal declared, "*this conventional banking approach is almost overnight seen to be a failure*, because it is defeating the whole object of development." Conventional banking stymied would-be borrowers who could not afford the costs of loans. Even more worrisome was the fact that the communist centers freely bestowed low-interest credits upon developing nations. Projects that went begging in Egypt and Afghanistan found both creditors and contractors in Moscow. How could the West counter communist efforts to obtain clients in the Third World unless it liberalized credit policies in Western money centers? Without loans, developing nations could not develop. Without generous terms, Soviet and Chinese aid filled the Third World void. Increasingly Washington stepped in to guarantee loans in return for interest rates so low as to almost qualify as grants. Robert McNamara, disillusioned by the course of the Vietnam War and intent upon stopping communism with dollars instead of bullets, forsook the Defense Department for development and the World Bank. In the "decade of development" big American bankers vied with each other to loan to Poland, Africa and South America—to demonstrate that capital ventured in developing countries was good business. However, most of the time it was not good business. Economic expansion proved minimal. In decades to come those loans would have to be written off as the revenues from anticipated development did not develop. Meanwhile, as Lilienthal observed, "The prudent banker concept is breaking down fast." Yes, and so too was the international New Deal concept.[1]

This is not to say that the New Deal was a developmental failure. On the contrary, all that those loan mistakes proved was that the Congo and Colombia are not like the American South and West. (For that matter, the credit revolution worked better in Texas than in Mississippi, although even the latter was better for it.) The American sunbelt is still a throbbing economic engine today, although its growth is uneven and excessive in certain places. Overall, the New Dealers built the world's largest middle-class society by following an experimental industrial policy that responded adroitly and speedily to the exigencies of the Great Depression and the threat of totalitarianism. As they wove together a fabric of sometimes contradictory initiatives during 1933–1940, the New Dealers' commitment to investment for growth eventually surpassed their instincts for stability and, in desperation, demonstrated that capitalist planning was both possible and preferable to totalitarian alternatives.

Expedience always is a part of American policy-making. In 1917–18, William G. McAdoo, Bernard M. Baruch and Herbert Hoover brought into being a previously unimagined state capitalism for expansion, buttressed by cartel combinations for stability—making free enterprise hearts sigh with either remorse or guilt over the cornucopia it engendered. As much as this trio later tried to expunge those legacies of a heroic industrial policy, they conferred upon the next generation of leaders a legacy that could not be ignored: the corporate state was a capitalist entity that could be creative. The moral disturbed Hoover, whose psyche could not accept the apothegm that the state represented community; therefore, as President he chose the politics of rugged individualism and inertia. Franklin Roosevelt came committed to the politics of a private-public partnership and action. To an extent, Jesse H. Jones and Louis D. Brandeis bridged a generational ideology gap—Jones for the sake of power, Brandeis for the sake of principle. Brandeis wanted all economic life to be experimental and fair—even when it abandoned supposedly sound capitalist principles. His creative iconoclasm mesmerized young lawyers. Felix Frankfurter, alienated intellectually from market practices, apotheosized the state as a market player where brilliant lawyers dictated to bumbling businessmen. Other lawyers—Thomas G. Corcoran, Benjamin V. Cohen, William O. Douglas, Jerome N. Frank and David E. Lilienthal—made themselves Brandeisians and carried the message to big capital: the state would bankroll alternative players in the market in the name of fairness and development. The New Dealers consciously broadened regulatory tactics they inherited from the populists and the progressives of 1890–1930 to ensure wider market opportunities and participation. The discontent of the depression provided the New Dealers with a brief interval in history when they might implement an experiment that success would sustain—and after dual revolutions in stabilization and credit, by 1939 they arrived at a consensus that the twenty-first century would remember them only for the latter—although Americans never foresook the former. The New Deal was a creator of markets.

For developing regions, markets and credit, the New Dealers were a godsend. That sterling trio of Texans Sam Rayburn, Lyndon Johnson and Wright Patman appreciated what Washington could do for Texas—or Oregon and Mississippi—as well as its political rewards. State capitalism was not an oxymoron for them; it boded abundance and creature comforts for their constituents. They became evangelists of state capitalism. They used the credit revolution to manufacture cheap power that brought opportunistic corporate capital and growth to the South and West. It would take decades to overcome Southern poverty and Western sparseness of population before growth would become a questionable addiction in parts of Florida and California, but by 1980 a national New Deal mentality had generated the sunbelt.

Most of all, the New Deal built the modern middle class. The old middle class had been commercial and professional, but the New Dealers gradually expanded it to include new ethnic groups and integrated much of the working class into capitalism through protected bargaining rights and a credit revolution that made home ownership desirable through affordability. New Deal state capitalism generated untold numbers of jobs in transportation, construction and electrical-related industries. The great dams at TVA and BPA and their examples of cheap rates made the sunbelt from Southern California to Southern Florida livable and workable through air conditioning. The New Deal credit revolution made electrical appliances a standard for progress and a decent standard of living. Through the RFC, FHA, REA and the Commodity Credit Corporation, and their imitators in the decades to come, the New Dealers made millions of renters homeowners and debt-burdened farmers entrepreneurs—thereby assuring economic growth. By offering low-cost money and competitive terms, the New Dealers warmed and entertained Americans in their homes.

However, in the half century that followed World War II, two disasters befell the New Deal economy. The first was the inflation and waste brought by the Vietnam War, and the second the gluttony of the 1980s that unproductively transferred wealth abroad and to the few. The integrity of the American economy could have withstood the first, as well as the oil shocks of the 1970s, had it not been for the 1980s' reaction against regulation and its preference for libertinism over liberalism. It was corporate and political leadership at its worst.[2]

The Vietnam War damage need not be reviewed extensively here; that agony will live with us for decades to come. New Deal liberals were partly responsible for its escalation in the 1960s after its inception in the 1950s; although Lyndon Johnson followed the example of his predecessors, he brought a misplaced can-do New Deal spirit to the enterprise. For all the talk about the freedom to build a TVA on the Mekong with which to enrich Indochinese lives, not all state enterprises are salutary. The war wasted humans and materials; in the end it proved that national resources were finite, national security was endangered by arrogance, and that national interests had been errantly and grievously defined. The depletion is measured in lost lives and dollars. "The preponderance of evidence supports the judgment that war, on balance, does not correlate positively with economic progress," an economic historian wrote at the height of the war. "Settlement by arms not only causes a great net waste of resources; it also retards industrial development and the division of labor. The illusion of progress remains, for the intensity of mortal combat spurs men and nations to great exploits in the areas that are deemed essential to military prowess. But it is not balanced growth nor advancement in speculative knowledge that the God of War seeds; it is merely the accelerated application of the already known for immediate purposes."[3]

Aside from confirming these generalizations the war in Vietnam, undertaken concomitantly with Johnson's Great Society's social programs, overinvested and overconsumed in national markets without the judicious restraints upon prices applied in World War II, and to a lesser extent during the Korean War. The silent tax of rising prices accelerated an unchecked and escalating inflation, eroding the affordability of New Deal gains for the middle class. It reduced the dollar's value, and in less than a decade after the war's economic mismanagement the United States found itself exporting jobs rather than goods and succumbing to the status of a debtor country for the first time since 1914—when war made the Europeans debtors to the United States. A quarter century's gains in living standards were reversed. Historical analogies are treacherous: Saigon was not Munich and 1965 was not 1940 for Lyndon Johnson.

Just as the Vietnam War began to define for most New Deal liberals the limits of state capitalism, supposedly conservative Republicans, led by Richard Nixon's "we are all Keynesians now," only began to understand its political magic and embrace the credit revolution. Bereft of a restrained and probing Eisenhower, Republicans aped New Deal rhetoric and credit initiatives. Nixon, perhaps correctly, equated Keynesianism with opportunism, but he lacked the leavening sensibilities of old-fashioned conservatives such as economist Arthur F. Burns. Worse, even Burns forgot the anti-inflation fiscal lessons he had taught Eisenhower and opted for controls—which Nixon applied with all the grace of a cover-up. The bicentennial decade turned to chaos amid Middle Eastern economic warfare in the form of an oil embargo. Oil cartelists got higher prices and Americans got costlier standards of living.

Economists moralize. In the 1970s they assured Americans that their frivolous standards of living needed to be reduced to European levels—even if that made the American way of life unexceptional. Ironically, the developed and the undeveloped worlds aspired to America's plentitude rather than the East's shared poverty. Amid the failure of government abroad, it became fashionable to speak of reducing government at home. Regulation was excessive, so went the argument. A Democrat, Jimmy Carter, ignored history and initiated deregulation, beginning with the airline industry. Others discovered a right-wing economic evangelist named Milton Friedman and a new monetarism that counted the money supply weekly. Years later the public, uncertain of what changes in the amount of dollars in circulation really signified, decided rightly it was of little consequence after all. Yet it also concluded the same concerning New Deal liberalism.

Enter Ronald Reagan, more escalating prices, more deregulation and more monetarism—with a twist of Keynesian fiscal magic espoused by "voodoo" economists who may never have read Keynes. Government was the problem, said the man who presided over it, and the solution was less of it. Deploring any industrial policy, the old actor allowed himself to forget that, as William Pfaff wrote, "The American era of unquestioned technological supremacy, from the 1940s to the mid-1970s, was produced by an industrial policy disguised as defense and space policy."[4] Nevertheless, he embraced exorbitant defense spending to combat an evil empire that rotted away before the unseeing eyes of American intelligence.

How to pay for it? "Supply-side" advocates found Reagan an easy mark. With the ease of scratching a simple diagram upon a restaurant napkin, they showed how reduced taxes would increase incomes and personal spending to elevate revenues; hadn't John F. Kennedy done that? Again, history proved to be a treacherous art. The supply-siders knew that their listeners wanted to believe that greed had social rewards, but the budgets that would be balanced were not. In fact, Reagan budgets made previous wartime deficits puny by comparison. Paradox abounded. Hustling state capitalism via innovative defense programs, the Reaganauts outdid New Dealers in broadening government's reach in the South and the West and thereby continued the boom that had begun in the 1930s. They radically rewarded foreigners too with the sale of vast quantities of American debt. They enriched themselves, failed to attain real economic growth, and dumped the cost for their splurge of paper upon future generations—the greatest sin as defined by conservatives contemporaneous to New Dealers. Inflation (diminished but not eradicated), insouciance to national health and infrastructural problems, and increasing debt service reduced budget flexibility, leaving a supply-side moral and economic disaster for Americans—a legacy that should be with us through the centennial of the New Deal.

Reagan inherited the oil shocks of the 1970s and the most horrendous peacetime inflation of the twentieth century, which reached 13 per cent per annum in 1980. The Carter administration had allowed interest rates to rise to the extent that many states had to abolish unenforceable usury laws. Not even government-encouraged usury deflated prices until 1982, when both inflation and unemployment crested at well into double digits. "Stagflation" was not new to American economic history—although its extent flattened the "Phillips curve," a shibboleth that inflation and unemployment were mutually exclusive consequences of one or the other. The consequences of this stagflation were momentous. While the jobless lines lengthened, many who still worked put aside dreams of home-owning until interest rates returned to what they had been. As of late 1991, even with persistent recession, mortgage rates remained above 8 per cent in most places and long gone were the days of 1967 when the purchase of a home was possible with a mortgage at 6.5 per cent. Increasingly the New Deal dream of broadening participation in capitalism was waning.

Accompanying the frenzy of high rates, banks and savings and loans paid premiums for money deposited with them. The Reagan administration lent a helping hand by deregulating the credit institutions. That is where the weak and the wicked moved in—as Franklin Roosevelt had warned when he accepted deposit guarantees with the proviso of regulation. The collapse of numerous savings and loans across America—because nonregulated sharpies looted them or they invested unwisely in real estate whose value dwindled in an overbuilt market—exhausted the Federal Savings and Loan Insurance Corporation (FSLIC). Congress created the Resolution Trust Company (RTC), an uninspired and unimaginative version of the old RFC, which promptly created a ponderous bureaucracy fueled by billions of dollars that were supposed to compensate depositors by selling off S & L assets to local promoters or corporations hungry for cheap assets.[5] By that time more banks failed annually, thanks to deregulation, than had failed in the nearly half century of FDIC regulation. Partly out of weakness and partly because it had become faddish, banks in the 1980s and into the early 1990s were merging. The American credit system, amid the greatest instability since the inception of the New Deal, underwent a second desperate credit revolution that might not have been necessary with regulation.*

State capitalism, as the RTC attested, was alive and well in America. But it had broadened to an extent undreamed of by New Dealers. In recent years Congress bailed out the Lockheed and Chrysler corporations, which along with Continental Bank in Chicago raise the question of whether certain business institutions are "too big to fail." The national interest does not permit their insolvency and passing from the market. That, in turn, raises another question: is it possible for a government or a governmental agency—federal, state or local—to fail? A few years ago the question might have been considered too outlandish to ask. No more. To pay for Reagan's warfare state and the transfer of dollars to owners of the national debt, the federals have increasingly shifted the burden of social services to state and local governments. Moreover, the economy sagged into a recession in 1990, from which it still had not recovered in 1992. On September 12, 1991, the city of Chelsea, Massachusetts, went into receivership. Philadelphia, the country's fifth-largest city, saw its bond rating downgraded in 1990 to the least creditworthy status and then could not pay its bills for several months in 1991. Although no municipalities had gone into bankruptcy, a spokesman for the National League of Cities reported that he anticipated "financial emergencies." "The biggest problem is that we've had decades of not paying attention to infrastructure," a Chicago expert on municipal finance declared. "It's clear now that the infrastructure that's 30 or 40 years old has to be replaced. [But] Municipalities are spending more time and money on social services—police, fire, the homeless, courts, health care and education. They are finding themselves more and more in a difficult situation."[6]

Furthermore, one careful Washington observer has noted that another savings and loan debacle might bring down one or more of the federal "state-sponsored enterprises" that lend or guarantee loans without proper

*Airline deregulation did not appear to suffer from chicanery so much as it suffered from competition. In November 1991 Midway Airlines, one of a host of new airlines launched in the wake of deregulation, went out of business. That left only one airline remaining of those begun since deregulation and an industry rapidly on the verge of losing old standbys such as TWA and Pan American. The surviving airlines were dominated by American, United and Delta—who were looking forward to an oligopolistic cartel to return them to the profitability they had known before deregulation.

regulation. Federal institutions in the business of guaranteeing mortgages such as the New Deal's Federal Home Loan Bank System and the Federal National Mortgage Association (Fannie Mae), or the state capitalist creatures of the Nixon 1970s such as the Federal Home Loan Mortgage Corporation (Freddie Mac) and the Student Loan Marketing Association (Sallie Mae)) are powerful bodies susceptible to market foibles for which the taxpayers would be liable. While nobody anticipates a federal filing for bankruptcy, should another disaster strike, federal debt service could escalate to a near-majority of the federal budget.[7]

The New Dealers did not intend to put the American taxpayer at risk for the stupidity or cupidity of bankers. Indeed, the system they erected in the 1930s would succeed today as it had for a quarter century if not for the excesses of war and fiscal policy. Clearly, government regulation was not the hobgoblin of small minds that is so often portrayed today. And just as certain is the fact that state capitalism is needed now to redevelop the sagging American infrastructure. "It is clearly within our means to do what we have to do," writes Felix Rohatyn, who has studied the RFC legacy: "increase our savings and investment rates; re-create a banking system which will adequately finance our business as well as our social needs; invest in an adequate public infrastructure to support our private and our public sectors."[8] It is too much to expect from our political system a neat corporatist solution to our economic woes, but honest men will have to agree to an industrial policy that reasserts the interests of the majority of the American people who do not labor in an intercontinental market. American power lies not in its military might; rather, it is best asserted in the still robust living standard that makes the United States the greatest market of the world—from which nobody would care to be excluded. However, Americans have to learn anew that they are only as good as their education, their health, and their markets. They are still capable of great projects; they are still capable of being New Dealers.

Acknowledgments

IN LIEU OF AN EXTENDED bibliographic essay on New Deal sources, I want to recommend to the general reader any of the writings of Arthur Schlesinger, Jr., William E. Leuchtenburg, Robert Dallek, Arthur Link, Sidney Fine, Frank Freidel, and Ellis Hawley. My intellectual debts begin with these historians and friends, none of whom has read this manuscript but all of whom have shared their ideas with me over the years. In all probability, however, if they had read any part of it they might have either disagreed with me or cautioned against some excesses. As it is, I want to thank them for being such stimulating friends and scholars of twentieth-century American political history. My gratitude also goes to all the scholars such as James S. Olson and Michael A. Bernstein whose monographs confirmed my thoughts that it was time for someone to pull their work together into a unifying theme on the political economy of the New Deal.

When the leadership of Northern Illinois University proclaimed me a Presidential Research Professor in 1985, it conferred upon me research benefits that immeasurably aided the completion of this project. That same year I became a Guggenheim Fellow for a not yet completed project; because the research for that project suggested the need for this one, this book is a spin-off of the Guggenheim investment.

Many people helped me along the way. The late Joseph L. Rauh, Jr., and David Ginsburg shared with me some of their experiences in New Deal Washington, and the late Ernest Cuneo lavished upon me his rich tales. Bill Leuchtenburg contributed a Lyndon Johnson quote that precedes the section on Texans. Arthur Schlesinger, Jr., was generous with his insights and his intellect, but most of all I value his friendship. John Ferris at the Franklin D. Roosevelt Library and several other curators there and diligent archivists such as Linda Hansen at the Lyndon Baines Johnson Library responded to all my claims upon their time and energies. Nancy Bressler is no longer at the Mudd Library at Princeton University, but she has done much to facilitate this book and my other writings. Kathleen Patchel shared with me her knowledge of lawyers and

Yale Law School. Richard Lowitt, Robert Himmelberg and Jeffrey Mirel reinforced many of my concepts of the New Deal. In addition to several enlightening lunchtime conversations about FDR at the Roosevelt Library some years ago, Ted Morgan got me together with the publisher-wise Tom Wallace who got me together with Ash Green and his editorial acuity. And when Humpty-Dumpty had a great fall, Sam Goldman put him together again—well, almost. Linda, who knows something about projects, sustained this one with her usual encouragement and love—as did Orrin and Jessica with theirs. In the end, however, nobody but the historian is responsible for this book.

Unpublished Sources

Manuscript Collections

Joseph Alsop Papers, Library of Congress
Arthur A. Ballantine Papers, Herbert Hoover Library
Bernard M. Baruch Papers, Mudd Library, Princeton University
Louis Bean Papers, Franklin D. Roosevelt Library
Adolf A. Berle, Jr., Papers, Franklin D. Roosevelt Library
Francis Biddle Papers, Franklin D. Roosevelt Library
Hugo L. Black Papers, Library of Congress
Charles C. Burlingham Papers, Harvard Law School Archives
John M. Carmody Papers, Franklin D. Roosevelt Library
Oscar Chapman Papers, Franklin D. Roosevelt Library
Raymond Clapper Papers, Library of Congress
Benjamin V. Cohen Papers, Library of Congress
Morris Llewellyn Cooke Papers, Franklin D. Roosevelt Library
Thomas G. Corcoran Papers, Library of Congress
Norman Davis Papers, Library of Congress
William O. Douglas Papers, Library of Congress
Stephen Early Papers, Franklin D. Roosevelt Library
Ferdinand Eberstadt Papers, Mudd Library, Princeton University
Mordecai Ezekial Papers, Franklin D. Roosevelt Library
Herbert Feis Papers, Library of Congress
Jerome Frank Papers, Sterling Library, Yale University
Felix Frankfurter Papers, Library of Congress
Edwin F. Gay Papers, Hoover Institution.
Richard V. Gilbert Papers, Franklin D. Roosevelt Library
Leon Henderson Papers, Franklin D. Roosevelt Library
Harry Hopkins Papers, Franklin D. Roosevelt Library
Cordell Hull Papers, Library of Congress
Harold L. Ickes Papers, Library of Congress
Robert H. Jackson Papers, Library of Congress
Lyndon Baines Johnson Papers, Lyndon Baines Johnson Library
Jesse H. Jones Papers, Library of Congress
Fred I. Kent Papers, Mudd Library, Princeton University
Julius A. Krug Papers, Library of Congress
Thomas Lamont Papers, Baker Library, Harvard University
David E. Lilienthal Papers, Mudd Library, Princeton University
Walter Lippmann Papers, Sterling Library, Yale University

Lower Colorado River Authority Papers, Lyndon Baines Johnson Library
Herbert Marks Papers, Franklin D. Roosevelt Library
Maury Maverick Papers, Barker Texas History Center, University of Texas at Austin
William Gibbs McAdoo Papers, Library of Congress
James H. MacLafferty Papers, Herbert Hoover Library
Eugene Meyer Papers, Library of Congress
Raymond Moley Papers, Hoover Institution
Henry Morgenthau, Jr., Papers, Franklin D. Roosevelt Library
George W. Norris Papers, Library of Congress
J.F.T. O'Connor Papers, University of California Library, Berkeley
Wright Patman Papers, Lyndon Baines Johnson Library
Drew Pearson Papers, Lyndon Baines Johnson Library.
Key Pittman Papers, Library of Congress
Stanley Reed Papers, University of Kentucky Library
Franklin D. Roosevelt Papers, PPF, PSF, OF, Franklin D. Roosevelt Library
Samuel I. Rosenman Papers, Franklin D. Roosevelt Library
James Rowe, Jr., Papers, Franklin D. Roosevelt Library
Beardsley Ruml Papers, Regenstein Library, University of Chicago
Alexander Sachs Papers, Franklin D. Roosevelt Library
Rexford Guy Tugwell Papers, Franklin D. Roosevelt Library
Jacob Viner Papers, Mudd Library, Princeton University
Henry A. Wallace Papers, University of Iowa Library
Harry Dexter White Papers, Mudd Library, Princeton University
Robert E. Wood Papers, Herbert Hoover Library

Oral History Research Office, Columbia University Project (COHC)

Lawrence Fly
Jerome Frank
Francis Perkins
Henry A. Wallace

Lyndon Baines Johnson Library, Oral History

Mary Rather
James Rowe

Doctoral Dissertations

Sally Hammond Clarke, "Farmers as Entrepreneurs: Regulation and Innovation in American Agriculture During the Twentieth Century," Brown University, 1987.
Robert Leslie Cole, "The Democratic Party in Washington State, 1919–1933: Barometer of Social Change," University of Washington, 1972.
Judith Kaaz Doyle, "Out of Step: Maury Maverick and the Politics of the Depression and the New Deal," University of Texas at Austin, 1989.
William Monroe Emmons, "Private and Public Responses to Market Failure

in the U.S. Electric Power Industry: 1882–1942," Harvard University, 1989.

William S. Forth, "Wesley L. Jones: A Political Biography," University of Washington, 1962.

Michael Abbot Goldman, "The War Finance Corporation in the Politics of War and Reconstruction, 1917–1923," Rutgers University, 1971.

Fred Greenbaum, "Edward Prentiss Costigan: A Study of a Progressive," Columbia University, 1962.

Walter Kraft Lambert, "New Deal Revenue Acts: The Politics of Taxation," University of Texas at Austin, 1970.

Monica Lynne Niznik, "Thomas G. Corcoran: The Public Service of Franklin Roosevelt's 'Tommy the Cork,'" University of Notre Dame, 1981.

Hugh James Savage, "Political Independents of the Hoover Era: The Progressive Insurgents of the Hoover Era," University of Illinois, 1961.

Janet Louise Schmelzer, "The Early Life and Early Congressional Career of Wright Patman: 1894–1941," Texas Christian University, 1978.

Dale Norman Snook, "William G. McAdoo and the Development of National Economic Policy, 1913–1918," University of Cincinnati, 1975.

Robert Hardin Van Meter, Jr., "The United States and European Recovery, 1918–1923: A Study of Public Policy and Private Finance," University of Wisconsin, 1971.

Notes

INTRODUCTION

1.. The astute business writer James Grant calls this credit expansion of the Federal Government, "socialization of risk." ***Money of the Wind: Borrowing and Lending in America from the Civil War to Michael Milken*** (New York: Farrar Straus Giroux, 1992) pp. 4, 181, 242, 261.
2. Unofficial Observer [John Franklin Carter], ***The New Dealers*** (New York: Simon and Schuster, 1934).

I Wilsonians

1 WILLIAM GIBBS MCADOO

1. Quoted in Mark Sullivan, "McAdoo's Chances for the Democratic Nomination," ***World's Work***, June 1923, 199; William Gibbs McAdoo, ***Crowded Years*** (Boston: 1931), pp. 501–02.
2. Walter Lippmann, "Two Leading Democratic Candidates," ***New Republic***, 23 (June 2, 1920), 10–11, reprinted in Lippmann, ***Men of Destiny*** (New York: 1927), pp. 112–19.
3. McAdoo, ***Crowded Years***, may be as honest a memoir as the genre allows. This profile also draws on John J. Broesamle, ***William Gibbs McAdoo: A Passion for Change, 1863–1917*** (Port Washington, N.Y.: 1973), Otis L. Graham, Jr., "William Gibbs McAdoo," ***The Dictionary of American Biography, Supplement Three***, pp. 479–82; and Dale Norman Snook, "William G. McAdoo and the Development of National Economic Policy, 1913–1918," unpublished doctoral dissertation, University of Cincinnati, 1975.
4. McAdoo, ***Crowded Years***, p. 220; Bernard M. Baruch, ***Baruch: The Public Years*** (New York: Holt, Rinehart & Winston 1960), pp. 6, 50–51.
5. Broesamle, pp. 26–31; Robert Watchorn, "The Builder of the Hudson Tunnels," ***Outlook*** 90 (December 26, 1908), 909–14; McAdoo, "The Soul of a Corporation," ***World's Work*** 23 (March 1912), 579–92.
6. William Gibbs McAdoo, "The Kind of Man Woodrow Wilson Is," ***Century*** 85 (March 1913), 744–53.
7. ***New York Times***, December 18, 1912; Snook, pp. 46–79, passim; Arthur S. Link, ***Wilson: The Road to the White House*** (Princeton, N.J. 1947), pp. 310–14; John Milton Cooper, Jr., ***Walter Hines Page: The Southerner as American, 1855–1918*** (Chapel Hill, N.C., 1977), pp. 235–46.

8. C. Vann Woodward, *Origins of the New South 1877–1913* (Baton Rouge, La., 1951), p. 471.
9. *New York Times*, February 23, 1899, February 23, 1900, February 23, 1901, December 15, 1904, December 10, 1908, December 15, 1910, December 17, 1911, December 18, 1912; Woodrow Wilson to William G. McAdoo, November 10, 1911, McAdoo Papers, Box 517.
10. Frances Wright Saunders, *Eleanor Axson Wilson* (Chapel Hill: University of North Carolina Press, 1985), pp. 268–72.
11. William G. McAdoo to Woodrow Wilson, October 1, 1913, McAdoo Papers, Box 518; McAdoo, pp. 253–55; for a different view, see James Livingston, *Origins of the Federal Reserve System: Money, Class and Corporate Capitalism* (Ithaca, N.Y.: Cornell University Press, 1986); for a recent attack on the Federal Reserve System, see William Greider, *The Secrets of the Temple* (New York: Simon and Schuster, 1987).
12. Broesamle, p. 171.
13. "The 'Greatest Secretary of the Treasury Since Alexander Hamilton,'" *Current Opinion* 66 (January 1919), 20–21; Norman Hapgood, "McAdoo," *Independent*, May 29, 1920, 282–84.
14. Cordell Hull, *The Memoirs of Cordell Hull* (New York: Macmillan, 1948), pp. 61, 74, 92; Nancy Shepherdson, "The First 1040," *American Heritage*, March 1989, 101–05; Jerold L. Waltman, *Political Origins of the U.S. Income Tax* (Jackson: University Press of Mississippi, 1985).
15. Jordan A. Schwarz, *The Speculator: Bernard M. Baruch in Washington, 1917–1965* (Chapel Hill: University of North Carolina Press, 1981), pp. 42–43.
16. Broesamle, pp. 167–85; George B. Tindall, *The Emergence of the New South 1913–1945* (Baton Rouge: Louisiana State University Press, 1967), pp. 33–38.
17. McAdoo to Wilson, August 27, 1915, H. B. Brougham memorandum of interview with the president, December 14, 1914, McAdoo Papers, Boxes 520 and 523; William G. McAdoo, "Wanted: American Ships," *Outlook* 113 (June 7, 1916), 326–30; McAdoo, *Crowded Years*, pp. 294–316; Broesamle, pp. 212–36; Samuel A. Lawrence, *United States Merchant Shipping Policies and Politics* (Washington, D.C.: The Brookings Institution, 1966), pp. 39n, 39–40; Robert Higgs, *Crisis and Leviathan: Critical Episodes in the Growth of American Government* (New York: Oxford University Press,1987), pp. 124–26.
18. On the railroads, see K. Austin Kerr, *American Railroad Politics 1914–1920: Rates, Wages, and Efficiency* (University of Pittsburgh Press, 1968), Albro Martin, *Enterprise Denied: Origins of the Decline of American Railroads, 1897–1917* (New York: Columbia University Press, 1971), and Gabriel Kolko, *Railroads and Regulation 1877–1916* (New York: Norton, 1965).
19. McAdoo to Wilson, December 6, 14, 15, Wilson to McAdoo, December 31, 1917, McAdoo Papers, Box 523; Kerr, pp. 39–143; McAdoo, *Crowded Years*, pp. 446–510.
20. McAdoo to Wilson, December 10, 1917, McAdoo Papers, Box 523; Michael Abbot Goldman, "The War Finance Corporation in the Politics of War and Reconstruction, 1917–1923," unpublished doctoral dissertation, Rutgers University, 1971, pp. 64–152; Higgs, p. 142.
21. Diary, November 18, 1926, Gay Papers; McAdoo to Wilson, August 2,

1917, May 16, July 10, 1917, McAdoo Papers, Boxes 522 and 523; David M. Kennedy, *Over Here: The First World War and American Society* (New York: Oxford University Press, 1980), p. 105; Milton Friedman and Anna Jacobson Schwartz, *A Monetary History of the United States 1867–1960* (Princeton, N.J.: Princeton University Press, 1963), pp. 189–239. On Keynes and World War II finance, see my discussion in *The Speculator*, pp. 396–408. Quote is from Charles Gilbert, *American Financing of World War I* (Westport, Conn.: Greenwood Press, 1970), p. xix. For another contemporary perspective, see Alexander D. Noyes, *The War Period of American Finance 1908–1925* (New York: Putnam, 1926).

22. "Letter to the President of the United States from the Secretary of the Treasury transmitting the Proceedings of the Pan American Financial Conference," September 6, 1915, McAdoo to Wilson, September 27, October 1, December 29, 1915, Wilson to McAdoo, October 5, 1915, McAdoo Papers, Box 520; Robert Hardin Van Meter, Jr., "The United States and European Recovery, 1918–1923: A Study of Public Policy and Private Finance," unpublished doctoral dissertation, University of Wisconsin, 1971, pp. 1–54; Snook, pp. 119–250.
23. McAdoo to Wilson, July 3, 1917, McAdoo Papers, Box 522.
24. Diary, November 22, 1918, Clapper Papers; Link, ed., *The Papers of Woodrow Wilson, 53, 1918–1919,* (Princeton, N.J.: Princeton University Press, 1986), pp. 401, 183, 468–69; McAdoo to Williams, March 11, 1920, Williams Papers, Box 45; Kerr, pp. 136–43, 204–27; also, see Diary, November 23, 1918, Anderson Papers; Diary, December 5, 1918, Hamlin Papers; "Why McAdoo Really Resigned," folder 106–17, Lamont Papers.
25. McAdoo to Wilson, March 23, 1918, McAdoo Papers, Box 524; Dewey W. Grantham, *Southern Progressivism: The Reconciliation of Progress and Tradition* (Knoxville: University of Tennessee Press, 1983), p. 408; George B. Tindall, *The Emergence of the New South 1933–1945* (Baton Rouge: Louisiana State University Press, 1967), pp. 33–69.
26. Diary, December 3, 1918, Williams Papers; Schwarz, pp. 107–10; McAdoo to Wilson, October 26, 1917, McAdoo Papers, Box 523; on Leffingwell, see Stephen A. Shuker, "Russell Cornell Leffingwell," *Dictionary of American Biography, Supplement VI, 1956–1960* (New York: Scribner, 1980), pp. 376–78.
27. Diary, December 5, 1918, Hamlin Papers; Diary, November 14, 1918, Long Papers; Diary, August 3, 1919, Auchincloss Papers; Diary, March 26, May 23, 1919; Morgenthau Sr. Papers; "Secretary McAdoo's Services," "Mr. McAdoo's Resignation," *Nation*, November 30, 1918, 646–47, 640.
28. Diary, November 27, 1916, Cummings Papers; Diary, January 7–10, July 3, 1920, Anderson Papers; Baruch to J. J. Donovan, January 29, 1920, to Robert Woolley, May 24, 1920, Baruch Papers, General Correspondence.
29. McAdoo to Wilson, May 12, 16, July 5, 6, 9, 1917, McAdoo Papers, Box 522.
30. Diary, May 31, July 3, 4, 1920, Cummings Papers; Wesley M. Bagby, *The Road to Normalcy: The Presidential Campaign and Election of 1920* (Baltimore: Johns Hopkins Press, 1962), pp. 54–78, 102–22, passim.; Daniel C.

Roper, *Fifty Years of Public Life* (Westport, Conn.: Greenwood Press, 1968), p. 211; for Cummings-Wilson correspondence, see Cummings Papers, Box 68; Burl Noggle, *Into the Twenties* (Urbana: University of Illinois Press, 19), p.

31. McAdoo to Williams, July 9, 1920, Williams Papers, Box 45; Baruch to Martin H. Glynn, July 12, 1920, Baruch Papers, General Correspondence; Roper, pp. 212–13.

32. On Franklin, see "Memorial of George Small Franklin," *The Memorial Book and Mortuary Roll, 1934–1935, The Association of the Bar of the City of New York 1935*, pp. 308–13. On Cotton, see Robert T. Swaine, *The Cravath Firm:* vol. 2 (New York, 1948), pp. 13–17; Cotton obituary in *New York Times,* March 11, 1931; Henry L. Stimson and McGeorge Bundy, *On Active Service in Peace and War* (New York: Harper & Bros., 1947), p. 161; Elting E. Morison, *Turmoil and Tradition: A Study of the Life and Times of Henry L. Stimson* (Boston: Houghton Mifflin, 1960), pp. 308–09, 354, Cotton quote on p. 121, original emphasis; Harlan B. Phillips, *Felix Frankfurter Reminisces* (New York: Reynal, 1960), pp. 108, 218–28; Michael E. Parrish, *Felix Frankfurter and His Times: The Reform Years* (New York: The Free Press, 1982), p. 71; *The Nation*, March 25, 1931, 315; *Survey*, March 15, 1931, 646.

33. Roper, pp. 213, 218; Robert K. Murray, *The 103rd Ballot* (New York: Harper & Row, 1976), pp. 37–50.

34. Roper, p. 258; Frankfurter to Newton Baker, April 16, 1923, Baker to Frankfurter, April 18, 1923, Frankfurter Papers.

35. Mary Synon, *McAdoo* (Indianapolis: Bobbs-Merrill, 1924), p. 187.

36. Schwarz, *The Speculator*, pp. 181–82; Arthur M. Schlesinger, Jr., *The Crisis of the Old Order 1919–1933* (Boston: Houghton Mifflin, 1957), pp.170, 181, 286, 293, 298, 307–10, 342, 347, 361, 376; Roper, pp. 258–60.

2 HERBERT HOOVER AND BERNARD BARUCH

1. Robert F. Himmelberg, "Business, Antitrust Policy and the Industrial Board of the Department of Commerce, 1919," *Business History Review* XLII (Spring 1968), 1–23; Jordan A. Schwarz, *The Speculator: Bernard M. Baruch in Washington, 1917–1965* (Chapel Hill: University of North Carolina Press, 1981), pp. 207–19.

2. Robert K. Murray, "Herbert Hoover and the Harding Cabinet," in Ellis W. Hawley, ed., *Herbert Hoover as Secretary of Commerce: Studies in New Era Thought and Practice* (Iowa City: University of Iowa Press, 1981), pp. 19–38; McAdoo telegram to Wilson, October 6, 1917, McAdoo Papers, Box 523.

3. Hawley, "Herbert Hoover and Economic Stabilization, 1921–1922," in ibid., pp. 43–79.

4. Sally Hammond Clarke, "Farmers as Entrepeneurs: Regulation and Innovation in American Agriculture During the Twentieth Century," unpublished doctoral dissertation, Brown University, 1987, pp. 35–37; Peter Fearon, *War, Prosperity and Depression: The U.S. Economy 1917–1945* (Lawrence: University Press of Kansas, 1987), pp. 28–30.

5. George B. Tindall, *The Emergence of the New South 1913–1945* (Baton

Rouge: Louisiana State University Press, 1967), pp. 111–42; Schwarz, *The Speculator*, pp. 227–41. For excellent evaluations of farmer grievances, see Clarke, pp. 44–66, and Fearon, pp. 28–41.

6. Joan Hoff Wilson, "Herbert Hoover's Agricultural Policies, 1921–1928," in Hawley, *Herbert Hoover as Secretary of Commerce*, pp. 115–47; also, Wilson, "Hoover's Agricultural Policies, 1921–1928," *Agricultural History* 51 (April 1977), 335–61.
7. Ellis Hawley, "Three Facets of Hooverian Associationalism: Lumber, Aviation and Movies 1921–1930," in Thomas K. McCraw, ed., *Regulation in Perspective: Historical Essays* (Cambridge, Mass: Harvard Business School, 1981), pp. 95–123; also, Hawley, "Secretary Hoover and the Bituminous Coal Problem," *Business History Review* 42 (Autumn 1968), pp. 253–70.
8. Schwarz, *The Speculator*, pp. 219–44; Preston J. Hubbard, *Origins of the TVA: The Muscle Shoals Controversy, 1920–1932* (New York: Norton, 1961), pp. 10, 82; Tindall, p. 241.
9. Ellis W. Hawley, "Herbert Hoover, the Commerce Secretariat, and the Vision of an Associative State," *Journal of American History* LXI (June 1974), 116–40; Evan Metcalf, "Secretary Hoover and the Emergence of Macroeconomic Management," *Business History Review* 59 (Spring 1975), 60–80; Joan Hoff Wilson, *Herbert Hoover: Forgotten Progressive* (Boston: Little, Brown, 1975), pp. 79–121; Robert F. Himmelberg, *The Origins of the National Recovery Administration: Business, Government, and the Trade Association Issue, 1921–1933* (New York: Fordham University Press, 1976).
10. Hoover quoted in Himmelberg, p. 113; Hawley, "Three Facets of Hoover Associationalism," pp. 112, 114; also, on the aviation industry, see Marylin Bender and Selig Altschul, *The Chosen Instrument: Juan Trippe and Pan Am* (New York: Simon and Schuster, 1982), pp. 65–176, passim; Samuel L. Lawrence, *United States Merchant Shipping Policies and Politics* (Washington, D.C.: Brookings Institution, 1966), pp. 42–44.
11. Michael Abbot Goldman, "The War Finance Corporation in the Politics of War and Reconstruction," unpublished doctoral dissertation, Rutgers University, 1971; James Stuart Olson, *Herbert Hoover and the Reconstruction Finance Corporation 1931–1933* (Ames: Iowa State University Press, 1977), p. 12.
12. David M. Kennedy, *Over Here: The First World War and American Society* (New York: Oxford University Press, 1980), pp. 345–46.
13. See, for instance, Numan V. Bartley, *The Creation of Modern Georgia* (Athens: University of Georgia Press, 1983).
14. Joe R. Feagin, *Free Enterprise City: Houston in Political and Economic Perspective* (New Brunswick, N.J.: Rutgers University Press, 1988), pp. 50–63.
15. See Beverley Bowen Moeller, *Phil Swing and Boulder Dam* (Berkeley: University of California Press, 1971); Joseph E. Stevens, *Hoover Dam: An American Adventure* (Norman: University of Oklahoma Press, 1988); John Fahey, *The Inland Empire: Unfolding Years, 1879–1929* (Seattle: University of Washington Press, 1986).
16. Erik N. Olssen, "Southern Senators and Reform Issues in the 1920s: A Paradox Unravelled," in Bruce Clayton and John A. Salmond, eds., *The*

South Is Another Land: Essays on the Twentieth-Century South (Westport, Conn.: Greenwood Press, 1987); Jordan A. Schwarz, *The Interregnum of Despair: Hoover, Congress, and the Depression* (Urbana: University of Illinois Press, 1971).

17. Gary Dean Best, *The Politics of American Individualism: Herbert Hoover in Transition, 1918–1921* (Westport, Conn.: Greenwood Press, 1975), pp. 54–69, Hoover quote on pp. 92–93, emphasis added; Schwarz, *The Speculator*, p. 225; Robert Skidelsky, *John Maynard Keynes: Hopes Betrayed 1883–1920* (New York: Viking, 1983), p. 399; Robert H. Wiebe, The Search for Order *1877–1920* (New York: Hill and Wang, 1967), p. 302.

18. Carolyn Grin, "The Unemployment Conference of 1921," *Mid-America* 54 (April 1973): 83–107; Peter Fearon, *War, Prosperity and Depression: The U.S. Economy* 1917–45 (Lawrence: University Press of Kansas, 1987), p. 138.

19. Harris Gaylord Warren, *Herbert Hoover and the Great Depression* (New York: Oxford University Press, 1959), pp. 168–87; Martin L. Fausold, *The Presidency of Herbert C. Hoover* (Lawrence: University Press of Kansas, 1985), pp. 106–12; Albert U. Romasco, *The Poverty of Abundance: Hoover, the Nation, the Depression* (New York: Oxford University Press, 1965), pp. 97–124.

20. Arthur A. Ballantine to Walter Lippmann, December 17, 30, 1931, Ballantine Papers, Box 14.

21. J. Joseph Huthmacher, *Senator Robert F. Wagner and the Rise of Urban Liberalism* (New York: Atheneum, 1968); William S. Forth, "Wesley L. Jones: A Political Biography," unpublished doctoral dissertation, University of Washington, 1962; Fred Greenbaum, Edward Prentiss Costigan: A Study of a Progressive," unpublished doctoral dissertation, Columbia University, 1962.

22. Ronald L. Feinman, *Twilight of Progressivism: The Western Republican Senators and the New Deal* (Baltimore: Johns Hopkins University Press, 1981), pp. 1–32; Hugh James Savage, "Political Independents of the Hoover Era: The Progressive Insurgents of the Senate," unpublished doctoral dissertation, University of Illinois, 1961.

23. David Burner, *The Politics of Provincialism: The Democratic Party in Transition, 1918–1932* (New York: Knopf, 1967), pp. 158–78; Erik N. Olssen, "Southern Senators and Reform Issues in the 1920s: A Paradox Unravelled," in Bruce Clayton and John A. Salmond, eds., *The South Is Another Land: Essays on the Twentieth-Century South* (Westport, Conn.: Greenwood Press, 1987), pp. 49–66. The research of Robert F. Himmelberg, unpublished at this writing, also suggests that the congressional Democrats were ripe for the New Deal.

24. Jordan A. Schwarz, *The Interregnum of Despair: Hoover, Congress, and the Depression* (Urbana: University of Illinois Press, 1970), pp. 64–65; Norman Davis to Cordell Hull, April 2, December 16, 1931, Norman Davis Papers, Box 27.

25. Schwarz, *The Interregnum of Despair*, pp. 78–94; Jacob Viner to John E. Galvin, October 30, 1931, Jacob Viner Papers, Box 34; James Stuart Olson, *Herbert Hoover and the Reconstruction Finance Corporation*, 1931–1933 (Ames: Iowa State University Press, 1977), pp. 24–46.

26. Urban A. Lavery to Franklin D. Roosevelt, December 17, 1932, PPF 5830.
27. James S. Olson, *Saving Capitalism: The Reconstruction Finance Corporation and the New Deal, 1933–1940* (Princeton, N.J.: Princeton University Press, 1988), pp. 14–20; Fearon, pp. 115–16, 109, 72, 102, 103, 111.
28. Diary, February 11, 16, 17, 1932, McLafferty Papers; Schwarz, *The Interregnum of Despair*, pp. 106–41; Mark Leff, *The Limits of Symbolic Reform: The New Deal and Taxation*, 1933–1939 (New York: Cambridge University Press, 1984), pp. 48–54; Fearon, pp. 121–24, 153, 157; E. Cary Brown, "Fiscal Policy in the 'Thirties': A Reappraisal," *American Economic Review* XLVI (December 1956), 868–69.
29. Fearon, p. 137; Olson, *Herbert Hoover and the Reconstruction Finance Corporation*, pp. 62–90
30. Diary, McLafferty Papers, May 19, 31, June 1, 28, July 2, 1932.
31. Schwarz, *The Interregnum of Despair*, pp. 179–200; Tindall, p. 388.
32. Norman Davis to Cordell Hull, April 2, 1931, to Walter Lippmann, August 22, 1932, Davis Papers, Boxes 27, 35; Russell Leffingwell to Walter Lippmann, October 27, 1932, Lippmann Papers, Box 84; Alexander Sachs to the Marquis of Reading, June 29, 1932, Sachs Papers, Box 60.

II Businessmen

3 JESSE H. JONES

1. "Business and Government: An Introduction to a Sequence of Articles about a Momentous Struggle," *Fortune* 17 (February 1938), 58, original emphasis.
2. Jones Papers, Box 32.
3. John A. Salmond, "Aubrey Williams: Atypical New Dealer?" in John Braeman, Robert H. Bremner, and David Brody, *The New Deal: The National Level* (Columbus: Ohio State University Press, 1975), p. 235; "Washington Notes," *New Republic*, January 27, 1935, 73.
4. Bascom N. Timmons, *Jesse H. Jones: The Man and the Statesman* (New York: Henry Holt, 1956), p. 67; Walter L. Buenger and Joseph A. Pratt, *But Also Good Business: Texas Commerce Banks and the Financing of Houston and Texas, 1886–1986* (College Station: Texas A&M University Press, 1986), p. 76. Much of the material in this chapter is taken from the Timmons biography.
5. Timmons, pp. 83, 81, emphasis added. On Chicago, see William Cronon, *Nature's Metropolis: Chicago and the Great West* (New York: Norton, 1991); On the history of the ship channel, see Marilyn McAdams Sibley, *The Port of Houston: A History* (Austin: University of Texas Press, 1968), and Buenger and Pratt, pp. 23–24.
6. Buenger and Pratt, p. 80; "Emperor Jones," *Time*, January 13, 1941, 11.
7. Buenger and Pratt, pp. 17–19, 44–45, 53, 61–63, 85–89
8. Arthur S. Link, ed., *The Papers of Woodrow Wilson* 53, November 9, 1918–January 11, 1919 (Princeton, N.J.: Princeton University Press, 1986), pp. 546–47.
9. Timmons, p. 117.
10. Woodrow Wilson to Jones et al., January 20, 1924, Edith Bolling Wilson

to Jones, June 21, 1924, Jones Papers, Box 27; Timmons, pp. 134–37; Bernard M. Baruch, *The Public Years* (New York: Holt, Rinehart and Winston, 1960), pp. 183–84; Jordan A. Schwarz, *The Speculator: Bernard M. Baruch in Washington*, 1917–1965 (Chapel Hill: University of North Carolina Press, 1981), pp. 183–84.

11. Timmons, pp. 148–49; Tom Connally as told to Alfred Steinberg, *My Name Is Tom Connally* (New York: Crowell, 1954), p. 131; Hogg quoted in Walter L. Buenger, "Between Community and Corporation: The Southern Roots of Jesse H. Jones and the Reconstruction Finance Corporation," *Journal of Southern History* 56 (August 1990), 496; on distrust of Jones, see Buenger, "Jesse H. Jones" pp. 490–91, Buenger and Pratt, pp. 54–56.
12. Buenger, "Jesse H. Jones," p. 500, banker quoted on p. 504; Buenger and Pratt, pp. 90–108, 83.
13. Buenger and Pratt, pp. 121–24.
14. Timmons, pp. 162–65; Buenger, "Jesse H. Jones," pp. 483, 506–10.
15. William Allen White, *A Puritan in Babylon* (New York: Macmillan, 1938), p. 439.
16. Russell Leffingwell to Walter Lippmann, January 4, 1933, Lippmann Papers, Box 84; to Eugene Meyer, January 9, 1932, Meyer Papers, Box 32; Jesse H. Jones, "Billions Out and Billions Back," *Saturday Evening Post*, June 12, 1937, 38.
17. Herbert Feis to Felix Frankfurter, February 25, 1932, Feis Papers, Box 33; Walter Lippmann to Eugene Meyer, April 22, 1932, Meyer Papers, Box 33; Jones quoted in James S. Olson, *Saving Capitalism: The Reconstruction Finance Corporation and the New Deal, 1933–1940* (Princeton, N.J.: Princeton University Press, 1988), p. 17.
18. Memoranda, December 24, 1932, January 7, 14, 21, 28, 1933, Thomas G. Corcoran Papers, Box 263, emphasis added.
19. Olson, pp. 25–41, 63–71.
20. Jesse Jones, "Billions Out and Billions Back," p. 40; Timmons, p. 187; Leffingwell quoted in Arthur M. Schlesinger, Jr., *The Coming of the New Deal* (Boston: Houghton Mifflin, 1958), p. 428. Eugene Meyer maintained that a widespread recognition of the need for capital existed well before Jones discovered it. See comments upon Jesse Jones's *Fifty Billion Dollars*, Meyers Papers, Box 30.
21. Robert E. Wood to Henry A. Wallace, February 23, April 13, George Peek, April 14, 1933, August 24, 1933, Wood Papers, Boxes 18, 12.
22. Jones's business files bulge with unhappy stories of businessmen, senators and representatives, not to mention public service agencies pleading for assistance for which the RFC guidelines did not make allowance. See Jones Papers, Boxes 35–50.
23. Hoover quoted in MacLafferty Diary, March 8, 1932; Roosevelt quoted in Frank Freidel, *FDR: Launching the New Deal* (Boston: Little, Brown, 1973), pp. 225, 215; Glass on bank guarantees in Ogden Mills memo, March 2, 1933, in President's Subject Files, Herbert Hoover Papers, Box 157; Timmons, pp. 194–95; Carter Glass to Jesse Jones, December 14, Jones to Glass, December 15, 1933, Jones Papers, Box 11. Also, see

Schwarz, *Liberal: Adolf A. Berle and the Vision of an American Era* (New York: The Free Press, 1987), pp. 86–87.

24. Timmons, pp. 198–205; Olson, pp. 137–140; Franklin D. Roosevelt to Jesse H. Jones, August 31, 1933, Jones Papers, Box 29; Tommy Corcoran to Felix Frankfurter, ca. late 1933, Corcoran Papers.
25. "Business and Government," *Fortune,* May 1940, 50.
26. Ray Tucker, "Texas Steerer," *Colliers,* September 22, 1934, 16; Jones quoted in Olson, p. 154.
27. Copy, Franklin D. Roosevelt to Jones, July 1, 1934, Morgenthau Diaries; Jones to John N. Garner, July 21, 1934, Jones Papers, Box 10; Russell Leffingwell to Walter Lippmann, January 4, 1933, Lippmann Papers, Box 84; Olson, pp. 119, 122–23; Jones, "Billions Out and Billions Back: The Bankers Boss the Railroads," *Saturday Evening Post,* June 26, 1937, 90, 92.
28. Jones to J.F.T. O'Connor, July 8, 1933, Jones Papers, Box 36.
29. Buenger, "Jesse H. Jones," pp. 506–07; Jones to John N. Garner, November 6, 1934, Jones Papers, Box 10; Timmons, pp. 213–17; Jones to Southern Pacific Company, June 16, 1933, to H. A. Scandrett, June 26, 1933, Jones Papers, Box 36; Jones to Stanley Reed, March 14, 1933, Box 35.
30. George Creel, "Hard-Boiled Jesse," *Colliers,* February 15, 1936, 42; Jones to Garner, July 21, August 24, 1934, Jones Papers, Box 10; Adolf A. Berle, Jr., to Franklin D. Roosevelt, July 25, 1934, PPF 1306; Jones, *Fifty Billion Dollars,* pp. 176–79.
31. Stanley Reed to the Board of Directors, June 27, 1934, Reed Papers, Box 4; Samuel Lubell, "The House That Jesse Built," *Saturday Evening Post,* December 7, 1940, 29; Tucker, p. 42; Jones to Herman P. Kopplemann, April 11, 1933, Jones Papers, Box 35.
32. McAdoo to President Wilson, May 16, 1917, McAdoo Papers, Box 523; Donald R. McCoy, "John Nance Garner," in John A. Garraty, ed., *Dictionary of American Biography: Supplement Eight 1966-1970* (New York: Scribner, 1988), pp. 205–07.
33. Ray T. Tucker, "Tiger from Texas," *Outlook and Independent* CLVI (November 26, 1930), 492–94; Schwarz, *The Interregnum of Despair,* pp. 65–66; Marquis James, "Poker-Playing, Whiskey-Drinking, Evil Old Man," *Saturday Evening Post,* September 9, 1939, 25; Samuel Lubell, "The House That Jesse Built," p.; Lubell, "New Deal's J. P. Morgan," *Saturday Evening Post,* November 30, 1940, pp. 9–11; Jones to Garner, July 21, August 24, November 6, 1934, Jones Papers, Box 10; William Bradford Huie, "Jesse Jones: Pawnbroker to the World," *American Mercury* 54 (April 1942), 433.
34. Roger Butterfield, "Silliman—He's A Wonder," *Saturday Evening Post,* November 23, 1940, 12–13.
35. William O. Douglas, *Go East, Young Man: The Early Years* (New York: Random House, 1974), p. 304.
36. P.F. to Tom, November 10, 1937, Thomas G. Corcoran Papers, Box 263.
37. Arthur Schlesinger, Jr., *The Coming of the New Deal,* p. 433; "Emperor

Jones," p. 12; Dwight MacDonald, "Reluctant Dragon, I," *Nation*, February 7, 1942, p. 158.

38. Olson, *Saving Capitalism*, pp. 162–86.
39. Ibid., pp. 45, 183, 195–96, 225; Ronald Tobey, Charles Wetherell, and Jay Brigham, "Moving Out and Settling In: Residential Mobility, Home Owning, and the Public Enframing of Citizenship, 1921–1950," *American Historical Review* 95 (December 1990), 1395–96, 1403–04, 1413–20; Michael A. Bernstein, *The Great Depression: Delayed Recovery and Economic Change in America, 1929–1939* (New York: Cambridge University Press, 1987), p. 74.
40. Peter Fearon, *War, Prosperity & Depression: The U.S. Economy 1917–1945* (Lawrence: University Press of Kansas, 1987), pp. 211, 224–26; Bernstein, *Great Depression*, pp. 63, 175–76. On the New Deal's power programs, see chapters 9, 10, and 11.
41. Morgenthau Diaries, 89:50–52, 90:111–16, 91:52–53, 104–5, 229–30, 293; Beatrice Bishop Berle and Travis Beale Jacobs, *Navigating the Rapids 1918–1971* (New York: Harcourt Brace Jovanovich, 1973), p. 142.
42. Morgenthau Diaries, 92:27–29, 93:11–12, 210, 213–214.
43. Morgenthau Diaries, 105:145–59, 106:339–45, 352–55, 111:214, 114:368–69; FDR to Jones, April 21, 1938, Jones Papers, Box 29; Jones, *Fifty Billion Dollars*, pp. 266–69.
44. Jones, *Fifty Billion Dollars*, p. 269, emphasis added; Douglas, p. 304.
45. Dwight MacDonald, "Jesse Jones, Reluctant Dragon, II," *Nation*, February 14, 1942, 187.
46. Franklin D. Roosevelt to Jesse H. Jones, July 7, 22, 1926, March 13, 1928, January 10, 1929, Jones to Roosevelt, July 14, 1926, March 26, 1928, January 14, 1929, Jones Papers, Box 29; Jones to Roosevelt, January 26, 27, 1933, PPF 703.
47. "Steve Early, September 9, [1938]," Also P. Papers; undated notes, FDR memo for Morgenthau, December 11, 1934, Morgenthau Papers, Box 4; "Jesse Holman Jones" *Current Biography*, p. 440–42; Jones to FDR, October 21, FDR to Jones, October 26, 1943, PSF 73.
48. Jones to FDR, December 14, 1935, Jones Papers, Box 29; FDR telegram to William Yeager, Jones telegram to FDR, November 1, 1936, PPF 703; William O. Douglas, *Go East, Young Man: The Autobiography of William O. Douglas* (New York: Random House, 1974), p. 305; Timmons, *Jesse H. Jones*, pp. 269–70, 333–43; Jones, pp. 262–63, 456–67.
49. First quote from Fearon, p. 180, other quote from Hammond, "Farmers as Entrepreneurs," pp. 104–05; also, on the Commodity Credit Corporation, see Olson, *Saving Capitalism*, pp. 143–47.
50. Morgenthau Diaries, 93:12, 128:47–48, 54–57, 133:193–197, 198:162, 202:118–19, 170–176, 205–07, 203:339–42, 204:28–32; Jones to B. M. Baruch, August 29, 1946, Jones Papers.
51. "Jinnee Jones," *Time*, April 13, 1942, 17; FDR to Jones, June 27, July 18, Jones to FDR, July 15, August 14, 22, 1939, Jones Papers, Box 29, PPF 703.
52. Jones to Garner, August 30, 1940, Jones Papers, Box 10; Turner Catledge, "New Deal's Man of Many Jobs," *New York Times Magazine*, October 6, 1940, 8, 18; Dwight MacDonald, "Jesse Jones, Reluctant Dragon,

I," emphasis added; Clifford J. Durr, "All the Power That Money Can Buy," *New Republic*, November 12, 1951, 17.

4 HUGH JOHNSON

1. Arthur Schlesinger, Jr., *The Coming of the New Deal* (Boston: Houghton Mifflin Company, 1958), pp. 103–05; Hugh S. Johnson, *The Blue Eagle from Egg to Earth* (Garden City, N.Y.: Doubleday, Doran, 1935), pp. 211, 208, original emphasis. On Johnson, see John Kennedy Ohl, *Hugh S. Johnson and the New Deal* (DeKalb: Northern Illinois University Press, 1985).
2. Jordan A. Schwarz, *The Speculator: Bernard M. Baruch in Washington, 1917–1965* (Chapel Hill: University of North Carolina Press, 1981), pp. 273–74.
3. Ibid., pp. 286–89.
4. See Thompson correspondence, Sachs Papers, Box 80.
5. Martin J. Sherwin, *A World Destroyed: The Atomic Bomb and the Grand Alliance* (New York: Knopf, 1975), pp. 26–27; Richard Rhodes, *The Making of the Atomic Bomb* (New York: Simon and Schuster, 1986), pp. 305–09, 312–15; Geoffrey T. Hellman, "The Contemporaneous Memoranda of Dr. Sachs," *New Yorker*, December 1, 1945, 73–80.
6. Alexander Sachs to the Marquis of Reading, June 29, 1932, Sachs Papers, Box 60. Most of the biographical information concerning Sachs comes from the finding aid for his papers at the Roosevelt Library.
7. Robert E. Wood to Henry A. Wallace, May 26, 1933, Wood Papers, Box 18; Sachs to Hugh Johnson, May 20, 1933, Sachs Papers, Box 37. The letter also can be found in Charles F. Roos, *NRA Economic Planning* (Bloomington, Ind.: The Principia Press, 1937), pp. 530–33.
8. Alexander Sachs to James N. Landis, January 25, 1934, to Edward S. Mason, September 17, emphasis added, to Franklin D. Roosevelt, January 23, to Charles F. Roos, January 22, 1935, July 23, 1935, Sachs Papers, Boxes 40, 45, 63.
9. Thomas G. Corcoran to Felix Frankfurter [undated, late 1933], Corcoran Papers, Box 198; Bernard Bellush, *The Failure of the NRA* (New York: Norton, 1975), pp. 40–44; Sachs to Charles F. Roos, July 23, 1933, April 21, 1936, Sachs Papers, Box 63.
10. Copy, FDR to Arthur Lehman, August 18, 1933, Sachs to Hugh Johnson, September 15, 1933, to Russell Leffingwell, October 2, 1933, to Isador Lubin, January 16, 1934, Sachs Papers, Boxes 63, 37, 40, 42; *New York Times*, August 27, October 1, October 14, 1933.
11. Sachs quoted in Roos, p. 84; FDR to Sachs, January 29, July 15, 1935, September 14, 1936, Sachs Papers, Box 63; to Jim Landis, January 22 [2], April 30, 1937, Sachs Papers, Box 40; copy, Thurston memorandum to Eccles, April 1, 1937, Patman Papers, Box 1508A.
12. Ohl, pp. 108–10, 151–57, 218–53; Schwarz, pp. 286–95.
13. Leon Henderson, "N.R.A." June 27, 1934, in Frank Papers, Box 12; Jacob Viner to John Dickinson, March 27, 1935, Viner Papers, Box 29.
14. Sachs to FDR, January 23, 1933 [1934], Sachs Papers, Box 63.
15. Ellis W. Hawley, *The New Deal and the Problem of Monopoly* (Princeton,

N.J.: Princeton University Press, 1966), pp. 111–46; Bellush, pp. 158–79; Theda Skocpol and Kenneth Finegold, "State Capacity and Economic Intervention in the Early New Deal," *Political Science Quarterly* 97 (Spring 1982), 25–78; Donald R. Brand, *Corporatism and the Rule of Law: A Study of the National Recovery Administration* (Ithaca, N.Y.: Cornell University Press, 1988).

III *Lawyers*

5 LOUIS D. BRANDEIS

1. Quoted in William E. Leuchtenburg, *Franklin D. Roosevelt and the New Deal* (New York: Harper & Row, 1963), p. 145.
2. Brandeis quoted in Melvin Urofsky, *Louis D. Brandeis and the Progressive Tradition* (Boston: Little, Brown, 1981), pp. 28.
3. On the significance of Brandeis and the New Freedom, see Thomas K. McCraw, *Prophets of Regulation* (Cambridge, Mass.: Harvard University Press, 1984), pp. 80–142.
4. Quoted in Thomas K. McCraw, "Louis D. Brandeis Reappraised," *American Scholar* 54 (Autumn 1985), 526.
5. Urofsky, p. 93; Richard M. Abrams, "Brandeis and the Ascendancy of Corporate Capitalism," Introduction to the Torchbook Edition, Louis D. Brandeis, *Other People's Money and How the Bankers Use It* (New York: Harper & Row, 1967), pp. xvi–xxvii. Also on Brandeis and Zionism, see Jerold S. Auerbach, *Rabbis and Lawyers: The Journey from Torah to Constitution* (Bloomington: Indiana University Press, 1990), pp. 123–49.
6. Brandeis quoted in Urofsky, p. 162; Bruce Allen Murphy, *The Brandeis/Frankfurter Connection: The Secret Political Activities of Two Supreme Court Justices* (New York: Oxford University Press, 1982), p. 139–47, 403–06; Thomas G. Corcoran to Felix Frankfurter, undated [ca. November 1933], Corcoran Papers, Box 198.
7. Joseph P. Lash, *Dealers and Dreamers: A New Look at the New Deal* (Garden City, N.Y.: Doubleday, 1988), p. 163; Adolf A. Berle to FDR, April 23, 1934, Berle Papers, Box 10; Jordan A. Schwarz, *Liberal: Adolf A. Berle and the Vision of an American Era* (New York: The Free Press, 1987), pp. 106–07.
8. *The Secret Diary of Harold L. Ickes: The First Thousand Days* (New York: Simon and Schuster, 1953), p. 363; Arthur Schlesinger, Jr., *The Politics of Upheaval* (Boston: Houghton Mifflin, 1960), p. 280; Michael E. Parrish, *Felix Frankfurter and His Times: The Reform Years* (New York: The Free Press, 1982), pp. 261–62; Frankfurter to Frank, June 10, 1935, Frankfurter Papers, Box 55.
9. FDR quoted in Philippa Strum, *Louis D. Brandeis: Justice for the People* (Cambridge, Mass.: Harvard University Press, 1984), pp. 393–94; Schlesinger, p. 651.
10. David E. Lilienthal to Calvert Magruder, November 17, 1942, Lilienthal Papers, Box 100; Schlesinger, p. 222.
11. Jerome Frank to Morris Ernst, September 30, 1939, Frank Papers, Box 21; Alexander Sachs to Eugene Meyer, July 12, 1935, Sachs Papers, Box 46.

12. Melvin I. Urofsky, "The Brandeis-Frankfurter Conversations," *Supreme Court Review* (1985), 303.
13. Philippa Strum, *Louis D. Brandeis: Justice for the People* (Cambridge, Mass.: Harvard University Press, 1984), pp. 132–45.
14. Ibid., p. 238.
15. Chaim Weizmann quoted in Robert A. Burt, *Two Jewish Justices: Outcasts in the Promised Land* (Berkeley: University of California Press, 1988), p. 134, n. 33; Strum, pp. 281–82.
16. Strum, pp. 287–89.
17. Untitled, unauthored biography of Benjamin V. Cohen in Cohen file, Corcoran Papers, Box 193.
18. Strum, p. 343.
19. See Richard P. Adelstein, " 'Islands of Conscious Power': Louis D. Brandeis and the Modern Corporation," *Business History Review* 63 (Autumn 1989), 614–56.

6 FELIX FRANKFURTER

1. Quoted in Philippa Strum, *Louis D. Brandeis: Justice for the People* (Cambridge, Mass.: Harvard University Press, 1984), p. 374.
2. Bruce Allen Murphy, *The Brandeis/Frankfurter Connection: The Secret Political Activities of Two Supreme Court Justices* (New York: Oxford University Press, 1982).
3. Joseph P. Lash, *From the Diaries of Felix Frankfurter* (New York: Norton, 1975), pp. 12, 25; Frankfurter to Eugene Meyer, June 6, 1936, Meyer Papers, Box 22; Michael E. Parrish, *Felix Frankfurter and His Times: The Reform Years* (New York: The Free Press, 1982), pp. 60–61.
4. Taft quoted in Parrish, *Frankfurter*, p. 82; Frankfurter to Newton D. Baker, January 4, 1918, Baker Papers; Memo of conversation with Felix Frankfurter, undated, Gay Papers, Box 2.
5. Max Freedman, ed. *Roosevelt and Frankfurter: Their Correspondence 1928–1945* (Boston: Houghton Mifflin, 1967), pp. 52, 57, 59; Lash, *Frankfurter Diaries*, p. 45.
6. Eugene Meyer to Felix Frankfurter, March 31, 1921, February 21, 1925, Frankfurter to Meyer, telegram April 2, 1921, February 19, 1925, Meyer Papers, Box 22; "F.F." Alsop Papers, Box 93.
7. Parrish, *Frankfurter*, p. 160; William O. Douglas, *Go East, Young Man: The Early Years* (New York: Random House, 1974), pp. 368–69.
8. Alger Hiss, *Recollections of a Life* (New York: Arcade Publishing, 1988), pp. 10–15; Marion Frankfurter quoted in Lash, *Frankfurter Diaries*, p. 30, Mrs. Howe quoted pp. 54–55, Pat Jackson quoted p. 76; Isaiah Berlin, *Personal Impressions* (New York: Viking Press, 1980), p. 85; Eugene Meyer to Frankfurter, June 19, 1936, Meyer Papers, Box 22.
9. Corcoran memo, "Re: New Men" to Reed, December 28, 1932, Corcoran Papers; Frankfurter to Reed, May 4, September 25, October 17, 30, November 12, December 8 telegram, 1935, Reed to Frankfurter, May 7, February 14, May 6, 1936.
10. Robert A. Burt, *Two Jewish Justices: Outcasts in the Promised Land* (Berkeley: University of California Press, 1988).

11. Joseph P. Lash, *Dealers and Dreamers: A New Look at the New Deal* (New York: Doubleday, 1988), p. 175; comment quoted in Leonard Dinnerstein, *Uneasy at Home: Antisemitism and the American Jewish Experience* (New York: Columbia University Press, 1987), p. 64; Alger Hiss, *Recollections of a Life* (New York: Arcade Publishing, 1988), p. 67.
12. Morton Rosenstock, "Are There Too Many Jews at Harvard?" in Leonard Dinnerstein, ed., *Antisemitism in the United States* (New York: Holt, Rinehart & Winston, 1971), pp. 102–08; Laura Kalman, *Legal Realism at Yale 1927–1960* (Chapel Hill: University of North Carolina Press, 1986), pp. 58–60; Parrish, *Frankfurter*, pp. 155–59.
13. Someone quoted from Geoffrey C. Ward, *A First-Class Temperament: The Emergence of Franklin Roosevelt* (New York: Harper & Row, 1989), p. 255; FDR quoted from Jerold S. Auerbach, *Unequal Justice: Lawyers and Social Change in Modern America* (New York: Oxford University Press, 1976), p. 187.
14. Frank Freidel, *Franklin D. Roosevelt: A Rendezvous with Destiny* (Boston: Little, Brown, 1990), pp. 295–96, 461, 531, 594–95; Richard Breitman and Alan M. Kraut, *American Refugee Policy and European Jewry, 1933–1945* (Bloomington: Indiana University Press, 1987), pp. 222–49, passim.
15. Friend and FF quoted in Stephen W. Baskerville, "Frankfurter, Keynes, and the Fight for Public Works," *Maryland Historian* 19 (Spring 1978): 1–2; Lash, *Frankfurter Diaries*, p. 166; copy, Frankfurter to Thomas G. Corcoran, October 1, 1941, Benjamin V. Cohen Papers, Box 8.
16. George N. Peek, "In and Out: The Experiences of the First AAA Administrator," *Saturday Evening Post*, May 16, 1936, 7; Lash, *Frankfurter Diaries*, p. 53.
17. Liva Baker, *Felix Frankfurter* (New York: , 1969), p. 13.
18. Frankfurter to Eugene Meyer, January 24, 1935, Meyer Papers, Box 22; Frankfurter to Jacob Viner, May 28, Viner to Frankfurter, June 1, 14, 1932, Viner Papers, Box 33; Arthur A. Ballantine to Frankfurter, June 9, 1932Ballantine Papers, Box 16.
19. Isaiah Berlin, *Personal Impressions* (New York: Viking Press, 1981), pp. 86, 89.
20. Powell and FF quoted in Michael Parrish, *Securities Regulation and the New Deal* (New Haven, Conn.: Yale University Press, 1970), pp. 2, 71; Harold J. Laski to William O. Douglas, April 10, 1934, Douglas Papers, Box 9; James Rowe, Jr., memorandum to Peggy Dowd, November 4, 1938, Rowe Papers, Box 10.
21. Lash, *Frankfurter Diaries*, p. 19.
22. Robert Skidelsky, *John Maynard Keynes: Hopes Betrayed 1883–1920* (New York: Viking Press, 1986), pp. 375, 381; Baskerville, pp. 6–12; Meyer to Frankfurter, June 19, August 25, 1936, Meyer Papers, Box 22.
23. "F.F.", Alsop Papers, Box 93; Joseph Alsop and Robert Kintner, "We Shall Make America Over," *Saturday Evening Post*, October 29, 1938, 76.
24. Lash, *Frankfurter Diaries*, pp. 35, 53; Frankfurter to Jerome Frank, September 29, 1933, Frank Papers, Box 12; Parrish, *Securities Regulation*, p. 42; Meyer to Frankfurter, June 8, September 19, Frankfurter to Meyer, September 13, 1934, Meyer Papers, Box 22.
25. Parrish, *Frankfurter*, pp. 244–45.

7 THOMAS G. CORCORAN

1. "The Janizariat," *Time*, September 12, 1938, 24.
2. Beverly Smith, "Corcoran & Cohen," *American Magazine* 124 (August 1937), 22; Eugene Meyer to Felix Frankfurter, May 18, 1938, Meyer Papers, Box 22.
3. "T. September 21, 1938," Alsop Papers.
4. "Thomas Gardiner Corcoran," *Current Biography 1940*, 192–94; Joseph P. Lash, *Dealers and Dreamers: A New Look at the New Deal* (New York: Doubleday, 1988), pp. 54–75, passim; Sheldon M. Novick, *Honorable Justice: The Life of Oliver Wendell Holmes* (Boston: Little, Brown, 1989), p. 479, n. 77; "T.—July 27, 1938," Alsop Papers, Box 93; Monica Lynne Niznik, "Thomas G. Corcoran: The Public Service of Franklin Roosevelt's 'Tommy the Cork,' unpublished doctoral dissertation, University of Notre Dame, 1981, p. 19; Frankfurter to Corcoran, February 23, 1932, Corcoran to Francis Biddle, April 26, 1946, Corcoran Papers, Boxes 198, 48.
5. Corcoran to Frankfurter, January 23, Corcoran to Frankfurter, ca. November, 1933, Corcoran Papers, Box 198; "T.—July 27, 1938," Alsop Papers, Box 93; Joseph Alsop and Robert Kintner, "We Shall Make America Over: The Birth of the Brain Trust," *Saturday Evening Post*, October 29, 1938, pp. 5–7, 74, 76, 77; astute reporter is Beverly Smith, p. 125, Niznik, p. 235.
6. Quoted in Niznik, p. 55.
7. Ibid., p. 79; "E.F.—August 10, 1938," Alsop Papers, Box 93; Wyzanski quoted in Lash, *Dealers and Dreamers*, p. 114; Niznik, pp. 90–91; Joseph L. Rauh, "Lawyers and Legislation of the Early New Deal," *Harvard Law Review* 96 (February 1983), 951. Also, see Felix Belair. Jr., "Two of the 'Selfless Six,'" *Nation's Business* 25 (July 1937), 25–26.
8. Lash, *Dealers and Dreamers*, pp. 9–54, passim.
9. Niznik, pp. 113–14; Lash, *Dealers and Dreamers*, p. 285; *The Secret Diary of Harold L. Ickes: The Inside Struggle, 1936–1939* (New York: Simon and Schuster, 1954), p. 389; C. C. Burlingham to Francis Biddle, October 21, 1941, Biddle Papers, Box 1; on Fahy, see Peter H. Irons, *The New Deal Lawyers* (Princeton, N.J.: Princeton University Press, 1982) pp. 235–39; Ben Cohen to Jerome Frank, May 13, 1939, Frank Papers.
10. Lash, *Dealers and Dreamers*, pp. 94, 130–36; Eugene Meyer to Felix Frankfurter, May 10, 1932, Meyer Papers, Box 22; Cohen quoted in Niznik, p. 69.
11. On the greater history of the Securities Act of 1933, see Joel Seligman, *The Transformation of Wall Street: A History of the Securities and Exchange Commission and Modern Corporate Finance* (Boston: Houghton Mifflin, 1982), pp. 1–100.
12. G. Edward White, "Recapturing New Deal Lawyers," *Harvard Law Review* 102 (1988), 513.
13. Foley résumé, James Rowe to Corcoran, April 1, 1937, Corcoran Papers.
14. Frankfurter to Frank, April 24, 1933, Frank Papers, Box 12; Alexander Sachs to Hugh S. Johnson, January 29, 1934, Sachs Papers, Box 37;

Corcoran to Frankfurter, ca. November 1933, Frankfurter to "Little Boys," May 15, 1934, Corcoran Papers, Box 198.

15. Lash, *Dealers and Dreamers,* p. 171; Niznik, pp. 93, 240–44; Corcoran to Harold L. Ickes, April 21, Corcoran to Clement Norton, July 25, Sam Rayburn to Corcoran, November 20, 1935, Edward C. Moran, Jr., to Corcoran, February 7, 1936, Corcoran to D. J. Driscoll, August 21, 26, 1936, Driscoll to Corcoran, April 3, May 16, 1937, August 4, 1938, Corcoran to Edward C. Eicher, September 19, December 21, 1936, Eicher to Corcoran, September 23, October 7, 8, December 15, 1936.
16. Corcoran to Isador Feinstein, September 8, 1936, May 14, July 14, June 2, 1937, Feinstein to Corcoran, May 28, 1936, August 20, 1937, "Monday nite" [late 1937], Peggy to Feinstein, August 28, 1937, June 11, 1938, Corcoran to Lincoln Filene, December 17, 1936, Corcoran Papers, Box 198.
17. Quoted in Lash, *Dealers and Dreamers,* p. 197; copy, George Roberts to Felix Frankfurter, February 27, 1936, Ben Cohen to Felix Frankfurter, March 9, 31, 1936, Cohen Papers.
18. Seligman, *The Transformation of Wall Street,* pp. 49–50.
19. Rayburn quoted in Seligman, pp. 66–67, Seligman, p. 97.
20. Seligman, *The Transformation of Wall Street,* pp. 127–29; Lash, *Dealers and Dreamers,* p. 201.
21. "B.—August 5, 1938," Alsop Papers, Box 98; Seligman, pp. 127–38, quote on p. 131; Rauh, 955–58.
22. Arthur M. Schlesinger, Jr., *The Politics of Upheaval* (Boston: Houghton Mifflin, 1960), pp. 316–18; Niznik, pp. 180–205; FDR to Corcoran, July 6, Corcoran to FDR, July 7, FDR to Corcoran, undated 1935, Corcoran Papers; "T.—July 27, 1938," Alsop Papers, Box 93; on the Jackson effort, see "Re: Converting one Robert Jackson into the Sweetheart of the Nation," by Morris Ernst in Corcoran Papers; "Cor-coran" story told to me by Democratic lawyer Ernest Cuneo; H. Dudley Swim to Corcoran, September 28, 1938, January 6, 1939, Russell W. Davenport to Corcoran, January 29, 1938, Claude Pepper to Corcoran, May 9, Corcoran to Lincoln Filene, May 17, to Samuel Zemurray, September 24, 1938, Corcoran Papers.
23. Eugene Meyer to Felix Frankfurter, May 25, 1938, Meyer Papers, Box 22; observer is Beverly Smith, p. 127; copy, Paul K. Read to Franklin D. Roosevelt, Cohen Papers; Henry A. Wallace, COHC, p. 533, 950–51, 990–91.
24. Corcoran to James Forrestal, May 2, 1939, Corcoran Papers; Arthur Schlesinger, Jr., "'Prich': A New Deal Memoir," *New York Review of Books,* March 28, 1985, 22; Blair Bolles, "Cohen and Corcoran: Brain Twins," *American Mercury* 43 (January 1938), 38–45; Walter Davenport, "It Seems There Were Two Irishmen," *Colliers,* September 10, 1938, 14, 76–79; Diary, July 5, 1940, Ickes Papers; Joseph Alsop to "Ma," November 15, 1938, Alsop Papers, Box 2.
25. Lash, *Dealers and Dreamers,* pp. 411–12, 445–52, 458–59, 461–63; James H. Rowe memo to Missy LeHand, January 14, Rowe memo for FDR, June 25, 26, September 24, 1941, Rowe Papers, Box 10; copy, Frankfurter to Corcoran, Cohen Papers, Box 8; W.O. Douglas to Grace [Tully], De-

cember 23, 1941, Douglas Papers, Box 367; Diary, January 18, March 1, 1942, January 13, 1945, Ickes Papers; John Morton Blum, ed., *The Price of Vision: The Diary of Henry A. Wallace 1942–1946* (Boston: Houghton Mifflin, 1973), p. 157; Alva Johnston, "The Saga of Tommy the Cork," *Saturday Evening Post,* October 13, 1945, 9–11+; Diary, July 21, 1943, August 31, 1944, Biddle Papers.

26. Lash, *Dealers and Dreamers,* pp. 452–55; Rowe memos for the President, August 1, 1941, October 2, 1941, Rowe draft of FDR letter, August 9, 1941, Rowe memo for Judge Rosenman, August 29, 1941, Rowe Papers, Boxes 10, 9; Diary, February 22, 1942, Ickes Papers; Diary, October 9, 1942, Biddle Papers; FDR to Ben Cohen, January 13, 20, Cohen to FDR, January 16, 1945, Cohen Papers, Box 12.

8 WILLIAM O. DOUGLAS

1. Quoted in Laura Kalman, *Legal Realism at Yale, 1927–1960* (Chapel Hill: University of North Carolina Press, 1986), p. 117.
2. Arthur Schlesinger, Jr., "The Supreme Court: 1947," *Fortune* 35 (January 1947) 201; for a different view of legal realism, see Morton J. Horowitz, *The Transformation of American Law, 1870–1960: The Crisis of Legal Orthodoxy* (New York: Oxford University Press, 1992).
3. Jordan A. Schwarz, *Liberal: Adolf A. Berle and the Vision of an American Epoch* (New York: The Free Press, 1987), pp. 50–68.
4. Quoted in Melvin I. Urofsky, *The Douglas Letters* (Bethesda, Md.: Adler & Adler, 1987), pp. 15–16; Julius Goebel, Jr., *A History of the School of Law, Columbia University* (New York: 1955), pp. 299–305; James E. Simon, *Independent Journey: The Life of William O. Douglas* (New York: Harper & Row, 1980), pp. 92–111, 125–30; George Creel, "The Young Man Went East," *Colliers,* May 9, 1936, 9; William O. Douglas, *Go East, Young Man* (New York: Random House, 1974), pp. 159–64; Bruce Allen Murphy, *Fortas* (New York: Morrow, 1988), pp. 11–13; Kalman, pp. 113, 261, n. 117, 129.
5. On Douglas's birthplace, see D. Jerome Tweton, *The New Deal at Grass Roots: Programs for the People in Otter Tail County, Minnesota* (St. Paul: Minnesota Historical Society, 1988), pp. 5–10; Simon, pp. 17–25.
6. McCloy quoted in Simon, *Independent Journey,* p. 81.
7. Simon, *Independent Journey,* pp. 218, 117–18; Murphy, pp. 19–20; Douglas, *Go East, Young Man,* pp. 167–69; "Dr. Wesley Sturges on Arnold" May 24, 1939, Alsop Papers, Box 37.
8. Thurman Arnold, *Fair Fights and Foul* (New York: Harcourt, Brace & World, 1965), pp. 3–37; Edward N. Kearny, *Thurman Arnold, Social Critic* (Albuquerque: University of New Mexico Press, 1970); Gene M. Gressley, ed., *Voltaire and the Cowboy: The Letters of Thurman Arnold* (Boulder: Colorado Associated University Press, 1977), pp. 1–94; Katz quote in Notes for *Saturday Evening Post* article on Thurman Arnold, May 1939, Alsop Papers, Box 37; Ellis W. Hawley, "Thurman Wesley Arnold," *Dictionary of American Biography, Supplement Eight 1966–1970* (New York: 1988), pp. 16–18; Kalman, pp. 31–32, 34–35, 119, 137–38, 273–74; Fortas, Rostow, and Levi on Arnold in *Yale Law Journal* 79 (1970), 983, 986,

988, 998; Wilson D. Miscamble, "Thurman Arnold Goes to Washington: A Look at Antitrust Policy in the Later New Deal," *Business History Review* 56 (Spring 1982), 1–15.

9. Kalman, pp. 49–50, 55–56, 119, 142; Glennon, *The Iconoclast as Reformer: Jerome Frank's Impact Upon American Law* (Ithaca, N.Y.: Cornell University Press, 1985), pp. 87–89.
10. Urofsky, p. 76; Joseph P. Lash, *From the Diairies of Felix Frankfurter* (New York: Norton, 1975), p. 175; Simon, pp. 128–30; Frank to Tugwell, May 4, 1933, Frank Papers, Box 16.
11. Douglas to Jerome Frank, December 4, 1933, April 28, 1934, Frank Papers, Box 11; Douglas to Frankfurter, December 8, 1933, Frankfurter to Douglas, January 16, February 5, 1934, Douglas Papers, Box 6.
12. Douglas, "Protecting the Investor," *Yale Review* 23 (1933), 521–33; Douglas to Jerome Frank, January 3, April 8, 1934, emphasis added; Douglas Papers, Box 6; Simon, p. 133.
13. Douglas to Frankfurter, February 19, 1934, Douglas Papers, Box 6.
14. Douglas to Frankfurter, March 28 ("never sent"). April 6, November 6, 1934, Douglas Papers, Box 6; Simon, pp. 134–36.
15. Simon, pp. 141–54; Urofsky, pp. 81–82; *Time*, January 27, 1936: 50.
16. Simon, pp. 154–56; Urofsky, p. 36.
17. William O. Douglas, "Termites of High Finance," *Vital Speeches of the Day* 3 (November 15, 1936), 86–93, emphasis added; "New SEC Chairman 'A Pretty Conservative Fellow,'" *Newsweek*, October 4, 1937, 37–38; William O. Douglas, "Your Securities: Their Future Protection," *Vital Speeches of the Day* 3 (May 1, 1937), 436–43; Simon, pp. 156–59.
18. Sachs to "Jim, Tom and Ben," March 9, 1934, Leffingwell to Sachs, January 9, 1935, Sachs Papers, Boxes 17 & 40; Joel Seligman, *The Transformation of Wall Street* (Boston: Houghton Mifflin, 1982), pp. 124–27, 138–55.
19. *Newsweek*, October 4, 1937: 37–38; *Time*, October 11, 1937, 61–68; Seligman, p. 155.
20. Seligman, pp. 156–60.
21. *Business Week*, September 25, 1937, 60; Max Lerner, "Wall Street's New Mentor," *Nation*, October 23, 1937, 429–32.
22. "Wall Street and Washington," December 1, 1937, Sachs Papers, Box 80; Simon, p. 184; Douglas to Frankfurter, January 14, 1938, Douglas Papers, Box 6.
23. Seligman, pp. 160–67, emphasis added; *Fortune* 17 (February 1938), 64–65, 120, 122, 124, 126.
24. Seligman, pp. 167–79; Ron Chernow, *The House of Morgan* (New York: Atlantic Monthly Press, 1990), pp. 421–29; "Stock Exchange, Saturday Evening Post article 1938, Charles R. Gay, March 28, 1938, William Harding Jackson, March 29, 1938, Eugene Lokey, March 31, 1938, Paul Shields, March 31, 1938, Alsop Papers, Box 37.
25. Douglas to FDR, June 23, September 19, November 10, FDR to Douglas, June 27, September 26, November 11, 1939, Douglas Papers, Box 367.
26. "J.F.—August 1, 1938, Alsop Papers, Box 93; Roosevelt to Douglas,

April 21, 1938, Douglas Papers, Box 367; "W.O.D.—August 11, 1938, Alsop Papers, Box 93.

27. *The Secret Diary of Harold L. Ickes: The Inside Struggle 1936–39* (New York: Simon and Schuster, 1954), p. 552.
28. Simon, pp. 189–94; Kalman, p. 140; Seligman, pp. 210–12; Ickes, *Inside Struggle*, pp. 588–89; *Time*, March 27, 1939, 12–13, *Newsweek*, March 27, 1939, 13–14; *Business Week*, March 25, 1939: 17.
29. William O. Douglas to Hugo Black, September 8, 1941, Black Papers, Box 59; Douglas to FDR, July 2, 1940, undated and marked "hold," Douglas Papers, Box 367; Diary, May 3, June 7, 1942, January 3, 1943, Ickes Papers; Arthur M. Schlesinger, Jr., "The Supreme Court: 1947," *Fortune* 35 (January 1947), 75; Simon, pp. 258–75.

9 JEROME N. FRANK

1. William O. Douglas, *Go East, Young Man* (New York: Random House, 1974), p. 182.
2. Robert Jerome Glennon, *The Iconoclast as Reformer: Jerome Frank's Impact Upon American Law* (Ithaca, N.Y.: Cornell University Press, 1985), pp. 9, 10, 15–17; Jerome Frank, COHC, pp. 14, 15–16, 52–53; *Current Biography 1941*, pp. 301–03; *Time*, March 11, 1940, 71–79.
3. For a useful summary of the ideas that motivated Frank and his circle of intellectual activists, see Richard P. Adelstein, " 'The Nation as an Economic Unit': Keynes, Roosevelt, and the Managerial Ideal," *Journal of American History* 78 (June 1991), 160–87.
4. Frank to T. L. Chadbourne, undated [ca. September 1931], to Felix Frankfurter, December 29, 1932, Frank Papers, Boxes 2 & 66.
5. Frank, COHC, 13–15; Frankfurter assessment of Frank quoted in Peter H. Irons, *The New Deal Lawyers* (Princeton, N.J.: Princeton University Press, 1982), pp. 121–22.
6. Irons, pp. 173–80; for Frank's version of the firing, see Frank to Eliot Janeway, September 12, 1938, Frank Papers, Box 30.
7. Quotes from Irons, pp. 126–28; Glennon, pp. 78–79; Joseph P. Lash, *Dealers and Dreamers* (New York: Doubleday, 1988), p. 218–19.
8. "J.F.—August 1, 1938," Alsop Papers, Box 93; Frankfurter to Frank, January 12, 1936, Frank to Frankfurter, January 18, 1936, Frank Papers, Box 12; Joseph Alsop and Robert Kintner, "We Shall Make America Over," *Saturday Evening Post* 211 (October 29, 1938), 80.
9. "According to Coyle," *Time*, October 24, 1938; Russell Leffingwell to Eugene Meyer, July 14, 1941, Meyer Papers, Box 32; Herbert Feis to Felix Frankfurter, June 15, 1932, Feis Papers, Box 33. For a sampling of Coyle's writings, see *Uncommon Sense* (Washington: 1936), *Waste* (Indianapolis: 1936), *Roads to a New America* (Freeport, N.Y.: 1937) *The American Way* (New York: 1938).
10. Irving Fisher to Jacob Viner, March 17, 1933, Viner Papers, Box 32; Wood Memorandum to the President, October 14, 1936, Wood Papers, Box 2; Frank Gannett to R.E. Wood, November 4, 1936, Wood Papers, Boxes 2, 31.
11. Edward A. Rumely to R. E. Wood, February 20, Wood to Rumely,

February 28, 1935, Wood Papers, Box 31; Lauchlin Currie, "Comments and Observations," *History of Political Economy* 10 (1978), 543; Sachs memorandum, November 28, 1934, Sachs Papers, Box 21. On Eccles, see Sidney Hyman, *Marriner S. Eccles* (Stanford, Calif.: Stanford University Press, 1976); Dean L. May, *From New Deal to New Economics: The American Liberal Response to the Recession of 1937* (New York: Garland Publishing, 1981), pp. 38–66.

12. R. G. Blakey to Jacob Viner, November 23, Viner to Blakey, November 26, 1935, Viner Papers, Box 22; Herbert Stein, *The Fiscal Revolution in America* (University of Chicago Press, 1969), pp. 35–36; Stein, "Wit and Wisdom in Economics," *Wall Street Journal*, June 3, 1991; Donald Winch, "Jacob Viner," *Dictionary of American Biography, Supplement Eight 1966–1970* (New York: Scribner, 1988), pp. 668–69.
13. Currie quoted in Stein, p. 165; L. B. Currie, "A Tentative Program to Meet the Business Recession," October 13, 1937, Richard V. Gilbert Papers; Lubin quoted in "I.L.—August 15, 1938," Alsop Papers, Box 93; Byrd L. Jones, "Lauchlin Currie, pump priming, and New Deal fiscal policy, 1934–1936," *History of Political Economy* 10 (1978), 507–22; Jones, "Lauchlin Currie and the Causes of the 1937 Recession," *History of Political Economy* 12 (1980), 303–09; Alan Sweezy, "The Keynesians and Government Policy, 1933–1939," *American Economic Review* (1972), 116–23; Alfred H. Bornemann, "The Keynesian Paradigm and Economic Policy," *American Journal of Economics and Sociology* 35 (April 1976), 125–36; James Tobin, "Hansen and Public Policy," *Quarterly Journal of Economics* 90 (February 1976), 32–37; John Kenneth Galbraith, *Economics, Peace and Laughter* (Boston: Houghton Mifflin, 1971), pp. 43–59.
14. On Ruml, see *Current Biography 1943*, pp. 647–50; Michael Drury, "Ruml," *Life*, April 12, 1943, 35–38; Alva Johnston, "The National Idea Man," *New Yorker*, February 10, 1945, 28–33; "Beardsley Ruml," *Fortune* 31 (March 1945), 135–38+; Robert M. Collins, *The Business Response to Keynes, 1929–1964* (New York: Columbia University Press, 1981), pp. 67–71; Broadus Mitchell, "Beardsley Ruml," *Dictionary of American Biography, Supplement Six 1956–1960*, (New York: Scribner, 1980) pp. 558–60.
15. FDR to Beardsley Ruml, December 18, 1935, Ruml Papers, Box 1.
16. B. Ruml to Jacob Viner, February 20, 1934, Viner to John E. Galvin, December 14, 1937, Viner Papers, Boxes 56, 34; Robert E. Wood to Henry A. Wallace, March 21, 30, 1938, to Harry L. Hopkins, July 22, 1938, Wood Papers, Boxes 18, 7; Alexander Sachs to Dorothy Thompson, January 3, 1938, J.M. Keynes to Sachs, April 30, 1938, Sachs Papers, Boxes 80, 39, his emphasis; copies, Frederic A. Delano to FDR, December 19, 20, 1938, Ruml Papers, Box 1; Kenneth D. Roose, *The Economics of Recession and Revival: An Interpretation of 1937–1938* (New Haven, Conn.: Archon Books, 1969).
17. R. E. Wood to E. A. Rumely, March 14, 1936, Wood Papers, Box 31; J. M. Keynes to Alexander Sachs, January 3, 1938, Sachs to Marriner S. Eccles, April 30, 1937, Sachs Papers, Boxes 21, 39.
18. "Policy in 1935: Paper Concerning Deficit Spending," Harry Dexter White Papers, Box 1, emphasis; Thomas W. Lamont to FDR, February 18, 1938, PPF 70; Robert E. Wood to Brendan Bracken, February 18,

1938, Wood Papers; see FDR file in Fred I. Kent Papers, Box 25; F. Eberstadt, "Where and How to Get New Funds For Plant Expansion," *Chemical & Metallurgical Engineering* 45 (February 1938), clipping in Eberstadt Papers, Box 173; F. Eberstadt to Robert A. Taft, April 20, 1939, Eberstadt Papers, Box 149; also see Eberstadt statements in Box 174.

19. Mordecai Ezekial to Jerome Frank, February 11, 1938, Ezekial Memorandum for members of informal discussion group, April 15, 1938, Frank Papers, Box 26; Ezekial, "Elements of Suggested Program for Action," March 15, 1938, Louis Bean Papers, Box 8; Warm Springs Memorandum, April 1, 1938, Ruml Papers, Box 1; Dean L. May, *From New Deal to New Economics: The American Liberal Response to the Recession of 1937* (New York: Garland Publishing, 1981), pp. 129–34; Jerome Frank to Tom Corcoran, May 27, 1938, Corcoran Papers, Box 198; Lauchlin Currie to Jacob Viner, June 13, 1938, Viner Papers, Box 28; Paul Appleby to Jerome Frank, July 28, 1938, Frank Papers, Box 21.

20. "Warm Springs Memorandum," April 1, 1938, "Compensatory Fiscal Policy," December 18, 1938, "The Twelve Trust Proposal," September 3, 1938, Ruml Papers, Box 1; Thomas G. Blaisdell memos to Jerome Frank, et al., July 9, September 27, 1938, Ruml, "The Retailer's Interest in National Fiscal Policy," Frank Papers, Boxes 22, 25, 38.

21. Copy, Paul P. Gourrich to Chairman Douglas, April 5, Frank to Gourrich, May 11, July 2, 21, August 1, 1938, original emphasis, Gourrich to Frank, July 20, October 3, 1938, Frank Papers, Boxes 27, 25, 28; Frank to Tom Corcoran, August 1, 1938, Corcoran Papers, Box 198; Elisha Friedman to Frank, November 3, 1938, Frank Papers, Box 27; Jacob Viner to Frank, February 24, 1939, Viner Papers, Box 33; also, see Frank to Benjamin V. Cohen, March 30, 1939.

22. Louis H. Bean to Frank, December 6, White quoted in Eliot Janeway to Frank, December 20, 1938, Frank Papers, Boxes 21, 30.

23. Joel Seligman, *The Transformation of Wall Street* (Boston: Houghton Mifflin, 1982), pp. 214–17; John Hanes to Frank, July 1, 1938, Frank Papers.

24. Frank to Elisha M. Friedman, May 7, June 1, October 24, 1938, Friedman to Frank, May 25, July 14, October 13, 1938, Frank Papers, Box 27; Frank to Thomas Corcoran, November 29, 1937, Corcoran Papers, Box 198; Seligman, pp. 218–37; "Holding Companies: Last Mile," *Time*, April 14, 1941: 79–81.

25. Mark Leff, *The Limits of Symbolic Reform: The New Deal and Taxation, 1933–1939* (New York: Cambridge University Press, 1984), p. 239.

26. Robert M. Collins, *The Business Response to Keynes, 1929–1964* (New York: Columbia University Press, 1981), pp. 46–47; Richard N. Chapman, *Contours of Public Policy, 1939–1945* (New York: Garland Publishing, 1981), pp. 34–59; John Morton Blum, *From the Morgenthau Diaries: Years of Urgency 1938–1941* (Boston: Houghton Mifflin, 1965), pp. 36–42; Jones, "Currie," 312; "Herbert Gaston—Dec. 23, 1938," "Harry White, July 12, 1939," Joseph Alsop Papers, Boxes 95, 34; "Business-and-Government," *Fortune*, May 1940, 132, 134, 136; telegram, Alexander Sachs to Dorothy Thompson, Sachs Papers, Box 80.

10 DAVID E. LILIENTHAL

1. Felix Frankfurter to David E. Lilienthal. January 10, 1934, Lilienthal Papers, Box 63.
2. Frankfurter to Lilienthal, January 10, 1934, Lilienthal Papers, Box 63.
3. For biographical sketches of Lilienthal, see *Current Biography, 1944*, pp. 413–15; Willson Whitman, *David Lilienthal, Public Servant in a Power Age* (New York: Henry Holt, 1948); Thomas K. McCraw, *Morgan vs. Lilienthal: The Feud within the TVA* (Chicago: Loyola University Press, 1970), pp. 18–23; Thomas K. McCraw, *TVA and the Power Fight 1933–1939* (Philadelphia: Lippincott 1971), pp. 43–46.
4. *The Journals of David E. Lilienthal*, vol. 1, *The TVA Years 1939–1945* (New York: Harper & Row, 1964), pp. 7–14, original emphasis; Lilienthal to Walsh, December 31, 1920, January 30, May 15, 1921, August 19, November 14, 1922, Walsh to Lilienthal, January 10, 1921, Lilienthal to Frankfurter, May 1, 1921, copy, Frankfurter to Donald Richberg, undated, Lilienthal Papers, Box 47.
5. Lilienthal, *The TVA Years*, pp. 6–7, 116, 147–48, 226, 594–95; *The Journals of David E. Lilienthal*, vol. 5, *The Harvest Years 1959–1963* (New York: Harper & Row, 1971), pp. 27–30.
6. Lilienthal to Donald R. Richberg, November 17, December 21, 1922, Lilienthal to Frankfurter, October 5, Frankfurter to Lilienthal, October 18, 1928, Lilienthal Papers, Boxes 47, 49; Thomas E. Vadney, *The Wayward Liberal: A Political Biography of Donald R. Richberg* (Lexington: University Press of Kentucky, 1970), pp. 53, 74; Lilienthal, *The TVA Years*, pp. 14–16; Ted Leitzell, "Uncle Sam, Peddler of Electric Gadgets," *New Outlook*, August 1934, 50.
7. Frankfurter to Lilienthal, October 10, 31, 1929, January 3, 1930, February 9, 1931, Lilienthal Papers, Boxes 49, 51; Lilienthal, *The TVA Years*, pp. 16–17; Remarks, "Realism in Regulation," by William L. Ransom, Lilienthal Papers, Box 52.
8. Frankfurter to Lilienthal, September 22, 1931, Morris Llewellyn Cooke, January 6, Cooke to Lilienthal, January 11, 1932, Lilienthal to Frankfurter, April 22, September 21, 1932, Lilienthal Papers, Boxes 51, 55, 57; Lilienthal, *The TVA Years*, pp. 24–28.
9. Lilienthal to Joseph Eastman, September 24, 1932, Frankfurter to Lilienthal, January 4, Lilienthal to Frankfurter, January 7, February 9, May 22, Lilienthal to Frankfurter, May 18, June 2, 1933, McNinch, February 6, 27, March 21, 1933, Lilienthal Papers, Boxes 55, 59, 60; Lilienthal, *The TVA Years*, pp. 32–36; McCraw, *Morgan vs. Lilienthal*, p. 22.
10. Lilienthal to Frankfurter, June 2, 9, 1933, Frankfurter to Lilienthal, June 6, 1933, Morris Llewellyn Cooke to Lilienthal, June 5, 1933, Lilienthal Papers, Box 59.
11. E. F. Scattergood to the President, May 27, 1933, copy in Corcoran Papers, Box 242; Roy Talbert, Jr., *FDR's Utopian, Arthur Morgan of the TVA* (Jackson: University Press of Mississippi, 1987), p. 92.
12. Roosevelt took with him to Muscle Shoals, in addition to Norris and Scattergood, Senators Clarence C. Dill of Washington, Hugo Black of Alabama, Kenneth McKellar and Cordell Hull of Tennessee, Represen-

tatives Lister Hill of Alabama and John J. McSwain of South Carolina, Frank P. Walsh of the New York Power Authority, and Frank R. McNinch of the Federal Power Commission. Judson King, *The Conservation Fight* (Washington, D.C.: Public Affairs Press, 1959), p. 267.

13. E. F. Scattergood, "Engineering and Economic Features of the Boulder Dam," *The Annals of the American Academy* 135 (January 1928): 115–22.

14. H.G. Butler, "Pools of Power," *Survey* 51 (March 1, 1924), 605–10; on electrical journal and northern California, see Thomas P. Hughes, *Networks of Power: Electrification in Western Society 1880–1930* (Baltimore: Johns Hopkins University Press, 1983), pp. 265–67, 281–84.

15. Kevin Starr, *Material Dreams: Southern California Through the 1920s* (New York: Oxford University Press, 1990), pp. 156–57; Robert M. Fogelson, *The Fragmented Metropolis: Los Angeles, 1850–1930* (Cambridge, Mass.: Harvard University Press, 1967), pp. 229–46.

16. Norris Hundley, Jr., *Water and the West: The Colorado River Compact and the Politics of Water in the American West* (Berkeley: University of California Press, 1975); Remi A. Nadeau, *The Water Seekers* (Garden City, N.Y.: Doubleday, 1950), pp. 137–218; Hoover quoted in William Hard, "Giant Negotiations for Giant Power," *Survey* 51 (March 1, 1924), 577.

17. Joseph Stevens, *Hoover Dam: An American Adventure* (Norman: University of Oklahoma Press, 1988), pp. 16–27, 31–34; Beverley Bowen Moeller, *Phil Swing and Boulder Dam* (Berkeley: University of California Press, 1971); Donald Worster, *Rivers of Empire: Water, Aridity, and the Growth of the American West* (New York: Pantheon Books, 1985), p. 211.

18. Stevens, *Hoover Dam*, pp. 20, 35–46, 117–58, 169–70, Englishman quoted on 188.

19. Robert Kelley, *Battling the Inland Sea: American Political Culture, Public Policy, and the Sacramento Valley, 1850–1986* (Berkeley: University of California Press, 1989), pp. 307–08.

20. John Fahey, *The Inland Empire: Unfolding Years, 1879–1929* (Seattle: University of Washington Press, 1986), pp. 90–98, 104–09, 163–69.

21. Robert L. Hill, "Power and Politics in Seattle," *Nation* 134 (March 2, 1932), 253–54; Ross quoted in Judson King, "Control by City Competition," *New Republic*, May 26, 1926, 33; clipping, "Greatness of J. D. Ross Recalled," *The Pacific Northwest*, in John M. Carmody Papers, Box 130.

22. William Edward Leuchtenburg, *Flood Control Politics: The Connecticut River Valley Problem 1927–1950* (Cambridge, Mass.: Harvard University Press, 1953), p. 13.

23. Jean Christie, *Morris Llewellyn Cooke: Progressive Engineer* (New York: Garland Publishing, 1983), pp. 1–67, passim; Edwin T. Layton, Jr., *The Revolt of the Engineers: Social Responsibility and the Engineering Profession* (Cleveland: Press of Case Western Reserve University, 1971), pp. 154–78.

24. Hughes, *Networks of Power*, pp. 297–313: Thomas P. Hughes, *American Genesis: A Century of Invention and Technological Enthusiasm 1870–1970* (New York: Viking Press, 1989), pp. 303–05; Thomas P. Hughes, "Technology and Public Policy: The Failure of Giant Power," *Proceedings of the IEEE* 64 (September 1976), pp. 1361–71; Christie, *Cooke*, pp. 68–94; Morris Llewellyn Cooke, "The Long Look Ahead," *Survey*, 51 (March 1, 1924), 601–04, 651; D. Clayton Brown, *Electricity for Rural America: The Fight for REA*

(Westport, Conn.: Greenwood Press, 1980), pp. 22–34; Leonard DeGraaf, "Corporate Liberalism and Electric Power System Planning in the 1920s," *Business History Review* 64 (Spring 1990), 12–22.

25. Pinchot quoted in DeGraaf, p. 28.
26. E. F. Scattergood to M. L. Cooke, December 18, 1924, Cooke Papers, Box 195.
27. Charles A. Gulick, Jr., "Holding Companies in Power," *New Republic*, May 26, 1926, 25–28; "Electric Power as an Issue in Politics," *New Republic*, October 6, 1926, 182–83; "Politics Discovers A 'Power Trust,'" *Literary Digest*, April 2, 1927, 12; Pinchot and *Times* quoted in "Fighting for Control of the 'Power Trust,'" *Literary Digest*, March 3, 1928, 8.
28. Felix Frankfurter, "Mr. Hoover on Power Control," *New Republic*, October 17, 1928, 240–43.
29. William Monroe Emmons, "Private and Public Responses to Market Failure in the U.S. Electric Power Industry: 1882–1942," unpublished doctoral dissertation, Harvard University, 1989, pp. 21–47; Langdon Post, "The Power Issue in Politics," *Outlook and Independent*, July 15, 1931, 332; H. M. Olmsted, "The Status of Municipal Electric Power Systems," *American City*, September 1929, 97–99.
30. Emmons, pp. 48–61; Frederick R. Barkley, "The Power Issue Emerges," *Outlook and Independent*, December 17, 1930, 614–16, 635–36; Fahey quoted in Leuchtenburg, p. 6; William Hard, "The Politics of Power," *World's Work* 60 (May 1931), 22–26.
31. Post, p. 332; Ronald Chernow, *The House of Morgan: An American Banking Dynasty and the Rise of Modern Finance* (New York: Atlantic Monthly Press, 1990), pp. 308–09.
32. Bernard Bellush, *Franklin D. Roosevelt as Governor of New York* (New York: Columbia University Press, 1955), pp. 208–42; Franklin D. Roosevelt, "The Real Meaning of the Power Problem," *Forum*, December 1929, 327–32; Morris Llewellyn Cooke, "Planning for Power, *Nation*, 134 (June 1, 1932), 621–24.
33. Post, p. 351; Floyd L. Carlisle, "Public Versus Private Ownership of Electric Power," *Current History*, August 1930, 894–97; Martin J. Insull, "The Real Power Problem," *Forum*, February 1930, 88–94.
34. John A. Piquet, "Why We Need an Enlightened Power Policy," *Industrial Management* 72 (December 1926), pp. 349–53.
35. Philip Cabot, "National Electrical Highways," *Survey* 51 (March 1, 1924), 581–83; McCraw, *TVA and the Power Fight*, pp. 6–15, 21–23; Morris Llewellyn Cooke, "Integrated Development of Power," *New Republic*, May 26, 1926, 18–20.
36. Preston J. Hubbard, *Origins of the TVA: The Muscle Shoals Controversy, 1920–1932* (New York: Norton, 1961); Roosevelt quoted in Richard Lowitt, *George W. Norris: The Persistance of a Progressive 1913–1933* (Urbana: University of Illinois Press, 1971), p. 568.
37. On Southern economic development in the 1920s, see James C. Cobb, *Industrialization and Southern Society 1877–1984* (Lexington: University Press of Kentucky, 1984), pp. 31–35 and George B. Tindall, *The Emergence of the New South 1913–1945* (Baton Rouge: Louisiana State University Press, 1967), pp. 219–84; Atlanta *Constitution* quoted in Blaine A.

Brownell, *The Urban Ethos in the South 1920–1930* (Baton Rouge: Louisiana State University Press, 1975), p. 128; Joseph Hyde Pratt, "In the Southern Appalachians," *Survey* 51 (March 1, 1924), 612; newspaper quoted in "Fighting for Control of the 'Power Trust," 9; Barkley, "The Power Issue Emerges," p. 616; also, see James C. Cobb, "Beyond Planters and Industrialists: A New Perspective on the New South," *Journal of Southern History* 54 (February 1988), 45–68.

38. Judson King, *The Conservation Fight: From Theodore Roosevelt to the Tennessee Valley Authority* (Washington, D.C.: Public Affairs Press, 1959), pp. 1–58, passim; also, see Wilmon Henry Droze, *High Dams and Slack Waters: TVA Rebuilds A River* (Baton Rouge: Louisiana State University Press, 1965), pp. 3–18.
39. Arthur E. Morgan, *The Making of the TVA* (Buffalo, N.Y.: Prometheus Books, 1974), pp. 38–52; Talbert, *FDR's Utopian*, pp. 22–38, quote on p. 37.
40. Talbert, *FDR's Utopian*, pp. 45–68; Morgan, *Making*, pp. 6–8; "Material Concerning Arthur E. Morgan," Alexander Sachs Papers, Box 47.
41. Morgan, *Making*, pp. 4–7.
42. McCraw, *Morgan vs. Lilienthal*, p. 12–16; Morgan, *Making*, pp. 20–21; Talbert, *FDR's Utopian*, p. 94, Arthur Morgan quoted on p. 184.
43. Morgan, *Making*, pp. 21–24; McCraw, *Morgan vs. Lilienthal*, p. 18; Talbert, *FDR's Utopian*, pp. 91–94.
44. Talbert, *FDR's Utopian*, pp. 101–35, Morgan quoted on p. 85, Bachman on p. 152.
45. Morgan quoted in Talbert, *FDR's Utopian*, p. 150; T.R.B., "Hatfields and McCoys in the TVA," *New Republic* 94 (March 23, 1938), 192.
46. Thomas K. McCraw, "Triumph and Irony—The TVA," *Proceedings of the IEEE* 64 (September 1976), 1372, 1380.
47. Jonathan Daniels, "Diagram for Democracy," *New Republic*, August 31, 1938, 96, emphasis added.
48. Lilienthal, *The TVA Years*, pp. 38–39; Lilienthal to Arthur Morgan, July 21, 1933, Frankfurter to Lilienthal, July 29, September 8, 1933, Lilienthal Papers, Boxes 60, 59.
49. Arthur Morgan memorandum to H. A. Morgan and David Lilienthal, August 14, Lilienthal memorandum, August 16, Lilienthal to George W. Norris, August 17, 1933, Lilienthal Papers, Box 60.
50. "General Considerations Concerning the Proposed Agency to Promote and Coordinate Industrial Expansion in the Tennessee Valley, The Tennessee Valley Associated Industries," April 1, 1934, "Reasons for the Specific Provisions in the Proposal for a Corporation to Promote and Coordinate Industrial Expansion in the Tennessee Valley, The Tennessee Valley Associated Industries," May 1, 1934, "Relations between Private Industry and Governmental Agencies. . . ," October 12, 1934, Lilienthal to Donald R. Richberg, November 3, 1934, Lilienthal Papers, Box 63; Morgan, *Making*, p. 73; Marguerite Owen, *The Tennessee Valley Authority* (New York: Praeger, 1973), p. 163.
51. Morgan quoted in Talbert, *FDR's Utopian*, p. 137.
52. For Arthur Morgan on Harcourt Morgan, see Morgan, *Making*, pp. 172–73.

53. David E. Lilienthal to Felix Frankfurter, June 22, July 13, 1933, Lilienthal Papers, Box 59; McCraw, *TVA*, p. 59; Morgan, *Making*, p. 22.
54. McCraw, *TVA*, pp. 60–66; Lilienthal to Frankfurter, July 27, 1934, Lilienthal Papers, Box 63.
55. McCraw, *TVA*, pp. 67–77; Lilienthal to Frankfurter, March 6, 1934, Lilienthal Papers, Box 63; engineer quoted in Jonathan Daniels, "Banner on a Yardstick," *New Republic*, August 24, 1938, 67–69.
56. Lilienthal to Frankfurter, September 12, 1935, Lilienthal Papers, Box 69; "Influence of Research, in Science and Engineering, on Reliability of Rendering Electric Service to Consumers of the Bureau of Power and Light, Los Angeles, California," by E. F. Scattergood, 9-25-33, with Scattergood to President Roosevelt, October 12, 1933, OF 42/12.
57. McCraw, *TVA*, pp. 85–86.
58. Memorandum, Arthur E. Morgan to Herbert S. Marks, October 21, 1935, Marks Papers, Box 5.
59. Morgan, *Making*, p. 29; Lilienthal, *The TVA Years*, pp. 47, 61–62; Lilienthal to George W. Norris, May 4, 1936, Lilienthal Papers, Box 74; Louis B. Wehle, *Hidden Threads of History: Wilson Through Roosevelt* (New York: Macmillan, 1953), p. 164.
60. Wehle, p. 164; Talbert, *FDR's Utopian*, p. 161, Morgan quoted on p. 183; Lilienthal, *The TVA Years*, p. 62.
61. Lilienthal to Frankfurter, August 2, 1936, Lilienthal Papers, Box 74; Scattergood to the President, June 4, 1934, Lilienthal to the President, June 9, 1934, OF 42–12.
62. Copy, Arthur Morgan to the President, May 18, 1936, Lilienthal Papers, Box 75; Morris L. Cooke to the President, July 7, 1936, Cooke Papers, Box 144; Lilienthal to Frankfurter, August 2, 1936, Lilienthal Papers, Box 74; Talbert, *FDR's Utopian*, p. 183, Roosevelt quoted on p. 163, Morgan quoted on p. 171.
63. Alexander Sachs to James M. Landis, February 6, 1934, to President Roosevelt, November 5, 6, 1934, Roosevelt to John Hancock, May 21, FDR to Sachs, September 17, telegram, Sachs to Henry Kannee, September 19, 1936, Sachs Papers, Boxes 40, 63; McCraw, *Morgan vs. Lilienthal*, pp. 67–70.
64. Lilienthal to Morris Llewellyn Cooke, April 19, 1935, to George W. Norris, May 4, 1936, Frankfurter to Lilienthal March 4, 1936, Lilienthal Papers, Boxes 69, 74; Morris L. Cooke to Lilienthal, May 8, 1936, Cooke Papers, Box 144; Russell Leffingwell to Walter Lippmann, February 27, 1936, Lippmann Papers, Box 84.
65. Lilienthal to Frankfurter, August 22, September 8, Memorandum to the President, September 9, to Senator Norris, September 14, to the Board of Directors, September 14, 1936, Lilienthal Papers, Boxes 74, 75.
66. Conference on Tuesday, September 22, 1936, Conference at Federal Power Commission . . . , September 25, 1936, Conference between Messrs. Basil Manly and Alexander Sachs, September 27, Sachs Papers, Box 63.
67. Wehle, pp. 164–66; McCraw, *TVA*, pp. 100–01; "Perspective on Tasks Arising from President's Power Pool Conference with Special Reference to the TVA and Commonwealth and Southern," Sachs Papers, Box 63.

68. Wehle, pp. 167–71; McCraw, *TVA*, pp. 98–99; McCraw, *Morgan vs. Lilienthal*, pp. 71–73; copy, George Fort Milton, to George W. Norris, November 4, 1936, Lilienthal Papers, Box 74; Morris L. Cooke to FDR, November 6, 1936, January 4, 1937, copy, Remarks of Arthur E. Morgan, December 30, 1936, Cooke Papers, Boxes 144, 147; Talbert, *FDR's Utopian*, pp. 172–74; "TVA: 'Napoleonic Madcap' Wins Tilt With a Mannerly Scholar," *Newsweek*, February 6, 1937, 12.
69. Wehle, pp. 171–75; McCraw, *TVA*, pp. 104–07; McCraw, *Morgan vs. Lilienthal*, pp. 77–80, 126, note 27; Lilienthal memorandum for the President, January 12, 1937, Lilienthal Papers, Box 80.
70. Sachs to Dorothy Thompson, February 2, 1937. Sachs Papers, Box 80; copy, statement of Mr. Wendell L. Willkie, February 2, 1937, Willkie to Lilienthal February 19, telegram, Willkie to Lilienthal, March 2, copy, Harcourt A. Morgan and Lilienthal to the President, March 5, Lilienthal to Frankfurter, March 25, Frankfurter to Lilienthal, March 31, May 19, 1937, Lilienthal Papers, Box 80; Talbert, *FDR's Utopian*, pp. 175–77.
71. Harcourt A. Morgan and Lilienthal to the President, November 19, 1937, Lilienthal Papers, Box 80; McCraw, *Morgan vs. Lilienthal*, pp. 90–98; Talbert, *FDR's Utopian*, pp. 179–81.
72. "Conference with Dr. Arthur E. Morgan," November 22, 1937, Sachs to Morgan, December 15, 1937, "Materials Concerning Arthur E. Morgan," Sachs Papers, Box 47.
73. Herbert Marks to Felix Frankfurter, December 28, 1937, January 1, 1938, Marks Papers, Box 2; McCraw, *Morgan vs. Lilienthal*, pp. 90–93, 97–99; Lilienthal to Frankfurter, January 28, 1938, to Frank R. McNinch, February 13, Lilienthal Papers, Boxes 83, 84
74. Lilienthal, *TVA Years*, pp. 69–74; Talbert, *FDR's Utopian*, pp. 186–89; McCraw, *Morgan vs. Lilienthal*, pp. 99–101.
75. Talbert, *FDR's Utopian*, pp. 189–93, Roosevelt quoted on p. 91; McCraw, *Morgan vs. Lilienthal*, pp. 101–03; Roosevelt quoted in Lilienthal, *TVA Years*, p. 114.
76. Untitled, "Sent to D. Thompson, March 18, 1938," Sachs to Arthur Morgan, March 22, 1938, Morgan to Sachs, January 23, 1939, Sachs Papers, Box 47, copy, Jerome Frank to Thompson, April 23, Thompson to Sachs, April 26, Sachs to Thompson, June 16, to Arthur Morgan, October 20, 27, 31, 1938, "A Man Stood Up," November 26, 1938, Sachs Papers, Box 80.
77. *Time*, June 6, 1938, 10–12; Joe Swidler to Herbert Marks, July 22, August 16, 1938, Marks Papers, Box 7.
78. Paul W. Ward, "Washington Weekly," *Nation*, November 28, 1936, 624.
79. Wendell Wilkie to Lilienthal, March 18, 1937, Lilienthal to Richberg, August 27, to the Editor of the *Atlantic Monthly*, September 14, to George W. Norris, November 13, copy, Harcourt A. Morgan to the President, November 9, 1937, Lilienthal Papers, Box 80; on Memphis, see Douglas L. Smith, *The New Deal in the Urban South* (Baton Rouge: Louisiana State University Press, 1988), pp. 117–20.
80. Lilienthal to George W. Norris, November 26, 1937, Lilienthal Papers, Box 80; Fred I. Kent to the President, December 10, 1937, February 7, 1938, Kent Papers, Box 25. Although Wall Street also accused the Public

Utilities Holding Companies Act of frightening investors into hiding, one scholar argues that it had the opposite effect "by reducing the risk associated with the pyramiding of securities." Emmons, p. 77.

81. Francis Biddle to Morris L. Cooke, October 24, 1938, Cooke Papers, Box 144; Lilienthal to Frankfurter, November 15, 1938, Lilienthal Papers, Box 83; Francis Biddle to Thomas Corcoran, November 5, FDR to Corcoran, November 28, 1936, Corcoran Papers.
82. "Telephone Conversation with the President re Commonwealth & Southern Corporation, 10 a.m. Saturday, February 4, 1939," "Stenographic Transcript of Telephone Conversation Between Messrs. David E. Lilienthal, Wendell L. Willkie, and J. A. Krug, February 4, 1939," Lilienthal Papers, Box 92.
83. Lilienthal, *TVA Years*, pp. 92–98, 107–08, 111–13, 119–20.
84. "T.V.A. Settlement and the Democratic Process," February 7, 1939, "T.V.A. Deal and Economic Reconstruction," undated, Sachs Papers, Box 80.
85. "Conference with the President, Wednesday Morning, July 19, 1939," Lilienthal memorandum for the President, July 14, Harcourt A. Morgan to the President, August 1, 1939, memorandum for the President, September 23, 1939, Lilienthal Papers, Box 92.
86. "The New Deal: Second Time Around," *Fortune* 17 (February 1938), 150, emphasis added; Joseph C. Swidler to Herbert Marks, July 22, 1938, Marks Papers, Box 7.
87. "Contest of the Corn-feds," Lilienthal Papers, Box 61; Paul W. Ward, "Washington Weekly," *Nation*, November 28, 1936, 624.
88. Lilienthal, "The TVA and Decentralization," *Survey Graphic* 29 (June 1940), 335, original emphasis; Jonathan Daniels, "Three Men in a Valley," *New Republic* 96 (August 17, 1938), 34–37.
89. Ted Leitzell, "Uncle Sam, Peddler of Electric Gadgets," *New Outlook*, August 1934, 50–53; Thomas K. McCraw, "Triumph and Irony—The TVA," *Proceedings of the IEEE* 64 (September 1976), 1375–76.
90. David E. Lilienthal, "The TVA Points Ahead," *Christian Century* 53 (October 7, 1936), 1318; Lilienthal, *TVA Years*, p. 88.
91. Michael A. Bernstein, *The Great Depression: Delayed Recovery and Economic Change, 1929–1939* (New York: Cambridge University Press, 1987), pp. 57, 29, 30.
92. Lilienthal to FDR, December 6, 1933, Lilienthal Papers, Box 60; W. A. Sutherland memorandum for Mr. Oliphant, Sutherland to M. H. McIntyre, December 18, 1933, OF 42B.
93. Copy, L. W. Douglas to Henry Morgenthau, Jr., December 14, 1933, OF 42B; Frankfurter to Lilienthal, January 10, Lilienthal to Frankfurter, February 14, March 6, April 29, 1934, Lilienthal to FDR, December 6, 1933, Lilienthal Papers, Boxes 63, 60; Gregory B. Field, " 'Electricity for All': The Electric Home and Farm Authority and the Politics of Mass Consumption, 1932–1935," *Business History Review* 64 (Spring 1990), 32–42.
94. Hugo L. Black to W. F. Broadhead, May 26, 1934, Black Papers, Box 189; M.H. McIntyre to Congressman Robert Ramspeck, June 9, 1934, OF 42B; Thomas G. Corcoran memorandum to Jesse H. Jones, July 20,

1934, Corcoran Papers. Box 249; Lilienthal to Frankfurter, August 7, 1934, Lilienthal Papers, Box 63; Lilienthal to the President, May 7, July 18, 1935, OF 42B.

95. Lilienthal, *TVA Years,* pp. 43–46; Joseph P. Lash, *Dealers and Dreamers: A New Look at the New Deal* (New York: Doubleday, 1988), p. 193; Lilienthal to FDR, December 3, 1934, Lilienthal Papers, Box 63; Lilienthal to Marvin H. McIntyre, December 11, 1934, OF 42B; EHFA Activities Review, December 12, 1934, Lilienthal to Tom Corcoran, April 23, 1935, Corcoran Papers, Box 249; Field, pp. 47–49.
96. Angus MacLean to FDR, June 1, 1935, OF 42B; Electric Home and Farm Authority Constitutionality, February 14, 1936, Corcoran Papers, Box 249; Lilienthal memorandum to the President, February 6, July 20, 22, 26, President to Lilienthal, July 20, 1935, Cooke, Cooksey and Corcoran to the President, July 31, OF 42B.
97. FDR memorandum, October 5, M.S. Eccles to FDR, November 4, 1935, OF 42B; "Memorandum: Re—Meeting to discuss RFC loans to Electric Home and Farm Authority: September 26, 1935," copy, Cooke to Stewart McDonald, October 24, 1935, Corcoran Papers, Box 249; Cooke to Lilienthal, October 14, 1935, Lilienthal Papers, Box 69; Cooke to the President, Cooke to Jesse Jones, November 18, 1935, OF 42B.
98. Cooke to Jesse Jones, November 18, 1935, Cooke to the President, January 16, 1936, Peter Grimm to Marvin McIntyre, December 26, A.S. Hewitt to Peter Grimm, December 16, 17, 1935, OF 42B. Philip J. Funigiello mistakenly attributes Cooke's complaints to Jones's tightfistedness and writes off EHFA before its time, *Toward a National Power Policy: The New Deal and the Electric Utility Industry, 1933–1941* (University of Pittsburgh Press, 1973), p. 158. In truth Jones was an advocate of EHFA's renewal in 1936. See Jesse H. Jones memorandum for the private files of things discussed with the President, December 31, 1936, Jones Papers, Box 29.
99. William A. Weaver to Thomas G. Corcoran, February 21, 1936, Corcoran Papers, Box 249.
100. Corcoran quoted in "Business-and-Government," *Fortune,* May, 1940, 124; Jesse H. Jones to FDR, March 24, 1934, April 24, 1936, Stanley Reed to Angus D. MacLean, December 16, 1933, Electric Home and Farm Authority Annual Report to Congress, June 30, 1936, OF 42B; "Electric Farm and Home Authority," Corcoran Papers, Box 249.
101. See EHFA file in Box 249, Corcoran Papers.
102. Unsigned, "Re: Electric Home & Farm Authority," March 21, 1938, OF 42B.
103. Copy, Jesse H. Jones to FDR, May 6, 1941, to Rep. Clifton A. Woodrum, July 9, 1941, Corcoran Papers, Box 151; Harold Smith memorandum for the President, FDR to Jones, September 16, 1941, copy, Harold Smith to Francis Biddle, October 3, Biddle to FDR, October 9, M.H. McIntyre to Smith, October 14, 1942, OF 42B.
104. For the record, his other two accomplishments were bringing bright young lawyers to Washington and the succesful establishment of the SEC. Notes for "We Shall Make America Over," in the *Saturday Evening Post,* Corcoran interview, July 27, 1938, Alsop Papers, Box 93.

105. Emil Schram to the President, September 16, 1937, "Operations for the Fiscal Year 1938," "Operations for the Fiscal Year 1939," "Summary of Operations for the Year 1940," Summary of Operations for the Year 1941," OF 42B.
106. Coppock, "Government as Enterpriser-Competitor," p. 196; William A. Weaver to Thomas G. Corcoran, March 12, 1936, Corcoran Papers, Box 249; "EHFA Summary of Operations for the Year 1940," OF 42B.

IV Texans

11 SAM RAYBURN

1. "Memorandum re Lyndon Johnson—Texas Situation," [ca. September 1940], Corcoran Papers; Lionel V. Patenaude, *Texans, Politics and the New Deal* (New York: Garland Publishing, 1983), p. 74–75, Stokes quoted on p. 63; also on the 1940 Democratic convention and Rayburn, see "George Stimpson," in Alsop Papers, Box 36.
2. On Rayburn, see *Current Biography 1940*, pp. 673–74; Alonzo L. Hamby, "Samuel Taliaferro Rayburn ("Sam")," *Dictionary of American Biography, Supplement Seven 1961–1965* (New York: Scribner, 1981), pp. 634–37; Robert A. Caro, *The Years of Lyndon Johnson: The Path to Power* (New York: Knopf, 1982), pp. 306–34; C. Dwight Dorough, *Mr. Sam* (New York: Random House, 1962); Anthony Champagne, *Congressman Sam Rayburn* (New Brunswick, N.J.: Rutgers University Press, 1984); Alfred Steinberg, *Sam Rayburn* (New York: Hawthorn Books, 1975).
3. Rayburn on Rayburn, Alsop Papers, Box 36.
4. "George Stimpson," "Jim Barnes," Rayburn file, Alsop Papers, Box 36.
5. Tom Connally, *My Name Is Tom Connally* (New York: Crowell, 1954), p. 91.
6. Marvin Jones, *Memoirs* (El Paso: Texas Western Press, 1973), p. 36.
7. Caro, pp. 321–25; Donald A. Ritchie, *James M. Landis: Dean of the Regulators* (Cambridge, Mass: Harvard University Press, 1980), pp. 43–48; Joel Seligman, *The Transformation of Wall Street* (Boston: Houghton Mifflin, 1982), pp. 55–70; Michael E. Parrish, *Securities Regulation and the New Deal* (New Haven, Conn.: Yale University Press, 1970), pp. 42–71; Joseph P. Lash, *Dealers and Dreamers* (New York: Doubleday, 1988), pp. 130–36.
8. James Rowe Oral History, LBJ Library I, pp. 18–20.
9. Seligman, pp. 73–100; Parrish, pp. 130–42; Lash, pp. 163–70; Caro, pp. 325–26; William O. Douglas, *Go East, Young Man* (New York: Random House, 1974), p. 410.
10. Philip J. Funigiello, *Toward a National Power Policy: The New Deal and the Electric Utility Industry, 1933–1941* University of Pittsburgh Press, 1973), pp. 32–97; Ellis W. Hawley, *The New Deal and the Problem of Monopoly* (Princeton, N.J.: Princeton University Press, 1966), pp. 329–37; Burton K. Wheeler, *Yankee from the West* (New York: Doubleday, 1962), pp. 307–13; Lash, pp. 191–214; Seligman, pp. 129–31.
11. Ray Tucker, "A Master for the House," *Colliers*, January 5, 1935; pp. 22, 49; "Leader Apparent," *Time*, December 14, 1936; "Rayburn," *Newsweek*,

December 26, 1936; "Deshler, two talks," "George Stimpson," Alsop Papers, Box 36.

12. "Steve Early," "Fred Vinson," "Sam Rayburn," Alsop Papers, Box 36.
13. Rayburn quoted in Champagne, pp. 48, 114; Caro, pp. 520–21.
14. D. Clayton Brown, *Electricity for Rural America: The Fight for REA* (Westport, Conn.: Greenwood Press, 1980), pp. 119, x, xiii–xv, 1–34.
15. Cooke to Key Pittman, August 14, 1935, Pittman Papers, Box 85; ibid., pp. 39, 22–58, passim; Fungiello, pp. 122–48; Jean Christie, *Morris Llewellyn Cooke: Progressive Engineer* (New York: Garland Publishing, 1983), pp. 145–89.
16. Brown, pp. 47–66.
17. Cooke to FDR, May 7, 1936, Cooke Papers, Box 147.
18. "REA Notes," July 9, 1958, Carmody Papers, Box 82.
19. Paul W. Ward, "Washington Weekly," *Nation,* March 27, 1937, 343–44; "REA Notes," July 9, 1958, M. R. Cooksey to Carmody, September 21, 1938, Carmody Papers, Boxes 82, 83; on Carmody, see undated "Washington Merry-Go-Round" clipping in Carmody Papers, Box 81; on Alabama loans, see REA file, Black Papers, Box 132; Carmody to Morris Llewellyn Cooke, October 31, 1938, Carmody Papers, Box 139.
20. D. Jerome Tweton, *The New Deal at the Grass Roots: Programs for the People in Otter Tail County, Minnesota* (St. Paul: Minnesota Historical Society Press, 1988), pp. 134–46.
21. John Robert Moore, "The New Deal in Louisiana," Michael P. Malone, "The Montana New Dealers," James F. Wickens, "Depression and the New Deal in Colorado," in John Braeman, Robert H. Bremner, and David Brody, *The New Deal: The State and Local Levels* (Columbus: Ohio State University Press, 1975), pp. 154, 247, 297; Carmody to Frank M. Wilkes, April 12, 1944, "Introduction to Scattered Notes on the Early History of REA, July 9, 1958," REA Experiences in Developing Rural Electrification in Arkansas," "The History of Generating Plants in REA," "Addenda to the History of Generating Plants in REA," "Alabama 21 Cherokee," Boyd Fisher to Carmody, February 21, 1940, *Rural Electrification News,* July 1939, Carmody Papers, Boxes 81, 82, 85.
22. E. J. Coil to Morris L. Cooke, May 12, 1939, Cooke Papers, Box 140; Carmody to T. F. Kelley, March 21, 1945, Carmody Papers, Box 84; copies, George W. Norris to the President, June 5, 1939, Roosevelt to Norris, June 7, 1939, Carmody Papers, Box 67; Brown, pp. 73–98; see Rowe memos for the President, January 29, 1940, February 12, 1941, Rowe Papers, Box 40.

12 LYNDON BAINES JOHNSON

1. Maverick quoted in Judith Kaaz Doyle, "Out of Step: Maury Maverick and the Politics of the Depression and the New Deal," unpublished doctoral dissertation, University of Texas at Austin, 1989, p. 252; also, on Maverick, see Richard B. Henderson, *Maury Maverick: A Political Biography* (Austin: University of Texas Press, 1970); Henderson, "Maury Maverick, *Dictionary of American Biography, Supplement Five 1951–1955* (New York: Scribner, 1977), pp. 480–81.

2. Stanley High, "The Neo-New Dealers," *Saturday Evening Post*, May 22, 1937, 10–11+; Maverick quoted in Doyle, p. 273.
3. Maury Maverick, "The South Is Rising," *Nation*, June 17, 1936, 770–72; Doyle, pp. 580, 582, 586; Maverick, "Let's Join the United States," *Virginia Quarterly Review*, January 1939, 64–77; Maverick, "Let's Join the United States," *Nation*, May 11, 1940, 592–94.
4. Doyle, pp. 1–4, 370, 342–43; Maverick to H. M. Aubrey, March 28, 1936, Maverick Papers, Box 2L22.
5. Maverick quoted in Doyle, p. 672.
6. Austin paper quoted in Doyle, p. 690.
7. Robert A. Caro, *The Years of Lyndon Johnson: The Path to Power* (New York: Random House, 1981), pp. 276–77, 281–83.
8. James H. Rowe, Jr., Oral History, Johnson Library, V:32–33, I:15, 7, V:5–6; Rowe quotes Johnson in Rowe to Tom Eliot, December 20, 1940, Rowe Papers, Box 12; Corcoran memorandum re Lyndon Johnson—Texas situation, ca. 1940, Corcoran Papers.
9. This portrait of Johnson and his family draws liberally from Caro, Robert Dallek, *Lone Star Rising: Lyndon Johnson and His Times 1908–1960* (New York: Oxford University Press, 1991), Paul K. Conkin, *Big Daddy from the Pedernales: Lyndon Baines Johnson* (Boston: Twayne Publishers, 1986), and Ronnie Dugger, *The Politician: The Life and Times of Lyndon Johnson, The Drive for Power from the Frontier to Master of the Senate* (New York: Norton, 1982).
10. Conkin, p. 46.
11. Dugger, pp. 197–98; Dallek, pp. 125–56.
12. Caro, pp. 448–49; Dallek, pp. 159–64.
13. John A. Adams, Jr., *Damming the Colorado: The Rise of the Lower Colorado River Authority 1933–1939* (College Station: Texas A & M University Press, 1990), pp. 3–15.
14. Autobiographical sketch attached to Mary Rather to Lyndon B. Johnson, December 29, 1939, LBJA, Box 36.
15. Caro, pp. 373–85, 392–95; Adams, pp. 16–70.
16. Johnson to Wirtz, July 12, August 9, 13, 1937, March 14, 1938, December 3, Wirtz to Johnson, August 4, 12, 17, November 30, 1937 (2), Sam Rayburn to Wirtz, March 9, 1938, LBJA, Boxes 36, 52.
17. Press release, March 17, 1938, attached to LBJ letter to Clarence McDonough, March 16, 1938, statement of Lyndon B. Johnson, April 12, 1938, LCRA, Box 26; Wirtz to LBJ, March 22, April 22, May 20, June 13, July 21, 1938, LBJA, Box 36; on the personal benefits of building public power to congressmen, see John E. Rankin to Johnson, December 3, 1938, LBJA, Box 52.
18. Wirtz to LBJ, April 22, May 18, December 22, 1938, "Austin Business Man" to Tom Miller, June 23, 1938, LBJA, Box 36; Johnson quoted in Caro, p. 472 and in Dallek, p. 182 Corcoran quoted on p. 501; Johnson to Corcoran, December 20, 1938, Corcoran Papers.
19. Caro, pp. 502–28.
20. Johnson to Corcoran, May 15, 1939, Corcoran Papers; George R. Brown, May 2, 1939, LBJA, Box 12; Max Starcke to LBJ, September 26, 1939, LBJA, Box 36; undated press release, LBJA, Box 72; copy of constituent

letter from LBJ attached to Corcoran to LBJ, October 11, 1939, Corcoran Papers.

21. Louis Johnson to James H. Rowe, December 17, 1938, Rowe Papers, Box 17; George Brown to LBJ, May 13, 1939, LBJA, Box 12; Memorandum, November 11, 1939, Johnson to Corcoran, December 8, 1939, Corcoran Papers; Harold L. Ickes, *Secret Diary: The Lowering Clouds* (New York: Simon and Schuster, 1954), pp. 94–95; undated press release, LBJA, Box 37; LBJ to George Brown, February 27, 1940, LBJA, Box 12; Caro, pp. 569–85.
22. Jesse H. Jones to John N. Garner, August 8, 1940, Jones Papers, Box 10; A. J. Wirtz to W. S. Gideon, August 16, 1940, LCRA, Box 25; Jones to FDR, August 23, 1940, PSF 73.
23. "Memorandum re Lyndon Johnson—Texas situation" [ca. September, 1940], Corcoran Papers, original emphasis; Diary, July 5, 1940, Ickes Papers; Caro, pp. 576–77, 619–26.
24. Memoranda for the President, October 18, 1940 [2], "The Political Line-Up as of October 18, 1940," by Louis Bean, LBJ to Rowe, October 25, 1940, Rowe Papers, Boxes 4, 17.
25. LBJ to Jim Rowe, October 25, 1940, with Honeyman drafts, Rowe Papers, Box 17; Caro, pp. 611–12, 632–33, 642–44, 655.
26. James Rowe memo for Lyndon Johnson, December 11, 1940, Johnson Papers, Box 32, Rowe Papers, Box 17; Johnson to FDR, February 19, 1941, Rowe Papers, Box 17; FDR to David E. Lilienthal, March 12, 1941, Lilienthal Papers, Box 98; Memo for Mr. Forster, re Defense Site Locations, June 6, 1941, Rowe Papers, Box 21.
27. George Brown to LBJ, March 5, 1940, LBJA, Box 12; A. J. Wirtz to W. S. Gideon, April 11, 1941, LCRA, Box 25.
28. Rowe memo for FDR, April 14, 1941, Rowe Papers, Box 17; FDR memo to Jesse H. Jones, April 30, May 23, 24, 1941 Jones Papers, Box 29, PSF73.
29. LBJ to Rowe, June 12, 1941, Rowe Papers, Box 17; on the 1941 race for the Senate in Texas, see Caro, pp. 675–740, passim.
30. Copy, Rowe memo to FDR, May 5, Jones to FDR, May 31, 1941, Jones Papers, Box 29; Rowe memo to Grace Tully, June 9, Rowe memos to FDR, May 5 [2], June 3, 5, Roosevelt to Rowe, June 10, 1941, Rowe Papers, Box 17, PSF 73.
31. Rowe memo to FDR, June 12, to Cordell Hull, June 21, to Alvin J. Wirtz, June 23, to FDR, June 21, to Harry Hopkins, June 26, 30, telegram to LBJ, June 30, 1941, Rowe Papers, Box 17. For Louis Bean's assessment of the election, see Rowe to LBJ, September 2, 1941, Rowe Papers, Box 17, LBJA, Box 32.
32. FDR telegram to Burnet R. Maybank, August 20, Rowe memos to FDR, August 20, 18 [2], 1, 1941, Rowe Papers, Box 21.

13 WRIGHT PATMAN

1. Hubert Kay, "The Warrior from Patman's Switch," *Fortune* 21 (April 1965), 183. A biography of Patman would be useful and should be significant, but I have had to depend upon the following for this portrait of him: Janet

Louise Schmelzer, "The Early Life and Early Congressional Career of Wright Patman: 1894–1941," unpublished doctoral dissertation, Texas Christian University, 1978.

2. Robert Sherrill, " 'The Last of the Great Populists' Takes on the Foundations, the Banks, the Federal Reserve, the Treasury," *New York Times Magazine,* March 16, 1969, 110; Kay, p. 185.
3. Kay, pp. 178, 183; Schmelzer, passim; *Current Biography 1946*, pp. 461–62.
4. Carl G. Ryant, "The South and the Movement Against Chain Stores," *Journal of Southern History* 39 (1973), 207–14; George B. Tindall, *The Emergence of the New South 1913–1945* (Baton Rouge: Louisiana State University Press, 1967), pp. 595–96; *Liggett* v. *Lee* (1932), 541, 544–86.
5. Hugh S. Johnson, *The Blue Eagle from Egg to Earth* (Garden City, N.Y.: Doubleday, Doran, 1935), p. 353; Copy, Albert Balanow to C. H. Janssen, March 21, George J. Schulte to Wright Patman, June 24, A. C. McCune to Patman, June 27, 1935, Patman Papers, Box 37C; Ellis W. Hawley, *The New Deal and the Problem of Monopoly* (Princeton, N.J.: Princeton University Press, 1966), pp. 59, 247–54; Broadus Mitchell, *Depression Decade: From New Era through New Deal, 1929–1941* (New York: Harper Torchbooks, 1969), pp. 261–63; Wright Patman, "Curbing the Chain Store," *Nation,* November 28, 1936, 624–26; Cecil Edward Weller, Jr., "Joseph Taylor Robinson and the Robinson-Patman Act," *Arkansas Historical Quarterly* (1989), 29–36; clipping, Charles F. Phillips, "Why laws to aid small stores are unnecessary, and full of economic dynamite," *Printers' Ink,* December 2, 1937, 11–13, in Eberstadt Papers, Box 173; Rowland Jones, Jr., to Wright Patman, February 25, 1937, Patman Papers, Box 1337B.
6. Hawley, pp. 254–58; Rowland Jones, Jr., to Patman, January 18, February 25, 1937, J. W. Dargavel to Patman, July 8 [2], Patman Papers, Box 1337B.
7. Wright Patman to Rowland Jones, Jr., July 16, Jones to Patman, August 6, 1936, Patman Papers, Box 1337B; clipping, *Farm-Town Hardware,* June 1938, Patman Papers, Box 37C; "Patman," *Current Biography 1946*, p. 462.
8. Patman, "Curbing the Chain Store," *Nation,* November 28, 1936, 624–26; Patman to Editor, *Nation's Business,* October 2, to Bruce Bliven, October 15, 1936, Patman Papers, Box 100B; "McKesson Case Curbs Patman Tax," *Business Week,* December 24, 1938, 30–31; " 'Sponsored' Patman," *Time,* December 24, 1938, 8–9.
9. Ryant, 216–22; Hawley, pp. 262–63; Jerome N. Frank to Morris Ernst, October 2, 1939, Frank Papers, Box 21; Statement, "Today, June 7, 1939 . . . ," Patman to George Schulte, October 17, 1939, Patman Papers, Box 37C.
10. Sherrill, pp. 110, 112; *Business Week,* July 8, 1939, 26–27, January 2, 1943, 52–53, April 24, 1943, 18–20, October 16, 1943, 22–23, October 28, 1944, 17–19; see Lone Star Steel file in Patman Papers.
11. Patman to Jack Lynch, December 14, 1946, *N.A.R.D. Journal,* November 7, 1960, 24–25, *Wall Street Journal,* March 21, 1963, clipping and Humphrey-Capehart press release in Patman Papers, Boxes 37C, 56, 119C.

V *New Dealers Abroad*

14 HENRY J. KAISER

1. The "New Western History" does not celebrate such economic development uncritically, but deplores the ravaging of the pristine West through the industrial exploitation of its resources. For a review of the literature of the New Western History, see William G. Robbins, "Laying Siege to Western History: The Emergence of New Paradigms," *Reviews in American History* 19 (September 1991), 313–31.
2. Clarence Avildsen to Tom Corcoran, May 24, 1938, Corcoran Papers, Box 189.
3. Publicist quoted in Vera Springer, *Power and the Pacific Northwest: A History of the Bonneville Power Administration* (Washington, D.C.: Department of the Interior, 1976), p. 39; Paul Kleppner, "Politics Without Parties, The Western States, 1900–1984," in Gerald D. Nash and Richard W. Etulain, eds., *The Twentieth-Century West: Historical Interpretations* (Albuquerque: University of New Mexico Press, 1989), pp. 328–29. The works of Gerald D. Nash on the twentieth-century West develop the theme of the West's colonial markets. See his *The American West Transformed: The Impact of the Second World War* (Bloomington: Indiana University Press, 1985), pp. vii, 3–14, and *World War II and the West: Reshaping the Economy* (Lincoln: University of Nebraska Press, 1990).
4. Springer, pp. 9, 12–13, 15–16; Robert Leslie Cole, "The Democratic Party in Washington State, 1919–1933: Barometer of Social Change," unpublished doctoral dissertation, University of Washington, 1972, pp. 121–24, 231–34, 247–51, 261–96; Robert E. Burton, *Democrats of Oregon: The Pattern of Minority Politics, 1900–1956* (Eugene: University of Oregon Press, 1970), pp. 64–69, 71–78, 82–88; Kleppner, pp. 318–24; Richard L. Neuberger, "Grand Coulee Opens Vast Area," *New York Times*, May 12, 1940.
5. On Kaiser, see Mark S. Foster, *Henry J. Kaiser: Builder in the Modern American West* (Austin: University of Texas Press, 1989); Foster, "Giant of the West: Henry J. Kaiser and Regional Industrialization, 1930–1950," *Business History Review* 59 (Spring 1985), 1–23; Foster, "Prosperity's Prophet: Henry J. Kaiser and the Consumer/Suburban Culture, 1930–1950," *Western Historical Quarterly* 17 (April 1986), 165–84; "Henry J. Kaiser," *Current Biography* 1942, pp. 431–35; Jordan A. Schwarz, "Henry John Kaiser," *Dictionary of American Biography, Supplement Eight 1966–1970* (New York: Scribner, 1988), pp. 307–10; obituary, *New York Times*, August 25, 1967.
6. Foster, "Giant of the West," p. 4; Foster, *Henry J. Kaiser*, pp. 57–61; "The Earth Movers II," *Fortune*, September 1943, 119.
7. Foster, *Henry J. Kaiser*, p. 63; Frank J. Taylor, "Builder No. 1," *Saturday Evening Post*, July 7, 1941, 9–11.
8. Foster, *Henry J. Kaiser*, pp. 65–67; "The Earth Movers II," pp. 220, 222.
9. T. H. Watkins, *Righteous Pilgrim: The Life and Times of Harold L. Ickes 1874–1952* (New York: Henry Holt, 1990), pp. 274–80; "H.I.—October 4, 1938," Alsop Papers, Box 36. Also, on Ickes, see Graham White and

John Maze, *Harold Ickes of the New Deal: His Private Life and Public Career* (Cambridge, Mass.: Harvard University Press, 1985).

10. "Ickes—TC" [Tom Corcoran] October 22 [1938]; "EF [Edward Foley] Oct. 24 [1938]," Alsop Papers, Box 36; "Harold Ickes—Memoir in re first marriage," Cohen Papers, Box 10.
11. Ibid.; *The Secret Diary of Harold L. Ickes: The First Thousand Days, 1933–1936* (New York: Simon and Schuster, 1953), pp. 37–38.
12. Springer, pp. 29–30, 32–33; FDR to Morris L. Cooke, January 16, B. H. Kizer to Cooke, January 22, 1937, Cooke Papers, Box 145; Minutes of President's Informal Committee on National Power Policy, January 19–April 30, 1937, Carmody Papers, Box 128; *The Secret Diary of Harold L. Ickes: The Inside Struggle 1936–1939* (New York: Simon and Schuster, 1954), pp. 59–61, 67, 86, 129–30, 137–38, 156, 165, 228.
13. Copy, Lawrence Lewis, et al., to Joseph J. Mansfield, June 7, copy, telegram, Ezra Scattergood to Mansfield, June 16, Key Pittman to Thomas G. Corcoran, June 18, to Mansfield, June 18, copy, Scattergood to FDR, June 19, Pittman to Corcoran, June 18, Scattergood to Corcoran, November 27, 1937, Corcoran Papers, Box 242; *The Inside Struggle*, p. 156.
14. Kaiser to Corcoran, June 4, 1941, Scattergood to Corcoran, March 10, 1938, May 20, 1939, Northcult Ely to Corcoran, July 7, 1938, Corcoran Papers, Boxes 496, 242.
15. J. D. Ross to Tom Corcoran, April 12, J. D. Ross Memo of Public Rate Hearings, March 26, 1938, Corcoran Papers, Box 242; Department of Interior press memo, November 9, 1939, National Power Policy Committee memo for the President, May 22, 1940, Carmody Papers, Box 128; Ben V. Cohen to Herbert Marks, August 23, 1939, Marks Papers, Box 1; also, see Charles McKinley, *Uncle Sam in the Pacific Northwest: Federal Management of Natural Resources in the Columbia River Valley* (Berkeley: University of California Press, 1952), pp. 157–72.
16. Taylor, 10.
17. "The Earth Movers II," p. 220; "The Earth Movers III," *Fortune*, October 1943, 193.
18. "Millions for Defense: Emergency Expenditures for National Defense 1933–1940" (Washington, D.C.: Federal Works Agency, 1940), found in Rowe Papers, Box 21; Lilienthal to Mrs. Roosevelt, May 9, 1945, Lilienthal Papers, Box 110.
19. "Marine Subsidies," "H.R. 8555." *Fortune*, September 1937, 65–67, 74–78; Samuel A. Lawrence, *United States Merchant Shipping Policies and Politics* (Washington, D.C.: Brookings Institution, 1966), pp. 44–79, Roosevelt quoted on p. 46; Laton McCartney, *Friends in High Places: The Bechtel Story* (New York: Simon and Schuster, 1988), pp. 56–58; Foster, *Henry J. Kaiser*, pp. 68–69.
20. "The Earth Movers II," pp. 119–22+; Foster, *Henry J. Kaiser*, pp. 68–89; Gerald D. Nash, *World War II and the West: Reshaping the Economy* (Lincoln: University of Nebraska Press, 1990), pp. 41–66.
21. Diary, August 8, 1942, November 24, 1944, Ickes Papers; Thurman Arnold memo for the Attorney General, September 10, 1942, Francis Biddle Papers, Box 1.

22. "Business-and Government," *Fortune,* May 1940, 42–43.
23. Gerald T. White, *Billions for Defense: Government Financing by the Defense Plant Corporation during World War II* (University, Alabama: University of Alabama Press, 1980), pp. 1–24; White, "Financing Industrial Expansion for War: The Origin of the Defense Plant Corporation Leases," *Journal of Economic History* 9 (November 1949), 156–83; David Ginsburg, "Re: Financing Increased Capacity," undated, Cuneo file, Corcoran Papers; draft of letter to Jesse Jones, May 24, 1940, Richard V. Gilbert Papers, Box 7; Jerome N. Frank to FDR, May 18, 1940, Frank Papers, Box 27.
24. White, *Billions for Defense,* pp. 26–49; "The War Goes to Mr. Jesse Jones," *Fortune,* December 1941, 91–93.+
25. Jesse Jones to FDR, FDR to Jones, August 3, 1940, Jones Papers, Box 29; "Jones' Bottleneck," *Business Week,* October 11, 1941, 15–16; "Jesse Gets Ruffled," *Time,* April 20, 1942, 15; Michael Straight, "Jesse Jones, Bottleneck," *New Republic,* December 29, 1941, 881–82; Diary, January 4, 1942, Ickes Papers; Drew Pearson to James Kerney, Jr., May 6, 1942, Pearson Papers, F158.
26. C. C. Burlingham to Ben Cohen, January 30, 1945, Cohen Papers, Box 6.
27. Henderson memo, Aluminum," undated, Rowe Papers, Box 15; Edward H. Levi memorandum for the Attorney General, August 4, 1944, Biddle Papers, Box 3; copy, Harold Ickes to Frank Knox, February 24, 1941, Hugo Black Papers, Box 34; George David Smith, *From Monopoly to Competition: The Transformation of Alcoa, 1888–1986* (New York: Cambridge University Press, 1988), pp. 214–24; White, *Billions for Defense,* pp. 72–73, 106–07; Foster, *Henry J. Kaiser,* pp. 90–98, 196–200; Nash, *World War II and the West,* pp. 117–21, 133–36; Jesse H. Jones with Edward Angly, *Fifty Billion Dollars: My Thirteen Years with the RFC* (New York: Macmillan, 1951), pp. 331–36; copy, E. F. Scattergood to Joseph A. Hartley, April 25, 1941, Corcoran Papers, Box 496.
28. "The Saga of Tommy the Cork," *Saturday Evening Post,* October 20, 1945, 24–25+; "Kaiser's Gamble," *Business Week,* October 18, 1941, 16; "The Earth Movers III," pp. 139–42; copy, Harold L. Ickes to Frank Knox, undated, thirteen point narrative, copy, Henry J. Kaiser, October 4, 1940, see 1941 material pertaining to Hansgirg, Todd-California Shipbuilding, and Magnesium, Corcoran Papers, Box 496.
29. Schwarz, "Henry J. Kaiser," p. 309.
30. Lilienthal, *TVA Years,* pp. 296–99, 302–05, 308, 316–17, 320, 322, 329, 332–38.
31. *The Journals of David E. Lilienthal: The TVA Years 1939–1945* (New York: Harper & Row, 1963), pp. 540, 549, 557; Memorandum re National Defense to FDR, June 12, 1940, Lilienthal Papers, Box 94.
32. Lilienthal to Louis D. Brandeis, October 12, December 8, 1939, "draft to FF," to Russell W. Davenport, March 27, 1940, "Joe" to Lilienthal, September 15, 1941, Lilienthal Papers, Boxes 91, 93, 96; David E. Lilienthal, "The TVA and Decentralization," *Survey Graphic,* June 1940, 335–67; George Stoney, "A Valley to Hold To," *Survey Graphic,* July 1940, 391–99; St. Louis *Post-Dispatch,* September 21, 1941; Lilienthal, *TVA Years,* pp. 125–42, 150, 156–58, 243–46, 254–55, 266–72, 278–79, 313,

338–42, 359–66, 375–77, 432, Ickes quoted on p. 137, FDR on p. 243, Cohen on p. 377; *The Secret Diary of Harold L. Ickes: The Lowering Clouds* (New York: Simon and Schuster, 1955), pp. 25–26, 45–46, 391–92, 399–401, 416, 440–41, 491, 585–87, 652; Diary, December 24, 1944, Ickes Papers.

33. FDR to Lilienthal, September 1, 1944, Lilienthal Papers, Box 106.

34. Copy, Clark Foreman memorandum for Mr. Mellett, May 25, 1938, Corcoran Papers, Box 198; Bruce J. Schulman, *From Cotton Belt to Sunbelt: Federal Policy, Economic Development, and the Transformation of the South, 1938–1980* (New York: Oxford University Press, 1991), pp. 3–8, 48–51.

35. The figures are drawn from Leonard Arrington, "The New Deal in the West: A Preliminary Statistical Inquiry," *Pacific Historical Review* 38 (1969), 311–16; Don C. Reading, "New Deal Activity and the States, 1933 to 1939," *Journal of Economic History* 33 (1973), 792–807.

36. Data in White, *Billions for Defense*, pp. 81–82.

37. Schulman, pp. 95, 98–111; George B. Tindall, *The Emergence of the New South 1913–1945* (Baton Rouge: Louisiana State University Press, 1967), pp. 694–95, 699.

38. Data in Bernard Weinstein and Robert E. Firestine, *Regional Growth and Decline in the United States: The Rise of the Sunbelt and the Decline of the Northeast* (New York: Praeger, 1978), pp. 52–53.

39. Gavin Wright, *Old South, New South: Revolutions in the Southern Economy since the Civil War* (New York: Basic Books, 1986), pp. 199, 236–41, 256–74; James C. Cobb, *The Selling of the South: The Southern Crusade for Industrial Development 1936–1980* (Baton Rouge: Louisiana State University Press, 1982), p. 36; Harvey S. Perloff, et al., *Regions, Resources, and Economic Growth* (Baltimore: Johns Hopkins Press, 1960), pp. 452–53; on highways, airports, and states, see Schulman, pp. 116–18; on Sears, see Schulman, pp. 90–91, 107; Faulkner quoted on p. 135. Also, see Harry N. Scheiber, "Federalism, the Southern Regional Economy, and Public Policy Since 1865," in David J. Bodenhamer and James W. Ely, Jr., *Ambivalent Legacy: A Legal History of the South* (Jackson: University Press of Mississippi, 1984), pp. 69–105, Cobb, *Industrialization and Southern Society 1877–1984* (Lexington: University Press of Kentucky, 1984), pp. 37–67, 136–164, and Numan V. Bartley, *The Creation of Modern Georgia* (Athens: University of Georgia Press, 1983), pp. 169–202.

40. Jack Temple Kirby, *Rural Worlds Lost: The American South 1920–1960* (Baton Rouge: Louisiana State University Press, 1987), p. 57.

41. Kirby, pp. 75–79; Numan V. Bartley, "The Era of the New Deal as a Turning Point in Southern History," in James C. Cobb and Michael V. Namorato, *The New Deal and the South* (Jackson: University Press of Mississippi, 1984), p. 139; also, on the New Deal impact upon Southern agriculture, Gilbert C. Fite, *Cotton Fields No More: Southern Agriculture, 1865–1980* (Lexington: University Press of Kentucky, 1984); David Goldfield, "Urbanization in a Rural Culture: Suburban Cities and Country Cosmopolites," in Paul D. Escott and Goldfield, *The South for New Southerners* (Chapel Hill: University of North Carolina Press, 1991), p. 85.

42. Thomas P. Hughes, "Senior Birdmen," *New York Times Book Review*, July 21,

1991, 6–7; James L. Clayton, *The Economic Impact of the Cold War: Sources and Readings* (New York: Harcourt, Brace and World, 1970), pp. 80, 187.

43. Nash, *World War II and the West*, p. 247, n. 62; "The Empire Kaiser Is Building," *Newsweek*, November 22, 1948, 64.

44. Edward H. Levi memorandum for the Attorney General, August 4, 1944, Biddle Papers, Box 3; "Kaiser Integrating," *Business Week*, December 30, 1944, 19–21; Mark S. Foster, "Giant of the West: Henry J. Kaiser and Regional Industrialization, 1930–1950," *Business History Review* 59 (Spring 1985), 1–23. For Kaiser's defense of his public financed ventures, see "Facts in brief about Henry J. Kaiser," published in 1946 by the Kaiser Companies, copy in Pearson Papers, F158.

45. Mark S. Foster, "Prosperity's Prophet: Henry J. Kaiser and the Consumer/Suburban Culture: 1930–1950," *Western Historical Quarterly*, April 1986, 165–84; "Adventures of Henry and Joe in Autoland," *Fortune*, March 1946 96–103+.

46. "The Empire Kaiser Is Building," *Newsweek*, November 22, 1948, 64–69; "Kaiser's Offsprings Settle Down," *Business Week*, December 9, 1950, 31–36; "The Arrival of Henry Kaiser," *Fortune*, July 1951, 68–73, 141–154; "Kaiser-Frazer: 'The Roughest Thing We Ever Tackled,'" *Fortune*, July, 1951, 74–77, 156–62; "Kaiserdom," *The Economist*, February 18, 1956, 464–65; "What Cooks with Kaiser—Across the Country, and Around the World," *Fortune*, July, 1956, 82–83; "Kaiser, 'Easing Up' at 75, Makes Hawaii Project Hum," *Business Week*, September 14, 1957, 152–62.

47. Kaiser manager quoted in Robert Sheehan, "Kaiser Aluminum—Henry J.'s Marvelous Mistake," *Fortune*, July, 1956, 175; Frank J. Taylor, "Builder No. 1," *Saturday Evening Post*, July 7, 1941, 9–11+; "This Is Henry J., 75," *Newsweek*, May 13, 1957, 96–98; "Henry J.'s New Paradaise, *Fortune*, March 1958, 106–09; "Springtime for Henry," *Newsweek*, May 21, 1962, 78–79.

48. Diary, January 13, 1945, Ickes Papers; Lilienthal to Felix Frankfurter, September 1, 1942, to Robert L. Duffus, June 10, 1944, to Judge Rosenman and Jonathan Daniels, [1945], copy, FDR to Estes Kefauver, March 2, 1945, Lilienthal Papers, Boxes 100, 103, 110; Lilienthal, *TVA Years*, pp. 435, 492, 511, 554–55, 560–61, 578–79, 592, 594–96.

49. Lilienthal, *TVA: Democracy on the March* (New York: Quadrangle Edition, 1966), xxi, some emphasis added.

50. Cooke to Lilienthal, May 10, 1944, Lilienthal Papers, Box 103; C. Herman Pritchett, "The Power and the Glory," *Virginia Quarterly Review* 20 (1944), 621–24; Julian Huxley, *TVA: Adventure in Planning* (London: Architectural Press, 1943), p. 135; Herman Finer, *The T.V.A.: Lessons for International Application* (Montreal: International Labour Office, 1944).

51. Tugwell quoted in William E. Leuchtenburg, *Franklin D. Roosevelt and the New Deal* (New York: Harper & Row, 1963), pp. 86–87; Philip Selznick, *TVA and the Grass Roots: A Study in the Sociology of Formal Organization* (New York: Harper & Row, 1966); Nancy L. Grant, *TVA and Black Americans: Planning for the Status Quo* (Philadelphia: Temple University Press, 1990); James C. Cobb, *Industrialization and Southern Society, 1877–1984* (Lexington: University Press of Kentucky, 1984), pp. 60–61.

52. Diary, January 11, 1942, Ickes Papers.
53. Diary, February 15, April 19, 26, 1942, Ickes Papers; Diary, May 7, 1942, Biddle Papers; John Morton Blum, ed., *The Price of Vision: The Diary of Henry A. Wallace 1942–1946* (Boston: Houghton Mifflin, 1973), pp. 69–70, 78, 137–38, 205–29.
54. Diary, May 9, 1943, Ickes Papers; Ernest K. Lindley, "Observations on the Wallace-Jones Feud," *Newsweek*, July 26, 1943, 40.
55. I. F. Stone, "Why Wallace Spoke Out," "Wallace Betrayed," *Nation*, July 10, 24, 1943, 34–36, 89–90; "Battle of Titans," *Time*, July 12, 1943, 19–21; FDR to Jones, August 9, 1943, PSF 73; Jesse H. Jones to John Nance Garner, July 14, 1943, Jones Papers, Box 10; "Mr. Wallace Walks the Plank," *New Republic*, July 26, 1943, 93–95.
56. Jones telegram to FDR, November 6, December 24, FDR to Jones, December 27, 1940, January 12, 1942, PPF 703, May 15, 1944, Jones Papers, Box 29.
57. Merritt H. Gibson to Drew Pearson, July 13, 1944, Pearson Papers, F158; Jones to FDR, July 6, 1944, E. R. memo for FDR, July 23, 1944, PSF 73; Jones to John Nance Garner, August 14, 1944, Jones Papers, Box 10; unsigned memo, "Texas Electors," August 29, 1944; Jesse H. Jones, *Fifty Billion Dollars: My Thirteen Years with the RFC* (New York: Macmillan, 1951), pp. 274–76.
58. Blum, *The Price of Vision*, pp. 382–83, 391, 396, 399, 401, 407–09, 412, 418, 420, 422, 426; Diary, November 24, December 9, 1944, Ickes Papers; Jones to FDR, January 11, 1945, FDR to Jones, January 20, Jones to FDR, January 20, 1945, Jones Papers, Box 29, PSF 73.
59. "My visit with the President," March 20, 1945, Jones Papers, Box 29; Jones, *Fifty Billion Dollars*, pp. 277–93; Bascom Timmons, *Jesse H. Jones* (New York: Henry Holt, 1956), pp. 349–55.
60. "Double-Trouble on Wallace," *Business Week*, January 27, 1945, 15–16; "Wallace's World," *New Republic*, February 5, 1945, 167; "Is F.D.R. Bent on Managed Jobs? Wallace Maneuver Gives a Clue," *Newsweek*, February 5, 1945, 36–40; "The Fight Against Wallace," *Time*, February 5, 1945, 15–17.
61. "Who's Conservative," *Time*, February 5, 1945, 15; "My visit with the President," March 20, 1945, Jones Papers, Box 29.
62. John Morton Blum, *From the Morgenthau Diaries: Years of Urgency, 1938–1941* (Boston: Houghton Mifflin, 1964), p. 57; H. D. White to Jacob Viner, January 11, February 7, 1940, Viner Papers, Box 66; White to Morgenthau, March 31, 1939, White to Hanson, March 27, 1940, White Papers, Box 6; Jordan A. Schwarz, *Liberal: Adolf A. Berle and the Vision of an American Era* (New York: The Free Press, 1987), pp. 212–17.
63. Memo of conference with FDR and Sumner Welles, April 10, 1940, FDR to Jones, September 27, October 10, 1940, Jones Papers, Box 29; Timmons, pp. 231–34; Morgenthau Diaries, May 14, 15, August 13, 1940, 262:200, 262:385–89, 292:113–14; "The War Goes to Mr. Jesse Jones," 92–93; Jones, *Fifty Billion Dollars*, pp. 214–30.
64. Schwarz, pp. 210–53.

65. Nash, *World War II and the West*, p. 119–20; Blum, *The Price of Vision*, pp. 335–37.
66. David E. Lilienthal, *Journals: The Atomic Energy Years 1945–1950* (New York: Harper & Row, 1964), pp. 593–94, 525–26.
67. David E. Lilienthal, *Journals: Venturesome Years 1950–1955* (New York: Harper & Row, 1966), passim; Lippmann quoted in Lilienthal, *Journals: The Road to Change 1955–1959* (New York: Harper & Row, 1969), p. 302; Lilienthal, *Journals: The Harvest Years 1959–1963* (New York: Harper & Row, 1971), passim; Lilienthal, *Creativity and Conflict 1964–1967* (New York: Harper & Row, 1976), passim; Lilienthal, *Management: A Humanist Art* (New York: 1967), pp. 47–48.
68. Beatrice Bishop Berle and Travis Beal Jacobs, *Navigating the Rapids 1918–1971: From the Papers of Adolf A. Berle* (New York: Harcourt Brace Jovanovich, 1973), pp. 542–43, 814; on Galbraith in India, see John Kenneth Galbraith, *Ambassador's Journal* (Boston: Houghton Mifflin, 1969); on Currie, see Lilienthal, *Creativity and Conflict*, pp. 287, 288, 289, 291, 296–97; on the Mekong, ibid., pp. 366–67.
69. Laton McCartney, *Friends in High Places: The Bechtel Story* (New York: Simon and Schuster, 1988), passim, and for quotes by Ribicoff and former Bechtel director, see pp. 104, 156; on Kaiser, see Foster, *Henry J. Kaiser*, pp. 250–53.
70. Thomas G. Paterson, *Meeting the Communist Threat: Truman to Reagan* (New York: Oxford University Press, 1988), pp. 147–58, 165; Walter LaFeber, *America, Russia, and the Cold War 1945–1990*, 6th ed. (New York: McGraw-Hill, 1991), pp. 58–63, 176–78.
71. Quoted in Dean Albertson, ed., *Eisenhower As President* (New York: Hill and Wang, 1963), p. 162, emphasis added.
72. James Tobin, "Defense, Dollars, and Doctrines," *Yale Review* 47 (Spring 1958), 325, 334.
73. Copy, Milton W. Harrison to Lauchlin Currie, October 16, 1940, Frank Papers, Box 24; Remarks before The National Association of Securities Commissioners on December 12, 1944, Eberstadt Papers, Box 174.

AFTERWORD

1. David E. Lilienthal, *Management: A Humanist's Art* (New York: Columbia University Press, 1967) pp. 50, 52, original emphasis.
2. See Kevin Phillips, *The Politics of Rich and Poor: Wealth and the American Electorate in the Reagan Aftermath* (New York: Harper Collins, 1989).
3. James L. Clayton, *The Economic Impact of the Cold War*, (New York: Harcount, Brace and World 1970), pp. 24–25; also, see Seymour Melman, *Our Depleted Society* (New York: Dell Publishing, 1965) and Anthony S. Campagna, *The Economic Consequences of the Vietnam War* (New York: Praeger, 1991).
4. William Pfaff, in Chicago *Tribune*, May 18, 1990.
5. See Martin Mayer, *The Greatest-Ever Bank Robbery: The Collapse of the Savings and Loan Industry* (New York: Scribner, 1990); "Behind the S&L Debacle," *Wall Street Journal*, November 4, 5, 1990.

6. Chicago *Tribune*, November 17, 1991.
7. Thomas H. Stanton, *A State of Risk: Will Government-Sponsored Enterprises Be the Next Financial Crisis* (New York: Harper Business, 1991).
8. Felix Rohatyn, "The New Domestic Order?" *New York Review of Books*, November 21, 1991, 10.

Index